Soviet and Post-Soviet Politics and Society
ISSN 1614-3515

General Editor: Andreas Umland,
Stockholm Centre for Eastern European Studies, andreas.umland@ui.se

Commissi London, mjł

EDITORIAL COMMITTEE*

DOMESTIC & COMPARATIVE POLITICS
Prof. **Ellen Bos**, *Andrássy University of Budapest*
Dr. **Gergana Dimova**, *Florida State University*
Prof. **Heiko Pleines**, *University of Bremen*
Dr. **Sarah Whitmore**, *Oxford Brookes University*
Dr. **Harald Wydra**, *University of Cambridge*

SOCIETY, CLASS & ETHNICITY
Col. **David Glantz**, *"Journal of Slavic Military Studies"*
Dr. **Marlène Laruelle**, *George Washington University*
Dr. **Stephen Shulman**, *Southern Illinois University*
Prof. **Stefan Troebst**, *University of Leipzig*

POLITICAL ECONOMY & PUBLIC POLICY
Prof. **Andreas Goldthau**, *University of Erfurt*
Dr. **Robert Kravchuk**, *University of North Carolina*
Dr. **David Lane**, *University of Cambridge*
Dr. **Carol Leonard**, *University of Oxford*
Dr. **Maria Popova**, *McGill University, Montreal*

FOREIGN POLICY & INTERNATIONAL AFFAIRS
Dr. **Peter Duncan**, *University College London*
Prof. **Andreas Heinemann-Grüder**, *University of Bonn*
Prof. **Gerhard Mangott**, *University of Innsbruck*
Dr. **Diana Schmidt-Pfister**, *University of Konstanz*
Dr. **Lisbeth Tarlow**, *Harvard University, Cambridge*
Dr. **Christian Wipperfürth**, *N-Ost Network, Berlin*
Dr. **William Zimmerman**, *University of Michigan*

HISTORY, CULTURE & THOUGHT
Dr. **Catherine Andreyev**, *University of Oxford*
Prof. **Mark Bassin**, *Södertörn University*
Prof. **Karsten Brüggemann**, *Tallinn University*
Prof. **Alexander Etkind**, *Central European University*
Prof. **Gasan Gusejnov**, *Free University of Berlin*
Prof. **Leonid Luks**, *Catholic University of Eichstaett*
Dr. **Olga Malinova**, *Russian Academy of Sciences*
Dr. **Richard Mole**, *University College London*
Prof. **Andrei Rogatchevski**, *University of Tromsø*
Dr. **Mark Tauger**, *West Virginia University*

ADVISORY BOARD*

Prof. **Dominique Arel**, *University of Ottawa*
Prof. **Jörg Baberowski**, *Humboldt University of Berlin*
Prof. **Margarita Balmaceda**, *Seton Hall University*
Dr. **John Barber**, *University of Cambridge*
Prof. **Timm Beichelt**, *European University Viadrina*
Dr. **Katrin Boeckh**, *University of Munich*
Prof. em. **Archie Brown**, *University of Oxford*
Dr. **Vyacheslav Bryukhovetsky**, *Kyiv-Mohyla Academy*
Prof. **Timothy Colton**, *Harvard University, Cambridge*
Prof. **Paul D'Anieri**, *University of California*
Dr. **Heike Dörrenbächer**, *Friedrich Naumann Foundation*
Dr. **John Dunlop**, *Hoover Institution, Stanford, California*
Dr. **Sabine Fischer**, *SWP, Berlin*
Dr. **Geir Flikke**, *NUPI, Oslo*
Prof. **David Galbreath**, *University of Aberdeen*
Prof. **Frank Golczewski**, *University of Hamburg*
Dr. **Nikolas Gvosdev**, *Naval War College, Newport, RI*
Prof. **Mark von Hagen**, *Arizona State University*
Prof. **Guido Hausmann**, *University of Regensburg*
Prof. **Dale Herspring**, *Kansas State University*
Dr. **Stefani Hoffman**, *Hebrew University of Jerusalem*
Prof. em. **Andrzej Korbonski**, *University of California*
Dr. **Iris Kempe**, *"Caucasus Analytical Digest"*
Prof. **Herbert Küpper**, *Institut für Ostrecht Regensburg*
Prof. **Rainer Lindner**, *University of Konstanz*

Dr. **Luke March**, *University of Edinburgh*
Prof. **Michael McFaul**, *Stanford University, Palo Alto*
Prof. **Birgit Menzel**, *University of Mainz-Germersheim*
Dr. **Alex Pravda**, *University of Oxford*
Dr. **Erik van Ree**, *University of Amsterdam*
Dr. **Joachim Rogall**, *Robert Bosch Foundation Stuttgart*
Prof. **Peter Rutland**, *Wesleyan University, Middletown*
Prof. **Gwendolyn Sasse**, *University of Oxford*
Prof. **Jutta Scherrer**, *EHESS, Paris*
Prof. **Robert Service**, *University of Oxford*
Mr. **James Sherr**, *RIIA Chatham House London*
Dr. **Oxana Shevel**, *Tufts University, Medford*
Prof. **Eberhard Schneider**, *University of Siegen*
Prof. **Olexander Shnyrkov**, *Shevchenko University, Kyiv*
Prof. **Hans-Henning Schröder**, *SWP, Berlin*
Prof. **Yuri Shapoval**, *Ukrainian Academy of Sciences*
Dr. **Lisa Sundstrom**, *University of British Columbia*
Prof. **Philip Walters**, *"Religion, State and Society"*, *Oxford*
Prof. **Zenon Wasyliw**, *Ithaca College, New York State*
Dr. **Lucan Way**, *University of Toronto*
Dr. **Markus Wehner**, *"Frankfurter Allgemeine Zeitung"*
Dr. **Andrew Wilson**, *University College London*
Prof. **Jan Zielonka**, *University of Oxford*
Prof. **Andrei Zorin**, *University of Oxford*

* While the Editorial Committee and Advisory Board support the General Editor in the choice and improvement of manuscripts for publication, responsibility for remaining errors and misinterpretations in the series' volumes lies with the books' authors.

Soviet and Post-Soviet Politics and Society (SPPS)

ISSN 1614-3515

Founded in 2004 and refereed since 2007, SPPS makes available affordable English-, German-, and Russian-language studies on the history of the countries of the former Soviet bloc from the late Tsarist period to today. It publishes between 5 and 20 volumes per year and focuses on issues in transitions to and from democracy such as economic crisis, identity formation, civil society development, and constitutional reform in CEE and the NIS. SPPS also aims to highlight so far understudied themes in East European studies such as right-wing radicalism, religious life, higher education, or human rights protection. The authors and titles of all previously published volumes are listed at the end of this book. For a full description of the series and reviews of its books, see www.ibidem-verlag.de/red/spps.

Editorial correspondence & manuscripts should be sent to: Dr. Andreas Umland, Department of Political Science, Kyiv-Mohyla Academy, vul. Voloska 8/5, UA-04070 Kyiv, UKRAINE; andreas.umland@cantab.net

Business correspondence & review copy requests should be sent to: **ibidem** Press, Leuschnerstr. 40, 30457 Hannover, Germany; tel.: +49 511 2622200; fax: +49 511 2622201; spps@ibidem.eu.

Authors, reviewers, referees, and editors for (as well as all other persons sympathetic to) SPPS are invited to join its networks at www.facebook.com/group.php?gid=52638198614
www.linkedin.com/groups?about=&gid=103012
www.xing.com/net/spps-ibidem-verlag/

Recent Volumes

264 *Dirk Dalberg*
Politisches Denken im tschechoslowakischen Dissens
Egon Bondy, Miroslav Kusý, Milan Šimečka und Petr Uhl (1968-1989)
ISBN 978-3-8382-1318-7

265 *Леонид Люкс*
К столетию «философского парохода»
Мыслители «первой» русской эмиграции о русской революции и о тоталитарных соблазнах XX века
ISBN 978-3-8382-1775-8

266 *Daviti Mtchedlishvili*
The EU and the South Caucasus
European Neighborhood Policies between Eclecticism and Pragmatism, 1991-2021
With a foreword by Nicholas Ross Smith
ISBN 978-3-8382-1735-2

267 *Bohdan Harasymiw*
Post-Euromaidan Ukraine
Domestic Power Struggles and War of National Survival in 2014–2022
ISBN 978-3-8382-1798-7

268 *Nadiia Koval, Denys Tereshchenko (Eds.)*
Russian Cultural Diplomacy under Putin
Rossotrudnichestvo, the "Russkiy Mir" Foundation, and the Gorchakov Fund in 2007–2022
ISBN 978-3-8382-1801-4

269 *Izabela Kazejak*
Jews in Post-War Wrocław and L'viv
Official Policies and Local Responses in Comparative Perspective, 1945-1970s
ISBN 978-3-8382-1802-1

270 *Jakob Hauter*
Russia's Overlooked Invasion
The Causes of the 2014 Outbreak of War in Ukraine's Donbas
With a foreword by Hiroaki Kuromiya
ISBN 978-3-8382-1803-8

271 *Anton Shekhovtsov*
Russian Political Warfare. Essays on Kremlin Propaganda in Europe and the Neighbourhood, 2020-2023
With a foreword by Nathalie Loiseau
ISBN 978-3-8382-1821-2

272 *Андреа Пето*
Насилие и Молчание. Красная армия в Венгрии во Второй Мировой войне
ISBN 978-3-8382-1636-2

273 *Winfried Schneider-Deters*
Russia's War in Ukraine
Debates on Peace, Fascism, and War Crimes, 2022–2023
With a foreword by Klaus Gestwa
ISBN 978-3-8382-1876-2

Rasmus Nilsson

UNCANNY ALLIES

Russia and Belarus on the Edge, 2012–2024

Bibliographic information published by the Deutsche Nationalbibliothek

Die Deutsche Nationalbibliothek lists this publication in the Deutsche Nationalbibliografie; detailed bibliographic data are available on the Internet at http://dnb.d-nb.de.

Bibliografische Information der Deutschen Nationalbibliothek

Die Deutsche Nationalbibliothek verzeichnet diese Publikation in der Deutschen Nationalbibliografie; detaillierte bibliografische Daten sind im Internet über http://dnb.d-nb.de abrufbar.

Cover picture: © Maksimermolaev54 via Wikimedia Commons. Licensed under CC BY-SA 4.0 (s. https://creativecommons.org/licenses/by-sa/4.0/deed.en)

ISBN (Print): 978-3-8382-1288-3
ISBN (E-Book [PDF]): 978-3-8382-7228-7
© *ibidem*-Verlag, Hannover • Stuttgart 2024
All rights reserved.

No part of this publication may be reproduced, stored in or introduced into a retrieval system, or transmitted, in any form, or by any means (electronic, mechanical, photocopying, recording or otherwise) without the prior written permission of the publisher. Any person who commits any unauthorized act in relation to this publication may be liable to criminal prosecution and civil claims for damages.

Alle Rechte vorbehalten. Das Werk einschließlich aller seiner Teile ist urheberrechtlich geschützt. Jede Verwertung außerhalb der engen Grenzen des Urheberrechtsgesetzes ist ohne Zustimmung des Verlages unzulässig und strafbar. Dies gilt insbesondere für Vervielfältigungen, Übersetzungen, Mikroverfilmungen und elektronische Speicherformen sowie die Einspeicherung und Verarbeitung in elektronischen Systemen.

Printed in the United States of America

Contents

Introduction...7

1	917-1991...	21

Kyivan Rus'...21

The Mongols...22

The Rise of Muscovy..25

The Russian Empire..29

The Revolution and the Bolsheviks...............35

Stalinism and War...46

Post-Stalinist Stabilisation.............................58

Stagnation and Fall of the Soviet Union.......69

2	1992-2011..	85

A New World Threatens..................................85

Putin's Ascendance.......................................101

Russia Returning...117

The Medvedev Interregnum.........................133

3	2012-2019..	149

A Man on a Mission.......................................149

Lukashenka Kicks Back.................................158

Belarus Considers Its Options......................176

Russian Militarisation...................................186

Return of the Cold War?...............................195

Putin confirms his position..........................204

Rise of the Russian World.............................214

4	2020-2024	223
	And the Streets Cried Out	223
	March towards the Edge	236
	The Reckoning	250
	Seeking Peace?	264
	Until the Bitter End?	278

Conclusion 287

Bibliography 291

Introduction

The Topic

The war in Ukraine shows no sign of ending. Now in its eleventh year the conflict has killed many thousands of people with civilians often bearing the brunt of Russian aggression. This has particularly been the case since February 2022, when the Kremlin unleashed its full-scale invasion on its neighbour. Russia's crimes have been assisted by Belarus. The smaller dictatorship along Russia's western borders has kept its own troops out of direct combat yet has been ready to offer its territory and resources to facilitate Russian attacks and to keep alive the possibility, if slight, of a renewed, land-based assault on Kyiv.

We are witnessing the most severe crisis in European security since the Second World War. The continent has frequently seen bloodshed over the last eight decades. Terrorist attacks have sought to disrupt societies, often through indiscriminate attacks and sometimes with the aid of individual governments. However, this is the first instance in Europe in which a country has officially chosen to break the fundamental principle of international law as it was established under the United Nations: that a state cannot engage in warfare without authorisation from the Security Council or due to the need of self-defence because of an imminent threat.

That the aggression has been perpetrated by Russia–a permanent, veto-wielding member of the Security Council–only increases the challenge to European and global order. For more than a decade the Russ ian regime has fostered militarisation within the country. It has promoted a Manichaean identity, believing in a struggle between absolute good and absolute evil. It has used historical tropes to further the narrative that Russia is under siege and that all true believers must be ready to sacrifice themselves so that the collective can live. In that sense, it is not an exaggeration to state that the regime, wittingly or unwittingly, is now promoting a death cult.

Into this maelstrom Belarus has been drawn. Ever since Aleksandr Lukashenka became president of Belarus in 1994 the country has been a close ally of Russia. Many analysts would argue that Belarus has been the closest ally. This is certainly what Lukashenka and his Russian counterparts have said. So, when Russia was going to challenge international order, was going to set Europe aflame again, it seemed inevitable that Belarus would follow. Yet is Belarus prepared to do so? And if Lukashenka decides to, or is forced to, stay close to Russia does this benefit the Kremlin or potentially make it more vulnerable?

The Russian leadership of today claims to be the vanguard of a civilisation, not a state. That Russian civilisation of which it speaks is the antithesis of a liberal democratic West. A West with powerful European and American backers which seeks to spread its totalising ideology and hierarchy across the globe. A West which is aggressive, subversive, and–ultimately–decaying. Against that egotistic individualism stands the Russian civilisation, centred on the Russian people but with Belarusians and true Ukrainians as brothers in arms. Ready to fight for a new world order in which traditional values and strong, masculine leadership rule over all.

For those of us who do not believe in the Russian elite and its values, who see the Kremlin and its allies as threatening us and the world, it is time to consider what can be done and what should be done in response. Yet in order to craft such a response we need to understand better the specific aims and motivations of Russia abroad. It is of particular importance to learn why and how Russia engages with allies, with those countries which seem to be fuelled by similar motivations and work towards similar aims. Such a country is Belarus.

The Argument

There are many similarities between Russia and Belarus and those similarities often stretch far back in time. Both countries are autocracies, which today offer almost no political or civic freedoms to their populations. Economic integration has been deep between the countries ever since Soviet days when the Russian and Belorussian Soviet republics were highly important to the Union. Military integration has picked up in recent years but has been pronounced for many decades if not centuries. And in terms of culture and identity many, and traditionally most, Russians and Belarusians see each other as part of the same community.

Nevertheless, a main point of this book is to show how Russia and Belarus also differ in numerous, important ways. True, they are both autocracies, but whereas the Russian autocrat seeks dominion over amorphous civilisation his Belarusian counterpart stands for statist sovereignty. Economically, they are closely integrated yet with increasingly diverging interests as Russia pulls away from Europe. Both Russia and Belarus are militarised, yet with a very different emphasis on the value of glorious conquest and stalwart defence. And while cultural links remain profound and are likely to last, Belarusian nationalism has become increasingly present in a form which is often incompatible with what Russia has become today.

Whether observers see Russia and Belarus as largely identical or not, there seems broad agreement that affairs in Belarus nowadays are largely controlled from Moscow. Particularly after 2020, when Lukashenka required economic and political assistance from Russia's Vladimir Putin to suppress and then largely suspend widespread popular domestic opposition to his rule. Even before that development, however, the Belarusian economy–indeed, its entire socio-economic system–was highly dependent on Russian help. A dependence which the Russian leadership learnt to very skilfully tie the smaller neighbour into a set of obligations reinforced by the presence of Russian military personnel in Belarus.

Unsurprisingly, war in Ukraine has strengthened Russian resolve to keep Belarus suppressed. Speculations continue about the viability of Belarusian independence, particularly when Lukashenka departs the stage. And yet, as this book will show it is remarkable how vigorously, and often very successfully, the Belarusian strongman has preserved manoeuvrability or reduced the Russian grip. By all accounts Putin and Lukashenka are not fond of each other and looking at their years of interaction it is not difficult to understand why. Their regimes are both fully deserving of condemnation—and yet, sometimes an observer can only laugh at the brazenness emanating from Minsk or the frustration clearly visible in Moscow.

It seems implicit in the above, and in most accounts of the bilateral relationship, that Belarus is an asset for Russia. Indeed, in many ways that is the case. As I mentioned, use of Belarusian territory and resources have enabled Russia to assault Ukraine. Belarus also offers credibility to Russian threats towards other neighbouring states. Furthermore, Minsk is offering Russia political support in international fora both for the invasion but also for attempts to keep the post-Soviet region close together. And while Belarus is much smaller and less wealthy than Russia it still has industrial assets and natural resources which Russian elites covet.

Yet there is also an argument to be made that Belarus is a threat to Russia–and that is an argument running through the narrative of this book. Gaining significant influence in, or even control over Belarusian territory also means that Russia has more territory to protect. In a wartime situation when Russian resources are stretched this could be a problem. In addition, while public protests have largely been removed from Belarusian public life there remains a widespread current of distaste or even anger directed towards the local leadership and that in Moscow. More insidious, however, is the presence of the uncanny in relations between Russia and Belarus.

The Uncanny

The idea of the uncanny arrives in psychology largely through the efforts of Sigmund Freud. By its German word "unheimlich", which can with some justification be translated as "un-homely", we see something clearly distinct from the personal and sacredly private sphere of the individual, yet still something in a relationship with that sphere.[1] Later, Jean Lacan builds on Freud's theory to develop his own understanding of "anxiety", which plays on the condition within human psychology that sees the individual torn

---

1   For a deeper engagement with the concept, see also Freud, 2003

between desires to move forward and to move back. Or, perhaps, torn between desires of freedom and of closure.[2]

Away from psychoanalysis, the uncanny also enters modernity through the arts. Arguably, this happens long before Freud. A straightforward example in literature is that of Mary Shelley's "modern Prometheus", better known as "Frankenstein", engaging with the interface between the possible and the permissible in an age when humanity overcomes what had seemed implacable natural obstacles.[3] Much older examples can be found of the uncanny in human productions (are grotesques on churches and in religious imagery there to remind us of what we are not or of what we can become?) yet there is something inherently transgressive in modernity which brings the uncanny into public consciousness.[4]

The uncanny, certainly, had always been present in human interaction if not necessarily been identified as so. Look to anthropologists such as Mary Douglas for the idea of that which is "taboo", by its nature unsuitable for society yet still holding a central role therein.[5] Or to religious historians such as Mircea Eliade who could view the "shaman" as an actor capable of straddling mutual untouchables, past and present, the material and the spiritual world, in order to assist the ordinary community's contact with that idealised past from which humans had strayed.[6]

Within interwar Europe Eliade had questionable inspirations. It does not take much effort to see links between his thoughts and palingenetic fascism. Still, the idealised state of nature and

---

2   Apart from going directly to Lacan's seminars on the topic of anxiety, a useful outline of his approach and its relationship with that of Freud can also be gleaned from Diatkine, 2006

3   And, of course, engaging with the interface of a young Mary Shelley between childhood and adulthood, between the premature death of several children and the birth of a celebrated literary monster (whether that monster is Adam, or Victor Frankenstein, or both is debatable). See also the extended quote in the excellent Moore, 2023: 41-42

4   The works of Friedrich Nietzsche would often be found in this landscape, notably viewing nihilism as inherently uncanny. On that, see also Nietzsche, 2017: book 1

5   Apart from Douglas' own works, there is a very clever approach to the interplay between taboo, disgust and morality by Giner-Sorolla and Sabo, 2016

6   For Eliade's thoughts on this, see Eliade, 2024

12   UNCANNY ALLIES

humanity's potential rebirth into it are central parts of allegedly progressive modernity and the Enlightenment. This is why Jean-Jacques Rousseau's understanding of democracy is, inherently, un-canny.[7] And it is why the Soviet Union, arguably one of the purest examples of putting (perceived) Enlightenment ideals into practice, could not avoid imparting premodern practices and thinking into the way in which the future was pursued. Be that, say, in the religious worship of Lenin or the fetishization of the personal, non-automatised interpersonal contact.[8]

From that Soviet heritage emerged Russia and Belarus and the identities through which their states are governed today. However, when I in this book refer to the "uncanny" I refer not simply to domestic affairs but to international relations, as well. To the assumption that perceptions and identities fundamentally matter for how states interact.[9] And to the assumption of social identity theory as transported to the international realm. Implying, therefore, that the interaction between those groups which we call states can be meaningfully analysed at a level beyond that of the individuals ruling or otherwise present in those states.[10]

That leads me back to the question of what, I will argue, is "uncanny" about the relationship between Russia and Belarus. Based on the above, I claim that what is uncanny for the subject, be that an individual or a state, is a conceivable alternate state, which is currently unrealised, yet which can be realised without the agency of the subject. This means that when I talk about an uncanny relationship between Russia and Belarus I am talking about a

---

7   In its relationship between general will and individual freedom, neither of which — in essence — can tolerate the other yet neither of which can be understood without its counterpart. On this point, I take note of the excellent counterargument by Thompson, 2017: 267, which argues for harmony between communitarianism and individualism in Rousseau's thinking, yet I would disagree that the individuals he describes can be called meaningfully "free."

8   In this context, the 1903 creation of the Bolshevik movement with its belief in revolution fundamentally independent from measurable, data-dependent socio-economic development seems to me pivotal. See also Janos, 1996: 3

9   Which is common for constructivist thinking in the discipline of International Relations, as discussed in a classic example by Guzzini, 2000

10   For a very helpful primer on the link between constructivism and social identity theory, see also Larson, 2012

relationship in which Belarus is viewed in Russia as the same "in essence" yet possessing a free will which can take it in a direction over which Russia does not have control. Now, the instinctive reaction of Russia to that danger is to dominate Belarus as far as possible. However, since Belarus is believed to essentially be the same as Russia the latter cannot put up a defence against anything in the former of which it disapproves. If there is not a clear distinction between subject and object in the Russian-Belarusian relationship there also cannot be a clear hierarchy between them.

This, in turn, points to a fundamental vulnerability in the nature of civilisation as understood within Russian policy thinking. The fact that the "Russian world" as interpreted under Vladimir Putin can be seen as potentially borderless, as arguably reaching into anything which has been deemed "Russian" by the leadership in Moscow, has been named as a threat to other groups everywhere. If anybody and any state can be a target for the Kremlin, then no one can feel safe. Perhaps, but that effect goes the other way, too. If Russia is to be potentially everything, then it is also potentially nothing. A state has a clearly defined structure (which may work more or less well in practice). Its constitution, or equivalent, sets out that structure and, even for those actors in the state who choose not to obey the constitution, it remains as a point of reference. There is no equivalent point of reference for the "Russian World". And if, say, Putin claims that reverence for the Soviet Union and its victory over Nazi Germany is essential to "Russianness", then he has a fundamental problem of status when a leader such as Lukashenka manages to commemorate those historic events at a time when Putin himself does not (as happened in 2020). If there is a public belief among those claimed by the "Russian World" that social welfare is a moral imperative, and if the Russian leadership cannot fulfil that imperative for its population as well as the Belarusian leadership can for the population under its daily administration then the Russian leadership risks suffering a fall in status incompatible with its understanding of Self. And if Russian elites outside the Kremlin begin to praise and even take lessons from the Belarusian regime then the masculine power around which Putin has constructed his mask is crumbling.

14   UNCANNY ALLIES

My claim, therefore, is that Belarus has the potential to be the doppelganger of Russia, and Lukashenka that of Putin. Whether it has achieved that aim is less important than the fact the risk exists, since the existence of that risk imbues the Russo-Belarusian relationship with a fundamental tension that cannot be overcome. Unless, perhaps, if one of the parties is utterly destroyed. However, as we saw in the analogous case of Yevgeny Prigozhin, even his untimely death could not turn attention away from the weakness which his rebellion had already exposed within the fabric of totalising Russianness.

The Method

My research for this book has been focused on the aim of understanding, rather than explaining. That distinction is fundamental to the social sciences and, ultimately, relates to the perceived nature of academic scholarship. It relates to the question of whether analysis of social affairs can, meaningfully, be compared to that of natural sciences.[11] When seeking to explain a social relation, such as that between states, a scholar begins deductively from theories the validity of which is then tested against empirical evidence. Conversely, when seeking to understand a social relation, the focus is on inductively beginning from the empirical material at hand to formulate analytical categories and conclusions.[12]

I seek to understand Russian relations with Belarus largely through textual analysis. The approach is discourse analysis, meaning that my research will be interpretative in nature. In practice, the individual messages and, occasionally, specific phrasings of texts, be those written or spoken will be analysed within the context of a

---

11   A foundational work on the differences between explanation and understanding, particularly in relation to international affairs, remains Hollis and Smith, 1990

12   While my analysis in this book does have constructivist assumptions (as noted above) those are not theories in the sense discussed here as they do not present predictions about cause and effect. In that sense the premises of this book align with the criticism of Alexander Wendt's positivism as presented by Kratochwil, 2000

broader political frame.[13] That context consists of material developments between the two countries. It also, however, considers global developments and, conversely, developments within each individual country. While the main focus here is on state behaviour that behaviour cannot be meaningfully understood without periodic involvement of domestic and wider international contexts.[14]

I have therefore consulted a wide array of secondary and primary texts. The first two main chapters are mostly based on secondary sources. Since an important function of these chapters is to provide support for what follows I have often built my findings here on existing scholarship, albeit reinterpreting and combining anew such prior analysis. The latter two chapters engage in-depth with the period between 2012 and 2024 and are therefore largely based on primary sources, chosen from a systematic search through the period covered of Russian and Belarusian nationwide media, governmental statements and the like as well as primary sources from other countries on a few occasions. Employing resources such as East View I searched Russian and Belarusian sources for relevant material, then sifting through the material found to include specific texts relevant for my topic and argument. Secondary research was here used for context and to assist efforts to ensure that no relevant texts or topics were omitted.

As I assembled and engaged with the sources used for the book I took inspiration from the approach of Ted Hopf. As outlined by Hopf, the aim was to categorise and, where this was deemed appropriate, re-categorise primary and secondary sources as my study progressed. Ultimately seeking to understand Russian and Belarusian identities as these developed separately and through constitutive interaction, my work aimed to define and distinguish tendencies within such identities only as the study progressed and always with the acceptance that such definitions and distinctions remained open to the interpretation, based on the sources used, of myself and of others.[15]

---

13   For textual analysis, see also Halperin and Heath, 2017: chapter 14

14   On levels of analysis in international relations, see also the engaging Temby, 2015

15   For the outline of Hopf's approach, see also Hopf, 2002: 23-38

To stress, such an approach does leave my findings open to challenge by those who either interpret the sources, which I used, in a different way, or decide that sources, which I left out, were relevant and necessary for the analysis at hand. The claim which I make to the validity of my findings, however, is based on the transparency with which I consult my sources and their meaning. That, I believe, is essential not only for interpretivist scholarship as such but also in an age where the impact of Artificial Intelligence on scholarship may be increasingly felt. To put it bluntly, when you, the reader, pay for this book with your money and your time you are not paying for access to one, unassailable truth about the topics at hand. You are paying to see into my mind as I grapple systematically with those topics. If you disagree with my findings, you will know the basis on which I made them and can challenge them accordingly. That, I would argue, brings an honesty and a meaning–central to the scholarly ethos–which texts written with input from Artificial Intelligence can never match.[16]

The Additional Literature

Beyond the works referenced in this book, the interested reader has a wide choice of English-language literature. Above, I have shown brief examples from existing scholarship on the uncanny and on social identity theory. In addition to works quoted there a reader interested further in topics of the uncanny might find interest in the chapters of The Monster Theory Reader, which does a fine job of showing the impact of the uncanny on social and cultural production through time.[17] Otherwise, anyone seeking to get "under the skin" of the uncanny would be well advised to consult literary giants such as Mary Shelley,[18] Edgar Allan Poe,[19] M.R. James,[20] Bram

---

16   Just as Artificial Intelligence cannot see the meaning in that eternal moment of Antonius Block and his strawberries with milk. For an excellent analysis of what Artificial Intelligence is, and is not, see Alang, 2024
17   On that work, see The Monster, 2020
18   Shelley, 2021
19   Poe, 2004
20   James, 2013

Stoker[21] or, indeed, a plethora of horror fiction from across the world.[22] As for social identity theory, Deborah Larson's above-mentioned chapter is a fine starting point. However, for an example of such theory linked to Russia the reader could also find much of use in Gulnaz Sharafutdinova's recent work[23] and, for a more international angle, Deborah Larson and Alexei Shevchenko's investigation of the Russo-Chinese relationship.[24]

Academic scholarship on Russia is enormous in quantity. As my book engages with questions of Russian identity–and presents historical background to understand the use and relevance of certain tropes used by elite actors today–a reader seeking to know more may consult Geoffrey Hosking's monograph on Russian history, still central of the field.[25] On the development of Russian identity, particularly under conditions of modernity, Vera Tolz offers a helpful guide.[26] A highly approachable comparative study of the Russian Empire is offered by Dominic Lieven,[27] while Nancy Kollmann specifically covers the empire's construction.[28] For the Soviet Union, an author who places that period in useful historical context is Robert Service.[29] Anyone seeking to understand the motives of the early Bolshevik elites could read Yuri Slezkine's epochal narrative.[30] And to understand where the Soviet Union headed, maybe consult Ronald Suny, who is also strong on how Soviet republics transformed into post-Soviet entities.[31]

In terms of Russian foreign policy, the English language work which still offers the broadest coverage is the overview produced by Robert Donaldson and Vidya Nadkarni.[32] There are also some useful insights about Russian foreign policy thinking to be gleaned

---

21   Stoker, 2021
22   A starting point may be Horror, 2012
23   Sharafutdinova, 2020
24   Larson and Shevchenko, 2019
25   Hosking, 2012
26   Tolz, 2001
27   Lieven, 2000
28   Kollmann, 2017
29   Service, 2020
30   Slezkine, 2017
31   Suny, 2010
32   Donaldson and Nadkarni, 2023

18   UNCANNY ALLIES

from the Routledge handbook on Russian international relations studies.[33] When it comes to Russian engagement with the post-Soviet region, the authors used in this book could well be complemented by those such as Johannes Socher[34] and Moritz Pieper,[35] as well as Kevork Oskanian and his unusual but quite thought-provoking conceptualisation of Russia's relationship to its surroundings.[36]

Belarus has increasingly become the focus of foreign academic attention in recent years. Apart from sources used in this book, a relatively new volume edited by Elena Korosteleva, Irina Petrova and Anastasiia Kudlenko offers fresh, varied perspectives.[37] Going back a few years, David Marples's work on Belarus and memory politics surrounding the Second World War remains relevant.[38] For Marples, it may also be worth the reader consulting his memoir on working with Belarus and Ukraine, which is a breezy, informative read.[39] As for Russian-Belarusian relations, such have mostly been covered by individual articles, although some important monographs by authors like Margarita Balmaceda are used in my work. For the reader who wants to understand the background of the more recent developments in the relationship, which I cover here, it might pay off to look at works by Ruth Deyermond[40] or by Alex Danilovich.[41]

The Structure

Apart from this introduction and the conclusion the book consists of four main chapters. These chapters are chronologically arranged. Chapter 1 takes the story of Russian-Belarusian relations, or relations between those territories part of Russia and Belarus today,

---

33   The Routledge, 2023
34   Socher, 2021
35   Pieper, 2021
36   Oskanian, 2021
37   Belarus, 2023a
38   Marples, 2014
39   Marples, 2020
40   Deyermond, 2007
41   Danilovich, 2006

from Medieval Kyivan Rus to the end of the Soviet Union. This background offered by the first part of this chapter shows how Russia developed relationships along its western borders with people living in modern-day Belarus but also in Poland. In fact, one significant take-away from this chapter is the role that Poland has historically played for Russia, particularly in and around the area where Belarus today can be found. Then, when the chapter moves to the Soviet era the reader can witness the development of a socialist Belarusian polity created partly by Russia-based Bolsheviks but also by local actors and developments which at times placed the interests and identities of Belarusian lands in conflict with those of the Soviet centre.

In chapter 2, the book then moves to the post-Soviet era as this developed until 2011. This is the chapter in which we see the arrival of Lukashenka as Belarusian president and the gradual rebuilding of Russia as a consistently significant foreign policy actor in the post-Soviet space and beyond. Whereas chapter 1 showed underlying themes on which contemporary Russian-Belarusian relations are build, this chapter very much brings the underlying importance of specific actors to the fore. In addition, there is an attempt in this chapter to engage with the question of why and how the potential for collaboration, even synchronicity between Russia and Belarus was often scuppered by domestic developments in the countries and diverging interests of the elites involved. In chapter 2 a subplot is also linked to the question of Western influence, or lack thereof, on the trajectory of Russia and Belarus and their international engagements. Particularly as we get to the latter part of Putin's presidency, and the interregnum under Dmitry Medvedev the question begins to be asked whether the West should have handled the two countries differently.

Chapters 3 and 4 then engage in-depth with the period, which is under particular scrutiny in this book. Here, the analysis gets quite detailed as it investigates how the Russo-Belarusian relationship moved through some of the most turbulent and violent years of modern European history. In chapter 3 we meet a Russia in a hurry. Putin's return to the presidency in 2012 begin the chapter and sees the Russian leader offer the West and the world a challenge from an assertive Russia. Since such assertion for Putin also involves sped-up integration in the post-Soviet space, Lukashenka is wary of how his power and Belarusian sovereignty may be undermined. At the same time, however, chapter 3 demonstrates the Belarusian regime's manoeuvrability in face of Russian pressure with Lukashenka and his supporters showing aptitude for the receival of benefits from Russia often without offering much in return. However, as the chapter progresses and as Russian foreign relations grow tense on the background of the invasion of Ukraine, Belarus appears to become increasingly constrained.

That development is even more evident after 2020 which is the year in which chapter 4 begins. This is the year during which Lukashenka faces widespread domestic protest following his presidential re-election and mishandling of the Covid-crisis. To survive, the Belarusian leader–with few other options for political survival–looks to Russia for help. Such help arrives, in economic and political terms and with a promise of military aid if need be. Locked in by Russia's influence in this way the Belarusian elite has little opportunity for deviation from Russia in 2022 when the full-scale invasion of Ukraine begins. Lukashenka's position as an accessory to the war is placed in even starker relief by the outspoken anti-war messages broadcast by his detractors, mostly from exile. However, chapter 4 also demonstrates how the Belarusian regime is keenly aware of broader public dissatisfaction in the country with the war in Ukraine and how the regime therefore frequently speaks for peace, albeit with little detail added. In mid-2024, when the narrative ends, Russia and Belarus remain aligned, yet it is clear that such alignment is based on immediate interest rather than deep-seated affinity between the regimes. The question of whether societies of Russia and Belarus still feel such affinity for each other is uncertain at time of writing.

1   917-1991

Kyivan Rus'

Medieval Europe was a fluid world. Following the dissolution of large parts of the Roman Empire, rulers on the continent spent centuries imposing order on their surroundings. Even when they succeeded, however, order was fleeting. Charlemagne's empire soon broke up; Augustine's ideal city was far away.[42] Into that world developed Kyivan Rus. Centred on the city of Kyiv, it was less a state–with unquestioned, central sovereignty–than an amalgam of principalities sometimes united yet often disparate. It was a trading realm, with principalities covering rivers and roads, which ferried goods between north and south.[43] And it was largely for pecuniary reasons that Volodymyr in 988 adopted Christianity as the official religion of Kyivan Rus. Volodymyr would not be the first Christian ruler of the land, and his personal piety is doubtful at best. Yet to the south lay the Byzantine Empire, Roman heir and centre of wealth.[44] Thus, becoming Christian was a way for elites in Kyivan Rus to signal their adherence to Byzantine ways. To the north of Kyiv, in Polatsk within modern-day Belarusian territory, Usiaslav soon learned the same lesson. In the mid-11th century, he built a cathedral to St Sophia meant to mirror the cathedral in Kyiv.[45]

That cathedral was meant as a signal to two constituencies. To rulers in Kyiv, and in other principalities within Kyivan Rus, Usiaslav stated his prominence. When he had finished building his cathedral, Usiaslav's forces would later battle forces belonging to his competitors and briefly rule the city of Kyiv.[46] More important than the variegated fate of Usiaslav, however, was the commitment he, together with other rulers in Kyivan Rus, had made to the church of Constantinople. After 1054, when that church split

---

42   For an overview of the period, see also Wickham, 2009
43   A useful depiction of Kyivan Rus is in Raffensperger, 2012
44   Franklin and Shepard, 1996, provides context
45   The entry and spread of the church in Kyivan Rus is described in McGuckin, 2020: 159-61
46   Dimnik, 2004: 256

22 UNCANNY ALLIES

decisively from its Roman counterpart, the principalities of Kyivan Rus seemed to be turned decisively southwards, rather than towards Central Europe.[47] The Belarusian lands would later become a borderland between Russia-dominated steppes and Central European powers. Kyivan Rus, in turn, would fall away as a centre of power. After its princes had reconfirmed their individual sovereignty relative to the centre through agreement at Liubech in 1097, the 12th century witnessed frequent infighting and dissolution.[48] Into that world of uncertainty Moscow appeared. Mentioned for the first time in chronicles in 1147, however, the later capital of Russia began as little more than a forested outpost. At that time, Moscow had none of the prominence of cities like Pskov or Ryazan, let alone the riches held by Novgorod.[49]

The Mongols

Or, indeed, the riches held by Vladimir, which in 1169 sponsored a raid on Kyiv, carrying plunder from there to the northeast. Formally, Kyiv would lose primacy in Rus only by 1299 when the metropolitanate was moved to Vladimir, yet that earlier raid had demonstrated conclusively the degradation of the centre.[50] Belarusian lands were similarly turbulent during the 12th century. The principality of Usiaslav, Polatsk, split into smaller domains fighting against each other, while also trying to regain influence in Kyiv. That aim remained elusive–partly because a unifying Polatsk was missing, but also because the Belarusian lands increasingly found themselves under external threat.[51] To the north, near the Baltic Sea, in 1201 was founded the city of Riga. Here, the rulers sought to Christianise Baltic pagan tribes, but they also–and often more vigorously–sought to colonise important trade routes and settlements along the Daugava and other rivers, bringing Germanic knights in

---

47 For an account of the schism and its protagonists, see also Khislavski, 2021
48 The gradual disintegration of Kyivan Rus is outlined in Martin, 2007: chapter 4
49 A brief summary of early Moscow is in Galeotti, 2022a: 6-14
50 A point also made in Subtelny, 2009: chapter 1
51 The gradual encroachment on Polatsk by neighbouring realms is mentioned by Plokhy, 2006: 95

direct conflict with Rus principalities.[52] That threat grew in 1226, when a Polish nobleman, Konrad, called into his lands the Teutonic Order. That knightly organisation had gained renown, and riches, from the Crusades and now turned against Prussian pagans. By mid-century, the Order had absorbed the knights of Riga, subsequently knows as the Livonian Order.[53]

The Teutonic Order and its allies would likely have conquered further lands to the east if not for a new ruler emerging from the city of Novgorod, Aleksandr Nevsky. Nevsky subjugated Vladimir and placed his son, Daniil, in charge of Moscow thus placing foundations for the importance of the latter.[54] And Nevsky kept back not only Teutonic Knights but also Swedes in semi-mythologised battles on Lake Peipus and the river Neva. Some later accounts have argued these battles entrenched divisions between West and East. That interpretation is overly deterministic, yet Nevsky's victories certainly gave Novgorod and its dependencies ability to consolidate regional primacy.[55] Or rather, the victories would have done so if not for a much greater threat now emerging across the Eurasian steppe. Decades earlier, advance raiding parties of Mongols had tested defences of Rus cities. Now, Batu's armies came back in greater numbers, conquering in less than a decade almost all of Kyivan Rus.[56] Most portentous of all was the destruction, in 1240, of the city of Kyiv itself. Unlike the earlier attack by Vladimir, now the metropolitan cradle was crushed under alien, seemingly unstoppable forces. Those princes of Rus, like Nevsky, who thrived under Mongol rule did so not through armed resistance but through diplomacy and servitude.[57]

---

52 Riga in the context of the northern crusades is described in O'Connor, 2019: chapter 2
53 The activities of the Teutonic Order in the Baltic Region are discussed in Knoll, 2008
54 A useful analysis of later Russian depictions of Alexander Nevsky is in Isoaho, 2006
55 Selart, 2015: chapter 3, provides good context for the military activity
56 A recent work on the Mongols is Favereau, 2021. Chapter 2 describes the conquest of Russian lands
57 Martin, 2006, shows the ways in which the Russian lands sought to adjust to Mongol dominance

24   UNCANNY ALLIES

Nowhere was that seen more clearly than in the rise of Moscow. Muscovite ruler Ivan controlled Vladimir by convincing the Mongol leadership of his dependability as a tax collector. Once in charge of Vladimir, Ivan moved the metropolitanate to Moscow, building a new church there and, from 1328, ruling as Grand Prince.[58] This placed Moscow well for subsequent domination of Russian lands. However, for now the Mongols remained in charge, readily sending armed forces to punish recalcitrant subjects. The Belarusian lands, in the meantime, were increasingly subject to growing pagan influence, consolidated under Mindaugas in the Grand Duchy of Lithuania.[59] Modern-day Belarusian historians have at times highlighted Belarusian influence in the Grand Duchy, partly through the temporary prominence of the city of Navahrudak. However, while that city was certainly notable within the Grand Duchy, it never gained the importance of Vilnius, made capital under Gediminas in the first half of the 14th century.[60] Gediminas, and Algirdas after him, spent the 14th century expanding Lithuania to the south and the east. A feat made the more remarkable by the plague, which otherwise ravaged European populations and economies at the time. By doing so, this growing state became a direct challenger to Moscow.[61]

More immediately, however, Lithuania clashed with the Mongols. Over a century after its entry on the European stage, the so-called Golden Horde was already strained from internal power struggles. And in 1362 it suffered its first significant military defeat in Europe to Algirdas' Lithuania at the Battle of Blue Waters.[62] Muscovite prince Dmitry Donskoy would have his own victory over Mongol forces eighteen years later. Yet not only had the internal decline of the Golden Horde developed further by that time, but Donskoy's victory proved fleeting with Moscow itself being sacked

---

58   For the transfer of authority in Rus to Moscow, see also Halperin, 2022: 12
59   Of course, the extent of Belarusian influence on Lithuania remains debated. See e.g. Astapenia, 2014
60   For the history of Navahrudak, see also Kananovich, 2016
61   A depiction of the territory of Lithuania and Poland in the 13th and 14th centuries can be found in Magocsi, 2018: 20-22
62   For the context to the battle, see also Mykhaylovskiy, 2019: chapter 4

in return by Mongol forces two years later.[63] Thus, if the late fourteenth century witnessed a potential successor to the Mongols' regional dominance that successor looked more likely to come from Vilnius than from Moscow. Particularly after 1386 when the marriage of Lithuanian Jogaila to Polish Jadwiga instituted a personal union between those two realms.[64] In a further flourish, the Teutonic Knights would be defeated in the Battle of Tannenberg in 1410 by joint Polish-Lithuanian forces. The Knights survived their defeat but would get little future support from Christian rulers, since the ruler of Lithuania by now had been Christianised through the personal union with Poland.[65]

The Rise of Muscovy

More pertinently, however, Christian Europe now had bigger problems than Baltic pagans. The Ottoman threat to Byzantium provoked the Council of Ferrara in 1438-39 where representatives of the Eastern Church formally accepted Papal sovereignty in return for promised military aid against the Muslim enemy.[66] The Russian envoy agreed to that deal yet was denounced upon returning to Moscow. The deal did little for Byzantium, too, which fell to the Ottomans in 1453. And within the Russian church, and society, now built a belief that the realm was–and perhaps should be–sealed off from a sinful world.[67] Here it was clearly important, as well, that the Kyivan metropolitanate in 1458–only five years after Byzantium's fall–declared itself independent of the Muscovite church. That split in the eastern church reached back some years, yet now had the immediate implication that even Orthodox believers within Lithuanian lands were separated from Muscovite believers.[68] Ivan

---

63   The changing fortunes of Moscow and the Rus' lands in relations with the Mongols are covered in de Hartog, 1996

64   Matters might, however, have been rather different had Jogaila instead become related to Donskoy. See also Christian, 2018: 75

65   The battle of Tannenberg and its context is covered by Hofbauer, 2010

66   The Council of Ferrara (and its continuation in Florence) is outlined in Chadwick, 2003: chapter 41

67   The fall of Byzantium is the subject of Crowley, 2005

68   See also Gudziak, 1998: chapter 3

III, ruler of Moscow from 1462, was keen to retain Russian connections to Europe. As the church increasingly championed the idea of Russia as a "Third Rome", the tsar was happy to link his image to that of Byzantium–notably by marrying Zoe Palaeologus, niece of the last emperor, in 1472.[69]

Beyond that eye-catching ceremony, Ivan III believed that international relevance would be based on expansion of his lands. Particular success was achieved during the 1470s, when Novgorod was defeated and subjugated. Not only did that provide access to rich resources; it also forced that important city away from the Lithuanians.[70] During the following decades, Moscow also took the cities of Tver and Pskov. Thus, by the early 16th century it was hard to see any serious challenge to Muscovite rule coming from inside the Russian lands. Even the Golden Horde was finally gone; after military victory in 1480 Russia no longer recognised its supremacy.[71] Yet to the West, Poland-Lithuania remained a barrier. Novgorod and its northern territories might now belong to Moscow, yet the latter otherwise found itself still further isolated from Central Europe. Some trade involved Moscow, such as through the Hanseatic League across the Baltic Sea, but a European great power Moscow was not.[72] So, Moscow was kept separate from some technological and cultural developments encompassing most of Europe. In contrast, the Belarusian lands were linked to such developments through Poland-Lithuania and the upcoming Habsburg Empire. Symbolically telling was the printing by a Belarusian-language bible in Prague by Francysk Skaryna in the early 16th century.[73]

In a world where political legitimacy still linked closely to religion–and where Protestants now pushed the vernacular into church services–such publicization of the Belarusian language could signal a definitive break by the Belarusian lands with

---

69   The development of the idea of the Third Rome is treated by Duncan, 2000
70   Arguably, though, Ivan III did not take full economic advantage of his conquest. See Martin, 2023
71   That change is described in Khodarkovsky, 2002: chapter 3
72   Relations with the Hanseatic League are shown in Tiberg, 1995
73   Skaryna remains under-exposed, although a defence of his importance is in Francysk, 2017

Muscovy and its entry into the cross-cultural, trade-heavy Central Europe.[74] Whereas Moscow now came under Ivan the Fourth, whose rule would be burdened by domestic power struggles–including the tsar's subsequently infamous techniques of terror–and protracted struggle against peoples of the steppe. Still, if Ivan the Fourth was largely excluded from European affairs this was of necessity rather than choice.[75] To the south, Ivan faced the Crimean Tatars, protected by the Ottoman Empire yet also a formidable force in their own right. In 1571 the Crimean Tatars even sacked Moscow. It was to prevent similar attacks, as much as for plunder, that Ivan conquered the steppe khanates of Kazan and Astrakhan.[76] Turning to the west, Ivan had little lasting success against Poland-Lithuania. Decades would be spent fighting over Livonia, through which Moscow hoped for stable access to the Baltic Sea and accompanying possibilities for trade. By the time of Ivan the Fourth's death in 1584, though, no such access had been acquired.[77]

Limited inroads had been made into the Belarusian lands early in the war with Poland-Lithuania. In the early 1560s the medieval city of Polatsk had been taken. However, consolidation of this and other gains was not achieved, with Ivan notoriously losing the services of Andrey Kurbsky, the successful military leader defecting to the enemy.[78] And Kurbsky appeared to have chosen wisely. The 1569 Union of Lublin transformed the personal union into a Polish-Lithuanian Commonwealth, institutionalising the Polish-Lithuanian Commonwealth. That Commonwealth placed itself on the frontline against Muscovite Russia, through its territorial ambition but also as a centre of the counter-Reformation with the Jesuit order consolidating in Vilnius.[79] While it was too late to eradicate Protestantism, the church in Rome now pushed back against the changes, often without the doctrinal flexibility earlier publicised

---

74   Confessional context is also provided in Eberhard, 1995
75   A classic account of Ivan IV's rule is de Madariaga, 2005
76   On these conquests, see also Perrie and Pavlov, 2003: chapter 3
77   Ivan IV's Baltic aims are described in Halperin, 2019: chapter 12
78   Kurbsky's correspondence with Ivan IV has been frequently debated. An outline of that debate is in Bogatyrev, 2012
79   On the Union of Lublin, see also Kiaupienė, 2001

28   UNCANNY ALLIES

by people like Erasmus. Facing Rome's advances, the church in Moscow needed allies and gained a boost with the visit and recognition from the Patriarch of Constantinople in 1589.[80] Such recognition was a domestic ideological boon for the otherwise enfeebled leadership of Fyodor, who had become tsar after Ivan the Fourth. Yet internationally the Patriarch's blessing did little for Russian influence. In the Belarusian lands, the 1596 Union of Brest instead saw local Eastern Orthodox churches declaring loyalty to the Pope.[81]

Although that Union might have had some foundation in religious belief it was clearly linked, too, to Muscovite political weakness. Over the following decades, indeed, the stability of that realm would come to breaking point, through the elite disputes marring the Time of Troubles.[82] After the disputed reign of Boris Godunov, no unified leader of Muscovy could be found. That power vacuum was exploited by Poland-Lithuania. First, it sponsored the so-called "False Dmitry" in his battle against Godunov and then, during 1605-06, his rule in Moscow and promotion of Catholicism.[83] Dmitry was soon killed, yet the new ruler–Vasily the Fourth–had little support from the nobility. By 1610 the Poles were again back in control, working with selected Russian nobility to place troops in Moscow and holding the realm by force. Deprivation and uprising followed, until the occupation was ended two years later.[84] This unedifying episode has been held up by later Russian historians and rulers as an example of the link between a strong Russian leader and stability–something gradually acquired under the Romanov dynasty from 1613 onwards–but also as a reminder that the western borderlands were a source of subversion.[85]

That sense of danger remained through the seventeenth century. Gradually, too, would rise the threat from Scandinavia and, particularly, from Sweden. As had previously been believed by

---

80   For this, see Goldfrank, 2020: 12
81   On the Union of Brest, see also Dmitriev, 2011
82   A dramatic recount of Ivan the Fourth's life and death is in Troyat, 2001
83   The reign of the False Dmitry would have long roots in Russian art and self-perception. For that, see Morris, 2018
84   A useful survey of the Time of Troubles is Dunning, 2004
85   For a conceptual and historical defence of that view, see Tsygankov, 2014: chapter 2

Ivan the Fourth, access to the Baltic Sea could circumvent Polish-Lithuanian terrestrial control, yet that advantage could not genuinely be sought until the rule of Peter.[86] During the early decades of the century, instead, the Romanovs consolidated their rule in Russia. Sweden was kept at bay with the 1617 Treaty of Stolbovo. Relations with Poland-Lithuania remained more volatile; a long truce between the countries, culminated in a few years of war during the 1630s.[87] Yet by mid-century Russian fortunes seemed mostly tied to the eastern steppes and Siberia. Then came the rebellion of the Ukrainian Cossacks under Bohdan Khmelnitsky against Poland-Lithuania, or, rather, for affirmation of rights for the local nobility. While the rebels were mostly found in modern-day Ukrainian lands, Belarusian lands, too, were affected.[88] It was in and through Belarusian territories that Polish-Lithuanian troops advanced on Khmelnitsky and his allies–and it was across that territory that Moscow and Warsaw fought after the Cossacks sought Russian assistance. Portentously, when that war was ended with the 1667 Treaty of Andrusovo, Russian borders had come westwards up to Belarusian lands.[89]

The Russian Empire

Two decades later, Russian relations with Poland-Lithuania would be further stabilised through the so-called "Permanent Peace". At the same time, Russia marked its intent to remain an important part of the European political scene by joining the Holy League, aimed against Ottoman control of the Balkans.[90] It would be almost a century before Russia could advance practically to the south. Yet symbolically the scene was set for Peter's promotion of Russia as a European great power. By the turn of the 18th century, the Russian tsar travelled across northern Europe, eager to learn from military and

---

86 Sweden's growing impact on the Baltic Sea region is shown in Kent, 2008: chapter 4
87 Lukowski, 2014: 92
88 Plokhy, 2012: 35-39, summarises the uprising
89 The Treaty led to local protests. See also Shiyan, 2011
90 Merriman, 2019: 270-71 notes the beginning of statist balance of power politics in Europe during this period

naval competitors.[91] And eager to defeat them in battle, too. Following early defeats to Sweden in what came to be known as the Great Northern War, Russian forces pushed forward decisively to the Baltic Sea. That advance was made permanent with the foundation in 1703 of a new capital, St Petersburg.[92] And it was supported, too, by a newly bureaucratised and cameralised approach to governance in Russia. Notably, seeking to take advantage of the large population in the country Peter introduced a permanent, standing army based on conscription among taxpayers. Thereby formalising the role of the population in biopolitical terms.[93]

The Belarusian lands were at the frontline of the Great Northern War and, thus, more influenced than most territories held by Russia. Sweden held territory there for a brief period, notably with the 1708 occupation of the city of Mogilev and would clearly have been central in any attempt to advance eastwards.[94] As it were, the Swedes under Charles XII would come decisively undone in the 1709 battle of Ukrainian Poltava. With that Russian victory, Russia had become a regional, if not quite a continental, great power. And he had seemingly halted attempts by enemies to use Russia's western borderlands as a springboard for attack.[95] Could the Russian gains be consolidated? Certainly, the outcome of the Great Northern War sought to do so. Following the 1721 Treaty of Nystad, Russia took control of the Baltic region. Peter had himself declared emperor and looked to spread Russia further afield, notably towards the Black Sea.[96] Yet for much of the eighteenth century, Russia would be preoccupied with domestic affairs. Peter's untimely death was followed by dynastic uncertainty. Even when Elizabeth and Catherine the Second managed to stabilise the realm, they found it prudent to retain limited involvement only in the major international conflagration that was the Seven Years' War.[97]

---

91   Hughes, 2002: chapter 3
92   For the Great Northern War, see Frost, 2001: chapters 9-10
93   Fuller Jr, 2006
94   Sweden's approach to the war is partly outlined in Ericson, 1997
95   Englund, 1992
96   Russian foreign policy advances under Peter are shown in Hughes, 1998: chapter 2
97   For that war, and Russia's hesitant participant, see Szabo, 2008

Catherine the Second, though, would prove willing to gamble abroad when resistance was limited. Apart from successes around the Black Sea, to the west Russia took advantage of increasing Polish politico-military paralysis by dismembering the historic enemy with Austrian and Prussian assistance. That process saw eastern Belarusian lands incorporated in Russia from 1772.[98] And all the while Russia was hovering over its neighbour, the latter was clearly seen by Catherine the Second as a bit of a Wild West. Not least after the second partition of Poland, in 1793, brought a substantial increase in the Jewish population under Russian sovereignty.[99] In this way, the newly acquired territories became symptomatic for Catherine the Second's conflicted view of burgeoning modernity. Corresponding with Enlightenment notables she may have been; still, the Russian ruler remained wary of rebellious tendencies, not least in the Belarusian lands now taken from Poland.[100] By the time of her death in 1796, Catherine controlled almost all of modern-day Belarus. She had not, however, succeeded in subduing nationalist sentiments of those Poles and other local groups who would be claiming local autonomy or even independence periodically throughout the following century, not least from educational establishments such as Vilnius University.[101]

Arguing that Belarusian nationalism was rather undeveloped at this time is missing the point. In the shadow of the French Revolution European elites were unsettled, fearing the turmoil which agitators like Napoleon could stir up. The 1807 Treaty of Tilsit did align Russia with France, but only temporarily.[102] Come 1812, French troops poured eastwards, using the Duchy of Warsaw and then Belarusian lands to reach Moscow. Famously, Russia soon

---

98   Subsequent history writing in the Russian Empire would depict Catherine the Second's gradual takeover of Belarusian lands from Poland-Lithuania as saving Belarusians from Polish oppression. See also Marples, 2005: 899
99   For context, see Polonsky, 2013: chapter 2
100   An engaging view on Catherine the Second's relationship with the Enlightenment is Zaretsky, 2019
101   For Vilnius at the end of Catherine the Second's reign and beyond, see Weeks, 2015: chapter 2
102   Adams, 2006: chapter 5 shows Russian vacillations regarding Napoleon's rise

32   UNCANNY ALLIES

expelled Napoleon, thereby precipitating his decline and fall a few years later. Nevertheless, as had been the case two centuries before Russia had seen its western borderlands allow passage of an existential threat.[103]Unlike before, though, this time Russia, too, could take advantage of those borderlands to spill westwards into Central Europe. The 1815 Congress of Vienna and its aftermath saw Russia in a dominant role, also leading in the conservative Holy Alliance and creating a Congress Poland to its liking.[104] Alexander then spent the last years of his rule clamping down on groups seen as a threat to future domestic stability. In a tendency, which would last throughout the nineteenth century, students in the Belarusian lands and elsewhere were targeted, including by measures preventing them from studying abroad.[105]

As supposed subversives the Jesuits were also expelled from the empire, removing their influence on education in the Belarusian lands and, particularly, from their historic base in Vilnius. By 1832, the university of Vilnius would be closed, followed soon after by edicts directing the exclusive use of Russian over Polish in schools.[106] That tightening of control over areas in and around Poland was linked to increasingly authoritarian governance in Russia overall under Nicholas, who had become emperor in turbulent circumstances in 1825, but more explicitly to the anti-Russian insurrection, which had shaken Polish, Belarusian and Lithuanian lands during the early 1830s.[107] Nicholas now saw threats even from smaller peoples in the empire, eventually banning even the use of Belarusian and Lithuanian as terms by 1840. The previous year, bishops in Polatsk had renounced the Union of Brest, taking the majority of the population in Belarusian lands into the Russian Orthodox Church.[108] Nicholas' conservative priorities seemed fitting to his activity abroad, where the Holy Alliance in 1849 had

---

103   A definitive work on Russia's war against Napoleon is Lieven, 2009
104   Zamoyski, 2007, offers a helpful overview of the Congress of Vienna
105   An outline of Alexander's complicated reign is in Rey, 2012
106   For details on how Russification now proceeded in the Empire, see Kappeler, 2001: chapter 7
107   The revolt magnified contemporary tension between ideas of unitary statehood vs empire in Russia; see also LeDonne, 2020: chapter 3
108   On that conversion and its nuances, see Skinner, 2019

motivated a Russian military expedition to assist Vienna against Hungarian rebels. Yet that triumph, and four decades of prominence in European politics, ended abruptly during the Crimean War, which exposed Russian military weakness.[109]

Recognising that outdated governance and social structures kept Russia behind modernising rivals, Alexander the Second used the aftermath of the Crimean defeat to catch up by widespread domestic reforms–most notably through the emancipation of serfs in 1861 and the so-called "zemstvo" reforms of local governance.[110] It proved difficult, however, to align such policies, and the urbanisation resulting from freed and impoverished peasants seeking employment in the cities, with continued emphasis on statist infallibility and control. Belarusian lands were in the midst of that dilemma. From 1862, their connection to imperial centres were ensured by railways.[111] First, the railway moving from St Petersburg to Warsaw and during the 1870s by a railway linking Moscow and Brest. Clearly, new transport links could aid local economic development, but it also facilitated the arrival of imperial troops called in to suppress, once more, local uprising in and around Belarus in the early 1860s.[112] And, of course, such railways were essential for Russian attempts at renewed assertion against European competitors. From the 1870s onwards, St Petersburg had somewhat overcome its post-Crimean irrelevance, notably on the Balkans, where the Ottomans were decisively defeated, and through alliances with first Germany and subsequently France.[113]

It is not inconceivable that a longer reign by Alexander the Second, and a less volatile Europe, could have seen Russia return to continental prominence and, perhaps, concomitant feelings of domestic security. As it were, however, the assassination of

---

109   For the Crimean War, see Figes, 2010
110   The economic impact of those reforms is discussed in Gregory, 1994: chapter 2
111   A clever take on how infrastructural developments made the empire both more capable and more vulnerable can be seen in Schenk, 2010
112   The uprising became an early focal point for statist defenders worried about links between the two subversive movements of modernity, socialism and nationalism. For this, see Kelly, 2016: chapter 20
113   Russia's foreign policy resurgence and limitations are analysed in LeDonne, 1997: chapter 12

Alexander the Second in 1881 sent imperial rule into a downward spiral.[114] The assassination was swiftly followed by renewed police repression of even obscure oppositional groups. Being placed, therefore, in a situation without realistic access to legal political power, organisations such as the Russian Social-Democratic Labor Party, founded in Minsk, sought wholescale societal transformation, arguably unlike contemporary socialists in Germany.[115] Into the twentieth century Russia was now ruled by Nicholas the Second, a man with little aptitude or vision for leadership. Following years of socio-economic malaise, and foreign policy fiasco, 1905 witnessed the beginning of state-wide unrest, which the regime could suppress militarily, yet without offering its population any long-term solutions.[116] The emperor did accept the creation in 1906 of a parliament, the so-called Duma, which included socialist representatives and Poles from Belarus and Ukraine. However, Nicholas the Second retained, and repeatedly used, the right to dissolve that and subsequent parliamentary assemblies, removing even the vestige of parliamentarianism and decentralisation.[117]

Partly through conviction and partly through expediency, Nicholas the Second increasingly appealed to Russian nationalism, provoking some backlash from minority nationalities, the cause of which was aided by growing literacy in the provinces. Among Belarusians, the journal Nasha Niva would become perhaps the first sustained centre of nationalist thought.[118] It may be fair to note that ordinary peasants and workers, still the clear majority of inhabitants in the Belarusian lands, saw limited attraction in Belarusian independence at this time. However, there was widespread resistance to imperial centralisation and overt Russification, notably as part of the agricultural reforms attempted by prime minister

---

114 While dealing with an earlier assassination attempt against Aleksandr the Second, the general confluence of terrorism and modernity in the context of the Russian Empire is illuminated well in Verhoeven, 2009
115 On that process, see also Riga, 2012: especially chapter 2
116 Lih, 2007, provides a helpful overview of views on this unrest and its aftermath
117 The potential, and repression, of the Duma is shown in Semyonov, 2009
118 For this, see also Ioffe, 2003a: 1247, even if the author somewhat downplays the importance of these events

Peter Stolypin.[119] Stolypin had understood that the Russian regime still required swift economic progress to prevent renewed widespread unrest or even revolution. But his assassination in 1911 reinforced the rudderless nature of the imperial elite, and less than three years later a complicated system of international alliances pulled Russia into the First World War.[120] For that cataclysmic event, the empire was ill-prepared. Following brief optimism at the onset of the conflict, the Russian army suffered decisive defeat against German troops at Tannenberg. By 1915, most of the Belarusian lands were under German occupation and would remain so throughout the war.[121]

The Revolution and the Bolsheviks

By the winter of 1916-17 the First World War showed no sign of ending and the Russian Empire saw little possibility of military success. Emperor Nicholas II had gone to the frontline, leaving his administration in the capital rudderless as unrest broke out before he was forced to abdicate in March.[122] The remainder of 1917 witnessed power struggles between parliamentary and extra-parliamentary forces in Petrograd, as well as frequent lawlessness across the Empire. By November, Lenin's Bolsheviks took power by default rather design, when the internationally recognised government under Aleksander Kerensky ran out of allies within both the working classes and the old elites.[123] However, having control in Petrograd was no guarantee of more wide-ranging success. Lenin could abolish the parliamentary system, yet he held little immediate credibility with peasants and the many non-Russian peoples of the Empire. Consequently, such peoples now declared sovereignty

---

119 Stolypin, though, saw Belarusian peasants as potential allies against Polish nobles. See Bushkovitch, 2011: 289

120 How Russia was drawn into the war is covered in detail by Lieven, 2015

121 A brief summary of military developments on the eastern front during the First World War is in Jukes, 2002

122 For the revolution of March (or February, according to the calendar then in place in Russia), see Hasegawa, 2017

123 The resultant "Russian Revolution" has been covered more than almost any other event in modern history. For a useful overview, see Wade, 2017

36   UNCANNY ALLIES

relative to the centre, as seen with the All-Belarusian Congress in Minsk that December.[124]

At that time the Congress, like similar national institutions elsewhere in the collapsing Empire, did not necessarily seek independence. If anything, protection from Petrograd against the German invaders was more prized in Minsk. Unfortunately, the Bolsheviks had neither ability nor inclination to defend frontier lands, which were abandoned in the Brest-Litovsk Treaty that March.[125] The Bolsheviks had hitherto expected their power grab to inspire worldwide revolution among the working classes. When such revolution remained absent, cessation of fighting with the Germans, even at the price of substantial losses of land, was seen by Lenin as necessary for regime survival. Belarusian elites, perhaps inevitably, felt abandoned and declared independence.[126] Yet from the outset Belarusian independence seemed doomed. German troops wanted to consolidate their gains in the east while preparing for a final push on the Western front. Consequently, any Belarusian hopes for genuine political autonomy were ill-starred. The Bolsheviks, in their turn, soon declared the Red Terror to defend and expand their gains anew.[127]

Over the following years, the Bolsheviks would consolidate their dominance in most of the territory of the former Russian Empire. Belarusian lands were an important part of Bolshevik plans, and after the First World War had officially ended the beginning of 1919 saw the creation of the Belorussian Soviet Socialist Republic (BSSR).[128] Yet although the BSSR had come into existence through co-optation of some Belarusian nationalists, tension between those and the Bolsheviks grew. The latter wanted to dominate the new political creation and when Belarusian lands that February were merged with Lithuanian areas in the so-called Litbel it appeared

---

124   An interesting comparative, historiographical view of the interplay between the Revolution and national movements is Semyonov and Smith, 2017
125   The Brest-Litovsk Treaty is covered in Chernev, 2017
126   Swain, 2022, discusses the Bolsheviks' hopes for world revolution
127   On the introduction of the Bolshevik Red Terror, see also Gerwarth and Horne, 2012
128   For a helpful account of the inconclusive peace brought to Eurasia by the end of the First World War, see Rieber, 2014: chapter 6

designed to weaken Belarusian (and Lithuanian) national coherence.[129] Nevertheless, both parties would soon have other concerns than those of power-sharing. The civil war, which had developed significantly during the previous year, now saw noticeable offensives by defenders of the old regime, the so-called Whites, answered by Bolshevik counter-offensives beginning late in the summer.[130]

The Bolsheviks would gradually come to dominate the civil war, partly due to superior logistics and partly to the substantial differences in aims and composition between various White armies and other, more local counterparts. What the Bolsheviks could not control, however, was turmoil in Central Europe and the reappearance of a Polish state.[131] The year of 1920 would experience protracted territorial battles between Bolshevik Russia and Poland with first Petrograd and then Warsaw threatened by invasion. October saw an armistice, which, with a peace treaty added in March 1921, consolidated borders for almost two decades and left about half of Belarusian lands under Polish control.[132] That the Bolsheviks compromised on ambitions for expansion proved a turning point for Leninist policy. Admittedly, world revolution had not been abandoned. The adoption of the 21 conditions by the Bolshevik-led Communist International (Comintern) in Moscow in the summer of 1920 stressed the primacy of world revolution and of Bolshevik leadership struggling against capitalism.[133]

The Comintern would come to play an important role in Bolshevik foreign policy. Its success would be measured on ability to subvert enemy regimes. Still, such subversion was not imminent in Poland or elsewhere. Conversely, the Bolsheviks worried that their own rule remained fragile–the Kronstadt rebellion of 1921 proved

---

129   The creation of the BSSR and later Litbel is summarised by Pipes, 1997: 150-54

130   Developments in the civil war are analysed well in Engelstein, 2017: 361-582

131   On the reappearance of Poland as an independent state after the First World War, see also Böhler, 2018

132   Borzęcki, 2008, offers a thorough account of the peace treaty and its consequences

133   The 21 conditions were meant to ensure discipline under Bolshevik leadership in the Communist International in a manner not dissimilar to "democratic centralism" in Russia. See also Vatlin and Smith, 2014

a reminder of this.[134] Now, Bolshevik Russia was institutionalised while domestic social groups were at least partly accommodated. In February 2021, a State Planning Committee, also known as Gosplan, was created to coordinate and develop economic strategies for Russia and allow that country's development to become an example to follow for populations elsewhere.[135] Additionally, the peasantry was offered the New Economic Plan–providing some economic freedoms for those seeking to sell wares on the private market. Clearly, beneficiaries might be found in Belarusian lands, but the policy was also an enticement to anyone living on the other side of the new international borders.[136]

The Bolsheviks believed it worth projecting, at least in parts, an image of their state as normalising. Mostly rebuffed by those governments victorious in the First World War–governments worried about revolutionary activity and demanding Bolshevik repayment of imperial-era debts–Russia used the 1922 Treaty of Rapallo to engage with fellow-outcast Germany.[137] Not only did that step remove possible tension between the two countries; it also allowed them to provide secret support for each other. The Bolsheviks remained on a war footing, as they would arguably remain until 1991, and would exploit any divisions in capitalist ranks, particularly as doubts of future leadership at home developed.[138] Arguably, the creation of the Soviet Union by December 1922 should be seen as an attempt both to ensure the regime would retain domestic as well as international coherence after Lenin. The Soviet Union was also, of course, an attempt to regularise and enmesh non-Russian regions in Moscow-led centralised rule.[139]

---

134 For the Bolsheviks' approach to that rebellion, see also Getzler, 2002
135 For context, see also Ellman, 2014: chapter 1
136 The New Economic Policy, and its controversy among Bolsheviks, is detailed in Smith, S., 2017: chapters 6-7
137 Indicating how the Treaty of Rapallo was important in processual as well as practical terms for Soviet foreign policy is also Bowring, 2017
138 From early 1922, Lenin's health began to markedly deteriorate. At the same time, Stalin gained the position of General Secretary and gradually built resistance to Lenin's expected heir, Trotsky. See also Fitzpatrick, 2022: chapter 2
139 Such regularisation also served, though, to tame the central government's extra-legal excesses after years of war communism. See Edele, 2019: chapter 4 for context

Internationally, the creation of the Soviet Union did not provide the Bolsheviks immediate benefits. They still found it difficult to receive recognition and partners in Western Europe and North America, from where the United States in March 1923 pointedly refused to offer diplomatic recognition to the new entity.[140] Constructing a new state also did little to change local power balances between Bolshevik-held lands and their capitalist neighbours. In April, Poland annexed parts of Lithuania, thereby consolidating control over Vilnius with at least tacit acceptance from the international community in the shape of the League of Nations.[141] Despite the recent peace treaty, the Bolsheviks feared future Polish designs on the neighbouring BSSR. So, over the coming years the territorial integrity of that Soviet republic was shored up by seeing substantial territories transferred to it from the Russian SFSR (RSFSR), around Mahilou and Vitebsk, and then Homel.[142]

It could also be claimed that the BSSR might have been particularly treasured by Bolshevik elites. Here was a republic created by the new regime, a showpiece for communism populated by a multinational and multilingual community, overcoming a history of tension between Belarusians, Jews, Poles and Russians. Promoting it was a communist duty.[143] The notion of the BSSR and post-Soviet Belarus as ideal examples of a political community would repeatedly return to the Russo-Belarusian relationship over the following century. Furthermore, that notion fit in well with the idea of "socialism in one country" as officially adopted by the 14th Congress of the Bolsheviks in 1925.[144] Whether "socialism in one country" implied a retreat from the idea of world revolution, as later charged by Trotsky and some outside observers, is questionable. Clear, however, was the investment now offered by the central leadership

---

140　An interesting, long-term analysis of Soviet diplomatic activity is found in Revell and White, 2002

141　Balkelis, 2018: chapter 7 outlines the war and its consequences for the Lithuanian nation, in particular

142　It should be noted, though, that the transfer of territory from the RSFSR to the BSSR could also be seen in a general context of demands for decentralisation in the USSR. See also Marková, 2022: 36

143　On this, see also the fascinating account in Bemporad, 2013

144　An incisive discussion of that policy is by van Ree, 1998

40   UNCANNY ALLIES

in state-building, institutionalisation and the creation of a Soviet national ethos.[145]

That context has to be kept in mind when discussing the policy of "indigenisation" carried out by the Bolsheviks in the decade following the civil war. Seeking to shore up alliances with nationalist elites across the Soviet Union, the Bolsheviks allowed for education and cultural promotion in non-Russian languages, especially in western regions.[146] Indigenisation clearly benefitted Belarusian nationhood. As discussed above, within the Russian Empire Belarusian identity had been nebulous. Consequently, support from Soviet authorities for Belarusian national projects had a substantial influence, which provided the foundation for a Belarusian self-understanding which, arguably, can be traced into the post-Soviet era.[147] Across the border, Belarusian elites were persecuted in Poland, as seen with the 1927 arrest of leaders within the Belarusian Peasant and Workers Party (Hramada). With some justification, Polish authorities feared collaboration between Hramada and the Bolsheviks would undermine the state, yet the arrests also indicated that interwar Poland was becoming increasingly authoritarian.[148]

If we only consider the factors above, it seems difficult to explain why the Soviet regime abruptly stopped indigenisation towards the end of the 1920s. That such a halt was called to the policy is clear, with nationalist and political elites in the BSSR and elsewhere suffering widespread persecution, prison sentences and execution.[149] In retrospect, this should not have been surprising. During the entire interwar period, the Soviet leadership saw itself as preparing for widespread battle. Following Lenin's death in early 1924, Stalin may have continued to view world revolution as the long-term aim, yet more immediate was the necessity to defend

---

145   Hidden in Trotsky's subsequent invective against Stalin's regime is a realisation of this. See Trotsky, 2004
146   The standout work on Soviet indigenisation remains Martin, 2001
147   A classic work on development of early twentieth-century Belarusian nationalism is Rudling, 2014
148   An explanation for the banning of Hramada with less focus on nationalist disagreements is in Fedorowycz, 2021
149   A useful overview of Belarusian nationhood in the interwar Soviet Union is in Savchenko, 2009: 77-96

against expected capitalist advances.[150] Also, however, conflict and violence were intrinsic to the Bolshevik system and Marxism-Leninism. During the civil war, Red Terror had been meaningful not for its result but for its process. Similarly, national elites were now hounded not so much for what they did as for the Marxist-Leninist system to reaffirm its identity through violence.[151]

The hunt for "subversives" and ritualistic use of violence became characteristic of Stalinism. Non-Russian national elites and entire peoples were victimised from the outset, and it was notable how Trotsky, Grigory Zinoviev, Nikolai Bukharin and other losers in the battle for power during the 1920s would repeatedly be accused of alliance with "alien" forces.[152] Yet the point to stress here is that anyone could be an "alien" in the eye of the Bolsheviks. The search for enemies was a constant preoccupation for the Soviet system, particularly after the 1928 Shakhty Trial, which unleashed the phenomenon of the Stalinist show trial.[153] Therefore, national elites in the BSSR or other republics could not secure themselves by pledging loyalty to communism or even to Stalin himself. What was likely to decide their fate was not what they did or did not do, but what they could potentially do in the eye of the centre.[154]

It is worth briefly stepping back from events to recognise that we are dealing here with the influence of the uncanny. From its inception, the Russian Empire had existed in a liminal state–chronologically, territorially, culturally. As such, the Empire was always vulnerable to that which was adjacent, yet essentially different–that is, "the uncanny".[155] Arguably, within the Empire Belarusian identity never reached such a status, which was instead fulfilled by Ukraine or, perhaps, Poland. Yet that changed in the Soviet Union,

---

150 Such Soviet fears being central to the claim that the Cold War began in 1917. See Haslam, 2011: chapter 1
151 The central place of violence in Soviet thinking is discussed in Holquist, 2003
152 On the fall of Trotsky, in particular, see also Rubenstein, 2011: chapter 5
153 The spirit of such turmoil, much more systemically fundamental than simple "paranoia" (with which lazy analysis has often labelled Stalinist violence), was illustrated by some, brave Soviet artists, as in Bulgakov, 2003
154 For another artistic view on how such individual, existential vulnerability functions we can turn, as so often is the case, to Orwell, 1989
155 A genuinely insightful understanding of this is in Sobol, 2022

where the BSSR could haunt the centre. Note that the uncanny would not, primarily, be found among Belarusian nationalists, but among those and that which had been Sovietised.[156] Because Soviet and Bolshevik narratives–fundamentals of Soviet and Bolshevik identity–could not be threatened by nationalist "others". Such others were central to narratives mired in conflict, as mentioned above. What was uncanny was an identity steeped in Soviet values–or, perhaps, neo-imperial values, as seen after 1991–yet not emanating from a Russian centre.[157]

The uncanny relationship between Russian and Belarusian actors shall reappear throughout the book. Going back to events of the late 1920s, though, it is clear that the Soviet leadership had concerns beyond those relating to identity. In 1928, the first five-year plan was instigated to quickly develop the economy.[158] Around the same time a decision had been made to introduce collectivisation for the vast majority of the peasantry. The immediate purpose of collectivisation was to optimise food production for expanding urban communities of workers and, at times, for export. Collectivisation also, however, aimed to catalogue and control the peasantry.[159] Over the following years, the disruption and violence accompanying collectivisation would be felt through famine across the Soviet countryside, particularly among Kazakhs, Ukrainians and those living in the Volga basin. While the BSSR was less severely impacted, there, too, private farming and subsistence outside state structures became impossible.[160]

Beyond immediate consequences for individuals, collectivisation and famine also dismantled civil culture across the affected

---

156 The idea of the Self conjuring its uncanny double is an ancient literary theme, never expressed better than by Andersen, 1997

157 Here we witness a reflection of the essential tension between stasis and revolution existing throughout Russian and Soviet history and self-understanding—as hinted at throughout Poe, 2003

158 Creating a five-year plan was, of course, also a ritual reaffirming the scientific infallibility of Marxism-Leninism. See Kenez, 2017: chapter 4

159 Documents highlighting the political nature of collectivisation can be seen in War, 2005

160 With millions of people dead from forced collectivisation and famine, debate continues regarding state motivation and guilt. A nuanced summary of that debate is in Nefedov and Ellman, 2019

areas. Consequently, any hopes of revitalised Belarusian national identity disappeared. In addition, atomising Belarusian society had the unintended consequence of weakening resistance to external incursion, an issue which would concern Soviet authorities to the coming of war and beyond.[161] Were the authorities aware of such a danger? In March 1930, Stalin famously penned an article entitled "Dizzy with Success", which warned against the haphazard way in which collectivisation had been promoted and stressed that any successes of that policy should be built upon systematically to further the Marxist-Leninist society.[162] Yet what the Soviet leader sought to preserve was not pre-existing national and local societies but a newly constructed, overarching Soviet society and Soviet man, which would be capable of carrying out those accelerated bursts of industrial production to which Stalinist rhetoric repeatedly returned during the following years.[163]

With the totalitarian pretensions of that society, Soviet authorities promoted physical and cultural ideals for its peoples to follow. Although it had many similarities to contemporary focus on bodily health, and bodily perfection, across European cultures, the Soviet idea of "fizkultura" in particular envisaged something valuable sculpted from unformed rather than pre-formed clay.[164] Society in the BSSR was influenced by such changes, too–gaining a 10,000-capacity stadium in Minsk in 1934–and by the centralisation of culture carried out through censorship and the abolition of local organisations, which were replaced by centrally approved unions, like the 1932 Union of Soviet Writers, within which membership for artists became mandatory.[165] Within that context, Belarusian culture had to be disassociated from prior bourgeois nationalism–particularly if the latter had a Polish tint. Here, it is interesting to see how the

---

161 Other research has similarly spoken of the "total distrust", which marked Stalinist society. See Hosking, 2014: chapter 1

162 Stalin, 1930

163 One of the most evocative depictions of Stalinist societal industrialisation remains Kotkin, 1997

164 An overview of the importance of "fizkultura" in Soviet self-understanding is in Schlögel, 2023: chapter 47

165 The purpose and development of the Union can be gauged through documents in Clark et al, 2007: chapter 10

44   UNCANNY ALLIES

1933 language reform, which aligned Belarusian orthography more closely to that of Russian, was overtly justified through Marxist-Leninist (and Russian) demands.[166]

Whether such policies were always likely to develop into the mass repression and terror seen across the Soviet Union during the second half of the 1930s is difficult to determine. What should be stressed, however, is that Stalin had fundamentally changed the system–perhaps less in an ideological than in an administrative sense.[167] Yet administrative initiatives obviously had ideological implications, too. For example, by introducing the internal passport in late 1932 Stalin not only enabled the state to quickly react to the emergency created by the assassination of Sergey Kirov two years later–it also mechanised and securitised individuals and peoples in the country.[168] Consequently, if we argue that contemporary leaders such as Vladimir Putin and Aleksandr Lukashenka are heirs to a statist-securitised (rather than a Marxist-Leninist) system, that worldview could arguably be traced back to the 1930s with its ever-present (or, ever-vocalised) threats and requirements for state expansion.[169]

Domestic securitisation should also be seen in an international context. As indicated earlier, emerging from the civil war the Bolsheviks had employed two kinds of foreign policy, promoting revolution through the Comintern, while also seeking traditional state allies, notably including Germany at Rapallo followed up by their trade agreement and non-aggression treaty in the mid-1920s.[170] To gain international respectability within European international society more broadly, by the late 1920s the Soviet Union publicly aligned with aims of peace initiatives such as the 1928 Kellogg-Briand Pact, pushing for the abolition of war. Being unwilling to disavow revolutionary subversion, however, the Soviet Union

---

166   Mayo, 1978: 26-27
167   A point well illustrated in Rosenfeldt, 2006: particularly chapter 9
168   The history of the Soviet passport is in Baiburin, 2021
169   The terror theatre, with its cast of defenders and destroyers of virtue, obviously also has clear links into modernity; see Shearer, 2013
170   For the context of Bolshevik foreign policy during the 1920s, see also Kocho-Williams, 2011: chapter 3

nevertheless largely failed to gain acceptance during that decade.[171] That would change in the early 1930s, partly due to successes in Soviet propaganda abroad and because some Western interlocutors became used to the Bolsheviks as just another interlocutor within an increasingly tense international situation. This might, for instance, explain how the Soviet Union eventually gained membership of the League of Nations in 1934.[172]

By that point, the League had already suffered numerous setbacks, though. Originally founded in 1920 with the aim to institutionalise and pacify international affairs, the organisation depended on widespread consensus among its members and had little answer to those regimes dissatisfied with contemporary power disparities in the world.[173] Such dissatisfaction was increasingly voiced by authoritarian or fascist regimes, beginning with Benito Mussolini's Italy, but soon also reaching Soviet borders in the shape of Japan, which in 1931 under flimsy pretexts attacked and invaded Chinese Manchuria, where the puppet state of Manchukuo was established the following year.[174] Now, the Bolsheviks had to pay attention to East Asia and the military risk to Siberia. Then, in early 1933 the spectre of a two-front war materialised with Adolf Hitler as German leader. While his longevity was not immediately recognised, he arrived on the basis of widespread militarisation and racialisation of the German polity.[175]

Hitler soon took specific policy steps to endanger European peace. Most portentous were his initiatives during 1935 to reintroduce German conscription and rearmament in direct contravention of provisions forced on the country following its defeat during the First World War and, clearly, aimed at threatening the continental

---

171   It is telling here how the Soviets, while publicly agreeing to the aims of peace, nevertheless kept clear of the Kellogg-Briand process. See also Cohrs, 2006: 466
172   For the move of the Soviets towards international collective security, see also Henry, 2020
173   The story of the League of Nations is outlined in Henig, 2010
174   How relations between the Soviet Union and Japan had turned sour even before this invasion is shown in Ferguson, 2008: 25-26
175   The authoritative account of Hitler's rise and public support—not least for his railings against "Judaeo-Bolshevism"—is Ullrich, 2016

status quo.[176] However, for Stalin danger had already been high-lighted the previous year through the German-Polish declaration of mutual non-aggression. While not unequivocally directed against Moscow, it appeared in the context of a mutual antipathy towards the Bolsheviks, thereby reinforcing the feeling of foreign threat to the BSSR and other western parts of the Soviet Union.[177] The Soviet leadership would soon seek to mitigate its isolation through diplomacy and agreements with other European regimes, notably France and Czechoslovakia. However, while such activity might help keep Germany, in particular, occupied elsewhere no illusions existed that the BSSR or western areas of the RSFSR would ever be defended by foreign troops.[178]

Stalinism and War

Then, in 1936 European danger seemed to move away from Soviet borders. Civil war broke out in Spain, where Francisco Franco's military rebellion was supported by fascist Italy and Germany, while the republican government got help from socialist movements, including some linked to the Soviet Union.[179] While Soviet aid was offered for a while, Moscow never fully committed to that conflict. Indeed, Soviet agents would focus more on undermining republican opponents than on battling Franco and the fascists. An unsurprising priority when considering that the Bolsheviks still viewed struggle for survival as fought simultaneously on internal and external fronts.[180] Thus, the relevance for my argument of the Spanish Civil War. Soviet action there became the perfect illustration of the nature of the Stalinist regime. Particularly as that regime simultaneously descended into brutalised disciplining at home

---

176 Placing German actions in the context of collapsing peace is Creswell, 2023
177 In post-Soviet Russia, that agreement would appear as part of a narrative of threats against the Soviet Union, helping to justify Moscow's policy against Poland in 1939. See e.g. Morozov, 2007
178 Contemporary Soviet diplomacy in Europe is shown in Carley, 2023
179 On Soviet involvement in the Spanish civil war, see Payne, 2004
180 The classic tale of discord on the republican side is Orwell, 2000

where the enforced change of party cards from early 1936 would signal the beginning of widespread repression and murder.[181]

As other well-populated regions of the Soviet Union, the BSSR would be severely harmed by this ensuing terror. Notably, the forested area of Kurapaty outside Minsk would become a notorious killing site with executions of hundreds of thousands of people; crimes which would resurface with the budding opposition movement under *glasnost* in the late 1980s.[182] To understand such and other crimes in their proper context it is pertinent, once more, to stress that they should not be seen as aberrations but as essential parts of Soviet Stalinist nature. While terror in the BSSR and elsewhere would often be driven by local dynamics its context remained central regime initiatives.[183] The terror became the apotheosis of Stalin's consolidation of power, symbolised also through the constitution of 1936, marking the Soviet Union as based on territory rather than movement. And thereby becoming ontologically vulnerable and penetrable along geographical borders, placing the BSSR in a frontier position less meaningful within the paradigm of world revolution.[184]

In a territorialised Soviet Union, furthermore, it made some sense to promote the role of the Russian centre, as Stalin now did. By spring 1938, it was decreed that Russian language had to be taught in every school, thereby formally beginning the process, which would eventually marginalise a language such as Belarusian.[185] This was less a matter of Stalinist Russian imperialism than an attempt at shoring up the centralised nature of a state perceived to be under threat. The regime now saw enemies everywhere, symbolised dramatically in the 1937 purging of those military leaders–

---

181 "Disciplining" here of course meant in a Foucauldian sense, as per Foucault, 2020

182 Recent research of the Kurapaty massacres is in Marples and Laputska, 2020

183 As seen, for instance, with the notorious NKVD order 00447 in the summer of 1937. For a genuinely insightful analysis of centre-regional interplay concerning the implementation of that order, see Ellman, 2010

184 The politics surrounding the 1936 constitution are outlined in Lomb, 2018. Whether the territorial reification of Bolshevism marked a historical turning point or a return to normal practice for a Russia-centred state remains moot

185 For the change in language education, see Pavlenko, 2013: 658-59

48   UNCANNY ALLIES

like Mikhail Tukhachevsky–on whom the defence of the realm had rested.[186] Now, Soviet military planning was cast into disarray–or at least not furthered in a timely fashion–at the same time as the country became increasingly isolated on the international stage. Isolation was highlighted in September 1938 by Moscow's exclusion from the Munich negotiations, yet that followed years of diplomatic failure.[187]

Years of conducting a dual foreign policy with an emphasis on subverting capitalist systems had alienated the Soviet Union from potential European allies. In retrospect, it was unsurprising that Stalin eventually found it necessary to ally with Germany at the cusp of the Second World War.[188] Born, partly, of desperation, the immediate consequences of that alliance nevertheless brought benefits to the Soviet Union and to the BSSR, the territory of which would effectively double from the invasion and annexation of interwar Polish theory two weeks following the Nazi onslaught on that country.[189] Clearly, the new territories were designed as a buffer zone insulating core Soviet territory from the growing intra-capitalist war. They also, however, signified renewed dismantling of a historical enemy and subversive element along the vulnerable western flank of the country, which–with the BSSR as its vanguard– could now spearhead Bolshevik influence into decadent "civilisation".[190]

Such influence would take violent form. Having warred with Poland less than two decades previously, Soviet security personnel now killed those believed to be pillars of Polish statehood. Named after the area where they were carried out, the Katyn massacres would long be blamed on Germany, until *glasnost* finally saw Soviet

---

186   The fall of Tukhachevsky is covered in Main, 1997
187   The sidelining of the Soviet Union in the Munich process is covered in Ragsdale, 2004
188   For the circumstances of the August 1939 Molotov-Ribbentrop agreement and its aftermath, see Moorhouse, 2016
189   Here, it is noteworthy how Soviet propaganda partly justified the invasion of Poland through tropes of "historical Russian lands". See also Głowacki and Lebedeva, 2015
190   For a personal history of such spearheaded influence, see also Wagner, 2020: chapter 3

authorities acknowledging their crimes.[191] Tellingly, though, post-Soviet Russian governments would increasingly place these crimes within securitised, contextualised logic emphasising the precarious status of international outsider held by the Soviet Union in 1939-40. Clearly, the western borderlands–much of which were absorbed into the BSSR–constituted a region where "special measures" could be justified.[192] Putin's regime would later present similarly assaults on Finland, the Baltic States and Bessarabia during 1939-41. History writing under Putin, especially concerning the Second World War, would relativise "sovereignty" and "rights" in ways directly linked to nineteenth-century European beliefs in the essential difference and ranking of nations–even to Social Darwinism and racialisation.[193]

Those observations are, of course, not intended to diminish the danger in which the Soviet Union found itself at the beginning of the 1940s. Although the German attack would eventually begin only in June 1941 it had been planned long beforehand and, as mentioned above, expressed an essential part of the Nazi German worldview.[194] In addition, there is no doubt that Soviet military ability and bravery was central to the eventual defeat of Nazi Germany and its allies. Soviet triumph, although hardly seen as such at the time, began over the winter of 1941-42 with the successful defence of Moscow at a time when little international assistance was available.[195] Subsequently, during 1942 and early 1943 the Battle of Stalingrad arguably proved the turning point–at least in terms of combat engagements–within the European theatre. Germany did fatally overextend itself, but that only became a problem because

---

191   A forensic look at the Katyn massacres is in Paul, 2010
192   Here, an obvious link can be drawn to Snyder's observation about the facilitation of violence through absence of acknowledged sovereignty. See Snyder, 2015
193   Petrov, N., 2021 offers useful detail concerning Russian debates on this topic
194   Operation Barbarossa, and Soviet failure to prepare adequately for the onslaught, is discussed in Ellis, 2015
195   Edele, 2021, shows well the conditions of total war in which the Soviet Union found itself

the Soviet regime was able to mobilise not only material resources but also public morale.[196]

Presenting the Second World War as a triumph–a vindication less of communism and more of great power strength emanating from a Russian centre–has guided post-Soviet Russian rhetoric. And, therefore, largely misrepresented that war. Partly, because that interpretation ignores the diplomatic concessions into which weakness had repeatedly forced Moscow before Germany attacked.[197] Partly, also, because the post-Soviet image of a Russian-led Soviet Union standing alone, or at least in the vanguard, against a threat to mankind as a whole conveniently ignores the material aid provided to Moscow by Western allies from 1942 onwards in what, for a while, was a genuine anti-fascist international alliance.[198] Yet, for the purposes of the argument made here by far the most significant omission made when presenting the war in a positive light is that such an interpretation obscures or even erases the experience of oppression, violation and chaos placed on individuals and communities particularly in the Soviet-German borderlands.[199]

That point becomes particularly pertinent when discussing events in the BSSR. If we here include the territory annexed to the BSSR from Poland in 1939, no other place on Earth suffered comparable human and material destruction. At least a quarter of the population died a violent death; cities were razed to the ground.[200] When Soviet troops retook Minsk in July 1944, the BSSR in effect had to be reconstructed. Consequently, the identity of the BSSR

---

196 The battle of Stalingrad and its human context was never more eloquently expressed than in Grossman, 2020
197 That weakness was not only visible in relation to European fascism. Arguably, the April 1941 neutrality agreement with Japan, and subsequent Japanese preoccupation away from Soviet lands, was necessary for the Bolsheviks to avoid committing unsustainable military resources to its Far East. That Japan might not have had to be so relatively accommodating towards the Soviet Union is explored in Ito, 2023
198 The diplomatic history of the Grand Alliance is discussed in Rise, 1995
199 That such experiences had been insufficiently covered was, of course, the theme of Snyder, 2011
200 Apart from stark figures, the most appropriate interpretation of the destruction in the BSSR remains that offered by Klimov, 1985

would–if anything–become even more Soviet than before. If the post-war Soviet Union as a whole existed in the shadow of the war, this was only more so for the frontline republic.[201] Yet the understanding of war would be different in Moscow and Minsk. Not only could Belarusians highlight their prominence in the war effort, their role as the first line of defence, but they were also aware that they had largely been sacrificed, even targeted, by the Soviet war effort.[202]

This was not just a matter of military necessity or callousness. Indeed, Soviet partisans and security forces would at times actively target civilian populations in the BSSR and surrounding areas in attempts to root out those who had locally collaborated with Germany or simply come to believe in local, rather than all-Union causes.[203] And as victory came closer, Soviet authorities took steps to consolidate territorial and political gains achieved before the German attack. Best known is the situation in Poland where the Red Army allowed for the failure of the Warsaw uprising and consequent demolition of Polish military potential, yet Soviet intent was similar across Central Eastern Europe.[204] While the war was ongoing, the Soviet leadership had also taken diplomatic steps to ensure postwar accommodation with its Western allies over Central Eastern Europe. An image had been projected of the Soviet Union as a civilised, reliable country, militarily capable yet no longer with revolutionary aims and belief in the world revolution.[205]

All of which meant that the outcome of the war in Europe could align with Soviet wishes. In February, the Yalta Conference

---

201 That the Soviet Union would remain in the shadow of war after 1945 is the theme of Lovell, 2010

202 In 1944, Operation Bagration became known as a decisive defeat of German troops, yet at the same time this Soviet advance showed little consideration for local Belarusian and other populations. See also Glantz and House, 2015: chapter 13

203 For analysis of how Soviet partisans forced civilians into resistance, and punished those unwilling to comply, see Statiev, 2014

204 A comparative study of how post-war Soviet-led consolidation took place is Applebaum, 2012

205 To promote that message should be seen also the official termination of the Comintern in 1943. For diplomatic engagement with Western partners during the war, see Reynolds and Pechatnov, 2018

confirmed the new territorial reality, acknowledging the transfer of territory from Poland to the BSSR while recompensing the former with regions taken from pre-war Germany.[206] At first glance, that summer the subsequent Potsdam Conference built upon similar principles and mutual understanding between the allies. However, by now it was becoming increasingly clear for the Soviet elite that the USA was unlikely to depart from Europe into interwar isolationism. Thus, a challenge to Soviet continental prominence remained.[207] At Yalta, in particular, Stalin benefitted from American aims to achieve Soviet participation in the coming United Nations. Assuming veto rights over significant security issues in that organisation, the Soviet Union agreed to join, while also securing separate memberships in the United Nations for the BSSR and the Ukrainian SSR.[208]

Under different circumstances the BSSR could be imagined linking lands dominated by Russians with Polish and German societies decimated by war and amenable to Soviet socialism. This world might have seen Bolsheviks promoting world revolution. That this did not happen tells us much about the nature of Soviet, and Russian, regime-building then and even today.[209] The Second World War may have ended in victory, and Stalin was convinced that internal contradictions remained within capitalism. Yet before such contradictions might result in another intra-capitalist conflict, the Soviet leader feared subversion of his state and attack on its

---

206 The Yalta Conference has been extensively covered. Plokhy, 2010, provides a readable account

207 Compared to Yalta, Potsdam has been seen as less consequential. However, Neiberg, 2015, shows understanding of the latter's important legacy

208 While this was partly a matter of prestige for the Soviet leadership, it was additionally yet another way to security international recognition for post-war territorial arrangements. See also Lubachko, 1972: chapter 13, for details of the Soviet diplomatic manoeuvres at the time, even if that source underestimates Soviet territorial concerns at the time

209 This is, of course, not to argue that Soviet authorities and their allies did not seek to remould occupied territories, as indicated by Applebaum above. It is, however, to claim that such efforts primarily intended to defend state security rather than promote transnational ideological influence. An interpretation famously expressed by X (George Kennan), 1946-47

severely weakened material and social structures.[210] The threat was certainly not just in the international sphere. Following the expulsion of German troops, militias resisted Soviet reimposition of control by force, particularly in the Baltic region and among Ukrainians, where local challenges would last until the early 1950s and retain the narrative of public resistance into the post-Soviet era.[211]

Soviet military control of the republics would not be seriously challenged under Stalin, or for many years following his death. For a regime promoting totalitarianism, however, military control could not be sufficient. During the late 1940s and early 1950s the Soviet Union witnessed renewed tightening of ideological control across society.[212] There also continued a streak of ethnic discrimination and even racism promoted by the regime. During the war, such attitudes had undoubtedly been part of the decision to deport entire peoples from Crimea and the Caucasus–and, indeed, from across the western borderlands, resulting in further depopulation of the already heavily impacted BSSR.[213] It seems plausible that repression and push for domestic ideological conformity would have increased had Stalin not died suddenly in March 1953. Whether such conformity would have become even more Russo-centric is less certain, yet as Stalin's successors also recognised, allying with the majority people of the Union created a useful core for statist stability.[214]

Such stability was of vital importance for the Soviet elite as the Cold War got under way. Debates on the causes of the Cold War and the nuclear arms race are, of course, ongoing. As indicated above, some post-war initiatives indicated Soviet self-belief and

---

210 However, for the alternate claim that Stalin might briefly have believed in the possibility of post-war collaboration with the West, see Roberts, 2007: chapter 10

211 While such militias did not particularly find a place in the BSSR, their existence in neighbouring regions compromised security in that republic, too. For an example of anti-Soviet militias, see Kaszeta, 2023

212 For the cultural expressions of such renewed repression, see Dobrenko, 2020

213 Soviet deportation and incarceration schemes of minority peoples of course existed within a broader narrative of biopolitics, as discussed in Prozorov, 2022: particularly chapter 5

214 The position of Russians in the Soviet Union is covered well by Hosking, 2006: chapter 7 notably looks at the wartime legacy

54   UNCANNY ALLIES

wish for power projection.[215] However, at least until the 1960s the Soviet Union found itself reacting to international events and perceived threats more frequently than it proved able to set the global agenda. True, from 1949 onwards a Soviet nuclear bomb existed, but that in itself was of little use without deployment mechanisms and other necessary military logistics.[216] Other forms of power projection traditionally favoured by communists–subversion of capitalist regimes through violence and propaganda–might have been more applicable to early post-war Soviet foreign policy, yet Stalin feared such activity might drag his country into a new world war, and fiercely resisted attempts to challenge his authority on the matter.[217]

Expelling Yugoslavia from the Cominform (and, thus, from the Soviet-led alliance) in 1948 could not undo damage already done. In 1947, referring to international sponsorship for the communist rebellion in Greece, the Truman Doctrine had cemented continued American involvement in Europe, thereby removing any Soviet hopes for a return to isolationist priorities in Washington.[218] What made matters worse for Moscow was the concomitant American use of its economic superiority to project influence. The Marshall Plan may have had altruistic elements involving American feelings of sympathy for European peoples in social despair, but it was also a direct attack on the most vulnerable flank of Soviet-sponsored regimes.[219] Sensing danger, Stalin forbade communist regimes from participating in the scheme and then counteracted by blockading access from the West to divided Berlin. Knowing that conquest of this city could precipitate conquest of divided

---

215   For a brief, yet nuanced discussion of the origins of the Cold War in Europe, see also McMahon, 2021: chapter 2
216   Focusing on nuclear weapons themselves as means to influence on international affairs is also to ignore the way in which the nuclear arms race threatened to become uncontrollable by any states involved, as memorably outlined in Ellsberg, 2019
217   The prominent example of Stalin's reticence on this matter relates to Tito's attempts to spread revolution on the Balkans and the subsequent Soviet-Yugoslav split in 1948. For the split and its aftermath, see also Kramer, 2014
218   The fundamental change in American foreign policy is shown in Kupchan, 2020: chapters 11-12
219   A useful overview of the Marshall Plan is in Holm, 2017

Germany, Stalin gambled that the West would pull back from escalation. Instead, the Berlin air lift created a public relations disaster.[220]

Not only did the USA and its allies continue to supply goods to erstwhile enemies in Berlin through a constant, airborne flow lasting over a year. They also interpreted Soviet actions as incompatible with a diplomatic solution of German, and by extension European, politico-military division and in 1949 formed NATO as an explicitly anti-Soviet alliance.[221] Germany itself seemed permanently divided after the creation in May that year of the Federal Republic of Germany. The Soviet Union responded the following October by sponsoring the foundation of the German Democratic Republic, yet that in itself could be seen as a defeat for Soviet ambition in Europe.[222] Instead of fostering a regime of "common European security", which could have been led, or at least kept in check, by Moscow and its allies, seemingly permanent tension now centred on Central Europe with military vulnerability piercing straight from the Germanies across Poland and the BSSR to Soviet heartlands.[223]

Attempts to pacify and isolate the European front from American influence through diplomacy and public calls for peace would continue to characterise Soviet and post-Soviet policies. It should be stressed, though, that Soviet and post-Soviet policies in that direction never aimed for a strong Europe, but a Europe divided piecemeal into manageable sovereignties.[224] That such a plan failed

---

220 The Berlin blockade and the airlift are discussed in Haydock, 1999
221 An account of the foundation of NATO is in Sayle, 2019: chapter 1
222 The development of two Germanies in the early post-war years is outlined in Schwarz, 2010
223 Stalin's foreign policy views of Europe at the time are well documented in Naimark, 2019
224 In that context, the 1951 Treaty of Paris creating the European Coal and Steel Community and leading the way for the European Economic Community (EEC) and, after the Cold War, the European Union, can be seen as portentous for Soviet and Russian hopes of being the/a continental great power. While an argument such as that advanced by Patel, 2017, may be quite correct in claiming that the EEC for a long time did little to promote peace beyond its borders, such an argument risks underestimating the EEC's ability to stabilise and coordinate developments within and between its members

56   UNCANNY ALLIES

forms an essential context even today for understanding Russian relations with Belarus. Continental conditions after the Second World War have never facilitated Russian acceptance of that neutralisation of the Belarusian space, which continues to form a central part of public identity emanating from Minsk.[225] It might, of course, still have been possible for postwar Moscow to build up fortifications around the BSSR and neighbouring territories, effectively cutting off the Soviet Union from regular involvement in European affairs and, instead, become a genuinely Eurasian power, taking advantage of the 1949 communist takeover in China and subsequent alliance-building with Beijing.[226]

In such a scenario, the BSSR and post-Soviet Belarus would still have mattered to Moscow. However, the region would then not have been as permeable to influence flowing between the Soviet Union/Russia and Europe–a permeability, which came to form an important part of Moscow's power projection, and its feeling of vulnerability.[227] That such developments never came to pass partly has to do with postwar events in Asia, which prevented that region from becoming a safe refuge for the Soviet Union. The Korean War ensured a permanent American military presence next to Soviet and Chinese borders, as did the Treaty of San Francisco.[228] And Soviet-Chinese relations would sour to the point of armed conflict during the 1960s, due to mutual mistrust of regional intentions, but also–and more importantly–due to fundamental disagreement on the future direction and leadership of the worldwide communist

---

225   The point here, and throughout the book, is not whether Soviet and Russian policy towards Europe is inherently aggressive or defensive (it can be both at different, or the same, times), but that neutralisation of (Central) Europe was and remains fundamentally incompatible with the ontological security of that Soviet and Russian state, which emerged after the war. For an example of how intractable that problem has proven to be, see also Akchurina and Della Sala, 2018

226   For the construction of that alliance, see Heinzig, 2003

227   Consequently, Soviet and Russian feelings of international vulnerability are not linked to geographical conditions, per se, but to political choices concerning those conditions. See also Bugajski and Assenova, 2016: especially chapter 3

228   The latter, of course, becoming a framework for Japan's alliance with the USA. For regional context, see also Li, 2017

movement with Moscow unable to countenance another (non-European) communist vanguard.[229]

So, for practical reasons the Soviet Union could not withdraw from Europe to Asian safety. However, such a course also remained impossible for ideological reasons. The victory of Marxism-Leninism in Russia had been the final victory of Westernisers in their centuries-long battle with Slavophiles over the principles on which the country should develop.[230] As an ideology, Marxism-Leninism was grounded in industrialised, European modernity within which the Bolsheviks wanted to belong. Of course, that version of modernity could and would be spread across the rest of the world, but with the Bolsheviks among the providers, not recipients, in that process.[231] Thus, the Soviet Union had to remain invested in Europe, for political and military security reasons, certainly, but also for reasons of ontological security and to have its status constantly reaffirmed by the only peers against which the Bolsheviks saw it narratively meaningful to measure themselves and their progress.[232]

That strategy remained after Stalin's death. His successor, Nikita Khrushchev, would gradually increase Soviet involvement in non-European affairs. Khrushchev would also, increasingly, promote the idea of "peaceful coexistence" and non-military competition with the West. Nevertheless, and partly due to the logic of the Cold War, the attraction and danger of Europe would not be abandoned.[233] Central to the Soviet view of Europe remained the German question. Early in his rule, Khrushchev supported the engagement of foreign minister Molotov in the 1954 Berlin Conference. That followed hints at Soviet-US détente, yet nevertheless failed to develop the necessary mutual trust required for progress on the

---

229 The Soviet-Chinese split is detailed in Lüthi, 2008
230 The Westerniser-Slavophile division being outlined in Tolz, 2010
231 One might even argue, the Bolsheviks had to see themselves as colonisers, not colonised, very much in a nineteenth century imperial mould as elsewhere argued by Buranelli, 2014
232 For the question of status, and the related concept of honour, in Russian relations with the West see also Tsygankov, 2012
233 A compelling account of Khruschev's engagement with Europe is in Zubok and Pleshakov, 1996: chapter 6

58   UNCANNY ALLIES

status of Germany.[234] The following year, Khrushchev himself took part in the Geneva Summit the avowed aim of which was continental, if not global peace. At Geneva, the Soviet leader advocated a European security community, centred on reunification of a neutral Germany and–implicitly–the gradual removal of the USA from European affairs.[235]

Post-Stalinist Stabilisation

The summit proved largely unsuccessful. Admittedly, participants could celebrate the re-assertion of Austrian sovereignty and neutrality, which became the outcome of the Austrian State Treaty signed two months prior. Yet, Austria had none of Germany's geographical importance for continental stability and would, like Finland, find itself saturated by mutual espionage in the decades to come.[236] That diplomatic resolution, though, had been overshadowed by the creation of the Warsaw Pact, a Soviet-led military organisation aimed at countering the US-led NATO. Khrushchev's purpose with the Warsaw Pact may have been founded primarily in a desire to retain socialist unity rather than repel capitalist aggression, yet the Pact did not invite international concord.[237] Arguably, sponsorship of the Warsaw Pact became symbolic of Soviet foreign policy under Khrushchev. Behind public bluster that the USA and its capitalist allies would be overtaken by the socialist promise remained Soviet feelings of vulnerability and, increasingly, of relative decline in the face of remarkable economic progress in the West.[238]

---

234   In this context, it should of course also be remembered that Soviet policy towards Germany in the years immediately preceding that conference had done little to promote Western (or German) trust. On this, see Wettig, 2017

235   For a more comprehensive view of Khrushchev's approaches to Germany, see also Zubok, 2000

236   International relations surrounding Austria between the end of the Second World War and the State Treaty are discussed in Carafano, 2002

237   The early years of the Warsaw Pact are well covered by Crump, 2015

238   A notable example of such progress was, of course, seen in West Germany, the relations of which with the Soviet Union is summarised in Sodaro, 1992: chapter 1

And such insecurity would feed back into Moscow's relationship with the BSSR. The late Stalinist regime promoted centralisation and, partly, cultural Russification. For Belarusians, this was seen, for instance, through the gradual removal of Belarusian language from the educational system, augured in 1951 by the cancellation of requests for Belarusian language tests in republican schools.[239] Republican demographics also changed with the inflow of ethnic Russians and other peoples. And unlike in some other western republics, such changes were less likely to be resisted locally since the removal of the pre-war population could be blamed on a now vanquished foreign enemy.[240] It helped, too, that the newcomers helped to rebuild the economy of the republic, rendering it one of the more advanced and industrialised Soviet republics. Eventually, the population of the BSSR would come to enjoy higher living standards than almost anywhere else in the Union.[241]

Yet relative prosperity came at a political price; Belarusian identity and nationhood was barely recognised in Moscow. After Stalin's death, security chief Lavrentii Beria had sought allies among local elites in the BSSR and other republics to gain support in the upcoming power struggle at the centre. Soon, though, Beria had been deposed and executed.[242] Having defeated Beria and other challengers, Khrushchev then set out his own governing profile in 1956 by denouncing Stalin and those purported deviations from Marxism-Leninism, which had allegedly held Soviet development back. What Khrushchev did not do, however, was to introduce more democratic governance in the Soviet Union or among allies.[243] Particularly after 1957, when he had removed all challengers through use of the broader Communist party membership and

---

239 See also Bekus, 2014: 46-47

240 Russification was particularly aimed at western BSSR, recently taken from Poland. For Soviet tactics there after the Second World War, see Ackermann, 2016

241 As an example of this, by 1980 consumption of foodstuffs such as meat and milk were higher per capita in the BSSR than anywhere else in the Soviet Union, with the exception of the Baltic republics. See Dronin and Bellinger, 2005: 317

242 For Beria's approach to BSSR elites, and the resistance he faced there, see Chernyshova, 2021

243 Smith, Kathleen, 2017, precisely indicates how Khrushchev's statements for change came to be misaligned with public expectations

60   UNCANNY ALLIES

populist rhetoric, Khrushchev's form of rule became personalistic and prone to far-reaching, and often unprofitable, economic experiments. In that context, developments in a republic like the BSSR very much became a means to a union-level end.[244]

Seeking to move away from imminent war with the West, Khrushchev promoted socio-economic modernisation abroad and at home–and what could be a more helpful illustration of Soviet progress than the regeneration of Belarusian lands recently devastated. For Moscow, the BSSR, and the Second World War, was a story of success, not of suffering.[245] However, local memory politics might disagree. After the war, Soviet military presence in Central Eastern Europe had been presented as "liberation" from fascism, a presentation accompanied by pervasive control and repression. And yet, shortly after Stalin's death Germans had unleashed widespread protests, refusing the narrative of unending gratitude.[246] Three years later, much more fundamental challenges to Soviet rule rose in Poland and then Hungary. Certainly, the 1956 protests, in particular, had profound nationalist elements. Anti-Russian slogans became particularly prominent among Hungarians where legitimacy was often sought from historical and modernist examples of national self-realisation.[247]

That Poland failed to erupt on a scale comparable to, or more damaging than, events in Hungary was in large parts due to the political revival of Władysław Gomułka. Previously communist leader in Poland and now reinstated in that position, Gomułka showed rare ability to combine communist orthodoxy with nationalist populism.[248] Consequently, while Khrushchev may have chafed at Gomułka's "insubordination", the latter's profile and skills were needed to prevent a wider, Polish uprising. Still, the aftermath of the crisis left the Soviet leadership in a dilemma. Having

---

244   The contribution of the BSSR to the overall Soviet economy and production line is summarised in Ioffe, 2004: 86-88
245   Khrushchev's leadership philosophy and style is presented in Thatcher, 2011
246   Soviet difficulties in handling the situation in Germany are shown in Harrison, 2003: particularly chapter 1 for developments during 1953
247   Such examples form a guide through much of the entrancing Sebestyen, 2006
248   Given Gomułka's composite political profile, his legacy has been complicated. See also Müller, 2022

accommodated Polish nationalism, even circumspectly, Moscow had lost certainty in the future of its European west.[249] For Belarusians, consequences of 1956 were complicated. For the Soviet centre, the value of the BSSR increased to insure the western front against Polish uncertainty. Yet after 1956 there was no appetite in Moscow for promoting Belarusian nationalism or cultural autonomy. And Belarusians now also had to face Polish mistrust as alleged Soviet stooges.[250]

It would, therefore, have been unsurprising if Khrushchev's reign had seen Belarusian identity fully absorbed into that of the Soviet Union as a whole. That, though, did not happen. Instead, local elites managed to coopt and, in part, take over the otherwise Russified and Russo-centric narrative of the Second World War promoted from Moscow.[251] The process began with the communist leadership of Kiril Mazurau (between 1956 and 1965), followed by that of Pyotr Masherau. Both had been prominent partisans during the war, and Masherau, in particular, proved adept at building a republican power base while also attracting increasing funds and attention to the BSSR.[252] As such, under Khrushchev and Leonid Brezhnev the BSSR distinguished itself very differently from its neighbours. The Baltics, and the Ukrainian SSR, would also remain under Soviet dominance until the late 1980s. However, by the late 1960s and early 1970s those republics saw the growth of a dissidence movement much less prominent among Belarusians.[253]

My argument here, then, is that the identity which now developed in the BSSR was less threatening to the Soviet Union than its

---

249 Here, it should of course be noted that communist authorities' accommodation to Polish conditions predated 1956. On this, see e.g. Kemp-Welch, 2008: 44-48 for how Stalinism moved between repressing and tolerating church activity in Poland

250 See here the telling recollections of Polish receptions of Belarusians on a "friendship visit" in September 1956, as described in Hornsby, 2019: 1216

251 The growing prominence of Belarusian politicians in that process until at least the mid-1970s is discussed in Kazakevich, 2022: 135-39

252 The importance of Masherau remains under-studied. However. Chernyshova, 2023, offers a useful attempt at remedying this

253 How the Baltic Republics and the western parts of the Ukrainian SSR remained somewhat apart from the rest of the post-war Soviet Union is discussed in Risch, 2015

Baltic and Ukrainian counterparts, but more threatening than the latter to a Russo-centric interpretation of said Union. Belarusian elites did not want to forsake the Union, they wanted to own it.[254] So, while Belarusian relations with the Soviet Union, and Russia, can be understood within a (post)colonial framework, the agency of coloniser cannot be assumed as fixed. We are back, therefore, at the uncanny relationship introduced above. With its wartime centrality and post-war modernisation, the BSSR, more consistently than the RSFSR, exemplified the communist story.[255] Some clarification, though, is in order here. I am not claiming that Belarusians did not suffer discrimination within the Soviet Union. For instance, following reforms of 1958 Belarusian language was increasingly removed from the educational sector leaving Minsk without any Belarusian-language schools by the early 1970s.[256]

And it must also be acknowledged that this "communist story" mattered profoundly to Russian identity in the decades leading up to, and following, the Soviet collapse. An important reason why Putin and Lukashenka could later profess alignment was the fact that both had been able to construct their regime legitimacy around Soviet-aligned tropes.[257] The point I am making here, however, is that Russian identity in the Soviet Union had other elements, too. Of particular importance here is the understanding of Russia as a civilisation. An entity without pre-determined geographic, and perhaps even ethnic, boundaries. And a centre for Eurasia as well as, arguably, the world.[258] An expansionist identity central to which is a belief not only in exceptionalism but also in the hierarchy of identities and of sovereignties–of the distinction

---

254 I would argue that such a thesis engages with the spirit, if not completely the empirical focus, of the post-colonial approach to the Soviet Union advocated by Annus, 2015: esp. 610

255 While largely focused on the RSFSR, Mijnssen's, 2021, work on "heroarchy" and hero cities would be applicable here to understand the ideological landscape within which the BSSR could situate itself

256 Kaiser, 1994: 255

257 For the importance of such building blocks for memory politics and memory regimes, see Bernhard and Kubik, 2014, even if that approach presupposes more plurality of debate than might currently be the case in Russia and Belarus

258 Malinova, 2020, provides a helpful historical overview of Russian civilisational thought

between "great powers" and "small powers", in short. Post-Soviet Belarusians would become increasingly uncomfortable with a moniker among the latter–something Lukashenka would adroitly exploit.[259]

I shall come back to this clash of identities in later chapters. For now, it is worth noting how great power identity manifested itself in Khrushchev's policies. At a global level, in 1957 the Soviet Union witnessed success in its competition with the USA when a satellite was sent into orbit.[260] For sure, the feat could have military implications, as could the successful ascent of Yuri Gagarin four years later, yet the main purpose of such triumphs was ideological and in terms of prestige. It was to show that Soviet man had overcome boundaries set by nature and, apparently, reached a new stage of evolution.[261] Down on Earth, Khrushchev's economic policies spreading crops like maize across lands previously (and subsequently) unsuited to such produce should be understood similarly. The Soviet leader remained in a constant race, at home and abroad, to prove his and his country's mastery of the situation.[262]

Despite ideological justification for his economic policies, a combination of poor execution and poor luck soon left him vulnerable to criticism. Such criticism also followed from the ambiguity of political tolerance. Even if Stalinism had caused widespread suffering, increasing limits to Khrushchev's "thaw" provoked popular frustration and uncertainty.[263] At times, tensions led to violence. For the Soviet system, it was one thing to suppress foreign countries or desperate Gulag prisoners. Yet when railway workers in Novocherkassk in 1962 protested for better living conditions the system panicked. Ideology did not permit Soviet workers to be dissatisfied,

---

259 Bowring, 2013, offers a thought-provoking approach to the importance of sovereignty in Russian political thinking, with chapter 10 particularly relevant for Putin's reign
260 The "Sputnik shock" shook Western beliefs in technological supremacy, as shown, humorously but also truthfully, by Kaufman, 1983
261 The importance of space exploration for Soviet identity is the topic of Gerovitch, 2015
262 The title and approach of Hale-Dorrell, 2021, is largely correct in this respect
263 Repression under Khrushchev is detailed by Hornsby, 2013

64   UNCANNY ALLIES

so they were shot instead.[264] No similar massacre took place in the BSSR, where–as previously indicated–living conditions were relatively tolerable. However, for elite views on the BSSR context matters. Moscow now saw a republic adjacent to Polish nationalist danger and defined by beleaguered ideology. If the BSSR had been constructed around a workers' dream, that dream was endangered.[265]

Ordinary Soviet citizens were somewhat unaware of Novocherkassk. And the leadership did recognise protesters had challenged the system to perform better (rather than challenge the system itself, as in Hungary). But a fear had now set in among elites–that the "social contract" of material progress for political quiescence bound patrons as well as clients.[266] That fear placed the Soviet centre on the defensive, at home and abroad. Similarly, the 1961 erection of the Berlin Wall had little to do with the putative risk of a Western assault and everything to do with a "workers' paradise" haemorrhaging workers to alleged capitalist exploiters.[267] Like the BSSR, East Germany had been reconstructed from the ground up to showcase socialist strength. Instead, it became a prison and centre for renewed international tension. With peace talks over the future of Germany in the past, autumn 1961 saw a military standoff in Berlin between Soviet and American troops.[268]

The dangers of Berlin were soon overshadowed by the Cuban Missile Crisis. Khrushchev partly provoked that crisis due to a wish for international status. If the Americans had rockets near the Soviet Union, as a fellow great power the latter should have rockets close to the American mainland, too.[269] Yet notice, too, how Khrushchev had been pulled back (and, absolutely, let himself be pulled back) into insecurity reminiscent of the Stalin era. Khrushchev did not seek world war, nor was he compelled to it through unchanging,

---

264   The events of Novocherkassk are shown in Baron, 2001
265   For an account of how some erstwhile elites were aware of the ideological danger in such developments see also Djilas, 1983
266   Hornsby, 2023: 279-80
267   The socio-economic difficulties besieging East Germany in the run-up to the construction of the Wall are shown in Wilke, 2014: chapter 12
268   Dramatically retold in Kempe, 2011
269   The Cuban Missile Crisis has been very widely covered. Plokhy, 2021, offers a recent, readable account

external circumstance. His fate became determined by the dream he had promised and failed to deliver.[270] Two years later, Khrushchev would be deposed as Soviet leader by an elite conspiracy led by Brezhnev. Khrushchev would spend his remaining years defending his break with Stalinism and professing hope in future Soviet generations–but in their ability to defend the country and the system rather than to expand it.[271]

It must be stressed that I am not arguing for the inherent peacefulness of the Kremlin. Or, that the West imposed conflict on Soviet and Russian leaders. I am arguing, though, that the emphasis on inherent insecurity in light of foreign threat and domestic subversion has been present throughout Soviet and post-Soviet Russian history.[272] And in that paradigm, the BSSR and Belarus have had a central place. Having largely failed to achieve global benefits under Khrushchev, Brezhnev's foreign policy continued to build up nuclear capability, but also used military superiority in Europe to threaten American allies, if less so America itself.[273] The BSSR was placed on the route from Soviet heartlands to Central Europe and also linking the main part of the RSFSR to Kaliningrad and the Baltic Sea. During the late 1940s, troops and non-military envoys from the BSSR had been used to populate that former German territory, forming a bridgehead towards the West.[274]

For a republic with only 9-10 million people, the BSSR had extensive involvement with the armed forces. Subsequent estimates placed at least 30% of the republican economy as linked to the military, with up to 200,000 military personnel stationed in the BSSR and twice that number working in the local military-industrial

---

270   Parallels with the post-Soviet era exist. To paraphrase Brian Stimpson, the Kremlin was never struck down by despair, it was struck down by hope, as suggested in Morahan, 1986. See also Yeltsin, 2000

271   See Khrushchev, 1971: 7

272   In this, I find inspiration from Skak, 2019, including conceptual links between leaders such as Yuri Andropov and Putin

273   Developments in military strategy within Europe during the early Brezhnev reign are discussed in Uhl, 2012

274   Involvement of people from the BSSR in the resettlement of Kaliningrad after the war is mentioned in Wójcik-Żołądek, 2023: 76

66   UNCANNY ALLIES

complex.[275] It was clearly a securitised place. And under Brezhnev, the BSSR would soon play a central role in foreign policy. In early 1968, nearby Czechoslovakia had chosen a new communist leader in Alexander Dubček. While a true communist believer, Dubček soon sought greater public engagement in his state.[276] While such a course might have been accepted by Khrushchev, Brezhnev's take-over of power in the Soviet Union and Soviet-lead Eastern Europe was marked by a marked resistance to socio-political change and after seeming initial vacillation by August 1968 Soviet troops led a Warsaw Pact invasion of Czechoslovakia, dismantling Dubček's re-gime.[277]

The BSSR played an important part in providing troops and access to the invasion, meaning that it would now also have a central role within the "Brezhnev Doctrine", promoted shortly after the Czechoslovak invasion to advocate Soviet rights to intervene abroad to defend its interpretation of socialism.[278] Although the situation in Czechoslovakia had been tamed, Poland would come to see violent unrest among workers again in 1970. At the cost of significant bloodshed, and the end of Gomułka's career, Polish communists got the situation under control, yet the socialist cause was clearly beleaguered.[279] To the northwest of the BSSR, during 1972 the Lithuanian SSR would experience riots in Kaunas after the self-immolation of Romas Kalanta, protesting against Soviet occupation. This unrest could be handled locally, yet it still reinforced the idea of the BSSR as surrounded by instability.[280]

Anyone in the BSSR unhappy with Soviet rule could also seek inspiration from dissidence movements among nationalist Ukrainians. Admittedly, compared to Belarusians Ukrainians had a much more detailed nation-building past to work from, yet their claim

---

275 Figures from Belarus, 1994
276 Dubček's policies are outlined well in Williams, 1997: chapter 1
277 An interesting account of the politico-legal context of the invasion can be found in Hafner, 2018
278 The Doctrine is discussed in Kramer, 1998: 167-70
279 The communist willingness to use violence against protesters in 1970 is detailed by Fajfer, 1993
280 The continued importance of Kalanta, and the riots accompanying his death, for anti-Soviet activity is described by Swain, 2015

that Russians were "outsiders" in the western parts of the Soviet Union could, in principle, appeal to Belarusians, too.[281] Nationhood had become a prominent topic in Soviet debate, even if the Soviet leadership did not approve. After Yuri Andropov had become head of the KGB in 1967, Soviet security forces were led by a man who as ambassador had come to prominence helping to crush Hungarians' uprising a decade earlier.[282] Yet even such a fearsome defender of the Soviet order did little to stem nationalism, which developed in reaction to statist policies whose consequences for society and for the environment were being felt not just in the minor republics, but even in the RSFSR, where "village prose" demonstrated fundamental unhappiness with centrist "progress".[283]

Gradually, the Soviet Union was moving towards post-modernity, towards a less centralised, more individualised society. In a sense, atomisation was back on the table, as it had been when totalitarianism was systemically promoted during the 1930s, but this time atomisation was promoted partly from below, on behalf of individuals and of non-statist groups.[284] Crucially, though, atomisation was now also promoted by the state through the "social contract"; the idea that material goods would be provided to the populace in return for political quiescence, for de-politicisation of ordinary sentiment. The system wanted to lose its potential critics, but– by doing so–lost its potential defenders, too.[285] And that matters for the purposes of this book not only because it foreshadows the collapse of the Soviet Union, but also because it gives an indication of the inherent brittleness of the post-Soviet Russian and Belarusian regimes. A brittleness of which leaders like Putin and Lukashenka

---

281 If nothing else, disaffected Belarusians could find inspiration from Ukrainian intellectuals' public criticism of the system. See, for instance, Ukrainian, 2021

282 Andropov's lessons from Hungary 1956 were somewhat ambivalent, however. See Sayle, 2009

283 Brudny, 1998, illustrates the identity battle developing between Marxism-Leninism and Russian nationalism

284 Obviously, here appear images conjectured by Jacques Tati's *Playtime*, or, from a slightly earlier date, Georgii Daneliia's *Walking the Streets of Moscow*. See also Oukaderova, 2010

285 The irony of that situation would have been well understood by Trotsky and Djilas, and by George Romero, 1978, too

would become painfully aware, thereby reinforcing the ontological insecurity persistently threatening their rule.[286]

More immediately, Soviet regime viability would be challenged by material problems. Hardships like those historically experienced would not reoccur under Brezhnev, particularly not in the relatively developed BSSR. Still, in retrospect it seems ominous both that ambitious economic reforms were undertaken early in Brezhnev's tenure, and that these were soon abandoned without replacement.[287] Instead, Brezhnev's regime sought to make its mark internationally. To the east, as indicated above, Soviet-Chinese relations had soured to the point of armed conflict by 1969. While all-out war was prevented, only three years later the American President's visit to China conjured the risk for the Soviet regime of a two-front conflict.[288] To mitigate this, during the early 1970s Brezhnev would strike several agreements with the USA. In itself, the most important agreement was the 1972 SALT I treaty limiting ballistic missiles and missile deployment sites for the parties, thereby seeking limits to the nuclear arms race. The ABM treaty could be seen in the same light.[289]

The Soviet Union employed softer means of influence, too, with Brezhnev visiting America in 1973 for the Washington Summit. Here, the Soviet leader ensured ample photo opportunities with his American counterpart, while also becoming the first Soviet leader to directly address the American public on television.[290] Also of priority–and, perhaps, more immediate priority–for the Soviet leadership was the political and security situation in Europe. Here, an international diplomatic triumph came in September 1971 when the victorious powers of the Second World War formally agreed on

---

286 Mann, 2013: 184, evokes the "shredding" of the governing ideology in the Soviet Union
287 The so-called "Kosygin Reforms", and the underlying political priorities rendering them unsustainable, are discussed in Feygin, 2024
288 For the Soviet role in American-Chinese rapprochement, see also Goh, 2005
289 While largely seen from an American point-of-view, Maurer, 2022, offers a useful timeline of the SALT I negotiations.
290 An engaging, if perhaps too sympathetic, reading of Brezhnev's motives for seeking personal engagement with Richard Nixon is in Raleigh, 2018

the status of Berlin and on access to it from Western Germany.[291] Finally overcoming an issue, which had dogged European (and Soviet) security since the Second World War, the agreement had materialised not least through the prior investment of West German Chancellor Willy Brandt, whose December 1970 visit to Poland and signature to the Treaty of Warsaw symbolised West German willingness to formally acknowledge postwar borders.[292]

Stagnation and Fall of the Soviet Union

Having taken such initiative, Brandt could engage directly with his East German counterparts. By late 1972, the "Basic Treaty" had set out a formal framework for relations between the two Germanies, thereby creating a lynchpin for European security, and by extension for the security of the western borders of the Soviet Union.[293] The following September, both Germanies had entered the United Nations, cementing their status in international law. Launched that year was also the Conference on Security and Cooperation in Europe (CSCE). With the status of Germany seemingly resolved, the Soviet Union and the USA for several years sponsored diplomatic negotiations on permanent, continent-wide stability.[294] The CSCE eventually formulated the 1975 Helsinki Accords. Covering a range of topics in European East-West relations, the Accords would subsequently become known for their human rights provisions. However, when signing the Accords the Soviet Union and other participants saw the main accomplishment as affirmation of post-war borders and of permanent peace in Europe.[295]

The Helsinki Accords appeared to place the BSSR in an advantageous position. Apart from having its political and territorial legitimacy reaffirmed, Minsk might also expect to take advantage of

---

291 The 1971 "Four Power Agreement" is summarised in Pittman, 1992: 33-35
292 Less dramatically, the treaty signed by Brandt in Moscow in August 1970 signified a similar stance. For a comparative analysis of Brandt's approach to the two treaties, see Gray, 2016
293 Developments in inter-German relations up to that point are outlined in Schoenborn and Niedhart, 2016
294 The long-term impact of the CSCE is shown well by Crump, 2016
295 For the significance of the Helsinki Accords see also Morgan, 2018

70   UNCANNY ALLIES

growing economic links between the Soviet Union and the West. As one of the most industrialised republics the BSSR might have expected a role to play.[296] Also, in the wake of the 1973 crisis endangering the supply of Middle Eastern energy to Western consumers, Brezhnev's administration sought to expand infrastructure for exports of oil and natural gas to Central and Western Europe. If that arrangement could become permanent, the BSSR was geographically well placed to take advantage.[297] That the Soviet centre might be willing to bet on an enhanced Belarusian role in energy exports was also shown by the 1975 establishment of an oil refinery in Mazyr, less than 400 kilometres from the border to Poland and, consequently, ideally placed for future value-added exports into Europe.[298]

Energy exports to Europe did increase through the Soviet collapse and always involved the BSSR and Belarus. However, at the same time the BSSR economy remained dependent on central support, while the Soviet economy overall became dependent on income from energy, the world prices of which began to drop significantly in the 1980s.[299] Even before that drop, however, economic difficulties of socialist Eastern Europe were becoming clear. Local regimes were increasingly unable to offer expected material progress, leading to widespread unrest not least in Poland, where renewed protests against price rises in 1970 saw widespread unrest, mass casualties, and the Soviet-approved replacement of Gomułka.[300] Unlike the Prague Spring here, and again in 1976, protesters appeared from the proletariat, the Bolsheviks' core constituency. Moscow seemed unable to offer allied regimes requisite economic support. Indeed, it appears that the Brezhnevite regime

---

296   Directing trade towards lucrative Western customers would also have been enticed Soviet leaders following their experience of difficult economic engagements with non-European countries before the 1970s. On this, see Sanchez-Sibony, 2014: chapter 6

297   The development of Soviet energy exports to Europe is analysed in Högselius, 2013

298   Balmaceda, 2013: 169

299   For the damage thus done to the Soviet economy, see also Ermolaev, 2017

300   Falk, 2003: 27-33 provides a fair outline of the immediate and medium-term consequences of these protests in Poland

might have had little intent on doing so–a political course then made explicit by the late 1980s.[301]

The BSSR itself did not suffer public unrest, yet political change came with the sudden death of Masherau in 1980. While officially caused by a car accident, speculation was rife at that time and later that the Belarusian leader had been killed to make way for increased Muscovite control over the republic and its resources.[302] Irrespective of the merits of that accusation, it is certainly true that Brezhnev's last years were marked by inter-factional fights within the Soviet elite. In a system severely damaged by corruption, actors in Moscow had widely differing views on what would benefit the country's, and their own, future.[303] For the purpose of this book, that development matters for two reasons. First, it reminds us that even under Brezhnev Soviet elites had concerns over the foundations on which their system rested. Second, in the context of such concerns even favoured republics like the BSSR suffered increased central control and exploitation.[304]

Given Kebich's subsequent comments on Masherau's death (as annotated above) it appears likely Belarusian elites remembered and resented such exploitation. For the Soviet centre at the time, though, republican elites could be kept in line as could the Belarusian population among which dissent remained relatively rare moving into the 1980s.[305] Dissent did exist, though, and gradually grew

---

301 This assumption is supported by the fact that the Soviet economy could likely have afforded much higher subsidisation of Eastern Europe, as demonstrated by Spechler and Spechler, 2009

302 One later proponent of the theory of assassination would be Vyacheslav Kebich, prime minister of Belarus between 1991 and 1994. For a summary of Kebich's thoughts on this, see also Fedorov, 2009

303 In a slightly sympathetic account of Brezhnev's end, the sense of decline and political confusion nonetheless shows clearly. See Schattenberg, 2021: chapter 9

304 Something Kebich clearly thought, too, as per the previous reference. See also Urban, 1989: chapters 5-6 for a detailed look at Soviet-era factionalism and patronage in the BSSR. Links to central Soviet power plays are described, for instance, on p. 111

305 One main reason for the quiescence of the BSSR population in the Soviet context was, of course, the significant proportion of veterans from the Second World War, whether Belarusian, Russian, or from another ethnicity, although—as discussed by Sinel'nikova, 2010: 253-56 that could, at times be a difficult constituency to fully satisfy

during the Brezhnevite era. It has been shown, for instance, that there was some sympathy for Czechoslovakia and the fate of the Prague Spring among intellectuals in the BSSR, who at the time themselves had briefly sought to exercise limited expression of freedom.[306] That the intelligentsia, and the Belarusian population more broadly, largely remained quiet in fear of repression does not mean that critique disappeared. One notable figure emerging under Brezhnev was Ales Adamovich, who worked within the Soviet system and considered himself socialist yet very much believed in the cultural "thaw" of the 1960s.[307]

Dissidence "from inside" the system existed elsewhere, too, in socialist Europe. Perhaps most dramatically, Andrey Sakharov — who had previously played a central role in developing the Soviet nuclear programme–had reinvented himself against the arms race, by 1975 achieving international stardom with receipt of the Nobel Peace Prize.[308] His was an unusually stark challenge to regime priorities, yet similar challenges from civil society were emerging elsewhere. In Czechoslovakia, Charta 77 was formed to take advantage of human rights provisions to which that country had signed up at Helsinki two years prior. De facto leader of that organisation became the playwright Václav Havel.[309] However, for the time being Sakharov and Havel could be overcome with relative ease. Neither had widespread following in society–it was, therefore, easy to place the two into temporary confinement or domestic exile. Potential imitators from the intelligentsia, like Adamovich, realised this and mostly kept their peace with political affairs, for now.[310]

Much more troublesome was the spectre of nationalism. Previously, I discussed how armed, nationalist partisans in the Baltic

---

306   For details on this, see also Astrouskaya, 2019: 64-71
307   On Adamovich's intriguing background and development, see also Isakava, 2017: 356-57
308   The development of Sakharov's thought and public profile under Khrushchev and Brezhnev is detailed by Bergman, 2009: chapters 6-13
309   Havel would become famous for his approach to non-violent resistance, as outlined in The Power, 2018
310   To give them their due, Havel and Sakharov were clearly aware of the challenges facing them, but saw their audience not so much in the regime as in a "liberated" public mind, to paraphrase Miłosz, 2001

republics and the Ukrainian SSR had been fought and defeated after the war, while retaining prominence among the intelligentsia through the 1960s. Sometimes nationalists did not challenge socialism, per se, but only its current iteration.[311] Arguably, in 1980 that became the case in Poland, too, where the birth of Solidarity–while of enormous historical consequence in the longer term–began on the basis of workforce disputes at the shipyards in Gdansk. Solidarity leader Lech Wałęsa was certainly ready for a fight, but he was hardly a "capitalist agent".[312] Yet Polish and Soviet leaders came to fear Solidarity above other challengers. As mentioned above, regime legitimacy centred on perceived socio-economic benefits for the working class. Consequently, challenges on that basis remained uniquely dangerous, as they would become decades later for Putin and Lukashenka, often mirroring their rule on perceived Brezhnev-era ideals.[313]

The socialist system never found a solution to Solidarity or to Wałęsa. Early, local protests in Gdansk soon spread nationwide and encompassed not only large parts of the working classes, but also a rejuvenated intelligentsia. Arguably, the protests developing during 1980 and 1981 showed better the potential of society-wide national protest than anywhere before.[314] Eventually, in late 1981 the Polish government introduced martial law. Wałęsa and other leading figures in Solidarity were imprisoned. There were even persistent rumours that a new Soviet-led military invasion aimed to crush resistance in the mould of 1968, or perhaps even 1956. That did not happen but would otherwise certainly have involved BSSR

---

311 This had been the case in 1956 in the Georgian SSR following Khrushchev's denunciation of Stalin and would reappear in that republic in 1978 protests against perceived linguistic discrimination in the new Soviet constitution. On the latter episode, see also Kaiser, 2022: 166-75

312 Remember here the inimitable appearance of Wałęsa in that delightful account of the socialist collapse, Sebestyen, 2009: chapter 4

313 In the Russian case, in particular, this is shown clearly by Crowley, 2021

314 That is, of course, a tendentious claim given developments of Hungary and Czechoslovakia, in particular, during previous decades. However, if Solidarity-led dissent is considered on the background of years of repeated unrest in Poland, and in the contest of developed, socialist modernity, its status as a breakthrough phenomenon may be argued. For claims to the uniqueness of the Solidarity phenomenon, see also Crampton, 1997: 368

participation.[315] In the event, repression could be handled by the Polish leadership without external assistance. Even if more difficulties had been foreseen, though, it is far from certain that the Soviet Union would have become military involved in what was a potentially very volatile situation, the consequences of which could have spilled into Soviet territory.[316]

Still, the Soviet leadership was deeply concerned about the consequences of regime change in Poland–or, indeed, the consequences of increased nationalism within regime and society at large. Already, the 1978 appointment of Karol Wojtyła as pope John Paul II had created a focal point of adulation easily rivalling that of communism.[317] Such a Catholic focal point could impact domestic affairs in the Soviet Union, too–in the Lithuanian SSR and among the population in the western BSSR. At the same time, some Polish intellectuals were gaining support by calling for closer relations between Poles and Belarusians with rhetoric somewhat similar to interwar expansionist Prometheanism.[318] Consequently, Soviet reluctance to allow political divergence among other socialist European states was not simply based in imperialism. Even after the seemingly definitive outcome of the Helsinki Accords, the western borders of the Soviet Union remained nebulous, prey to ontological insecurity. In the perception of Moscow, that pattern would remain after 1991.[319]

By the early 1980s, though, the Soviet leadership had more wide-ranging international problems. Détente had declined from the mid-1970s and now appeared moribund if not deceased. Arguably, an early sign of this malaise had been the 1977 arrival of

---

315 For indication that such an invasion into Poland from the BSSR had long been considered, see also Mastny, 1999: 205

316 As also argued by Gompert et al, 2014: 146-47

317 John Paul II's visit to Poland in 1979 did not help the communist cause, either. See Felak, 2020: chapter 1

318 Important here was the 1980 publication by Bohdan Skaradziński entitled *Belarusians-Lithuanians-Ukrainians: our enemies-or brothers?* On that, see also Turkowski, 2023: 682-83

319 Here it is worth remembering that we are dealing with "territories" and "borders" as constructions rather than empirical givens—just as the nature of "Russian Empire" (let alone its extent) has changed persistently over time. A fine overview of that process remains Longworth, 2005

Jimmy Carter as American president on a platform of human rights partly aimed at socialist dictatorship.[320] At the same time, to the east Chinese instability following the death of Mao Zedong was being resolved in favour of Deng Xiaoping who would gradually reform the country's economy if not its autocracy. That change did nothing to reassure Brezhnev's elites, who–perhaps understandably–could fear increased collaboration between its two great power enemies.[321] So, towards the end of Brezhnev's reign global politics appeared unpropitious. Still, the Soviet Union managed to make a bad situation worse. Most notable was the invasion of Afghanistan in late 1979, which not only undermined relations with the West but fatally challenged the work done by Moscow within the Third World over preceding decades.[322]

Entering the 1980s, the Soviet Union therefore found itself isolated to a greater extent than had long been the case. It did not help that the invasion itself was bungled, coming only after protracted instability within Afghanistan itself and quite understaffed and -equipped for the task of pacifying and "normalising" the Central Asian state.[323] And while the worsening crisis in Afghanistan did not directly threaten the viability of the Soviet state, it did highlight the inadequacy of the system as a whole, not least through the growing number of young men returning from the conflict dead or gravely wounded with little success to show for such sacrifice.[324] I

---

320   Carter's focus on repression in the Soviet Union and Central Eastern Europe would be continued under his successor, although the reasons for such continuity have been contested. See also Hartmann, 2001

321   That Deng at this point was eager to acquire support against the perceived Soviet threat is shown in Vogel, 2011: chapter 9

322   The problem for the Moscow leadership, at the time of the invasion and when departure was later planned, was that any policy towards Afghanistan seemed designed to damage Soviet prestige in the Third World. This is well pointed out by Kalinovsky, 2009: 70

323   The details of the immediate debates and activities surrounding the Soviet invasion are well presented by Braithwaite, 2011

324   There is a broader point to be made here that the failed conflict in Afghanistan could be said to be a starting point for the de-masculinisation of Soviet — and later Russian — society with failures in Chechnya and (more prosaically) socioeconomic conditions to follow for beleaguered "male-ness". Such a development has been well outlined by Eichler, 2012: particularly chapter 1, and would

76 UNCANNY ALLIES

mention this here to set the context for the neurotic foreign policy of Brezhnev's late reign and of his short-reigning successor, Andropov. Remember also that this was an age of revolutionary activity. Contrasted to so much political virility, as in Ruhollah Khomeini's Iran, an impotent Soviet Union looked ever more a country of yesteryear.[325]

In this situation, Soviet foreign policy might have benefited from activities marking continued great power status. However, by the late 1970s such status had already been slipping away. The great advances in arms control achieved with the USA earlier in the decade had slowed down, to be halted fully by Washington after the Afghan invasion.[326] Of less military yet much symbolic consequence was the subsequent boycott of the 1980 Moscow Olympics by America and several of its allies. During the post-war era, communist regimes had increasingly used sports to showcase ideological triumph–the Moscow Olympics would have been a crowning glory, now partly taken away.[327] Afterwards, there was little likelihood of the international situation improving for the Soviet Union. In January 1980 Ronald Reagan became American president on an avowedly anti-communist programme. Having made a career as an actor, Reagan had then hitched his political profile closely to the fight against communist subversion.[328]

And although Reagan may have been aged, in public he retained vigour–unlike the Kremlin leaders which he opposed. By the early 1980s Soviet elites were dying or effectively becoming incapacitated with age. Brezhnev himself passed away in late 1982 and

---

starkly contradict, too, a Soviet and Russian understanding of "great power" status.

325 Of course, the Soviet leadership briefly hoped for some sort of alliance with the new Iran, without much chance of success. For a summary of Soviet relations with Iran at the time, see Westad, 2005: 296-99

326 The collapse of arms negotiations during the late 1970s was of course shown through the aborted SALT II. See also Ambrose, 2018: chapter 6

327 A very useful overview of the political context in which the 1980 Moscow Olympics existed is Chepurnaya, 2016

328 The build-up of Reagan's public profile against communism is a theme of Kengor, 2007: part I

had been increasingly feeble over the preceding decade.[329] Brezhnev's successor, Andropov, was of starker ideological bent as shown in his lengthy KGB tenure and posting in Hungary, as mentioned earlier. Andropov was very much in favour of centralisation, being perhaps less concerned with immediate foreign policy gains than with shoring up support for the system at home, including in republics like the BSSR.[330] The new General Secretary needed resources, though, which a stagnating economy could not provide. Problems with discipline arose among the Soviet workforce and with materiel, too–both issues recently showcased to the world in Afghanistan and, less dramatically, in incidents such as the infamous "Whiskey on the Rocks" submarine beaching by Sweden in 1981.[331]

Reagan sought to take full advantage of Soviet weakness. Building on the principles of the Helsinki Accords, the American president repeatedly chastised Soviet breaches of their citizens' human rights. For now, focus remained on high-profile individuals, such as Andrey Sakharov, yet Soviet national groups, too, could take notice.[332] Still, Soviet leaders would have been happy if American pressure had concentrated on political or cultural issues. Instead, Reagan increasingly pushed a military advantage against his opponent, buoyed by advisers convinced that the Cold War could only be finished through the absolute and overt defeat of either side.[333] Whether Reagan wanted all-out conflict was unclear, but he certainly appeared more inclined for such a possibility than had most, if not all, of his postwar predecessors. As he incautiously joked about the destruction of the Soviet Union in 1984, many

---

329 For a brief, but convincing summary of the decrepitude increasingly marring Brezhnev's tenure, see also Crump, 2013: chapter 13

330 Andropov and his leadership remain under-exposed in scholarship. An idea of his priorities, though, can be gleaned from Sell, 2016: chapter 8

331 Although of limited military importance, this event gained great publicity abroad for its symbolism. For how the matter was handled in the West and specifically by Sweden, see also Stern and Sundelius, 1992

332 Reagan's strategy of using human rights to challenge the Soviet Union is covered by Peterson, 2012

333 The background for such a worldview is the topic of Robin, 2017

78   UNCANNY ALLIES

observers–and not just within communist regimes–believed the joke belied deeper intent.[334]

Such belief was supported by events over a previous year arguably more dangerous for peace than any other after 1945. In March of 1983 Reagan had launched his "Star Wars" programme, seeking technological capacity to counter the Soviet nuclear arsenal. That realisation of this programme might be decades into the future did not reassure Moscow.[335] They knew that Reagan had previously stated intent to abolish all nuclear weapons but saw little reason to trust that. Distrust soon had fatal consequences when a South Korean civilian plane was shot down by the Soviet air force in September, most likely due to suspicion of espionage.[336] As horrific as that incident was, though, worse could have happened shortly after. In a separate incident, Soviet early warning systems mistakenly alerted the military to alleged incoming American nuclear missiles. Only the initiative–or, pointedly, the lack of response from a local Soviet commander prevented possible conflagration.[337]

Soviet forces were clearly rattled by perceived Western, notably American, intent. That November once again danger developed when the NATO-exercise Able Archer appeared to some Soviet analysts to shroud an intended surprise attack. Soviet fears were still not realised in pre-emptive strikes, yet without some trust-building hot war could soon break out.[338] And that outbreak might well take place in Europe, along the Soviet western borders. Apart from more general disagreements over arms control, the late 1970s had also seen Europe become stage for a crisis centred on shorter-range missiles presented by both sides, potentially enabling surprise attacks and, arguably, nullifying Soviet continental advantages in conventional arms.[339] Although the missile standoff never fully realised,

---

334 Soviet apprehension was also stoked by Reagan's previous moniker of the "Evil Empire". On that, see Rowland and Jones, 2016
335 The Soviet response to "Star Wars" is the topic of Podvig, 2017
336 The shooting down of the South Korean airlines, and the tension building between the superpowers across that year, is masterfully rolled out in Downing, 2018
337 This incident has received some coverage over the last decade, and very engagingly so by Anthony, 2014
338 On Soviet perceptions of Able Archer at the time, see Barrass, 2016
339 Bange, 2016, provides understanding of the military aspects of the missile crisis

the BSSR again appeared on a major front line in world affairs–despite the recent promises from Helsinki. After Andropov's death, the brief tenure of Konstantin Chernenko did little to help matters. The interim leader was gravely ill throughout and, in any case, never minded for renewed détente.[340]

Matters would prove different with Chernenko's epochal successor, Mikhail Gorbachev. Although Gorbachev did not appear as an elite outlier from the onset–indeed, he very much rose as Andropov's protégé–he was of a relatively younger generation and clearly of the belief that personal diplomacy mattered.[341] A few months before officially becoming Chernenko's successor in 1985 Gorbachev had a fruitful photo opportunity with the UK prime minister, who may have had fundamental ideological differences with her guest but understood–and showed the world–that the new generation of Soviet leader might augur a more hopeful world.[342] This should not be taken to imply that Gorbachev started his tenure as General Secretary with intent to end the Cold War through Soviet concessions. Indeed, at his inaugural standoff with Reagan in Geneva Gorbachev repeatedly pushed for American abandonment of Star Wars and appeared quite prickly on criticism levelled at his domestic political system.[343]

Yet at least the Soviet leader had shown willingness–as well as capacity–to meet with Reagan and demonstrate a wish to overcome the dangerous impasse of preceding years. Gorbachev had also made clear his understanding of the significant domestic challenges facing his country, indicating he might wish international stability to focus on domestic priorities.[344] Soon, Gorbachev would

---

340 There is even less literature on Chernenko's reign than on that of Andropov, which is unsurprising given the lack of developments under the former. However, for the legacy left to Gorbachev when he took over, see Wilson, 2014: chapter 4

341 Such traits are prevalent in most writings on Gorbachev. A classic here is Brown, 1996: especially chapter 7

342 Subsequently somewhat mythologised, those seeking helpful context for this meeting should read Brown, 2008

343 Tension surrounding this early encounter between Gorbachev and Reagan is clear from Service, 2015: chapter 14

344 That, of course, was also a main message of Gorbachev, 1987

80 UNCANNY ALLIES

have a fatal reminder of such priorities. In April 1986 a partial meltdown of the UkSSR Chernobyl nuclear power plant caused widespread radioactive pollution, substantial casualties and international condemnation, not least regarding the paucity of information released by Moscow regarding the incident.[345] Chernobyl was located close to the borders of the BSSR, which received around 70% of the fallout. In response, Belarusian intellectuals, including Ales Adamovich, directly warned Gorbachev of a "spiritual extinction" of Belarus–due to the radioactive fallout but also to the neglect of Belarusian identity signified by callous official response to the accident.[346]

Gorbachev proved partly receptive to criticism over the Chernobyl catastrophe. Although the Soviet leader always remained resistant to admitting personal responsibility, for him the nuclear accident showed a creaking economic system and inadequate command systems across the Soviet state. Soon, Gorbachev instituted "perestroika" and "glasnost" the two policies for which he would become best known.[347] Abroad, glasnost–the push for increased openness in public debate–was most remarked upon. However, Gorbachev made explicit from the outset that glasnost was there to support the prime policy of perestroika–the restructuring of the Soviet economy against perceived bureaucratic resistance. Gorbachev was not seeking systemic change; he was a populist seeking systemic reinvigoration.[348] While that aim found some public sympathy, increasingly domestic challengers would appear. Nationalism would come to present one vocal challenge. For that, the BSSR might not seem an obvious place, given the earlier mentioned scarcity of national institutions. As elsewhere in the Soviet Union,

---

345 The Chernobyl accident, and the context which facilitated it, is the topic of the persuasive Plokhy, 2018
346 Adamovich's plea to Gorbachev on behalf of Belarus is reproduced in Adamovič, 2006
347 For the interplay of perestroika and glasnost, see also Zimmerman, 2016: chapter 6
348 The question of whether Gorbachev's populism was simply a ploy for power or managed to entrance himself as much as his audience is well covered by Zubok, 2002

though, ordinary Belarusians began to take an interest in their past.[349]

In the summer of 1988 that interest concentrated on Kurapaty, the above-mentioned forested area near Minsk where was now found widespread remains of Stalinist repression victims. By that autumn the notion of Belarusians as victims of Soviet, even Russian, aggression had become public with police repression of groups like the newly formed Belarusian Popular Front.[350] That notion was of course not held by everyone, or even by a majority in the BSSR. Particularly regarding depictions of Russians, it mattered that the republic, on linguistic and other indicators, remained among the most Russified outside the RSFSR. Notably, such Russification had arguably spread to western BSSR, as well.[351] It also mattered that republican living standards remained among the best in the Soviet Union. However, given such relative advantages for the status quo it becomes even more remarkable that dissent now spread ever more publicly. By February 1989 thousands were allowed to march in Minsk to advocate preservation of the Belarusian heritage.[352]

The following month witnessed elections to the Soviet Congress of People's Deputies, a new legislative assembly instituted by Gorbachev and–for the first time–including genuine opponents of the elite. In the BSSR prominent communist politicians lost their elections, as did young Lukashenka, albeit very narrowly to Viacheslau Kebich who had much administrative resource.[353] Kebich would become prime minister of the BSSR by June 1990, at a time when the Soviet Union as a whole was undergoing fundamental changes. Most notably, that same month Boris Yeltsin led the

---

349   An overview of the so-called "Informal Groups" emerging under Gorbachev and seeking to circumvent official institutions is provided by Shubin, 2006

350   On the discoveries at Kurapaty providing impetus for the creation of the Belarusian Popular Front, see also Temper, 2008: 253-54

351   See Szporluk, 1979: 87 for evidence of how Belarusian-language media had been largely subdued even in the western parts of that republic by the later years under Brezhnev

352   The protests were, of course, also motivated by renewed public disclosures of the damage done by Chernobyl to the territory and population of the BSSR. See the comment on this by Rich, 1990: 197

353   See also Wilson, 2021: 148

82   UNCANNY ALLIES

RSFSR to declare republican sovereignty, giving official recognition of the challenge to centralisation which would increase until the Union's demise.[354] In July, Kebich took the BSSR on the same path, declaring republican sovereignty in turn. Note, though, that "sovereignty" at this point was not intended to lead to a dissolution of the Soviet Union. Neither the BSSR leadership nor that of Yeltsin wanted full-fledged independence; they wanted additional resources for their local power bases.[355]

That power base appeared secure in the BSSR. When elections for the BSSR Supreme Soviet took place in March 1990, the communists gained 84% of seats. Certainly, the electoral system was rigged in their favour, yet the security of the BSSR leadership contrasted with the increasing challenges faced by Gorbachev and the Soviet centre.[356] And the situation of the BSSR in the Soviet Union seemed to have substantial public backing. In March 1991, Gorbachev called a Union-wide referendum on whether the Soviet Union should be continued under the same fundamental principles as before. To that, a significant majority of voters in the BSSR agreed.[357] True, republican dissenters had by now become highly vocal. No one was more so than Zianon Pazniak, who had made his name in the disclosure of the mass graves at Kurapaty and who had formally led the Belarusian Popular Front ("Rebirth") from the summer of 1989, when the Belarusian Language Society was also established.[358]

Admittedly, that society had its founding conference in the neighbouring Lithuanian SSR, taking advantage of more propitious political conditions there. Yet the language initiative at least managed to get some formal traction. At the beginning of 1990 Belarusian was made the official language of the BSSR, planned to phase

---

354   Yeltsin, in addition, swiftly sought alliance with other republican leaders on the issue of decentralisation, e.g. in December 1990 treaty with the UkSSR. On this, see Dunlop, 1993: 60
355   See also Smith, 2013: 276-78
356   For a comparison of the BSSR election with that of other Soviet republics in 1990, see Montgomery and Remington, 1994
357   The referendum, and its context amid republican counter-referendums, is well detailed by Walker, 2003: chapter 3
358   Bogdan, 2011, investigates Pazniak's political rhetoric and aims at the time

out Russian over a decade.[359] It is likely, however, that Belarusian nationalist gains would have reached no further if not for developments moving the entire Soviet Union to its end. When the 1991 August coup sought to oust Gorbachev on behalf of regressive challengers the BSSR leadership offered its support then fell with their patrons as the coup collapsed.[360] Taking over, then, in the republic was Stanislau Shushkevich who as parliamentary chairman led the BSSR to its declaration of independence, in the process changing the name, flag and state symbols from the now obsolete communist past. The BSSR was no more; yet its replacement was mired in uncertainty.[361]

---

359   As pointed out by Woolhiser, 2014: 96, the BSSR was among the last republics to pass such a language law
360   The August Coup continues to be discussed. A concise, useful summary of the coup and its immediate aftermath is in Beissinger, 2002: 425-30
361   That uncertainty across the soon-to-be former Soviet space is the *leitmotif* running through Plokhy, 2014

2 1992-2011

A New World Threatens

As the end of 1991 approached, Soviet republican elites found themselves in a dilemma. Apart from the Baltic republics, and arguably Georgia, there was little appetite for complete separation from existing economic or inter-personal networks. Soviet institutions had been designed to make such separation difficult and costly; this now showed.[362] When Yeltsin, Shushkevich and Ukrainian president Leonid Kravchuk in December signed the Belovezhskaya Pushcha agreement (which soon became the basis for the Commonwealth of Independent States, or CIS) this became a contingency solution following the referendum confirming Ukrainian independence. For Russia, the CIS was seen as a means to retain some influence in neighbouring states.[363] The Belarusians, in turn, accepted the necessity of continued collaboration with Russia, in particular, but saw their country's role in the medium term as linking the post-Soviet area and Europe. Indeed, Shushkevich himself was hoping that his Belarus over the years would be able to bring those two regions closer together.[364]

Should that plan succeed, it might provide Belarus with an international identity it had hitherto lacked. Although the First World War had seen limited attempts at organising the Belarusian space (or parts thereof) politically the resultant institutions, as well as any economic infrastructure left from the Russian Empire had quickly been dominated by the Bolsheviks.[365] Some groups in the BSSR had done well from their time in the republic. However, the latest incarnation of such people had just seen their Soviet Union dissolve with little input from Belarusian elites or even from the Belarusian

---

362   Some of the economic consequences seen by the post-Soviet states when breaking out of the Soviet system are analysed in Suesse, 2018

363   For Belarusian intent at the Beloveshskaya Pushcha negotiations, the reader can find much illumination in Shushkevich, 2013, even if the author perhaps over-emphasises his importance at the event

364   See also Chafetz et al, 1996: 741

365   For that, see Horowitz, 2003: 31

86   UNCANNY ALLIES

opposition which, albeit highly vocal at times, had been unable to take advantage.[366] Some people in Belarus, notably Lukashenka, would later use the emasculation of the Soviet collapse to advocate a return to Sovietised values. At first, though, leaders of the independent state adopted some of the rhetoric of the erstwhile opposition, presenting their polity as heir to a millennial-old Central European imperial legacy.[367]

Pazniak and the Belarusian Popular Front wanted to take advantage of that rhetoric. From its inception in the late Soviet Union, the Front had called for Belarus to completely break free from Soviet economic structures, instead linking up with the free-market global economic system, perhaps similar to idealised medieval trade networks across Central Europe.[368] In that aim the leaders of Belarus agreed, in principle. Partly to that end, in June 1992 Shushkevich signed a Friendship Treaty with Poland. In doing so, Shushkevich stressed the close ethnic links between Poles and Belarusians in rhetoric which might have provoked consternation among Russians still reeling from the loss of much historical territory.[369] However, Russia itself was eagerly seeking economic and political contacts abroad. Also–unlike in the Baltic States or Central Asia–Russians did not broadly perceive a threat from Belarusian national self-construction with almost half of all Russians in Belarus believing in the value for themselves of Belarusian national rebirth.[370]

It was not as if most Belarusians, or the Belarusian state, wanted to break all relations with Russia. Despite the entreaties of opposition figures like Pazniak, the above-mentioned Friendship Treaty with Poland had quickly been followed by an agreement with Russia aimed towards increased political and military collaboration in future.[371] Shushkevich, in particular, did not want to

---

366   This is also the point of Gel'man, 2008: 167-68
367   As that legacy incorporated Lithuanian narratives, too, it was unsurprising that the latter offered differing interpretations. For an example of this, see also Lagerspetz, 1999: 385
368   An approach noted in Abdelal, 2002: 473
369   See also Burant, 1993: 407-08
370   For that, see Marples, 1999b: 574
371   On developments in Belarusian foreign policy at this time I have to slightly disagree with the point made by Martinsen, 2002: 402, that early post-Soviet

choose sides for Belarus. And for most Russians the danger was not Belarusian strength, but Belarusian weakness. Russian elites knew that they retained several avenues of influence in Minsk. Notably, Belarusian security forces–including the KGB–were rumoured to remain closely linked to their erstwhile colleagues in Moscow.[372] Also, the Belarusians pledged conciliatory intent. From parliament even came early pledges that the country wanted to model itself after Denmark in international affairs. As the Scandinavian country–not known for belligerence–had only 27,000 troops with a 5m population so would Belarus with 10m people allegedly only have 54,000 troops.[373]

Unlike Denmark, Belarus had inherited nuclear weapons: 81 ICBMs (holding 81 warheads). However, that number was dwarfed not only by Russia's arsenal but by those of Ukraine and Kazakhstan. Minsk held 7% of warheads in Ukraine, and 8% of warheads in Kazakhstan. And unlike them (and Russia) it had no bombers to delivers nuclear weapons.[374] Nevertheless, as with Ukraine and Kazakhstan Russia swiftly sought international support to put pressure on Belarus for the hand-over of nuclear arms to its territory. Indeed, Moscow conditioned its support for the vaunted START I treaty–widely hailed in the USA and elsewhere–on the accession of its three neighbours to the Nuclear Non-Proliferation Treaty.[375] Back in late 1991 the three countries had agreed to joining this Treaty and to swiftly returning all tactical nuclear weapons to Russian soil. That process was completed within the first few months on 1992 (apart from nuclear weapons held with the Black Sea Fleet on Crimea).[376]

Belarus was not seeking non-alignment; although, perhaps "multi-alignment" could be a more helpful term

372 As mentioned in Way and Levitsky, 2006: 405

373 The suggested comparison taken from Chafetz, 1993: 142

374 This was pointed out by Drezner, 1997: 76

375 An observation made in Rublee, 2015: 150

376 Zagorski, 1992: 28. Incidentally, this observation is also worth remembering when discussing the counterfactual case of whether Ukraine, in particular, should have held on to nuclear weapons to protect itself against future Russian aggression. That option was not considered by anyone at the time, let alone the Ukrainians who may have held on to strategic nuclear weapons while

By May 1992, the link between the START I treaty and the non-nuclear commitment of Belarus, Ukraine and Kazakhstan was made explicit in the Lisbon Protocol, according to which the latter three would remove all nuclear arms and facilities for arms production from their territory, while pledging not to gain such capacity again in future.[377] In pushing for that solution (and by its subsequent work leading up to the 1994 Budapest Memorandum) Russia had not sought to remove military challengers but to better manage the threat posed by over 40,000 nuclear weapons and around 1.5m kilos of plutonium and highly enriched uranium stored across the four post-Soviet states.[378] Such management was partly a matter of prestige for Russia. Control of nuclear weapons was seen as one aspect of great power status carried over from Soviet times. Also, of course, a country now allowed to participate in the G7 (thereby moving the organisation towards a G8) needed to show some control of its neighbourhood.[379]

Particularly since such control was otherwise spectacularly lacking. As the consequences of Soviet disintegration rolled across the region, unrest was emerging everywhere around Russia. A vicious, but short-lived civil war in Moldova was overshadowed by international warfare in the South Caucasus and what would prove to be a protracted conflict in Tajikistan.[380] Inside Russia itself, Yeltsin faced prolonged uncertainty from a "parade of sovereignties", which witnessed local powerholders holding as many resources as possible away from Moscow's control. Worst was that problem in the North Caucasus republic of Chechnya, which is 1992 declared its independence from Russia with great uncertainty on how that would proceed.[381] An even more existential security problem

---

compensation and aid was sought, but had been quick to hand over the potentially much more militarily flexible and useful tactical nuclear weapons.

377   Yost, 2015: 510-11
378   Galeotti, 2022b: 46
379   That the prestige offered by G7 mattered to Russia could repeatedly be seen in official statements and articles, such as Razumovskii, 1996
380   Offering a detailed description of how Soviet collapse could spill into post-Soviet conflict, particularly in the case of Tajikistan, is Scarborough, 2023
381   That event, with all the uncertainty surrounding it in the Russian political space, is the topic of Gall and de Waal, 1997: chapter 6

would then develop during 1993 around the central Russian state itself, culminating in the autumn when Yeltsin had parliament targeted by tanks before running a constitutional referendum, seemingly providing legal legitimacy for a substantial clarification, and consolidation, of presidential powers.[382]

All this is mentioned not to excuse Russian (in)action abroad, but to place the latter in context. Given such multiple sources of local instability, the Kremlin was not planning world domination. Certainly, Russia spearheaded the formation of the Collective Security Organisation (CSO) in May 1992, yet that signalled a rearguard action rather than expansionism.[383] There was conviction among Moscow elites that other post-Soviet administrations–including in Minsk–were incapable of handling their own affairs and that their inevitable failure within military security affairs in particular would rebound on Russian stability. That states like Belarus were very quick to set up their own armed forces did little to reassure Moscow.[384] Unlike some other post-Soviet states, though, in Belarus some elites wanted to retain international military links. Above was mentioned the bilateral agreement from mid-1992 promising future Russo-Belarusian collaboration. Shushkevich would have preferred to remain non-committal, yet towards the end of the following year the Belarusian legislature forced through the country's membership of the CSO.[385]

Pushing for CSO membership had been Kebich, then still considered Shushkevich's main challenger in the upcoming Belarusian presidential election. With such support inside Belarus Russia had

---

382 For the momentous influence of these events on Russian political trajectories, see also Gel'man, 2023

383 Çakmak and Özşahin, 2023: 977. The point here is particularly to push back against any retrospective notion that the CSO was meant as a challenger to NATO. Instead, the organisation was an attempt to handle security concerns (and increasingly non-military concerns at that) within and among member-states; a development also seen when the CSO further institutionalised a decade later.

384 Russian attempts to salvage some military unity in the former Soviet space are discussed in Odom, 1998: chapters 15-16. An obvious point to make here is that Russia showed little ability to handle its own military security. The colonial attitude in Moscow's stance towards its neighbours is clear, too.

385 The treaty that Belarus thereby signed up to can be found as Collective, 1992

90   UNCANNY ALLIES

also secured continued presence of its own troops within that country, thereby offering Moscow a military forward position in the west and next to Poland.[386] Such a position mattered for Russia not only given historical concerns about Polish intentions (which have already been referred to), but also because it reduced the risk of the exclave of Kaliningrad being marooned should Poland and the Baltic States move closer to the West.[387] Belarus–despite fervent wishes of the opposition and partly Shushkevich–was not likely to have such options. From the early 1990s it seemed unlikely that Belarus (and other post-Soviet states, apart from the Baltic Republics) would be invited to join NATO or the new European Union, even if those post-Soviet states tried to improve themselves.[388]

So, for reasons of Belarusian domestic politics–as well as those belonging to international affairs–by the early 1990s Russia seemed able and happy to keep its neighbour within its military reach. Whether Russia wanted to keep Belarus within economic reach, as well, remained more doubtful, since Russian society was rocked by socio-economic instability.[389] Facing such difficulties, the Kremlin was not keen on safeguarding the socio-economic fortunes of its neighbours, too. For some Belarusians distancing was welcome. Shushkevich highlighted how economic confederation was not needed for Belarus and would be against its constitutional international neutrality. Kebich, in turn, stressed that his country's development needed Russian aid.[390] At first, a sort of compromise between those approaches was sought. In April 1992 a Belarusian rouble was introduced. However, at the same time Russian currency

---

386   Yost, 1993: 103
387   While discussions on NATO-enlargement did not pick up speed until the middle of the decade, Poland and other Central European countries had early on made clear their interest in Western security guarantees. Their request also had notable identity implications, as discussed in Kuus, 2004
388   Notice, for instance, how Romania was formally presented with the future possibility of EU membership, despite the country at this time being seen as less democratic than Belarus. On that, see Way and Levitsky, 2007: 57
389   The difficulties faced by Russia when emerging from the Soviet era have been covered widely. An informed, comparative account of the policies followed and their immediate consequences in Russia and other post-communist states can be found in Åslund, 2012: particularly chapters 1-8
390   These contradictory positions are shown in Tsygankov, 2000: 117

was freely circulating in the country. Given high inflation barter trade was also prevalent, leaving neither the Russian nor the Belarusian central bank with fiscal control.[391]

Eventually, by August 1993 Russia announced the end of the rouble zone. Having intended to keep the rouble as a common currency across much of the post-Soviet space, the Russian central bank–and the Russian government–had suffered from increased inflation pushed by short-term bailouts sought by neighbouring states.[392] With that option now being removed, regimes outside Russia had to go elsewhere for support or suffer further calamity. In Belarus, the latter seemed more likely. Kebich and Shushkevich tried to blame each other for the difficult transition. Both chose to use as their medium for the attack Lukashenka, known already for railing against corruption.[393] The idea was that either Kebich or Shushkevich would fall under Lukashenka's onslaught. In return, that medium could be offered an important role in the victor's administration following the presidential election. Soon, indeed, Shushkevich was forced from his position in January 1994, having already–as mentioned above–been defeated over the question of CSO membership.[394]

Come March, the post-Soviet Belarusian constitution was adopted. Like most other post-Soviet states after 1991 Belarus had been left with an amalgam of laws based on the Soviet constitution of 1977. While a new legal framework understandably had taken time to create, the legal limbo had left the polity vulnerable to

---

391 Indeed, barter would prove persistent in the region, for simple financial reasons but also due to protracted institutional weakness. On causes of barter, see also Ledeneva and Seabright, 2000

392 Granville, Brigitte (2016) "Lessons from the Collapse of the Ruble Zone and the Transferable Ruble System", *CESifo Forum*, vol. 17, issue 4

393 Later, official Belarusian sources would present Lukashenka's early life and career not unlike that of Jimmy Stewart, coming from the genuine people in the countryside to offer genuine values in the cesspit of the capital. On this, see Astapova, 2016b, and consider, perhaps, that the "swamp" is a more central image in Belarusian than in American imagery.

394 Shushkevich would later stress the reforms he could have introduced if he had retained power and implied Lukashenka was a "pathetic plebeian", who had "enslaved himself before Russia." On this, see Shushkevich, 2004: 65

power struggles.[395] With that framework now in place and Shushkevich out of the way, the path should have been prepared for Kebich to take advantage. That February, he appealed directly to the Russian connection by highlighting not only economic connections between the states but also alleged "spiritual bonds." Polish media even showed Kebich mirroring Soviet presentations.[396] The extent to which Kebich was assisted by Russian actors is unclear. It has, for instance, been claimed by people involved in creating the new constitution that the prime minister had flown in Belarusian legislators, who had in the meantime become Russian citizens, to help ensure the new constitution could get through parliament.[397]

Clearly, that had worked. The constitution gone through while being more skewed in favour of the executive than almost any other post-Soviet constitution. Comparing specific competencies, the Belarusian constitution offered the presidency more than most other of the new constitutions outside of Central Asia, bar those of Georgia and Russia from late 1993.[398] President Kebich, therefore, might have completed a takeover of Belarus. However, such a president never became reality. Instead, Lukashenka took advantage of compromising material on Kebich previously offered him by Shushkevich to place himself as representative of the public will to overcome political rot in the country. By July, Lukashenka had won a comprehensive victory.[399] Crucially, Lukashenka had not won by promising a wholly new Belarus. In the election there had been calls for a complete break with the Russia-focused past and a decisive turn to the West. But such calls had come from

---

395 That became a common problem in post-Soviet states, as seen above in the Russian case. One partial exception, though, could be found in the Baltic States. For more, see also Partlett, 2019

396 Burant, 1995: 1136

397 Way, 2012a: 637

398 Frye, 1997: 542

399 Watching Lukashenka addressing crowds following his victory, there is presented the image of a humble man, dressed in slightly dowdy clothes, linking very carefully to the "authentic" countryside. For a brief impression, see Belorussia, 2015

Pazniak and the Popular Front who had been far from victory with their message.[400]

The future of Belarus would be the past–or, at least, an idolised vision of that past. After only a month in the job Lukashenka went on a television broadcast across the post-Soviet space to declare that the Belarusian people was eager–even more eager than their politicians–to reunify with the Russians.[401] And when part of that Belarusian people forgot what it really wanted, Lukashenka proved ready to remind it of its true allegiance. Already by that autumn, riot police would begin to be deployed in order to stop nationalist groups commemorating historical victories over Russian invaders.[402] This might have been expected to appeal to the Russian leadership. Belarus would stay within Russia's orbit or even get closer to Russia. Fears of a Belarusian alliance with Poland, which would have increased the vulnerability of Kaliningrad, could be largely ignored, even if Poland for a while kept hopes up for such an alliance.[403]

More immediately, Lukashenka gained admiration among some Russians for the courage of his convictions compared, for instance, to his Ukrainian counterpart. When gaining power around the same time as Lukashenka, Leonid Kuchma had used his inauguration speech to appeal to historic bonds between Ukrainians, Russians and Belarusians–until nationalist outcries forced him to recant.[404] No such backtrack for the moustachioed man of the people who proved very attractive to Russian nationalists. Having been temporarily subdued in the autumn of 1993, vocal opposition to Yeltsin had returned in the Russian parliament and in Russian political debate more broadly over the coming year.[405] During 1994

---

400   Marples, 2006: 359
401   Tsipko, 1994: 444
402   Lukashenka proved unashamed about overt repression almost from the beginning of his tenure. For an overview, see also Marples, 1999a: chapter 4
403   For instance, Poles had previously noted with satisfaction that communist-era narrative staples on the mistreatment of Belarusians within interwar Poland had largely disappeared among Belarusian historians. See also Sanford, 1997: 67
404   See also Wilson, 2002: 38
405   An idea of the themes and nationalist presence in the December 1993 election and subsequent Russian parliament can be gained from Wyman et al, 1995

94   UNCANNY ALLIES

growing machismo in the Russian polity was also due to deepening tensions in the North Caucasus, where Chechnya in particular became ever less governable. Many Russian elites advocated a military solution to that problem–and were then dismayed when the December invasion quickly placed ill-prepared Russian troops in a quagmire.[406]

There had also been domestic disquiet in the summer of 1994 as Yeltsin let Russia join the Partnership for Peace programme (PfP) under NATO. Admittedly, Lukashenka's Belarus had followed suit half a year later, but at least the Belarusian self-image did not depend on status equality with NATO, unlike the self-image of many Russians.[407] Worse still, as the Balkan Wars moved towards Western military intervention and Serb defeat, Yeltsin could only rail impotently against developments, while pointedly supporting the Americans on every important decision; or at least doing nothing to prevent implementations of steps to further the dissolution of Yugoslavia.[408] Whereas Lukashenka, despite leading a much smaller country with much more limited resources not only called for help for "Serbian brothers" but also, allegedly, offered to provide a place of exile for Bosnian Serb militia ideologue Radovan Karadžić, as the latter contemplated life after defeat.[409]

Given all this, by the beginning of 1995 there were not many Russians opposed to the idea of renewed cooperation with Belarus, including in the form of economic engagement even if the Russian economy remained somewhat feeble and not necessarily capable of propping up the welfare of aligned states.[410] That January Russia

---

406   Continuing with the theme of political (de)masculinisation, overcoming Russian impotence in Chechnya would become a central pillar in statist political narratives under Putin, placing the latter in competition for "manliness" with Lukashenka. See also Eichler, 2006
407   All Moscow got when joining the PfP was a recognition that it had "weight" in Europe. See also Deni, 1994
408   Yeltsin's (arguable) duplicity on the Balkans is the topic of Surovell, 2012
409   Allegedly, Yeltsin would later tell the French president that Karadžić had been flown to Minsk to see if Minsk appealed to him. It did not, and Karadžić returned home. On that story, see Borger, 2016: 267
410   To illustrate this point, fragility runs through the account of Johnson, 2016: particularly chapter 6, on the road to establishing a financial market within Russia.

and Belarus signed a memorandum preparing a future customs union between the countries. There was no reason, as such, why this should be controversial–already, Belarusian goods were mostly directed to Russia with subsidised energy resources heading the other way. So, the memorandum offered no new direction for bilateral relations.[411] Still, its confirmation of existing relations came at a crucial moment. By the mid-1990s the EU was developing Partnership and Cooperation Agreements (PCAs) with Russia, Belarus and neighbouring post-Soviet states. Rhetoric surrounding this process, and the wording within the agreements themselves, indicated that Brussels was hoping for ever better market access in partner countries.[412]

In the case of Belarus such hope did not last long. For other post-Soviet states, including Russia, relations with the EU remained active and holding some promise. However, following rapid and comprehensive democratic deterioration under Lukashenka, his regime would see negotiations with Brussels effectively frozen within a few years.[413] During the latter half of the 1990s Belarus also failed to acquire membership within the Council of Europe. Seen as symbolising European values and identity, the Council had seen Belarus apply for membership. The relationship had survived Lukashenka's arrival as president yet fell away after the probity of the May 1995 parliamentary elections was questioned.[414] Undoubtedly, criticism was fair. The conduct of the regime during these elections set the tone for the political values (or lack thereof) promoted by Lukashenka over coming decades. While the nationalist opposition, being only a small part of the previous parliament, now lost parliamentary representation altogether.[415]

---

411   In addition, the bilateral memorandum followed a CIS-declaration from the previous year, already conveying similar intent. See also Soglashenie, 1994
412   For comments on the unusual wording of these agreements, see also Hillion, 2000: 1216
413   That development was also outlined by Smith, 2005: 760
414   The failure of Belarus' attempt to join the Council of Europe is discussed in Pridham, 2001: 73-74
415   As would be pointed out by Way, 2005: 254. Part of the point made by Way, though, is also — rightly — that the Belarusian nationalist opposition had never managed to properly organise.

96   UNCANNY ALLIES

That the Belarusian leader could scupper his relationship with the Council of Europe in return for domestic political control is not surprising. Possibly, though, creating a fight with the Council could have been the plan all along. To make clear that Belarus did not share the view of "Europe" held by its neighbours.[416] If so, Lukashenka would have intended that message partly for domestic consumption. In his public appearance and his rhetoric, the Belarusian president had sought to evoke images of the Soviet era. Not so much in its communist aspect, which now had relatively few adherents, but in its representation of stability and a modicum of welfare.[417] And if his state sought ideals in the past, it could not coexist easily with a European Union clearly seeking ideals in the future. Better to break with Brussels and note with self-satisfaction that the socio-economic model built in Belarus was much better at promoting equality than those of almost all EU countries.[418]

Why the country had such relative socio-economic success was not something Lukashenka publicly queried, however. In fact, during the last years of its Soviet existence and up to the mid-1990s the BSSR and then Belarus had been quite slow to adjust economic course, consequently picking up little outside economic interest or investment.[419] So, if Belarus had been able to avoid the worst consequences of the Soviet collapse this was not due to any radical governance or particular initiatives abroad. Instead, politicians like Kebich (partly backed by Shushkevich) and now especially Lukashenka had done their utmost to gain Russian subsidies and

---

416   An exciting contextualisation of such a view within the framework of "Central Europe" is explored by Hagen, 2003

417   For the summary of Lukashenka's brand during the beginning of his tenure, see also Karbalevich, 2001

418   A claim which Lukashenka could make with some justification. As he came into the presidency, Belarus had a Gini coefficient (measuring inequality) of only 28. Admittedly higher than the 23 of the BSSR yet still lower than that of all other post-Soviet states (with Russia's coefficient now being 48). See also Bunce, 1999: 765

419   Thus, relative to its GDP until 1995 Belarus had less Foreign Direct Investment than all other countries, bar conflict-ridden Armenia and Georgia. On a similar parameter, Belarus had been among the post-Soviet countries receiving relatively least in loans from international providers such as the World Bank Group. For these points, see also Fish, 1997: 38

easy market access whenever possible.[420] Lukashenka was aware that his government could take more initiative to safeguard his country's economic future. It is, for instance, noticeable that Belarusian citizenship laws around this time offered easier acquisition for ethnic Belarusians. Not an uncommon post-Soviet practice yet a sign that Minsk wanted to build up its population and tax base.[421]

Such measures, though, would only have effect in the longer term. Right now, Lukashenka needed Russia. So, together with the 1995 parliamentary elections he presented a public referendum promoting economic integration with Russia, the introduction of Russian as an official language, and new state symbols, including a flag similar to that of the BSSR.[422] All the suggested changes passed with a clear majority showing Moscow Lukashenka's intent and capabilities for domestic control. Such a Belarusian president held some allure for Yeltsin and would be even more popular with the new Russian parliament being elected by the end of 1995 and dominated by nationalist and great power sentiments.[423] As indicated above, until this time Yeltsin had been careful to present Russia as a responsible power abroad. Lukashenka's blunt measures and rhetoric might be tolerated, but at first Moscow had made sure the West knew that any belligerence towards the West did not come from Russia.[424]

Yet Yeltsin was learning. That the European security landscape would not be changed to his benefit. That Russia would remain in socio-economic difficulty. And that domestic opposition,

---

420   As I have already indicated, such Belarusian policy did not start with Lukashenka. Although someone like Shushkevich may have talked of forging policies apart from Russia he did not do much to live up to that ideal. Consequently, even before Lukashenka's presidency developed outside observers expected Belarus might be absorbed in Russia. On that, see e.g. Medish, 1994

421   On Belarusian citizenship law at the time, see also Shevel, 2009: 273

422   The components of this referendum are also discussed by Astapova, 2016a: 716-18

423   On the outcome of the Russian parliamentary election, see also König, 1996

424   To repeat, this was a major point of Russian insistence that nuclear weapons had to be sent to it from Belarus, Kazakhstan and Ukraine. That such insistence had been valued by America, in particular, could be seen through continued Western assistance towards that aim during the mid-1990s. See also Sarotte, 2021: 235

98   UNCANNY ALLIES

indirectly aided by Lukashenka, would take advantage of his trouble before the upcoming Russian presidential election. Now, increasingly, the Russian president mirrored Lukashenka's pushback against the West.[425] How should such Russian foreign policy change be interpreted? Some observers have argued, cogently and often convincingly, that Moscow's increased insistence on its difference and rightful status as a great power now emerged from ideological tendencies held by substantial political forces and rooted in the country's historical and sociological fabric.[426] Others have claimed, again with arguable validity, that Russian foreign policy began to change because it did not witness reciprocity from the West, and particularly from America. That it was not so much a matter of Russia pulling itself away as the West pushing Russia away.[427]

Still, the domestic politics to which I alluded above surely matter, too. After the parliamentary elections of late 1995, Yeltsin only had half a year to turn around dismal popularity ratings against Gennady Zyuganov who as Russian communist leader had public cut through with cries against inequality and for punishment of the oligarchy.[428] Zyuganov was never as radical as he himself or his detractors would claim. It is worth noting that this politician would easily find himself a role in the Russian political establishment later under not only Yeltsin but also Putin. In early 1996, his popularity was real, though, as was his nationalism.[429] The Russian president got out of his trouble through oligarchic sponsorship, energetic public relations and ill-concealed hints that a Zyuganov victory might not be allowed. Yeltsin also, though, turned to Lukashenka.

---

425   Yeltsin and his government had infrequently challenged the West before Lukashenka became president. Now, though, Russia could take advantage of Lukashenka's remoulding of Belarus to suggest that Russia might return nuclear weapons to Belarus in response to NATO-enlargement. For this, see Splidsboel-Hansen, 2002: 386
426   This logic is seen in Light, 1996
427   On that claim, see also Tsygankov, 2022b: chapter 3
428   That Zyuganov had a real chance of overcoming Yeltsin was certainly the view of many international observers at the time. See, for instance, Powell, 1996
429   For a more complete impression of the message promoted by Zyuganov, see also Zyuganov, 1997

Only 22% of Russians believed their country was doing well; in Belarus the corresponding proportion was 50%. Lukashenka was clearly doing something right.[430]

And so it was that the Russian leadership turned the Belarusian way, preparing the path for Putin. By the spring of 1996, even relative moderates within the Russian elite–such as the advisory Council for Foreign and Defence Policy–were pushing for integration with Belarus and with Ukraine on national as much as economic grounds.[431] Lukashenka's above-mentioned referendum was intended to show such elites that he was listening and ready to reciprocate Russian steps for closer relations. Indeed, the referendum accompanied his agreement with Yeltsin for closer economic relations, including a future common currency, signed that spring and seemingly providing content to declarations from the previous year.[432] That accord also followed a quadripartite agreement entered into in March by Russia, Belarus, Kazakhstan and Kyrgyzstan on plans for a single economic space, eventually with supranational institutions and with a possible supranational cultural element, too, in a manner seemingly inspired by the relatively novel European Union.[433]

Instead of these agreements challenging each other or the institutional framework constructed by the CIS, the Russian government saw them as steps on a path to unity. New foreign minister Yevgeny Primakov hoped that some countries in the CIS could form an example to follow for the rest, with Belarus towards the very front.[434] Other Russian politicians went further. That same March the Russian parliament adopted a resolution declaring the 1991 Belovezhskaya Pushcha agreement invalid. Which meant that they, in effect, declared the Soviet dissolution to be legally invalid. Although Yeltsin was free to ignore that consequence, he was left

---

430 These public opinion figures can be found in Blanchflower, 2001: 384

431 Proponents for such a course included figures like Sergey Karaganov who would develop foreign policy views in tandem with the presidency over the following decades. See also Tolz, 2002: 240

432 The agreement and its link to the Belarusian referendum is mentioned by Liu et al, 2017: 55

433 That quadripartite agreement was outlined further by Metcalf, 1997: 539

434 Primakov's expectations were recorded in Smith, 2016: 178

in no doubt that his domestic challengers wanted more.[435] From Belarus, Lukashenka saw his possibilities with Russia. Ensuring that domestic challengers would be nullified, in November he pushed through constitutional changes, curtailing legislative oversight. Local elite and public protests ensued, but the president was helped by the direct intervention of Russian prime minister Viktor Chernomyrdin. Lukashenka's political gamble had paid off.[436]

Economically, relations were looking promising, too. Russia signed a long-term deal for the delivery of natural gas with PGNiG, the Polish state-owned monopoly. That agreement, which envisaged some gas being forwarded to the lucrative German market, would involve building the Yamal-Europe pipeline crossing Belarus and ensuring substantial benefits for the regime in Minsk.[437] Belarusian energy fortunes were not immutable. At the same time as Yamal-Europe was getting ready, political disagreements between Russia and Latvia led the Kremlin to threaten termination of the oil pipeline running across Belarus to Ventspils, instead building up its own ports for delivery to the world markets.[438] A reminder that Lukashenka was not always in control of his own fate. Sometimes, too, he could overreach. Clearly aiming to please his sympathisers in Russia, the Belarusian president suggested to Poland a direct route should be allowed for Russians to pass directly between Belarus and Kaliningrad. The Poles quickly shut that suggestion down.[439]

Still, no real harm done. Many Russians liked Lukashenka's chutzpah. And he was clearly capable of thinking ahead on issues of more direct importance to him. While Yeltsin was handing over swathes of the Russian economy to oligarchs, the Belarusian president moved towards nationalisation. Possibly in preparation for

---

435　On this parliamentary declaration, see also Wise and Brown, 1998: 131
436　For further details on the referendum and Chernomyrdin's appearance, see Way, 2015: 697
437　The natural gas deal and the place of Belarus in relation to it is mentioned by Bouzarovski and Konieczny, 2010: 8
438　That spat and the Russian threat are discussed in Balmaceda, 1998: 283
439　Lukashenka's suggestion and the Polish reaction are mentioned in Snyder, 1998: 31

further exposure to Russian business.[440] Such economic control was mirrored on the ideological front by the creation of Direct Action, an organisation intended to link Lukashenka directly to younger Belarusians. Thus, the institutionalisation of Belarusian populism was born, in a pattern which Putin's Russia would later follow, most notably a decade later as a reaction to the Coloured Revolutions.[441]

Putin's Ascendance

Yeltsin's re-election as president appeared to have doused the challenge from the nationalist opposition. For his run-off against Zyuganov, the Russian leader had co-opted the recognisable and widely respected figure of Aleksandr Lebed–a lieutenant general who had come to fame forcing a halt to the Moldovan civil war.[442] Subsequently supporting the executive's assault on parliament in 1993 Lebed had come a solid third in the first round of the presidential election. He then endorsed Yeltsin's bid and was rewarded, briefly, with the post of secretary in the Security Council before being unceremoniously dumped, eventually becoming a Siberian governor.[443] Yeltsin had won his battle for power. He was destined to lose the war, however, being on his second and constitutionally last term. Even if that might have been tweaked, the president's health was giving way. A bit into his new term, the question was whether Yeltsin might complete his allotted time in office.[444]

Who waited in the wings to take over? Before adopting its post-Soviet constitution, Russia had briefly had a vice-president, but that experiment ended in acrimony with the office holder, Aleksandr Rutskoy, briefly imprisoned. Then there was the prime minister since 1992, Viktor Chernomyrdin, an experienced manager

---

440 This tendency in Lukashenka's economic policies, and how they differed from previous policies under Kebich, is described by Matsuzato, 2004: 244-45

441 The introduction of Direct Action is the topic of Silvan, 2020: 1318

442 For the involvement of Lebed and his 14th Guards Army in the Moldovan conflict, see also Haynes, 2020: 158

443 The tale of Lebed's ultimately unsuccessful bid for power is in Elletson, 1998

444 Yeltsin himself would discuss some of those health concerns in Yeltsin, 2000

and trusted by Yeltsin but with little public support.[445] Primakov would briefly take over as prime minister and was much more of a political figure and thinker than Chernomyrdin. He was also relatively popular with the nationalist opposition due to his willingness to call out what he saw as Western breaches in the mutual relationship.[446] That was the reason why Yeltsin would call Primakov to lead the government. However, it was also an indication that Yeltsin would never become comfortable with a man who was clearly able and willing to carve out an independent political profile with allies in Moscow and also across the regions.[447]

Here was an opening for Lukashenka. If a Union State could gain real powers, the Belarusian leader hoped to take overall control or, at least, veto Russian decisions impacting on his regime. As the Union Charter was signed in May 1997 Lukashenka's triumphant tone was unmistakable, as was the fact that Yeltsin followed suit.[448] The Kremlin was on a foreign policy roll that spring. Apart from the Union Charter, Yeltsin also managed to sign a high-profile Friendship Treaty with Ukraine as well as coming to a long-term agreement on the stationing of the Russian Black Sea Fleet in Crimea, as well as the division of that fleet.[449] Even more importantly, a Russia-NATO Treaty was concluded. In Moscow, this step was presented as a conclusion to years of uncertain relations between those two parties. As NATO-enlargement into Central Europe looked set to go ahead, the Treaty was supposed to give Russia a

---

445 Long after his time in office, and even his death, Chernomyrdin would be periodically highlighted by the Putin administration as a example to follow of a selfless servant of the state — less a reflection of Chernomyrdin's achievements than of his reluctance to challenge for the top job. For his posthumous image in Russia, see also Frolov, 2018

446 Surovell, 2005, intelligently explores Primakov's impact (or lack thereof) on Russian foreign policy

447 On that relationship, see also the comments by Medvedev, 2000: chapter 11

448 Details of the Charter and the presidential rhetoric surrounding it are offered by Sakwa and Webber, 1999: 397-98

449 A thorough analysis of the Black Sea Fleet accords and the Russian motivations surrounding them is offered by Sherr, 1997

veto on further enlargements or similarly wide-ranging decisions. Argued Yeltsin, anyway.[450]

That interpretation was certainly also the one on which his political opponents insisted. Politicians like Zyuganov saw little reason to hope for permanent peace abroad and instead wanted Russia to build up a defensive ring in neighbouring regions like Belarus to the west, as well as the Caucasus and Kazakhstan to the south.[451] That attitude fitted well within Lukashenka's plans. The Belarusian president was now openly betting on the Russian vector. I noted above how he had caused the EU and Council of Europe to distance themselves. Then Belarus effectively forced the Soros Foundation out of the country, leading the American ambassador to be recalled.[452] Having triumphed in the constitutional amendments the previous year, Minsk hounded private institutions or individuals it could not easily control. Consequently, not only were Western investors being chased off, so were private investors within the country. Lukashenka might have wanted more Belarusians in the country, as I noted previously, but they should work for him.[453]

With medium-size companies being increasingly challenged if not demolished in Belarus the economy focused on a few state companies, but also–specifically–on provisions from Russia. Notably, Lukashenka's regime relied ever more on cheap energy prices, both for domestic consumption and for the lucrative re-export of refined oil products.[454] The Belarusian president wanted the best of all worlds. While lauding ever deeper cooperation with Russia he had promised his parliament that Belarus would never lose sovereignty in a Union with Russia, that it would benefit at least equally with its greater partner and that Belarusian soldiers would never be sent

---

450 At the time, Russian elites still hoped NATO could become gradually obsolete and replaced by the OSCE in European security institutionalisation. On that, see e.g. Shustov, 1997

451 Zyuganov's comments on that topic can be found in Erickson, 1999: 263

452 The tax scheme used by Belarus to hound the Soros Foundation is outlined by Rich, 1997

453 To see how state practice was impacting on private investment in Belarus, see also Radnitz, 2010: 140

454 As noted in Connolly, 2008: 594, 597

to serve abroad.[455] That attitude played well in Belarus but was not what the Kremlin wanted. Tension also appeared from differences in tolerance. Russia was hardly a democracy, yet still allowed more open debate than Belarus. As Russian journalists critically covered demonstrations against Lukashenka they were thrown out of Belarus, to the official consternation of the Russian leadership.[456]

The Belarusian leader began to suspect conspiracy against his Union. Even after the Charter had been signed, he spoke darkly about forces of sabotage. Charges which grew more vehement when Russian reportage that summer rightly questioned whether a putative borderless relationship would be jeopardised by Belarusian inability to ensure control with traffic from third countries.[457] Lukashenka's fear was not that the Union would stop in its tracks. Yeltsin and his government had already pledged allegiance to it as a central aim of Russian foreign policy. Indeed, by late 1998 Russia and Belarus would, once more, declare that the Union State would be realised before the end of the following year.[458] Yet if Lukashenka's image was tarnished, if his supporters in Russia were no longer convinced that he could provide security or identity benefits to their cause the Union might not favour him. A regime perceived as weak might even risk Russian encroachment on Belarusian sovereignty, perhaps on behalf of Russians living there.[459]

Or, more prosaically, Moscow could simply stop funding its ally. While Russia had been doing well, Belarus had benefited from handouts to avoid taking unpopular socio-economic decisions at home. What would happen to Belarus if money stopped flowing from Russia was shown in August 1998, however, as the Russian

---

455 Lukashenka gave such promises in February 1997, provoking some concern among Russian observers. See e.g. Diatlikovich, 1997
456 This spat was covered by Markus, 1997: 60
457 The incident in question, during which journalists filmed themselves crossing the Belarusian-Lithuanian border without any control by Belarus, is discussed by Sasunkevich, 2016: 94
458 This declaration received mostly sympathetic coverage in Russia, such as by Karelin, 1998
459 Not that many self-identifying Russians in Belarus wanted such protection from Moscow, though. For surveys indicating this, see also Barrington et al, 2003: 311

government defaulted on its debts.[460] Within a few years the country's fortunes, and its ability to assist allies, would return. However, in the immediate months following the default consequences rippled across not only Russian economic life but also that of Belarus. Towards the end of the year, reports noted that Belarus was suffering from rationing of food and other essentials.[461] Conditions were not much better for other countries in the vicinity of Russia. The Baltic States were at least on a path towards EU-membership, even if that would not arrive for a while. But Ukraine, which had only recently agreed to increase economic cooperation with Russia, might now regret that choice.[462]

Further abroad, the default came at a very inopportune time for Yeltsin. Only that May had Russia finally managed to become a full member of the G8, thereby taking its place in a somewhat informal club which, nonetheless, gathered some of the world's most important leaders.[463] True, Russian membership largely had a political rather than an economic character, but a default severely damage its prestige and the prestige of the Yeltsin government which from now on would be seen as being in inevitable decline. Primakov's arrival as prime minister, and Igor Ivanov as foreign minister, did little to change that.[464] The new government could play on anti-Western sentiment in Russia. At the end of 1998, when American and British airplanes bombed an Iraq allegedly in violation of its security commitments to the UN, Russia demonstratively withdrew its ambassadors to the two aggressor countries. This only served to underline Russian impotence, though.[465]

---

460 Details of that default are covered by Gilman, 2010
461 Such suggestions are mentioned in Hillman and Ursprung, 2000: 205
462 The agreement on economic cooperation between Russia and Ukraine from February 1998 is also discussed by Ilchenko, 1998, who also points out (with some justification although also with much entitlement on behalf of Russia) that Ukrainian attraction to Russia will only last as long as economic benefits are received.
463 The accession of Russia to the G8 is detailed in Penttilä, 2003: 69
464 Russian observers understood well the difficult hand dealt to Primakov. See, for instance, Latsis, 1998
465 And to stress to Middle Eastern regimes that Russia would be of limited practical use to them. See also Freedman, 2001: 216

And it undermined Russian strategy for wider international relevance. The previous year, in April, Yeltsin had followed up successful collaborative declarations with Belarus by meeting with Chinese leader Jiang Zemin and together declare the birth of a multipolar world order, a direct response to concerns about an America-led unipolar system.[466] Similar ambitions had shone through the new Russian national security concept approved in December 1997. Here, the ambition and necessity of having Russia return not only to great power status but to a position of a pole in such a multipolar world order was made explicit.[467] For the plan, Russia needed allies. This was the reason why China had been approached. Beijing might not yet be a great power, but it was undoubtedly heading that way. Then, Primakov also included India in what looked like a Eurasian pole in world politics, offering an alternative to US-dominance.[468]

No rhetorical flourishes could hide Russian material weakness, though. And it was not as if Belarusian material assets would significantly add to what Russia already had. But Lukashenka could be a loud cheerleader demonstrating to other countries in the region what Russia had to offer them and, perhaps, becoming a model to emulate.[469] For many Russians it was a bonus that Lukashenka so actively pushed away potential alternatives in the West. Whereas the Belarusian president had previously alienated Western governments through his domestic anti-democratic practices, during the summer of 1998 he upped the stake by expelling diplomats from their residences under dubious pretences of required refurbishment.[470] That governments in the EU, and then the USA, on the basis of such treatment decided to issue visa bans to leading members of the Belarusian regime was only a bonus for those seeking to build Russia as a great power in world politics.

---

466 The text of the Russo-Chinese declaration can be found in China-Russia, 1997
467 Three years later, Putin's national security concept largely echoed that worldview. For that continued theme, see also Godzimirski, 2000: 82
468 Primakov's suggestion that Russia, China and India constituted a power pole in world politics was reported by Skosyrev, 1998
469 It also helped that Lukashenka's Belarus invested significantly in CIS-markets, sending about a quarter of all trading activity that way and thereby showing belief in this region as a viable economic entity. See also Filatotchev et al, 1999: 1024
470 That spat was described by Karpekova, 1998

Now, Belarus had few realistic options other than staying with Russia.[471]

If Lukashenka could not diversify his global contacts, though, he could diversify them within Russia. The president was close to Moscow mayor Yuri Luzhkov, one of the more powerful figures in Russia, who spoke up for the Belarusian against Western sanctions. In heavily industrialised parts of Russia could Lukashenka find allies, too.[472] They, too, were gearing up for a time after Yeltsin and found a sovereign ally in Minsk politically helpful. Economically, on the other hand, Lukashenka's offers were more limited. It was telling that his relations with Russian regions, as with the Russian central administration, remained more focused on declaration than on specifically value-adding projects.[473] This would not change during the last year of Yeltsin's reign. Just before Russia's first president resigned a Union Treaty was finally signed. And while that Treaty envisaged great aims for the Union centred on supra-state structures there remained little detail and even less hard deadlines on which to build such structures.[474]

The next Russian leader would be aware of such a problem of non-commitment. In his short-lived capacity of secretary of the Russian Security Council during April 1999 Putin had stressed that strategic and economic circumstances, presumably international as well as domestics, required Russia and Belarus to speed up their plans for mutual reinforcement.[475] At this point it did some appear likely that Putin would remain satisfied with the Belarusians simply stringing Russia along. On that, Putin was far from a political outlier. Even self-ascribed liberal opposition figures and parties in the country, like Yabloko or Anatoly Chubais, now wanted real

---

471 Lukashenka's rapid transformation into a pariah for American and European countries was covered by Iusin, 1998

472 Such contacts are described further in Balmaceda, 1999: 7

473 See here also the perceptive observation by Alexseev and Vagin, 1999: 60-61, that while the Pskov governor chose to engage with Lukashenka over his Baltic counterparts for Pskov civil servants it was much more common to meet with Estonian and Latvian counterparts than with Belarusian ones.

474 For the signing of the Union Treaty see also Kolossov and Turovsky, 2001: 154

475 Putin's comments on this point were shown by Ambrosio, 1999: 83

Union with Belarus.[476] And there was increasing public regret over the Soviet collapse. By 1999, in surveys almost 70% of Russians surveyed stated they were "very upset" over the collapse. Tellingly, the same proportion of respondents in a contemporaneous poll had Lukashenka as their best-liked foreign leader. It was hardly a stretch to see those attitudes as linked.[477]

The Belarusian regime certainly did so and ever more openly used the Soviet Union as its model. However, as I noted above, that was not the model of ideologically stringent communism but of welfare provisions and of security. Despite being a country in peacetime, Belarus was swiftly becoming one of the most securitised post-Soviet regimes.[478] Partly to enable Lukashenka to keep control but clearly also as an identity marker at home and abroad. Not dissimilar, in fact, to the way Putin would soon mark himself as a leading candidate for the Russian presidency by avenging terrorist attacks allegedly committed by Chechens through a restart of the Chechen War.[479] And in both the Belarusian and the Russian case overt demonstration of the continued relevance of these countries and the regime types they contained. It is not coincidental that Putin's and Lukashenka's increased militarisation at home came shortly after their demonstrable inability to assist Yugoslavia against NATO in the Kosovo dispute.[480]

By promoting militarisation, therefore, Putin and Lukashenka could complement each other. However, the rise of a younger, more vigorous Russian president also harmed Lukashenka's prospects. More than ever a Belarusian takeover of Russia via the Union State

---

476 For the broad appeal of union with Belarus within Russian political classes, see also McFaul, 1999: 28-29

477 These survey data are analysed in Dunlop, 2000: 9

478 See for instance the proportion of military personnel relative to overall population, which at this point was higher in Belarus than in Russia and all other post-Soviet states, apart from Armenia and Azerbaijan, who constantly prepared for mutual hostilities. Admittedly, the proportion of military personnel in Belarus had gone down under Lukashenka but nowhere as much as in Russia. See also Miller and Toritsyn, 2005: 327

479 How Putin came to "own" that conflict is the topic of Evangelista, 2002: chapter 4

480 The clash between Russia and NATO is the topic of Norris, 2005. As that clash was playing out Lukashenka would often appear to side with the most vociferously anti-NATO forces in the Russian elite.

now seemed unlikely, even if the prospect of Lukashenka as vice-president in such a construction remained a possibility.[481] Perhaps for such an eventuality did the Belarusian regime stress its political and identity links to Russia whenever possible. In February, for instance, did the government openly admit to censoring history books to remove alternative, Belarusian nationalist interpretations of the twentieth century. In Russia, sympathisers with such interpretations took note.[482] Once again, we see Russia absorbing from Belarus practices and ideologies for which Putin would later become infamous. And such absorption was facilitated by the clear societal similarities between Belarus and Russia. If Lukashenka's country otherwise appeared like a Russian province, means employed by the regime there should be applicable within the Russian Federation, too.[483]

Following that logic it also becomes informative to consider the techniques and choices of alienation made by Minsk. Although most people in Belarus declared themselves to be Belarusian, something the state had been happy to accept through citizenship laws (as shown above), they still largely spoke Russian in everyday life.[484] Belarusian, conversely, was the language of choice for ethnic Poles living in the country. Therefore, when Lukashenka at this time denigrated Belarusian language and customs he was aiming more at Poles in the country than at Belarusians, per se, making his increasingly frequent celebrations of Belarusian sovereignty in later years less of a fundamental change.[485] Also, and unlike the situation for Russians living in Belarus which I mentioned above, many Poles were geographically concentrated, specifically in the country's southwestern part. This meant activity undertaken by them could

---

481 This was a scenario feared by Brown, 1999: 11-12
482 On Belarusian governmental acknowledgment of such censorship, see also Belarusian, 1999
483 Lukashenka, of course, did not see himself a ruling a "Russian province." However, he could not deny that Belarusian society throughout the country was influenced by ethnic Russians, thereby giving the country very much a Russian provincial feel. On that point, see also Rowland, 2003b: 260
484 As frequently confirmed through opinion polls, such as shown in Arel, 2002: 239
485 For the frequent use of Belarusian language by ethnic Poles in Belarus, see also Rowland, 2003a: 538

110   UNCANNY ALLIES

be presented by the regime as physically separate from the rest of the population, or as realistically seeking to separate themselves.[486]

It also matters that post-war western Belarus and eastern Poland had remained largely devoid of significant settlements, with the partial exception of Brest. Demographic similarity had manifested itself in pervasive linguistic links. It became difficult to hear the end of one population and the beginning of the next. And that made their disciplining difficult.[487] Particularly as the Belarusian regime worked within a Soviet-era worldview. True, under socialism Poland had been an ally but an ally with a known nationalist streak which was recognised as so dangerous that it could not be easily defeated by communism but instead often had to be accommodated.[488] If it were to be overcome this would only happen by socialist modernity moving heavy industry and urbanisation into the backwards countryside. That was classical Marxism-Leninism, and it was eerily similar to Lukashenka's assault on a largely rural western Belarus where, so the Belarusian regime indicated, ancient enemies roamed.[489]

Not dissimilar, incidentally, to the distrust of the provinces historically imprinted on Russian centre-periphery relations and only becoming more pronounced later under Putin. Such distrust would become a main reason for the gradual disappearance of federalism in Russia and for the engrained tension between Moscow and Minsk in years to come.[490] For now, Lukashenka did not want any differences with the Kremlin highlighted but used the "Polish issue" to deepen divisions with the rest of Europe. While countries like Poland complained the Belarus did not want to be part of a

---

486   The regional, rural character of the Polish demographic group in Belarus around this time is discussed by Eke and Kuzio, 2000: 533-34

487   The point of linguistic similarity brought on by common rurality is from Ioffe, 2003b: 1038-39

488   Or, as I previously indicated, had even led to nationalism being used to legitimise communism in Poland. See Zaremba, 2019

489   It should be stressed, though, that — for Lukashenka — the countryside was not inevitably bad; it just had to be "tamed". On the Soviet model for this, and some problems inherent in that model, see also Bekus, 2010

490   Incidentally, in the case of Russia this is a point at which Loftus, 2019 arguably hints, particularly in chapter 2

progressive "Central Europe", Lukashenka's regime claimed dividing lines had been promoted by the West.[491] And, therefore, that it was not up to Belarus to solve any disputes which had occurred. Instead, it would enjoy Russian goodwill. The arrival of Putin as president largely coincided with increased world market prices for energy. And by the turn of the millennium the before-mentioned Yamal-Europe pipeline was fully operational.[492]

So, not only could Russia send more natural gas to Europe, but it could take advantage of transit across Belarus to be less dependent on Ukraine. That Minsk would take advantage of this situation was inevitable. Changing its tax regime Russia tried to limit Lukashenka's profiteering but with limited success.[493] Still, since Yeltsin's exodus had been dominated by the default, when Putin came in he was more concerned with quick economic turnaround overall than with whichever benefits Lukashenka could scrape together. So, Belarus would be allowed to gain not only from energy transits, but from hosting substantial trade transit streams between Russia and the EU.[494] Being a relatively inexperienced leader, and mostly familiar with operating through bureaucracy and relative anonymity, it was unsurprising that Putin would not start his foreign policy course around a high-profile spat with an ally. At least partly therefore were Lukashenka and his subsidies left relatively unscathed while Putin found his feet.[495]

---

491 While Lukashenka's criticism of ill-treatment by the West was often without foundation, on some occasions during the 1990s the West did seem to hold Belarus to different standards than other post-communist states. Earlier, I noted how Brussels in the early 1990s had held out the prospect of future EU-membership to Romania even though that country was then seen as less democratic than Belarus. That the West was relatively slow to support civil society, too, in Belarus could be seen by the much more generous funds sent from Western donors like USAID to Slovakians than to Belarusians, even though the two countries struggled with similar democratising problems. See also Jang, 2024: 241

492 This development is elaborated on by Kropatcheva, 2011: 562

493 Details of such fiscal attempts by Russia are further detailed in Tabata, 2002: 625-26

494 For a breakdown of the transport of goods between Russia and the EU, and the Belarusian role herein, see also Laurila, 2003: 49

495 Observers of Russian foreign policy during Putin's first presidential term frequently commented on such alleged pragmatism. I would argue this was

112   UNCANNY ALLIES

This meant, though, that Lukashenka would come to interpret his new interlocutor as weak. As someone still so focused on carrying forward the idea of a union and re-integration in the post-Soviet space that he would let the Belarusian leader get away with much more than would in reality be the case.[496] Perhaps Lukashenka's misperception of Russia's intentions had been exacerbated by the haphazard way in which Yeltsin had left office. A dramatic resignation on the last day of the millennium had been very much in Yeltsin's flamboyant style. However, the tone of regret in his final address did not indicate a tone of triumph or optimism.[497] Putin stepped into the breach as interim president and, a few months later, easily won his election. As he stepped into that position, Putin openly agreed with his predecessor that Russia had many domestic problems, including Chechnya, and concluded that expansive foreign policy projects could wait. A seemingly sensible outlook which appealed to Russians.[498]

It also mattered that the new leadership had easily been able to see off Primakov. In a potential alliance with Luzhkov, the populist former prime minister had indicated anti-corruption campaigns at home and a vigorous foreign policy standing up for Russia and challenging America, in particular, where possible.[499] Such was not Putin's strategy. He built connections with Europe, including Germany where he addressed parliament in German. And with America, too. When Putin hosted Bill Clinton in Moscow it might seem inconsequential–an incoming leader hosting an outgoing one. However, just a year after NATO's bombardment of Yugoslavia it indicated eagerness to retain relations.[500] Russia would not foster

---

    indicated, for instance, in Black, 2004: including in chapter 9 on relations with Belarus

496   Lukashenka might have done better to consider the tone of Ivanov, 2002: chapter 1, which indicated a Russia that viewed itself very much as embodying the spirit of the great power of the past.

497   Yeltsin's farewell to the nation can be found at Statement, 1999

498   After Chechnya, foreign policy was the issue where Putin was seen as most competent by the public. See also Colton and McFaul, 2003: 195

499   For an idea of the political course Primakov might have followed as president, see Daniels, 1999

500   This was also the impression with which the American president was left. See Baumgartner, 2016

division in Europe; this was the message. And that left Belarus in an awkward position. I suggested above that Lukashenka might have seen Putin as inexperienced and weak, a patsy for the West. As product of a country which had consistently underperformed during the 1990s.[501]

If Moscow would now crawl to the West, it might do so over the welfare of Belarus. Lukashenka would not have that. So, while Putin was settling in the Belarusian leader called out to the West, to NATO, saying that he was ready for normal relations as long as these were founded on mutual respect.[502] The EU would become a target, too, for Belarusian schmoozing. Unlike among the Russian public, where recent years of hardship had promoted a narrative of Western exploitation of Russia which also damaged the image of the EU, surveys in Belarus showed the organisation and its activities were well respected.[503] Therefore, Lukashenka was unlikely to suffer domestic criticism as he stressed the need for "kind" relations and genuinely all-European integration processes. The president would also point out that his country was at the centre of Europe and therefore, so it might seem, essential for any genuinely European movement.[504]

Lukashenka would take low-cost opportunities for collaboration within the continent. Engaging in administrative exchange or sign non- or barely-binding multilateral declarations which showed that Belarus was ready to be part of European society without having to pay for it. Ecological affairs became one prominent example of this.[505] To demonstrate its alleged goodwill, his regime

---

501 The already indicated economic problems of Russia, culminating in the 1998 default, had seen Russia's real GDP consistently underperform that of Belarus. On this, see Glenn, 2003: 129

502 This call for détente came in a speech to the Belarusian parliament. See also Löwenhardt et al, 2001: 610

503 For a comparison of attitudes towards the EU in Russia and Belarus around this time, see also White et al, 2002b: 190

504 See such comments from Lukashenka's New Year's address at Klinke, 2013: 130

505 There is, for example, an account of how Belarus made sure to join the Aarhus Convention on transparency in environmental administration in Zaharchenko and Goldenman, 2004: 229, 231. Notice how Putin, still early in his tenure, kept Russia out only learning later how international environmental causes could help to greenwash his country's reputation.

then permitted a smidgen of political tolerance in parliamentary elections of October that year. Certainly, parliament was becoming an irrelevance in Belarus and the opposition only got two seats in it anyway. Yet the regime wanted to signal to America and the EU that repression might not worsen.[506] Russia did not care about repression and readily certified the election. Instead, Moscow considered what benefits Belarus could offer for the economic subsidies received. Secretary of the Security Council Sergey Ivanov saw military benefits in collaboration between Belarus and Kaliningrad– not so much against the West as to assist local security and anti-crime endeavours.[507]

Practically necessary, perhaps, but also foreshadowing the wider institutionalisation of post-Soviet security cooperation which would come in a couple of years later. Similarly, Putin's Kremlin was happy to have Belarus as the lynchpin for post-Soviet multilateral economic cooperation in the Eurasian Economic Community, which was included three Central Asian states.[508] And if Putin wanted a central place for Belarus within post-Soviet integration this could work well for Lukashenka. His value for Russia would be to offer political support at the same time as the Kremlin could offer Belarus economic support in an economic exchange broadly supported by ordinary Belarusians.[509] Then, if that deal worked out well for Belarus other countries in the neighbourhood might move in a similar direction. Ukraine was a longer-term objective, but what about Moldova? Here, the April 2001 parliamentary election saw the communist party gain a clear majority of seats on a manifesto suggesting inclusion in the Russia-Belarus Union.[510]

---

506 Of course, that signal was somewhat undermined by the election boycott called for among the Belarusian opposition. For an interesting analysis of the run-up to the election, and an indication that the EU, in particular, was not ready to take Lukashenka on good faith, see also Lindner and Sahm, 2000

507 As noted by Blank, 2002: 156-57

508 The place of this development in the sequence of economic collaboration within the post-Soviet space is detailed by Stevens, 2020: 1154

509 Unlike in nearby Moldova and Ukraine, at this time the public in Belarus viewed economic progress as linked to Russia rather than the EU. On that point, see White et al, 2002a: 143

510 On the 2001 manifesto of the Moldovan communists, see also March, 2007: 605

Given that the communists, under new prime minister Vasile Tarlev, had distinguished themselves from other parties in that election by refraining from supporting EU integration for Moldova, it did appear the country might pivot decisively towards Russia. Lukashenka could claim part of the honour for that accomplishment.[511] The Russians acknowledged his value in post-Soviet integration. Building his political profile in speeches to the Russian public and Russian legislators, Putin explicitly linked the Russo-Belarusian Union to his country's manifest destiny of developing as a centre of Eurasia while also remaining also a part of Europe.[512] A moment of reflection is required. Unlike the historical and future role of Belarus as bulwark for Russia against Europe or as vessel for Russian power projection there, might Russia in this moment have accepted Belarus as sovereign? As a genuine ally for that "liberal empire" of which Russian elites like Anatoly Chubais spoke?[513]

Answers to such questions clearly illumine Russian foreign policy as a whole. Because if answers here are in the affirmative the implication is a Russia capable of change, capable of post-imperial existence. And if that is assumed, then a follow-up question must be why that post-imperial Russia did not come into being?[514] Did the West miss its chance for international harmony? 2001, after all, would become known as the year of 9/11. Of the epochal terror attacks on American soil, inaugurating the "War on Terror", which Putin immediately joined despite apparent risks to his support among American-sceptic Russian elites and general society.[515] Seeking to deflect international criticism of Russian conduct in Chechnya, while also realising security and political benefits

---

511 Although it likely mattered more that Russia had widespread economic and political contacts among Moldovan elites, as well as a stranglehold over Transnistria. On Russia's involvement in the election, see also Korosteleva, 2010: 1280

512 On that point, see for instance Putin's words to the Federal Assembly in 2001, which were recorded by Ambrosio and Vandrovec, 2013: 448

513 Discussions around a Russian "liberal empire" can also be found in Gerasimov, 2003

514 Leading us back to that perennial query of "who lost Russia?" As discussed in recent years by Conradi, 2022: where chapters 9 and 10 are particularly relevant for this period.

515 Putin's dilemma at the time is summarised in Antonenko, 2001

acquired from closer collaboration with America, Putin saw his security services link well with those of George Bush. The Russian president might even argue the West had come to see the world through his eyes.[516]

And that should give Russia space to operate without interference in its post-Soviet neighbourhood. Or so, at least, was the assumption in the Kremlin. But working with Russia and tolerating Russia was not the same as trusting Russia in a context when American foreign policy soon centred on the spread of liberal democracy.[517] And that priority would not work well with Putin, at all. Soon, in the Middle East America would remove an ally of Russia in Iraq's Saddam Hussein, thereby introducing more than a decade of instability across the Middle East and underlining Russian impotence in world affairs.[518] Closer to home, the EU was preparing for its ever-widest enlargement round that would bring the organisation to Russian borders. Consequently, Central Eastern Europe would be formally carved up between "insiders" and "outsiders." By 2001, citizens of Visegrád countries gained easier access to the EU, while Belarusians and Ukrainians were kept at arm's length.[519]

That did not imply the West had forgotten about Belarus and Russia. Indeed, Western organisations were putting still more money into their democratisation. In Minsk, Lukashenka gained re-election that autumn with an ostensibly clear majority and very respectable turnout. Russian-led observers from the CIS were complementary about the election, but the OSCE highly critical.[520] Knowing that Belarusian elites were unable, let alone highly unlikely, to constrain or remove Lukashenka Western organisations

---

516 The increased security collaboration between Russia and America within the early "War on Terror" is analysed in Lieven, 2002

517 How an ideological push for democracy played a role in American foreign policy even during the early stages of the War on Terror is covered by Woodward, 2002

518 Russia's failed attempt to prevent the US invasion of Iraq in 2003 is analysed in Golan, 2004

519 The change in EU visa-policies for the Czech Republic, Hungary, Poland and Slovakia — but not for Belarus and Ukraine — is the topic of Hormel and Southworth, 2006: 620

520 For international reaction to the 2001 Belarusian presidential election, see also Morrison et al, 2024

ramped up sponsorship of civil society. The intention was to train a new generation of political activists transforming Belarus in a liberal democratic image, which could then gradually change the political culture of the country.[521]

Russia Returning

That might have been intended as a longer-term, organic way of transforming Belarus. Lukashenka did not see the initiative in that light. He had come to understand the battle for power as a zero-sum game, within which any opponents would destroy him, perhaps physically, if they got the chance.[522] Since the Belarusian opposition had limited sympathy for Russia, Putin, too, was uncomfortable with developments. His government had wanted Lukashenka to be re-elected in 2001 and to that end had provided the Belarusian leader with large sums of money for his campaign, albeit these were officially designated as a stabilisation loan for the Belarusian economy.[523] Lukashenka would have won the election without Russian funds–the opposition remained too disorganised and the security services too loyal to the regime for any other outcome to be realistic. Nonetheless, public discord had been brewing–surveys showed democracy being favour by a clear majority of the population, even more so after the presidential election.[524]

So, Russia had at least helped to keep things quiet. Now, it wanted to recover some funds. Focusing on energy, state gas company Gazprom wanted to charge Belarusian customers more. Minsk resisted but promised to partly sell its national gas company Beltransgaz. Putin, still new to Lukashenka, believed that promise

---

521 An example of such civil society funding came through the Pontis Foundation, founded to train Belarusian and Ukrainian democratic activists. See also Bunce and Wolchik, 2006: 299

522 Lukashenka's fear would not have been helped by the incendiary rhetoric offered against him and his Russian allies by parts of the Belarusian opposition, including Pazniak. On that, see also Gapova, 2002: 655

523 Russian funding of Lukashenka's re-election campaign is mentioned in Nikolayenko, 2015b: 473

524 Survey results for this can be found in Haerpfer, 2008: 417-18, 421

and the dispute remained civil.[525] There is no indication that Lukashenka ever intended to make good on the deal. This was partly for practical reasons. Suffering from Russian default, Belarus had begun to sell some of its companies to foreign investors, in a partial break with the protectionist attitude existing during much of the 1990s (and which I described previously).[526] However, the energy sector was a different matter. The hydrocarbons industry formed the bedrock of Lukashenka's political power. If he handed part of that sector to outside interests, the president would have less funds to distribute to clients and would no longer be able to do it as discreetly as was currently the case.[527]

Better to play for time. As indicated before, Belarus saw itself as central to Putin's project for post-Soviet unity. Years of summits on the institutional nature of that project would require Moscow to keep the Belarusians happy. Occasionally some agreement would be secured–in spring 2002 the Collective Security Treaty Organisation (CSTO) was inaugurated.[528] Now, Lukashenka could present as a security provider, as he had done within the organisation's less institutionalised predecessor. Sure, there would be some domestic disquiet. Ordinary Belarusians saw the ongoing Russian assault on Chechnya and feared Belarusian soldiers might now be dispatched there. But Minsk quickly legislated against sending its troops to combat zones.[529] So, Lukashenka had tamed Putin. Taking over the Union State might no longer be viable, but at least the Belarusian could use Russia to stay strong at home and project power abroad. Push against neo-imperialist ambitions of the EU, flush on expected

---

525   For the price disagreements and the Belarusian promise, see also Svoboda, 2011: 28

526   On how Belarus had now begun to invite foreign investors (relatively more so than Russia), see also Epstein, 2008: 881

527   The Belarusian economy was considered highly opaque and corrupt by international organisation. So much so, in fact, that the IMF would soon request the Belarusian government to place funds gained through privatisation in a transparent account supervised by the legislature. Although, given the increasingly supine nature of parliament such measures might have had limited effect. See also Kaltenthaler et al, 2006: 2

528   The foundation and development of the CSTO is the topic of Davidzon, 2021

529   For Belarusian public opinion and legislation, see also Kuzio, 2003: 441

enlargement and soon instigating plans for a "Wider Europe" spreading its ideas eastwards.[530]

Lukashenka knew from experience that the EU would not allow him to contribute to those ideas. His calls for collaboration the previous year had largely been ignored by Brussels–particularly following his re-election in late 2001–with the West expecting nothing but trouble and instability from Belarus and its neighbour Ukraine.[531] That sentiment spilled over to upcoming EU members. We saw how Brussels had begun to distinguish its treatment of Visegrád countries with that of their eastern neighbours. The next step, unavoidable in EU logic but damaging for Central European cohesion, was the request that countries like Poland must impose visas on Belarusians, Russians and Ukrainians.[532] The Baltic States were in a similar situation. Of course, visa requirements could be locally interpreted. Lithuanians were notably prepared to keep borders permeable, but Riga showed how the cover of EU requests could be used to politicise the issue. Longstanding Latvian annoyance over illegal migrants from Russia and Belarus led to stricter visa control.[533]

Subject to such treatment, Lukashenka thought he would find it easy to convince his population that their future lay to the east. Collaboration between sub-state regions in Belarus, Russia and Ukraine began to take official form with "Slobozhanshchyna" an early example hereof in September 2002, even if that project did not take off.[534] Still, there was clearly still wariness among local populations that integration could go too far too quickly. To show one example of this, in March Ukrainian parliamentary elections had seen parties openly advocating integration with Russia and Belarus

---

530   On "Wider Europe" and its potential for neo-imperialism, see also Bosse, 2010: 1297

531   Evidence that this was the case can be seen in contemporary communication between Britain and Spain predicting instability in those two post-Soviet countries and considering steps that, years later, would result in the European Neighbourhood Policy. See also Browning and Joenniemi, 2008: 547

532   The introduction of visa requirements by Poland is mentioned in Fritz, 2005: 205

533   Baltic approaches to EU visa requirements vis-à-vis Belarus and Russia are outlined in Galbreath, 2006: 456

534   For the formal instigation of that region, see also Zhurzhenko, 2004: 502

120   UNCANNY ALLIES

get very low vote shares in proportional voting across the country.[535] While the neighbouring Moldovans, who had only recently supported political forces openly advocating desire to move closer to Russia, had begun to reconsider their choices given what might, one day, be available from the EU. If not for themselves then indirectly through Romania, which was likely to become an EU member before long.[536]

To avoid losing further ground to the EU, the Kremlin ramped up plans for post-Soviet integration. What the West, and Lukashenka, had not considered in their complacent view of Putin was that the Russian president never viewed great power status as negotiable or international relations as fundamentally collaborative.[537] Yes, during these years ideas of a "liberal empire" gained currency in Russian elite rhetoric but Putin only bought into that framework in terms of methods, not aims. If his country could control the neighbourhood through money rather than guns that was all fine. But control was not negotiable.[538] Consequently, it was never likely that the Kremlin would leave EU expansion unanswered. And here we may need to turn prevalent wisdom on its head. Analysts have frequently noted that Russia viewed the EU as much less of an existential threat than NATO until, at least, Putin's return as president in 2012.[539]

Yet particularly within the context of the War on Terror we might need to reverse that idea. Not only could Russia work with NATO against perceived terrorism, it genuinely had value-adding capabilities to offer. Whereas in relations with the EU Russia was seen as little more than an energy provider expected to

---

535   The meagre results for such pro-union parties were recorded by Chudowsky and Kuzio, 2003: 281
536   Surveys in Moldova showing how that population no longer equated support for the communists' domestic policy priorities to support for its avowed foreign policy course are discussed in Cantir and Kennedy, 2015: 411
537   Oldberg, 2005, summarises that attitude well.
538   Here, it is also worth recounting the perceptive analysis of Tsygankov, 2006, even if the titular "soft power" seems misleading.
539   A distinction made also in Russian official foreign policy documents such as the first foreign policy concept adopted under Putin. For this, see Foreign 2000: 9-11

democratise.[540] We may even bring in a bit of World-Systems Theory at this point. In which case Russia sees itself as relegated to the international periphery by an EU wanting to take its resources and then, ideally, produce luxury and other goods which could be sent back to Russia for profit from Russian consumers.[541] I am not claiming this was the case, or even the conscious intention of the EU. I am claiming, however, that this was the analytical frame within which Putin was coming to view the EU. In a world of power politics, the EU would inevitably seek to dominate through its main asset, its economic strength.[542]

Putin's Russia would therefore have to do the same. That explains why Moscow pushed post-Soviet economic integration and deliberately modelled such integration on that of the EU. Wealth was never the main point, institutional power was, creating a situation—as in the EU—where participants would find it nigh impossible to retract from the centre.[543] Not dissimilar, incidentally, to Russian motivations behind institutionalisation in the CSTO at this time. And that placed Belarus in a tricky position. Certainly, Russians still looked at Belarusians as close relations, as brothers and sisters more trusted and sometimes more valued than other populations abroad.[544] They were particularly inclined to see Belarusians as similar in culture; in perceptions of history and in perceptions of religion, too. Emerging from the Soviet Union, religion had slowly

---

540 Such an EU attitude towards Russia was, in fact, engrained in the PCA from 1994, where the expected subordination of Moscow was clear from the preamble onwards. See also Pavlova, 2021: 144

541 World-Systems Theory was of course developed by Immanuel Wallerstein. If applying it to Russia, however, consulting Kagarlitsky, 2015, might be more fruitful

542 If this all sounds awfully similar to pre-1992 thinking that is perhaps to be expected. Putin was (no longer a) communist but he had grown up with an understanding that economics was simply another avenue to power. Geoeconomics, at least as much as geopolitics, was central to his worldview. For geoeconomics as distinct from geopolitics in the case of Russia, see also Wigell and Vihma, 2016

543 For an example of how Russia modelled its economic integration of the post-Soviet space on the EU see also Dragneva and Wolczuk, 2016: 686

544 Surveys taken in Russia confirmed this tendency on a consistent basis. Identity links were particularly highlighted among respondents. For an example, see O'Loughlin and Talbot, 2005: 36

gained traction in Russia and now Putin was beginning to use the Russian Orthodox Church to build a Russian nation and a "Russian world."[545]

The Russian president was seldom religious in a liturgical sense. He was, however, a believer in the church as an instrument of state power, seen at least since the days of Emperor Peter. That was certainly also Lukashenka's understanding when he made the Belarusian Orthodox Church the state church of Belarus in October 2002.[546] To be clear, Lukashenka was not confirming subordination to an instrument of Russian state power but signalling his expectation that the Church coordinated its activities with him. If it failed to listen, he would, and at times did, readily circumvent it by direct populist appeals to the Belarusian population through religious settings or tropes.[547] Why did Lukashenka feel the need to control the religious scene in the country? Partly, that wish for control existed within his broader authoritarian streak. Crackdowns on all aspects of civil society were forthcoming. From 2003, NGOs had to seek official permission before taking funds from abroad.[548]

This restriction was motivated by a fear within the Belarusian administration of foreign subversion. Subversion which in the best Soviet tradition was seen as hiding under the guise of civic–and religious–organisations. In previous years it had been noted with concern that American Evangelicals seemed relatively focused on activities in Belarus.[549] And from parts of Russian media came warnings that imminent EU enlargement should actually be understood in historical and religious terms. That the enlargement constituted an inevitable alliance of Lutherans and Catholics against the

---

545   For the place of religion in the project of the "Russian world", see also Hurak and D'Anieri, 2022: 128

546   A decision also mentioned by Kuzio, 2005b: 46

547   One high-profile example of this came shortly into 2003 at the funeral of Soviet-era musician Vladimir Mulyavin, allowing Lukashenka also to present himself as a unifier of Belarusians and Russians. See also Lonkin, 2024: 406

548   This step was analysed in Christensen and Weinstein, 2013: 85. There are similarities between such a policy in Belarus and laws coming to Russia later against "foreign agents." Another example, perhaps, of Moscow learning from Minsk.

549   As seen also from data supplied by Wanner, 2004: 740

righteous Orthodox and the cohesiveness among peoples which religion had promoted within the Russian World.[550] Admittedly, and along the lines of my previous comments, in terms of direct funding of civil society Belarus had actually received rather less in proportional terms than other post-Soviet states. But that might just be a sign of how carefully Western funding to Lukashenka's enemies was being funnelled.[551]

Or it might be a sign that Belarus was not a high priority for the West. If so, perhaps the danger to the country came not from America and the EU but from Russia. In June 2002, Putin had made clear that he expected a future Union State to have a single, unified state apparatus.[552] Lukashenka did not really like the centralising sound of this and sniffed that Putin did not seem very serious about the Union. Very well, then. Later than summer the Russian president let it be tersely known that he would be happy to receive Belarus as a Russian region with Lukashenka demoted to provincial governor.[553] Que wailing and gnashing of teeth in Minsk. This was absolutely not what Lukashenka had envisaged. All of a sudden that plan of "stringing Russia along" seemed unsustainable. Sure, keep fleecing Russia when possible, but take heed of Putin's jibe about the popularity of Russia in Belarus and start building up Belarusian national identity post-haste.[554]

It is telling, perhaps even a little amusing, that it was just around this time that the Belarusian educational authorities remembered that Belarusian textbooks could be promoted in schools and that specifically Belarusian geography and history could be taught. Before, those subjects had been looked down on. Now, they

---

550   See a selection of such Russian fears in Von Seth, 2018: 428. There is a lot to unpack here—not least the historical and religious ignorance of anyone believing Lutherans and Catholics find it easy to collaborate on anything (or even coordinate activities among themselves).

551   A comparison of American funding for post-communist civil society between 1990 and 2004 shows Belarus receiving less than several other post-Soviet states. For this, see Bunce and Wolchik, 2010: 65

552   Details of this were provided by Deyermond, 2004: 1198

553   A helpfully blunt presentation of Putin's position is offered by Plugatarev, 2002

554   That nation-building can be fostered by (perceived) external threats is of course a frequent observation. For useful considerations of nation-building, see also Talentino, 2004

mattered.[555] So, this was the dilemma for Lukashenka's Belarus. It could not push Russia away for it still needed Russian money and occasional political support. On the other hand, whenever Russians turned up to offer such support–say, in times of elections–they did so with a proconsular glint in their eyes.[556] And so affairs rolled on to 2004 and that big election–Putin's re-confirmation as big boss in Russia. In Belarus, this was the year when presidential term limits were abolished. Putin was not at that stage, yet. Nonetheless, he had no intention of facing even moderate electoral competition.[557]

He was duly re-elected with over 70% of votes. However, turnout in the election was down indicating perhaps waning public enthusiasm for the ruler. Around this time the European Values Survey also indicated that respondents in Russia, and in Belarus, were relatively less likely to be proud of their country than re-spondents from elsewhere.[558] That, though, did not imply respond-ents were ready to disavow their country or the part of the country from which they came. In fact, separate surveys within Russia and Belarus alike showed a clear identification with the country or more local region from which a respondent originated.[559] A tendency that seemed to jar with Putin's plans for post-Soviet integration. It did not, though, jar as clearly with Lukashenka's attempts to cobble to-gether a Belarusian national identity. Acknowledging that Belarus-ians historically had been closest to Russians, the president still ad-monished Moscow for trying to force specific developments on Bel-arus.[560]

---

555 The glut of Belarusian educational initiatives is summarised in Leshchenko, 2004: 343

556 Here, it is perhaps worth noting the creation, in 2003, of the Russia-led CIS Election Monitoring Organisation. Ostensibly there to give rhetorical support to scolded autocrats, it was also a way for Russia to ensure elections were car-ried out "properly" according to Moscow' wishes. For this organisation, see Yakouchyk, 2016: 206

557 For the abolition of presidential term limits in Belarus, see also McAllister and White, 2016: 363

558 Discussion of the findings from this Survey is in Shulman, 2005: 34

559 A breakdown of such responses is provided by Korosteleva and White, 2006: 197

560 What is designated as "Creole nationalism" by that analyst is outlined in Ioffe, 2007a: 369

Prior and future developments in Belarus, it was made clear, should be decided by Lukashenka's regime only. Most common was it for it to turn the country's public image further towards an idealised Soviet lens, with major squares and road in Minsk being renamed in that spirit.[561] There was, though, also increasing space to promote a pre-Soviet–and, by implication, less Russian–presentation of the country. From the past a medieval Minsk was conjured with emphasis of how the city had once been under that quintessentially European Magdeburg Law. This spoke of a sovereign land, and of a land open for business.[562] That last point was linked to EU-enlargement taking place. Encompassing ten countries, the enlargement saw the EU moving right up to Belarusian and Russian borders. Lukashenka made clear he had no interest in being used as a buffer between the EU and Russia but also that he expected Belarus to join the EU one day.[563]

Quite the statement considering those above-mentioned Russian concerns about the EU and its ideology. And a very different attitude than that being expressed during 2004 to the south by Ukraine's prime minister and presidential candidate Viktor Yanukovych. Expected by Russia to take over after Kuchma, Yanukovych was all for joining Russia-led economic institutions.[564] In fact, in the run-up to the Ukrainian presidential election one opinion which did unite the main candidates, Yanukovych and Viktor Yushchenko, was the need to retain good relations with Russia (and, accordingly, with Belarus) even if Yushchenko was much the keener on eventual integration with the West.[565] Such similarity was later overlooked in Russian and Belarusian accounts of the "Orange Revolution" which saw Yushchenko overcome election fraud. The event became a perennial source of anxiety for Russian

---

561 Details of how that happened and how some non-Soviet Belarusian names were pushed to the suburbs are provided by Bekus, 2017b: 802

562 Despite its undoubted value for memory politics, "Magdeburg Law" had been a more malleable concept than Lukashenka was suggesting. On this, see Malloy, 2022: 57

563 That prediction was presented in White et al, 2010: 348-49

564 Yanukovych's attitudes to foreign policy were noted by Kuzio, 2005a: 39

565 On Yushchenko's political priorities before the election, see also Kuzio, 2010: 10

elites, while their Belarusian counterparts noted the calls among some Ukrainian protesters for spreading revolution to Belarus.[566]

That did not happen. It might even be argued that the revolution did not spread to Ukraine, despite Yushchenko's subsequent presidential term. Nonetheless, supporters and beneficiaries of current political structures in Belarus and Russia extended their gratitude to the Belarusian leader whose firm grip on power had allegedly prevented turmoil there.[567] Belarus had held its own parliamentary election during that autumn. Easily dominated by candidates supportive of the regime, the event took place simultaneously the with earlier-mentioned referendum abolishing presidential term limits. Perhaps that was why some Russian politicians not only hailed the election but also suggested Lukashenka could be made leader for life.[568] That was not going to happen, yet, but did indicate grudging admiration for the Belarusian president. After all, and unlike in Belarus, he had created a country in which people did not rebel–partly due to fear of repercussions but also since they considered their living standards to be tolerable.[569]

Tolerable largely due to Russian economic assistance, as we have repeatedly seen, and that would now seem set to continue. The previous winter, in a renewed dispute over payments, Gazprom had briefly shut off gas to Belarus, leading an angry Lukashenka to denounce them as "terrorists."[570] Such a spat now seemed less like to occur. After all, the Russians did not want to risk popular Belarusian dissatisfaction leading to further spread of coloured revolution, precisely at the time when the EU had responded to the Belarusian election with another round of sanctions against

---

566 A call which was remarked upon in Beissinger, 2007: 266
567 Such praise for Lukashenka can be found in Herd, 2005: 8
568 A suggestion from Pavel Borodin, whose job was to promote the Russia-Belarus Union. He may, admittedly, have stated this with a hint of irony and certainly with awareness of Russian self-importance. See also Vanderhill, 2014: 272
569 In that respect, it was noticeable that support for Lukashenka in Belarus did not appear to significantly correlate with support for return to the socialist past. Unlike in Russia and Ukraine, the Belarusian leader was perceived to have created a present good enough to dull longings for the past. See also Gherghina and Klymenko, 2012: 63
570 For further details on the spat, refer also to Rutland, 2008: 209

the regime.[571] And in a year when Poland had swiftly proven its intent to influence EU foreign activity. Not only was its government prepared to partake in sanctions against its neighbour, but the country also began hosting hundreds of young Belarusians, Russians and others from post-Soviet Europe, teaching them how to organise civil society movements.[572]

Belarus tried to push back against Poland but would find over the coming year that an EU member state had greater resources to bring. In the summer of 2005, the Polish minority in Belarus suffered harassment from Minsk with three Polish diplomats also expelled from the country.[573] In return, though, apart from bilateral protests the Polish government also pursued the matter in its multilateral forum, managing to quickly escalate it within Council of the European Union. While Poland's efforts did not have significant immediate repercussions for Belarus, they did reinforce the theme of human rights as something central to EU-Belarus relations.[574] As well as the theme of Lukashenka as a serial violator of such rights and the Belarusian regime as unreliable. Until the Belarusian presidential election of 2006 tension between Minsk and Brussels would increase. Arguably, the EU could have been better at using incentives as well as threats toward Belarus.[575]

Not necessarily to change Lukashenka's mind but to show Belarusians a realistic alternative to their current situation. Beyond the above-mentioned interaction with politicised youth activists there was probably a need for broader engagement with a society which, in both Belarus and Russia, had learnt to tolerate autocracy in return for welfare goods.[576] More effort might have been made to make clear to ordinary Russians and Belarusians that their socioeconomic systems were not, after all, doing particularly well. That incomes might be going up but that long-term investments on

---

571 Those EU sanctions are also highlighted by Hellquist, 2019: 416
572 This took place within the framework of the "Study Tours to Poland" programme. On that, see also Pospieszna and Galus, 2020: 221
573 That spat being summarised in Galbreath and Lamoreaux, 2007: 124
574 A thematic development covered by Copsey and Pomorska, 2010: 317
575 This point was also taken up by Merheim-Eyre, 2017: 105
576 For the continued impact of this "social contract" on societal quiescence in both Russia and Belarus, see also Finkel and Brudny, 2012: 8

assets such as fiscal institutions and infrastructure was lacking and that, therefore, more should be expected of their leaderships.[577] Particularly within Belarus a more proactive European Union might have found a receptive audience for that message and the idea that Brussels could help. Unlike in Russia where surveys showed a steady decline in the proportion of people identifying themselves with Europe, in Belarus such people become more common around the 2006 election.[578]

And continuing such thoughts, the mid-2000s might have been the ideal time to convince Lukashenka that a break with Russia was desirable and feasible. We have previously seen how Belarusians felt close to Russia but now, at least, surveys were showing a marked drop in support for a union.[579] Similarly, perhaps Lukashenka did not have to worry about his people placing their allegiance with Putin? Whereas the early presidency of Putin had seen the Russian's popularity among Belarusians soar ahead of his Belarusian counterpart, increased authoritarianism in Russia and a botched Russian response to the Ukrainian Orange Revolution had helped push Putin's popularity low.[580] We might, therefore, be seeing here a window of opportunity during which the European Union could, potentially, have convinced Lukashenka to break with Russia. Of course, formidable obstacles for such a break remained. Putin might have lost popularity in Belarus yet could still count on widespread affinity for Russian culture.[581]

---

577   The problem of delayed socio-economic development was now worse in Belarus than in Russia, yet both countries were storing up problems for the future, something at times overlooked by analysts of the day. However, for useful points on this, see also Fortin, 2012: 911

578   These survey results were shown by White et al, 2008: 225

579   With such a union being supported by only 12% of respondents in 2005. See also Buhr et al, 2011: 428

580   An indication of the fluctuating relative popularity among Belarusians of Putin and Lukashenka during these years is offered by Ioffe, 2007c: 41

581   And, indeed, for Russian language. Despite the recent changes to increase the presence of Belarusian language in the educational system it would clearly take many years for such changes to have noticeable effect. For data on the continued importance of Russian language in Belarus, see also Comai and Venturi, 2015: 888

The Belarusian elite might be less swayed by cultural links to this neighbour. As we know from other post-Soviet states after 1991 elites tended to globalise through language and economic links in the West. Tellingly, if they went to work abroad educated Belarusians were more likely to go to the European Union than to Russia.[582] Particularly in terms of business, there was an impression among Belarusian businesspeople that Russia was a "hard" place to engage economically, often marred by criminality and by deals working to a zero-sum principle. This could make the Russian economy, as a whole, come across as somewhat repulsive to Belarusians.[583] It was also, however, a source of opportunity for those with ambition. Through competent use of informal practices great profits could be made without having to suffer under the institutionalised power of something like the European Union. Learning in Russia might prepare Belarusians for engagement with the West and elsewhere.[584]

None of those reasons, however, bound Belarusian and Russian elites together as much as did developments in Ukraine. Despite plenty of evidence to contrary, the narrative remained that the West had instigated Yushchenko's triumph. And that activists doing the Western bidding were now moving across the post-Soviet region.[585] In response to such perceived aggression the regimes in Russia and Belarus quickly built up their own supportive populist organisations, particularly focusing on youth activism. We saw previously how such efforts had existed in Belarus through most of Lukashenka's tenure, now his Republican Youth Union was accompanied by higher-profile Russian efforts, primarily Nashi.[586] Furthermore, the Russian authorities took inspiration from their

---

582 That tendency was in contrast, incidentally, to Ukraine from where the preferred destination for educated emigrants seemed to be Russia. On that, see also Danzer and Dietz, 2014: 193

583 Interesting comments on that point from Belarusian respondents can be gained from Miazhevich, 2007: 1343

584 The idea of Russia as a conduit for Belarusians' modernisation, and possibly even Westernisation, is discussed by Miazhevich, 2009: 190

585 The Ukrainian Orange Revolution had certainly inspired democracy activists from countries like Belarus, where the idea of an upcoming "denim revolution" at the presidential election of 2006 took hold. See also Hale, 2006: 317

586 The institutionalisation of pro-regime support in Russia and Belarus around this time is debated in Hellmeier and Weidmann, 2020: 76

Belarusian colleagues and instituted early narratives and legal propositions against so-called "foreign agents", the idea that some people in the population had to be uncovered as effectively fifth columnists ready to work with foreigners to subvert the state.[587]

There was also an uptick in the Sovietisation of official nationalism within the two countries. Lukashenka, in particular, could reach to the Second World War not only because it was a historical memory on which Belarusians, mostly, could agree, but also because it reinforced the narrative of a foreign incursion which had to be resisted.[588] Minsk did not fully jettison efforts to build a non-Soviet (and non-Russian) Belarusian identity. Indeed, we shall come to see repeatedly how that identity later grew as a means of resistance against Russia. However, spooked by the coloured revolutions Lukashenka did reach to a Soviet identity for which he knew there was public sympathy.[589] And instead of reaching towards the West, Lukashenka's Belarus now made a public display of its eastwards reach. 2005 became the year when Belarus applied for observer status in the Shanghai Cooperation Organisation. Indicating that even if the country did not want to be beholden only to Russia, a Chinese alternative might be sought.[590]

At least in the medium term. The Chinese economy was still some way from full capacity. Also, Beijing could not send energy to Belarus. Putin had become more adept at energy negotiations with Lukashenka and secured agreement on gradually increasing prices for gas deliveries as well as Russian partial ownership of Belarusian energy infrastructure.[591] When timing its demands, though, Russia was careful. The push on energy pricing and ownership only came at the end of the year, long after the March 2006 Belarusian

---

587 For Russian parliamentarians' call for measures to be taken against "foreign agents" — and for similar rhetoric in Belarus — following the Orange Revolution, see also Chaudhry, 2022: 561

588 On the uptick of commemorations of the Soviet era during the aftermath of the Ukrainian Orange Revolution, see also Marples and Laputska, 2022: 33

589 As shown through numerous opinion polls, but also open to multiple interpretations as by Lewis, 2018: particularly chapter 5

590 Contemplation of the Belarusian application to the Shanghai Cooperation Organisation is found in Lanteigne, 2006-07, 621

591 Details of this are offered by Browning and Christou, 2010: 115

presidential election, the run-up to which had seen Lukashenka's popularity benefit from Russian short-term promises of energy prices lower than for even some Russian customers.[592] Funds sent from Russia helped Lukashenka to increase Belarusian public sector wages just before the election. Such funds would also play their part in retaining the picture of Belarus as a relative egalitarian society. That was not just a matter of the population's welfare but of its impression of what Lukashenka and his Belarus meant.[593]

Equality was part of Belarusian identity. It spoke to a communitarian belief which arguably was much stronger here than in Russia. It would become widely accepted among Russian nationalists that their country, or civilisation, was communal much more so than the individualist West. That seemed a much more convincing claim for the Belarusians to make.[594] And a problem for the Belarusian opposition became its relative inability to promote such communalism and societal harmony. Among leading opposition figures before the election there was open disagreement about how to frame "Belarusianness". Alyaksandr Milinkevich, nominated to lead the opposition charge, was harshly criticised for refusing to break with Russia should he win.[595] Particularly vociferous in his criticism was Pazniak's Conservative Christian party which during the year ramped up accusations against Russia, and against Lukashenka as Russia's toady, of "ethnocide" against the Belarusian people in a "fascist" tendency linking back to Stalin-era crimes, such as in relation to the mass executions at Kurapaty.[596]

---

592 On Russian economic support for the Belarusian regime before this election, see Tolstrup, 2015: 684

593 That Belarus remained a relatively egalitarian society can be seen when comparing its Gini-coefficient with that of other post-Soviet countries, as done in Gugushvili, 2015: 728

594 For a brief illustration of this, note how it was much more common for people in Belarus than people in Russia to be member of a trade union. Of course, that difference was also impacted by degrees of state involvement, but that is sort of the point — Lukashenka was constructing (at least on the surface) the collectivist society of which Putin spoke but did not do much to further. On comparisons over trade union membership, see White and McAllister, 2007: 590

595 On Milinkevich being accused of being "pro-Russian", see also Marples, 2007: 63

596 For these acidic accusations, see Goujon, 2010: 20

132 UNCANNY ALLIES

That approach was never appealing to a majority of people in Belarus seeking to get by and likely to have connections in Russia. The Kremlin knew this and sent leading ministers to Minsk to highlight those exciting projects in which the two countries could engage as long as Belarusians made the sensible choice of Lukashenka.[597] Undoubtedly, the official election result–which saw Lukashenka re-elected with 84% of votes–was marred by fraud and widespread protests against the authorities did briefly break out in the capital. However, those protests were not significantly replicated elsewhere, and a repetition of the Ukrainian scenario never looked likely.[598] Western actors, including the European Union, had tried to keep a close eye on the election. The Belarusian regime had hardly been welcoming and had, for instance, spent some effort trying to keep members of the European Parliament out of the country so that they could not function as election monitors.[599]

Predictably, the conduct of the election would be widely criticised by European and North American states and institutions. The European Union announced new sanctions but was at pains to stress that those were directed specifically against the leadership, not the Belarusian people. All fine and well, but still lacking specific incentives, as I mentioned before.[600] Some commentators also pointed to Western hypocrisy regarding Belarus. Claimed that Lukashenka retained public support, that he had handled socio-economic affairs well, and that he was being treated differently from other non-Western dictators. Questionable claims, certainly, but one to which Western regimes still lacked a practical, constructive answer.[601] The Russians were more proactive. That summer

---

597 Further detail of visits by Russians such as defence minister Sergei Ivanov and prime minister Mikhail Fradkov are offered from Ambrosio, 2007: 243

598 The limited impact of post-election protests in Belarus in 2006 is discussed in Way, 2012b: 442

599 That obstruction being noted as part of a longer-term pattern by Goode, 2016: 880

600 For statements from the European Union following the Belarusian election, see Portela, 2016: 919-20

601 An example of such claims can be gained from Sussman, 2006: 27-28. Clearly, the attitudes presented in that article go far beyond what most Western commentators would state (and, indeed, far beyond what the author of this book argues). Still, such attitudes would always find publicity absent a clear

they celebrated the retention of Lukashenka in military exercises under the aegis of the CSTO and hosted by Belarus. Participants were not subtle in their signalling–according to the exercises Belarus called for help from "Dneprovia" against a "Bugia" seeking to take western Belarus away.[602]

Politically, murmurings were heard amongst Russian elites for an increasingly ambitious Russo-Belarusian Union. Following the loud argument a few years prior Moscow was careful about ambitions within the Union. Externally, though, Russia considered whether the Union might take on board de facto states like Transnistria. Surely, an aim on which Lukashenka could agree.[603] He would be less happy about the Russian push for economic advantage and could not completely avoid the pressure. The president did, though, muse about nuclear power to offset hydrocarbons dependency. Symbolically, quite a statement considering the Chernobyl legacy. Practically, however, as would become clear, not necessarily something to take him further away from Russia.[604]

The Medvedev Interregnum

Soon, Lukashenka would find out why he might want distance from Russia. The two countries may have reached an agreement on natural gas in late 2006 yet soon they were sparring over oil. In particular, Russian company Transneft charged Belarus with illegally siphoning off oil from pipeline and briefly stopped transit during January 2007.[605] While outside observers had sympathy with the Russian position, taking such drastic measures rebounded on energy supplies for the European Union. In response to this and

---

Western strategy towards Belarus (and towards Russia, too), including a clear endgame.

602 The point being that the Dnepr is a river shared between Russia, Belarus and Ukraine, while the Bug forms a border between Belarus and Poland. On this, see also Silitski, 2010: 348

603 Some Russians mentioned the Georgian de facto states of Abkhazia and South Ossetia in the same vein, in prophetic terms considering the war two years later. For all of this, see March and Herd, 2006: 372-73, 375

604 For Lukashenka's considerations of nuclear power, presented in connection with the December 2006 negotiations with Gazprom, see Marples, 2008a: 221

605 That dispute being covered by Tekin and Williams, 2009: 341

134   UNCANNY ALLIES

similar problems between Russia and Ukraine the year before the European Commission instigated new energy policy measures marshalling institutional power against external deliverers over the coming decade.[606] Brussels would become prepared to take punitive economic measures against Russia if it did not receive contracted energy deliveries. Moscow had no interest in, and limited capacity for, such a fight. Blaming transit countries for the spats, the Kremlin instead invested in pipelines under the Baltic Sea going directly from Russia to the European Union.[607]

The European Union was persuaded by that plan. Yet it left Belarus (and Ukraine) with a problem. If transit territory became less valuable to the Russians, then Lukashenka would have less leverage in the bilateral relationship. He was likely to receive less subsidies and hence be unable to retain a still relatively comfortable socio-economic situation.[608] It would also make it more difficult, if not impossible, for him to promote Belarus to the West and globally in a quest to seek partnership alternatives to Russia. Realistically, Lukashenka could not build a case on democratic credentials as there was broad agreement among observers of the still increasing autocratic tendencies in his regime.[609] However, some foreign analysts remained impressed, or at least satisfied, with the society and daily life that Lukashenka had built. Everybody understood that funds from Russia had played a significant part in this project, yet it was also about how the project was carried out, how oligarchy, while certainly present, remained low-key.[610]

This, therefore, looked like a society quite different from that of Russia. It allowed parts of the Russian elite to highlight their own populist credentials. Zyuganov argued Belarusian societal stability

---

606   The beginning of this EU process is outlined in Bosse, 2009: 223
607   Developments of the so-called Nord Stream project are discussed in Bosse, 2011: 529
608   On measurements such as poverty and unemployment, for instance, Belarus remained somewhat ahead of Russia, even after years of energy-fuelled growth in the latter. For the data, see Rasizade, 2008: 12
609   And the increasing autocratic tendencies of Russia. For discussions of such autocracy, see also Rivera and Rivera, 2009: 603
610   An example of how the approach by the Belarusian regime might contrast favourably with that of Russia in the eyes of outsiders is seen in Ioffe, 2007b: 71

showed an example to follow for Putin while professional firebrand Vladimir Zhirinovsky praised Lukashenka's robust rebuttal of Western critique.[611] Some prominent Russians went further. Well-known nationalist and writer Aleksandr Prokhanov scolded the Kremlin for having forced an increase in energy prices on a "loyal ally" like Belarus, making clear that Russia could not afford to alienate those who remained ready to participate in the Greater Russia project.[612] This came as Putin's second presidential term was heading towards the end. Speculation remained about his succession or possible ways of staying in post. In the wake of the coloured revolutions, the Russian leader was also moving to a more assertive position abroad, with 2007 witnessing partial suspension of Russian participation in European arms control.[613]

This was a poor time for Putin to be showed up by the Belarusians. It did not help that Lukashenka kept talking publicly about how he could help the European Union. So, there followed some tart comments from Putin on Russian television about how his country was funding more than 40% of the Belarusian budget.[614] However, the Belarusian regime was ready to stand its ground. Partly because it wanted to see who, if anyone, might succeed Putin and whether that person could prove more malleable. Also, though, since Lukashenka knew that standing up for Belarusian interests against Russian pressure played well with the domestic, Belarusian audience.[615] Minsk was ready to milk that popularity. With his re-election long secured, in March 2007 Lukashenka felt sufficiently confident in his domestic control to officially celebrate, for the first time, the anniversary of the 1918 Belarusian state. Thereby seeking to overshadow the opposition's commemoration, but also to send a

---

611   The opinions of those Russian politicians are provided by Suslov, 2012: 582

612   Prokhanov's critique was provided within Tsygankov, 2008: 52, 55

613   The reference here being to Russian suspension in participation within the Treaty on Conventional Armed Forces in Europe. Far from a total negation of arms collaboration with the West yet an unprecedented step, nonetheless. See also Wilcox, 2011

614   For Lukashenka's attempted seduction of the European Union, and Putin's response, see also Bosse and Korosteleva-Polglase, 2009: 155-56

615   Look, for instance, at surveys taken in Belarus in the wake of the early 2007 spat with Russia over oil deliveries. As analysed by Balmaceda, 2014a: 525

signal to Russia.[616] And among continued rumblings within the Russian elite about a takeover of Belarus through the Union State, Lukashenka pushed back. When visiting Siberia in 2007, he even told local representatives that any attempt to force Belarus into Russia would create a new "Chechnya" to the west of Russia.[617]

A pointed comment considering Chechnya's years of bloody fighting. And a reminder that the Russian brand was linked to martial values. Maybe that could change. In 2008, Putin's presidency did end. He was replaced by Dmitry Medvedev's focus on modernisation and on the economy. A focus the new leader openly wanted into relations with Belarus.[618] If a strategy of legal fairness and transparency succeeded, perhaps Russia and Belarus could avoid further disagreement? That would be in the Russian interest with energy prices remaining high and a substantial, if still minority, proportion of deliveries to the lucrative EU market still going through Belarus.[619] From the Belarusian point of view, and despite all the problems surfacing during Putin's presidential terms, the deal offered by Russia was still quite lucrative. For a start, despite the previously mentioned bilateral agreement to gradually increase energy prices for Belarus, at the time of Medvedev's accession those prices were still relatively low.[620]

And such subsidisation helped the Belarusian economy in numerous ways. The comment by Putin noted above had perhaps exaggerated Russian assistance to its neighbour. Nevertheless, if we combine the direct energy discounts offered, together with lucrative energy on-sell by Belarus and fees for energy transit it the fillip for Belarusian engagement with Russia remained clear.[621] Under Putin, it had increasingly seemed as if Moscow expected

---

616 Official events in Belarus for this anniversary are mentioned in Marples, 2008b: 33

617 This comment was registered by Libman, 2011: 1341

618 See, for instance, Russian remarks to that effect by mid-2008 in Korosteleva, 2009: 239

619 In the case of natural gas, for instance, data on that can be gleaned from Dimitrova and Dragneva, 2009: 865

620 For a snapshot, see also the helpful comparison between prices for Russian natural gas in several post-Soviet states, as offered by Tolstrup, 2009: 935

621 A discussion of these different ways in which Russian energy helped the Belarusian economy is provided by Alieva and Pikulik, 2023: 1180

Lukashenka to choose between its wares and those of the EU. Now, though, there was hope that Medvedev would be more flexible. So, Lukashenka tested his options with Brussels by releasing political prisoners and duly got visits from Brussels.[622] Belarus had previously eased repression in return for an EU response. Yet this was a test to see if Russia would react negatively. And it did not. Even when Brussels announced it wanted to coordinate energy transfers with Belarus–a step which some in Russia might see as excluding their input–Moscow was restrained.[623]

Perhaps Medvedev wanted to gradually offload Belarus to the European Union? After all, he had arrived as president with a mission firmly focused on domestic affairs, on rebuilding Russian financial and manufacturing capacity, dragging the country away from its dependency on hydrocarbons and the risk of Russia developing Dutch Disease.[624] The new Russian president very prominently spoke out against corruption and the chaotic, personalised business world of the Yeltsin and Putin eras. Admittedly, Putin, too, had complained about corruption but seemed to tolerate it within the system of informal practices he dominated. Medvedev's message was much starker, set to inaugurate a new Russia.[625] In which case there was not really space to humour Lukashenka's economic desires. Energy subsidies was one problem, but potentially unfair competition from Belarusian producers of machinery and foodstuffs was another. If Minsk wanted closer relations with the EU market then let them face that challenge.[626]

That, anyway, would have been the logical progression of Russian-Belarusian relations if Medvedev had been a clear break

---

622 That blatant quid pro quo is mentioned by Kazharski and Makarychev, 2015: 334
623 On that suggestion of EU-Belarus collaboration on energy transfers, see also Bosse, 2012: 376
624 Medvedev's profession of such aims, and a discussion of whether he tried to pursue them, is a theme of Black, 2015
625 Nowhere was that ambition set out with more symbolic clarity than in Medvedev, 2009
626 Already a majority of Belarusian exports went to the EU. And even if statistics were heavily influenced by energy trade, Lukashenka frequently argued his manufactured goods, too, could find a place in European markets. For trade statistics by 2008, see also Bechev, 2011: 422

with Putin. But he was never intended to be. The two had followed each other closely since the 1990s and Putin had handed the presidency to a person he saw as subservient. His evaluation largely proved correct.[627] The world was given an early warning that Putin as prime minister still retained control in Russia with the invasion of Georgia in August 2008. With the war partly due to NATO comments in April that Georgia and Ukraine would one day become members, Western hopes of a changed Russia were comprehensively disabused.[628] Particularly since Russia then officially recognised parts of Georgia as independent, on alleged parity with Kosovo. From Moscow there was a hope, leaning towards an expectation, that Belarus would support its course. And Lukashenka did indeed later send a fact-finding mission to the disputed territories of Abkhazia and South Ossetia.[629]

But he had no intention of following Russia's lead anytime soon and instead let the question drag on in the Belarusian parliament. At the same time, Minsk saw an opportunity in Georgia and soon developed a framework for economic and scientific collaboration with the Caucasian state.[630] Not a particularly friendly gesture towards Russia, since Georgia was still led by Mikheil Saakashvili, who was very much vilified in Moscow. Yet certainly a strategy in line with Lukashenka's presentation of Belarusian identity as an amalgam of many cultures and guided by many interests.[631] With Medvedev distracted first by domestic affairs and now by war, Lukashenka was happy to build his profile with Georgians and with other post-Soviet populations as a tough leader who was

---

627   On the clear links between the foreign policies, in particular, of the two Russian presidents, see also Sagramoso, 2020: chapter 10

628   A useful work on the Russo-Georgian war and its context is Asmus, 2010

629   There were even suggestions that the Russians later tried to bribe Lukashenka to support recognition of the territories' independence, as mentioned in Cooley and Mitchell, 2010: 72

630   Lukashenka's initiative on the matter is the subject of Kakhishvili and Kupatadze, 2023: 125

631   That image also afforded evocative description by Belarusian philosopher Valiantsin Akudovich, as cited in Pershái, 2010: 394

ready to take decisions for the benefit of his people and without taking direction from Moscow or anywhere else.[632]

Given all the speculation, moving towards certainty, that Medvedev had been doing Putin's bidding regarding Georgia (and other high-profile policies) Lukashenka was also sending a none-too-subtle signal to the Russians. He knew that many Russian elites still favoured unification with Belarus (arguably even more so than with Ukraine).[633] And if Russia now decided to move in a more martial direction than Medvedev's presidency had indicated at first, then Lukashenka was ready to follow suit. He was already paying for Russian soldiers stationed in his country, unlike the attitude of other post-Soviet states, such as in Kazakhstan.[634] Still, Belarus had to be seen as Russia's equal–perhaps even more so in this than in other fields. Commemoration, even celebration, of the Second World War had continued in Medvedev's Russia but the Russian war was not that of Belarus and now cultural products from Minsk, like movies, frequently highlighted Belarusian specificity.[635]

There was some background in late Soviet culture for doing this (as I mentioned in chapter one) and some Russian movies, like the acclaimed documentary "Kiselev's List," were still prepared to present a Second World War as different in Belarus than elsewhere, not least due to overwhelming presence of the Holocaust.[636] Yet in the heady wake of the Russo-Georgian War, and with martial values having been increasingly promoted under Putin, the Kremlin had indicated a willingness to turn Russia, and its allies, into a symbol of large-scale warfare and glory–without space for Belarusian, or any other localised specificity.[637]

632　A profile that seemed to build well in both countries of the region, judging from the comments gathered by Person, 2016: 343

633　That comparison, with additional data, offered by Zimmerman, 2009: 202

634　A point made by Kramer, 2008: 14 and perhaps particularly telling considering how eager the Belarusian regime otherwise was to get payouts from Russia.

635　As an example, see the television series "In June '41" shot in Belarus from 2008 and depicting a war with local conditions including Belarusian language and customs and even a Polish element. On that, see Bekus, 2017a: 255

636　A core topic for "Kiselev's List" as also mentioned by Waligórska, 2016: 358

637　There is a very interesting analysis of this development in Russian attitudes to war, particularly the Second World War, by Carleton, 2017: chapter 3, culminating in prophetic words on p. 112

I mention this here to foreshadow developments in Russian policy thinking seen clearly after 2014. The West swiftly moved past Russia's assault on Georgia. As Medvedev spent his presidency seeking to convince the West of his modernising credentials he found a receptive audience, keen to collaborate to escape the global economic shock now developing.[638] This meant that Medvedev would find it easier to present an image and a legacy of modernisation and economic rationalisation than was warranted by the destruction with which his time in office had begun. When Putin later stepped up aggression in Ukraine Western observers were, therefore, more shocked than they should have been.[639] Conversely, Lukashenka was quickly disabused of any notion that Medvedev would be more pliable than Putin. Indeed, as Russia was beginning to feel the effects of the global economic crisis, dissatisfaction rose over perceived exploitation by Belarus. Not least since the latter country, unlike Russia, avoided recession during 2009, even if growth fell precipitously.[640]

The Belarusian president showed initiative to keep economic hardship from the population where possible. He could not avoid some socio-economic problems, like a rise in unemployment, which was exacerbated by the economic crisis in Russia to which many Belarusians had become used to travel for work.[641] He could, though, use the public sector to retain welfare benefits for all people in Belarus, whether they were in employment or not. A prime example of this remained the healthcare sector, key data for which remained much more positive than was the case for Russia or

---

638 A recession which, of course, also curtailed any foreign policy ambitions which Medvedev might have had. To get an impression of the difficulties which Russia seemed to be in at the time, see also Goldman, 2009

639 An example of how the time of Medvedev was misunderstood in the West is Treisman, 2011. Although in many ways an excellent academic study it works from the assumption, I would argue, that Medvedev fundamentally wanted strategic collaboration with the West. That is indeed what Medvedev said — not so much what he did.

640 On the Belarusian ability to avoid recession, see also Connolly, 2012: 357

641 In fact, looking at Belarusian emigration as a whole (and not just in terms of highly skilled migrants as previously discussed) Russia at this time was a relatively much more popular destination than for people from Moldova and Ukraine. On data for this, see Brunarska et al, 2014: 136

Ukraine.[642] Notice also how the Belarusian state, in the midst of a financial crisis, pushed large-scale industry in the country not only to uphold but to increase their commitment to the welfare of their employees. Very much a Soviet tradition and something Putin had, periodically, promoted, too, but not as consistently as the Belarusians.[643]

As I have noted before, such policies can and have been used to present Lukashenka as a "benevolent dictator." That remained a misnomer. He was adept at political survival and realised a minimum of welfare was required to keep Belarusians relatively quiet. Such welfare required Russian funding, so he had to remain acceptable to Moscow.[644] As I have hinted at before, there even remained among some Belarusian elites a belief that further developments in relations between Belarus and third countries, such as in the EU, could only take place through Russian mediation. That it was only with the help of Moscow that Belarus could be remembered and taken seriously abroad.[645] Such Russian sponsorship was periodically suggested. In the middle of 2009, notably, prime minister Putin declared that Russia would drag Belarus (and Kazakhstan) with it into the World Trade Organisation (WTO) membership of which Russia had negotiated for years. Problematically, however, Putin's outburst was largely born with frustration over the slow accession process.[646]

It confused and rather scared many Russian elites who were eager for the perceived economic benefits from the WTO and, perhaps rightly, saw Putin's comments as a way to slow membership negotiations down. In a rare case of public disagreement with his mentor, Medvedev also quickly contradicted Putin, making clear

---

642 As shown through UN data from 2009 and summarised in Ioffe and Yarashevich, 2011: 766
643 In this respect it is telling that social contributions within the costs of Belarusian industry under Lukashenka rose not only in absolute terms but as a proportion of the budget. Data on this are in Yarashevich, 2014: 1714
644 For further detail, see also the Belarusian balancing act outlined in Balmaceda, 2014b: 148-54
645 For the slightly contradictory sentiments on this topic among Belarusian elites, see Korosteleva, 2011: 253
646 On Putin's statement, see Sakwa, 2011: 965

142   UNCANNY ALLIES

Russia was seeking entry alone.[647] And that episode, following from war in Georgia, signalled to Lukashenka that days of easy gains from Russia were over. Within global economic crisis Medvedev did not pursue the "liberal empire", respecting and assisting neighbouring countries' progress. He pursued competitive mercantilism in which countries like Belarus would only be tolerated through reciprocal benefits.[648] Consequently, there is a broader point to be noted regarding Russian foreign policy. From 2012, Putin would often be accused of mirroring such policy after the 19th-century Russian empire, disregarding sovereignty of Belarus and other smaller states in a world which "rightfully" belonged to so-called great powers.[649]

Medvedev was thinking that, too. He believed some states had more rights than others. He was prepared to bully his neighbourhood. He was more willing than Putin to use institutional rather than coercive power, but only as a means, not as an end. That is what Lukashenka understood, and that is what the West missed.[650] Knowing that Medvedev would not make his life easier, the Belarusian president pushed back. First, in a discrete but important step, from 2009 Belarusian authorities circumscribed access by Russian media to Belarusian consumers. Pushing Russian television onto Belarusian state-controlled channels made censorship easier in case of future bilateral spats.[651] Such a spat duly appeared. In May, Putin visited Minsk to negotiate a loan which he tied to Russian takeover of Belarusian dairy companies, and–so claimed Lukashenka–to Belarusian recognition of Abkhazia and South

---

647   Medvedev's counter to Putin's statement is offered by Connolly and Hanson, 2012: 489

648   Such as in the growing IT-industry, where Belarus seemed to be following the Baltic States, particularly Latvia and Estonia, in monetising the new media in a way from which Russia could and would learn over the following years. On Belarusian advances in the IT-sector, see also Warf, 2009: 567-68

649   A logic sometimes taken up among Western analysts, too, with O'Hanlon, 2017, as a consistent if controversial example hereof.

650   Of course, one reason why Russia lost interest in focusing on institutional power was that it encountered the master of such power in the shape of the European Union. For an incisive analysis of that meeting, including a useful primer on types of power, see also Casier, 2018

651   This media manoeuvre is very well explained by Szostek, 2018: 321

Ossetia. Following Belarusian refusal on both counts, Russia then sanctioned dairy imports from Belarus.[652]

Ostensibly, sanctions were warranted on grounds of food sanitary standards–reasoning which Russian authorities would continue to use over the coming decade, including against Ukraine as shall be seen in the next chapter. Few were convinced by that explanation, though, including an incandescent Lukashenka who duly boycotted participation in the upcoming CSTO-summit held in Moscow.[653] Soon, the "milk war" ended. Yet fundamental disagreements persisted. As I noted earlier in this chapter, the Belarusian regime had never been comfortable with privatisation and, with the exception of Turkmenistan, by 2010 still had the second-lowest rate of privatisation in the post-Soviet region. So, business takeovers by Russian elites were not welcome.[654] Having failed to force Lukashenka's hand, such elites were growing increasingly frustrated not just by the risk of missed economic opportunities but also by the cheek shown by the Belarusian "peasant" in resisting them. During 2010, Russian hostile measures grew so blatant that even some Russian Communists called it out.[655]

Clearly, admiration for Lukashenka's "hard man" image continued among sections of the Russian polity. While neither Putin nor Medvedev held him in high regard, Russian regional leaders could see the Belarusian as an example of how to marry power imbalances with a need for self-preservation within a Moscow-centred hierarchy.[656] The Kremlin had to make an example of Lukashenka. So, mid-2010 saw energy disputes break out into open conflict. Gazprom was allowed to raise prices to Belarus and cut deliveries; in

---

652 The so-called "milk war" is well described by Silitski, 2009, even if he overstates Russia's interest in getting rid of Lukashenka.

653 For Lukashenka's boycott of the CSTO summit, see also Locoman and Papa, 2022: 284

654 Comparisons of privatisation rates can be found in Junisbai, 2012: 897, which also shows privatisation rates in Russia around the average for the post-Soviet region.

655 That Russian defence of Lukashenka's position is shown in Dawisha, 2011: 352

656 Such regional leaders would occasionally consult him for direct lessons, an example being the visit to Belarus of the governor of Ivanovo Region. On this, see Obydenkova and Libman, 2012: 376

144   UNCANNY ALLIES

turn, Belarus threatened to stop oil deliveries to Europe if it did not receive allegedly outstanding fees for energy transit and tariffs.[657] Knowing that Russia was unlikely to relent, at least in the longer term, Lukashenka at the same time sped up his search for alternative energy partners. Apart from tentative links from the EU, China offered help with fiscal stability, while Venezuela stated it could guarantee supplies of natural gas for 200 years.[658]

Most importantly, given Russian-Belarusian tension Kazakhstan saw a chance to circumvent Russia in the race for Belarusian energy assets. From the Kazakh side, oil infrastructure was the bigger target. In principle, Minsk had already agreed on the sale of such to Russia, but now the Kazakhs appeared with a counteroffer.[659] Kazakhstan mainly wanted was to gain leverage over Russia in separate bilateral energy negotiations and was never likely to take Russia's place in Belarus. Yet Lukashenka's actions were provoking insubordination among Russia's alleged "inferiors", and he knew it. In July he appeared publicly with Saakashvili in what could be described as epic trolling.[660] And in a slightly more ambiguous act Belarus took in as a refugee Kurmanbek Bakiyev, who as Kyrgyz president had been overthrown and forced to flee. Russia was notedly uncomfortable with any sort of executive overthrow, yet it had worked to undermine Bakiyev, so might not be wholly comfortable with his continued presence next door.[661]

Lukashenka was happy to keep Russians on edge. Moscow wanted to hit back and in August broadcast "The Godfather", a television documentary sharply criticising Belarusian economic dependence on Russia, its authoritarianism and unexplained disappearances while also presenting the Belarusian president as little more than a local thug.[662] Appearing only a few months before the

---

657   Further details of this clash can be found in Stulberg, 2012: 832
658   Presumably in liquified form and somewhat impractical given the distance between the countries. See also Monday, 2011: 829
659   Kazakh attempted involvement in the Belarusian energy sector is discussed by Zabortseva, 2014: 319
660   The mutual support offered between Lukashenka and Saakashvili is mentioned in Padhol and Marples, 2011: 4
661   The arrival of Bakiyev in Belarus is the topic of Cameron and Orenstein, 2012: 23
662   This so-called "media war" is further detailed by Vieira, 2014: 564

next Belarusian presidential election the documentary could have been damaging if it had offered new information or effectively circumvented Belarusian state propaganda. As it was, this Russian initiative came to be little more than a frustrated outburst which Lukashenka would remember bitterly but could overcome.[663] In December, the Belarusian president was re-elected with over 80% of the vote, a bit down from his official vote share at the last election yet a clear sign of his political dominance. As before, Western actors decried voting fraud while Medvedev quickly stepped in to offer his congratulations.[664]

Despite all the animosity over the past summer, the Russian leadership knew that Belarus still had few other potential allies to which it could turn. The economic model on which Lukashenka had so far thrived did not appear sustainable and Moscow were optimistic they would eventually reel him in.[665] The post-electoral crackdown in Belarus did little to change Russian optimism, for as Lukashenka's riot police cracked skulls in the snow in Minsk (including those of losing presidential candidate Andrey Sannikau) chances of the European Union reaching out to the Belarusians in the foreseeable future noticeably diminished.[666] And if this was the repressive course which Lukashenka's Belarus would take in future then it could be an example for other post-Soviet regimes in a way which Medvedev and Putin could find useful. Already, it was

---

663 That Russia did not want to overthrow Lukashenka may also be guessed by the fact that little attempt was made to use non-traditional media to get the character assassination across. By the end of 2010, the Russia-led CSTO would use post-electoral unrest in Belarus to warn against the subversive dangers of the internet. If that was really their opinion, it is telling that the internet was not further employed when Russia attacked Lukashenka. On the subsequent CSTO-warnings against the internet, see also Lysenko and Desouza, 2015: 639

664 Medvedev's support for Lukashenka's re-election is in Tudoroiu, 2011: 419

665 For an example of upcoming economic problems for Belarus, its trade deficit had grown precipitously during the past decade. On this, see Yarashevich, 2013: 212

666 In its treatment and protracted incarceration of political opponents like Sannikau and Milinkevich, who had lost the previous presidential election, Belarusian authorities were showing the way for Russia to persecute individuals like Aleksey Navalny over coming years. For that comparison, see also Evans, 2024: 345

noticeable that Yanukovych, who had finally snuck in to the Ukrainian presidency, refused to criticise his Belarusian colleague.[667]

There was little doubt that the Yanukovych administration wanted to go the Belarusian authoritarian way, if possible. Ukraine was still a bit circumspect on the matter to avoid alienating other European countries yet the following year the Ukrainian ambassador to Minsk praised Lukashenka for bringing "stability."[668] So, as Medvedev moved towards the last year of his term his Russia could look at its neighbours with some comfort. Ukraine remained at a slight length from Russia yet under Yanukovych remained a "brother." While smaller Belarus, awkward as it could sometimes be, was still mentioned by Medvedev as part of the Russian nation.[669] Not, he had made clear, that this entailed such countries to special treatment. But that it bound them to Russia and the fate of Russia as it prepared to make more overt use of the financial and other resources it had built up over the last decade to retake its rightful place in the world.[670]

A recent institutional aide for that aim was the Customs Union, which Russia had inaugurated in 2010 together with Belarus and Kazakhstan. We have already seen how such institutional trappings did not prevent competition between those three states. However, since he remained convinced of the importance of economic power such an institution mattered to Medvedev.[671] In principle, removing customs barriers between these countries should bring transparency and favour larger Russian companies in deals between them and their Belarusian counterparts. Some success was

---

667 On the lack of official Ukrainian condemnation of the post-electoral crackdown in Belarus, see also Dimitrova and Dragneva, 2013: 671
668 That comment being noted in Kuzio, 2015: 178
669 For Medvedev's rhetoric in this regard, see also Valenza, 2023: 412
670 If the fate of Belarus and Ukraine was to assist the Russian mission, then the implication was that refusal to provide such assistance might constitute betrayal. The potential crudity in that message could come out in unexpected ways, as in the wholly misguided (and quickly retracted) campaign by authorities in Perm, which used a quote from Hitler to imply a fascist essence to non-Russian sentiments in Belarus and Ukraine. See also Goode, 2012: 13
671 The beginning of the Customs Union is discussed in Korolev, 2018: 903

seen, notably when a deal was finally agreed in 2011 for Russia to build a nuclear power plant in Belarus.[672] By the end of that year, while Russian domestic politics were becoming increasingly unruly due to public dissatisfaction with Putin's stitched-up return to the presidency, Medvedev and Lukashenka built on existing economic collaboration to present a Declaration on Eurasian Economic Integration accompanied with Russian takeover of some Belarusian energy infrastructure.[673]

In return for which the Belarusians not only saw some of their energy subsidies restored but also benefitted from the release of the second part of a $3bn loan which would be crucial to keep the Lukashenka regime fiscally afloat and avoid serious public unrest.[674] Apart from immediate benefits conveyed by such deals and the Customs Union they would also make it more complicated for Belarus to integrate with the European Union, should Lukashenka seek to do so. Not that this seemed immediately likely. After the repression of December 2010, the Belarusian had less trust than ever in Brussels.[675] There were widespread calls for release of Belarusian political prisoners, something which some countries in the European Union took up as a cause célèbre even more so than had been the case after 2006. Indeed, one of the Belarusian presidential candidates, Ales Mikhalevich, received asylum in the Czech Republic.[676]

It seemed Lukashenka now had little place other than Russia to go. Putin would come back as Russian president and had already indicated that he would push a more uncompromising line against Europe and America. So, why did the Belarusian leader keep talking about his desire for closer relations with the European Union

---

672 As outlined in more detail by Miller and Volpe, 2023: 1325
673 Further details on this offered by Frye, 2011: 748
674 That loan is also mentioned in Clem, 2011: 795
675 Thus, for instance, in June 2011 the European Union instigated an arms embargo on Belarus, something Russia would face, too, but only after the Crimean invasion of 2014. See also Kranz, 2016: 978
676 On that asylum, see also Weiss, 2018: 184

and NATO?[677] And why, in the summer of 2011, did he publicly squabble with the Russian government over the state of his economy, refusing to accept there was any sort of crisis while now also pushing for alternative oil suppliers in the form of the ambitious Azerbaijanis?[678] Lukashenka did so because he knew conditions could change. He knew that many people in Belarus, perhaps even a majority, still viewed him as a tough but fair leader who would do his utmost to steer the country through current difficulties in order to retain long-term stability.[679]

Furthermore, Lukashenka knew that support within Belarus for unification Russia, let alone absorption by the bigger country, had fallen significantly in recent years. Clearly a more assertive Russia was finding it difficult to keep friends and influence attitudes abroad, even in a country as similar as Belarus.[680] And he could look at protests developing in Russia and reflect that these might say something more fundamental about Russia. Putin would re-emerge as president, yet his people were dissatisfied, angry, fearful. Not all of them but enough that it made sense for Lukashenka to wait and see what might be around the corner.[681]

---

677 As he did, for instance, in April 2011, when he planned for Belarus to integrate with those organisations while also "flirting" with Russia. See also Gnedina, 2015: 1010

678 The unhelpful interaction between Lukashenka and Russian foreign minister Sergei Lavrov as well as the plan for cooperation with Azerbaijan are covered in Saivetz, 2012: 409

679 It was telling here that surveys at this time showed a clear decrease in the proportion of respondents in Belarus seeing public officials as corrupt, in a clear difference with public sentiments in Russia and Ukraine. For this, see McAllister and White, 2015: 86

680 Surveys showing attitudes in Belarus towards integration with Russia are in White et al, 2016: 19

681 Public pessimism in Russia (and Ukraine) at the time was shown by White, 2011: 803. The source also shows how there was more optimism in Belarus.

3 2012-2019

A Man on a Mission

Coming into 2012, Vladimir Putin was raring to go. He had recently announced his return to the presidency; a post he likely regretted ever vacating. His stand-in, Dmitry Medvedev, had advocated "liberalisation" yet with little to show for it–at home, where street protests now called out for a complete change of regime, or abroad.[682] Russia had proven military capacity in Georgia, but only partly, while the West largely ignored Russian wishes–particularly outside the post-Soviet region. This, certainly, was the narrative promoted by Putin, who now prepared for his presidential return by having articles published in national media setting out his plans for assertive domestic and foreign policy.[683] In those plans, Belarus appeared to fit well. Notably, Minsk kept promoting ideas of regional integration. For instance, at the beginning of the year Lukashenka prepared for the return of Putin by reintroducing the idea of a common currency between Russia, Belarus and Kazakhstan–a currency he likened with clear ideological intent to the Euro.[684]

Later that year, in July Lukashenka would use his address for Independence Day to stress how Eurasian integration would not cause a loss of Belarusian independence but would provide "independence of a new type" enabling linkage between global economic centres in the East and West.[685] The Belarusian president argued that regional integration was an inevitable consequence of contemporary globalisation and a logical way for the country to protect its interests within capitalist competition. Even if the interests of individual companies might sometimes lose out to a delegation of sovereignty made in the national interest.[686] Music to the Kremlin's

---

682 Comprehensive evaluation of Medvedev's foreign policy is in Pacer, 2016
683 A summary of Putin's messages in the separate articles, including on foreign policy, is offered by Rojansky and King, 2012
684 On this see Belarusian, 2012c and also Shchipanov, 2012
685 The text of the address is in Lukashenko, 2012a
686 This was reported in President, 2012a. Not that all Russian observers were convinced Lukashenka's optimism would carry the day. See also Trushkov, 2012

ears, one might think. The Belarusian leader had made very clear, however, that integration should not mean subordination to Russia. Indeed, he specifically warned that the Eurasian great powers of Russia and China should keep Belarus closely engaged in their initiatives.[687]

And Lukashenka repeatedly went out of his way to praise China for its potential investments in his country, such as a proposed technology compound to produce cars, as well as the country's ability to take advantage of global expertise in its search for perennial economic growth.[688] In fact, during 2012 the Belarusian regime would repeatedly, and pointedly, stress China as a model to follow. By the autumn, the president was highlighting how Beijing had managed to combine communist values with capitalist methods. That was also, of course, a covert slight against Russia following years of Medvedev's vaunted "modernisation."[689] So, if Putin wanted to use Belarus to support Russo-centric Eurasian integration he might be disappointed. Also, integration remained of limited material impact. In July a major Russian newspaper analysed the Customs Union between Russia, Belarus and Kazakhstan, pointing out that it had little economic value for Russia, despite government statements to the contrary.[690]

Consequently, the incoming Putin administration might be better served through bilateral links with Belarus. After his reinstatement as president, Putin made his first trip abroad went to Minsk. There, he talked of the "great future" for the relationship, while Lukashenka stressed all the programmes run between the governments and between Belarus and individual Russian regions.[691] All good and well, perhaps, but no specific gains were announced at the meeting. And for a Russian leadership very much intent on strengthening the "power vertical" inside the country

---

687   For that reminder by Lukashenka, see Minsk, 2012
688   For Lukashenka's statements to Chinese media, see also Interv'iu, 2012. Notice also, though, misgivings by the Kremlin as Belarus lured Chinese companies to produce cars there rather than in Russia. That was the subject of Russia, 2012
689   As reported in President, 2012b
690   For this analysis, see Rudakova, 2012
691   The tone of bonhomie which the two presidents wanted to convey is well conveyed by Gamov, 2012

(and inside the post-Soviet region more generally) having Lukashenka build up his own networks in the Russian provinces was not exactly welcome.[692] There were some successes in the relationship during 2012, particularly within the military sector. In February, Medvedev had an accomplishment late in his presidency when Russia acquired formal rights to conduct aerial patrols along Belarusian borders with NATO member-states, even as some Belarusian commentators complained about the consequent loss of sovereignty.[693]

The regime in Minsk pushed back strongly against such complaints. It stressed its role of security provider whenever possible. Vadim Zaitsev, head of the KGB, declared his country to be a "barrier" against all sorts of extremist and otherwise criminal activity and hinted at the importance of Belarus for the security of the European Union.[694] Such hints at Belarusian international importance were common. As was the implication that instability was foisted on Belarus from outside, including from Russia. An implication made even more clearly half a year before by the interior ministry warning about increased drugs flows from Central Asia and Russia as a result of the Customs Union.[695] Or shown indirectly during the repeated incidents when Belarusian authorities prevented Russian agricultural goods including seeds and livestock from entering the country, due to pathogens and other alleged results of ineffective

---

692 Clearly, the Belarusians were conscious of the value of having such administrative and economic links circumventing the Kremlin. Witness, for instance, the official outcry from state airline Belavia that Russian administrative restrictions following disputes over flights were preventing it from keeping in touch with Russian cities other than Moscow. See Belarusian, 2012a. On the block of Belavia flying to most Russian cities, see also Cherkasova, 2012

693 That complaint lodged in Lukashenka, 2012

694 For this, see KGB, 2012. Not that such reassurance helped Zaitsev who would be fired in early November ostensibly following the suicide of a subordinate but more likely connected to security failures over the previous year. See also Vasil'eva, 2012

695 The claim was reported in Drug, 2012. That summer, a large-scale anti-drugs operation hosted by the Russian-led CSTO was likely an answer to such Belarusian concerns. See also Aleksandrov, 2012

Russian practices and lack of expertise; claims Russia found more fitting to be made against less able countries than itself.[696]

The Belarusians were likely correct in their criticisms, which did not help relations. Nor did Lukashenka's reminders that Belarusian security provisions, benefiting Russia as well as Belarus, were expensive. In October, he noted that NATO itself considered the Belarusian army the strongest in the post-Soviet region. And then asked for Russian cash for its upkeep.[697] In Moscow they were increasingly exasperated by Lukashenka's pleas for money, as shall be shown again shortly. Russian commentators pointed out, though, that the new Putin administration clearly saw much to emulate in Lukashenka's administration–not least in its attitude towards domestic opponents, recently so vociferous when protesting against Putin's return.[698] Thus, the fact that Putin's first presidential visit to Minsk had failed to yield tangible results did not matter much. Important instead was the signal sent by that visit, showing the company in which Putin wanted to find himself and the political direction in which he was travelling.[699]

Even when the Belarusian president in December 2012 exhorted workers to work as if they were in a situation of war, it might have been a crude response to genuine economic difficulties faced by the country in the wake of global economic crisis–but for sympathetic Russian elites Lukashenka's approach sounded a bit like Andropov.[700] Only in rare cases did Lukashenka's authoritarian regime cause the Russian state discomfort. When two Belarusians were executed following a terror conviction the act was widely condemned in Europe–and even the Kremlin had to consider domestic disgust over these acts. Still, even here official reaction was

---

696 For an example of Belarusian checks on Russian livestock, see Belarus, 2012e. An overview of the dispute is also offered by Kirpichevskaia, 2012

697 On that request for money, see also Rynochnuiu, 2012

698 On the new Russian administration's preference for identifying with the policies of Lukashenka, see also Galimova et al, 2012

699 A point also made that summer by former deputy prime minister and now opposition stalwart Boris Nemtsov. See Boris, 2012

700 In a similar spirit, Lukashenka decreed that workers could only resign from a company with permission from their superiors, as reported by Val'samaki, 2012

muted.[701] And far from all Russians were against the death penalty–let alone other authoritarian practices. Indeed, some Russian nationalists deliberately sought towards Belarus, concerned about Putin's public disavowal of nationalist political parties and believing a more friendly reception could be gained in the smaller country to the west.[702]

Putin would soon become more adroit in accommodating nationalists. And although nationalism was perhaps not something learnt from Lukashenka (who himself was experimenting with that ideology) populist approaches to governance arguably was. Repeatedly, opposition commentators in both countries would note how poorly the two leaders got along.[703] Indeed, not long after Putin's supposedly successful early summer trip to Minsk did Medvedev, now Russian prime minister, get time with Lukashenka, being offered the best smiles and parades the Belarusians could muster. Certainly, Belarus wanted economic favours, but it was a reminder to Putin that he was not the only Russian politician valued abroad.[704] A few months later, at a CIS summit in Turkmenistan Putin had individual meetings with several colleagues yet appeared to snub Lukashenka. Apart from any longer-held grudges that snub might also have stemmed from the Belarusian's incautious comments on Putin's alleged health issues (let alone snipes about the latter's height).[705]

Lukashenka appeared quite able to get under the skin of Russian elites. He had cultivated the balance between seeking and offering protection; being on the border between ally and alien. Constantly reminding Russians and Belarusians that he may not be an ideal solution, but that he would always be better than an alternative.[706] Witness his above-mentioned flirtations with China–in the

---

701   As noted by Russian foreign minister Sergey Lavrov in Glava, 2012
702   This was reported in Nationalist, 2012. How Putin's motives could still be mistrusted by some Russian nationalists is clear from Stepanenko, 2012a
703   For an example of that by the time of Putin's presidential return, see Khalezin, 2012
704   On Medvedev's visit, see Netreba, 2012
705   Although this longer analysis comes from a domestic opponent of Lukashenka, other accounts at the time appear to corroborate it. See Lebed'ko, 2012
706   A waspish but incisive take on Lukashenka's craft was offered by Radzikhovskii, 2012

face of potential Russian insecurity. Or look at how he invited Japan to build a nuclear power plant in Belarus. Less than a year after the Fukushima disaster. And knowing quite well that the Russians–already contracted to build one plant in Belarus–would not welcome competition.[707] The Belarusian leadership was always seeking multiple economic partners. Although years of political divergence had complicated relations with the European Union, in particular, Minsk and Lukashenka had kept calling for "dialogue" with the Western organisation without offering much specific or consistent to Brussels in the way of compromise or concessions.[708]

More feasible than achieving change in relations with the EU– or convincing major economic powers like China and Japan–was taking advantage of the post-Soviet marketplace. In March, Belarusian prime minister Mikhail Myasnikovich pointed out that only 6% of food exports currently went to non-Russian CIS states and that this imbalance should be rectified.[709] Even if this did happen, though, by far the main impact on the Belarusian economy would remain related to energy resources. And, thus, to Russia. By 2012, decades of price disputes showed no sign of stopping. True, Russia had gradually moved onto Belarusian assets, most recently buying 50% of gas pipeline operator Beltranshaz.[710] Minsk had hoped such agreement would secure long-term low prices for Russian oil and natural gas, yet by the end of the year familiar disputes, as well as questions about how much natural gas Russia should actually export to, as opposed to through, Belarus, and how much oil should go to Belarusian customers.[711]

---

707 Lukashenka's invitation was mentioned by Kriat, 2012
708 This was, again, done by Lukashenka when answering questions in connection with his annual address to parliament and people, as reported in Niama, 2012
709 Myasnikovich's comments were reported in Belarusian, 2012b. For analysis of Belarusian trade imbalances and differences in outlooks among the elites at this time, see Suzdal'tsev, 2012
710 Details of that agreement, including Russian contingency plans if the Belarusian side reneged again on its obligations, came out in early 2012. For this, see Belarus, 2012c. Overall, the deal was a step which Russian officials claimed was really meant as a favour to the Belarusian economy, without the Belarusians agreeing. See also Khodasevich, 2012b
711 As usual, disagreement started to spill out into public space as autumn commenced. For more, see Rossiiskie, 2012

2012-2019   155

At stake was also how much oil Belarus should receive for re-fining and on-sale. A 2010 agreement saw Belarus getting Russian oil duty-free in return for revenues for export duties collected on petroleum products made from Russian crude. By March 2012 such duties were raised 4.4% after Minsk had first tried to lower them.[712] It had never been likely that returning Putin would accept being out of pocket. Not simply because of his distrust of Lukashenka but given the increased state interference in economic affairs to which he and his new government explicitly tied itself. A political course marked by the renewed prominence of Sergey Glazyev and statist capitalism.[713] Indeed, in the run-up to Putin's inauguration political commentators in Belarus, including Shushkevich, foresaw that the new Putin presidency would be even more hands-on than in its prior incarnation four years before and determined to centralise not just the Russian Federation but the post-Soviet space; a task for which energy links and dependencies were ideal.[714]

At the same time, Russian reporters were noting that contin-ued difficulties of the Belarusian economy. The Belarusian National Bank consistently refuted any risk that the country would become unable to fulfil its debt obligations. Experts from the Russia-led EEC, though, seemed to disagree and were demanding stricter con-ditions for further credit.[715] Minsk, in return, scrambled around for additional funding from other international financial bodies, among which the most notable was the IMF. However, it was never likely that the IMF–known for its inflexibility towards debtors–would prove more amenable to Belarusian wishes than any Rus-sian-led provider.[716] Many observers, therefore, expected Minsk to gradually adjust to Russian wishes by offering Moscow a greater share of profits from its sale of refined oil products, and by

---

712   Presumably, Belarus wanted to lower export duties to increase sales, which would go into its own budget. For the raised export duty, see also Belorussiia, 2012. And for the initial lowering of the duty, see Belarus, 2012b

713   See Åslund, 2013

714   See also Stanislav, 2012

715   See Khodasevich, 2012a

716   Belarusian financial authorities periodically returned to the idea of IMF fund-ing, reported e.g. in Belarus, 2012d. The options for funding for Belarus are also discussed in Gabuev, 2012

providing Russian investors with easier and more widespread access to privatised state assets in Belarus; access for which Russian representatives repeatedly asked.[717]

The Belarusians proved prickly, though, particularly Lukashenka. The president noted that any agreements reached with Russia on energy pricing was not a "hand-out" but a fundamental precondition of the Single Economic Space with Russia and Kazakhstan. If there was a substantial energy price difference between customers within that Space free and fair competition was impossible.[718] In a similar vein, after Putin had visited Minsk that summer (and, presumably, made clear to his counterpart that Russia expected more concessions in return for its oil and gas) the Belarusian government stressed that it had always stuck to agreed contracts, by paying in full and in a timely fashion.[719] Whatever the merits of that claim, the Belarusians had frequently moved away from the spirit of contracts and informal arrangements between the countries. While Belarus officially remained Russia's closest ally in efforts of post-Soviet integration, research suggested that it was also a leading country in erecting non-tariff barriers for Russian goods entering Belarus.[720]

Consequently, the Russian government had come to see its counterpart as hustlers. In June, the ambassador noted Belarus was importing more petroleum products (solvents and diluents) than it needed for domestic consumption. As indicated above, if Belarus was re-exporting such products for profit, it should send export duties collected to Russia–which was not happening.[721] The following month that problem was escalated to governmental levels when prime minister Medvedev instigated an investigation into the alleged defraud of Russian state coffers. Belarusian prime minister

---

717 Such requests for Belarusian privatisation would periodically come from the Russian ambassador to Belarus, Aleksandr Surikov, as reported, for instance, in Russian, 2012 and by Kagan, 2012
718 As reported by Stepanenko, 2012b
719 See the comments by Belarusian First Deputy Prime Minister Uladzimir Syamashka in Belarus, 2012a. For a summary of the manoeuvrings by Russia and Belarus around the energy question see Sheremet, 2012
720 On that fairly persuasive claim, see Libman and Vinokurov, 2012: 868
721 This was reported in Prokshin, 2012

Myasnikovich sympathised, but offered no indication that he or his administration would do much to assist Russian inquiries.[722] Soon, the Belarusians sought to put Russia on the back foot. If Moscow was so keen to get its hands on the Belarusian energy sector, including, perhaps its refineries, then Belarus would like access to natural gas and oil extraction within Russia itself, as had been offered to other foreigners.[723]

More generally, Lukashenka made clear he was happy to welcome investors from abroad–including Russia–as long as these were "decent". Belarusians had built up the state's economic assets, so the president noted, and he would not allow foreigners to arrive picking off individual bits exclusively to their own liking.[724] Here, as elsewhere, in Lukashenka's words was a hint that Russians were (latent) criminals, facilitated by a weak regime. He could offer that accusation more directly–soon after, Lukashenka claimed he had resisted selling the state-owned potash company Belaruskaliy even though a "Russian businessman" had offered him a $5bn bribe to do so.[725] Brave Lukashenka standing up for his country. And clearly sensing a public mood in his country. Six years earlier, when offered the choice between unification with Russia and joining the EU, 57% of Belarusians surveyed had chosen Russia, opposed to 29% for the EU. Now, the proportions were equal–38% support for either option.[726]

And that change in public mood within Belarus had happened during a time when the EU had shown its true colours as a direct competitor for influence within Russia's "near abroad"–those neighbouring countries, which Russia as a self-ascribed great power would expect to dominate.[727] Tellingly, and in a change from previous Russian foreign policy practice, there was increasingly less distinction in Moscow being made between the activities of

---

722 As reported by Medetsky, 2012
723 For that suggested trade-off, see also Kravchenko, 2012
724 This was noted in Belarusian, 2012d, and offered context in Khodasevich, 2012c
725 As quoted in Lukashenko, 2012b
726 Ioffe, 2013: 1269
727 This point being forwarded by some Western commentators, as well, including Zielonka, 2012: 518

158   UNCANNY ALLIES

NATO and of the EU in Central Eastern Europe. Countries were being "bribed" to move from their historic bonds with Russia to an alien, hyper-liberal West.[728] Now, through Putin's return Russia pushed for continental primacy and primacy of its ideas in defining the nature of "Europe"–to ensure that this included Russia, and that Russia would no longer be on its borders but be central in it. If that happened, the liminal position of Belarus, too, would be fundamentally changed.[729]

Lukashenka Kicks Back

Russia entered the fateful 2013 with self-confidence. Putin had been back as president for almost a year, so could present a new foreign policy doctrine. This highlighted changes in the international order brought on by the global economic crisis and showed how Russia and its near allies would be well placed in the new world.[730] During Putin's second presidential term his government had already indicated that educational materials would be employed in service of a state-led narrative. In 2013, standardised history textbooks were now being distributed–with simple answers on the theme like the Second World War and relations with Belarus and Ukraine.[731] And Kremlin-approved messaging would be well placed to reach a country like Belarus. The Russian state was keen to use television to spread its ideology and the Belarusian market was saturated with Russian channels, assisted by Belarusian state policies and notable subsidisation to make such channels hard to avoid for viewers.[732]

Minsk still had very weighty economic reasons for supporting Russian policies. As in the cases of other post-Soviet states, like Ukraine and Moldova, as indicated above Belarusian exports remained dependent on the Russian market in what appeared still

---

728   For an overview of how that process had come about, see also Maass, 2017
729   An excellent account of Russian attempts to redefine "Europe" is Neumann, 2017
730   For the text, see Foreign, 2013: section 48 for mention of Belarus.
731   On those books, see also Krawatzek and Frieß, 2023: 1340
732   The conditions supporting Russian television in Belarus are detailed in Szostek, 2015: 124

after-effects of Soviet-era industrial location, specialisation and general infrastructure.[733] Belarusian economic links to Russia certainly did not only take intergovernmental form. Indeed, one of the most important benefits Belarus was gaining from its neighbour stemmed from remittances averaging around \$1bn annually entering its economy from workers in Russia–a very important socio-economic safety valve.[734] And then there remained the energy benefits, of course, which still offered the country prices comparable to those presented to domestic Russia customers. Thus, from 2013 prices in Belarus for Russian natural gas were agreed to equal those in the major gas producing Russian region, Yamalo-Nenets (plus a bit for transport and infrastructure).[735]

As indicated previously, analysts noted that such dependence on cheap Russian energy could move Belarus towards a rentier economy and "Dutch disease". Yet that did not appear to have happened; or not yet anyway. Look for instance at the World Bank's "Doing Business" global survey, which saw Belarus moving up substantially between 2006 and 2013.[736] So, the country seemed to have potential for healthy economic development. But was that because of Russia, or in spite of it? Public surveys showed cooling towards closer relations with Russia among respondents in Belarus. Over recent years proportions supporting close links to Russia and to the EU had moved to the same size.[737] Concerning for the Kremlin was also that such sentiments seemed to spread elsewhere, too. Look at Ukraine, for instance, where a survey from April 2013 had a clear plurality of respondents (44% support) choosing EU-integration over integration with the Russia-led Customs Union (33%

---

733 A point pursued in Lankina et al, 2016: 1606
734 Details can be found in Ash, 2015: 1038
735 This point is noted by Jirušek and Kuchyňková, 2018: 843. What these authors do not explore, though, are the symbolic underpinnings of such a deal. In effect, Belarus is equated to a region critical for Russian energy security — yet in the case of Belarus, sovereignty has been removed from the Kremlin (and arguably from the power vertical)
736 And, in that survey, Belarus now ranked clearly above Russia (and, for that matter, Ukraine). On this, see Kulakevich, 2014: 894
737 A plurality of respondents now wanted to work with both partners, instead of exclusively going to one or the other side. See Korosteleva, 2016: 686

support). Arguably, Belarus was unhelpful in selling that organisation.[738]

The Belarusian regime did declare enthusiasm for integration with Russia–mostly, anyway. Indeed, together with its Kazakh counterpart Minsk stated it wanted more genuine integration by having more input in the Customs Union and other intergovernmental bodies and by directing these towards practical, economic issues instead of the more declarative slant sometimes offered by Russia.[739] One example of a quite practical economic step might be the complete alignment of customs rates, as highlighted by former Belarusian prime minister Syarhey Sidorski and clearly in the spirit of any genuine Customs Union or, as was supposed to be soon introduced, full-blown economic union.[740] More generally, the Belarusian government was concerned that Russia-led integration had previously been moving at such a speed that necessary regulation and institutionalisation had not been adopted. Consequently, the countries involved still produced their own products instead of uniting around the production of genuinely international goods.[741]

In terms of the Russia-Belarus Union, Lukashenka complained that the steps earlier agreed to had not been carried out. The Belarusian president hinted that he might have welcomed a constitution for the Union supported by a popular referendum, although he provided little detail on what such a constitution might have entailed.[742] Perhaps it could have promoted specific identities showing the "spiritual depth" of Russians and Belarusians? Lukashenka

---

738 Orlova, 2017, 226-27
739 Belarusian complaints that integration was being carried out in the wrong manner are shown in Krickovic, 2014: 521
740 This is from Belarus, 2013. As Sidorski would repeatedly make clear, a genuine Customs Union should have no barriers to free trade. See also Sidorskii and Siul'zhina, 2013
741 The comments can be found in Belarusian, 2013a. As pointed out by the Belarusian First Deputy Prime Minister, his country was happy for the Customs Union and Single Economic Space to be expanded at the expense of the CIS countries. See also Borisova, 2013
742 This being noted in Belarusian, 2013c. Towards the end of the year, Russian media would suggest that Lukashenka's idea of a referendum might just be another way of getting money from Russia, i.e. that he should be paid to ensure Belarusians voted "the right way." On that suggestion, see Paratunin, 2013

was now very happy to laud the values promoted by the Russian Orthodox Church, to which the Belarusian Orthodox Church remained subordinate. Contrasting that Church, too, with a deepening crisis of the West.[743] All of which tallied well with Russian policy. By early 2013, Putin had become bullish regarding the prospect of post-Soviet integration and openly challenged any outsiders not to interfere with that process. The Russian president warned against subversive steps taken to "lure away" integration partners from his country.[744]

Putin's political allies expected integration to proceed at pace. In May, shortly before the annual affirmation of state power that was Victory Day, parliamentarian Vyacheslav Nikonov lauded a "stronger, stabler, smarter and richer" Russia under the returned Putin. Russia was being criticised by the West, but only because the latter felt Moscow's growing might.[745] Nikonov was not subtle–he was appropriately chairman of the parliamentary committee for education. But he was not the only actor showcasing Russian ability. Putin himself talked about a whole host of benefits Russia could bring its partners–including something as detailed as healthcare benefits to Belarusians still marked by the Chernobyl disaster.[746] A very particular set of benefits, perhaps, but well suited–one would think–to a population for the identity of which that disaster retained central importance. Or, it would have been well suited if Belarusians had not, over the years, lost faith in Russian willingness and ability to clean up after Soviet-era errors.[747]

Such a charge could have practical policy consequences for the bilateral relationship. The Belarusian government remained committed to building a nuclear power plant and, despite periodic

---

743 For this, see Belarusian, 2013b. Another example of Lukashenka's alignment with the Russia-led church is reported by Chinkova, 2013

744 See here Putin's comments to the Russian security services in Smirnov, 2013

745 As written by Nikonov, 2013

746 Stated by the Russian president in a joint press conference with Lukashenka. See also Vystupleniia, 2013

747 Over the years official Belarusian media had repeatedly castigated Russia for abandoning its smaller neighbour to the consequences of the Chernobyl disaster—a charge easily expanded to cover any Russian irresponsibility. See also Zhukova, 2017: 496

162   UNCANNY ALLIES

entreaties to other providers, was set to use Russian companies for the construction. Not an appropriate solution for the many protesters denigrating Russian safety standards and levels of corruption.[748] That criticism could also reach into periodic disputes over agricultural trade, as briefly mentioned above. Witness, for instance, the ill-concealed charge against Russian radiation safety presented by Belarusian official media when discussing acceptable food standards in the two countries in the context of free trade.[749] Given that attitude, Minsk unsurprisingly still resisted Russian attempts to politicise phytosanitary means. Over the summer of 2013, for instance, as Russia was increasing its attempts at forcing Ukraine away from the EU and towards a Russian-led economic union its stop for Ukrainian exports on alleged health grounds were overtly refused by Belarus.[750]

Periodically, too, would continue Russo-Belarusian disputes over agricultural standards. On several occasions Russia would refuse entry to Belarusian goods–or search them thoroughly despite formally free trade–with Belarus retaliating. Late in the year, there were even suggestions that the removal of the Russian chief public health officer was directly linked to pressure from Lukashenka.[751] Such a charge was impossible to prove. However, the mere idea that the Belarusian president could exert such influence on Russian sovereignty indicated vulnerability of the latter. Defence commentator Aleksandr Golts argued that Lukashenka had repeatedly exploited Putin's abject desire for allies–a desire only increased as the Russian president was shunned across the globe.[752] As illustration for this Golts pointed to the most spectacular fall-out between the two states during 2013–the arrest in August by Belarus of Russian businessman Vladislav Baumgertner. The latter was head of the Russian potash company Uralkaliy, which had shortly before

---

748   As discussed in more detail by Nikolayenko, 2015a: 232-33
749   That example is provided by Zhukova, 2018: 1067
750   Kazakhstan, too, was dismissive of Russian accusations against Ukraine. See Svoboda, 2019: 1695-96
751   That interpretation was presented by Yulia Latynina. For this, listen to Latynina, 2013
752   These dismissive points can be found in Golts, 2013

terminated its alliance with Belaruskali, creating significant turbulence in global potash markets.[753]

When Baumgertner was arrested it caught Russian authorities by surprise. After initially offering muted criticism, Russian first deputy prime minister Igor Shuvalov denounced the arrest as "unacceptable" and "strange". The businessman had been arrested following a meeting the Belarusian prime minister and Russian parliamentarian Leonid Kalashnikov more than hinted the arrest was akin to kidnapping.[754] If so, it was a well-executed crime. Russian analysts claimed Uralkaliy had sought to dominate the potash relationship and had refused Lukashenka's price for a sale of Belaruskali. That was not a new dispute, however. Why had it exploded now? Arguably, the Putin regime was in a hurry to consolidate gains abroad.[755] That aim, though, was not shared by Lukashenka. If Russia was going to widen its own sovereignty it could well encroach on the sovereignty of its neighbours. So, the Belarusian president reminded Russians that his regime was no more ready to abandon power to them than to the West.[756]

More bluntly, foreign minister Uladzimir Makei suggested that Belarus balance between Russia and the EU. Perhaps not a novel appeal–as mentioned earlier Minsk had long taken pride in linking East and West. The timing was interesting, though. As Makei spoke in mid-November relations were turning increasingly bitter between Moscow and Brussels.[757] At stake was the future of Ukraine. For years the latter had sought closer EU relations. Despite friendly policies towards Russia under presidents Leonid Kuchma and Viktor Yanukovych, in particular, Kyiv was keen on economic benefits from Western trade. And Russia had largely accepted this, even when Viktor Yushchenko accelerated EU-friendly policies

---

753 The immediate economic consequences of the split are reported by Filatova, 2013
754 That budding Russian outrage was reported by Russian, 2013b. For a similar take on the arrest of Baumgertner, and worries about a weak Russian response, see Terent'eva, 2013
755 A useful take on the background of the case is by Vardul', 2013
756 For instance, making that point to Belarusian university students, as reported in Belarusian, 2013d
757 Makei's comments were reported by Minister, 2013

164   UNCANNY ALLIES

during his term.[758] However, as mentioned above by 2013 Russia had come to equate threats from the EU and NATO. So, President Yanukovych was reminded of the support offered him by Moscow over the years. A new natural gas pipeline through Belarus, "Yamal-2", was mooted to take even more of Russian energy to Europe away from Ukrainian transit.[759]

That plan was soon scuppered on Polish unwillingness to participate. A memorandum previously co-signed by Moscow and Warsaw was rejected by the latter in July. This certainly did not end Russian options for circumventing Ukrainian territory in its energy deliveries–Nord Stream and, potentially, South Stream, could be used–but it made such tactics more expensive.[760] And upcoming was the November EU-summit in Vilnius. Here, Ukraine–with Armenia, Georgia and Moldova–were planned to sign association agreements with the EU, leaving Russia (and Belarus) without realistic possibility of absorbing those three countries into Russia-led economic union. Such loss of status (and, with Ukraine, economic possibilities) was impossible for Russia to accept.[761] In the months before the summit, Putin had enjoyed only partial success scuppering the agreements. Georgia and Moldova had, perhaps slightly surprisingly in the latter case, ignored the Russian plea. Conversely, following a meeting with the Russian president in September Armenia's leader tersely noted that Armenia had decided to join Russia's Customs Union.[762]

But that was all small fry from a Russian point-of-view. Pressure on Kyiv increased with multiple carrots and sticks presented. Before, Belarus had largely supported the Russian cause, agreeing Ukraine could lose access to lucrative Eurasian markets. By early October, though, Myasnikovich was suggesting his country could benefit well from Ukrainian-EU free trade.[763] And as Yanukovych

---

758   An acceleration outlined by Larrabee, 2006
759   A threat to Ukrainian energy security discussed, with perhaps a hint of glee, by Maksimov, 2013
760   Poland's rejection of "Yamal-2" was written about by Gavrish and Serov, 2013
761   A brief yet poignant summary of tensions leading up to the summit is by Morris, 2013
762   See also Leal-Arcas et al, 2015: 282
763   On this, see also Ivzhenko, 2013

gave in to Russian incentives, and protesters came to central streets and squares of Kyiv, in particular, Belarusian state media did not try to hide the problem. Making direct links to the Orange Revolution served as a warning about the opposition, but also about a feckless Ukrainian dictatorship.[764] That fecklessness would remain. Over the winter of 2013-2014 Ukrainian authorities repeatedly, and cackhandedly, tried to frighten their detractors into submission. Russia offered support for this, wishing for even more brutality to be employed. Eventually, conflagration would ensue in February with hundreds of deaths proving a gateway to a new age in Russia's foreign policy.[765]

Before events had fully unfolded, however, Russia was getting ready. In the south we now know (and might have expected) that Moscow was looking for gains on Crimea. To the north, in December Russian airplanes began patrolling Belarusian airspace while a Russian airbase in the country was announced for 2014.[766] Discussions about such an airbase had been ongoing since the spring and it was clearly prompted now both by Russian broader concerns about its neighbourhood slipping away and by Belarusian concerns that a protracted, increased crisis to the south might spill across its borders and set off instability there.[767] By that point, some solutions had also seemingly appeared on the bilateral issue of Baumgertner and the potash business. Indeed, by the end of 2013 Surikov, a man who perennially seemed to find himself in headlights, stated that while mistakes had been made on both sides the Russians had made most of them.[768]

And very telling it was, indeed, to see Moscow playing so nice with Belarus just as it was about to breach core principles of international law in the case of Ukraine. There was, indeed, in Putin's

---

764 Also see how Belarusian reporters linked chaos in Kyiv to unjustified slanders on the socialist past, as in Chuden, 2013

765 The unfolding of events in Ukraine over that winter and early spring are outlined with detail and verve by Wilson, 2014

766 The announcement on the airbase being reported in Russian, 2013a

767 Russian commentators were quick to highlight the claim crimes by Ukrainian nationalists had historically reached into Belarusian territory. See for instance Ostanovit', 2013

768 As reported in Russia, 2013

third term developing an increasingly ambiguous, perhaps at times self-contradictory, attitude towards international behaviour, norms and law.[769] Rapprochement with Belarus had not come all that smoothly, though, during the last months of 2013. Having already grabbed Baumgertner, Minsk then presented an arrest warrant for Suleyman Kerimov–a major stakeholder in Uralkaly and the man in whose place Baumgertner had allegedly flown to Minsk for his fateful August meeting.[770] What made the chase for Kerimov potentially more problematic was the fact that the latter was well placed among Russian elites. He was a parliamentary representative for Dagestan–representatives from the North Caucasus being particularly chosen for their loyalty to the federal centre–and allegedly close to prime minister Medvedev himself.[771]

So, was Kerimov losing status in Russian politics or was Medvedev himself falling away? Either way, Russian elites really did not want Lukashenka to make that call, or even influence it. As mentioned earlier, the previous summer the Russian prime minister had been received with great fanfare in Minsk. Now, the moustache had apparently turned.[772] Admittedly, a bit of silly imagery presented there. However, silly imagery tied to the deliberate and constant projection of (toxic) masculinity offered by Lukashenka and conflicting directly with Russian masculinity as increasingly projected by the regime at home and abroad. The context for position of top dog (or, rather, male dog) was a constant.[773] Immediately following Baumgertner's arrest, Russian deputy prime minister Arkady Dvorkovich had suggested that Lukashenka's actions might frighten off other Russian businesspeople from investing in the Belarusian economy. Suggesting that the absence of a solution

---

769   A good place to start learning more about that tendency in Russian foreign policy might be Allison, 2020

770   Following a Belarusian referral, Kerimov was quickly placed on Interpol's wanted list. See Interpol, 2013

771   As outlined by Peremennaia, 2013

772   Obviously, observers had long suspected Medvedev's relative weakness in the Russian political hierarchy. For a nuanced take on the presentation of that issue during Medvedev's presidency, see also Duncan, 2013

773   For the masculinisation of Russian foreign policy around this time, see also Riabov and Riabova, 2014

would necessitate a "civilised divorce" hinted not only at the potash companies but to the bilateral relationship overall.[774]

The Kremlin was not likely to take matters that far yet come October the Belarusian president himself readily talked about how Baumgertner's arrest had been politicised. Claiming himself, with some support from Russian commentators, that this was at heart an economic case, Lukashenka now directly linked reductions in Russian oil supplies to the matter.[775] The Belarusian leadership was always ready to complain about its (lack of) energy deals with Russia. Yet using the current dispute to do so also allowed Lukashenka to play on Russian fears for future Eurasian integration. If Belarus could persuade countries like Kazakhstan that Russia was pushing supranational politicisation, resistance to Russia might build up.[776] And such resistance would build on Russia's increasing Ukrainian woes. Even before demonstrations in Kyiv had started, even as Yanukovych began to appear susceptible to Russian pressure, Russian commentators openly worried that the Kremlin had squandered the opportunity to attract a regional circle of allies. Optimism from early that year was slowly draining away.[777]

War Returns to Europe

Back in 2007, the Russian city of Sochi had been named as host of the 2014 Winter Olympics. That triumph had been the result of a concerted effort by a leadership and a country on the rise. Now, the event was set to symbolise Russian great power status.[778] And despite persistent stories of corruption–and some of construction failures–on their own terms the Olympics largely succeeded. Sporting arenas proved more than adequate, while Russian athletes came top of the medal table to great local and international acclaim. Very costly they may have been, but the games proved excellent at sportswashing.[779] Or, they would have been if their later days had

---

774 Dvorkovich's comments were reported by Russian, 2013c
775 Reported in Minsk, 2013
776 In Kazakhstan, often a supporter of further integration, Lukashenka might find a receptive listener. See, for instance, Nazarbayev's concerns as reported by Kazakh, 2013
777 For an example of such commentary, see Pugaiushchie, 2013
778 For the intended symbolic importance of the games, see Petersson, 2014
779 Whether that is the most accurate moniker is debated, though. See also Skey, 2023

not been completely overshadowed by events in Ukraine. As the final day of the games approached violence in Kyiv and elsewhere increased, culminating around February 22 with hundreds of casualties, largely among anti-government protesters, and a Russian press increasingly alarmed by developments.[780]

The courage of ordinary people in Ukrainian cities inspired international opinion–not least since Ukrainians seemed much more united against Yanukovych and for a Western future than had been the case a decade earlier. Such sentiments might grow, too, in Belarus, where surveys now showed 45% support for EU-membership versus 37% for unification with Russia.[781] For obvious reasons, Lukashenka did not want his population to take inspiration from the protests in Ukraine. While stating that events there were none of his business (unless participants wanted to involve him), the Belarusian president blamed the instability on Ukrainian "clans" and, implicitly, the lack of a strong, centralising leader like himself.[782] However, in early 2014 he also allowed his government to open negotiations with the EU on issues of visa facilitation and readmission agreements. Having suffered setbacks with Yanukovych during 2013 and seeing little progress with Belarus since 1995, Brussels now wanted to regain initiative in the region. Lukashenka, always looking for more options, readily agreed.[783]

And there were signs that the EU could increase its offerings to Belarus and other countries in the neighbourhood. Some member-states openly advocated such a course. In early February, Poland and Sweden pushed to reinvigorate the Eastern Partnership. Regarding Belarus they wanted more use of soft power and, perhaps, sub-governmental interaction.[784] Such an offensive fed into Russian worries of getting caught out, of being ill-prepared for

---

780 A polemic and interesting take on Russia's stake in the Ukrainian revolution of 2013-14 can be gained from Shevtsova, 2014
781 Survey data summarised in The Most, 2015
782 Lukashenka's criticism of Ukrainian clans was mentioned in Reaktsiia, 2014
783 1995 of course being the year when the soon-suspended Partnership and Cooperation Agreement between Belarus and the EU was signed. For Belarusian negotiations with the EU in January 2014, see also Delcour and Fernandes, 2016: 1265, 1270
784 As reported by Słojewska, 2014

unexpected developments in the post-Soviet region. Some commentators saw Russian domestic political arrangements as a source of problems abroad; Russian foreign policy could not engage constructively with non-state actors or the general population in allied countries.[785] Analysts closer to the Russian state described Ukraine as a symptom of Russia losing out to the West on powers of attraction and highlighted the need for a more active promotion of Russian benefits to Ukrainians (and other post-Soviet peoples) while waiting for hostile opponents to be overcome by incompetent governance.[786]

Such analysts, or other observers, did not expect military Russian intervention in Ukrainian affairs. Yet such intervention was coming. Beginning on February 27, soldiers without military insignia occupied key infrastructure, military and political sites on Crimea. The Russian state disavowed direct involvement yet much sympathy for these "defenders" of ethnic Russians against purported Ukrainian extremism.[787] The occupation of the peninsula was soon completed and with relatively minor bloodshed. Local inhabitants (well, those allowed on television, anyway) declared themselves overjoyed by developments, and after only a good two weeks a referendum was set up confirming Crimean independence from Ukraine, swiftly followed by the official incorporation of this region into Russia.[788] Some international reaction followed. The vast majority of countries in the world refused to recognise the annexation. There was widespread concern that the referendum had been preceded by the expulsion of all credible observers and had taken place in the shadow of armed soldiers. Western sanctions were introduced yet in a limited, somewhat ineffective form.[789]

Some Belarusian observers were cautiously optimistic about the meaning of it all for their country. Practical aspects of the

---

785 A weakness highlighted by Trudoliubov, 2014
786 The analysis offered by Bordachev, 2014
787 For an instructive, if frequently chilling, account by Russian observers of how the invasion of Crimea took place, see Brothers, 2014
788 A detailed view of these developments is offered by D'Anieri, 2023b: 217-22
789 Barron, 2022, is scathing yet largely on-point in his evaluation of EU-sanctions, in particular.

Crimean annexation might have been completed, but the symbolic role of the peninsula remained in play. Minsk might offer its political support for the EU or the Russian position, depending on who could pay the most.[790] A great plan, for sure, if the Belarusian regime could pull it off. Clearly, Lukashenka did not feel so confident. The Belarusian president was not prepared to bluntly denounce the Russian offensive, not least because indications existed that the Crimean annexation had proven quite popular with many people within Belarus as well as Russia.[791] Lukashenka did, though, denounce Russia's step as a "dangerous precedent" in world affairs. He specifically pointed to the 1994 Budapest Memorandum (of which he was a co-signatory), castigating participants there for not adhering to promises then given to preserve Ukrainian territorial integrity. Now, he said, aggression of other countries might be emboldened.[792]

Like other regional leaders, Lukashenka was also concerned about Russian plans to potentially move into other parts of Ukraine, as–indeed–would soon be the case around Donbass. Unlike his peers, though, the Belarusian president showed his disquiet even further by allowing Ukrainian interim president Oleksandr Turchynov to visit Minsk. A visit noted in Russia.[793] It was also noted that Lukashenka spoke directly against the idea of "federalising" Ukraine–an idea for decentralisation in that country, which was becoming popular in Russia since it could allow Russian de facto representatives in Ukraine to gain a veto over the further domestic and, particularly, foreign policy trajectory of that country.[794] What the Belarusian leader rarely said openly–yet remained clear to all–was a fear by his regime that successful "federalisation" by Russia in Ukraine might soon lead to the appearance of soldiers

---

790   This was the attitude presented by Martinovich, 2014
791   Opinion polls now supporting closer relations between Belarus and Russia were reported in Bulletins, 2015
792   The Belarusian president would return to that narrative periodically, see e.g. A.G. Lukashenko, 2014
793   See, for instance, how that choice by Lukashenka was highlighted by Dubnov, 2014
794   Russian commentators understood clearly the link between Lukashenka's aversion to Ukrainian federalisation and to Russian intent, as shown by Khodasevich, 2014b

without military insignia turning up in Belarusian provinces such as Homel and Mahileu, moving the latter away from his control.[795]

As with Ukraine, Lukashenka could be confident that Western countries would not come to his defence against Russia. And not simply because of their reluctance to engage Russia militarily. Among leaders in countries such as Germany there remained a residual equation of (most of) the post-Soviet space with Russia.[796] So, the president knew he was on his own. Lukashenka now denigrated Yanukovych's weakness, allegedly facilitating the Ukrainian revolt. Already, it has been noted how the Belarusian president railed against Ukrainian political "clans"–he also made clear he would not run away like Yanukovych and that armed (Russian) incursions into his country would be resisted.[797] Lukashenka would claim in his state of the union address that his government could quickly mobilise half a million men and would give a higher budget to the military. Russian nuclear weapons would certainly not be hosted by Belarus. While Makei noted how engagement with the West–particularly the EU–would proceed apace.[798]

Beyond such belligerent talk, the Belarusian regime now sped up initiatives highlighting an independent national identity. In his address on the Day of the Republic Lukashenka partly spoke Belarusian, explicitly linking the language to nationhood. The presence of Belarusian language in education and media was increased.[799] It was not very likely that Belarusian language would come to dominate public space–indeed, that was unlikely to be Lukashenka's wish. Yet Belarusian society was witnessing the growth of *trasianka*, somewhat of a mixture between Belarusian and Russian which, in itself, marked the region out as different from its eastern neighbour.[800] Monuments, too, could show the historical legacy of Belarusians as different from that of Russia. One telling example came

---

795 That fear was discussed by Hall, 2023: 12
796 Or, perhaps more accurately, with "that which was controlled from Moscow." On this point, specifically regarding Germany, see also Portnov, 2015: 724
797 Such points being mentioned by Allison, 2017: 533
798 All these points being gathered by Sejersen, 2019: 513
799 These observations were made by Astapova et al, 2022: 14
800 On the prevalence of *trasianka*, see also Cheskin and Kachuyevski, 2019: 15

172 Uncanny Allies

that June with a statue of Duke Alherd on horseback being erected in his former home of Vitebsk. Close to the Russian border. Alherd had sometimes cooperated with Muscovy; he had also besieged it.[801]

And in May Lukashenka used the hosting of the Ice Hockey World Cup to promote a Belarusian national idea. He made explicit that the international focus and prestige gained could build up the national brand–important, although he did not say this explicitly, when many abroad still saw him as an ally of Russian aggression.[802] At the same time, the Belarusian leadership remained wary of ideas taking over in Russia. In March, upon officially annexing Crimea, Putin had spoken to the Russian houses of parliament about the historical, cultural and, above all, religious values tying together Russia, Belarus and Ukraine.[803] In itself, that was a sentiment with which Belarusians could potentially get on board. Their problem was that the Kremlin was becoming increasingly Manichean in its worldview. There was no longer space for compromise between the Russian civilisation and that of the West (or, of any other non-Russian civilisation, at the end of the day).[804]

This, therefore, presents us with another example of the uncanny in the Russo-Belarusian relationship. Russian, and Soviet, identity had historically been linked to (the possibility of) expansion. Although empires were partly built through the overpowering of enemies, they were also built through their assimilation. The multicultural, admittedly under one ruler, was the whole point.[805] This is not, by any means, to imply that Russian or Soviet empires were always–or even predominantly–tolerant towards minorities. The lands of some Siberian peoples were razed, the Jewish population was subjected to horrific pogroms, and punitive expeditions

---

801   For more on the erection of the statue of Alherd (with pretty pictures, too, and — indeed — an impression of how the statue now dominates the view of the Orthodox Resurrection Church), see U Vitsebsku, 2014
802   On Belarus hosting the championships, see Rojo-Labaien, 2018: 1104
803   A fair analysis of the context for this speech is offered by Plokhy, 2023: 119
804   Although he seems loath to place blame for this on Russia, that binary view of Europe, in particular, is otherwise identified by Sakwa, 2015: chapter 2
805   See e.g. Kivelson and Suny, 2017

were repeatedly used against villages and towns of the Caucasus.[806] There is also nothing laudable about the expansionary nature of Russian (or other) empires. But perhaps what can be distinguished is the concept of "imperialism" from that of "colonialism". The latter emphasises the transformation of an "outer" region on behalf of an "inner" region. The former emphasises the transformation of both.[807]

Again, this is in no way meant as a praise of empire. It is a reminder that someone like Lev Gumilev has often been at odds with nationalist and racist forces in modern-day Russia, since Gumilev stressed that "Russia" by its nature was an amalgam of peoples, open to the steppes and Eurasia more broadly.[808] Ideas like those of Gumilev had previously filled much of post-Soviet Russian official rhetoric. Witness frequent references to Russia as a "bridge" linking Europe and Asia, culturally and economically. Witness, too, promotion of Russia as a "liberal empire", attracting surrounding countries through a positive narrative exuding from the Kremlin.[809] All fine and well–Belarusians had certainly bought into that idea, expecting investment from both the EU and China. Now, though, Minsk was increasingly being told it had to choose between Russia and non-Russia. That it was placed in a new Cold War, led by Putin's idolisation of Andropov's policies.[810]

And that non-Russian states in the post-Soviet region should be careful not to challenge Russia. Or, indeed, as Konstantin Zatulin stated on television in early May, since Russia had already "saved" its neighbours within the Soviet framework, and then "allowed" those neighbours to gain independence, they should not scheme against Russia.[811] In response the Belarusian regime could say it

---

806 Such collective punishment obviously continued in the Soviet Union. For recent scholarship on the adaptation and memorialisation of such, see Finnin, 2022

807 There is the beginning of discussion on such themes in the excellent Kumar, 2021: 1-5

808 Bassin, 2016: chapter 7 sets out well the complicated relationship between Gumilev and Russian nationalists.

809 A classic example of Russian academic thinking in that vein would be Trenin, 2002

810 An aspect of Putin's psychology much remarked on in the West, but also by Russian commentators such as Karavaev, 2014

811 Comments presented in Russkii, 2014: 29m, 27s

was not trying to hinder Russia; it was living up to ideals of multi-directional engagement which had–formally, at least–until recently been promoted from Moscow. If Russia now wanted to promote binary, exclusionary policies then it was the Kremlin, not Lukashenka, that had changed its tune.[812] And that is where the uncanny appears. Belarus had not turned into the opposite of Russia–it had remained what Russia used to project. No matter Lukashenka's unprincipled selfishness. No matter Russia claiming a changing world. Russia was changing, too. Back to the zero-sum thinking, which Moscow had purportedly given up around the 1975 Helsinki-Accords.[813]

Such changes in Russian foreign policy led numerous analysts–not least among Western academics–to highlight the advent of a "new Cold War". The comparison did not quite work–today no two all-encompassing ideologies battled for domination–yet mutual intolerance certainly gave the lie to globalist optimism from the 1990s and perhaps even 2000s.[814] Belarusian identity could jar with Russian aggression in unexpected ways. Witness the slightly bizarre Russian TV-show *Chernobyl: exclusion zone* broadcast from 2014. Here, conspiracy, not shoddiness, caused the accident, while an alternative universe made the catastrophe American. Leading to American, not Soviet, collapse. Inventive, if not very respectful to victims of the real incident.[815] Lukashenka, though, could not straightaway change that trajectory in Russian thinking. Instead, he continued trying to profit from it. In May, together with Kazakhstan, Russia and Belarus signed up to the long-negotiated Eurasian Economic Union, to take effect from 2015. Almost immediately,

---

812 And such exclusionary policies by the Russian leadership appeared in tune with Russian public opinion, as shown by polls such as by Otnoshenie, 2014, which demonstrated a sharp increase in public hostility to Ukraine and the West.

813 Or at least by the arrival of Gorbachev. Notice here the repeated refrain about Belarusian readiness to do deals with any country as long as its interests were being respected. As, for instance, stated in Kononovich and Kriat, 2014 — although events the previous day in the skies over Ukraine had made the international environment even more hostile than before.

814 Give and take the "War on Terror". For an example of literature purporting a "new Cold War", see also Lucas, 2014

815 A more complete take on that TV-series, which unsurprisingly gained some popularity in Russia, is by Feldberg, 2023: 1601

Makei complained that the agreement, as signed, really did not offer enough integration.[816]

That was another way for Minsk of saying that it really should receive more money for its support for Russian-led regional integration. Even though by the terms of the prior customs union the Belarusian economy had done significantly better than other participants who had broader opportunities for extra-union trade.[817] And even though Belarusian trade was about to enter into a long-term, very beneficial relationship with the pattern of sanctions being exchanged by Russia and the West. For instance, as some Western foodstuffs were officially kept out of Russian shops, seafood from land-locked Belarus rose to unprecedented, even incredible heights.[818] Then, as Ukraine entered into closer economic relations with the EU, Russia tried to get Belarus (and Kazakhstan) to jointly introduce customs duties on the runaway post-Soviet state. Minsk had little interest in this and instead allowed Ukrainian producers to send their goods through Belarus from where entry into the Russian market was largely free.[819]

Towards the end of the year, it appeared Russia elites were tiring of the schemes from Belarus. First, by November Putin approved new legislation aimed to increase taxes on the extraction of oil, potentially severely denting Belarusian profits from their refinement and re-export and provoking harsh rebuke from Lukashenka.[820] That same month Russia blocked the transport of more than 360 tonnes of fruit and vegetables from Belarus. The latter had officially been allowed to transfer goods from the EU through Russia to Kazakhstan. Now, Russian authorities publicly noted that such goods had been illegally sold in Russia, instead, and had decided to stop it.[821] In addition, Russian phytosanitary institutions also banned several Belarusian meat and dairy producers

---

816 Makei's complaints being reported by MID, 2014
817 A point made well by Hartwell, 2022: 318, 326
818 See the example of Norwegian fish moving through Belarusian distributors to Russia, offered by Weber and Stępień, 2020: 3021
819 This profitable role as middleman for Belarus was mentioned by Libman and Obydenkova, 2018: 1041
820 See also Roberts and Moshes, 2016: 557
821 That message being reported in RF, 2014

from selling their goods in Russia on grounds of alleged health violations committed due to laxer standards within the smaller country, knowing very well how damaging that would be to a core constituency backing Lukashenka.[822]

The Belarusian leadership declared themselves outraged with Lukashenka himself speaking up. Then, in early December, Belarusian authorities apparently introduced checks of goods travelling between the two countries. Minsk denied this was a customs check, but noted, in passing, that its agents had detected multiple shipments of Russian goods not conforming to Belarusian health standards.[823] The dispute rumbled on through the end of 2014. Governments became directly involved without solving the matter. Surikov, in turn, repeatedly went on the airwaves to calm relations and take blame away from Belarus as he had done before. Why the seemingly annual ritual? Because the Russian government knew that they needed Belarusian goodwill.[824] And that such goodwill might otherwise become in limited supply as a more stressful international political environment developed, at the same time as continued frailty of the global economic system–including the possibility of falling oil prices–might begin to directly impact Belarus and any other country directly dependent on trade with Russia.[825]

Belarus Considers Its Options

By early 2015, Russia primarily looked to Belarus for moral support regarding the war in Ukraine. In mid-2014 fighting in eastern Ukraine had escalated following the election of Petro Poroshenko as Ukrainian president. Then, in July international attention on the conflict–and on Russian culpability–was magnified by the downing

---

822 For data illustrating the dependence of such Belarusian producers on the Russian market, see Wengle, 2020: 925
823 The story being described in Gamova, 2014, noting that Russian control posts were quickly set up in response
824 For an example of Surikov's approach, see Nedelia, 2014: from 29m 24s
825 Russian economic woes, including weakness of its currency, also impacted revenue gained by Belarusian companies from re-selling refined oil on the Russian market. See also Recknagel, 2014

of a passenger airline.[826] The aftermath of this crime saw a substantial increase in Western sanctions laid on Russian actors and their allies (although sanctions remained noticeably less thorough than would be the case eight years later). Russian countersanctions were placed on goods, particularly foodstuffs, otherwise being sent from the EU to Russian markets.[827] However, despite its aggressive pushback the Kremlin also realised it had to be seen to offer some solution to the war in Ukraine. So, peace talks were suggested–with the participation of Russia, Western interlocutors and warring parties from inside Ukraine. And the host for such talks became Belarus.[828]

When the MH17-airplane was shot down, Belarusian authorities and media had largely refrained from commenting. However, the leadership had advocated peace in Ukraine from the onset of the conflict and could clearly see status gains from hosting meetings which, on paper, sought to resolve the matter.[829] From a Russian point-of-view it was desirable to have a close ally as an ostensibly "neutral" mediator. During the rest of the year, Russian elites periodically praised the Belarusian input to the peace talks, even if Lukashenka still refused to recognise the independence of the Donbass and the Russian annexation of Crimea.[830] Nonetheless, coming into 2015 Belarus still found itself closer to Russia's position in the Ukraine conflict. Whether alignment would remain, though, was a different question. Russian commentators were noting that the Kremlin continued to push neighbouring countries away–if not

---

826 Despite repeated denials by Russian authorities (and by some Western observers) legal authorities have determined beyond any reasonable doubt that the individuals responsible for the atrocity were directed and assisted by the Russian state. For the court judgment to that effect, see also Summary, 2022

827 For a sense of the push for more Western sanctions in response to the shooting down of the aircraft, see e.g. MH17, 2014.

828 On the so-called Minsk Process, and a suggestion on why it ultimately failed, see also D'Anieri, 2023a.

829 For Lukashenka's rhetoric on this, see e.g. Manilyk, 2014

830 Lukashenka had previously indicated that Russian annexation of Crimea had a link to imperialism and noted, pointedly, that Belarus had historically held parts of the territory of the Russian Federation, as reported by Khodasevich, 2014a. He had also noted that the Ukrainians had given Russia an excuse for taking the peninsula, particularly by not fighting for Crimea. As reported in Smirnov, 2014

178   UNCANNY ALLIES

directly through military action, then by blatant, ineffective attempts at bribery.[831]

As mentioned above 2015 was supposed to inaugurate a more economically institutionalised relationship between Russia and its neighbours through the introduction of the Eurasian Economic Union (EEU) which came into effect at the beginning of the year and was supposed to be the culmination of decades of attempts at post-Soviet international economic regularisation.[832] Russia might continue to bribe countries like Belarus for support, but such bribery would attain a legal veneer. And when Minsk asked for funds in future (as it surely would) Russia could leave that to be decided (at least in public) by a supranational body for which other member-states also had to take responsibility.[833] In principle, the EEU remained ideal for the Belarusian economy. By 2015, Belarus was only sending about 7% more of its exports to Russia than it was sending to the EU. However, its import figures were much more skewed, at 33% difference, particularly due to its continued dependence on energy imports for consumption and re-sale.[834]

Research indicates that Belarus had previously benefitted more than other core participants in Eurasian economic integration. Between 2010 and 2013 for Belarus trade with Russia and Kazakhstan went up relatively much more than for those other countries. Notably, though, that relative advantage had begun to disappear in the run-up to the EEU inauguration.[835] As indicated above, Russia had grown wise to Belarusian attempts to take advantage of the relationship and now pushed back, also due to effects of global economic crisis, which limited the interest in economic openness within Kazakhstan, too. While the EEU might remedy this through increased free trade, such changes would take time.[836] Minsk also foresaw difficulties with the way the EEU would function. If free

---

831   Such a downbeat analysis was offered by Zhuchkova, 2015
832   For the background of the Eurasian Economic Union, see also Sakwa, 2024
833   The legal set-up for the EEU remained subordinated to member-state agreement and consensus, though, leaving Russia with the ability to stop any decisions to which it objected. See also Ginsburg, 2020: 246
834   These data presented by Shyrokykh, 2022: 448
835   This research being presented by Adarov, 2023: 470
836   A point spelled out in detail by Knobel', 2015

trade between member-states was supposed to develop then different economic models had to converge. Here the founding documents of the EEU favoured the relative fiscal stringency of Russia and Kazakhstan over the looser monetary policy on, say, public spending favoured by Lukashenka.[837]

So there currently remained a discrepancy between possibilities for economic integration and the aims of political integration to which Russian and Belarusian elites periodically returned. Indeed, Putin himself stated in March that a purpose of the Russo-Belarusian Union was to prepare the post-Soviet region as a whole for moving closer together.[838] Since such political integration was unlikely to offer Lukashenka any increased influence, he was unlikely to share Putin's political aims. In terms of economic collaboration, over the last year or so the Belarusian regime had become increasingly troubled by Russian economic contraction moving onto the Belarusian economy.[839] Minsk was increasingly willing to let some Russian companies be prominent on the Belarusian market. One very visible example of this was the presence of the oil company Lukoil, which developed a large downstream presence in the energy sector of Belarus, just as it had done in Moldova and elsewhere in Central Eastern Europe.[840]

A presence in quite a sensitive sector, one might have thought, given the protracted disagreements over energy affairs which had marred Russo-Belarusian relations in recent years. Lukashenka, though, could dole out love for Russian investors when it suited him–he also hinted that Belarusian settlements could be named after their Russian benefactors.[841] The problem was that even ostensibly private Russian investment brought political and maybe

---

837 Details on provisions agreed to within the EEU are offered by Moldashev and Hassan, 2017: 227
838 As reported by Rossiia, 2015
839 For instance, in June Lukashenka noted to prime minister Kabyakou that Belarus had lost almost \$3bn due to shrinking Russian demand and the effect of sanctions. Whether that figure was correct was less important than the signal for more economic openness, which the president clearly wanted to send. See also Doklad, 2015
840 Balmaceda and Westphal, 2024: 374
841 An example offered by Vuolteenaho and Basik, 2024: 461

180   UNCANNY ALLIES

military baggage. Previously, a booming Russian economy had indicated this might be tolerable. If Russia offered the world enough money, perhaps the world could change international practice in its favour? Yet Russia had reached too far, too quickly.[842] After the annexation of Crimea, the Belarusians accelerated attempts to find investors elsewhere. One option might be China, which had begun the Belt and Road Initiative. Bilateral collaboration would centre on the "Great Stone" economic cooperation zone, which the Chinese president placed within the Belt and Road Initiative on his visit to Minsk in 2015.[843]

It was the first time in almost a decade and a half that a Chinese leader had visited Belarus and clearly Xi Jinping envisaged further opportunities. He notably invited increased collaboration between sub-state political and economic actors. Given the substantial capabilities of many Chinese provinces such collaboration might offer great benefits for the Belarusian economy.[844] Shortly after, Belarus became an observer in the Shanghai Cooperation Organisation. (Belarus would eventually join in 2024.) This institution often focused on political and military, as much as economic matters, and it had also included Russia from the beginning. So, as with Chinese economic investment in Belarus, Moscow did not have immediate cause for concern.[845] Circumstances were different with growing EU interest in Belarus. Earlier, I noted how Russian aggression towards Ukraine in 2014 had contributed to Poland and Sweden suggesting accelerated investment in the Eastern Partnership and Belarus. Such priorities remained in place for many EU countries in 2015, with Russian commentators now highlighting initiatives from the Baltic States.[846]

Belarus also saw ways in which its economy could benefit further from collaboration with Baltic neighbours. With a nuclear

---

842   A point made in much more detail by Inozemtsev, 2015
843   The project and visit being detailed by Cheng, 2020: 795-96
844   This event was covered by Khodasevich, 2015
845   Belarusian observer status in the Shanghai Cooperation Organisation was reported by Sozaev-Gur'ev, 2015
846   As Latvia held the EU Presidency during the first half of 2015, Russian observers saw Riga trying to pull Belarus into membership of the Council of Europe and regenerated involvement in the Eastern Partnership. See also Sinitsyn, 2015

power plant being built, Minsk reached out to Lithuania for future collaboration on energy storage. The Lithuanians, long worried about safety at the Belarusian plant, declined the engagement.[847] As for Poland, 2015 saw a change of government. The Law and Justice party came back to power with a mix of welfare populism and nationalism. In foreign policy it politicised memories of those eastern regions, which had historically belonged to Poland and, as with much of Belarus, only been taken away 70 years before.[848] Politicisation fell on fertile ground. Over the previous decade Belarus had often been central to Polish discourse and had been a major recipient of Polish economic support. In fact, by receiving a total of $143 million in Polish bilateral development aid, Belarus had been third among all recipients (and above Ukraine).[849] Furthermore, 2015 saw the centennial commemoration of the "bieżeństwo"–the forced removal by Russian authorities during the First World War of millions of people from the frontline. Such commemorations were uncontroversial in Poland and among local Belarusian groups. In Moscow, on the other hand, this was exactly the kind of transborder Polish-Belarusian activity to avoid.[850]

Investment by the Polish state and society offered Lukashenka's Belarus a credible alternative to Russia in the medium-term. Minsk did not suggest that relations with Russia should be severed, and in February Lukashenka himself even had to reassure nervous Russian journalists that Belarus was not about to leave the EEU, which it had just joined.[851] Their worries were, though, comprehensible when considering repeated complaints and challenging behaviour emanating from Minsk over the years. Only the previous month, the Belarusian president had stated that "Yes, Russia is our brother and our friend. But you see how they sometimes

---

847   Lithuanian observers believed a coming nuclear power plant in Kaliningrad might have similar need for Lithuanian assistance. See also Fuks, 2015

848   For the narrative place of the "Kresy Wschodnie" in Polish political discourse, see also Lewis, 2019: 523-24

849   For data on this, see also Opršal et al, 2021: 284

850   For buy-in to the commemorations by the Belarusian minority in Poland, see also Niziołek, 2022: 357

851   However, Russian media was quick to point out that Lukashenka had been less clear on the subject in January. See also Gushchin, 2015

behave. Therefore, we need to be sure to diversify, whatever the cost."[852] Lukashenka had also denounced Russia's blockade of Belarusian goods specifically as being against the principles of the EEU. The sentiments otherwise coming out from Minsk similarly seemed to indicate that the organisation, while officially established, could only be expected to work after a decade, given Russian obstruction.[853]

Hardly reassuring signals from what was supposed to be Russia's closest partner. Particularly at a time when Russian commentators and, arguably, Putin and other Russian elites were periodically hinting at all-out conflict between Russia and its enemies in the West and elsewhere, up to and including mention of a "third world war" during prime time.[854] At the same time, Russia also took specific steps to undermine post-Cold War European continental stability. As mentioned in the previous chapter, back in 2007 Russia had suspended its participation in the Treaty on Conventional Armed Forces in Europe (CFE). Now, the government suspended participation even in meetings to discuss the future of the Treaty.[855] And if the Kremlin did plan to deploy non-nuclear weapons where this had previously been in breach of the Treaty, Belarus could well become involved. In fact, Belarusian observers noted how Russian high-tech offensive military equipment was being moved to their state–ostensibly for Victory Day parades, but arguably as a test-run for future escalation.[856]

A putative offensive could, of course, also involve a takeover of control in Belarus itself. Throughout 2015, Lukashenka would periodically return to concerns about territorial sovereignty. Possibly in preparation for the presidential election that autumn, in January Belarus introduced new legal guidelines for martial law in a step clearly envisaging hostile foreign involvement.[857] The

---

852   As quoted from Johnson and Köstem, 2016: 211
853   On Belarusian dissatisfaction with Russia's approach under the EEU, see also Vieira, 2016: 575
854   Such discussions on world war were, for instance, entertained on Vremia, 2015: from 30m 22s
855   Analysis of Russia's step is offered by Sukhov, 2015
856   For such concerns, see also Dynko, 2015
857   A point that Russian observers did note. See also comments by Ekspert, 2015

Belarusian leader could hint at such concerns, too, in a subtler way. When he visited Georgia that April Lukashenka was on overtly friendly terms with his Georgian counterpart. And he pledged, once more, not to recognise the independence of Abkhazia and South Ossetia, as Russia (but almost no other countries) had done.[858] Admittedly, Russia had been on reasonable terms with the Georgians since the 2013 removal of Mikheil Saaskashvili, yet Lukashenka was clearly out to mark a sovereign position. He did so again, more openly, in August when he mocked the idea of the "Russian World", even suggesting he had made that notion fall out of fashion.[859]

This only a year after Putin had legitimised his conquest in Ukraine specifically through reference to such a World. And at a time when the Kremlin, as already hinted at, systematically tried to promote its vision of the world across Eurasia and elsewhere, spending substantial effort–and sums–in the process.[860] It almost appeared as if Lukashenka was goading his Russian counterpart into a reaction. Quite brave, given that the Belarusian presidential election was only a few months away. In the end, both leaderships knew that a realistic alternative to Lukashenka would not be found, and Putin did indeed congratulate the latter on his re-election.[861] It should be noted, though, that before the election the two leaders had held a meeting in Sochi which the Russian administration openly linked to the fate of the upcoming election. While it is not clear what was said in private, Putin's aide had indicated the importance of the meeting in advance.[862]

And apart from being more diplomatic in public afterwards, Lukashenka did also throw a few morsels to the Russians. Witness, for instance, the November announcement that the Belarusian Orthodox Church (institutionally subordinate to its Russian

---

858 Lukashenka's confirmation of Georgian territorial sovereignty was reported by Dvali, 2015
859 This was reported by Kononovich, 2015
860 Where this process stood by the summer of 2015 was summed up by Kamakin, 2015
861 As reported in Putin, 2015
862 These comments were reported by Ushakov, 2015

counterpart) would now help to ensure cultural conformity of school materials.[863] During Putin's third presidential term, the Russian Orthodox Church was increasingly central to the construction of national identity. And leading figures within the Church frequently talked of the "Russian World" and links between Russians and Belarusians (and Ukrainians). So, Lukashenka's gesture was symbolically meaningful if not designed to significantly change Belarusian education.[864] Similarly, the Belarusians signalled some concession to Russia by being a bit more circumspect in their relations with other potential partners. After visiting the United Nations together with Makei, Lukashenka was happy to repeat his wish for better relations with the West, but he stressed that no U-turn was coming.[865]

Then in December, after a European Union official had noted that the long-negotiated visa facilitation and readmission agreement between Belarus and the EU was ready to be signed, the Belarusians dampened expectations. A simple misunderstanding, perhaps, yet Minsk was fully aware that the Russians, sharing freedom of movement with Belarus, observed such negotiations keenly.[866] From Moscow there was also acute awareness that Lukashenka remained reluctant to give up any material benefits to Russia. Problems remained with bilateral trade. In November, Russia stated it would impose a food embargo against Ukrainian goods from the start of the new year in retaliation for Ukraine joining Western sanctions on Russia.[867] Unsurprisingly, the Belarusians spotted an opportunity. Swiftly, the Belarusian ministry for agriculture and food noted that the country would exploit the resultant gap on the Russian market, sending Belarusian goods in to replace their Ukrainian

---

863 This was noted in V Belarusi, 2015
864 For the growing links between Russian nationalism and religion during this period, see also Mitrofanova, 2016
865 On Lukashenka's statements on the topic, see also Lukashenko, 2015. And the quite scathing evaluation of the Belarusian president's manoeuvrings by Portnikov, 2015
866 The Belarusian statements were reported by Minsk, 2015
867 A summary of the dispute reported by Vorotnikov, 2015

counterparts'. This would help alleviate loss of income from globally falling food prices and take advantage of a coming rise.[868]

Of course, the Belarusian administration was also very aware and respectful of the Russian position in the difficult circumstances within which Moscow found itself, burdened by sanctions. So, the head of the Belarusian State Customs Committee guaranteed his Russian counterparts that Belarus would faithfully work to keep Ukrainian goods from the Russian market.[869] You could almost hear a scream coming out from Moscow. Over the previous twenty months, Belarusians had made a good living out of sanctions-busting the Russian market. And now Minsk was going to be all law-abiding. Right-o… Russia responded that by early December import of Belarusian dairy products and vegetables would be limited.[870] Obviously, this was insufficient to halt Belarusian schemes of "re-packaging" Ukrainian goods. But it sent a signal, as in previous years, that Russia was no longer prepared to simply let Minsk earn money on Russian goodwill. Lukashenka was addressing his domestic economic problems by warning against "experiments" foisted upon Belarus by outsiders, like Russia.[871]

Not the words of a man who was about to let his economic assets be taken over by uncontrollable outsiders in the name of the EEU. Problematic, though, was the fact that an unreformed economy seemed closely linked to falling living standards in Belarus. This, notably, was the message from vigilant Belarusian researchers.[872] Consequently, the Belarusian domestic socio-economic position was likely to become still more complicated during the coming year. Which meant that Lukashenka might become even more concerned about losing control over his population and, in return, even more recalcitrant in his relations with the EEU and Russia.[873]

---

868   See a similar observation made by Alexei Dzermant in Polemika, 2015
869   On this, see also Belorusskie, 2015
870   The Russian announcement was mentioned by Wegren et al, 2017: 58
871   For Lukashenka's warning, see also Kriat, 2015
872   As reported in Progressing, 2015
873   On Lukashenka's difficulties in retaining his domestic "social contract" during these years and his consequent thoughts on remoulding it, see also Wilson, 2016

Russian Militarisation

There was one further issue on which Lukashenka had pushed back against Russia during the second half of 2015 and that related to military affairs. As mentioned in the previous chapter, Russia had held a military presence in Belarus since 1995, with Russian airplanes also patrolling Belarusian air space for several years.[874] Since 2013, Russia had pushed for an additional airbase in Belarus–something to which Minsk intermittently agreed. Eventually, come September 2015 Putin authorised the Russian ministry of defence to sign a 15-year agreement for an air base in Belarus. Given the durability of other Russian military bases abroad, that agreement might well be extended.[875] However, widespread protests against such a base then took place on the streets of Minsk during October. Tellingly, independent Belarusian media noted that protesters were largely left alone by the police, indicating at least tacit official sympathy for their complaints. Or, perhaps, a test by the administration to see whether Russia would react.[876]

As no immediate reaction was forthcoming, Lukashenka had felt sufficiently emboldened to state on television that Belarus would welcome Russian aircraft but had plenty of Belarusian pilots to man these. Such patriotism could be seen in light of the upcoming election, yet the president and his supporters continued in a similar vein.[877] The dispute lasted into 2016 with no immediate sign of solution. By the time of mid-spring, Makei did promise that Belarus might return to consider the option of a Russian military air base in the country if international circumstances were to change but he clearly did not see that as imminent.[878] Some opposition analysts in Belarus still thought that Russia could seek to hasten such insecurity for Belarus by preventing it from developing its own

---

874 Russia, Belarus and other CSTO member-states had even spoken about a joint air force. See also Kucera, 2013
875 Putin's order to the ministry of defence was recorded in Rasporiazhenie, 2015
876 The demonstration in the centre of Minsk, and the fact it was allowed to last for several hours, was reported in Hundreds, 2015
877 See, for instance, Lukashenka's confirmation of this position as reported by Nasha, 2015
878 Makei's comments on this topic were reported by MID, 2016

armed forces, effectively waiting for Belarusian-owned aircraft to become so old that they were no longer workable and Russian air-power was needed.[879]

Arguably, Russia did not need to use such underhand methods to keep tabs on the military power of its neighbour. And the Belarusians had never denied the need for security collaboration. In fact, moving into early 2016 Lukashenka complained about insufficient developments in the CSTO, stressing the need for protection of member states.[880] Note, though, that Minsk–by appealing to strengthen the CSTO–was specifically not asking for Russia to take more responsibility for Belarusian security. It was asking for such responsibility to be delegated away from Moscow, with Belarus having a veto not only on military decisions but on measures taken against non-military threats, too.[881] Such non-military threats played an important part in the Belarusian military doctrine, which came into force in July 2016. Apart from references to hard security threats, the doctrine also referred to ideology and propaganda which might undermine the constitutional order of Belarus and, arguably, could as easily come from Russia as from the West.[882]

In fact, over the summer of 2016 such Russian propaganda provoked some public protest within Belarus. In May, it emerged that schoolchildren from eastern and northeastern Belarus had visited military sports camps within Russia, where they had received training from prominent figures within the Russian neo-Nazi movement.[883] Not only was their involvement criticised by figures within Belarusian civil society and political opposition–institutions loyal to Lukashenka got involved, too. In early June, pro-government media decried the trainers as mercenaries who sought to corrupt Belarusian children and, in the longer term, undermine state

---

879   See such accusations presented by Harbatsevich, 2015
880   As reported by Kriat, 2016
881   Kuleszewicz, 2017, provides a useful overview of the central position, which the Belarusian authorities at this time aimed to obtain within the European security landscape.
882   For speculations along such lines, see also the comments by Ambrosio, 2022: 1714
883   This was also highlighted by Yudina and Verkhovsky, 2019: 740

stability more generally.[884] A couple of months later, state television reported on the attempts by neo-Nazis to recruit Belarusian teenagers for their organisations. Crucially, in the report neo-Nazism was explicitly tied to ideas of the "Russian world" and the organisation Russian National Unity, which was said to seek abolition of Belarusian sovereignty like German Nazis had done.[885]

Such imagery meant that the Belarusians here were not simply trying to highlight Russian civil (or state) aggression towards their state. They were using the threat to confirm the role of Belarus as a perennial, cross-generational defender against fascism in all its forms and on behalf of a law-abiding world.[886] In addition, the Belarusians were making a point out of the fact that they were the true heirs to the Soviet victory in the war, just as sovereign statehood–and not more expansionist, amorphous ideas about "civilisations" and the like–was the morally correct choice.[887] So, we find quite a radical, even brave, attempt by Belarusian society and state to push away Russia–or at least the "Russia" developing during Putin's third presidential term–from Belarusian identity and from the territorially-bound (as opposed to nation-bound) understanding of Eurasian and, indeed, Soviet heritage.[888]

This means that from the slightly incidental issue of Russian-sponsored youth activities in Belarus we can use Belarusian reaction to more fundamentally distinguish between types of nationalism promoted. First, Belarusian nationalism under Lukashenka is rooted in current territorial arrangements, whereas Russian nationalism is rooted in a (semi-mythological) territory alternative to that currently held.[889] Second, under Lukashenka Belarusian nationalism arguably became geopolitical rather than biopolitical, whereas

---

884   Such charges were laid out by Tsarik, 2016

885   The report was by ONT Television and was summarised by Harbatsevich, 2016

886   Belarusian promotion of such an identity has, of course, been a leading narrative throughout this book. For an analysis arguing similarly around this time, see also Zadora, 2016

887   An insightful analysis of the interplay of sovereignty and Belarusian memory politics can also be gleaned from Bekus, 2023

888   On the practice of "nation branding" in conditions of the contemporary world it may also be instructive to read Aronczyk, 2018

889   A distinction also hinted at by Klymenko, 2016: 43

under Putin for Russia the opposite was the case. The sum of these two points, therefore, is that for Belarus territory had become something to be defended. Whereas for Russia population had become something to be expended.[890] It is worth noting here that my analysis therefore implicitly criticises findings elsewhere which claim that Russian foreign policy became a combination of biopolitics and geopolitics. The problem, as I see it, is that such scholarship understands these as different, non-exclusive means of control, whereas I view them as fundamentally incompatible sources of identity.[891]

There are lengthy ways in which those comments can be expanded–regarding Russian foreign policy in general and regarding the nature of these two concepts. That is not the purpose for a book which focuses on a bilateral relationship. However, it helps the narrative of this book by, again, moving focus to the uncanny.[892] Belarus cannot be a threat to Russia if it follows Russia's lead. Conversely, Lukashenka's regime can be a threat at the level of identity (the foundation for policy-thinking and -making) if it presents itself as acting in a way correct for an heir to the Russo-Belarusian joint memory font that is the (perceived) Soviet heritage.[893] And it was not just from the Belarusian regime that the difference could be perceived. Look at some very interesting focus groups run in Minsk during 2015, where participants were probed on their understanding of Belarusian distinctiveness. After some gallows humour they

---

890 Literature on geopolitics and biopolitics is legion and, frequently, of limited quality. For a breezy, yet valuable starting point on (critical) geopolitics, see Dodds, 2019. An outline of biopolitics and its various socio-political manifestations is offered by Rentea, 2016

891 For an example of the scholarship with which I here disagree, see Makarychev and Yatsyk, 2017

892 If we are really going to be interdisciplinary here, we can also see the geopolitical/biopolitical difference linked to the uncanny in the arts. One example— Bram Stoker's Dracula is the uncanny reflection of humanity at the threshold of modernity (what with crumbling castle, rail timetables, etc.). And he is first and foremost a *boyar* (the vampiric is incidental) but is he a master of lands or of people? Is his essence bound to the brides (and Mina Harker) or the soil in the coffins? Such ambiguity helps to make the book a masterpiece. For the uncanny in *Dracula*, see also Senf, 1979

893 By saying this, I am also challenging—at least in part—the rational actor assumptions underlying much excellent scholarship on memory politics. An obvious example might be Kubik and Bernhard, 2014

190   UNCANNY ALLIES

moved unfailingly to territorial traits (and, specifically, the marshes).[894]

But back to Russo-Belarusian interstate relations in mid-2016. At this point, the Russian state (perhaps frustrated by lack of Western recognition of its Ukrainian territorial gains) increasingly highlighted the possibility of conflict with the West. In light of the above-mentioned suspension of the CFE the Russian military was relocating to answer perceived initiatives from NATO.[895] Over the summer there were reports from Russian observers that the military was building up its forces along its Western borders, including along its border with Belarus. Such was, admittedly, denied by Putin's spokesman Dmitry Peskov, yet the narrative fit with pre-existing images in Russia and Belarus of the latter as a vanguard against invaders.[896] Lukashenka stressed that Belarusian armed forces could repel enemies partly through Russian assistance. However, it was noticeable that as the Belarusian president talked specifically about the ability of Belarusian forces to enjoy rapid mobility as a militia it reminded not only of partisans in the Second World War but also of Ukrainian resistance to Russia.[897]

And that autumn, during parliamentary elections in Belarus, the president celebrated by stating–as he had done before and would do again in the years to come–that his country needed both Russia and the West as partners. So, he explicitly rejected his country's place exclusively on the Russian side of a new continental division.[898] Around the same time Russian media investigated how Belarusian armed forces were reinforcing their positions along the border. Mind you, not the border between Belarus and NATO, but the border between Belarus and Russia. Sources explicitly noted continued fear in Minsk of a "Crimean scenario" engulfing the

---

894   Webbed feet ahoy — this is pure Puddleglum! Yet Puddleglum was, of course, a great hero. On the focus groups, see Rohava, 2018: 650, 655
895   This being reported in Rossiia, 2016. For a Russian view of how Russia should stand strong against NATO, see Evstaf'ev, 2016
896   Claims of military build-up, and Peskov's denial in relation to the Belarusian border, were reported by Kukushkina, 2016
897   For the focus on military self-defence in Lukashenka's speeches around the 2016 Belarusian Independence Day, see also Khodasevich, 2016b
898   This was reported in West, 2016

eastern parts of the country.[899] And towards the end of the year, Belarusian opposition media highlighted how governmental and military elites from the country visited both Latvia and the United States discretely but quite possibly with a view to retaining a working relationship with NATO at the same time as this organisation and Russia were effectively pushing each other away.[900]

Officially, Russian remained eager to emphasise the stability and potential inherent in relations with Belarus. Late 2016 saw the publication of a new Russian foreign policy concept. Bearing the mark of the conflict in Ukraine, and therefore frequently alluding to a conflictual international environment, the concept nonetheless again placed Belarus as a crucial ally.[901] Russia needed such allies in the precarious position it still found itself in, with numerous Western sanctions remaining and the focus of international organisations remaining on Russian (mis-)governance in the occupied territories. On this, Belarus was mostly reliable for the Kremlin–for instance helping to push back against a high-profile UN-resolution that November.[902] And that vote was not a one-off in terms of Belarus's stand in international fora. Back in July, the Belarusian representative had abstained from voting on a similar resolution condemning human rights abuses on Russia-occupied Crimea, when that resolution was presented to the parliamentary assembly of the OSCE.[903]

So, it was probably not likely that Minsk would join the West anytime soon. Unless, of course, the incentives were sufficient. Neighbouring Poland kept showing great interest in Belarusian developments, which in the context of the EU Eastern Partnership were highlighted as a priority in the 2016-20 Polish Development Cooperation Programme.[904] And while the Polish government officially continued to tie any funds to democracy and good

---

899   Such investigation was published by Lavnikevich and Khodarenok, 2016
900   These and similar findings were outlined by Iakovlevskii, 2016
901   See the text of the concept at Foreign, 2016: particularly sections 50-51
902   The resolution condemned Russian human rights abuses on Crimea and was voted against by Belarus in a move causing some consternation among Ukrainians and parts of domestic Belarusian opposition. For the vote, see also Misiia, 2016
903   That resolution being described in Tbilisi, 2016: 39-44
904   For that, see also Pospieszna and Pietrzyk-Reeves, 2022: 533

192   UNCANNY ALLIES

governance in Belarus, it was noteworthy that the Polish foreign minister went out of his way to stress to his Belarusian counterpart, and to Polish media, that Warsaw was seeking democratic evolution, not revolution, under Lukashenka.[905] Perhaps Brussels could be equally "understanding" towards the oft-called "last dictatorship in Europe"? During 2016 the EU continued to hint to Lukashenka that a non-Russian future was possible. Notice how sanctions, long around given the Belarusian regime's egregious human rights abuses, were not renewed in February 2016.[906]

At the same time Brussels, together with Washington, also removed the vast majority of the personalised sanctions and asset freezes, which had previously been in place against specific members of the Belarusian regime, including Lukashenka himself, who were accused of direct culpability for human rights breaches.[907] Lukashenka also liked being personally thanked for any support he provided. Russian elites could do that, yet often seemed to take him for granted. Not so the Turkish president who in November went out of his way to thank Lukashenka for support during the difficult year Turkey had just endured with Russia.[908] Partly in return for such Turkish delight did the Belarusian president invite his counterpart to send investment into Belarus. While not the size of the Russian economy, numerous Turkish businesses still retained expertise and capital sufficient to benefit the Belarusian manufacturing sector, in particular, within a still-mooted privatisation.[909]

And then there remained the Chinese. As mentioned earlier, in 2015 President Xi had visited Minsk and Chinese projects there. Still, as Lukashenka reciprocated that visit during September 2016, he could reflect that the Chinese state may be more generous than Russia, but it mainly sought to invest in its own companies

---

905   Those comments were reported by Łomanowski and Szoszyn, 2016
906   As well pointed out also by Hellquist, 2016: 1014
907   This was further discussed by Marples, 2016: 928
908   Such Russian-Turkish tension had followed the downing of a Russian military jet by Turkish air defence in 2015. President Recep Erdoğan's gratitude to Lukashenka was expressed during a bilateral meeting, as analysed by Krivosheev, 2016
909   Lukashenka's invitation to Turkish investors was mentioned in Osipov, 2016

abroad.[910] Hence the dilemma. Unlike Russia (let alone the EU), China did not seek Belarusian political concessions. However, for its cash Beijing wanted guarantees of profitability. And Minsk needed that cash. Problems with a slowed-down Russian retail market were compounded by falling oil prices, resulting in a fall of 39% y-o-y revenue from Belarusian oil exports.[911] True, in the foreseeable future the Belarusian economy was supposed to receive a boost from the (Russian-funded and Russian-built) nuclear power plant currently being constructed in the Astravets district in the northwestern part of the country. We saw earlier, though, that mooted energy collaboration with the Lithuanians had not been achieved.[912]

Furthermore, the plant remained unpopular, too, among large parts of the Belarusian population. Given the history of nuclear fallout from Chernobyl, any safety issues during the construction would be noticed and that was, indeed, what happened in July with an accident involving a reactor pressure vessel, which then had to be replaced by the Russians.[913] The Russian contractors said that it barely was an accident with the vessel just falling a few metres while being moved before barely touching the ground, but they of course wanted to be considerate to the Belarusians. Little could be done, though, to alleviate more fundamental concerns regarding the plant and its slightly precarious location.[914] Other sectors of the Belarusian economy were challenged, as well. World Bank figures outlined a depressing tendency for the country. Whereas back in 2010 GDP growth in Belarus had been measured to be as high as

---

910   A point also noted by some Russian commentators, like Lavnikevich, 2016

911   For context, the problems of the Belarusian economy by mid-2016 are discussed in Natsional'naia, 2016

912   And remained unlikely to be so. Lithuania consistently proffered concerns about the safety of the coming power plant—quite an issue for Vilnius after it had been forced by the EU to close down its own Ignalina plant. On concerns in Lithuania and in Belarus, see e.g. Brown, 2016

913   An entertaining account of problems at the nuclear plant is by Popova, 2016

914   For a list of perceived safety issues with the nuclear plant from an (admittedly not wholly neutral) source, see also Fundamental, n.d.

8% that figure had dropped precariously to 1.6% in 2014, before moving to negative growth over the following years.[915]

It was difficult to see how Russia would help Minsk move out of that negative spiral. The EEU still did not seem capable to working to its full potential or–more worryingly perhaps for Belarus–its full potential was not sufficient to make up for the limitations placed on the Belarusian economy by state-driven intervention.[916] Economic potential within a Russia-Belarus Union State remained held back by mutual miscomprehension. Both Moscow and Minsk had severely procrastinated on the fundamental issue of power distribution between them. Remembering that this question had been central even to relations between Yeltsin and Lukashenka, it was remarkable that no resolution had been found by 2016.[917] On specific avenues for bilateral economic collaboration diverging narratives also appeared. See, for instance, the protracted debates during the spring of 2016 on Belarusian military-industrial production. Russian prime minister Medvedev was angling for an opening of the Belarusian economy to outside influence, particularly by moving some of this production to Russia.[918]

A few days later, Belarusian prime minister Andrey Kabyakow then reminded the Russians that they understood the nature of "integration" differently from Belarusians. While trying to make it sound as if this was about Belarusian self-understanding as much as pure economics, Kabyakow was–diplomatically–telling Moscow not to push its economic imperialism.[919] Later that month Lukashenka would use his annual address to parliament to push his own kind of diplomacy by telling the Russians that Belarus was

---

915   Such data being presented by De Vogel, 2022: 20

916   The limited economic, as opposed to political, nature of the EEU also being stressed by Russian commentators, such as Faliakhov, 2016

917   This kind of misunderstanding and procrastination was also hinted at by Romanchuk, 2016

918   A message partly backed up by Surikov, who highlighted to the Belarusians advantages of uniting Russian and Belarusian production in Surikov, 2016. On the same day, the Russian ambassador also warned Belarus about the potential pitfalls of joining the WTO, although whether this was a sop to Belarusian protectionism or an attempt to keep away competitors from third countries remained ambiguous. For this, see Rossiiskii, 2016

919   See also the Belarusian prime minister's comments as reported in Belarus', 2016

not an "errand boy" for Moscow and that Russia really should consider selling one of its oil fields to him.[920] He was not really going to change and would end 2016 by demonstratively staying away from EEU and CSTO meetings in Russia, brandishing displeasure with Russian offers on energy pricing while believing that Putin could still be pushed to offer him a better deal. That attitude would not change much in the immediate future.[921]

Return of the Cold War?

During the year of 2017 the most published event in Russian-Belarusian relations would be the joint Zapad 2017 military exercises taking place in September. Ostensibly, these exercises signalled the strength of the bilateral relationship, the willingness of the regimes to protect each other against domestic and foreign enemies.[922] Instead, though, the event provoked concern in Belarusian society and across Europe, without seemingly bringing Russia and Belarus closer together. Indeed, it might have been difficult for the relationship to suddenly improved given other sources of tension, which marred it both before and after early autumn.[923] First came ill will transferred from Lukashenka's non-attendance at the EEU and CSTO meetings in Russia at late 2016. Speculation was brandished that the Belarusian president might have stayed at home in fear of an attempted coup in his absence. More likely he saw the event as a chance to reaffirm Belarusian independence and importance.[924]

Perhaps that was not just done to stoke Lukashenka's ego. He clearly worried about the continued fighting and destruction in

---

920   As presented with more than a hint of criticism by Khodasevich, 2016a

921   Lukashenka's push for better deals was also the topic of Klaskovskii, 2016

922   The Zapad exercise, which had last been carried out four years prior, was officially designated against "terrorists" threatening territorial sovereignty of the Union State. As reported by Tikhonov, 2017

923   Tension which might have as much to do with the evolving nature of Russia's international profile as with anything done by Belarus. Early in 2017, Russian media pointed out that opinion polls indicated not only that Russians now saw their country as feared abroad, but also that Russians largely welcomed such an image. For this interpretation, see also Novoprudskii, 2017

924   Such petulant motivation for Lukashenka was proposed in Russia by Feduta, 2017

Ukraine plus Russian unwillingness to withdraw from the situation. By late January, the Belarusian president openly stated that Ukraine was fighting for its independence and noted how lucky his country had been in comparison.[925] Now, Belarus might be tempted to seek closer relations in the West, irrespective of any further deterioration in relations between Russia and the West. Indeed, Lukashenka specifically called out Putin for having previously suggested that Belarus should make friends again with the West and then scolded the Belarusian government when it chose to do this.[926] Across the year, the Belarusian government would repeat warnings against a renewed arms race between Russia and NATO with Makei, for instance, noting that frequent, direct contacts between military and political elites from both sides were required to keep tensions and dangerous misunderstandings at bay.[927]

This did not appear to have much impact of Russian-Western relations, though. As had been the case the previous year, the Russian government accused NATO rearmaments, particularly within the Baltic region, as well as hostile rhetoric of forcing Russia to carry out military build-ups within its western regions.[928] Subsequently, Russian media would use the run-up to the Zapad 2017 exercises in September to denigrate NATO for deliberately stoking unfounded fears about these exercises among Central Eastern European countries, and within the Baltic States, in particular. However, given the protracted escalatory rhetoric emanating from Moscow Western reaction was always likely.[929] Ukrainian authorities were similarly concerned that Zapad 2017 might cover a move of Russian forces to Belarus in preparation for an attack from the north on Kyiv (something which would, indeed, be happening a few years later). During

---

925 Lukashenka's comments on Ukrainian independence are in Bratskie, 2017
926 Those complaints by Lukashenka were recorded by Kriviakina, 2017
927 The Belarusian foreign minister emphasised such confidence building steps to media in Belarus before visiting his Russian counterpart, as reported by Makei, 2017d
928 Those accusations and justifications for Russian behaviour were presented by Russian defence minister Sergey Shoigu as outlined in Andreev, 2024
929 An example of Russian commentators accusing NATO of irresponsible scaremongering would be the roundtable discussion reported by Bozh'eva, 2017

the summer the Ukrainian military responded by setting up local defence forces across the country.[930]

Subsequently, Ukrainian president Poroshenko specifically warned against such a scenario. Concern stemmed partly from the sheer size of Zapad 2017, but also from the fact that specific figures on the number of troops involved varied widely in information provided. Poroshenko also noted that Russian provocations might seek to stoke a pretext for an attack.[931] That seemed borne out shortly afterwards. Russian special forces lured the son of a Ukrainian military officer away from the country before capturing him and transferring him to custody in Russia awaiting trial for alleged terrorism offences. From a Belarusian point of view, the problem was that the man had been kidnapped from Belarusian territory.[932] This appeared to put paid to months of Belarusian attempts to downplay any dangers to other countries from Zapad 17 (and, by extension, from Russia). Back in July, during a televised conversation with Poroshenko, Lukashenka had explicitly assured his counterpart that Belarusian territory would not be used to attack Ukraine, now or in future.[933]

As shown above, that reassurance was clearly insufficient for the Ukrainians as Zapad 2017 grew closer. Inside Belarus, too, Lukashenka was not able to calm all of public opinion. Within the political opposition, individuals and organisations had protested against Zapad 2017 since spring and, often, against the mere presence of Russian troops in the country.[934] A system of coordinated repression could keep overt Belarusian resistance to the event down. Nevertheless, as Zapad 2017 rolled out its opponents moved onto the internet where they began to identify with "Veishnoria"– the fictional enemy state against which the military exercises were

---

930   Following legal initiatives such as Uriad, 2017
931   As written in Safarov, 2017
932   Russian confirmation that it had, indeed, carried out this abduction was reported in Solovei, 2017
933   See also Ivzhenko, 2017
934   For an example of such disgruntlement, and its frequent link to animosity towards Lukashenka, see Na Kastrychnitskai, 2017

supposedly directed.[935] Clearly, there was quite a bit of good-natured mockery displayed. Yet internet commentators also used Veishnoria to project the idea of a peaceful state, assaulted by Russian (and Lukashenka's) brutality, pointing out that Zapad 2017 had placed this fictional state in an area taken during the Second World War and central to post-Soviet political opposition.[936]

Soon, the exercise was finished, and Russian troops were withdrawn from Belarus. Or at least that was the claim from Moscow and Minsk whereas the administration in Kyiv and some Western observers claimed that military personnel and equipment had been left in Belarus awaiting potential use against Ukraine.[937] Beyond military personnel, some Russian civilians in Belarus also promoted links to Putin. In an eye-catching example of that, while the exercises were ongoing Belarusian opposition media reported the boisterous presence of Russian far right activist on the streets of Minsk drawing attention to themselves and their allegiance to Putin.[938] Clearly, these activists wanted to draw attention to themselves and their cause at a time when Zapad 2017 had drawn mixed reaction within Belarusian society. Tellingly, a couple of weeks after that event Belarusian authorities noted stricter requirements of Belarusian citizens and hotels for having any foreign guests registered with the authorities.[939]

Now, the new rules might of course not be particularly directed against Russians. Being a regime prone to securitisation, the Belarusian administration could well be concerned about undue influence from Western or other foreign actors. Notice, though, how Lukashenka–in repeated warnings throughout 2017–had not

---

935 A summary of how "Veishnoria" received its own map, flag and applications for citizenship from Belarusians (and Russians) on the internet is offered by Agius and Edenborg, 2019: 59

936 On similarities between the designated "Veishnoria" and areas providing main support for oppositional and nationalist candidate Pazniak in the 1994 presidential election, see for instance the comment and map provided by commentator Chaly, 2017

937 Such suspicion was shared by NATO. See also Jozwiak, 2017

938 This was reported by Pochemu, 2017

939 That announcement, and its potential impact on Russians, was discussed in U Militsyi, 2017

always specified the origins of "subversives".[940] And as we remember the above-mentioned hints in the Belarusian military doctrine from the previous year regarding threats from means of influence favoured by Russia, it is also worth noting (the Belarusian regime certainly did so) that well-connected Russian analysts had recently called for a change in relations with Belarus.[941] Much blunter were the televised warnings against Belarusian "nationalism", which were broadcast from Moscow in late March. Tellingly, the claim forwarded was that ordinary Belarusians remained closely attached to their Russian heritage, but that the Belarusian regime and its ostensible political opposition had effectively joined forces to promote nationalist distance from Russia.[942]

How had such hostile rhetoric against the Belarusian regime been able to emerge from an ostensibly close ally? As we have seen before, hostility might stem from increasing differences in post-Soviet identity. For instance, among young adults the intolerance against bodily autonomy (e.g. on same-sex marriage) was substantially more pronounced in Russia than in Belarus.[943] That indicated divergence in educational and cultural context within which new generations were being raised. Look also at the view of history. Amidst the ontological insecurity of post-Soviet societies and regimes, memory politics had become important, as indicated previously. Indeed, Russia–and Belarus, too–had introduced laws to protect specific narratives on the Soviet past.[944] Still, although many Belarusians retained some sympathy for Soviet times yet with awareness of the damage and death that repression had caused.

---

940   In the spring of 2017, large-scale protests and repression had led some Russian observers to argue that Lukashenka sometimes lashed out in blind fury. See also Khodasevich, 2017b

941   Arguably a change to which there was only one "correct" answer. Witness Fyodor Lukyanov's slightly ominous comments in February about the economic opportunities for Belarus in Russian-led integration and how standing in-between Russia and the EU was really an outdated thing to do. See Luk'ianov, 2017

942   These and similar accusations were broadcast in Bukhgalteriia, 2017

943   As found by a Pew survey from 2017 and highlighted by Frear, 2021: 1470. It should be noted, though, that support for same-sex marriage in Ukraine was as low as in Russia, and that even in Belarus support remained at only 22%.

944   As outlined by Nuzov, 2017: 138-39

200   UNCANNY ALLIES

Such awareness was becoming ever less part of Russian socio-political consciousness–some commentators in Russia now even made a living out of minimising and relativising Soviet failures and crimes.[945]

I highlight such seemingly disparate examples because they illuminate how Belarusian expressions of national and other kinds of self would jar with the kind of Russia being now constructed. At the same time, of course, Belarusians drew on similar memories and tropes as Russians, thereby making any difference of interpretation starker.[946] Having noted traits in Russian ideologies predisposing that country to mistrust any deviations in thought by Belarusians it should be noted, too, that specific policies from Minsk kept damaging relations. At the beginning of 2017 Belarus suddenly introduced a five-day visa-free regime for tourists from 80 countries.[947] Despite having freedom of movement with Russia–and therefore no border control between the two countries–Belarus did not consult its partner before taking the step. Officials like Makei explicitly linked this relaxation of visa rules to the country's attempts to obtain concessions from the EU.[948]

And to act as a trust-building step when discussing other visa- and migration-related matters. By the summer, Minsk and Brussels seemed on the way finally to agree on a readmissions scheme, which would enable Belarus to collaborate with the EU's border regime in handling illegal migrants coming through the country.[949] That agreement was important for Lukashenka who sought to burnish his domestic and international reputation as a reliable security provider and a benevolent host for refugees. He had already contrasted favourably Belarusian hospitality with that of Russia and the EU. Consequently, visa and migration agreements with the EU

---

945   Such Russian proponents of the Soviet era could be very intolerant of Belarusian memories of repression. See, for instance, how a writer like Aleksandr Dyukov received Russian state funds to consistently minimise and even belittle Belarusian casualties, as shown in articles such as Dyukov, 2017

946   The angry defensiveness present in public Russian ideology at the time also being well presented by the examples offered by Walker, 2018

947   Introduction of that policy is discussed by Matveeva, 2018: 727

948   As reported in Khodasevich, 2017a

949   Agreement on the draft readmissions deal was reported by Evropeiskie, 2017

had symbolic as well as practical implications.[950] Therefore, not only were the Belarusians ready to ignore Russian safety concerns–they openly did it on behalf of an institution to which Russia increasingly saw itself opposed. Having learned of this plan, Russian security services quickly prepared "border zones" within which entrants from Belarus could be supervised and, if necessary, detained.[951]

Such a step was not necessarily done in panic–although the Russian leadership had undoubtedly been angered by Lukashenka's initiative–but became the latest expression of the constantly politicised manoeuvrings by two regimes, which still needed each other albeit for different purposes. Manoeuvrings which put paid to any spirit of security community between them.[952] Bilateral relations were not about to improve. Russia had proposed that a meeting within the Union State take place in Moscow that February, ostensibly to discuss energy relations but clearly with a view for wider-ranging issues. However, that meeting was abruptly cancelled, ostensibly due to "scheduling differences" but likely for Lukashenka to reaffirm his status.[953] The Russian government was not happy about that behaviour or by Belarusian unwillingness to either pay fair energy prices or offer greater political concessions to Russia. In March, Medvedev openly accused Minsk of blackmail, threatening to delay further integration until yet more energy discounts had been received.[954]

Eventually, in April, the two presidents did finally meet and negotiate their energy affairs. Russia would return oil deliveries for Belarus to prior levels in return for Belarusian recognition of its natural gas debts. However, as Putin promised this debt would be restructured, Belarusian commentators worried about what price

---

950　For analysis of how Lukashenka promoted his security and humanitarian credentials on the migration question, see also Vieira, 2021: 310

951　As discussed by Khodasevich, 2017c

952　For the politicised nature of the changes in Russian and Belarusian border arrangements in early 2017, see also Khimshiashvili et al, 2017

953　For what the meeting might have entailed, see also Sozaev-Gur'ev, 2017

954　Medvedev's angry comments—including a pointed if insincere reminder that the Belarusians could just go their own way if they so chose—were summarised in Medvedev, 2017

might be requested.[955] And as for the agreement itself, Belarusian officials clearly did not expect it to be of benefit for their country in the longer run. Only a month later, the head of Belnaftakhim, the state-controlled petrochemical organisation, stressed that new, non-Russian sources of oil had to be found.[956] Energy disputes seemed certain to recur later in the year. Not just due to Belarusian duplicity and greed. The recalcitrant behaviour stemmed also from belief that Russian-led economic integration was not working–at least not working as well as it had been advertised. Hence Lukashenka's repeated suggestions that the EEU and EU should interact further.[957]

It was never quite clear how such interaction might work–the question alone of primacy of regulation appeared insurmountable. Yet the Belarusians persisted and made the issue quite existential in nature. Witness Makei's comments in July 2017 to Spanish media that closer links with the EU would strengthen Belarusian sovereignty and political independence.[958] A few months later Makei provided a highly positive evaluation of the Eastern Partnership summit in Brussels, clearly presenting it no longer as a threat but as an opportunity for his country. Throughout the foreign minister's account shone satisfaction with being treated respectfully by the EU.[959] Contrast that with Makei's growing complaints on collaboration with Russia. Economic integration within the EEU was potentially promising but did not work when one party (i.e. Russia) constantly took unilateral, protectionist steps, allegedly to protect against goods from third parties, while being too slow to open for investment from Europe and from Asia.[960]

Lukashenka knew that the later the EEU market would integrate properly with outside partners the later regulations of that market would be implemented consistently. For now, engaging

---

955   An example of such concerns was the article by Klaskovskii, 2017
956   This was reported in Belneftekhim, 2017
957   Indeed, the Belarusian foreign ministry suggested economic cooperation with the EU while keeping closer to Russia on foreign political issues. On that point, see Nitoiu, 2018: 700
958   As reported in Makei, 2017a
959   Makei's summary of the event was presented by Makei, 2017c
960   On this, see also Makei, 2017b

through informal practices could work for Belarus–numerous energy discounts bore witness to that–yet it left the country's economy in constant danger of blunt Russian pressure.[961] A prime example of this still consisted of agricultural trade. Over the winter of 2016-17 Russian health authorities repeated and in parts enlarged previous bans on goods from Belarus–and particularly meats–being imported into Russia. The Belarusian regime, perhaps understandably, denounced the step as politicised.[962] The problem being, however, that apart from complaints Minsk had little recourse to force products through. As discussed previously, through talks with Putin Lukashenka had previously seemed able to overcome Russian bureaucracy. Now, though, the Kremlin showed ever less willingness to talk and the EEU, by its own admission, had no relevant powers to assist.[963]

Ill will from such economic spats carried on through the year. Even when Zapad 2017 supposedly showed a united front against the West Putin and Lukashenka largely presented separately. Reactions from neighbouring countries, while concerned, seemed to perceive Minsk as much as a hostage of Moscow as an aggressor in its own right.[964] Clearly, Russian elites had limited respect for Belarusian sovereignty. Following the above-mentioned Belarusian participation in the Eastern Partnership meeting in Brussels Russian television presented the neighbouring state as a "prostitute", selling itself to the highest bidder. A charge which, unsurprisingly, brought a furious response but from official Belarusian media and not just the opposition.[965] Arguably, a disrespectful television segment could have been ignored, but over the following days Minsk

---

961 Hence, for instance, the threat of countermeasures by Belarus if Russia continued its refusal to recognise goods certificates issued in other EEU member-states. See also Belarus', 2017

962 The dispute also being mentioned by Svoboda, 2021: 71

963 As also pointed out specifically relating to the 2016-17 meat dispute by Roberts, 2017: 430

964 See, for instance, Latvian fears that Russia might seek to bind Belarus so closely to its military machine that the Lukashenka regime would not be able to avoid involvement in warfare (as arguably would happen from 2022). This was mentioned by Lasmanis, 2017

965 Prominent here was Karpovich, 2017

showed no sign of letting go. Belarusian state television criticised Russian "hysterics" and admonished the authorities to ban the producers of the offensive Russian segment from the country in perpetuity.[966]

Why such a severe reaction? At the time, some observers in Belarus and elsewhere suspected that the Belarusian leadership had been genuinely offended by the Russian jibes. After years of largely supporting Russian annexation of Crimea (or at least refraining from overt criticism) more Russian gratitude and understanding had perhaps been expected.[967] At the same time, it was also abundantly clear by late 2017 that the Belarusian authorities were becoming increasingly weary and wary of the Russia emerging in Ukraine and elsewhere. Putin was gearing up for re-election in 2018 through increasing belligerence and decreasing reference to Belarus as a mediator in any sort of peace negotiations.[968] Certainly, Russia had not given up on its image in the West, what with the branding within the upcoming football World Cup and profitable economic linkages. As 2018 approached, though, Minsk was concerned that such an image might survive further aggressive moves against Belarus with no one in the West caring very much.[969]

Putin confirms his position

In December 2018 Lukashenka reached the end of his tether. Possibly. For the time being, anyway. The Belarusian president had a history of public histrionics–frequently when addressing Russia, as

---

966   As discussed by Pankovets, 2017

967   For a useful take on Belarusian attitudes to the Crimean annexation it might be worth also looking at Mudrov, 2020, where the author indicates (as I did previously in this chapter) that there had been quite widespread understanding within Belarusian society for the annexation.

968   Apart from the earlier reference to D'Anieri's take on the eventual failure of the "Minsk process", see also an article such as Pogodina, 2017. Not to agree with it, but to notice how this Moscow-faithful piece declares the process very much alive while spending the vast majority of words on decrying Western perfidy, while only mentioning Belarus once — ominously (in light of my comments in the text above) in the context of the Eastern Partnership.

969   Whereas analysts supporting the Belarusian opposition believed this was precisely the time to put pressure on Minsk. See e.g. Moshes, 2017

I have demonstrated. But now it was all over. According to him, the two countries were no longer brotherly nations–they were simply trading partners.[970] And even if Lukashenka would soon ask for Russian favours again, renouncing the foundations of the relationship outright was not something he was in the habit of doing. So, what had led him to this point? Why did he now almost seem to take the Ukrainian side in their battle with Russia.[971] The proximate cause for Lukashenka's ire was Medvedev. Towards the end of the year, the Russian prime minister had stressed that future Russian economic assistance to Belarus would have to be linked to specific steps on wider political, economic and likely military integration between the countries.[972]

A week and a half before his outburst, Lukashenka had gathered his government to discuss the Russian threat to Belarusian independence. Anonymous sources indicated that Russia might pursue its agenda through the media, and the president himself argued in public that Russian wishes for further integration would mean a takeover of his country.[973] He still went for talks in Moscow late in the month but with little to show for it. Some analysts noted that the Belarusian regime said little about the contents of that meetings afterwards, indicating it had not gone as Lukashenka might have wished for it to go.[974] Analysts assumed that he had asked for money–in the form of loans, credit or subsidies–and for Russia to offer Belarusian trade full or improved access to the Russian market. This was, after all, how Lukashenka had behaved before. But would it work this time? That seemed uncertain given Russian behaviour during 2018.[975]

For Russia the most important event of the year was the reelection of Putin as president in March. Not because it was ever in doubt whether Putin would stand or, for that matter, whether he

---

970   This particular outburst was from a government meeting and reported Lukashenka, 2018b

971   As recorded by Sharipzhan, 2018

972   A summary of Medvedev's approach was offered by Nizhnikau and Silvan, 2022: 1216

973   This was argued in Lukashenka, 2018a

974   On this observation, see Khalip, 2018

975   For such expert comments, see also Drakakhrust, 2018

would win–and win by a large margin to the next contestant.[976] Similarly, there were widespread suspicions that his victory, when it came, had been at least artificially inflated in its magnitude. Over the years to come such an interpretation appeared to be confirmed through the use of statistical analysis, which demonstrated suspicious patterns in numerous voting results.[977] Why did the regime bother with an election? Partly, it was for the benefit of an international audience–as shown also by the subsequent World Cup the Kremlin still wanted such branding. Yet Putin's re-election also provided him with a partly accurate opinion poll (in unannounced figures) on his statist, assertive/aggressive policies since 2012.[978]

Belarusian observers understood that Putin's re-election might not augur well for their country. Unsurprisingly, the official message from Minsk was one of support and confirmation not only of Putin but of the entire political process and, by extension, Russian ability to carry out such an event as well or better than Western comparators.[979] Yet from Belarusian opposition commentators came warnings that Russian pressure would not relent. Indeed, it was suggested that–by the time of the next Russian presidential election six years into the future–the Lukashenka regime better be prepared to fight for the independence of Belarus, as Russia might have abandoned any support for it.[980] Some Belarusian commentators went further. They argued the Russian regime was turning into a "cult of personality" around Putin with that president likely to change the Russian constitution and potentially stay in power all his life. On such a path, of course, Russia would follow Belarus and the choice Lukashenka had made years before.[981]

---

976 A summary of the election result was offered by Roth, 2018
977 For a background on how such analysis was carried out, see Petrova, 2024
978 For more on authoritarian regimes' reasons for holding elections, see Miller, 2017: 20
979 Accompanied with proud information about how polling station in Belarus had helped Russian citizens there to take part in the process. See also Prezidentskie, 2018
980 This was suggested by Pavel Usov in Zaprudskii, 2018
981 Whether there was a "cult of personality" around Putin was debated by some Russian analysts in the run-up to the election. Particularly interesting approaches to that question came from Kiva, 2018, from Tuliakov, 2018, and from Davydov, 2018

It might appear such a political course would have only consequences for domestic Russian politics. However, the identity around which Putin had by now settled his regime required a spread of the so-called "power vertical" beyond the state–and perhaps even beyond the nation–to a Russian civilisation.[982] Within such a civilisation, clearly, Belarus and Belarusians would play a central part. Russia was now showing becoming mono-religious–in fact if not quite in law–and church leaders including Patriarch Kirill himself used religious and state holidays and commemorations to restate the organic unity of the "Eastern Slavs."[983] Somewhat by coincidence such rhetoric became more frequent and vociferous in the aftermath of Putin's re-election. In April, Poroshenko and Ukrainian church leaders asked the Orthodox Ecumenical Patriarch in Constantinople for autocephaly. At first, the Russian-lead church denounced the application as a stunt made for domestic electoral consumption and bound to fail.[984]

Russian perceptions did not improve when Poroshenko encouraged Moscow to support the call for autocephaly as a way to seek absolution for Russian crimes in Ukraine. As the year progressed it seemed increasingly likely that autocephaly would be granted. The Belarusian Orthodox Church, subordinate to Moscow but clearly with Lukashenka's blessing, sharply criticised Constantinopolitan interference.[985] Eventually, autocephaly would be granted in October leading the Russian Orthodox Church to move away from its erstwhile theological superior. For the purposes of Russo-Belarusian relations, however, it is noteworthy that the break with Constantinople provided impetus for Putin and his allies to inject their policies with quasi-religious purpose.[986] As I

---

982   On the nature of such civilisational discourse and how it frequently acquired religious meaning during Putin's third presidential term, see also Shnirelman, 2020

983   A helpful overview of how Russia was becoming a mono-religious state (if not society) is by Flake, 2021

984   Ukrainian parliamentary approval for church autocephaly followed swiftly, though, as reported in Ukrainian, 2018

985   For the message from the Belarusian Orthodox Church, see also Obrashchenie, 2018

986   The grievances laid against the Ecumenical Patriarch by the Russian Orthodox Church is set out in Statement, 2018

pointed out in Chapter 1, there was historical precedence for such a step. In the 15th century the idea of the "Third Rome" had been promoted by the Russian Orthodox Church as a means of isolation and conservation following Constantinople's agreement of formal subordination to erstwhile "schismatics" in Rome.[987]

Now, the new Russian nationalism, or civilisationism, could centre on a similar image of exclusivity and isolationism. In order to do so, however, it needed to gather peoples (or souls) around it to dedicate their existence to defence of the true faith–a faith the high priest of which was Putin himself.[988] This became a prime purpose of the so-called Immortal Regiment–participants in celebrations for victory in the Second World War displaying photographs of relatives who had fought, and often died, for protection of the Soviet lands. The message was clear–true patriots would lay down their life for protection of the common cause.[989] Not all analysts agree with this essentially statist and belligerent interpretation of the Immortal Regiment, instead viewing it as partly civic and perhaps even pacific in nature–and as an expression of incomplete Russian nation-building. At a societal level such claims may have some validity–yet hardly when it came to the Kremlin's intent.[990]

And this placed Lukashenka in a dilemma. As in Russia, the Immortal Regiment was present during Belarusian Victory Day celebrations. Participants clearly demonstrated allegiance to Russia. The Belarusian president chose first to ban the Regiment and then allow it to march, seeking to disrupt the activity without looking like an opponent of the Russian World.[991] Yet that hardly mollified either Russophiles or Russophobes in the country. Lukashenka also

---

987 An event with which Putin was well familiar. On that point, see Drost and de Graaf, 2022

988 Linking Putin's rule to the Third Rome had arguably developed since 2012, with antecedents from ideological tendencies during his first two terms. See also Østbø, 2016

989 It is apposite here to remember that references to "resurrection" (certainly in the context of the Old Testament) relate to peoples, not individuals. On that point, see also Ehrman, 2021: particularly chapter 3

990 For a prominent example of such an alternative interpretation of the Immortal Regiment, see also Kurilla, 2023

991 This tactic was observed by Anton, 2018

used his speech on Victory Day to point out that the war had been fought and won by all the Soviet peoples together and that no one nation–by which he was clearly referring to the Russians–should monopolise the triumph.[992] He would come back to that topic the following month when he explicitly countered Russian accusations that Belarus and Belarusians were betraying historical links to Russia. Calling his country a "memorial to the war", Lukashenka also drew attention to the unequalled casualties suffered by the population there.[993]

Whether such classical tropes would work now was questionable. In Belarusian opposition media were being published stories about how multiple websites had been found spreading pro-Russian narratives inside Belarus ostensibly on behalf of Belarusian regional actors, yet in reality being funded from Russia. Their message would not support Lukashenka's belief in distinct Belarusian memories.[994] Consequently, unease built between Belarusians and Russians throughout 2018. Then, in October, when the Ukrainian Orthodox Church did receive autocephaly, the Russian Orthodox Church held a synod in Minsk. That was very much meant to signal that people in Belarus belonged to Kirill's congregation. In response, Lukashenka offered no support for sovereign Belarusian clergy.[995] Instead, he held a widely covered meeting with Kirill, afterwards stressing his understanding for the position of the Orthodox Church. Lukashenka criticised splits between co-religionists with direct reference to external interference in the name of so-called democracy. His public comments throughout echoed closely what might have been heard from the Kremlin.[996]

And they certainly did not bring him closer to Ukraine. Back in February Lukashenka had openly called for a swift end to fighting in Donbass. Then he had stated explicitly that he was not

---

992 Lukashenka's speech was recorded as Lukashenka, 2018c
993 Such comments were recorded on Lukashenko, 2018c
994 For the reports on Russian-funded websites seeking to influence the Belarusian socio-political landscape, see also Harbatsevich, 2018a
995 The lack of Belarusian participation in the synod was also noted by Harbatsevich, 2018b
996 These comments were reported by Kriat, 2018

taking sides in the fighting but believed that Belarusian mediation was required to bring "brotherly peoples" to stop their feud.[997] As had sporadically been the case in previous years, Lukashenka had also repeated his offers that Belarusian troops could be sent to Donbass as peacekeepers, thereby possibly moving away from his long-standing, and quite public, aversion to sending Belarusians to any kind of conflict area.[998] In previous years such an offer might have received a hearing in Kyiv, given Lukashenka's at times assiduous courting of Poroshenko, despite risks to his own relationship with Putin. Now, though, the Ukrainians firmly asked Belarusian troops to stay away, ostensibly due to Belarusian participation in the CSTO and thus military alliance with Russia.[999]

The Ukrainian government mentioned continued faith in Belarusian goodwill but was aware that the Minsk Process by late 2018 enjoyed limited domestic support, at best. When Russian troops could be found in Belarus and more might arrive in coming years, Lukashenka would have had to go out of his way to reassure his southern neighbour.[1000] So why had Lukashenka not sought to use Kirill's visit to underline Belarusian sovereignty and an identity separate from that of Russia? And why did he, also in mid-October, openly welcome Putin to the "Russian cities"–as Lukashenka called them–of Mogilev and Vitebsk? Some concession, given the above-mentioned emphasis on geopolitics in Belarusian identity-making.[1001] Some Belarusian commentators suggested that the Belarusian leader was reacting to increased Russian pressure for

---

997   As recorded at Lukashenko, 2018a
998   From the West, too, came repeated support for a peacekeeping mission in eastern Ukraine and on an expedited basis. See for instance Germany, 2018
999   That Ukrainian explanation also being presented by Hadano, 2020: 217
1000 At times, Lukashenka's attempts to reassure Ukrainians of his peaceful intent were less than elegant, though — as, for instance, when he suggested Belarusian troops turn up as peacekeepers on the frontline in Ukraine. See also Lukashenko, 2018d
1001 And, indeed, considering the architectural reaffirmation of Vitebsk as Belarusian just a few years prior, as mentioned above. Here, it may also be worth recalling that Lukashenko himself is from the region of Vitebsk and went to school in the region of Mogilev. For the official story on that, see also Hometown, 2024, which (tellingly) includes a prominent picture of Lukashenka with Putin.

unification–which seemed plausible–and that he was promoting the image of Belarusians as virtually similar to Russians and therefore not a people to be further challenged or even exploited.[1002]

Would such a tactic work? Russian authorities were certainly prepared to keep Belarusians close–and make sure they did not go anywhere else. See the silky-smooth assurances offered in October that the Belarusians should not worry about any foreign threats, as they were under Russia's protection.[1003] Those comments were uttered by Mikhail Babich, who had recently arrived in Belarus as Russian ambassador, taking over from the hard-toiling (and, arguably, long-suffering) Surikov. Babich had appeared on stage apparently holding more powers than his predecessor, being carefully picked and entrusted by the Russian president himself.[1004] Why had Moscow decided to upgrade their ambassador? It might well bode ill for any attempts at Belarusian autonomy. Within Belarusian media and public debate there were stories about Babich's links to the Russian secret services and military, although his experience as an administrator was likely more relevant.[1005]

Then there were rumours circulating that the Belarusian government was being remade to appease Russian wishes. Around the time of Babich's arrival in the country, Lukashenka had installed a new prime minister–Siarhei Rumas. The latter had a history of advocating for economic restructuring and privatisation in Belarus–something likely to appeal to Russian business.[1006] As was to be expected, Lukashenka had insisted that no one decided official appointments apart from him. At the same time, though, the president was concerned about the horrible way in which Russia was treating Belarusian companies. His country had been lured to integrate and

---

1002 That could certainly be an interpretation of the story presented by Kolesnikov, 2018a, although that presenter seems to find it difficult to take Lukashenka (and perhaps the Belarusian people) seriously.
1003 As reported in Minsk, 2018
1004 The strengthened position of Babich relative to his predecessor was discussed by Nezhdanskii, 2018
1005 The background of Babich is detailed by Gryl', 2018
1006 For the opposition media's take on Rumas as he entered public consciousness in 2012, see also Gorbachev, 2012

212 Uncanny Allies

now its people were being discriminated against.[1007] Lukashenka's complaints were nothing new (as evidenced throughout this chapter) but the danger was now more acute. In September, he went to Sochi for talks with Putin. State television reported fruitful discussions, about economic issues and question on further political integration. Lukashenka repeatedly stressed his fight for the Belarusian position but without conveying much optimism.[1008]

Within Belarusian opposition media now spread rumours that Lukashenka would leave power. That he would not stand in the upcoming Belarusian presidential election scheduled for 2020. Admittedly, that guess was based on little more than the downcast reaction by Lukashenka following the meeting as well as the dearth of official Russian comments.[1009] But that might be misunderstanding the Russian position. If the Kremlin could get its way with Belarus–by exerting targeted pressure–then it would absolutely be in the Russian interest to retain Lukashenka. Any alternative leader would, as a minimum, need time to consolidate domestic power, delaying further integration with and concessions to Russia.[1010] And the Belarusian regime had, after all, done well from collaborating with the Kremlin. In its foreign trade Minsk had access not only to the Russian market (when absent Russian trade barriers) but also polities dependent on Russia, such as–notably–Crimea and the Donbass.[1011]

Apart from personal benefits accruing to elites, the Belarusian state and society from such trade, all of these continued to live quite well, too, on Russian subsidies–World Bank data of 2018 showed the country with a higher GDP/capita than even oil rich and increasingly self-confident Azerbaijan.[1012] So, when October saw the

---

1007 For an example of such complaints by Lukashenka in the summer of 2018, see e.g. Khodasevich, 2018
1008 Lukashenka's summary of the meeting was also reported by Lukashenko, 2018b
1009 For speculation about the end of Lukashenka's time in power, see Nezygar', 2018
1010 A Russian tactic also outlined by Orenstein, 2019: chapter 4
1011 An example of how coal from Donbass was being rerouted through Belarus to international markets is provided by Marandici and Leşanu, 2021: 344-45
1012 That comparison being made by Buscaneanu, 2021: 634

Russian government give notice that the country would pause deliveries of petroleum products to Belarus–thereby preventing the latter from re-exporting it for substantial profits–then that should quickly impact Belarusian policies. By now, Russia was not even trying to hide its intentions.[1013] Similarly with Medvedev's above-mentioned address on integration. He had simply laid out two scenarios for future relations, linking any sort of preferential economic treatment for Belarusians to political concessions on their part. The Kremlin expected that to be no choice since Lukashenka had no other potential benefactor ready to let him dictate conditions of collaboration.[1014]

Russian commentators largely saw the situation in a similar light. Some commentators believed Moscow would gain benefits irrespective of what Lukashenka chose to do. Either it would get firmer control over Belarus, or it would be able to reduce expenditures, which it found it increasingly difficult to defend in more economically austere times.[1015] Others expected Lukashenka to fight on for political relevance, even as his rule could never survive the liberalisation which would inevitably follow putative Russian withdrawal. His problem was, though, that integration for Russia was now likely linked to constitutional manoeuvres keeping Putin in power after 2024. So, more than ever the "power vertical" was non-negotiable.[1016] And that seemed to place a clear time limit on any delaying tactics or other machinations, which Lukashenka could produce. Quite possibly, 2019 would see more compromises and short-term deals being struck over energy and other bilateral trade relations. Yet, as things stood a reckoning was coming.[1017]

1013 The Russian announcement was outlined in Korsunskaya et al, 2018
1014 For analysis of Medvedev's approach on this matter, see also Kłysiński et al, 2018
1015 This point-of-view being noted by Ruvinskii, 2018
1016 These topics were covered by Kolesnikov, 2018b
1017 On the possibility of renewed compromise being achieved, for the time being, see Sozaev-Gur'ev, 2018

Rise of the Russian World

As 2019 began, which priorities was the Russian leadership chasing? Ideologically moving Russia towards a religious social conservatism, the Kremlin had little new to say on socio-economic measures, despite a visibly worsening budgetary position. Russian commentators suggested that the elite now just wanted to retain power, in any way possible.[1018] However, public dissatisfaction in Russia was increasing. The previous year attempts to reform the Russian welfare and benefits system had led to widespread, public protests among a demographic which had largely been among the Kremlin's supporters, accepting Putin's narrative that his reign should be compared to the chaos under Yeltsin.[1019] And while the reform was carried through, some underlying dissatisfaction remained in society. Given potential economic challenges ahead, nationwide media suggested that the question of incomes and personal wealth would be central to coming elections, with support for Putin now suffering noticeable declines in opinion polls.[1020]

It seemed possible, however, that such public malaise would move to apathy rather than anger. The Russian leadership had been careful to provide support for numerous regional stakeholders, who could keep prominent protesters down. If the remainder of the populace then chose to disengage from the political protest this might be acceptable for the Kremlin.[1021] However, the chance of public anger was certain to increase if people in Russia could see neighbouring societies, otherwise similar to their, living more comfortably. And that would be a problem with Belarus. When Lukashenka asked for subsidies or loans, in Putin's view this was not simply economically problematic, but ideologically challenging, as well.[1022] So, the Russian administration did not resist further

---

1018 For an example of such analysis, see Svanidze, 2019
1019 The welfare reform on which these protests were centred is detailed by Logvinenko, 2020: 109
1020 On this, see also Rost, 2019
1021 As also suggested by Ruvinskii, 2019
1022 A reminder is suggested by the research of Walker, 2022, that a loss of income and employment could also lead to a crisis of masculinity among Russian young men, thereby challenging the masculinisation of political overall.

integration, as Lukashenka would periodically claim, but sought integration on terms that would reduce Belarusian exploitation of Russian support and goodwill. Medvedev, for one, was now quite scathing about the Belarusian president's rhetorical deflections from the core economic issues at hand.[1023]

In a similar vein, the Russian prime minister and his government were increasingly unwilling to entertain Belarusian suggestions on integrative principles and declarations, or for that matter on longer-term initiatives, like a common currency. As Medvedev himself made clear, such discussions should wait until agreements on day-to-day economic affairs had been reached.[1024] It may seem strange that such agreements had not yet been fleshed out within the EEU–an organisation which had now existed for four years, after all. Certainly, Lukashenka had sometimes held further EEU integration back. However, it was also the case that Russia knew the EEU–like some of its predecessors–disproportionately favoured Belarus.[1025] This might not have been a problem if Russians and Belarusians had simply been concerned with economic benefits for their own country. However, as I indicated above the Russian leadership (and, arguably, the Belarusian leadership, too) knew it had to be seen to live up to welfare and other societal standards offered across the border.[1026]

Once more, therefore, we see an example of the uncanny in the Russian-Belarusian relationship. If an essential part of the identity of both regimes was statist socio-economic welfare and progress, neither could afford for the other to show it up on that issue. It would leave the laggard open to largely justified charges of oligarchy.[1027] That ontological underpinning had been present in bilateral disputes ever since Putin's return as president yet was becoming particularly noticeable after Putin's re-election in 2018. Some

---

1023 For a statement on this, see Medvedev, 2019a
1024 This suggestion was recorded by Medvedev, 2019b
1025 Data on this were provided in Knobel et al, 2019: 179-80
1026 Arguably, therefore, Russia and Belarus were in a "zero-sum game" on developments in public welfare. See also Hort and Zakharov, 2019: 293
1027 Similarly, in his highly published expose of Putin's riches Russian opposition leader Aleksei Navalny knew very well he was striking at a central pillar of the Putin mystique. For that expose, see also Putin's, 2021

216   UNCANNY ALLIES

Russian commentators even hinted that Russia was picking on countries like Belarus because its economic capacity had proven unable to keep up with great powers elsewhere in the world.[1028] And there was no doubt that Lukashenka's age-old habit of complaining about alleged ill-treatment on the side of Russian providers was wearing thin in Moscow. Witness, for instance, Peskov's curt dismissal in April of any Belarusian attempt at "blackmailing" Russia by threatening to block Russian oil deliveries to Europe.[1029]

Back in January, the Russian ambassador to Belarus had already suggested that his host country should begin to find its oil elsewhere as it, apparently, could not afford Russian deliveries. Babich was being most condescending as he also noted how "free competition" within the EEU would have to benefit Russian as well as Belarusian actors.[1030] It might be argued that Babich was making the best of developments. The previous year Belarus had already explored the option of oil deliveries from Kazakhstan and there was little to suggest that such exploration would halt. Indeed, Lukashenka led a visit to Kazakhstan in late May and early June partly for that purpose.[1031] Eventually, late in the year the two regimes declared themselves strategic partners while also setting out framework agreements for oil deliveries from Kazakhstan–deliveries thought likely to start the following year. True, Russia would have been practically able to stop such collaboration, yet doing so overtly could have sunk the EEU.[1032]

So, it was easier for the Russian ambassador to pretend the plan had Russia's blessing, all along. Babich did not have to be so obnoxious about it, though. Elsewhere, he openly provoked Belarusians, telling them their country was only stable due to Russian aid while offering plenty of data to back that up.[1033] Not long after, when asked about the price of the Russia-built nuclear power plant

---

1028 That was certainly hinted at by Rossiia, 2019
1029 Peskov's telling-off was recorded by V Kremle, 2019b
1030 On that, see also Bibikov, 2019
1031 For official Belarusian presentation of Lukashenka's visit, see also Lukashenko, 2019a
1032 On the news that Belarus and Kazakhstan agreed in principle on oil deliveries to the former, see also Dogovor, 2019
1033 That bit of diplomacy came in Mikhail, 2019

Babich near Astravets, Babich directly accused a Belarusian member of parliament of falsely quoting him on a specific number and dismissed as groundless Lukashenka's comments on the topic in his state of the nation address.[1034] In response the Belarusian ministry of foreign affairs scathingly accused Babich of behaving as if he had been sent to a Russian federal region where he could give orders without any concern for local rights or input. Dismissed as "emotional", Babich was presented as little more than a bully.[1035]

Russian diplomacy in Belarus had changed since Surikov's tenure. A solution was needed and soon Babich was moved on. Russian observers did not, however, expect essentials to change in Russian policy. Moscow had decided to be a bit more tactful, making it less likely that the Belarusian establishment would automatically unite against Russia in protest.[1036] Would it work? Well, after the second half of 2018, in particular, had proven very difficult for Lukashenka he had shown some willingness to smooth relations over. In February, for instance, he had congratulated in effusive language Kirill on the latter's ten-year anniversary as head of the Russian Orthodox Church.[1037] Those comments were only offered, though, after Metropolitan Pavel had started the year by explicitly setting out the Russian claim to the church in Belarus, warning it against moving towards autocephaly like the Ukrainians had done. That Pavel was also speaking on behalf of the Russian state and about the Belarusian state was undoubted.[1038]

So, Lukashenka was reacting to Russian initiatives from the beginning of the year and that pattern mostly stayed the same throughout 2019. From the Russian side the rhetorical offensives were clearly coordinated. There were warnings from state media that ethnic hatred against Russians could now be seen in Belarus.[1039] Babich, then still in post, warned his hosts to distinguish carefully between a policy of gradually introducing elements of Belarusian

---

1034 The Belarusian answer to Babich's complaints was recorded by MID, 2019
1035 The ministry's confrontational message can be found in Otvet, 2019
1036 For such a take on the ambassadorial replacement, see also Aptekar', 2019
1037 This was reported in Lukashenko, 2019c
1038 Pavel's comments appeared in Glava, 2019
1039 As suggested in Segodnia, 2019: from 16m, 30s

218   UNCANNY ALLIES

culture into public life and then seeking to remove Russian elements from the country. While the former course was acceptable, the latter could damage Belarusian long-term interests.[1040] Such messages seemed eerily similar to statements produced against Ukraine in the run-up to the invasion of that country in 2014. And Belarusian society was, if anything, even more susceptible to Russian propaganda than its southern neighbour had been–Russian media dominated television and some internet media.[1041]

The Russian authorities guarded their information dominance in Belarus carefully. As they saw matters, the threat did not directly come from Western media even if an increasing proportion of young Belarusians spoke English. However, Belarusian opposition media was a different matter–Belsat was even marked by Babich (who else?) as an information threat.[1042] Minsk had no wish to defend Belsat, yet still had to worry about what would happen to its room for manoeuvre should Russia come to fully dominate media in Belarus. All of a sudden, Lukashenka had some understanding, perhaps even respect for the situation in which Ukraine had found itself.[1043] And, as it would happen, 2019 then became the year when Ukraine got a new leader. While elected on a platform of challenging oligarchic structures and bringing peace to his country, new president Volodymyr Zelensky had more than a hint of the outsider's populism about him.[1044]

That was the kind of profile which resonated with Lukashenka. Admittedly, the two leaders were from different generations and had different understandings of state and of democracy, yet they both sought to create a direct link to their respective populations and were thus similarly vulnerable to Russian attempts at severing that link.[1045] So, Lukashenka welcomed Zelensky

---

1040 Those warnings were reported by Ivanov, 2019
1041 For an overview of this, see also Tsarik, 2019
1042 As discussed by the ambassador in Babich, 2019
1043 On the media situation in Belarus at the time, for the reader it might also be worth consulting Manaev, 2018
1044 Useful analysis of Zelensky's background can be found in Onuch and Hale, 2022: chapters 4-5
1045 For the populist streak in Zelensky and his party Servant of the People, see also Yanchenko and Zulianello, 2024

as president and at times seemed to aim for a bit of a bromance. For instance, when speaking to presumably bemused schoolchildren in September the Belarusian leader claimed he himself had given up riding a bike to office just because Zelensky had gotten their first. And that was apparently just marvellous.[1046] Lukashenka had a history of physical bonding (e.g. ice skating with Putin) and might therefore be predicted to stretch himself this way for Zelensky. Putin would not follow suit. Note, though, that Zelensky's arrival had been met with some Russian hope, while Western analysts briefly wondered if he could be a Kremlin plant.[1047]

Early in his presidency, Zelensky suggested the convocation of a peace conference for Donbass. As he wanted this conference to be in Minsk, Lukashenka was very much in favour. Tellingly, though, the Belarusian president also helped Zelensky to push for the inclusion of American, German, French and British leaders to support the Ukrainian cause.[1048] Lukashenka knew that the Kremlin would not support widening responsibility for conflict resolution away from Russia, so why did he go with Zelensky on the matter? Likely because it offered the Belarusian president a chance to mark himself as sovereign, but also as someone genuinely committed to lasting regional peace and stability.[1049] The Russians did not believe him–or, at least, could not allow Belarusians to take the lead on the matter. On the whole, Moscow was increasingly minded to keeping Belarus out of Ukrainian affairs. Lukashenka's renewed suggestion that Belarusian troops could provide peacekeeping in eastern Ukraine was given short shrift from Russia.[1050]

Russia could not, though, stop the Belarusian leader from travelling to Ukraine for a high-profile meeting with Zelensky in early October. Ostensibly meeting on the topic of cooperation between their domestic regions, the two leaders declared each other

---

1046 That statement was televised on Lukashenko, 2019d
1047 For Russian reactions to Zelensky's electoral victory, see also Dobrokhotov, 2019
1048 For more on this, see also Busygina and Filippov, 2021: 483
1049 Lukashenka's call for regional peace was also made in his remarks to an Independence Day parade as recorded by Lukashenko, 2019b
1050 As witnessed by the statements of Peskov, recorded in V Kremle, 2019a

best of friends now and in future.[1051] Afterwards, Belarusian and Ukrainian observers were very complementary about the meeting. It was seen as a sign that Belarus was serious about promoting a multi-vector foreign policy, while at a more specific level opportunities could now be spotted for profitable economic collaboration between the two countries and their manufacturing sectors.[1052] The Russian elite was uncomfortable with this. The Kremlin's ire was aroused further by Lukashenka's insistence that Russia was part of the Donbas conflict. Long accepted as a given by most of the world, the Russian leadership still clung to a position that this was a domestic Ukrainian conflict which they just wanted to mitigate.[1053]

Then Lukashenka took his support for Ukraine one noteworthy step further. At the CIS summit of Ashgabat, the president specifically advocated that the solution to the conflict in Ukraine should be found collectively between the organisation's members. That Zelensky could be invited to a future summit and talk matters out with one president after another.[1054] That idea was dead in the water. Russia absolutely did not want other post-Soviet states to have a stake in Ukraine's future. So, why the suggestion? Lukashenka's wanted as many countries as possible actively involved in the region's future. So that Belarus, one day, would not be all alone with its Russian "Big Brother."[1055] To avoid such a fate, he would seek allies in surprising places. Suddenly, Minsk was visited by American guests–and not just any guests but Donald Trump's national security adviser John Bolton and, in early 2020,

---

1051 The very positive sheen placed on this meeting can still be viewed on Volodymyr, 2019
1052 Particularly on that economic point, see also Palivoda, 2019
1053 Much evidence clearly contradicts Russia's argument here. It should be noted, though, that some scholars have detected a kernel of violence in eastern Ukraine separate of Russian involvement. See also Arel and Driscoll, 2023, although it must be stressed that this work does not in any way exonerate or ignore Russian meddling in Ukraine before or after 2014.
1054 Russian media largely preferred to ignore Lukashenka's uncomfortable suggestion and instead highlighted how the Ukrainians themselves had decided to stay away for reasons founded on arrogance. See also Panfilova, 2019
1055 See also Lukashenka's warning to Russians earlier in the year that they should prepare themselves for what real integration would entail—namely a change of their state rather than simply a takeover of Belarus. As reported in Lukashenko, 2019e

secretary of state Mike Pompeo. Two of the most prominent foreign policy hawks, keen to project American power abroad.[1056]

The Russian administration made clear that this, really, was no big deal. When Bolton arrived in Minsk in late August this was just an internal affair of Belarus, according to Peskov. Nothing to see here and, by the way, if Belarus would buy American oil as rumour had it then that was their business.[1057] Lukashenka himself went out of his way to defend his reasons for seeking better relations with the Americans. It was not as if the Trump administration had ignored the Russians, so now it was the Belarusian turn. It was simply prudent for a small, geographically exposed country like Belarus to seek friends where possible.[1058] That argument persuaded no one. In Moscow, it was clear that the Belarusian regime was ready to disavow any part in imperial or Soviet history whenever victimhood became more convenient. Medvedev noted as much in stark comments that November, complaining against notions in Minsk that "foreign powers" had fought wars on that territory.[1059]

Belarusian state media was furious. Never had the country's population or leaders started any wars or profited from them. Instead, Belarus had repeatedly been a victim of great power aggression including on behalf of the Soviet Union and its capital, which would surely have fallen to Nazi Germany if not for brave Belarusian resistance.[1060] Since Masherau authorities in Minsk had pursued this narrative, but never before in such an aggressive tone. If we here also look back to the dispute from two years prior regarding the unilateral decision to open Belarus to Western visitors, we can see a conflict not over specifics but over which regime best comprehended "security."[1061] That dispute had simmered in the

---

1056 For more on this, see also Gould-Davies, 2020: 189
1057 On this, see also Burchakov, 2019
1058 A sentiment also expressed in Belarus', 2019
1059 Medvedev's complaints that the Belarusian regime seemed to be disavowing its own history was reported by Medvedev, 2019b
1060 For the rather grumpy Belarusian answer, see Medvedev, 2019a
1061 Informal practices could, though, sometimes undermine Belarusian claims of being infallible security providers and border protectors. A genuinely hilarious anecdote showing Belarusian "flexibility" towards security commitments

222   UNCANNY ALLIES

background of the bilateral relationship ever since. The Russians were not only, or even primarily, concerned about Western infiltration through Belarus but that this country could be used as a gateway into Russia for illegal economic migrants and other "undesirables" from the Global South.[1062]

This, though, was just one of many problems between Russia and Belarus as 2019 moved to its end. Lukashenka was slowly getting ready for his expected re-election the coming year. Putin still wondering how to prolong his own tenure. The much-vaunted Union State, while seemingly supported by both, in reality satisfying neither.[1063] And the Belarusians apparently seeking a way out of the relationship sooner rather than later. Signing a high-profile loan deal with China for more than $500 million that December, in an overt attempt to call the Russians' bluff and get another patron into the region, something Beijing had seemed willing to across Central Eastern Europe.[1064] So help us, Minsk now even declared its willingness to participate in joint military exercises with NATO, that bête noire of Russia. Continued Belarusian professions of "strategic partnership" with Russia were clearly insufficient to guarantee future alliance. Moscow would have to find some new way to bind its neighbour once and for all in 2020.[1065]

---

is provided by Wolfe, 2023: 831-32. Without retelling the story here, it can just be noted that this is exactly the sort of Belarusian behaviour which the Russian authorities did not welcome.

1062 Avakov, 2019, and its quote from Russian parliamentarian Konstantin Zatulin shows clearly Russian uneasiness with Belarusian border management.

1063 A longer analysis of the condition of the Union State at this time was by Il'iash, 2019

1064 For the loan deal, see also Belarus', 2019

1065 The head of the Belarusian military expressed willingness for joint exercises with NATO on Belokonev, 2019

4 2020-2024

And the Streets Cried Out

When protesters went on the streets of Minsk, Russian reactions were halting. Officially, Lukashenka had won the Belarusian presidential election of 2020 with 81% of the votes. Albeit that number was slightly down from five years prior, the re-election seemed convincing. Particularly given an official turnout of 84%.[1066] However, the victory was swiftly challenged by observers within Belarus and abroad. Svitlana Tsikhanouskaya–standing instead of her husband and without political experience–was likely to have run Lukashenka very close or even beaten him. Tellingly, distrust in the official result was seen, too, within Russia where regime-faithful members of parliament openly talked of fraud.[1067] Indeed, while the Russian state and its supporters would soon come to praise Lukashenka's victory in the face of Western machinations, early reaction among the Russian elite was much more varied. Not only about the result itself, but also about the nature of the protesters in Belarus.[1068]

The Kremlin later noted that the dramatic events in Belarus could and would not occur in Russia. Peskov spoke about the countries having different cultures, including political cultures, and political scenography. A surprising claim, one might have thought, given the many years in which the Russian elite had stressed how similar the two countries were.[1069] The Russian leadership had good reason, though, to distance the country from events in Belarus. Already Russian commentators had pointed out that conditions facilitating protest were common to Russia and Belarus; that the unrest might be founded in youth dissatisfaction and awareness of better conditions elsewhere in the world.[1070] Certainly, academic analysis

---

1066 See Ob Itogakh, 2020
1067 Also see V Gosdume, 2020
1068 See the illuminating overview of Russian elite opinion offered by Kozlova, 2020
1069 These statements were reported in Peskov, 2020a
1070 On that, see Gontmakher, 2020

of the background of the protesters as they appeared in Belarus offered many similarities to previous cases of protesters in Russia. In both cases, the most active protesters appeared urbanised from what might be seen as a middle class of individuals with secure income based on substantial cultural, educational and intellectual capital.[1071]

Matters had not been improved by the failure of the Russian state to attract Belarusians to its actions or even its image. Russian observers were concerned that putatively allied populations elsewhere, on the Balkans, say, or in Central Asia, were watching events in Belarus to see what, if anything, Moscow would or could do.[1072] If the Russian administration could not attract foreigners it might struggle to attract ordinary people in Russia. Protests had erupted in the Russian Far East over the replacement, by Moscow, of a locally popular governor, accused of serious crime. Now, his defendants on the streets were openly linking their protests to those seen in Belarus.[1073] Links between these protest movements, and sympathisers elsewhere, were a concern for Russian authorities, not least since such links were frequently facilitated by Russian actors and institutions. Telegram–to which I linked for the information above–was a well-known instrument for protesters. While increasingly controlled in Russia, Belarusian authorities clearly did not have a grip.[1074]

And the leadership of Telegram, knowing this, readily promoted the internet service to protesters in Belarus. They pointed out that Telegram had already been tried and tested by Russian opposition movements and that the service could easily be accessed in Belarus, given the free economic space between the two countries.[1075] Lukashenka was aware of that danger, yet needed Russian support to counter it. So, he tried to sell the story of Telegram, and that of social media more broadly, as one of Western-sponsored

---

1071 Presented also by Greene, 2022: 90
1072 As observed by Bondarenko, 2020
1073 The inclusion of pro-Belarusian rhetoric was mentioned by observers, such as Khabamol'sk, 2020
1074 For details see Kuznetsova, 2023: 10-11
1075 Noted by Robertson, 2022: 148

subversion, undermining not only the political order of Belarus and Russia, but also the mental and, arguably, spiritual health of their populations.[1076] The Kremlin needed little encouragement to believe in the danger of infection from abroad. Russian state-controlled media, and the Russian ministry of foreign affairs, even spoke about a Polish threat to take military control of some Belarusian regions with Polish minorities, apparently inventing Polish elite statements for that purpose.[1077]

Beyond such peddling of unsubstantiated fears, as August progressed Moscow also increasingly tried to offer Minsk practical assistance in handling the unrest. Apart from social media, Lukashenka's regime also had problems from some printed media, circumventing domestic restrictions to have newspapers and other material created by sympathetic printing houses in Russia.[1078] As the authorities systematically suppressed its opposition media, increasing numbers of staff working for state-owned media resigned. Here, Moscow saw a chance for influence and sent its own media people to help. Regrettably, though, these propagandist soon misrepresented protesters to such an extent that their messages became scarcely credible and consequently had limited public resonance.[1079] More effective, perhaps, were the scarcely veiled threats by Putin that Russian military and other security forces could be sent to assist Lukashenka's attempts to bring order to the streets. While certainly capable of bringing fear to the Belarusian opposition, Putin's "offer" seemed just as much a threat to Lukashenka himself.[1080]

It is illustrative that the issue of CSTO intervention in Belarus was never seriously considered. The involvement of this or any other international organisation would have further highlighted Lukashenka's loss of domestic sovereignty. At the same time, from

---

1076 Details of Lukashenka's rhetoric are in Wijermars and Lokot, 2022: 138
1077 For Russian media reporting on such alleged threats, see Mukhin, 2020
1078 This being pointed out by Way, 2020: 21
1079 The paradox as noted by Giles, 2024: 162
1080 Officially, the leaders presented the matter as Lukashenka asking Russia for the potential of military assistance. In reality, the publication of such an offer was, as a minimum, closely coordinated with Putin and, likely, initiated by the latter. See also Roth, 2020

the Russian point of view, a multilateral solution was likely to diminish Russian control over the situation.[1081] Not that such control was in any way secured, as things stood by September. Admittedly, the brutality on the streets of Minsk and some other Belarusian cities was slowing down the challenge to Lukashenka. Even by the standards of prior Belarusian, or indeed Russian, official practice, tactics used in Belarus were grim.[1082] This was done to demolish opposition networks and to bind Belarusian security forces closer to the state. The violence also, however, served a political purpose. Lukashenka's Belarusian supporters now had reaffirmed that their leader would use any means to prevent the fall of the centre and the rise of alternative, oligarchic and potentially criminal challengers.[1083]

From a Russian perspective, the problem with such a presentation was twofold. First, Lukashenka was implicitly returning to the narrative of Belarus being somehow "purer" and "more orderly" than Russia, widely seen in Belarus–and in Russia–as a source of banditry under Yeltsin and, perhaps increasingly again, under Putin.[1084] Second, because the imagery offered by Lukashenka only worked with a select part of his population. The more his state became identified with violence, the better non-violent protesters could plausibly construct their movement–and their version of Belarus–around anti-violent norms of civil society, in contrast to the president and to Russia, as well.[1085] Then there was the feminine aspect of the Belarusian protest movement. With women being particularly prominent among the oppositional leadership (Tsikhanouskaya being foremost among these) their visibility and agency threatened regime-authorised understandings of the feminine in need of protection. And, by extension, threatened the understanding of the masculine protector.[1086]

1081 This question is partly considered by Libman and Davidzon, 2023: 1301
1082 For a summary of the viciousness presented, see also Situation, 2023
1083 An observation made by Hervouet, 2021: 67-68
1084 Not helped, obviously, by Russian public perceptions of inequality on the rise. See e.g. Walker, 2017
1085 See the helpful analysis on this by Korosteleva and Petrova, 2022: 146
1086 These points derived from Lozka and Makarychev, 2024: 7.

Prominent women within the Belarusian protest movement were aware of possibilities inherent in that threat. Sometimes, especially younger women could use their physicality in direct opposition to police. On camera, and sometimes while being dragged away to police vans, such women would rip masks of burly security personnel, forcing responsibility upon the latter.[1087] Thus, there were highly practical aims with such unmasking. However, the symbolics of female physical manifestation also derived from examples seen in Ukraine and, indeed, Russia. The organisation Femen had long carried out happenings in Ukraine and abroad, involving mostly younger women often partly naked and covered by fake blood and other symbols of violence.[1088] More famous, perhaps, had become Pussy Riot–the Russian female-fronted group which carried out in the Cathedral of Christ the Saviour in Moscow a public protest against the Putin leadership and its backers in the Russian Orthodox Church, following which several members were subjected to a trial seemingly based on accusations of blasphemy.[1089]

In particular among younger women such direct challenge to state-sponsored masculine ideology was transnational–uniting the supposed powerless in Russia, Belarus and Ukraine against the status quo. And if physical challenges were beaten down, cultural resistance could remain alive. The prime Belarusian example of such was arguably Nobel Prize winning author, Sviatlana Aleksievich.[1090] Other advocates of cultural-behavioural differentiation from Belarusian (and Russian) state practice turned further from reminders of physical trauma and force, instead using tropes of

---

1087 For an example of such activity, see Women, 2020. Notice the appearance of Belarusian national dress early in the video, the collective encirclement around the (clearly worried) police and the high-pitched battle cries pushing in on the thugs. And first of all, notice the bravery shown by slightly built women well aware of the potential risks to themselves of beatings and worse.

1088 A sense of the insurgent ideals from which Femen sprung can be seen in Aitkenhead, 2013

1089 The best work on that trial and its context remains Gessen, 2014

1090 Aleksievich was directly involved in criticising the Belarusian state and its violence but had a long history of telling stories of the officially marginalised such as in Alexievich, 2017

irony and humorous subversion to highlight not only the inhumanity of their opponents but also the frequent ridiculousness of the latter.[1091] It is important to stress, too, that while oppositional activity often centred around redefinition of the feminine (and thereby the political) it was not necessarily tied to women. Indeed, a famous proponent of non-violent resistance was Václav Havel–with links to his thoughts and 1989 frequent in Belarusian and Russian opposition activity.[1092]

Thus, even more so than their Russian counterparts, Belarusian resistance leaders sought to identify with the mass of protesters. Whereas the Russian opposition movement had often remained hierarchical in nature, centred on specific individuals (e.g. Navalny) in Belarus agency was handed over the public organisationally but also rhetorically.[1093] And that was quite a problem for Putin as well as for Lukashenka. If the dissatisfied in Russia and Belarus would come to operate as networks rather than hierarchies, they would be much more difficult to target, repress and remove. So, it was in both regimes' interest to stop and to discredit the Belarusian resistance.[1094] Hence the reference to "alien influences", which was briefly mentioned above. Certainly, such influence could be claimed from abroad. Statist media in Belarus and Russia (and sympathetic media in other countries, too) placed Tsikhanouskaya as a stooge of the West and well-known civil society sponsors like George Soros.[1095]

The claim of a malevolent West influencing proceedings in Belarus got support from some external observers. If not directly accusing secret services of nefarious activity, such support focused on the failure of the USA or Europeans to accommodate Russian and Belarusian viewpoints, instead seeking maximalist gains for an

---

1091 A prime example of such use of irony (albeit with a jester's bite attached) is from the incomparable Marharyta Liauchuk. For this, see Krasnaia, 2021
1092 On links between the uprising in Belarus and 1989, see also Bekus, 2021
1093 This is shown in very insightful detail by Gabowitsch, 2021: 3
1094 A useful conceptual introduction to the interplay between civil society and networks is Diani, 2015: chapter 1
1095 Thereby also offering an anti-Semitic tinge to the smears. See also Gentile and Kragh, 2022: 978-79

exclusivist definition of "democracy."[1096] A few foreign leaders might buy into that explanation. See, in particular, how Hungarian prime minister Viktor Orbán used the uprising in Belarus to present himself as an invaluable "mediator" between authoritarianism and democracy–between the "Russian world" (apparently including Belarus) and promoters of liberal democracy.[1097] Not many countries supported that Hungarian claim, though. In fact, a secondary consequence of longer-term importance became the split arising between Orbán and his Polish colleagues. Previously, these regimes had largely united against "EU overreach" and in favour of "illiberalism"–now, Poland became a foremost critic of Lukashenka's violence.[1098]

So, interestingly and unexpectedly among the fall-out of Russian support for Belarusian protest suppression was the splintering of what might have been a powerful alliance inside the EU offering sympathy when the increased assault on Ukraine began in 2022. Arguably another example of how Russian propensity for reaction, rather than action, damaged its strategic aims.[1099] Not that Lukashenka's administration, for that matter, was ready to consider long-term interests. Among the numerous victims of police arrests after the election were journalists from Russian media. Russian foreign minister Sergei Lavrov had to publicly remind Makei that the journalists did hold accreditation and should be released forthwith.[1100] Another Russian citizen who found himself in trouble with the Belarusian state was the head of the Russian Orthodox Church in Belarus, Metropolitan Pavel. After Pavel had expressed some concern about the treatment of protesters his foreign origins became expedient in having him relocated back to Russia.[1101]

It was telling, therefore, that the Belarusian "fight against foreign subversion" might rebound on relations with Russia. Notably,

---

1096 An example of such an argument is by Tsygankov, 2022a: 1567
1097 This is pointed out by Yanık and Subotić, 2021: 258
1098 As noted by Petrova and Pospieszna, 2021: 533
1099 That was a popular theme, too, within sections of the Russian press at the time. I have previously alluded to examples of this, another might be Tsipko, 2020
1100 A day prior, Russian foreign ministry spokeswoman Maria Zakharova issued similar sentiments in less temperate language. See also Ne Po-Bratski, 2020
1101 As shown by Elsner, 2023: 773

230 UNCANNY ALLIES

Tsikhanouskaya and the Belarusian opposition movement had largely refrained from that course, with the opposition leader largely conversing in Russian and staying away from divisive nationalist symbols while stressing the necessity of continued links to Russia.[1102] That message seemed to fit with the persistent rhetoric offered by Lukashenka over the years. Yet, as shown in the previous chapter, after 2014 the president had become ever more worried about Russian assaults on Belarusian sovereignty and his power base, talking earlier in 2020 about Russian aims to dissolve the Belarusian state.[1103] In fact, the run-up to the presidential election had been dominated by just such fears after the arrest in Belarus of more than 30 current and former members of the Wagner Corps, a Russian private military company. Russian authorities had quickly dismissed involvement and hinted at a Ukrainian plot against Russo-Belarusian relations.[1104]

And while Lukashenka might like that story the Russians could have been more reassuring. Some of the Russian pro-regime politicians who would later challenge the validity of Lukashenka's victory described the arrested militants as simply having been "on holiday"–very much the rhetoric used by Russia regarding the presence of Russian soldiers in eastern Ukraine.[1105] Not really what was needed for warmer bilateral relations. Russian commentators quickly picked up on the political implications of such arrests as well as on the way in which they–or at least the news presenting and detailing them–had been carefully stage-managed by Minsk.[1106] The question remained how the Kremlin would react to the arrests. On this point, some mainstream Russian media believed that the Belarusian leader might well have provoked unprecedented long-term distrust between the two countries by implicating

---

1102 This is the point also made by Bedford, 2021: 814
1103 That was noted by Way and Tolvin, 2023: 788
1104 Some subsequent reports indicated this might have a grain of truth. See also Larsen, 2023: 431
1105 These unfortunate comments were noted by Avakov and Zelenskaia, 2020
1106 A helpful example here is Khalip, 2020, who surmises that Lukashenka might have wanted to notify Russia and the West that he was very much the only wielder of sovereign violence in Belarus.

his neighbours in overtly criminal activity–a far cry from simple economic disputes.[1107]

There were even arguments among Russian opinion-makers that Lukashenka needed to be taught a lesson. It was pointed out, with some justification, that Lukashenka had a history of ignoring or deliberately challenging norms for friendly or simply tolerable relations with the West, but that the thuggish behaviour shown here demanded an answer.[1108] Even for those Russian observers who were less certain about the pre-meditated nature of the arrests widespread agreement existed that he now found himself in a difficult situation. Would he prosecute the mercenaries? Or send them to Ukraine from where a request for extradition had been sent? Neither would help Belarusian relations with Russia.[1109] The most helpful resolution, according to some Russian state media, might be if Russia and Belarus carried out joint investigation of the matter. After all, since private military companies were–ostensibly–outlawed in Russia, it would be in the official interest of the Russian government, too, to clarify the case.[1110]

Would Lukashenka compromise with Russia? Clearly, the president did whatever possible to keep the case high-profile until the election. Addressing security services on television, the Belarusian leader stated that the country was being targeted in hybrid warfare yet chose not simply to pin the blame on the West or Ukraine, naming Russia as another suspect.[1111] The Russians were, unsurprisingly, not pleased. Fears appeared that Lukashenka would hand over the mercenaries to Ukraine. If he did so, some commentators suggested, the Belarusian president would become a traitor to the "Russian world" by handing over what were effectively Russian "hostages" to Ukrainian "terrorists."[1112] Others saw some possibility that Lukashenka might resolve the situation without

---

1107 For that analysis and warning, see Rostovskii, 2020
1108 An opinion expressed within Mishutin, 2020
1109 This is the dilemma presented by Krivosheev and Shimanov, 2020
1110 For such an attempt at putting formal veneer on the bilateral talks which were already ongoing in private, see Bainazarov, 2020
1111 As reported in Idet, 2020
1112 These accusations were presented by Popov, 2020

carrying through such an extradition to Ukraine and noted that he had called for representatives of both Russian and Ukrainian law enforcements to appear for consultations in Minsk–a possibilities which such analysis also, tellingly, saw if the opposition somehow won the elections.[1113]

If the Russian government did not wish to humour Lukashenka, it could decouple from his regime. However, Russian commentators warned that an economic split might be quite expensive, as this would likely entail Lukashenka's refusal to pay debts and might hamper Russian energy transfers to Europe (let alone Russia's military presence in Belarus).[1114] So, it might be necessary for the Russian leadership to ensure Belarusian compliance by other means. Speculation began to circulate in Russian opposition media that military force could conceivably be used against Belarus if the crisis dragged on or even worsened following the expected re-election of a bullish Lukashenka.[1115] In terms of a counterfactual, it might have been interesting to witness bilateral developments had Lukashenka's re-election been seamless. As it were, the Belarusian regime needed help from Russia and, consequently, became much more amenable to wishes from the Kremlin. Before the mercenary spat and the election suggestions had existed Russia was losing Belarus.[1116]

Now, it seemed much more likely that Belarus could be kept, although Lukashenka was still expected to extract as high a price as possible for his favours. Could Russia convince him towards comprehensive, genuine integration of the countries? Perhaps, but would such a situation be acceptable to Belarusian society?[1117] Public opinion figures from early 2020 might offer Putin some hope. After all, in Belarus the personal popularity of the Russian president had proven to be higher than in most other post-Soviet states outside Russia, standing at over 70%. For a country not directly

---

1113 For all this, see Krivosheev, 2020
1114 Such potential difficulties were foreseen by Sergeev, 2020
1115 Considerations that military confrontation might be conceivable were expressed by long-term security expert Pavel Felgengauer. See Fel'gengauer, 2020
1116 An example of this was offered by Rostovskii, 2020
1117 All questions asked by Russian state media. See Radzikhovskii, 2020

controlled by him, this seemed an impressive figure.[1118] Around the same time, over 60% of respondents to another survey in Belarus had also agreed or strongly agreed with the proposition that they were part of a Russian civilisation. This, therefore, seemed to provide a useful base not only for closer bilateral relations, but for relations on Russian, civilisationist terms.[1119]

However, support for Russia at an identity level might not imply support at a practical and political level. The Belarusian government's long-standing rhetoric favouring relations with both Russia and the West had support from almost half of Belarusian respondents in a third survey, while almost 80% favoured an official status of neutrality for the country.[1120] In addition, it has to be reiterated that survey results were from early 2020–before the presidential election and Russian support for Lukashenka's repression. The surveys had also largely been carried out before the Covid-19 pandemic–that almost unprecedented health crisis which would put the governance of both Russia and Belarus under severe strain.[1121] Available data would later show that both countries, like most countries in the world, would suffer greatly from the disease. However, particularly during 2020 Russia and Belarus both presented data on infection and particularly death rates, which seemed relatively (or even highly) benign compared to data seen in the West.[1122]

Were the regimes in Moscow and Minsk providing manipulated figures? Perhaps, although it had to be considered that no standard method of measuring the health impact from Covid-19 existed. Until excess death rates would become available at a later date, differences in how countries measured what counted as death caused by Covid-19 significantly skewed comparisons.[1123] Also, the

---

1118 The data comes from O'Loughlin et al, 2024: 5
1119 This figure was taken from Bakke et al, 2023: 230, 240
1120 This information is from O'Loughlin and Toal, 2022: 51
1121 Socio-economic impacts of the pandemic will of course be the subject of research for years to come. For an overview of its global spread and casualty rates, see Covid-19 Dashboard, 2023
1122 As pointed out by Åslund, 2020: 542
1123 For the difficulties of measuring death rates caused by Covid-19, see also Msemburi et al, 2023

healthcare response of Russia and Belarus could have benefitted from the san-epid system of Soviet healthcare, which prioritised large-scale sanitary and epidemiological projects over individualised care and, thus, might have been rather poor at improving individual welfare yet was, in principle, appropriate for a mass event like Covid-19.[1124] However, despite such a potential advantage Russian and Belarusian pandemic responses suffered from political choices. Putin chose to delegate responsibility for healthcare measures to ministries and local authorities, likely to avoid receiving personal blame for failings. By doing so, however, the Russian effort became disjointed and often hampered by rumours and fears among the public.[1125]

In Belarus, Lukashenka was much keener to retain control. He did so partly since it corresponded to the nature of his regime, and partly in the hope of improving his personal image among Belarusians (and Russians) relative to that of Putin who could be indirectly portrayed as more aloof from the population at large.[1126] However, the pandemic soon became a liability for the Belarusian president due to his protracted efforts to ignore its effects. Having registered the first Covid-19 case in late February, the authorities did nothing to limit social interactions. Schools remained open and anyone taking precautions, like wearing masks, could even be ridiculed by the leadership.[1127] When Lukashenka did offer remedies against the disease he tended to fall back on nationalist tropes, like drinking vodka or visiting the sauna. This was done to reinforce his own image of masculinity but also to show his nation as a rural, even "pure" community in contrast to the urbanised (and, by extension, corrupt) Russia.[1128]

The Russian regime might have ignored Lukashenka's idiosyncrasies if not for the fact that the populations of the two

---

1124 A comprehensive view of Soviet healthcare is also offered by Grant, 2022
1125 Russian pandemic governance, and its contrast with Belarus, discussed by Leukavets et al, 2023: 550
1126 On the Russian president, Lukashenka probably had a valid point. See also Dettmer, 2020, on Putin's (and other autocrats') attitude to disease
1127 As mentioned by Aktürk and Lika, 2022: 5
1128 These tropes were shown by Givens and Mistur, 2021: 218

countries enjoyed freedom of movement. The Belarusian leader openly refused border closures from the outset, leaving Moscow concerned, since Belarus also (as mentioned before) in recent years had allowed increased visa-free travel from third countries.[1129] Understandably, the Russians then introduced some border control with Belarus, resulting in scathing comments from Minsk and increasingly irate criticism by Russian state newspapers and television over Lukashenka's policy of simply ignoring the healthcare catastrophe. In response, by mid-April Belarus introduced epidemic control for people arriving from Russia.[1130] Lukashenka's coup-de-grace in this propaganda war was to let Victory Day parades go ahead, while Putin had sensibly postponed the event in Russia. The Belarusian president made no secret of the fact that he saw this contrast as signifying Belarus as the true heir to the Soviet Union and victory in the Second World War.[1131]

I mention all of this to provide background to the Belarusian presidential election and the months following that. Not only did Lukashenka's neglect of public health help to fuel dissatisfaction with his rule, but relations with Russia were also more tense than previously given his repeated attempts to upstage his Russian counterpart.[1132] So, when the Belarusian president received Russian help after the election Moscow expected some gratitude. Earlier that summer Putin had carried through amendments to the Russian constitution in a public referendum, largely to overcome existing presidential term limits. Now, the Russian leadership were eager for Lukashenka to carry out his own constitutional changes.[1133]

1129 The problem of border control is touched on by Walker, 2023: 357-58

1130 Despite being a highly passive-aggressive move, made even more intolerable to Russia as it was medically justifiable, still provoked a quick Russian promise of increased collaboration with Belarus on the epidemic, as mentioned in Raseia, 2020

1131 A helpful overview of the contrasting approaches to Victory Day is provided by Melnichuk, 2020

1132 Relations were really not helped, either, by Lukashenka's attempts to blame domestic dissatisfaction on the machinations of Russian "oligarchs" — a charge met with a curt denial by Peskov, as reported by Peskov, 2020b

1133 Constitutional changes which Lukashenka himself had stressed as necessary, before any new elections in Belarus could be held. This was stated in Peremeny, 2020

236 Uncanny Allies

Why did Moscow promote such changes? Partly, it was realised that even small concessions might reduce the risk of further public unrest. More pertinently, though, the Russian elite realised that a weakening of Lukashenka's powers might allow for the strengthening of other Belarusian actors, easier to control.[1134]

By September, when his security forces had mostly gained control of public space, Lukashenka tried to slow down his earlier promotion of constitutional changes. Putin, though, would not agree to this and seemed to blindside his colleague by stating–at a mutual event–that these constitutional changes were certainly coming.[1135] The issue would remain contentious into 2021. As indeed would long-lasting economic disputes. If Lukashenka were to reverse his fortunes in the public eye, he had to retain Russian subsidies, particularly on the energy front, which had been threatened repeatedly in recent years. For this winter, though, Russia tided him over.[1136] And, of course, it also helped him to finally commission the first unit of the nuclear power plant at Astravets, which was connected to the electricity grid in November. This would not swiftly strengthen Belarusian energy independence or the economy, but it perhaps marked some sign of progress and modernity after a difficult year.[1137]

March towards the Edge

On September 17, 2021, the Russian state celebrated its collaboration with Nazi Germany during the Second World War. On social media the foreign ministry commemorated the 82nd anniversary of the Soviet invasion of Poland carried out following agreement with

---

1134 For the claim that Russia was now seeking to slow down integration with Belarus until society there had calmed down and Lukashenka could allow himself to be less defensive, see also Kamakin, 2020

1135 This being outlined by Suzdaltsev, 2023: 136

1136 However, the Belarusian president still also insisted that the Kremlin had to fulfil a decade-old promise to offer energy (particularly natural gas) to Belarus at the same price as it offered it to Russian customers–a request unlikely to be permanently solved anytime soon. See also Lukashenko, 2020

1137 Getting the nuclear power plant up and running is discussed by Nukusheva et al, 2021: 658

Adolf Hitler. How did Russia get to this point and what would it mean for Belarus?[1138] As we have previously seen, politicisation of history by Russia was nothing new. Parallels with the Second World War and the Cold War were easily drawn, while fears were presented by politicians and in Russian media that the country had to fortify itself against surprise or subversive assaults by the West.[1139] The foreign ministry accused Western actors, led by the USA, or seeking to remodel the entire post-Soviet region, dismember existing unity there and peel away layers of protection–territorial but primarily biopolitical–offered to the Russian core. While Russia faced that danger in all directions, its hold on Belarus might be particularly precarious.[1140]

After all, Belarusian borders had been secured less than 70 years before, following protracted, bloody warfare. Lukashenka had proven himself adept at highlighting alleged threats to his sovereignty from Poland and from Poles living in Belarus. During 2021, too, historically inflected disputes between those two countries continued.[1141] Belarusian state television readily accused its western neighbour of seeking to restore interstate borders as these had existed until the Molotov-Ribbentrop Treaty and subsequent invasion by Soviet troops in 1939. Therefore, Russian media and state narratives was always likely to gain official Belarusian support for commemoration of Stalin's "recovery" of peoples from interwar eastern Poland.[1142] And for more widespread attempts to put pressure on Poland. During the first half of 2021, Polish commentators worried that the Law and Justice government had weakened the country's ability to resist Russian and Belarusian pressure and had made the

---

1138 The tweet in question is MID Rossii, 2021. The date had been declared to be "National Unity Day" in Belarus by decree that summer
1139 For a summary of such attitudes, see also Sakhnin, 2021b
1140 An example of Russian foreign ministry rhetoric on the matter is Baikova, 2021
1141 Such as during the spring of 2021, over the arrest of Poles in Belarus charged with inciting ethnic hatred and promoting Nazism. On Belarusian coverage of that dispute, see also Osipov, 2021
1142 Suggestions by Belarusian media that Poland was motivated by territorial revanchism are seen in Glavnyi, 2021

238   UNCANNY ALLIES

country seem like a vulnerable chink in the armour of the EU and NATO.[1143]

Later in 2021 Russia and Belarus would seek to exploit such perceived Polish weakness through the high-profile issue of migration. Particularly since 2015, increased numbers of migrants in an economically challenged environment had made this issue subject of vigorous, often hostile debates across the EU member states.[1144] In few countries had the topic conjured as much animosity as in Poland, particularly under Law and Justice. It was unsurprising, therefore, that Moscow would now assist Minsk in pushing migrants from third countries across the Polish border, forcing Warsaw to either accept the newcomers or to return them forcibly in contravention of international law.[1145] As Poland and its allies understandably complained about this policy, the Russian government was quickly out to offer its support to Belarus. Quickly, the issue was liked to Western contemporary and historical behaviour which had created instability in the Global South and, therefore, facilitated conditions for today's migratory trends.[1146]

Subsequently, Russian commentators would largely offer support for such rhetoric and tactics. It was hinted, with some justification, that European decision-makers had been caught unawares by the renewed influx of migrants. There were suggestions, too, that Brussels might use the crisis as a excuse to further hostilities towards Belarus and Russia.[1147] Russian and Belarusian media became adept at emphasising the genuine humanitarian catastrophe developing along the Belarusian-Polish border while at the same time uncritically referencing the political framing of the crisis as presented by authorities in Moscow and in Minsk. In this way, the aim was to build domestic and foreign support for a favourable resolution.[1148] There were, though, some warnings that an impetuous

---

1143 Such sentiments were expressed by Rzeczkowski, 2021
1144 The broader issue of migration within contemporary European history is well covered by Gatrell, 2019
1145 The basics of that plan being outlined by Bachmann et al, 2023: 861
1146 This was the message offered by the foreign ministry in Brifing, 2021
1147 This was hinted at by Petrov, G., 2021a
1148 A prime example of such journalism, ethically justifiable and ethically suspect at the same time is Postnikova, 2021

Lukashenka might escalate the migrant crisis to the detriment of Russia. For instance, when the Belarusian president now warned that he might see increased Western sanctions as a reason to block energy deliveries to Europe, this was not in Russia's interest.[1149]

It was even suggested that such a problem existed within a wider pattern where Lukashenka increasingly dragged Moscow into conflict with the West. Whereas in previous years we witnessed the Belarusian administration fighting for a position of international neutrality, now—allegedly—it wanted to go further into confrontation than Russia did.[1150] And yet, was that really what was happening now? Let us step back for a moment to consider who was leading whom? Perhaps think about this as if of different tones being moved towards harmony. But who was the mover? And what would be the harmony?[1151] Earlier, I indicated that Russia more than Belarus had seen humans (rather than territory) as resources. Now, however, Belarusian policies were gaining a biopolitical edge, too. Think back to Lukashenka's corporal take on Covid-19—his implied (and explicit) belief that only un-real unhealthy people (i.e. not "real" Belarusians) had anything to fear.[1152]

Or, arguably, think back to the nature of the Belarusian regime itself. While its paternalistic brand had historically offered to secure the welfare of its people against external threats (a territorial point of view) paternalism also implied an elite monopoly on deciding the nature of the beneficial for the population.[1153] From there, the step to viewing the general public as consisting of "bare life" was not far. As an example, see the tax on "social parasites", which had been introduced (and vigorously challenged) in 2015 to punish those individuals allegedly sponging on the state. So, inherent

---

1149 That problem was outlined by Strokan', 2021
1150 As suggested by Rostovskii, 2021
1151 That particular image inspired by the genius interplay in act 1, scene 3 of Mozart's Don Giovanni. For a good recording of this, see Mozart, 2023, particularly from 38m 38s onwards and listen to the shifting tonality more than the libretto. Also see Brown-Montesano, 2007: 68
1152 As shown by Lukashenka's attitude to the Victory Day parade and, by his measures to combat the virus, as per Traktor, 2020
1153 On that conceptual logic, see also Kazharski and Makarychev, 2021: 2

individual rights were missing.[1154] In May 2021, Lukashenka demonstrated that attitude, once more, to international uproar. A civilian airplane, carrying passengers from Athens to Vilnius across Belarusian airspace, was forced to land by Belarus under false pretences in order for Belarusian security forces to arrest two passengers wanted for working with the political opposition.[1155]

Understandably, such modern piracy and blatant disregard for the safety of those foreign citizens who had been on the plane was immediately met by Western condemnation and suggestions of further sanction against the Belarusian regime. From Russia, however, came accusations of hypocrisy and a list of similar actions taken by other countries.[1156] That, too, became the message from some commentators and academics linked to the Russian state. Apart from making similarities to other cases (including, tellingly, activity by Ukraine) they argued that the severe Western reaction showed the importance of the people arrested and disappointment that Belarus was now placed unequivocally within the Russia-led camp.[1157] Lukashenka had only reduced his international options. As part of any consequences which would follow, it seemed clear from the outset that Western airlines would halt routes to Belarus. As the earlier vaunted visa-free regime had depended on foreigners flying in, rather than travelling by land, the country would be largely isolated apart from Russia.[1158]

To reinforce the partnership, Putin made sure to meet with his Belarusian counterpart a few days later in Sochi. Here, the two leaders were frequently photographed together. A material token of Russian support became a promise than a delayed loan of $500m would soon be released. Also, Russia stated it would increase flights to Belarus.[1159] Finally, the Russian authorities seemed to show imitation of their allies as a form of flattery. A few days after

---

1154 For the "parasite tax", see also Gray and Cameron, 2019
1155 A detailed account of how the plane was forced to land is offered by Eccles and Sheftalovich, 2022
1156 That official message was Kommentarii, 2021.
1157 See quotes on this in Poplavskii, 2021
1158 On the expected closing of airline routes, see Atasuntsev, 2021
1159 These details are found in Kulakevich and Kubik, 2023: 833

the Belarusians had forced the Ryanair plane to land, Russian authorities dragged an activist from Open Russia off an airplane. Admittedly, this plane was on the ground yet still ready for take-off.[1160] Yet the alignment between the Russian and Belarusian regimes was now clear. Did such alignment exist between the populations? Perhaps in parts. Certainly, among Russians Belarus remained a close ally. And even after the crackdown against protesters the previous year, 38% of Russian respondents still believed Lukashenka to be in the right.[1161]

Yet in Belarus ambiguity still reigned. In a pattern similar to that seen across the previous decade (and arguably a lot longer) respondents there still sought international neutrality for their country. By the summer of 2021, just over half viewed the EU positively, with the figure being similar for Russia.[1162] Perhaps unsurprisingly, it would seem that participation in post-election protests correlated significantly with attitudes towards Russia. Data taken among Belarusian protesters during 2020 and 2021 showed 43% viewing Russia as the biggest threat, while 41% wanted to join the EU and only 2% wanted to join Russia.[1163] Such figures should be placed in context, of course. As noted previously, for the vast majority of protesters Russia had been a relatively minor concern. During the half year after the election, and after Russia had openly propped up Lukashenka, less than 3% of protesters primarily cared about the international direction of Belarus.[1164]

However, even if Belarusians largely wanted to focus on domestic developments alignment with Russia now dragged the country into international tension. Even if that might not be in Russia's own interests — even if Moscow might have benefitted from having a neutral buffer between itself and the West — Russian elites no longer recognised that.[1165] The latter stressed that a

---

1160 That case is mentioned in Henry and Plantan, 2022: 288
1161 Such data being taken from Blackburn and Petersson, 2022: 306
1162 As shown through the research of Burlyuk et al, 2024: 914
1163 This information was gathered by Onuch and Sasse, 2022: 66
1164 For more on this, see Onuch et al, 2023: 756
1165 On the self-fulfilling prophecy of international animosity increasingly enveloping Russian political culture, see also Martynov, 2021

confrontation with the West was looming along Belarusian borders. In June, defence minister Sergei Shoigu stated as much when he directly accused NATO of conducting exercises to prepare for offensive operations near Belarusian borders in an international climate more dangerous than the Cold War.[1166] The Russian state stressed it was ready for confrontation. Some of its critics believed the state had prepared itself for a long time. That squandering to the tune of many trillions of roubles of energy-fuelled income had carried on for a couple of decades to shore up Russia's position in Belarus and across the world.[1167]

In general, this might be true—as shown previously in this book, the post-Soviet Belarusian economy had frequently been subsidised. However, by 2021 Moscow wanted more for its money. Recent events in Belarus, coupled with a slowing Russian economy, left the regime with some security concerns over the status quo.[1168] The Kremlin viewed foreign policy partly, sometimes primarily, as a means to retain power at home. This meant that Russian elites, like their Belarusian counterparts, would be inclined to see any Western criticism as attempts at subversion and that they tended to view public protests in post-Soviet countries as part of a coordinated movement.[1169] It was time to strike back. To place Belarusians in a more consistent, strategic framework for a decades long military standoff with NATO. In March, such a framework was given corporeal form with the bilateral Strategic Partnership Initiative, envisaging the creation of three joint military training centres in Belarus.[1170]

Around the same time, the Belarusian administration changed several military and security leaders. Local observers suggested that Lukashenka had chosen to bring in a new head of the general staff, new regional commanders and a new deputy defence minister

---

1166 Shoigu's remarks were linked to the Moscow Conference on International Security and its focus on Western military threat, as discussed at length in Alekseev and Moskovchenko, 2021
1167 On such an argument, see also Titova, 2021
1168 Something which was pointed out by Magid, 2021
1169 Such as during 2020 when protests in Belarus and the Russian Far East partly overlapped. See also Lipskii, 2021
1170 Further details on the Initiative are offered by Götz, 2024: 213

to improve chances of military integration with Russia.[1171] These appointments and the Initiative became opening salvos to increased military collaboration during the rest of the year. In September, the Zapad 2021 exercises received slightly less attention than had been the case four years prior, yet this time the parties were much more explicit about responding to perceived NATO aggression.[1172] Even more ominously, this time some troops deployed to Belarus as part of the exercises did not return to Russia after Zapad 2021 had officially finished, instead remaining in Belarus, presumably to work on further coordination of Belarusian forces within a Russian framework, but also developing a potential joint front for Ukrainians to worry about.[1173]

And worry the Ukrainians certainly did. After 2020, Russian elites had worked hard to separate Belarusians and Ukrainians. Scarcely veiled threats, by the state administration but also by allied institutions like the Russian Orthodox Church, told Belarusians that they could expect domestic radicalisation and conflict—as in Ukraine—if they did not obey their government.[1174] As before, Lukashenka reinforced that message whenever possible. More noteworthy, however, was that he now veered away from the role of mediator in the Russo-Ukrainian war to a role of Russian supporter. No longer did the Belarusian president hint Russia was a party to the war, but instead urged parties within Ukraine to negotiate.[1175] Lukashenka was happy to continue hosting negotiations in Minsk but not by endangering relations with Russia. And he explicitly ruled out making Belarus develop in a way similar to Ukraine— with increased access for European goods and individuals—even though this, allegedly, was what the Western countries had tried to force him to do.[1176]

1171 Something also indicated in Khodasevich, 2021b
1172 See, for instance, Putin's comments on the matter as reported in Glava, 2021
1173 That development after Zapad 2021 was also noted by Gustafson et al, 2024: 402-03
1174 Patriarch Kirill's words on this were reported by Patriarkh, 2021
1175 As seen, for instance, in the summary from Rabochii, 2021
1176 Lukashenka was quoted on this in Lukashenko, 2021b

244 UNCANNY ALLIES

That isolationist streak was novel. Belarus had always resisted political implications accompanying the Eastern Partnership, for instance. Yet previously the regime had stressed that economic collaboration should not depend on political attitudes. Tellingly, even by 2021 World Bank data still rated Belarus much higher than Russia on its ability to trade across borders.[1177] Until now, therefore, the regime in Minsk had kept alive a foreign policy previously espoused by Russia, too. A foreign policy largely centred on economic priorities and a traditional understanding of state sovereignty with states in the international landscape being potentially positive-sum competitors, rather than necessarily zero-sum enemies.[1178] This was no longer the way in Russia viewed the world and, as a geographical neighbour with an intertwined identity, Belarus could not be allowed to diverge. And since the Russian project, as we saw above, did not overly appeal to the Belarusian population, Lukashenka was increasingly isolated from his people and dependent on Russia.[1179]

Such dependence seemed destined to grow. Because of Lukashenka's relative weakness, perhaps, but more because of the Manichean worldview emanating from Moscow. With increasing candour, in his public appearances Putin espoused the view that domination and autocracy not only mirrored the way the world worked but that way it should work.[1180] Clearly, something Schmittian had come to rule in Russia. But whereas the German had primarily been concerned with command of the state of emergency within the domestic polity, the Russian regime also sought command of the state of emergency abroad. Making that link was most straightforward when this abroad was close to home — like Belarus.[1181] And that gets us to the article. That article. Which Putin penned in July of 2021, espousing the "historical unity" of Russians,

---

1177 For World Bank data, see also Defraigne, 2021: 666
1178 This idea being derived from the framework developed in Wendt, 1999: chapter 6
1179 On the difficulties faced by the "Russian project" in Belarus, see also Sakhnin, 2021a
1180 The development in Putin's public persona is also discussed by Gol'ts, 2021
1181 For an example of scholarship linking Carl Schmitt to Russian foreign policy, see also Auer, 2015

Belarusians and Ukrainians—and the spiritual unity, too. With the western parts of the two latter countries subject to alien invasions and cultural subjugation by the Poles.[1182]

Subsequently, Putin's article has been widely described by analysts as providing the ideological underpinnings for Russia's February 2022 full-scale invasion of Ukraine. In that context, a frequent theme has been the importance of Ukraine (and, to a lesser extent, Belarus) for Russian self-perception particularly in its imperial guise.[1183] Scholars Western, Ukrainian and Russian have outlined in detail the multiple intrinsic links which Ukraine and Russia are reported to have in official or at least public discourse, before doing a fine job of critically analysing or completely demolishing the nature of those links and their implications as claimed by Putin and his allies.[1184] A well-meant and, indeed, a necessary job. Yet missing the bigger picture. Under Putin, particularly from 2012—and, even more so, from 2018—Russia pushed foreign policy aggression not for a specific aim or as a specific reaction, but as an essential process. Violence and its self-enforcing reproduction became the nature of the beast.[1185]

This had implications for Ukraine, but certainly also for Belarus. If Russia was to be increasingly militarised then a Belarus within its orbit would have to develop similarly. A new Russian national security strategy was introduced with the West presented as a threat not because of what it did but what it stood for.[1186] With the Russian world standing alone, isolated (despite professions of friendship with countries like China and India) due to a damaging combination of messianic grandiosity and persecutory inferiority now the basis not only for the national security strategy but for Russian self-image. Into this world Belarus was being dragged.[1187] Into

---

1182 The text of this article can be found in Putin, 2021
1183 On the link between the sentiments expressed in the article and the full-scale invasion, see also Reid, 2022
1184 A recent, impassioned example of this approach is Zygar, 2023
1185 Some perceptive observers of the Russian regime have depicted this well–Sorokin, 2018, is a useful example
1186 As pointed out by Petrov, G., 2021b
1187 The nature of Russian (foreign) policy identity was similarly explored by Kunadze, 2021

this world the Belarusian regime was being dragged. The Russian leadership pushed Lukashenka to fully commit to their cause through the politically very important issue of Crimea. By the middle of 2021, the Russian presidential administration was openly pushing for Belarusian recognition that the peninsula belonged to Russia.[1188]

Previously, the Belarusian president had been circumspect about Crimea. While acknowledging Russian command of that region, Lukashenka noted Russian businesspeople were loath to engage there. Perceiving correctly that such reticence stemmed from fear of international sanctions, the Belarusian leader under such circumstances saw no reason while he should risk the latter.[1189] By late 2021, Lukashenka did eventually take that risk. Speaking on Russian television, the president not only reiterated previous comments that Crimea belonged to Russia *de facto* but also that it belonged to Russia *de jure*. As such, he supported inter-state violence as a legitimate means to change state borders in the modern world.[1190] That was a change from the Belarus of old. The principle of sovereign inviolability had not only underpinned Lukashenka's autocratic governance but also his national identity. Tellingly, he tried to cling on to such a self-image a bit longer — claiming he had prevented international interventions and "world war" by holding out the previous year.[1191]

At the same time, on the anniversary of his disputed re-election, Lukashenka also stated to the cameras that Belarus would never abandon its sovereignty. That integration with Russia would continue, but that this had to be based on equality between the parties. That supranational means to do so were unlikely to work.[1192] A month later the prime ministers of Russia and Belarus signed 28 programmes for integration. These programmes were overwhelmingly connected to economic sectors and seemed designed to tie Belarus not only into the Russian economy but also into the social

---

1188 Russian state rhetoric in this matter is detailed in Khodasevich, 2021c
1189 Lukashenka's attitude being detailed in Hansbury, 2023: 220, 300
1190 The televised comments by Lukashenka were mentioned by Giusti, 2023: 1245
1191 Such comments were presented in Belarusi, 2021
1192 All of which was mentioned in Lukashenko, 2021a

welfare policies presented by the Kremlin.[1193] This development indicated that Russo-Belarusian integration was very much back on the agenda for two main reasons. First, because the programmes presented — while leaving much work to be done — were more specific than previous high-flying declarations. Second, because precisely economics and socio-economic affairs had always been central to Lukashenka's legitimacy.[1194]

At the same time, parts of the Russian press noted that the Belarusian leadership might have signed on to these programmes in the hope that the EU or other Western actors might appear with a counteroffer to reduce or remove Russia's increased advantage in Belarus.[1195] If so, Minsk had lost the gamble. The Belarusian economy, and its social stability (such as it was after 2020) was endangered not simply by sanctions but also by inability or unwillingness to carry out economic reforms. Any actor now assisting the country would take advantage of that situation, as Russia now prepared to do.[1196] In that context, it was quite right to note — as analysts did over subsequent days and weeks — that the Russian leadership remained circumspect about the speed with which Russo-Belarusian state integration would now take place. The more important point being, however, that such speed (or lack thereof) did not matter if the direction was set.[1197]

So, this is the story (is it not?) of Russian triumph — of how Moscow methodically reeled in its smaller neighbour, eventually using economic and political means to bind Belarus as closely as was the intent for Ukraine. And for Ukraine, of course, Russia and Belarus could now promote military integration, too.[1198] The following month, Belarus extended the lease by Russia of its military facilities in the country. This was quite similar to what Russia had done in 2010 when extended lease of Black Sea Fleet facilities in

---

1193 The declaration on these programmes is Sovmestnoe, 2021
1194 Similar analysis was expressed by Panteleev, 2021
1195 This was suggested, for instance, by Khodasevich, 2021a
1196 That outlook, and the lack of Western interest in competing for the attention of the Belarusian government, is outlined in Boiko et al, 2021
1197 For an analyst noting that Russia was slightly downplaying prospects of integration, see Shraibman, 2021
1198 This prediction being made at the time by Karbalevich, 2021

Ukraine and sent a signal — to Belarusians and the world — that Moscow would again fight to protect its bases.[1199] Soon, the Russo-Belarusian Union State updated its military doctrine. The two regimes viewed the international landscape — and its sources of threat — in a similar manner. The doctrine also used phrases indicating that war might be imminent. That doctrine became the basis for the joint military exercises immediately before Russia's full-scale invasion of Ukraine in 2022.[1200]

Russian triumph over Belarus, therefore. Or perhaps not? In that literary masterpiece by Truman Capote, *In Cold Blood*, while attempting to understand the murderers an important point is that they were mutually constitutive. That neither would have killed without the other's presence. Such toxic mutual reinforcement can be seen in our case, too.[1201] Remember how this section started. With the Russian state praising its collaboration with Nazi Germany. Collaboration necessary to protect Belarus and the Russian World. Belarus is not something to gain for Russia, it is something to lose. And that loss, should it occur, would leave the core of "Russia" — the land and the idea — vulnerable.[1202] So, Belarus must be neutralised, right? Well, no — as I indicated above. If Russia simply wanted protection, it could fortify its borders. It could retreat into military, political — perhaps even economic isolation. Historically, such a strategy has had some supporters in Russia. Some believers that isolation brought purity.[1203]

But Putin's Russia did not seek isolation, did not seek purity. Whether it had ever done so was doubtful. Instead, the state had constructed an identity in which conflict, danger and the constant risk of imminent catastrophe were not simply tools to keep the

---

1199 The wider military framework within which that happened was described in Tikhonov, 2021

1200 The adoption of this updated doctrine is mentioned in Douglas, 2023: 860

1201 This is indicated in Capote, 2000: e.g. 247, 291-94

1202 The historical background for Russian fears for its western flank were outlined earlier in this book. In contemporary thinking, such fears have been popularised by "geopolitical" thinkers, such as Aleksandr Dugin. See also Clover, 2022: perhaps particularly chapter 11

1203 Such thinking of course potentially linked to messianism. For a conceptual link between purity and the political, see also Douglas, 2002: particularly chapter 7

population in check but were essential elements of this identity.[1204] So, Belarus was important for Russia. For cultural and historical reasons, certainly, but also because Belarusian lands brought Russia all the way in where it mattered. All the way into the centre of Europe where great power identities had been won and lost in imperial days. Moscow wanted to win. But it had to play.[1205] And while it is accurate, therefore, to say that Belarus helped Russia to play this game of great powers it is equally accurate to say that Belarus in this action enabled Russia to enact self-harm on numerous parameters. To claim that Russia could have gone in no other direction is, unquestionably, a fallacy.[1206]

Agency matters. And the agency of Putin and Lukashenka, of the Russian and Belarusian regimes, had now brought their countries, and the European continent, to the brink of war. Was this where they wanted to go? Or had they been dragged unwillingly there by a world seemingly prizing separation over unity?[1207] I do not think so. In Russia, Putin was of a generation raised under Brezhnev and Andropov, as the Soviet communist state became the Soviet security state. While far from inevitable, it is not surprising that the Russian president, largely surrounded by elites from that same generation, viewed glory in martial terms.[1208] For the Belarusians it was admittedly different. Lukashenka had viewed himself as a local leader, building fiefdom on a tale of stability. Pushing away "alien pollutants" like dissidents or disease. Russia had been the chosen ally of convenience. Yet that alliance had become ever

---

1204 How this began to be seen in Russian popular culture even before Putin's return to the presidency is intriguingly demonstrated by Carleton, 2010

1205 With a friendly thought to Belkar Bitterleaf and Burlew, 2008. The point I make in the main text here also links back to my earlier reference to Buranelli and Russia in the nineteenth century. See further thoughts on the matter of Russian international status by Šćepanović, 2024

1206 Plenty of analyses, scholarly or otherwise, have presented Russia as bound to follow age-old patterns in foreign policy–because of the perceived nature of Russia or because of the perceived nature of the international system. An example of the former is Kotkin, 2016. An example of the latter is Mearsheimer, 2015. Unsurprisingly, this book vehemently disagrees with both of those analytical angles.

1207 That is a *leitmotif* running through Hill, 2018, and many other, lesser accounts.

1208 On this, see also the intriguing hint at the dynamic nature of security thinking under Andropov in Adamsky, 2023: 166

more entangled and now stability was about to come crashing down.[1209]

The Reckoning

"A więc wojna! Вранці Путін оголосив про ведення спеціальної військової операції на Донбасі. Z dniem dzisiejszym wszelkie sprawy i zagadnienia schodzą na plan dalszy. Росія збйснила удари по нашій військовій інфраструктурі та наших прикордонниках. Całe nasze życie publiczne i prywatne przestawiamy na specjalne tory — weszliśmy w okres wojny. У багатьох містах України було чутно вибухи. Cały wysiłek narodu musi iść w jednym kierunku. Ми вводимо воєнний стан по всій території України. Wszyscy jesteśmy żołnierzami. Слава Україні. Musimy myśleć tylko o jednem — walka aż do zwycięstwa."[1210]

This has nothing to do with us. No one from our military is involved in the fighting. We are just trying to protect our citizens, our land. Are we our brother's keeper? Such, or thereabouts, was the message of the Belarusian government a few weeks after Russia unleashed death across Ukraine.[1211] After all, Lukashenka had warned — had he not — that conflagration was coming. That the European continent was close to all-out conflict affecting every state. And all because of the irresponsible behaviour of the "others". Those who were pushing Ukraine to go far beyond, to claim far more, than it should have rightly considered.[1212] Yet those warnings were not heeded. Very soon, Belarus would find itself on the frontline of warfare by volume unprecedented in Europe since the Second World War. How did it get there? Did Russia drag Belarus to its side? Did Belarus try to resist? What was the endgame for either separately or for both?[1213]

1209 Recently, Lukashenka had of course also gone along with Putin's belligerence against Ukraine in an attempt to diverge Russia from focusing on constitutional and other domestic changes in Belarus. See also Whitmore, 2021

1210 Polskie, 2023; Rossiia, 2022a

1211 See for instance the televised message from a representative of the Belarusian ministry of defence, on Khotiat, 2022

1212 The Belarusian president noted this shortly before Russia's all-out war in Ukraine following talks with Putin. See My Vpervye, 2022

1213 This is not the book to give a blow-by-blow account of Russia's war in Ukraine–nor could such be done satisfactorily while the war remains ongoing. For specific military updates on a daily basis, see Ukraine, 2024

Warnings of conflict had come not just from Belarus, but from the USA, too. They, though, expected aggression from Russia with Belarusian aid. In a mirror image of fears from Zapad 2017 concern centred on Russo-Belarusian military exercises and tens of thousands of Russian troops remaining in Belarus, near Ukraine's northern border and Kyiv.[1214] The idea that Belarus held an increasingly special place in Russian foreign policy strategy was underlined also by the appointment, in January, of a new ambassador to Minsk — Boris Gryzlov. Formerly interior minister and head of United Russia, Gryzlov now came from the post of parliamentary speaker.[1215] He was a trusted, senior ally of the Kremlin. And he arrived in Minsk when the Russian government had just seen rejected by the US and NATO wide-ranging blueprints for European security. The Kremlin wanted clear recognition of its special status, its dominance in a neighbourhood where NATO would not expand or militarise.[1216]

That request was not accepted by the Americans or by NATO. It came down to different types of power with which the two sides believed themselves to be endowed. Although a military organisation, NATO saw itself as adept at wielding institutional power, enmeshing Russia and other third parties in diplomacy, declarations and agreements.[1217] The Russian leadership, on the other hand, wanted recognition of their hard security concerns — and capabilities. Over the winter of 2021-22, when it became clear that no such recognition was forthcoming — Russian commentators warned that a war of nerves was underway, even if they did not yet suspect full-scale to break out.[1218] If anything dramatic or destructive were to happen, the Russian point of view clearly was that this would be the fault of the adversary. That military options were not only available but actively considered by the Russian leadership. That

---

1214 On that worry, see also Atzili and Kim, 2023: 658

1215 Gryzlov's appointment was covered in Boris, 2022

1216 An introduction to the different positions on this held by Russia and NATO is in Gasiuk, 2022

1217 A classic account of how such institutional power was wielded by NATO relative to Russia is Pouliot, 2010

1218 As discussed for instance in Chernenko, 2022

Moscow would not sit idly by while NATO reinforced its positions along Russian borders.[1219]

In retrospect, the possibility of a full-scale Russian attack on Ukraine should have been more widely considered. Not only were Russian military manoeuvres clearly pointing in that direction, but so, too, was Russian rhetoric. Lavrov himself argued that NATO had lost touch with reality and had sabotaged the peace process in Ukraine for years.[1220] Time was clearly running out. Russian media suggested NATO troops were, and would continue to be, deployed to the eastern flank of the organisation in ever increasing numbers. And Ukrainian forces were clearly getting stronger year by year, making any future clash with them increasingly costly for Russia.[1221] Among Russian observers there was much attention offered to the fact that Western diplomatic personnel was now being withdrawn from Ukraine. Some suggested this was simply another political step, with Western countries escalating the crisis without wanting to make an unambiguously aggressive step against Russia.[1222]

Others, perhaps more hopefully, viewed confusion among European countries, in particular. And indicated that whereas the USA had clearly decided to increase pressure on Russia, its European allies — while broadly sympathetic to that aim — were not sure how to accomplish that aim, for instance through sanctions.[1223] In addition, and perhaps most tellingly, some Russian observers were constructing the narrative that any military conflict — should it come — would be in American, but not in Ukrainian interest. That the Ukrainians, in fact, very much preferred to stay with the status quo, avoiding unnecessary bloodshed and inching towards some resolution between domestic interest groups.[1224] I mention all of this not to agree with it or, indeed, to claim anything about intent

---

1219 All of which is touched on by Postnikova and Baikova, 2022
1220 Following reporting by Petrov, G., 2022
1221 A problem warned about in Moiseev, 2022
1222 The implication, for instance, offered by Lakstygal and Mishutin, 2022
1223 This potential for internal conflict among Western decision-makers was touched on by Strokan', 2022
1224 As was mentioned by comments to Bainazarov, 2022

by the commentators. Russian rhetoric on Ukraine had been mendacious at least since 2014. Notably, to suggest that Ukrainians might be able to accept the status quo deliberately ignored the thousands of frontline deaths over the preceding decade.[1225]

Or to claim that Russia had not been an essential part of the bloodshed. So, there is no agreement with the Russian position here. There is, however, a focus on the narrative building up to full-scale warfare and, particularly, with the Belarusian position herein. Did Minsk add to tension or try to reduce it?[1226] Here, we can certainly refer to specific, seemingly unambiguous comments indicating that Lukashenka was with the Russians, come what may. On television, in early February the president made clear that upcoming military exercises with Russia aimed to scare the Ukrainians (and to scare NATO, as well, if required).[1227] And if a war occurred, the Ukrainians would not stand a chance. Fighting would last only a few days, with Kyiv unable to offer meaningful resistance and its supposed Western allies being too slow and ineffective to make a difference. That, of course, could be seen as a warning to Baltic States, too.[1228]

And yet, the more meaningful message to take away from the Belarusian pre-war stance does not relate to specific predictions. It relates, instead, to the regime's normalisation of and identification with a state of war. Whereas before Belarus had been presented as an object of sovereign defence, now it was a subject of sovereign offense.[1229] See, too, how that Belarus had presented itself in the context of unrest breaking out in Central Asia at the beginning of 2022 when Belarusian forces were dispatched to Kazakhstan.

1225 For a reminder of this, see also the perceptive–frequently heartbreaking– Khromeychuk, 2021

1226 A question made no less intriguing by Lukashenka's comments in late 2021 when he assured listeners both that Belarus was not seeking war with Ukraine and that Belarus might join Russia in an attack on Ukraine to defend Donbas, despite both Russia and Belarus at that time officially viewing Donbas as part of Ukraine. See also O Vragakh, 2021

1227 See also the Belarusian president's comments in Belarus', 2022

1228 Lukashenka's comments on this were stated to infamous Russian TV-host Vladimir Solovev and reported by Ukraina, 2022

1229 The gist of a novel Belarusian narrative around the normality of war is the subject of Karbalevich, 2022

Admittedly, this followed an official request by the latter to the CSTO, yet previously Minsk had stated clear unwillingness to participate in such missions.[1230] Concerned Belarusian observers saw the mission as another sign that Belarusian foreign policy had become beholden to Russian interests after 2020. Whereas previously the Belarusian president had been quick to state that unrest abroad never concerned his country, even if in a neighbouring state like Ukraine, now he got involved.[1231]

Yet listen to the wide-ranging, and more ominous conclusions drawn by the chairman of the Belarusian Helsinki Committee Aleh Hulak. He would soon pass away but here managed to speak of consequences outlasting him — of a region and world where armed intervention was conducted by autocracies against "external threats" claimed and defined by them.[1232] Lukashenka, perhaps inadvertently, quickly confirmed that attitude and its regional relevance. Referring to the arrival of the CSTO to quell unrest in Kazakhstan, the Belarusian president suggested neighbouring Uzbekistan might also like to join the organisation as insulation against future dangers. Uzbek commentators, unsurprisingly, saw that as a veiled threat.[1233] But that January Lukashenka was not really talking to them. Or even to the Ukrainians. Instead, he was talking to the Russians and to himself, speechifying the idea of permanent threat and, perhaps, permanent warfare. To protect himself against enemies foreign and domestic, for sure. But also to reconstruct meaning.[1234]

As Russian troops spilled into Ukraine from Russian and Belarus territory international condemnation and countermeasures

---

1230 For the declaration that Belarusian troops would be sent to Kazakhstan, see also Ofitsial'noe, 2022

1231 That was the argument presented, for instance, by Hurnevich, 2022

1232 As mentioned in Prinimat', 2022

1233 The spat escalated quickly. By mid-January Uzbek president Shavkat Mirziyoyev more than hinted Lukashenka should keep quiet and that Tashkent could handle challenges alone. See also Etarli, 2022

1234 Soon, when Lukashenka claimed that Russia had struck pre-emptively against Ukraine, that Kyiv (and NATO) had prepared to attack Russia and Belarus, he linked that directly to the Second World War. The message was clear–the war had never truly finished, and the mistake of 1941 would not be repeated. On this, see Ne My, 2022

quickly followed. Sanctions against the two aggressor countries were led by America and the EU, soon striking not only Belarusian defence and financial sectors but the economy and the elite more broadly.[1235] Existing sanctions, particularly from the EU, were adjusted in a manner championed by Latvia to more specifically target individuals and to make it more difficult for Russian and Belarusian citizens to have ownership of, or significant involvement in, defence and other sensitive economic sectors in the West.[1236] For Russia and Belarus, the invasion had symbolic costs, too. Almost immediately after full-scale warfare against Ukraine had begun, the International Olympic Committee called for all international sporting events to be moved from the two countries and for participants from those countries to be excluded from competitions, wherever possible.[1237]

Would such pressure work? In the longer run, perhaps, but for now the Belarusian regime seemed determined, or maybe destined, to support the Russian position. Partly, that could be down to the sanctions-regime itself. A restricted flow of Western goods to Russia could see an increase in the market share there of Belarusian producers.[1238] More fundamentally, if Russia was at least partly cut off from normal access to global trade the leadership and its allies in the business world would have to depend on informal mechanisms, understandings and trust. The Kremlin hardly trusted Lukashenka yet knew his autocratic centralised governance ensured some predictability absent formal rules.[1239] So, the Belarusian president could be fairly confident Russia would do little to challenge his sovereignty, as opposed his suzerainty. Against such potential benefits of the war, Belarus and Russia also faced significant

---

1235 Further details on sanctions can be found in United, 2022: 622-23
1236 As mentioned by Herranz-Surralles, 2024: 16-17, 31
1237 This was detailed in Kobierecka and Kobierecki, 2023: 1329, 1333
1238 That unintended consequence of trade embargoes was pointed out by Mahlstein et al, 2022: 3352
1239 Regarding agricultural goods, that point was also indicated by Dragneva and Hartwell, 2022: 99

problems. Primarily, after it became clear that the war had no end in sight the lack of a realistic aim was clear.[1240]

Ironically, therefore, it could be said that Putin had learnt from Lukashenka — learnt all the worst lessons, that is. Learnt that issues and those with whom one interacted should just be strung along, solutions delayed, reforms avoided. Just keep doing what you are doing, and the world will adapt. Well, it no longer did.[1241] And we had seen, again, the influence of the uncanny. An increasingly autocratic Belarus had offered Moscow a model of how to resist Western expectations of normative alignment. An increasingly belligerent Russia had offered Minsk a model of how to turn such resistance into violence. They had succeeded together and would now fail together.[1242] Sensing the danger, as the fighting kept grinding on and Russian forces woefully underperformed Lukashenka periodically made clear his impatience. By early May, he was complaining about how slow Russian operations had been while at the same time alleging his own role in providing the prospect of a negotiated solution.[1243]

At that point, Lukashenka had, indeed, used media appearances to stress how the conflict had to be settled peacefully. When making that argument, the president had returned to the incarnation of Belarus as inherently peaceful and neutral — in so far as it argued any differences could be settled without the total subjugation of either party.[1244] Unlike the Russian leadership, which insisted on talking about its "special military operation", Lukashenka was ready to call Russian activity in Ukraine a war. And to stress, at home and to Western press, that no one would benefit from a

---

1240 That Lukashenka, at least officially, had expected a brief war was suggested above. For expectations in Russia–and most of world–that Ukraine would quickly lose, see also Eckel, 2022

1241 A similar point is made in a scathing, yet persuasive manner by Gould-Davies, 2022: 40, 42

1242 This is where the "black knight" assumption falls short–influence between putative patron and client is mutual. Just as a company's branding has internal as well as external resonance. For an example of analysis involving the "black knight" assumption see Kulakevich and Augsburger, 2021

1243 These points were brought up by Ramani, 2023: 298

1244 One example of Lukashenka's rhetoric on this point is from Belorusskii, 2022

widening conflict and that nuclear weapons really should not be used.[1245] That last statement was more noteworthy than it sounded, as it came following persistent Russian discourse promoting use of such weapons. Throughout the year, the Belarusian leader would repeatedly bring up the danger of a nuclear clash. Sometimes by hinting that Russians decision-makers might be ready to use such weapons rather than lose in Ukraine.[1246]

That threat, popular too among some Russian media personnel and even government representatives, did have limited success abroad. It was likely to have been one factor holding back more direct American intervention in Ukraine, while some analysts promoted the nuclear risk as a legitimate reason to override the suzerainty of Ukraine and neighbouring states.[1247] However, such ponderings did little to end the war. So, Lukashenka's regime increasingly stressed the possibility that the West, particularly the Americans, planned to use nuclear weapons not only against Russia, but against Belarus, as well. Allegedly accompanied by small groups of special military forces taking over provincial cities.[1248] That claim appeared to tally with the long-standing distrust shown particularly towards Polish policies. In May and again in June Lukashenka warned outright that the Poles, with American help, were planning to assault Belarus. The president then used that unsubstantiated possibility as a reason why Belarusian forces should not be moved to Ukraine.[1249]

A more likely danger to Lukashenka's regime, though, would be his own population among whom involvement with Russia's war in Ukraine unsurprisingly proved unpopular. During the spring, opinion polls showed that 70% of respondents disagreed with the use of Belarusian territory by Russian troops attacking Ukraine, while 40% opposed the war overall.[1250] With such figures

---

1245 See here a summary of Lukashenka's long interview with AP at Phillips, 2022
1246 Such was hinted, for instance, in Lukashenko Otvetil, 2022
1247 And, likely, Ukrainian sovereignty, too, since anything less than unconditional military victory for Ukraine would almost certainly leave parts of its territory in Russian hands. For analysis in this vein, see e.g. Doyle, 2022: 218
1248 On that warning, see also V KGB, 2022
1249 Such reasoning by Lukashenka was outlined in Miarka, 2024: 90
1250 The survey data can be found in Korosteleva and Petrova, 2023: 882

appearing under conditions of severe political and policing repression, it was likely resistance to the war could be even higher. Even before Russia had initiated its full-scale invasion, in January hackers and other saboteurs had damaged Belarusian infrastructure to delay its use by Russia.[1251] After the invasion had begun, the Belarusian political opposition sought alliance with Ukraine. Arguing that both Belarus and Ukraine were victims of Russia occupation, albeit brought on by different means, Sviatlana Tsikhanouskaya claimed that not only she but many other Belarusians actively damaged Russian war efforts, materially or through counterpropaganda.[1252]

Pointedly, like Lukashenka Tsikhanouskaya, too, viewed the war as intrinsically connected to the fate of Belarusian politics. Unlike him, however, she viewed brave Ukrainian resistance and future establishment of improved post-war governance as examples to follow essential for the progress of Belarus. Gone was any of the equivocation towards Russia seen in 2020.[1253] Her words tended towards the measured and succinct. Other Belarusian commentators were more openly agitated. Decades of promises about stability and safety for Belarusians had now been jettisoned for reasons that had never been satisfactorily explained. Not only ordinary people, but also Belarusian elites might soon query benefits of such unwavering support for Moscow.[1254] And some would do much more than query. On the battlefield began to turn up not just individual Belarusians fighting for Ukraine but also entire contingents proudly identifying themselves as Belarusian. One well-known example became Pahonya, a group which explicitly linked Lukashenka's fall to a Russian defeat and also argued for "de-Russification" of Belarusian society.[1255]

1251 That early Belarusian involvement in anti-war efforts was described by Brantly and Brantly, 2024: 490
1252 Tsikhanouskaya stated this in Tikhanovskaia, 2022
1253 On the Belarusian opposition's unequivocal distancing from Russia, see also Jalalzai and Jurek, 2023: 125
1254 Such were the thoughts expressed in Bagdzevich, 2022
1255 Pahonya is detailed much further by Josticova and Aliyev, 2024: 213

Precisely that, which Russia had long claimed was the danger inherent in a "Ukrainianised" Ukraine. And now, seemingly, growing out of Lukashenka's back garden seeking to strangle him. That danger was not likely to diminish while the war was ongoing. And Belarus was bound not only to the war but to a militarised Russia.[1256] Apart from the presence of Russian soldiers in Belarus, and the informal means undoubtedly used to keep Lukashenka (relatively) in check, Belarus had been linked to Russia through several recent, formal initiatives. In the wake of the invasion, amendments to the Belarusian constitution had removed the country's neutral, non-nuclear identity and international status.[1257] Opposition leaders like Tsikhanouskaya displayed no particular support for the old version of the constitution, given that the regime had hardly lived up to its provisions about "democracy", yet noted that the changes now introduced could turn the country, under Lukashenka's leadership, into a threat for all of Europe.[1258]

Western actors would listen carefully to such warnings from the Belarusian opposition and from Ukraine. Indeed, that autumn president of the European Commission Ursula von der Leyen regretfully noted that the EU had failed to heed their warnings against Putin's belligerence. Now, Lukashenka might expect his Western image to be moulded perpetually by his detractors.[1259] And while the constitutional amendments had, allegedly, been supported by a clear majority of the population on a very respectable turnout, opposition commentators pointed out that—apart from any artificial inflation of the data—many Belarusians who had turned up to polling stations did so primarily to publicly declare opposition to the war in Ukraine.[1260] Nevertheless, the amendments passed. As did a new military doctrine for the Russo-Belarusian Union State published shortly before the Russian full-scale invasion

---

1256 That the war was further militarising Russian state and society has frequently been pointed out by analysts. See, for instance, McGlynn, 2023: chapters 3 and 8 may be particularly relevant here

1257 Thereby moving formally away from the entire tradition of post-Soviet Belarusian foreign policy. For details, see also Stykow, 2023: 815

1258 See Tsikhanouskaya's comments on the matter at Eto Izmena, 2022

1259 Von der Leyen's comment was mentioned in Floyd and Webber, 2024: 1166

1260 As outlined (with substantial photographic evidence) in Protesty, 2022

began. With this doctrine Belarusian armed forces might be on the way to complete integration within the Russian military. In such a situation, eventually, Belarusian deployments abroad might circumvent elites in Minsk.[1261]

Albeit such coordination would exceed anything the Russians currently appeared capable of. At the beginning of the war, the intention had been to overwhelm Ukrainian forces from several directions, capture or kill Zelensky's leadership, and declare a Crimea-like fait accompli. As already mentioned, this plan spectacularly failed.[1262] Russia did not fare much better when trying to sway international public opinion. True, some of the most powerful countries outside the West, including China and India, refused to directly challenge Putin on his "de-Nazification mission" in Ukraine, instead merely insisting that they wanted peace as soon as feasible.[1263] So, Russia tried to buttress its cause by appealing to the Global South through the UN. That plan had limited success, at most. Around a week after the launch of Russia's full-scale invasion the General Assembly overwhelmingly supported Resolution ES-11/1, condemning the Russian attack on Ukraine.[1264]

Admittedly, a few countries had failed to turn up to the vote and among the 35 countries actively abstaining were—as indicated above—China and India as well as some other regionally significant states. Voting against the resolution, Belarus found itself in the company of not only Russia but also Eritrea, North Korea and Syria.[1265] None of those countries were international heavyweights,

---

1261 Although that had not quite come to pass yet. A thoughtful analysis of the new doctrine and its implications can be gained from Dyner, 2022

1262 Thereby also removing one of the most likely reasons why the international community could have tolerated Russia's de facto takeover, as had happen after the largely bloodless attack on Crimea. For an (admittedly quite stark) example of how some circles in the West could be very receptive to such an argument, see e.g. Scaliger, 2022

1263 To underline the moral ambiguity of whom such "peace-mongers" might include and what "peace" might entail, one of the first regimes to call for calm after the Russian full-scale invasion had begun was that noted beacon of tolerance, the Afghan Taleban. On that, see Taliban, 2022

1264 For details of voting on the resolution, see Resolution, 2022

1265 It was notable, therefore, that no other post-Soviet state apart from Belarus had supported Russia. As pointed out by Zaporozhchenko, 2024: 16

pretty much all of them were dependent on Russian goodwill. So, the strength of Russia's argument seemed to have convinced no one. In response, Russia and its few allies tried to promote a resolution condemning (allegedly Ukrainian-led) attacks on civilians in Ukraine but gained little traction.[1266] Then, when seeking to avoid concrete institutional consequences of the war, Russia specifically called on Belarusian assistance. When debating whether Russia should be suspended from the UN Human Rights Council the Belarusian delegate argued that would be the thin end of the wedge, encouraging rising intolerance emanating from the West. Russia, however, was suspended.[1267]

Overall, therefore, Russia did not have much diplomatic success over the war. This, though, did not prevent the Putin regime from doubling down on pre-war narratives. A multipolar world order was rising within which the Kremlin would turn to allies in the south and east — allies of rising power and resisting Western interference.[1268] That foreign policy course also entailed, unsurprisingly, ever more visible borders with Europe — an insistence that in-depth collaboration with that part of the world had become impossible, at least for now. Some Russian commentators even invoked Cold War imagery, talking of a renewed Iron Curtain, erected by the hatred for Russia "engrained" in Europe.[1269] Another Cold War trope prominent in Russian foreign policy rhetoric remained the idea that America and its allies wanted to expand their influence to contain Russia's rightful interests and power. By the end of the year Russia was making clear that even failure in Ukraine would not prevent NATO from pushing against Russia elsewhere.[1270]

Russia also returned to a view that any possible institutionalised progress in Europe could only happen within the framework

---

1266 That attempt at changing the dominant public narrative is mentioned by Allison, 2024: 279

1267 Although against the suspension voted 24 countries, including four post-Soviet Central Asian states as well as Belarus. The Belarusian arguments for this vote are mentioned by Simonyan, 2024: 76

1268 Putin laid out his vision for a multipolar world e.g. on Tseremoniia, 2022

1269 This kind of narrative was promoted by Baranov, 2022

1270 A much-expanded exposition on this was offered by Lavrov in Press-Konferentsiia, 2022

of the OSCE. Considering the fields of expertise held by the organisation it was hardly going to address any military security concerns of the Kremlin yet became a useful forum for Russia to air political grievances.[1271] We have seen how Moscow enlisted Belarus for support within the UN and the approach to the OSCE just highlighted was made with its ally, too. More had been expected of Lukashenka. Even if the initial take-over of Ukraine had been swift, Belarus could have shored up Kaliningrad's security or aggression towards the Baltics.[1272] Into March, opposition accounts did suggest that Belarusian troops had briefly moved onto Ukrainian territory, but that they had been pulled back as military personnel refused to fight in the war. That made them a potential liability for Russia, prone to surrendering or rebelling against their commanders.[1273]

It was, in any case, doubtful whether direct military intervention on behalf of Russia by Belarusian troops would have made a significant difference to the war. Given the high casualty rates, shifting part of the damage onto Belarusians would, of course, have lessened the burden placed on Russian troops.[1274] Taking such massive casualties, however, would almost certainly have increased the rate by which Belarusian soldiers deserted the battlefield and possibly left for Ukrainian ranks. In addition, we have already covered the issue of pro-Ukrainian Belarusian militias; Lukashenka had no need for such militias gaining extra recruits and equipment.[1275] And the president's fear of armed rebellion at home might well leave him to seek distance from Russia, even rapprochement with its enemies. Admittedly, that course would be difficult as long as Russian troops remained in Belarus, yet a combination of Lukashenka's

---

1271 The strategy for Russia to follow in the OSCE is laid out in Rossiia, 2022b

1272 Russian-led aggression in that direction was a concern of Belarusian commentators in February. See also Klaskovskii, 2022

1273 For these accounts, see also Belorusskie, 2022

1274 Although, whenever we consider casualty rates in the war some care is required due to severe methodological difficulties. For a thoughtful piece on this, see also Dagorn, 2022

1275 For the likely inability of Belarusian forces to conduct effective operations in Ukraine, see also the analysis by Chalyi, 2022

desperation and their vulnerability in Ukraine might conceivably create a window of opportunity.[1276]

So, to minimise the risk of such a scenario developing Russian interests seemed better served by the use of Belarus as a base from where Russian forces could operate. At the beginning of the war, it might have been possible to have Belarusian troops inserted behind the frontline in northern Ukraine to, say, guard Chernobyl.[1277] Once that frontline had dissipated, though, Russia did not want to risk its use of Belarusian territory. Also, in somewhat of a parallel with the Belarusian domestic landscape after 2020, the primary aggressor benefitted from gathering even partial accomplices as these would be increasingly loyal the more their participatory guilt was established.[1278] Finally, it might be helpful for Russia to retain Belarus as an option to host future peace negotiations with Ukraine. While few now believed in Belarusian neutrality, forcing Ukraine to have talks there might be easier than having such talks in Russia, while at the same time symbolically underlining Russian superiority and ensuring friendly surroundings.[1279]

Lukashenka understood this and periodically reached out to Ukrainians. He repeated the refrain that only Ukrainian elites were "Nazis", while ordinary people were fine. Not that different from some Russian statements, perhaps, although the president did extend his alleged trust to west Ukrainians, too, who had regularly been grouped together as inveterate enemies by Russia.[1280] But witness Lukashenka's bizarre greeting to Ukrainians on their day of independence commemorating their parliamentary vote exiting the Soviet Union. True, he did refer to "brotherly peoples" and similar ideas of Putin's. But celebrating an independence Russia was openly trying to take away hinted at continuing disparities between Russian and Belarusian policy strategies.[1281]

1276 This was speculated on, albeit in fairly general terms, by Shraibman, 2022
1277 An option suggested by Karbalevich, 2022
1278 That point was indicated, at least in part, by Vadim Mozheiko in O Chem, 2022
1279 For thoughts along those lines, see Edinstvennoe, 2022
1280 Such rhetoric by Lukashenka is visible in Umpirovich, 2022
1281 Lukashenka's independence greetings to Ukrainians can be found at Lukashenko Pozdravil, 2022

Seeking Peace?

Lukashenka had always liked guests. He had invited foreign dignitaries to visit him — a Serb ideologue here, a Central Asian president there — and ordinary people to see the land he had preserved. Sometimes, he liked guests to stay longer than they had intended. Now a new tourist was in town. A chef called Yevgeny Prigozhin.[1282] Prigozhin was an old ally of Putin. Having held a wide range of business interests, including within the food industry, during Putin's third presidential term Prigozhin had become known for his sponsorship of the Wagner Group, a private military company with profitable activity in Africa, among other places abroad.[1283] Then, with Russia's full-scale invasion of Ukraine proving surprisingly difficult Prigozhin's fighters had been called in to help with some of the hardest fought battles. Offering relatively good pay to experienced personnel and with little concern for the lives of civilians or its own fighters, the Wagner Group had some success.[1284]

However, disputes with the Russian military had flared up during battles around the city of Bakhmut. Exceptional levels of bloodshed severely damaged the ranks of the Wagner Group. This led Prigozhin, now often seen among his soldiers, to accuse his military counterparts of incompetence and worse in appearances growing ever more dramatic.[1285] Eventually, in June 2023 something snapped. Seeking to oust the military leadership Prigozhin led the Wagner Group from southern Russia towards Moscow, even briefly battling Russian forces on the way. Although Prigozhin claimed that he did not seek to challenge Putin personally, the Russian president could never ignore the

---

1282 The Belarusian president may thus be said to have engaged in "place branding" over the years. For that, see also van Ham, 2008: particularly 128-32

1283 For an illustration of how Putin's Russia used the Wagner Group, see also Marten, 2019

1284 The nature of the Wagner Group's activity in Ukraine is also shown by Nordstrom, 2023

1285 As illustrated by Wagner, 2023

insubordination.[1286] Although Prigozhin was not officially denounced by name, the rebellion was called out by Russian elites including Putin himself as a "betrayal" against the regime, but also against the country itself and the stability and security which the president had, allegedly, worked all his career to entrench.[1287]

At its core the uprising was about sovereignty and who would control the state of emergency. When Russian state identity had increasingly taken a Schmittian turn, as noted previously, any challenge on such grounds had to be taken seriously. Even if Prigozhin could not win, his attempt damaged the raison d'être of the regime.[1288] Despite such concerns, though, after the rebels had been persuaded to stop before Moscow, the Kremlin seemed surprisingly magnanimous. Prigozhin could keep his Wagner Group and at least some of his fortune. Yet given the animosity he had stirred up, the oligarch had to be removed from the Russian domestic political scene.[1289] Enter Lukashenka. Pro-Kremlin media had sought to downplay Prigozhin's activities, stressing that the situation had always been under control. Nevertheless, even such media had to admit that significant bloodshed might have ensued. And they noticed that in the negotiations, which stopped the Wagner Group's march, Lukashenka had played an important part.[1290]

One particular advantage of Lukashenka's intervention had been that it enabled the Russian leadership to handle the case in an extra-legal, informal manner by involving a foreign politician—and someone with decades of experience handling oligarchs. Thus, the Belarusian intervention could accompany well efforts from such domestic troubleshooters as Yunus-Bek Yevkurov.[1291] But what should happen now? Prigozhin was persuaded to leave Russia for

---

1286 An overview of the Wagner rebellion and its ultimate failure is in Arutunyan and Galeotti, 2024: chapters 8-10
1287 These accusations were reported by Tikhonov et al, 2023
1288 Considerations along such lines were in Rostovskii, 2023
1289 For the trouble Prigozhin had placed Putin in relative to the Russian public, see also Skrypchenko, 2023
1290 Such grudging acceptance of Lukashenka's participation is seen in Grishin, 2023
1291 The extra-legal advantages of Belarusian intervention are hinted at by Remchukov and Rodin, 2023

residence in Belarus, together with those many members of the Wagner Group, who remained loyal to their commander. This solution provoked fear among ordinary Belarusians, who thought the Wagner Group would drag the country more actively into the war.[1292] That many respondents also saw the newcomers as a support structure for Belarusian authoritarianism was, obviously, not so much of a concern for Lukashenka. Indeed, as Wagner Group personnel were arriving the president openly talked about handling them and using their battlefield experience to train the Belarusian military (and, likely, domestic security forces, too).[1293]

Soon, the Belarusian government advertised contributions of the Wagner Group to the security of the state. For instance, the Ministry of Defence offered brief footage of Belarusian recruits being quite enthusiastic about the training the newcomers could offer. Such messages projected control over a disruptive force and, not least, aimed to increase Belarusian military morale.[1294] So, that relationship worked well — for about a week. Then, Belarusian state media began reporting on Lukashenka's frustrations with his guests, who were — apparently — eager to move westwards, threatening Poland in revenge for prior encounters with Polish military equipment provided to Ukrainian forces. The president stressed this was unacceptable and that he was in control.[1295] That control seemed unquestionable soon after when Prigozhin died. Ostensibly the victim of a freak airplane accident, few if any observers doubted that the explosion of Prigozhin's airplane was something other than a murder commissioned by Putin. It appeared that the Wagner leader had overestimated his credit with the Russian president and elite.[1296]

Was that good news for Lukashenka? No longer would he have to consider the risk that Prigozhin could lead Wagner soldiers

---

1292 As stressed by numerous respondents to Poteria, 2023
1293 Lukashenka's attitude on this point was reported by Lukashenko, 2023
1294 An example of such footage can be found at Instruktory, 2023
1295 Claims of Lukashenka's dissatisfaction were reported by Nas, 2023
1296 An anonymous Russian intelligence officer subsequently claimed the murder of Prigozhin was ordered by Nikolai Patrushev, secretary of the Russian Security Council. On that allegation, see Butler, 2023

(and perhaps Belarusian soldiers) against Lukashenka's wishes. Yet, had that ever been a serious danger? After his march on Moscow, Prigozhin had largely remained outside Belarus, for instance in Russia engaging with African diplomats.[1297] In terms of his relations with Lukashenka, one could argue that Prigozhin had owed the Belarusian president a favour. Instead, as Tsikhanouskaya tartly but correctly pointed out, the "security guarantees" offered by Belarus to Prigozhin had proven to be little worth. Leaving Lukashenka's use as host for future prominent visitors doubtful.[1298] Even worse for the Belarusian leader, and for any other elites still beholden to goodwill from the Kremlin, the killing of Prigozhin had demonstrated graphically what might happen to those who challenged the "power vertical" emanating from Moscow. And that any informal agreements seemingly mediated by Lukashenka for Prigozhin ultimately had little traction with Putin.[1299]

There were even suggestions from some that Putin might hold Lukashenka personally responsible for what had happened in June. That the Russian president might believe his peer to have been involved in Prigozhin's mutiny. Even if there was not much evidence for this, it did represent another lingering tension in the presidential relationship.[1300] For the time being, though, could Belarusians take over Wagner Group personnel and equipment in Belarus? Some commentators argued that members of the private military company might now be rudderless and seek new leadership. Yet there was no obvious reason why such leadership should be Belarusian rather than Russian.[1301] In addition, if the assets of the Wagner Group were now going to be split up between various members of the Russian state and larger companies ensuing tension might well be something the Belarusian president wanted to keep out of

---

1297 As suggested by Hülsemann and Busvine, 2023
1298 Tsikhanouskaya made her comment in Tsikhanouskaya, 2023
1299 A perceptive comment with potentially very broad implications offered by Aliaksandr Marozau. See Drakakhrust, 2023
1300 That theory was presented in Putin, 2023
1301 The ambiguous results of Prigozhin's death for Lukashenka were also pointed out by commentators in Smerts', 2023

his country to avoid the development of situations he could not control.[1302]

Over the following days and weeks, Lukashenka would periodically deny that the Wagner Group personnel were going anywhere. And that, in fact, his state would be able to gather 10,000 militants on his orders at short notice against anyone threatening Belarus. State media faithfully disseminated that claim.[1303] It is more likely, though, that Lukashenka was happy to see the back of the Wagner Group. Together with regular Russian troops in Belarus, the Group could have challenged the primacy of Belarusian forces. The president had never overcome concerns that state sovereignty might be taken away—by Russia as well as the West.[1304] And even if Wagner troops in Belarus had turned their aggression on other countries, notably Ukraine, this might have damaged Lukashenka. The Belarusian population remained opposed to direct involvement in the war. Consequently, society might have reacted poorly if local authorities had been unable to prevent Russian militants bringing the fighting to Belarus.[1305]

Throughout the year, polls showed respondents in Belarus overwhelmingly against the war in Ukraine or, at least, overwhelmingly against participation in this by Belarusian troops. Interestingly, whereas before Prigozhin's rebellion support for close relations with Russia had been clear (as seen by the previous source) by late 2023 attitudes on this were more ambivalent.[1306] Direct conclusions cannot be drawn from this. Nevertheless, based on the earlier mentioned Belarusian concerns when the Wagner Group transferred briefly to that country it seems probable that Lukashenka could see a calmer country easier to govern without the Wagner Group's presence. Particularly as long as Prigozhin's demise had

---

1302 That a piecemeal splitting up of the Wagner Group could now take place was suggested by some analysts like Aliaksandr Frydman. See also Lukashenku, 2023

1303 As for instance in Kriat, 2023

1304 An example of such concerns can be found in his speech as reported by Konoga, 2023

1305 For an opinion poll showing Belarusian resistance to participation in the war, see Belarusy, 2023

1306 As shown by Konsolidatsiia, 2023

not been conclusively determined.[1307] The Belarusian leadership clearly sought calmer conditions as 2023 moved on. Previously seen calls for peace in Ukraine would periodically reappear, as they had done the previous year. Sometimes in the shape of individual comments or asides, but frequently also as official diplomacy, from the president or the Ministry of Foreign Affairs.[1308]

Not only were such calls in themselves not novel, they were also not very surprising. However, compared to 2022 Belarusian concerns about the war had increased. Suggestions flourished about splits in the Belarusian leadership with the General Staff notably against the Russian full-scale war from the outset, as — apparently — had been the now late Makei.[1309] Obviously, such claims should be considered critically. They came from opposition media without verification. Their claims of military prescience hinted that Belarusian armed forces in hindsight disassociated themselves from Russia's blunder. And yet Belarusian troops had stayed away from fighting. Lukashenka himself now admitted that he had been surprised by the full-scale invasion.[1310] Was he trying to show Belarus as victim of circumstances? Well, yes, but that hardly placed Lukashenka in an impressive light. By his admission, the Belarusian president had stated he had been unable to control the dispatch of lethal force from his own territory. Showing Russia in control of the operation.[1311]

Why does that matter? Because it indicates, perhaps, that this was not Lukashenka "going rogue", disassociating himself from Russian belligerence. But that, instead, he was set up by the Kremlin to test out possibilities for a negotiated solution. Seeking peace

---

1307 While most observers accepted Prigozhin's death from the outset, some suggested he might have survived in hiding, allowing the Kremlin to remove him from the scene without actually killing him. Never a very likely theory yet certainly something to concern Minsk, if the Wagner Group had stayed put in Belarus. See also Pertsev, 2023

1308 An example of the latter being Vystuplenie, 2023a

1309 Details of such alleged elite splits appeared in Kto v Okruzhenii, 2023

1310 As picked up following a televised interview in August by Navumchyk, 2023

1311 A point perhaps inadvertently gained from Lukashenka by a journalist who had clearly turned to Russian sympathies, undoubtedly to the cost of Lukashenka's prestige if need be. On the background of the journalist, see also Ruskiia, 2023. For the entire interview, see also Chem Zakonchitsia, 2023

270   UNCANNY ALLIES

could work with Lukashenka's brand, while Putin supposedly uncompromising principles could be publicly retained.[1312] That explanation seemed eminently plausible. By the summer of 2023 the Russian state was certainly feeling the burdens of war. And in domestic politics Putin had long used parliamentarians and the like to present suggestions for legislative bills the support for which the Russian president could then offer or withhold depending on the public mood.[1313] Other indications existed that Russia was looking to use Belarus as a medium for peace talks. The latter country was highlighted by the Russian government as a country also unfairly treated in Europe, for instance by being discriminated against by the OSCE, an organisation which Russia had otherwise presented as an institutionalisation of peace.[1314]

So, Belarus was presented by Russia as a fellow sufferer from Western ill intent. This should convey public legitimacy Lukashenka push for peace. And Russia was often careful to show Belarus as an equal partner in search for continental stability, even one time setting out joint conditions for peace in Ukraine with its smaller neighbour.[1315] Yet if Russia and Belarus were "equal partners" did that mean they were searching for the same peace? Officially yes, yet Russia was still not prepared to accept anything other than Ukrainian submission (e.g. loss of suzerainty and at least some sovereignty) and that could well be the first step to the absorption of Belarus.[1316] So, Lukashenka's interest could be served by supporting calls for peace in Ukraine but not by total Russian triumph. What to do? By all accounts, the Belarusian president now sought to move focus away from Ukraine—a conflict he could not control—to Poland, a conflict where he might take a leading role.[1317]

1312 This was also the analysis presented by Klaskovskii, 2023a
1313 A useful conceptual framework here may be that of "outbidding". See also White, 2024
1314 For Russian comments on the OSCE, see also Vystuplenie, 2023b
1315 That joint peace proposal was presented in Sovmestnoe, 2023
1316 As mentioned already in the beginning of the year by Fridman, 2023
1317 A role which the Russians seemed primed to accept. See, for instance, Lavrov's declaration of Belarus as a "barrier" against NATO in K Predstoiashchemu, 2023

For the Belarusians it became a matter of inflating disputes to the point where they could plausibly demonstrate their own importance to Russia. In response to an increase in Polish military infrastructure along its borders with Ukraine and Belarus, security officials in Minsk took upon themselves to defend the entire CSTO from such "provocation."[1318] Belarus had previously complained about Poland — and Russia had mostly agreed. Yet the point is that in 2023 Belarusian complaints appeared to become much more frequent and largely ahead of any Russian involvement. This might be understandable to Moscow if a given dispute was localised, say over border crossings.[1319] Or if the Polish authorities went out of their way to seek confrontation with the Belarusian regime. In May, for instance, a former deputy defence minister in Poland called for his country to prepare support for a Belarusian popular overthrow of Lukashenka. The Russian leadership could not let that pass by without comment.[1320]

But if the Kremlin could accept that the Belarusian administration complained harshly against such obviously unfriendly Polish comments, what to do when Lukashenka decided to escalate problems in that relationship with Warsaw? What, in short, to do when the Belarusian regime threatened Poland with nuclear weapons?[1321] How did that happen? Conversations about the stationing of Russian nuclear weapons in Belarus had existed for some time. That was why, as I mentioned previously, the Belarusian constitutional amendments of 2022 had removed the country's non-nuclear status. Now, ostensibly in response to Western arms build-up, Russia was moving tactical nuclear weapons across the border.[1322] By late

---

1318 That was a task undertaken by Alyaksandr Valfovich, secretary of the Belarusian Security Council. See also Vol'fovich, 2023
1319 In February, when Poland announced a significant reduction in options for crossing the border from Belarus, even journalists sympathetic to Poland saw past any official explanations and as politically motivated bilateral punishment. See Hurnevich, 2023
1320 The Polish statement was in Gen. Skrzypczak, 2023
1321 As Belarusian state television seemed to be doing in April, not least by indicating (in a style reminiscent of Soviet times) that Polish politics were guided by interwar imperial ambition. See also Glavnyi, 2023: 19m 20s onwards
1322 As argued approvingly by Popov, 2023

March, commentators in Moscow were outlining how that step would bring significant tactical advantages for Russia in the context of a renewed arms race in Europe. An arms race, such commentators hastened to add, which was solely the fault of the Americans and their aggressive Polish and Baltic allies.[1323]

There was very much a Cold War vibe to Russian statements now appearing that nuclear weapons placed in Belarus would be just retaliation for American nuclear-armed installations close to Russian territory. And that nuclear weapons in Belarus would be able to reach all of Europe.[1324] Analysts in Moscow gleefully noted, as well, that the Belarusian armed forces would now become fully integrated with their Russian counterparts. It was openly suggested — and clearly as a means of praise — that such military integration of Belarus would be a reminder of the days of the Warsaw Pact.[1325] True, the Russian military-strategic position in Europe might now be exposed to countermeasures by NATO and the Americans. Tactical nuclear weapons might be transferred to Poland or even to Ukraine from where, it was perhaps indicated, their transfer to active use on the battlefield might not be far off.[1326]

Still, among Russian observers there was largely agreement that the benefits of tactical nuclear weapons in Belarus would be worth such risks. Even those few who saw the deployment as having largely political, rather than military, importance supported the move and stressed that Russia and Belarus were doing nothing to exacerbate continental tension.[1327] The Russian presidential administration very much seconded that opinion. In early April Peskov claimed without qualification that the transfer of nuclear weapons to Belarusian territory was in response to NATO aggression and a step taken in order to preserve security across the entire European continent.[1328] It was, perhaps, slightly difficult to see how such professions in favour of international peace were compatible with

---

1323 That being the gist of information offered by Val'chenko, 2023
1324 Both lines of argumentation present in Baranets, 2023
1325 This was claimed by Frolov, 2023
1326 Warnings of potential Western countermeasures appeared in Mukhin, 2023
1327 Such argumentation could be found in Kulagin, 2023
1328 That claim was recorded by Kreml', 2023

decades-long Russian attempts to circumvent or ignore longstanding arms treaties—let alone compatible with Russian suspension in February 2023 of participation with America in the New START treaty.[1329]

Such seeming lack of consistency did not bother Belarusian state-affiliated media. Here, there was little belief in the security offered by international institutionalisation, possibly as a consequence of the apparent uselessness of the 1994 Budapest Memorandum. No, the only thing that could keep Belarus out of wars was, it seemed, holding nuclear weapons.[1330] There was rejoicing, furthermore, that the country could respond adequately and with resonance to Western attempts at "nuclear blackmail"—seen through the stationing of nuclear weapons in Western Europe and the use of depleted uranium shells on the battlefield. If the enemy was ready to break norms of war, Belarus could now retaliate.[1331] This sounded like statements offered in Russia. So, transferring tactical nuclear weapons to Belarus was all part of Russia's plan? Well yes, but that is only part of the explanation. As I mentioned earlier, Russia and Belarus reinforced each other's aggression—that became very clear now on the issue of nuclear weapons.[1332]

Such mutual reinforcement implied that any deployment of tactical nuclear weapons to Belarus came with risks. If the Belarusians had been able to operate such weapons on their own initiative, as some military officers had seemed to indicate previously, any danger could have been magnified through unpredictable chains of command.[1333] However, such autonomy was never on the cards. Russian military doctrine (and common sense) spoke against it. Not that Lukashenka necessarily noticed. That he claimed nuclear

---

1329 A step also linked to the transfer of nuclear weapons to Belarus by Ponzio and Siddiqui, 2023: 202

1330 That being the opinion, for instance, of parliamentarian Oleg Gaidukevich. See also Osipov, 2023b

1331 This logic was presented in Osipov, 2023a

1332 Albeit through slightly emotive language, former deputy foreign minister of Belarus Andrei Sannikov understood this mutual reinforcement well. See Sannikov, 2023

1333 For the implicit claim by Belarusian officers, see also Kristensen et al, 2023b: 191

weapons would not be fired from Belarus without is say-so could, just, be plausible. That the weapons belonged to Belarus, which he argued that June, was less so.[1334] The Belarusian president was not about to overpower Russian military personnel or run away with nuclear weapons. Yet notice the remarkable change in his approach. Only a few years prior, Lukashenka had forsworn nuclear weapons as antithetical to his country. Now, he saw them as essential.[1335]

There had, admittedly, been a few years when Belarus took an intermediary position. Just the previous September Lukashenka had accepted that if the Americans were to place nuclear weapons within Poland, then Belarus would, reluctantly, have to consider Russian nuclear arms. Yet by 2023 Poland remained non-nuclear. And yet Lukashenka was welcoming nuclear arms.[1336] Concern spread within the Belarusian political opposition. One obvious problem was that the presence of nuclear weapons in the country might make it a target for preventive strikes. That issue was only exacerbated by the weapons in question being tactical and, therefore, potentially seen by enemies as more difficult to monitor.[1337] At the same time, that risk — whether significant or not — could be used by the Russian leadership to keep Belarus under close control. Even if cross-border attacks against the Russian nuclear bases in Belarus were unlikely, Moscow could always argue its increased surveillance was motivated by the danger from domestic sabotage in Belarus.[1338]

Soon after the plan to transfer nuclear weapons to Belarus had been announced rumours about Lukashenka's health began. Having appeared unwell when visiting Moscow for Victory Day, the

---

1334 These statements by Lukashenka are in Kristensen et al, 2023a: 402

1335 There is some merit here to Shraibman's claim that Lukashenka and Putin increased their nuclear threats across 2023 since blackmail with lower-key threats had not worked. However, for Belarus nuclear threats had not been the habit previously. And for Russia any time Lukashenka engaged in rhetorical escalation Moscow almost inevitably had to follow. See also Sever, 2023

1336 This was covered well by Shraibman, 2023

1337 On the issue of complexity and tactical nuclear weapons in a Russian context it may also be worth consulting Zysk, 2017

1338 A potential excuse for Russian increased surveillance as predicted by Klaskovskii, 2023b

Belarusian president inadvertently forced his population to consider what might happen without him. Many showed little sympathy to a man responsible for mass repression.[1339] Others noted that Lukashenka was aging and plagued by many ailments typical for his age and generation. There were even speculations that the leader had suffered for years from a heart condition, the consequences of which were becoming visible. Given the secrecy surrounding his health, comparisons with decrepit members of the Soviet Politburo seemed inviting.[1340] Yet if Lukashenka suddenly died, who would be the "Gorbachev" — or even the "Khrushchev" — to take over? Most considered it unlikely that the regime would simply collapse. The security services were likely to take over. In which case, an unspoken assumption might have it, security connections to Russian elites could become prominent.[1341]

For now, Lukashenka survived. His health improved. As we have seen, over the summer he was fresh enough to issue threats based on his ownership of nuclear arms. On September 17, National Unity Day, the president and his media took time to harangue the Poles for their alleged aggression, incompetent leadership and poor welfare.[1342] That tone would remain through the rest of the year. After Donald Tusk had returned as Polish prime minister in mid-December, regime-friendly analysts in Belarus confidently predicted trouble with cohabitation (and, by implication, political compromise and democracy) clearly not leading to stability or progress. There were hopes, though, that Ukraine would receive less help.[1343] Belarusian hostility towards Poland was matched by that towards Lithuania. Here lived many members of the Belarusian opposition.

1339 Someone whose methods opposition media would compare to those of Stalin. See also Klaskovskii, 2023c

1340 The suggestion that Lukashenka might be suffering from heart disease was seen in Parad, 2023

1341 In that context, the Belarusians might not be reassured by analyses emerging from Russian governmental publications stressing the unity between Russia and Belarus created through a joint understanding of state security. See also Abramov, 2023

1342 For examples of this, see e.g. Lukashenka's list of historical grievances caused by the Poles in Belarus', 2023b

1343 As mentioned in Lisenkova, 2023

Here, also, was an elite which in recent years had gone great lengths to challenge Minsk—on the war in Ukraine, but also, say, on that nuclear power plant in Astravets, which Vilnius continued to denigrate.[1344]

The relevance of such increased tension between Belarus and its non-Russian neighbours (NATO-member Latvia was also little-favoured) was that Lukashenka remained dependent on Russia. At times, this had made him look very weak—at the Victory Day parade in Moscow, say, or when forced to be a polite visitor at Moscow's vassals in eastern Ukraine.[1345] That might be unavoidable. However, it was one thing to be obviously inferior to an ascendant great power. It was something quite different to get tied to a Russia seemingly unable to escape war in Ukraine and losing—perhaps in perpetuity—its status in the international system.[1346] Or a Russia where the economy felt the strain of warfare and sanctions. I previously noted how sanctions against Russia could benefit Belarusian companies operating there, and that remained the case. But only to a point. If sanctions slowed down investment, access to capital and technology for Russian business that would impact Belarusian counterparts, too.[1347]

International commentators would argue that sanctions had enjoyed limited, if any, effects on Russian power and ability to conduct warfare. In the short run, there was some truth in this. Yet it overlooked the vulnerable position from where the Russian economy had started, and the Belarusian one too, following years of missed or misguided reforms.[1348] Russia and Belarus could perhaps promote greater economic efficiency, but that would damage elite

---

1344 Most notably as part of National, 2023

1345 By going as an official guest Lukashenka had effectively recognised the legitimacy of local east Ukrainian regimes. As noted by Aleksandr Klaskovskii in Shavel', 2023

1346 For the consequences of the war in Ukraine on Russia's international position, see also Kříž, 2023

1347 An overview of sanctions following Russia's full-scale invasion of Ukraine is in Abely, 2023

1348 Despite its much broader remit, underlying tension between Russia and modernity, which directly impacted on its economic and socio-economic prospects, is convincingly envisaged in Etkind, 2023. Unsurprisingly, findings from that work would often be relevant for Belarus, too.

interests and loyalty. Alternatively, a new source of funds could be found. For Russia, as long as hydrocarbons and other natural resources were available, customers could probably be found, if not necessarily customers willing to pay a high price.[1349] Belarus, however, did not have that option. So, 2023 had seen Lukashenka go — almost begging bowl in hand — to find backers other than Russia. We have noticed how Europe was being pushed away. Iran could perhaps be a helpful partner, but that would mainly be in the defence industries.[1350]

That left China. Lukashenka's visit to Beijing in December was, officially, a great success. The political symbolism of the meeting between Lukashenka and Xi Jinping was taken by Belarusian state media to signify yet another affirmation of multipolar world order with alliances stretching across Eurasia.[1351] Chinese media was, unsurprisingly, upbeat too. However, this did not obscure the fact that Belarus for China had a primary role of transit country. One of Beijing's major gripes with the Russian war in Ukraine had been its damage to trade flows between China and Europe — and, thus, damage to the Belt and Road Initiative.[1352] If goods could not flow through Ukraine they would go via Belarus to Poland and the Baltics. Xi expected Lukashenka to keep borders open for that purpose, and Lukashenka readily agreed. Yet with continued European tension — brought on not least by Lukashenka's own behaviour — whether his guarantees would persuade Chinese partners remained to be seen.[1353]

1349 In the long run, skewing the economy further towards sales of hydrocarbons would bring further problems, though, as noted by Kluge, 2022
1350 Lukashenka did visit Tehran in March 2023, where several bilateral agreements were signed. However, those agreements were largely scant on detail and commitment. For the visit, see also Kononovich, 2023
1351 For a paean to the Belarusian president's trip, see also Gigin, 2023
1352 That problem for China set out well by Mendez et al, 2022
1353 For analysis of this and other issues discussed during Lukashenka's visit to China, see also Peramovy, 2023

Until the Bitter End?

Is it a bird? Is it a plane? No, it is a Russian drone flying over Belarus. It is the summer of 2024 and explosive-laden kamikaze drones launched by Russia are forcing Belarus to scramble fighter jets. Local analysts speculate Russia seeks to cow Lukashenka, to remind him that he shall not escape the war.[1354] If so, that threat has been timed well—to coincide with the 30-year anniversary of his reign. This first and so far only president of Belarus has saved the country, building institutions and stability. Making the country respected abroad and engaging the broader public. Says state media.[1355] As he was growing up, Lukashenka was a sensible child, ready for hard work and never dreaming that he would run the country. But he witnessed the hardship of fellow villagers and like a reverse Cincinnatus, asked by no one but apparently desired by all, rose to the foremost office of his land.[1356]

Putin offers warm congratulations to his colleague. Lukashenka has stuck around and that should be respected. As long as "Daddy" from Minsk understands his place. Within the bilateral relationship, true, but also in a reinforced Union State where Russia and Belarus are with each other—all the way.[1357] Will Lukashenka be obedient? Many Belarusian analysts fear so. They fear that their country is being pulled away not only from security and progress but from European society, instead following Russia into the "anti-West"—a domain defined only by that which it is not and by the direction in which it is not going.[1358] Belarus can no longer hope to get profit from working with Europe. So, the regime runs around across the world to see if anyone wants to do deals with it. Selling some potash here. And some machinery there.

1354 This was suggested by Vasilevskii, 2024

1355 A telling example of that–including fetching pictures of Lukashenka–is offered by Spasatel'nyi, 2024

1356 Lukashenka's rise from humble beginnings is the theme of Kurak, 2024 among a selection of commemorative media pieces.

1357 As Putin points out in his unsubtle greeting on the Belarusian Independence Day. See also Aleksandru, 2024

1358 A similar argument is echoed by Karbalevich, 2024

Maybe a bit of weapons. All in the knowledge that dependence on the Russian market inevitably remains.[1359]

And is Russia now about to take away even such vestiges of sovereignty? Maybe not while Lukashenka remains in the presidency — that was clearly a subtext of the media paeans mentioned above. The current ruler in Minsk and his domestic allies have stakes in staying separate from Russia.[1360] But when they go, or are gone, is there any Belarus left to keep the Russian state at bay? We have seen examples of how not only the Belarusian regime, but also ordinary Belarusians could stand up for their independence. Not least in the summer of 2020. Is that still the case come 2024?[1361] What happens with future generations of Belarusians, and of Russians too, when state-sponsored slogans and education promotes "patriotic" ideology, unity, uniformity in the two states? Putin can easily congratulate Belarus on its Independence Day, if Belarus has simply received the freedom to return to its Russian home.[1362]

If Belarus is to stay ever closer to Russia it should also benefit from this. Its lands should be protected. It has been suggested by analysts that, early in 2024, the Belarusian military doctrine was updated to highlight the role of nuclear weapons in national defence.[1363] If that is, indeed, the case such priorities fit with the international context provided by the state and its loyal media to the doctrine. Context of a world apparently filled with threat from the West, its military preparations and hybrid attempts to destabilise, dismember and destroy Belarus.[1364] Suddenly in February, Belarusian Defence Minister Viktar Khrenin is talking about a massing of over a hundred thousand Ukrainian troops near the Belarusian border. At a time when Ukraine is supposed to be fully occupied with

---

1359 Klaskovskii, 2024, details such problems further, although that article is perhaps more disparaging of non-European trading options than is helpful

1360 This was also pointed out in Drakakhrust, 2024

1361 An argument also pursued by former Russian politician Mark Feigin in Feigin, 2024

1362 See also Putin's rhetoric promoting patriotic education in Russia and Belarus in Videoobrashchenie, 2024

1363 This claim was offered by Kristensen et al, 2024: 124

1364 A substantial theme in articles such as Buzin, 2024

Russia in the east. What are the Ukrainians up to? Belarus better keep alert — with nukes at the ready.[1365]

Soon after, elections are coming up. In Belarus, in late February delegates are chosen for national and local legislatures. Chosen by whom? Well, by moustachioed machismo, of course — it looks less like ever before as a meaningful public choice and more like slightly flaccid grand guignol.[1366] The Russian state is quick to congratulate Minsk on how well it has performed. Not just on the result but on the ability to make an election run smoothly under such constant pressure from the wicked West with its frequent attempts to interfere in Belarusian sovereign affairs.[1367] Woe betide such outsiders if they even consider disrupting Putin's party the following month — his re-re-re-re-election as president of Russia with a modest 88% of votes. A triumph made slightly less inconvenient by the sudden demise in February of Navalny and, with him, the figurehead of any widespread domestic opposition.[1368]

Obviously, Lukashenka congratulates his significant other. Yet, does the election actually matter for Belarus? In 2012 Putin returned energised, stretching Russia abroad. After 2018 that energy seemed to turn rancid, suspicious of everything "out there". There is no indication that the election of 2024 will make Putin look differently at the world.[1369] What might happen, though, is that "out there" changes — comes closer and closer to the Kremlin. Just look at the aftermath of the terror attack near Moscow later that March. When armed militants assault and murder more than a hundred civilians, ordinary visitors to a concert.[1370] The so-called "Islamic State" quickly takes responsibility. Apparently, the assailants are apprehended by Russian security forces. And then humiliated. Tortured. Mutilated. After the concert hall massacre public anger is

---

1365 Khrenin's claim was reported in Khrenin, 2024
1366 Bedford, 2024, is appropriately cynical about the spectacle.
1367 Official Russian congratulations on the Belarusian elections are at Zaiavlenie, 2024
1368 Circumstances of the 2024 Russian presidential election are offered by Gozzi and Scarr, 2024
1369 As suggested also in Lutskevich, 2024
1370 The immediate aftermath of the terror attack is covered by Atkinson, 2024

great in Russia, understandably. Does that explain public support for barbarism? Does that explain statist pride in violence?[1371]

Or should reasons for such pride, such support rather be found in more than a decade of anger, of frustration, of war? Of the state showing the up-and-coming generations how to stand up straight, march in line and start for that dawn of nothing? Of obeying the Z?[1372] If so, maybe Lukashenka can find novel use in post-2024 Putin's Russian world. For the Belarusian leader has long shown he has no qualms about using violence to combat violence. To cleanse the polity. To undo those glitches in that perfect security, which his state was supposed to have had.[1373] Now, call upon the expertise of Belarus. Let them tell us how they shoot people in the back of the head. Let us, perhaps, send the terrorists over there — for justice. So, say Russians, the public and the elite alike, after the Crocus has wilted. And Moscow and Minsk strengthen each other's resolve to kill.[1374]

After the attack, Russian authorities had sought to draw public attention to Ukrainian involvement in the atrocity. Sought to argue that the terrorists had fled from the scene of the crime towards Ukrainian territory where, so it was suggested, their Ukrainian handlers prepared to give them free passage.[1375] That such a plan would, by necessity, have involved the terrorists getting through Russian military lines first seemed to slip the Kremlin mind. And the Russian public mind, too, as it appeared that these gory if unsubstantiated theories had support within the Russian general

---

1371 Questions taken up by Roth and Sauer, 2024

1372 What has happened to (some) Russian youth under Putin is carefully investigated by Garner, 2023

1373 For instance, Sweeney, 2012, shows proceedings not that dissimilar in essence from what happened in Russia in 2024, although Belarusian state violence was less overt.

1374 The death penalty has been suspended in Russian law since 1996. Within Europe, Belarus remains the only country actively using such punishment. See also Tragediia, 2024, for the example of Russian parliamentarian Maria Butina suggesting Belarusian provisions on the death penalty could be employed against the Crocus City Hall assailants, since the victims of the attack included Belarusian citizens.

1375 Reasons for that approach by the Russian state are offered by Rosenberg, 2024

public.[1376] So, why did Lukashenka suddenly muddle that narrative? Why did the Belarusian leader note that, actually, the terrorist at first had fled not towards Ukraine but towards his country. Where they were thwarted by the excellent Belarusian security forces and by the handle he himself had taken of the situation.[1377]

So, now Putin cannot even have the terror attack and its aftermath for himself. Lukashenka just had to become involved and show everybody — and Putin — how important Minsk is for keeping everything secure. Unlike, of course, the Russian security forces who blatantly failed at the concert.[1378] The Belarusian president is always there, ready to step in when the Kremlin cannot. In April Ukrainian drones appear to have struck critical infrastructure in Russia's Oriol Region. That is just a few hundred kilometres from Belarus and Lukashenka is ready to step in, to look after Russian civilians.[1379] As he had been in February when visited by the governor of Russia's Briansk Region, even closer to Belarus than Oriol. Connections between Belarus and Briansk went back into the Soviet era, so the Russians should just tell him if they needed anything, anything at all. That went for Russian-occupied territories in Ukraine, too.[1380]

In principle, this should please Putin. The Belarusian leadership is professing loyalty and support for Russia in its hour of need. Yet it does not quite work for the Russian president's public image to have Lukashenka turning up as the man in control. To sell himself as the security provider.[1381] Now, apparently, with added

---

1376 Opinion polls taken indicated half of Russian respondents might agree with the blaming of Ukraine. See also Stognei, 2024

1377 Those remarks by the Belarusian president are recorded in Lukashenko, 2024d

1378 As some observers, particularly in Ukraine, pointed out the Russian elite had a longstanding reputation for creating insecurity rather than security, including inside Russia itself. For perhaps the most famous, still murky case of this– the apartment bombings of 1999 — see also the unparalleled investigation in Dunlop, 2012

1379 That offer being reported by Lukashenko, 2024c

1380 Lukashenka's profession of relevance was covered by Lukashenko, 2024e

1381 And, for that matter, a security provider to the EU as well as Russia. Lukashenka's professed vigilance in stopping the Crocus City Hall terrorists had been for the benefit of the West as well as Moscow. Of course, Lukashenka would not stop people just on the say-so of the West–something on which he would often publicly reflect. See also Lukashenko, 2024a

nuclear weapons. Nuclear weapons which might be held by Russian soldiers, but which really, legitimately, belong to Belarus. At least according to the Belarusian administration, which talks about the "return" of these weapons to the country, rather than their "deployment" from Russia.[1382] The capacity for a big bang is coming back to Belarus, a potential destroyer of worlds. The military point of nuclear weapons is mostly minor. The political point, however, is essential. And if the ownership of nuclear missiles conveys great power status it matters when Belarusian public life starts issuing nuclear threats.[1383]

When Belarusian elites can say that "simply, humbly, without bragging…What is that thing you call an atom bomb? You have it and we have it!". Ok, so that quote was provided from the Soviet Union on the occasion of the confirmation of a Soviet nuclear bomb, but you get the gist.[1384] If Putin wants to drag Belarus with him back to the Soviet security state, if he wants that to be the basis for the Union State, then that is alright with Minsk. In such a case, however, the Belarusians are owners of this past just as much as are the Russians.[1385] So that, when Putin and Lukashenka meet in January 2024 to jointly commemorate the lifting of the siege of Leningrad during the Second World War, and to erect a monument to this near St Petersburg, the Belarusian president still points out that, actually, the Belarusians suffered uniquely during the war.[1386]

That is not incorrect — as I pointed out in a previous chapter, the territory of modern-day Belarus suffered proportionally more casualties that anywhere else on Earth. And as long as the Kremlin keeps talking about its "fascist" enemies in Ukraine and the West,

---

1382 That friendly message from Minsk was reported in Minoborony, 2024
1383 "Normal Americans, Frenchmen, Germans and Poles don't want to burn in a nuclear flame", as Belarusian analyst Aleksei Beliaev so charmingly put it. On that, see Bareiko, 2024
1384 For the quote, see also Yemel'ianenkov, 2020
1385 On this point, Tsikhanouskaya is partly right–Lukashenka does look back to a Soviet state (defined by military security and corporatism, rather than communism), although being part of a single state with Russia is less of the direct appeal. See also Sviatlana, 2024
1386 That observation appeared in Lukashenka's speech for the occasion, as reported in Otkrytie, 2024

Lukashenka's rhetoric only helps.[1387] However, it does become another example of the Belarusian leader's insistence that the Soviet heritage must be interpreted on its terms, or at a minimum not contrary to its terms. And that, again, creates tension when the Soviet heritage to be interpreted and reconstructed is, from its roots, inconsistent.[1388] For instance, should such heritage centre of the provision of welfare, of physical security, of international status? With increasing consistency Russia seems to veer towards the last option, but that cannot be the attraction of the Soviet Union for Lukashenka or his allies, since they would not be allowed by Moscow to marshal such status.[1389]

Yet, if the Soviet heritage is to be reconstructed as welfare, as the provision of goods and everyday comforts to the general population, then the Russian heir is failing. So is Belarus but given the smaller economy and strategically timed servility towards the Kremlin Lukashenka hoped his failings on this point could be masked.[1390] Today, Russia neither can nor wants to help him in this regard, beyond doing the bare minimum to secure against unplanned regime change. As I mentioned above, Minsk seeks additional economic partners, or sponsors, with increasing febrility yet still with limited results as of the middle of 2024.[1391] Yes, there remains the Chinese option. However, as I noted previously the relationship between Belarus and China has, particularly of late, been marked more by grand declaration than by specific economic deals

---

1387 For a recent example of Putin's equation of the Ukrainian regime with that of Nazi Germany, see again the commemoration of the end of the siege of Leningrad and his comments on that occasion, in Putin Repeats, 2024

1388 An inconsistency well known to anyone seeking to understand the Soviet Union, with Remnick, 1993, being a telling, early post-Soviet example.

1389 Unless, perhaps, Belarus can use its influence in an international organisation-like the CSTO–to enhance its status. For an example of such logic concerning the power of smaller states, see also Hornát et al, 2023

1390 For the importance of welfare provisions for Belarusian state legitimacy, and the consequent necessity for the Belarusian state to centralise welfare policies to a more significant degree than in Russia, see also Bindman and Chulitskaya, 2023: 241

1391 A problem to which the Belarusian administration at times is admitting. See also Sakovich, 2024

or, for that matter, by much evident Chinese belief in the continued relevance of Belarus.[1392]

Absent significantly increased Chinese interest is Belarus doomed to fall under Russia's spell? If so, what will the impact be should Russian material capabilities fall significantly in the time to come? Will increased Russian influence insulate Belarusian exposure to socio-economic decline, or will it hasten that decline?[1393] What happens if the Belarusian military is, eventually, dragged across the border into Ukraine? If the Ukrainian military attack Belarus? Or, perhaps most intriguingly, if the Ukrainian and Belarusian leadership comes to some mutual accord? Not a likely scenario, admittedly. Yet one that Putin, given years of experience with Lukashenka's vagaries, cannot completely rule out.[1394]

1392 For a sign that this relationship might be more promising than I indicate here, observers could point to Belarus' accession to the Shanghai Cooperation Organisation as a full member in mid-2024; an accession for which Lukashenka pointedly thanked Russian assistance. See also Lukashenko, 2024b

1393 Just as Russia does not have unending supply of soldiers, it also does not have unending supply of money. And the war in Ukraine is costly. See also Shatz and Reach, 2023

1394 Particularly after the Prigozhin rebellion. On speculations about Lukashenka's loyalty towards Russia relative to the war in Ukraine, see also Rad, 2024

Conclusion

We need to talk about death. Specifically, about the eventual demise, political or physical, of Putin or Lukashenka. What happens then? After all, as the preceding chapters have laid out Russian-Belarusian relations in the post-Soviet era have often been personalised, guided by the foibles and ambitions of those two leaders. Should Putin pass first from the public scene it is likely that Russian politics would be dominated, even consumed, by the search for his successor. Or even by temporary collective rule. In such a case it seems probable that relations with Belarus would be somewhat ignored, as—indeed—might all foreign policy. If, however, Lukashenka departs first Belarus would find itself in a precarious position. To state that is not to praise the current regime which for years has fought the spectre of domestic dissatisfaction with brutal suppression and economic mismanagement. It is, however, to acknowledge that an obvious heir to the president does not exist. Consequently, it does not seem a stretch to suggest that a Belarus without Lukashenko might witness security services rally together to manage his succession in a manner perhaps similar to what has been seen in Central Asia. Under such circumstances, existing personal and profession links to Russian security personnel could well prove important.

That assumption rests on a wider belief that Russian relations with Belarus shall remain close. That irrespective of whichever people constitute the elites of the two countries mutual interdependence shall remain prominent. Partly, that foreseeable development might be based on interest as regimes in Moscow and Minsk see few likely allies elsewhere. They also understand each other well. Partly this has to do with the personalised autocracies established, where Putin and Lukashenka, and many of their followers, have spent decades encircling each other, working with and sometimes against each other's purposes. At times, alliances, too, have been created across borders against domestic rivals. Mutual understanding does not only come from direct interaction, though. It also very much comes from that post-Soviet heritage which has persistently been promoted and remoulded by the memory politics of Russia and Belarus. Battling to revisit a perceived golden past, often the two leaderships have reinforced each other's narratives. It is not so much that they want to return to communist rule. Today, that ideology has few adherents. In fact, looking at the discrete, almost embarrassed way in which the centenary of the Russian Revolution was celebrated it seems clear that few, if any, actors of importance have Lenin as their lodestar.

What does remain prominent, though, is the image of strength and of stability, which the Soviet Union is claimed to represent. Putin, Lukashenka and elites around them came of age during the reign of Brezhnev, as the public focus on the ideology of communism transformed into a focus on statist security. For people in both the Russian and the Belorussian Soviet republics those years saw normality return. The hardships of the Second World War faded as did the immediate fear that aggressor states just across the border might try to seize territory through violence or credible threat. At the same time, though, this was the height of the Cold War when the Soviet Union had reached effective military parity with the United States. That had security implications and it had ideological implications, too, as elites in Moscow and many ordinary Soviet citizens took pride in great power status. Following the Soviet collapse, and the socio-economic difficulties which hit Russia, in particular, it was not surprising that ordinary citizens and elites might judge the Soviet past less harshly. However, to understand why some aspects of that past gained particular prominence we have to turn to the agency of post-Soviet leaders.

Putin was never a communist, but he was a statist working within the security services. Unsurprisingly, therefore, as he became president in 2000 Putin promoted that heritage for his country, finding a ready audience for his claims that Russia had to be rescued from oligarchic greed and Western perfidy. Lukashenka, too, believed in the strong state. And he certainly developed structures to enhance the security of that state and, particularly, of himself. However, an image of great power status would never sell in Belarus as well as would an image of welfare and sovereign stability. That, consequently, became the brand promoted in Minsk. The different paths chosen by Putin and Lukashenka might have been compatible. Particularly after 2020 when the domestic danger facing the Belarusian president made it easy for him to accept Russian claims of a dangerous West. In the face of widespread international sanctions, the two countries now have more reason than ever to stay close. At the same time, the two presidents should be able to find comfort in each other's presence. By now, both have been leaders for decades. Both have created personalist, populist regimes depending on their masculine centrality. Both know that they are unlikely to ever peacefully hand over power.

So, why the persistent unease with which Russian and Belarusian elites engage? Partly, it can be explained through personal relations, or lack thereof. Despite public displays of bonhomie, Putin and Lukashenka never got along well, seeing each other—with some justification—as arrogant and untrustworthy. Nevertheless, despite the impact of the two leaders this unease reaches deeper. For Belarus, Russian expansionism and centralisation are perennial threats. Given material and ideological links between the two countries it was always likely that Russian foreign policy ambition would reach first towards the smaller neighbour to the west. Conversely, from the Russian point-of-view the behaviour of Belarus has long been a source of frustration. Across the Russian population there is a belief that the Belarusians ought to be more grateful for all the support they have received from Moscow. That Belarus should offer support to a Russia besieged on all sides. Such a belief is not, however, simply founded on abstract notions of fairness or on a rational cost-benefit analysis. It is founded on a belief that Russians and Belarusians, ultimately, are the same people. On a belief that the two nations are similar heirs to a Soviet and, before that, imperial heritage.

And this, eventually, is where we come back to the meaning of the uncanny within the relationship between Russia and Belarus. During the twentieth century, and before, developments in the two territories were intimately linked. In the post-Soviet era Russian and Belarusian leaders faced similar challenges and, frequently, made similar choices. As this book has shown, however, the positions of the two countries did not always align. It would be common for elites in Moscow and in Minsk to engage in one-upmanship with each side seeking to prove to themselves and the world that they knew best how to carry their country and the region forward. Even when Russian and Belarusian policies did not differ much in practice their very similarity held dangers for the relationship. For if Belarusians admitted that they were just doing what the Russians did, their sovereignty would be endangered. And if Russians admitted they followed a Belarusian lead, status as a great power became questionable. Some argue that tension has been resolved. That Lukashenka, after 2020, has lost the battle. He and his people are certainly more in need of Russian aid than before. And yet, as I showed, the Belarusian regime keeps pushing, keeps manoeuvring for sovereign space. As long as that manoeuvring continues, tension shall remain.

Bibliography

Abdelal, Rawi (2002) "Memories of Nations and States: institutional history and national identity in post-Soviet Eurasia", *Nationalities Papers*, vol. 30, issue 3

Abely, Christine (2023) *The Russia Sanctions: the economic response to Russia's invasion of Ukraine*, Cambridge: CUP

Abramov, S. (2023) "The Ideological Security of the Union State of Russia and Belarus", *International Affairs (Moscow)*, vol. 69, issue 6

Ackermann, Felix (2016) "Autosovietization: migration, urbanization and social acculturation in western Belarus", *Jahrbücher für Geschichte Osteuropas*, vol. 64, issue 3

Adamovič, Ales' (2006) "Nicht nur ein AKW: ein Brief an Mikhail S. Gorbačev", *Osteuropa*, vol. 56, issue 4

Adams, Michael (2006) *Napoleon and Russia*, London: Bloomsbury

Adamsky, Dmitry (2023) *The Russian Way of Deterrence: strategic culture, coercion, and war*, Stanford, CA: Stanford UP

Adarov, Amat (2023) "Eurasian Economic Integration: impact evaluation using the gravity model and the synthetic control methods", *Review of World Economics*, online first

"A.G. Lukashenko: Ia Ochen' Ser'ezno Pogruzhen v Situatsiiu v Ukraine" (2014) *Sovetskaia Rossiia*, October 9

Agius, Christine and Edenborg, Emil (2019) "Gendered Bordering Practices in Swedish and Russian Foreign and Security Policy", *Political Geography*, vol. 71

Aitkenhead, Decca (2013) "Femen Leader Inna Shevchenko: 'I'm for any form of feminism'", *The Guardian*, November 8. https://www.the guardian.com/world/2013/nov/08/femen-leader-inna-shevchenk o-interview (accessed July 16, 2024)

Akchurina, Viktoria and Della Sala, Vincent (2018) "Russia, Europe and the Ontological Security Dilemma: narrating the emerging Eurasian space", *Europe-Asia Studies*, vol. 70, issue 10

Aktürk, Şener and Lika, Idlir (2022) "Varieties of Resilience and Side Effects of Disobedience: cross-national patterns of survival during the coronavirus pandemic", *Problems of Post-Communism*, vol. 69, issue 1

Alang, Navneet (2024) "No God in the Machine: the pitfalls of AI worship", *The Guardian*, August 8. https://www.theguardian.com/news/artic le/2024/aug/08/no-god-in-the-machine-the-pitfalls-of-ai-worship (accessed August 8, 2024)

Aleksandrov, Aleksandr (2012) "'Kanal' protiv Narkotikov", *Krasnaia Zvezda*, June 20

"Aleksandru Lukashenko, Prezidentu Respubliki Belarus'" (2024) *Kremlin.ru*, July 3. http://www.kremlin.ru/events/president/letters/74447 (accessed August 11, 2024)

Alekseev, Anton and Moskovchenko, Ol'ga (2021) "Otkrytyi i Zainteresovannyi Dialog v Interesakh Mira", *Krasnaia Zvezda*, June 25

Alexseev, Mikhail and Vagin, Vladimir (1999) "Russian Regions in Expanding Europe: the Pskov connection", *Europe-Asia Studies*, vol. 51, issue 1

Alexievich, Svetlana (2017) *The Unwomanly Face of War: an oral history of women in World War II*, New York: Random House

Alieva, Leila and Pikulik, Alexei (2023) "Rent Distribution Modes in Azerbaijan and Belarus: implications for the opposition", *Europe-Asia Studies*, vol. 75, issue 7

Allison, Roy (2017) "Russia and the Post-2014 International Legal Order: revisionism and *realpolitik*", *International Affairs*, vol. 93, issue 3

Allison, Roy (2020) "Russian Revisionism, Legal Discourse and the 'Rules-Based' International Order", *Europe-Asia Studies*, vol. 72, issue 6

Allison, Roy (2024) "Russia's Case for War against Ukraine: legal claims, political rhetoric, and instrumentality in a fracturing international order", *Problems of Post-Communism*, vol. 71, issue 3

Ambrose, Matthew (2018) *The Control Agenda: a history of the Strategic Arms Limitation Talks*, Ithaca, NY: Cornell UP

Ambrosio, Thomas (1999) "The Geopolitics of Slavic Union: Russia, Belarus, and multipolarity", *Geopolitics*, vol. 4, issue 3

Ambrosio, Thomas (2007) "Insulating Russia from a Colour Revolution: how the Kremlin resists regional democratic trends", *Democratization*, vol. 14, issue 2

Ambrosio, Thomas (2022) "Belarus, Kazakhstan and Alliance Security Dilemmas in the Former Soviet Union: intra-alliance threat and entrapment after the Ukraine crisis", *Europe-Asia Studies*, vol. 74, issue 9

Ambrosio, Thomas and Vandrovec, Geoffrey (2013) "Mapping the Geopolitics of the Russian Federation: the Federal Assembly addresses of Putin and Medvedev", *Geopolitics*, vol. 18, issue 2

Andersen, Hans (1997) "The Shadow" in *The Complete Fairy Tales*, London: Wordsworth

Andreev, Oleg (2017) "Minoborony RF Priblizilos' k Granitsam NATO", *Nezavisimaia Gazeta*, June 22

Annus, Epp (2015) "The Ghost of Essentialism and the Trap of Binarism: six theses on the Soviet empire", *Nationalist Papers*, vol. 43, issue 4

Anthony, Peter (2014) *The Man Who Saved the World*, Statement Film, WG Film and Ego Media

"Anton Matol'ka Zaklikau Ne Dapuskats' Razdachy Heorhieuskikh Stuzhak na Buduchykh 'Nesmiarotnykh Palkakh'" (2018) *Nasha Niva*, May 10. https://nashaniva.com/209402 (accessed August 10, 2024)

Antonenko, Oksana (2001) "Putin's Gamble", *Survival*, vol. 43, issue 4

Applebaum, Anne (2012) *Iron Curtain: the crushing of Eastern Europe 1944-56*, London: Allen Lane

Aptekar', Pavel (2019) "Posol na Vykhod", *Vedomosti*, May 6

Arel, Dominique (2002) "Interpreting 'Nationality' and 'Language' in the 2001 Ukrainian Census", *Post-Soviet Affairs*, vol. 18, issue 3

Arel, Dominique and Driscoll, Jesse (2023) *Ukraine's Unnamed War: before the Russian invasion of 2022*, Cambridge: CUP

Aronczyk, Melissa (2018) "Nation Branding: a twenty-first century tradition" in *Nation Branding in Modern History*, New York: Berghahn; eds. Carolin Viktorin, Jessica Gienow-Hecht, Annika Estner and Marcel Will

Arutunyan, Anna and Galeotti, Mark (2024) *Downfall: Prigozhin, Putin and the new fight for the future of Russia*, London: Ebury

Ash, Konstantin (2015) "The Election Trap: the cycle of post-electoral repression and opposition fragmentation in Lukashenko's Belarus", *Democratization*, vol. 22, issue 6

Åslund, Anders (2012) *How Capitalism Was Built: the transformation of Central and Eastern Europe, Russia, and Central Asia* (2nd ed.), Cambridge: CUP

Åslund, Anders (2013) "Sergey Glazyev and the Revival of Soviet Economics", *Post-Soviet Affairs*, vol. 29, issue 5

Åslund, Anders (2020) "Responses to the COVID-19 Crisis in Russia, Ukraine, and Belarus", *Eurasian Geography and Economics*, vol. 61, issue 4-5

Asmus, Ronald (2010) *A Little War That Shook the World: Georgia, Russia and the future of the West*, Basingstoke: Palgrave Macmillan

Astapenia, Ryhor (2014) "The History of the Great Duchy of Lithuania: Belarus' medieval origins", *Journal of Belarusian Studies*, vol. 7, issue 2

Astapova, Anastasiya (2016a) "Counter-Hegemony in Today's Belarus: dissident symbols and the mythological figure of Miron Vitebskii", *Nationalities Papers*, vol. 44, issue 5

Astapova, Anastasiya (2016b) "Political Biography: incoherence, contestation, and elements of the hero pattern in the Belarusian case", *Journal of Folklore Research*, vol. 53, issue 2

Astrouskaya, Tatsiana (2019) *Cultural Dissent in Soviet Belarus (1968-1988): intelligentsia, samizdat and nonconformist discourses*, Wiesbaden: Harrassowitz

Atasuntsev, Aleksandr (2021) "ES Nachal Gotovit' Vozdushnuiu Izoliatsiiu Belorussii", *RBC.ru*, May 24. https://www.rbc.ru/politics/24/05/2021/60ab71a39a7947736ef492a7?from=column_2 (accessed July 18, 2024)

Atkinson, Emily (2024) "Moscow Attack: day of mourning after 137 killed at Crocus City Hall concert", *BBC News*, March 24. https://www.bbc.co.uk/news/world-europe-68646380 (accessed July 26, 2024)

Atzili, Boaz and Kim, Min (2023) "Buffer Zones and International Rivalry: internal and external geographic separation mechanisms", *International Affairs*, vol. 99, issue 2

Auer, Stefan (2015) "Carl Schmitt in the Kremlin: the Ukraine crisis and the return of geopolitics", *International Affairs*, vol. 91, issue 5

Avakov, Artur (2019) "Predel Soiuznogo Gosudarstva", *Moskovskii Komsomolets*, November 15

Avakov, Artur and Zelenskaia, Dar'ia (2020) "Za Lukashenko Prishli Rossiiskie Boeviki", *Moskovskii Komsomolets*, July 30

"Babich Rasskazal, Chto Budet, Esli Belarus' Zakhochet v Evrosoiuz" (2019) *Belsat*, February 10. https://belsat.eu/ru/news/babich-rassk azal-chto-budet-esli-belarus-zahochet-v-evrosoyuz (accessed July 12, 2024)

Bachmann, Sascha-Dominik; Putter, Dries and Duczynski, Guy (2023) "Hybrid Warfare and Disinformation: a Ukraine War perspective", *Global Policy*, vol. 14, issue 5

Bagdzevich, Viktar (2022) "'Na Yakuiu Khaleru Bylo Leztsi va Ukrainu? Narmal'na zh Zhyli': pra shto mauchats' belaruskiia chynouniki", *Nasha Niva*, March 10. https://nashaniva.com/?c=ar&i=286125 (accessed July 21, 2024)

Baiburin, Albert (2021) *The Soviet Passport: the history, nature, and uses of the internal passport in the USSR*, Cambridge: Polity

Baikova, Tat'iana (2021) "'Vidii Stremlenie Zapada Perekroit' Postsovetskoe Prostrastvo': Zamestitel' Ministra Inostrannykh Del RF Andrei Rudenko—o krizisakh vblizi rossiiskikh granits", *Izvestiia*, February 10. https://iz.ru/1122605/tatiana-baikova/vidim-stremlenie-zapada-per ekroit-postsovetskoe-prostranstvo (accessed July 18, 2024)

Bainazarov, El'nar (2020) "Delo — Bremia: otkrytie granitsy s Belorussiei mogut otlozhit' iz-za skandala", *Izvestiia*, July 31. https://iz.ru/1042143/elnar-bainazarov/delo-bremia-otkrytie-granitcy-s-belorussiei-mogut-otlozhit-iz-za-skandala (accessed July 16, 2024)

Bainazarov, El'nar (2022) "Yazyk iz Kieva Uvedet: zachem Zapad evakuiruet diplomatov s Ukrainy", *Izvestiia*, January 24. https://iz.ru/1281638/elnar-bainazarov/iazyk-iz-kieva-uvedet-zachem-zapad-evakuiruet-diplomatov-s-ukrainy (accessed July 21, 2024)

Bakke, Kristin; Rickard, Kit and O'Loughlin, John (2023) "Perceptions of the Past in the Post-Soviet Space", *Post-Soviet Affairs*, vol. 39, issue 4

Balkelis, Tomas (2018) *War, Revolution, and Nation-Making in Lithuania, 1914-1923*, Oxford: OUP

Balmaceda, Margarita (1998) "Gas, Oil and the Linkages between Domestic and Foreign Policies: the case of Ukraine", *Europe-Asia Studies*, vol. 50, issue 2

Balmaceda, Margarita (1999) "Myth and Reality in the Belarusian-Russian Relationship: what the West must know", *Problems of Post-Communism*, vol. 46, issue 3

Balmaceda, Margarita (2013) *Politics of Energy Dependency: Ukraine, Belarus, and Lithuania between domestic oligarchs and Russian pressure*, Toronto: UTP

Balmaceda, Margarita (2014a) "Energy Policy in Belarus: authoritarian resilience, social contracts, and patronage in a post-Soviet environment", *Eurasian Geography and Economics*, vol. 55, issue 5

Balmaceda, Margarita (2014b) *Living the High Life in Minsk: Russian energy rents, domestic populism and Belarus' impending crisis*, Budapest: Central European UP

Balmaceda, Margarita and Westphal, Kirsten (2024) "Cross-Regional Production Chains, Competitive Regionalism, and the Deepening of Regulatory Fault Lines in Euro-Asia", *Review of Policy Research*, vol. 41, issue 2

Bange, Oliver (2016) "SS-20 and Pershing II: weapon systems and the dynamization of East-West relations" in *The Nuclear Crisis: the arms race, Cold War anxiety, and the German peace movement of the 1980s*, New York: Berghahn; eds. Christoph Becker-Schaum, Philipp Gassert, Martin Klimke, Wilfried Mausbach and Marianne Zepp

Baranets, Viktor (2023) "Zachem Rossiia Razmeshchaet Iadernoe Oruzhie v Belorussii: dostanem do liuboi strany NATO v Evrope", *Komsomol'skaia Pravda*, March 26. https://www.kp.ru/daily/27482.5/4738925/ (accessed July 24, 2024)

Baranov, Andrei (2022) "Zheleznyi Zanaves Vosstanovlen: Evroparlament ob"iavil Rossiiu sponsorom terrorizma", *Komsomol'skaia Pravda*, November 23. https://www.kp.ru/daily/27475/4682136/ (accessed July 22, 2024)

Bareiko, Irina (2024) "Belarus' i Rossiia Kak Nasledniki Pobeditelei Natsizma Prodolzhaiut Bor'bu s Nim v XXI Veke — Beliaev", *Belarus' Segodnia*, July 2. https://www.sb.by/articles/belarus-i-rossiya-kak-nasledniki-pobediteley-natsizma-prodolzhayut-borbu-s-nim-v-xxi-veke-belyaev.html (accessed July 26, 2024)

Baron, Samuel (2001) *Bloody Saturday in the Soviet Union: Novocherkassk, 1962*, Stanford, CA: SUP

Barrass, Gordon (2016) "*Able Archer 83*: what were the Soviets thinking?" *Survival*, vol. 58, issue 6

Barrington, Lowell; Herron, Erik and Silver, Brian (2003) "The Motherland Is Calling: views of homeland among Russians in the Near Abroad", *World Politics*, vol. 55, issue 2

Barron, Kiegan (2022) "The Annexation of Crimea and EU Sanctions: an ineffective response", *The Arbutus Review*, vol. 13, issue 1

Bassin, Mark (2016) *The Gumilev Mystique: biopolitics, Eurasianism, and the construction of community in modern Russia*, Ithaca, NY: Cornell UP

Baumgartner, Pete (2016) "Bill Clinton in 2000: Putin 'could get squishy on democracy'", *Radio Free Europe/Radio Liberty*, January 8. https://www.rferl.org/a/bill-clinton-putin-could-get-squishy-on-democracy/27477287.html (accessed July 30, 2024)

Bechev, Dimitar (2011) "Of Power and Powerlessness: the EU and its neighbours", *Comparative European Politics*, vol. 9, issue 4-5

Bedford, Sofie (2021) "The 2020 Presidential Election in Belarus: erosion of authoritarian stability and re-politicization of society", *Nationalities Papers*, vol. 49, issue 5

Bedford, Sofie (2024) "The 2024 Parliamentary Elections in Belarus Were Nothing More Than an Illusion", *LSE*, March 11. https://blogs.lse.ac.uk/europpblog/2024/03/11/the-2024-parliamentary-elections-in-belarus-were-nothing-more-than-an-illusion/ (accessed July 26, 2024)

Beissinger, Mark (2002) *Nationalist Mobilization and the Collapse of the Soviet State*, Cambridge: CUP

Beissinger, Mark (2007) "Structure and Example in Modular Political Phenomena: the diffusion of Bulldozer/Rose/Orange/Tulip revolutions", *Perspectives on Politics*, vol. 5, issue 2

Bekus, Nelly (2010) "Nationalism and Socialism: 'phase D' in the Belarusian nation-building", *Nationalities Papers*, vol. 38, issue 6

Bekus, Nelly (2014) "Ethnic Identity in Post-Soviet Belarus: ethnolinguistic survival as an argument in the political struggle", *Journal of Multilingual and Multicultural Development*, vol. 35, issue 1

Bekus, Nelly (2017a) "Constructed 'Otherness'? Poland and the geopolitics of contested Belarusian identity", *Europe-Asia Studies*, vol. 69, issue 2

Bekus, Nelly (2017b) "Ideological Recycling of the Socialist Legacy: reading townscapes of Minsk and Astana", *Europe-Asia Studies*, vol. 69, issue 5

Bekus, Nelly (2021) "Echo of 1989? Protest imaginaries and identity dilemmas in Belarus", *Slavic Review*, vol. 80, issue 1

Bekus, Nelly (2023) "Reassembling Society in a Nation-State: history, language, and identity discourses of Belarus", *Nationalities Papers*, vol. 51, issue 1

"Belarus Defence Industry Begins Switch to Civilian Production" (1994) *Central European*, vol. 4, issue 9

"Belarus Has No Debts for Gas, Electricity Imports, Says Deputy Premier" (2012a) *Belapan*, June 22

Belarus in the Twenty-First Century: between dictatorship and democracy (2023a) Abingdon: Routledge; eds. Elena Korosteleva, Irina Petrova and Anastasiia Kudlenko

"Belarus Lowers Export Duty on Crude Oil, Petroleum Products" (2012b) *Belapan*, February 1

"Belarus May Have to Buy Back Pipeline Operator if Deal with Gazprom Breached" (2012c) *Belapan*, January 10

"Belarus' Ne Iskliuchaet Vvedeniia Otvetnykh Mer na Deistviia FTS po Nepriznaniiu Sertifikatov EAES—Sen'ko" (2017) *Belta*, May 17. https://www.belta.by/economics/view/belarus-ne-iskljuchaet-vv edenija-otvetnyh-mer-na-dejstvija-fts-po-nepriznaniju-sertifikatov-eaes-senko-247718-2017/ (accessed August 10, 2024)

"Belarus' Ne Sobiraetsia Druzhit' s Zapadom protiv Rossii" (2019) *Belta*, September 26. https://www.belta.by/president/view/lukashenko-bela rus-ne-sobiraetsja-druzhit-s-zapadom-protiv-rossii-363468-2019/ (accessed August 10, 2024)

"Belarus' Podpisala s Bankom Razvitiia Kitaia Soglashenie o Kredite na 3,5 Mlrd Iuanei" (2019) *Belta*, December 16. https://www.belta.by/econ omics/view/belarus-podpisala-s-bankom-razvitija-kitaja-soglashen ie-o-kredite-na-35-mlrd-juanej-372991-2019/ (accessed August 10, 2024)

"Belarus' Poidet na Sovmestnye s Moskvoi Voennye Deistviia v Sluchae Nastupleniia Ukrainy na Donbass" (2022) *Zerkalo Nedeli*, February 6

298 UNCANNY ALLIES

"Belarus' Radi Druzhby s Pol'shei Pereshagnula cherez Boli, No za Bugom Priniali Eto za Slabosti" (2023b) *Belta*, September 17. https://www. belta.by/president/view/lukashenko-belarus-radi-druzhby-s-polsh ej-pereshagnula-cherez-bol-no-za-bugom-prinjali-eto-za-slabost-588 591-2023/ (accessed August 11, 2024)

"Belarus Seeks 5bn Dollars from IMF" (2012d) *Interfax*, January 30

"Belarus to Launch Veterinary Checks of Russian Pork after Disease Outbreak" (2012e) *Belapan*, August 8

"Belarus' v Integratsionnykh Proektakh s Rossiei Razvitie Predpriiatii Stavit Vyshe Vladel'cheskikh Voprosov — Kobiakov" (2016) *Belta*, April 1. https://www.belta.by/economics/view/belarus-v-integra tsionnyh-proektah-s-rossiej-razvitie-predprijatij-stavit-vyshe-vladel cheskih-voprosov-187970-2016/ (accessed August 9, 2024)

"Belarus Wants Domestic Customs Rates to Apply to Goods Moving in Russia-led Bloc" (2013) *Belapan*, May 31

"Belarusi Udalos' Ne Dopustit' Nachala Novoi Mirovoi Voiny" (2021) *Belta*, August 9. https://www.belta.by/president/view/lukashen ko-belarusi-udalos-ne-dopustit-nachala-novoj-mirovoj-vojny-454555 -2021/ (accessed August 11, 2024)

"Belarusian Airlines Warn Russian Flights Ban Cuts Sole Link with Regions" (2012a) *Belapan*, April 6

"Belarusian Authorities to Revise Textbook on History" (1999) *Radio Free Europe/Radio Liberty Newsline*, February 25. https://www.rferl.org/ a/1141851.html (accessed July 29, 2024)

"Belarusian First Deputy Premier Sees Flaws in Russia-led Trade Blocks" (2013a) *Belapan*, June 6

"Belarusian Premier Urges Food Export Diversification" (2012b) *Belapan*, March 14

"Belarusian President Lauds Russian Church, Sees 'Spiritual Crisis' in West" (2013b) *Belapan*, July 29

"Belarusian President Notes Failure to Fully Implement Union State Treaty" (2013c) *Belapan*, March 18

"Belarusian President Urges Russia to Respect Country's Sovereignty" (2013d) *Interfax*, October 17

"Belarusian President Wants Regional Economic Bloc to Have New Currency" (2012c) *Belapan*, January 19

"Belarusian President Welcomes 'Decent' Russian Investors" (2012d) *Belapan*, September 3

BIBLIOGRAPHY **299**

"Belarusy Ne Khochuts' Vaiavats' va Ukraine, ale Ne Suprats' Saiuza z Rasiiai" (2023) *Euroradio.fm*, June 20. https://euroradio.fm/belarusy-ne-khochuc-vayavac-va-ukraine-ale-ne-suprac-sayuza-z-rasiyay (accessed July 24, 2024)

"'Belneftekhim' Vedet Peregovory po Diversifikatsii Postavok Nefti" (2017) *Belta*, May 5. https://www.belta.by/economics/view/belnef tehim-vedet-peregovory-po-diversifikatsii-postavok-nefti-245941-20 17/ (accessed August 10, 2024)

"Belokonev: Nashi voennye mogut otpravit'sia v Livan v Sostave Ital'ianskoi Mirotvorcheskoi Missii" (2019) *Nasha Niva*, December 9. https://nashaniva.com/?c=ar&i=242440&lang=ru (accessed July 12, 2024)

"Belorussia—Lukashenko Addresses Crowds" (2015) *YouTube*, July 21 (https://www.youtube.com/watch?v=HDnZ-bkC83Q) (accessed on June 28, 2024)

"Belorussiia Povyshaet Eksportnye Poshliny na Neft' i Nefteprodukty", *Vesti.ru*, February 29. https://www.vesti.ru/finance/article/19061 84 (accessed August 6, 2024)

"Belorusskie Soldaty i Ofitsery Massovo Otkazyvaiutsia Voevat' protiv Ukrainy" (2022) *Xartyia '97*, March 5. https://charter97.org/ru/ne ws/2022/3/5/457699/ (accessed July 22, 2024)

"Belorusskie Tamozhennye Organy Iz''iali Bolee 1 Tys. t Tovarov pri Popy-tke Ikh Nezakonnogo Vvoza v Rossiiu" (2015) *Belta*, September 15. https://www.belta.by/economics/view/belorusskie-tamozhenny e-organy-izjjali-bolee-1-tys.-t-tovarov-pri-popytke-ih-nezakonnogo-vvoza-v-162753-2015/ (accessed August 9, 2024)

"Belorusskii Narod Nikakoi Voiny, Nikakogo Konflikta Ne Priemlet" (2022) *Pul Pervogo*, April 8. https://t.me/pul_1/5210 (accessed July 21, 2024)

Bemporad, Elena (2013*) Becoming Soviet Jews: the Bolshevik experiment in Minsk*, Bloomington, IN: OIU

Bergman, Jay (2009) *Meeting the Demands of Reason: the life and thought of Andrei Sakharov*, Ithaca, NY: Cornell UP

Bernhard, Michael and Kubik, Jan (2014) "A Theory of the Politics of Memory" in *Twenty Years after Communism: the politics of memory and commemoration*, Oxford: OUP; eds. Michael Bernhard and Jan Kubik

Bibikov, Vladimir (2019) "V Dele Nuzhen Sovet", *Soiuz Belarus'-Rossiia*, January 24

300 UNCANNY ALLIES

Bindman, Eleanor and Chulitskaya, Tatsiana (2023) "Post-Soviet Policy Entrepreneurs? The impact of nonstate actors on social service reform in Russia and Belarus" in *Lobbying the Autocrat: the dynamics of policy advocacy in nondemocracies*, Ann Arbor, MI: UMP; eds. Max Grömping and Jessica Teets

Black, J. (2004) *Vladimir Putin and the New World Order: looking East, looking West?* Lanham, MD: Rowman and Littlefield

Black, J. (2015) *The Russian Presidency of Dmitry Medvedev, 2008-12: the next step forward or merely a time out?* Abingdon: Routledge

Blackburn, Matthew and Petersson, Bo (2022) "Parade, Plebiscite, Pandemic: legitimation efforts in Putin's fourth term", *Post-Soviet Affairs*, vol. 38, issue 4

Blanchflower, David (2001) "Unemployment, Well-Being, and Wage Curves in Eastern and Central Europe", *Journal of the Japanese and International Economies*, vol. 15, issue 4

Blank, Stephen (2002) "Putin's Twelve-Step Program", *Washington Quarterly*, vol. 25, issue 1

Bogatyrev, Sergei (2012) "Normalizing the Debate about Kurbskii?" *Kritika*, vol. 13, issue 4

Bohdan, Siarhei (2010) "Nezalezhnasts' i Zneshniaia Palityka: viziia belaruskikh natsyianal-demakratau, kanets 1980-kh — 1995 hh. (pryklad Zianona Paz'niaka)", *Palitychnaia Sfera*, vol. 15, issue 2

Böhler, Jochen (2018) *Civil War in Central Europe, 1918-1921: the reconstruction of Poland*, Oxford: OUP

Boiko, Anastasiia; Ageeva, Ol'ga; Mil'kin, Vasilii; Mishutin, Gleb and Grinkevich, Dmitrii (2021) "Edinstvo Ekonomicheskoi Prirody", *Vedomosti*, September 13. https://www.vedomosti.ru/economics/artic les/2021/09/13/886291-ofitsialnaya-belorussiei (accessed July 19, 2024)

Bondarenko, Oleg (2020) "Minskie Uroki dlia Moskvy", *Moskovskii Komsomolets*, August 13

Bordachev, Timofei (2014) "Izvlech' Uroki, Stat' Sil'nee", *Izvestiia*, February 24

Borger, Julian (2016) *The Butcher's Trail: how the search for Balkan war criminals became the world's most successful manhunt*, New York: Other

"Boris Gryzlov Naznachen Poslom RF v Belorussii" (2022) *Interfax*, January 14. https://www.interfax.ru/russia/815463 (accessed August 11, 2024)

"Boris Nemtsov: Putin Khochet Vsekh Obezvrevidt' po Primeru Lukashenko" (2012) *Khartyia '97*, August 25. https://charter97.org/ ru/news/2012/8/25/57368/ (accessed August 6, 2024)

Borisova, Tat'iana (2013) "SNG v Povestke Dnia Evraziiskie Perspektivy Postsovetskoi Integratsii Sotrudnichestvo", *Belarus' Segodnia*, March 21

Borzęcki, Jerzy (2008) *The Soviet-Polish Peace of 1921 and the Creation of Interwar Europe*, New Haven, CT: Yale UP

Bosse, Giselle (2009) "Challenges for EU Governance through Neighbourhood Policy and Eastern Partnership: the values/security nexus in EU/Belarus relations", *Contemporary Politics*, vol. 15, issue 2

Bosse, Giselle (2010) "The EU's Relations with Moldova: governance, partnership or ignorance?" *Europe-Asia Studies*, vol. 62, issue 8

Bosse, Giselle (2011) "The EU's Geopolitical Vision of a European Energy Space: when "Gulliver" meets "white elephants" and Verdi's Babylonian King", *Geopolitics*, vol. 16, issue 3

Bosse, Giselle (2012) "A Partnership with Dictatorship: explaining the paradigm shift in European Union policy towards Belarus", *Journal of Common Market Studies*, vol. 50, issue 3

Bosse, Giselle and Korosteleva-Polglase, Elena (2009) "Changing Belarus? The limits of EU governance in Eastern Europe and the promise of partnership", *Cooperation and Conflict*, vol. 44, issue 2

Bouzarovski, Stefan and Konieczny, Marcin (2010) "Landscapes of Paradox: public discourses and policies in Poland's relationship with the Nord Stream pipeline", *Geopolitics*, vol. 15, issue 1

Bowring, Bill (2013) *Law, Rights and Ideology in Russia: Western reform, Byzantium or messianic identity?* Abingdon: Routledge

Bowring, Bill (2017) "Yevgeniy Pashukanis, His Law and Marxism: a general theory, and the 1922 Treaty of Rapallo between Soviet Russia and Germany", *Journal of the History of International Law*, vol. 19, issue 2

Bozh'eva, Ol'ga (2017) "NATO Beret Pribaltiku na Ispug", *Moskovskii Komsomolets*, September 1

Braithwaite, Rodric (2011) *Afgantsy: the Russians in Afghanistan, 1979-89*, London: Profile

Brantly, Aaron and Brantly, Nataliya (2024) "The Bitskrieg That Was and Wasn't: the military and intelligence implications of cyber operations during Russia's war on Ukraine", *Intelligence and National Security*, vol. 39, issue 3

"Bratskie Manevry" (2017) *Zerkalo Nedeli*, January 28

"Brifing Ofitsial'nogo Predstavitelia MID Rossii" (2021) *Facebook.com*, July 9. https://www.facebook.com/watch/live/?ref=watch_permalink&v=227155412561960 (accessed July 18, 2024)

Brothers Armed: military aspects of the crisis in Ukraine (2014) Minneapolis, MN: East View; eds. Colby Howard and Ruslan Pukhov

Brown, Archie (1996) *The Gorbachev Factor*, Oxford: OUP

Brown, Archie (1999) "Russia and Democratization", *Problems of Post-Communism*, vol. 46, issue 5

Brown, Archie (2008) "The Change to Engagement in Britain's Cold War Policy: the origins of the Thatcher-Gorbachev relationship", *Journal of Cold War Studies*, vol. 10, issue 3

Brown, Jonathan (2016) "Controversial New Nuclear Plant Ignites Belarus", *Al Jazeera*, October 18. https://www.aljazeera.com/featur es/2016/10/18/controversial-new-nuclear-plant-ignites-belarus (accessed July 7, 2024)

Brown-Montesano, Kristi (2007) *Understanding the Women of Mozart's Operas*, Stanford, CA: University of California

Browning, Christopher and Christou, George (2010) "The Constitutive Power of Outsiders: The European Neighbourhood Policy and the eastern dimension", *Political Geography*, vol. 29, issue 2

Browning, Christopher and Joenniemi, Pertti (2008) "Geostrategies of the European Neighbourhood Policy", *European Journal of International Relations*, vol. 14, issue 3

Brudny, Yitzhak (1998) *Reinventing Russia: Russian nationalism and the Soviet state, 1953-1991*, Cambridge, MA: Harvard UP

Brunarska, Zuzanna; Nestorowicz, Joanna and Markowski, Stefan (2014) "Intra- vs Extra-Regional Migration in the Post-Soviet Space", *Eurasian Geography and Economics*, vol. 55, issue 2

Bugajski, Janusz and Assenova, Margarita (2016) *Eurasian Disunion: Russia's vulnerable flanks*, Washington, DC: Jamestown Foundation

Buhr, Renee; Shadurski, Victor and Hoffman, Steven (2011) "Belarus: an emerging civic nation?" *Nationalities Papers*, vol. 39, issue 3

"Bukhgalteriia Druzhby" (2017) *TV-Tsentr*, March 27. https://www.tvc.ru/channel/brand/id/20/show/episodes/episode_id/49097 (accessed August 10, 2024)

Bulgakov, Mikhail (2003) *The Master and Margarita*, London: Vintage

"Bulletins 'IISEPS News' No 1" (2015) *IISEPS*, n.d. http://www.iiseps.org/?p=2106&lang=en (accessed August 7, 2024)

Bunce, Valerie (1999) "The Political Economy of Postsocialism", *Slavic Review*, vol. 58, issue 4

Bunce, Valerie and Wolchik, Sharon (2006) "International Diffusion and Postcommunist Electoral Revolutions", *Communist and Post-Communist Studies*, vol. 39, issue 3

Bunce, Valerie and Wolchik, Sharon (2010) "Defeating Dictators: electoral change and stability in competitive authoritarian regimes", *World Politics*, vol. 62, issue 1

Buranelli, Filippo (2014) "Knockin' on Heaven's Door: Russia, Central Asia and the mediated expansion of international society", *Millennium*, vol. 42, issue 3

Burant, Stephen (1993) "International Relations in a Regional Context: Poland and its eastern neighbours—Lithuania, Belarus, Ukraine", *Europe-Asia Studies*, vol. 45, issue 3

Burant, Stephen (1995) "Foreign Policy and National Identity: a comparison of Ukraine and Belarus," *Europe-Asia Studies*, vol. 47, issue 7

Burchakov, Anatolii (2019) "Pogovorili o Suverenitete: zachem Bolton priezzhal k Lukashenko v Minsk?" *BBC News Russkaia Sluzhba*, August 29. https://www.bbc.com/russian/features-49511381 (accessed August 10, 2024)

Burlew, Rich (2008) "The Philosophy of Chaos", *Giant in the Playground*, n.d. https://www.giantitp.com/comics/oots0606.html (accessed July 19, 2024)

Burlyuk, Olga; Dandashly, Assem and Noutcheva, Gergana (2024) "External Democracy Promotion in Times of Internal Rule-of-Law Crisis: the EU and its neighbourhood", *Journal of European Public Policy*, vol. 31, issue 3

Buscaneanu, Sergiu (2021) "Tertium Datur: multi-attribute reference points and integration choices between the European Union and Eurasian Economic Union", *The British Journal of Politics and International Relations*, vol. 23, issue 4

Bushkovitch, Paul (2011) *A Concise History of Russia*, Cambridge: CUP

Busygina, Irina and Filippov, Mikhail (2021) "Russia, Post-Soviet Integration, and the EAEU: the balance between domination and cooperation", *Problems of Post-Communism*, vol. 68, issue 6

Butler, Alexander (2023) "How Wagner Chief Evgeny Prigozhin's Death Was 'Orchestrated by Putin's Oldest Ally'", *Independent*, December 24. https://www.independent.co.uk/news/world/europe/russia-ukraine-prigozhin-putin-wagner-b2469030.html (accessed July 24, 2024)

Buzin, Nikolai (2024) "Chto Vkliuchaet v Sebia Obnovlennaia Kontseptsiia Natsional'noi Bezopasnosti", *Belarus' Segodnia*, January 18. https://www.sb.by/articles/sozidanie-i-razvitie-a-ne-razrushenie-i-unichtozhenie-glavnye-orientiry-belorusskogo-obshchestva.html (accessed July 26, 2024)

Çakmak, Cenap and Özşahin, M. (2023) "Explaining Russia's Inertia in the Azerbaijan-Armenia Dispute: reward and punishment in an asymmetric alliance", *Europe-Asia Studies*, vol. 75, issue 6

Cameron, David and Orenstein, Mitchell (2012) "Post-Soviet Authoritarianism: the influence of Russia in its 'near abroad'", *Post-Soviet Affairs*, vol. 28, issue 1

Cantir, Cristian and Kennedy, Ryan (2015) "Balancing on the Shoulders of Giants: Moldova's foreign policy toward Russia and the European Union", *Foreign Policy Analysis*, vol. 11, issue 4

Capote, Truman (2000) *In Cold Blood*, London: Penguin

Carafano, James (2002) *Waltzing into the Cold War: the struggle for occupied Austria*, College Station, TX: Texas A&M UP

Carleton, Gregory (2010) "Victory in Death: annihilation narratives in Russia today", *History and Memory*, vol. 22, issue 1

Carleton, Gregory (2017) *Russia: the story of war*, Cambridge, MA: Belknap

Carley, Michael (2023) *Stalin's Gamble: the search for allies against Hitler, 1930-1936*, Toronto: UTP

Casier, Tom (2018) "The Different Faces of Power in European Union-Russia Relations", *Cooperation and Conflict*, vol. 53, issue 1

Chadwick, Henry (2003) *East and West: the making of a rift in the church – from apostolic times until the Council of Florence*, Oxford: OUP

Chafetz, Glenn (1993) "The End of the Cold War and the Future of Nuclear Proliferation: an alternative to the Neorealist perspective", *Security Studies*, vol. 2, issue 3-4

Chafetz, Glenn; Abramson, Hillel and Grillot, Suzette (1996) "Role Theory and Foreign Policy: Belarussian and Ukrainian compliance with the nuclear nonproliferation regime", *Political Psychology*, vol. 17, issue 4

Chaly, Serge (2017) "Karta Vrazhdebnoi Shvambranii", *Facebook*, August 29. https://www.facebook.com/sergechaly/posts/10210112960485 114 (accessed on July 8, 2024)

Chalyi, Sergei (2022) "Na Litse Ministra Oborony Belarusi Khrenina Chitaetsia Zastyvshaia Maska Uzhasa", *Khartyia '97*, June 30. https://charter97.org/ru/news/2022/6/30/504520/ (accessed July 22, 2024)

Chaudhry, Suparna (2022) "The Assault on Civil Society: explaining state crackdowns on NGOs", *International Organization*, vol. 76, issue 3

"Chem Zakonchitsia Voina v Ukraine?" (2023) *YouTube*, August 17. https://www.youtube.com/watch?v=XzSCMh2ITyE (accessed July 24, 2024)

Cheng, Zhangxi (2020) "Building the Belt and Road Initiative? Practices en route", *The Pacific Review*, vol. 33, issue 5

Chepurnaya, Olga (2016) "The Moscow Olympics, 1980: competing in the context of the Cold War and state dirigisme" in *Routledge Handbook of Sport and Politics*, Abingdon: Routledge; eds. Alan Bairner, John Kelly and Lee, Jung

BIBLIOGRAPHY 305

Cherkasova, Mariia (2012) "Belorussiu Ne Pustiat v Rossiiskie Regiony", *Kommersant*, April 6

Chernenko, Elena (2022) "Bez Osobogo Vostoka", *Kommersant*, January 26. https://www.kommersant.ru/doc/5182806 (accessed July 21, 2024)

Chernev, Borislav (2017) *Twilight of Empire: the Brest-Litovsk Conference and the remaking of East-Central Europe, 1917-1918*, Toronto: UTP

Chernyshova, Natalya (2021) "De-Stalinisation and Insubordination in the Soviet Borderlands: Beria's attempted national reform in Soviet Belarus", *Europe-Asia Studies*, vol. 73, issue 2

Chernyshova, Natalya (2023) "Between Soviet and Ethnic Cultural Policies and National Identity Building in Soviet Belarus under Petr Masherau, 1965-80", *Kritika*, vol. 24, issue 3

Cheskin, Ammon and Kachuyevski, Angela (2019) "The Russian-Speaking Populations in the Post-Soviet Space: language, politics and identity", *Europe-Asia Studies*, vol. 71, issue 1

"China-Russia: joint declaration on a multipolar world and the establishment of a new international order", *International Legal Materials*, vol. 36, issue 4

Chinkova, Elena (2013) "Aleksandr Lukashenko-Patriarkhu Kirillu: 'Belarus' Budet Tikhim Domom dlia Pravoslaviia", *Komsomol'skaia Pravda*, July 30

Christensen, Darin and Weinstein, Jeremy (2013) "Defunding Dissent: restrictions on aid to NGOs", *Journal of Democracy*, vol. 24, issue 2

Christian, David (2018) *A History of Russia, Central Asia and Mongolia: Inner Eurasia from the Mongol Empire to today, 1260-2000*, Chichester: Wiley

"Chuden Kiev v Dekabre" (2013) *Belarus' Segodnia*, December 10

Chudowsky, Victor and Kuzio, Taras (2003) "Does Public Opinion Matter in Ukraine? The case of foreign policy", *Communist and Post-Communist Studies*, vol. 36, issue 3

Clark, Katerina; Dobrenko, Evgeny; Artizov, Andrei and Naumov, Oleg (2007) *Soviet Culture and Power: a history in documents, 1917-1953*, New Haven, CT: Yale UP

Clem, Ralph (2011) "Going It Alone: Belarus as the non-European European state", *Eurasian Geography and Economics*, vol. 52, issue 6

Clover, Charles (2022) *Black Wind, White Snow: Russia's new nationalism* (new ed.), New Haven, CT: Yale UP

Cohrs, Patrick (2006) *The Unfinished Peace after World War I: America, Britain and the stabilisation of Europe, 1919-1932*, Cambridge: CUP

"Collective Security Treaty (1992)" in *Russian Foreign Policy in Transition: concepts and realities* (2005) Budapest: Central European UP; eds. Andrei Melville and Tatiana Shakleina

Colton, Timothy and McFaul, Michael (2003) *Popular Choice and Managed Democracy: the Russian elections of 1999 and 2000*, Washington, DC: Brookings Institution

Comai, Giorgio and Venturi, Bernardo (2015) "Language and Education Laws in Multi-Ethnic De Facto States: the cases of Abkhazia and Transnistria", *Nationalities Papers*, vol. 43, issue 6

Connolly, Richard (2008) "The Structure of Russian Industrial Exports in Comparative Perspective", *Eurasian Geography and Economics*, vol. 49, issue 5

Connolly, Richard (2012) "Climbing the Ladder? High-Technology Export Performance in Emerging Europe", *Eurasian Geography and Economics*, vol. 53, issue 3

Connolly, Richard and Hanson, Philip (2012) "Russia's Accession to the World Trade Organization", *Eurasian Geography and Economics*, vol. 53, issue 4

Conradi, Peter (2022) *Who Lost Russia? From the collapse of the USSR to Putin's war on Ukraine*, London: Oneworld

Cooley, Alexander and Mitchell, Lincoln (2010) "Engagement without Recognition: a new strategy toward Abkhazia and Eurasia's unrecognized states", *The Washington Quarterly*, vol. 33, issue 4

Copsey, Nathaniel and Pomorska, Karolina (2010) "Poland's Power and Influence in the European Union: the case of its eastern policy", *Comparative European Politics*, vol. 8, issue 3

"Covid-19 Dashboard" (2023) *Johns Hopkins Coronavirus Resource Center*, March 10. https://coronavirus.jhu.edu/map.html (accessed July 16, 2024)

Crampton, R. (1997) *Eastern Europe in the Twentieth Century — and after (2nd ed.)*, London: Routledge

Creswell, Michael (2023) "The Collapse of the Versailles System" in *The Oxford Handbook of World War II*, Oxford: OUP; eds. G. Piehler and Jonathan Grant

Crowley, Roger (2005) *Constantinople: the last great siege, 1453*, London: Faber and Faber

Crowley, Stephen (2021) *Putin's Labor Dilemma: Russian politics between stability and stagnation*, Ithaca, NY: Cornell UP

Crump, Laurien (2015) *The Warsaw Pact Reconsidered: international relations in Eastern Europe, 1955-1969*, Abingdon: Routledge

Crump, Laurien (2016) "Forty-Five Years of Dialogue Facilitation (1972-2017): ten lessons from the Conference on Security and Cooperation in Europe", *Security and Human Rights*, vol. 27, issue 3-4

Crump, Thomas (2013) *Brezhnev and the Decline of the Soviet Union*, Abingdon: Routledge

Dagorn, Gary (2022) "War in Ukraine: why it is so hard to estimate the number of dead?" *Le Monde*, September 26. https://www.lemonde.fr/en/les-decodeurs/article/2022/09/26/war-in-ukraine-why-it-is-so-hard-to-estimate-the-number-of-dead_5998268_8.html (accessed July 22, 2024)

Daniels, Robert (1999) "Evgenii Primakov: contender by chance", *Problems of Post-Communism*, vol. 46, issue 5

D'Anieri, Paul (2023a) "Commitment Problems and the Failure of the Minsk Process: the second-order commitment challenge", *Post-Soviet Affairs*, vol. 39, issue 4

D'Anieri, Paul (2023b) *Ukraine and Russia: from civilized divorce to uncivil war (2nd ed.)*, Cambridge: CUP

Danilovich, Alex (2006) *Russian-Belarusian Integration: playing games behind the Kremlin walls*, Aldershot: Ashgate

Danzer, Alexander and Dietz, Barbara (2014) "Labour Migration from Eastern Europe and the EU's Quest for Talents", *Journal of Common Market Studies*, vol. 52, issue 2

Davidzon, Igor (2021) *Regional Security Governance in Post-Soviet Eurasia: the history and effectiveness of the Collective Security Treaty Organization*, Basingstoke: Palgrave Macmillan

Davydov, Ivan (2018) "Vozhd' Beloe Pero: obraz Putina v detskikh predvybornykh risunkakh", *Republic (Slon)*, February 15

Dawisha, Karen (2011) "Is Russia's Foreign Policy That of a Corporatist-Kleptocratic Regime?" *Post-Soviet Affairs*, vol. 27, issue 4

De Hartog, Leo (1996) *Russia and the Mongol Yoke: the history of the Russian principalities and the Golden Horde, 1221-1502*, London: British Academic

De Madariaga, Isabel (2005) *Ivan the Terrible: first tsar of Russia*, New Haven, CT: Yale UP

De Vogel, Sasha (2022) "Anti-Opposition Crackdowns and Protest: the case of Belarus, 2000-2019", *Post-Soviet Affairs*, vol. 38, issue 1-2

Defraigne, Jean-Christophe (2021) "The Eurasian Economic Union and the Challenge of the BRI: a comparison of their respective impacts on economic development and Russia's regional leadership", *Eurasian Geography and Economics*, vol. 62, issue 5-6

Delcour, Laure and Fernandes, Sandra (2016) "Visa Liberalization Processes in the EU's Eastern Neighbourhood: understanding policy outcomes", *Cambridge Review of International Affairs*, vol. 29, issue 4

Deni, John (1994) "Russia Signs PFP Accord Despite Absence of 'Special Relationship'", *Arms Control Today*, vol. 24, issue 6

Dettmer, Jamie (2020) "From Putin to Bismarck, an Autocrat's Fear of Germs", *Voice of America*, June 19. https://www.voanews.com/a/covid-19-pandemic_putin-bismarck-autocrats-fear-germs/6191402.html (accessed July 16, 2024)

Deyermond, Ruth (2004) "The State of the Union: military success, economic and political failure in the Russia-Belarus Union", *Europe-Asia Studies*, vol. 56, issue 8

Deyermond, Ruth (2007) *Security and Sovereignty in the Former Soviet Union*, Boulder, CO: Lynne Rienner

Diani, Mario (2015) *The Cement of Civil Society: studying networks in localities*, Cambridge: CUP

Diatkine, Gilbert (2006) "A Review of Lacan's Seminar on Anxiety", *The International Journal of Psychoanalysis*, vol. 87, issue 4

Diatlikovich, Viktor (1997) "Rossiia Snova Khodit v Dolzhnikakh u Lukashenko", *Izvestiia*, February 21

Dimitrova, Antoaneta and Dragneva, Rilka (2009) "Constraining External Governance: interdependence with Russia and the CIS as limits to the EU's rule transfer in the Ukraine", *Journal of European Public Policy*, vol. 16, issue 6

Dimitrova, Antoaneta and Dragneva, Rilka (2013) "Shaping Convergence with the EU in Foreign Policy and State Aid in Post-Orange Ukraine: weak external incentives, powerful veto players", *Europe-Asia Studies*, vol. 65, issue 4

Dimnik, Martin (2004) "Kievan Rus', the Bulgars and the Southern Slavs, c. 1020-c. 1200" in *The New Cambridge Medieval History (vol. 4): c.1024-c.1198, part II*, Cambridge: CUP; eds. David Luscombe and Jonathan Riley-Smith

Djilas, Milovan (1983) *The New Class: an analysis of the communist system*, San Diego, CA: Harcourt Brace

Dmitriev, Mikhail (2011) "Conflict and Concord in Early Modern Poland: Catholics and Orthodox at the Union of Brest" in *Diversity and Dissent: negotiating religious difference in Central Europe, 1500-1800*, New York: Berghahn; eds. Howard Louthan, Gary Cohen and Franz Szabo

Dobrenko, Evgeny (2020) *Late Stalinism: the aesthetics of politics*, New Haven, CT: Yale UP

Dobrokhotov, Roman (2019) "Russia Was Too Quick to Celebrate Zelenskyy's Victory in Ukraine", *Al Jazeera*, April 26. https://www.aljazeera.com/opinions/2019/4/26/russia-was-too-quick-to-celebrate-zelenskyys-victory-in-ukraine (accessed July 12, 2024)

Dodds, Klaus (2019) *Geopolitics: a very short introduction (3rd ed.)*, Oxford: OUP

"Dogovor o Postavkakh Nefti v Belarus' Mozhet Byt' Zaklyuchen v Nachale 2020 Goda—Aset Magauov" (2019) *Kazinform*, December 6. https://www.inform.kz/ru/dogovor-o-postavkah-nefti-v-belarus-mozhet-byt-zaklyuchen-v-nachale-2020-goda-aset-magauov_a3592222 (accessed August 10, 2024)

"Doklad" (2015) *Belarus' Segodnia*, June 2

Donaldson, Robert and Nadkarni, Vidya (2023) *The Foreign Policy of Russia: changing systems, enduring interests (7th ed.)*, Abingdon: Routledge

Douglas, Mary (2002) *Purity and Danger: an analysis of concepts of pollution and taboo*, Abingdon: Routledge

Douglas, Nadja (2023) "Belarus: 'securitization' of state politics and the impact on state-society relations", *Nationalities Papers*, vol. 51, issue 4

Downing, Taylor (2018) *1983: the world at the brink*, London: Little, Brown

Doyle, James (2022) "Building a Nuclear Off-Ramp Following the War in Ukraine", *Bulletin of the Atomic Scientists*, vol. 78, issue 4

Dragneva, Rilka and Hartwell, Christopher (2022) "The Crisis of the Multilateral Order in Eurasia: authoritarian regionalism and its limits", *Politics and Governance*, vol. 10, issue 2

Dragneva, Rilka and Wolczuk, Kataryna (2016) "Between Dependence and Integration: Ukraine's relations with Russia", *Europe-Asia Studies*, vol. 68, issue 4

Drakakhrust, Yurii (2018) "Vyniki Sustrechi Lukashenki i Putsina i Perspektyva Belaruska-Raseiskikh Adnosinau", *Radyio Svaboda*, December 29. https://www.svaboda.org/a/29683167.html (accessed July 10, 2024)

Drakakhrust, Iury (2023) "Yakimi Buduts' Nastupstvy Merkavanai Hibeli Pryhozhyna dlia Belarusi? Tlumachyts' palitoliah Aliaksandr Marozau", *Radyio Svaboda*, August 24. https://www.svaboda.org/a/32562030.html (accessed July 24, 2024)

Drakakhrust, Iury (2024) "Iakaia Spadchyna Zastanetstsa Pas'lia Lukashenki? Pohliad Artsioma Shraibmana", *Radyio Svaboda*, July 10. https://www.svaboda.org/a/33028395.html (accessed July 26, 2024)

Drezner, Daniel (1997) "Allies, Adversaries, and Economic Coercion: Russian foreign economic policy since 1991", *Security Studies*, vol. 6, issue 3

Dronin, Nikolai and Bellinger, Edward (2005) *Climate Dependence and Food Problems in Russia 1900-1990: the interaction of climate and agricultural policy and their effect on food problems*, Budapest: Central European UP

Drost, Niels and de Graaf, Beatrice (2022) "Putin and the Third Rome: imperial-eschatological motives as a usable past", *Journal of Applied History*, vol. 4, issue 1-2

"Drug Trafficking across Belarusian, Russian borders Expected to Increase" (2012) *Belapan*, February 7

Dubnov, Arkadii (2014) "Skelety 'Slavianskogo Shkafa': chast' vtoraia", *Gazeta.ru*, April 1. https://www.gazeta.ru/comments/2014/03/31_x_5971109.shtml (accessed August 7, 2024)

Duncan, Peter (2000) *Russian Messianism: Third Rome, revolution, communism and after*, Abingdon: Routledge

Duncan, Peter (2013) "Batman and Robin? Exploring foreign policy differences between Putin and Medvedev during the Medvedev presidency", *CEPSI Working Paper 2013-03*, London: UCL

Dunlop, John (1993) *The Rise of Russia and the Fall of the Soviet Empire*, Princeton, NJ: PUP

Dunlop, John (2000) "Sifting through the Rubble of the Yeltsin Years", *Problems of Post-Communism*, vol. 47, issue 1

Dunlop, John (2012) *The Moscow Bombings of September 1999: examinations of Russian terrorist attacks at the onset of Vladimir Putin's rule*, Stuttgart: ibidem

Dunning, Chester (2004) *A Short History of Russia's First Civil War: The Time of Troubles and the founding of the Romanov dynasty*, University Park, PA: PSUP

Dvali, Georgii (2015) "Aleksandr Lukashenko Proiavil Mirnuiu Initsiativu", *Kommersant*, April 24

Dyner, Anna (2022) "New Military Doctrine of the Union State of Belarus and Russia", *The Polish Institute of International Affairs*, February 15. https://www.pism.pl/publications/new-military-doctrine-of-the-union-state-of-belarus-and-russia (accessed July 21, 2024)

Dynko, Aliaksandra (2015) "Vaiskovy Ekspert: Na Menskim Paradze Raseia Adpratsouvae Perakidvan'ne u Belarus' Vaiskovai Tekhniki", *Radyio Svaboda*, May 7. https://www.svaboda.org/a/27000242.html (accessed August 9, 2024)

Dyukov, Alexander (2017) "The Death Toll in the Kuropaty Massacre", *International Affairs (Moscow)*, vol. 63, issue 5

Eberhard, Winfried (1995) "Reformation and Counterreformation in East Central Europe" in *Handbook of European History, 1400-1600: late Middle Ages, Renaissance, and Reformation (vol. 2)*, Leiden: Brill; eds. Thomas Brady Jr., Heiko Oberman and James Tracy

Eccles, Mari and Sheftalovich, Zoya (2022) "Inside the Control Room of Belarus' Hijacked Ryanair Flight", *Politico*, October 25. https://www.politico.eu/article/belarus-hijack-minsk-ryanair-athens-to-vilnius-control-room/ (accessed July 18, 2024)

Eckel, Mike (2022) "Russian Officials Predicted a Quick Triumph in Ukraine: did bad intelligence skew Kremlin decision-making?" *Radio Free Europe/Radio Liberty*, March 11. https://www.rferl.org/a/russia-invasion-ukraine-intelligence-putin/31748594.html (accessed July 21, 2024)

Edele, Mark (2019) *The Soviet Union: a short history*, Hoboken, NJ: Wiley Blackwell

Edele, Mark (2021) *Stalinism at War: the Soviet Union in World War II*, London: Bloomsbury

"Edinstvennoe Mesto, Kuda Soglasitsia Vyekhat' Putin dlia Peregovorov s Zelenskim—Eto Belarus'" (2022) *SN-Plus*, March 12. https://www.sn-plus.com/2022/03/12/edinstvennoe-mesto-kuda-soglasitsya-vyehat-putin-dlya-peregovorov-s-zelenskim-eto-belarus/ (accessed July 22, 2024)

Ehrman, Bart (2021) *Heaven and Hell: a history of the afterlife*, London: Oneworld

Eichler, Maya (2006) "Russia's Post-Communist Transformation: a gendered analysis of the Chechen Wars", *International Feminist Journal of Politics*, vol. 8, issue 4

Eichler, Maya (2012) *Militarizing Men: gender, conscription, and war in post-Soviet Russia*, Stanford, CA: SUP

Eke, Steven and Kuzio, Taras (2000) "Sultanism in Eastern Europe: the socio-political roots of authoritarian populism in Belarus", *Europe-Asia Studies*, vol. 52, issue 3

"Ekspert: Belorussiia Gotovitsia k 'Gibridnoi Voine', Khotia Chto Eto Takoe, Nikto Ob''iasnit' Ne Mozhet", *Regnum*, January 26. https://regnum.ru/news/1888388 (accessed August 9, 2024)

Eliade, Mircea (2024) *Shamanism: archaic techniques of ecstasy*, Princeton, NJ: PUP

Elletson, Harold (1998) *The General Against the Kremlin: Alexander Lebed—power and illusion*, London: Little, Brown

Ellis, Frank (2015) *Barbarossa 1941: reframing Hitler's invasion of Stalin's Soviet empire*, Lawrence, KS: UPK

Ellman, Michael (2010) "Regional Influences on the Formulation and Implementation of NKVD Order 00447", *Europe-Asia Studies*, vol. 62, issue 6

Ellman, Michael (2014) *Socialist Planning (3rd ed.)*, Cambridge: CUP

Ellsberg, Daniel (2019) *The Doomsday Machine: confessions of a nuclear war planner*, London: Bloomsbury

Elsner, Regina (2023) "Praying Instead of Protesting? The Belarusian churches and political protest after the 2020 presidential election", *Nationalities Papers*, vol. 51, issue 4

Engelstein, Laura (2017) *Russia in Flames: war, revolution, civil war, 1914-1921*, Oxford: OUP

Englund, Peter (1992) *The Battle of Poltava: the birth of the Russian Empire*, London: Gollancz

Epstein, Rachel (2008) "The Social Context in Conditionality: internationalizing finance in postcommunist Europe", *Journal of European Public Policy*, vol. 15, issue 6

Erickson, John (1999) "'Russia Will Not Be Trifled With': geopolitical facts and fantasies", *Journal of Strategic Studies*, vol. 22, issue 2-3

Ericson, Lars (1997) *Lasse i Gatan: kaparkriget och det svenska stormaktsväldets fall*, Lund: Historiska media

Ermolaev, Sergei (2017) "The Formation and Evolution of the Soviet Union's Oil and Gas Dependence", *Carnegie Endowment*, March 29, https://carnegieendowment.org/posts/2017/03/the-formation-and-evolution-of-the-soviet-unions-oil-and-gas-dependence?lang=en&center=global (accessed on June 11, 2024)

"Etarli Kuch Va Salokhiiatga Egamiz" (2022) *Telegram*, January 13 https://t.me/Press_Secretary_Uz/1148 (accessed July 21, 2024)

Etkind, Alexander (2023) *Russia against Modernity*, Cambridge: Polity

"'Eto Izmena Gosudarstvu, Izmena Narody': Tikhanovskaia prokommentirovala voinu i referendum" (2022) *Zerkalo*, February 28. https://news.zerkalo.io/economics/10608.html (accessed July 21, 2024)

Evangelista, Matthew (2002) *The Chechen Wars: will Russia go the way of the Soviet Union?* Washington, DC: Brookings Institution

Evans, Anthony (2024) "Competitive Authoritarianism, Informational Authoritarianism, and the Development of Dictatorship: a case study of Belarus", *Public Choice*, vol. 198, issue 3-4

"Evropeiskie Partnery Zainteresovany v Zakliuchenii Belarus'iu i ES Soglashenii po Readmissii i Vizam—Makei" (2017) *Belta*, June 22. https://www.belta.by/politics/view/evropejskie-partnery-zainteresovany-v-zakljuchenii-belarusjju-i-es-soglashenij-po-readmissii-i-vizam-254028-2017/ (accessed August 10, 2024)

Evstaf'ev, Dmitrii (2016) "Po Moshcham i Elei", *Izvestiia*, May 11. https://iz.ru/news/613038

Fajfer, Luba (1993) "The Polish Military and the Crisis of 1970", *Communist and Post-Communist Studies*, vol. 26, issue 2

Faliakhov, Rustam (2016) "Kto Predast Rossiiu", *Gazeta.ru*, January 12. https://www.gazeta.ru/business/2016/01/11/8015273.shtml (accessed August 9, 2024)

Falk, Barbara (2003) *Dilemmas of Dissidence in East-Central Europe: citizen intellectuals and philosopher kings*, Budapest: Central European UP

Favereau, Marie (2021) *The Horde: how the Mongols changed the world*, Cambridge, MA: Belknap

Fedorov, Konstantin (2009) "Krest'ianin, Direktor, Prem'er-Ministr", *Svobodnaya Mysl'*, April 30

Fedorowycz, Daniel (2021) "Beyond Ideology: reassessing the threat of Belarusian opposition in interwar Poland", *Nationalities Papers*, vol. 49, issue 5

Feduta, Aleksandr (2017) "Novogodnie Strashnye Sny Belorusskogo Rukovodstvo", *Ezhednevnyi Zhurnal*, January 3. https://www.ej.ru/?a=note&id=30576 (accessed August 9, 2024)

"Feigin pra Belarus', 30 Strachanykh Gadou i Shanets Pas'lia Lukashenki" (2024) *YouTube*, July 16. https://www.youtube.com/watch?v=ndET4vqtu6I (accessed July 26, 2024)

Felak, James (2020) *The Pope in Poland: the pilgrimages of John Paul II, 1979-1991*, Pittsburgh, PA: UPP

Feldberg, Olya (2023) "From Dinosaurs to Nuclear Fallout: multiple temporalities of scale in memory studies", *Memory Studies*, vol. 16, issue 6

Fel'gengauer, Pavel (2020) "Ne Brat'ia po Oruzhiiu: chto belorusskaia armiia mozhet protivopostavit' rossiiskoi", *Novaia Gazeta*, August 6. https://novayagazeta.ru/articles/2020/08/06/86546-ne-bratya-po-oruzhiyu (accessed July 16, 2024)

Ferguson, Joseph (2008) *Japanese-Russian Relations, 1907-2007*, Abingdon: Routledge

Feygin, Yakov (2024) "Choosing Stagnation: the Kosygin Reforms and the rise of Brezhnev's stagnationary coalition", *Europe-Asia Studies*, vol. 76, issue 1

Figes, Orlando (2010) *Crimea: the last crusade*, London: Allen Lane

Filatotchev, Igor; Wright, Mike; Buck, Trevor and Dyomina, Natalya (1999) "Exporting and Restructuring in Privatised Firms from Russia, Ukraine and Belarus", *The World Economy*, vol. 22, issue 7

Filatova, Irina (2013) "Potash Giants End Alliance, Market in Turmoil", *The Moscow Times*, July 30. https://www.themoscowtimes.com/2013/07/30/potash-giants-end-alliance-market-in-turmoil-a26291 (accessed August 7, 2024)

Finkel, Evgeny and Brudny, Yitzhak (2012) "No More Colour! Authoritarian regimes and colour revolutions in Eurasia", *Democratization*, vol. 19, issue 1

Finnin, Rory (2022) *Blood of Others: Stalin's Crimean atrocity and the poetics of solidarity*, Toronto: UTP

Fish, M. (1997) "The Determinants of Economic Reform in the Post-Communist World", *East European Politics and Societies*, vol. 12, issue 1

Fitzpatrick, Sheila (2022) *The Shortest History of the Soviet Union*, Exeter: Old Street

Flake, Lincoln (2021) *Defending the Faith: The Russian Orthodox Church and the demise of religious pluralism*, Stuttgart: ibidem

Floyd, Rita and Webber, Mark (2024) "Making Amends: emotions and the Western response to Russia's invasion of Ukraine", *International Affairs*, vol. 100, issue 3

"Foreign Policy Concept of the Russian Federation" (2000) *International Affairs (Moscow)*, vol. 46, issue 5

"Foreign Policy of the Russian Federation" (2013) *Beijing.Mid.Ru.* https://beijing.mid.ru/en/countries/rossiya/kontseptsiya_vneshney_politiki_rossii/ (accessed August 6, 2024)

"Foreign Policy Concept of the Russian Federation" (2016) *Interkomitet*, December 1. https://interkomitet.com/foreign-policy/basic-documents/foreign-policy-concept-of-the-russian-federation-approved-by-president-of-the-russian-federation-vladimir-putin-on-november-30-2016/ (accessed August 9, 2024)

Fortin, Jessica (2012) "Is There a Necessary Condition for Democracy? The role of state capacity in postcommunist countries", *Comparative Political Studies*, vol. 45, issue 7

Foucault, Michel (2020) *Discipline and Punish: the birth of the prison*, London: Penguin

"Francysk Skaryna, the Martin Luther of Belarus" (2017) *Economist.com*, January 31

Franklin, Simon and Shepard, Jonathan (1996) *The Emergence of Rus 750-1200*, London: Longman

Frear, Matthew (2021) "'Better to Be a Dictator Than Gay': homophobic discourses in Belarusian politics", *Europe-Asia Studies*, vol. 73, issue 8

Freedman, Robert (2001) "Russian Policy toward the Middle East under Yeltsin and Putin from 1991 to 2000", *Jewish Political Studies Review*, vol. 13, issue 1-2

Freud, Sigmund (2003) *The Uncanny*, London: Penguin

Fridman, Aleksandr (2023) "V Sluchae Pobedy Kremlia v Ukraine Belarus' Mozhet Rastvorit'sia v 'Istoricheskoi Rossii'", *Telegra.ph*, January 9. https://telegra.ph/V-sluchae-pobedy-Kremlya-v-Ukraine-Belarus-mozhet-rastvoritsya-v-istoricheskoj-Rossii-01-09 (accessed July 24, 2024)

Fritz, Verena (2005) "New Divisions in Europe? East-East divergence and the influence of European Union enlargement", *Journal of International Relations and Development*, vol. 8, issue 2

Frolov, A. (2018) "Viktor Chernomyrdin: man, politician, diplomat", *International Affairs (Moscow)*, vol. 64, issue 4

Frolov, Andrei (2023) "Porazitel'nye Perspektivy", *Izvestiia*, March 27. https://iz.ru/1488962/andrei-frolov/porazitelnye-perspektivy (accessed July 24, 2024)

Frost, Robert (2001) *The Northern Wars: war, state and society in Northeastern Europe, 1558-1721*, Abingdon: Routledge

Frye, Timothy (1997) "A Politics of Institutional Choice: post-communist presidencies", *Comparative Political Studies*, vol. 30, issue 5

Frye, Timothy (2011) "Belarus and Its Implications for the Study of Transition Economies: an introduction", *Eurasian Geography and Economics*, vol. 52, issue 6

Fuks, Erika (2015) "Rusijos ir Baltarusijos Atominės be Kruonio — Nė iš Vietos?" *Delfi*, November 24. https://www.delfi.lt/verslas/energetika/rusijos-ir-baltarusijos-atomines-be-kruonio-ne-is-vietos-69587914 (accessed August 8, 2024)

Fuller Jr., William (2006) "The Imperial Army" in *The Cambridge History of Russia (vol. 2): imperial Russia, 1689-1917*, Cambridge: CUP; ed. Dominic Lieven

"Fundamental Problems of the Astravets Nuclear Power Plant under Construction in Belarus" (n.d.) *Ministry of Foreign Affairs of the Republic of Lithuania*. https://www.urm.lt/en/news/928/fundamental-problems-of-the-astravets-nuclear-power-plant-under-construction-in-belarus:33485 (accessed July 7, 2024)

Gabowitsch, Mischa (2021) "Belarusian Protest: regimes of engagement and coordination", *Slavic Review*, vol. 80, issue 1

Gabuev, Aleksandr (2012) "Pered Nami Eshche Lezhit Polosa Volatil'nosti", *Kommersant*, February 10

Galbreath, David (2006) "Latvian Foreign Policy after Enlargement: continuity and change", *Cooperation and Conflict*, vol. 41, issue 4

Galbreath, David and Lamoreaux, Jeremy (2007) "Bastion, Beacon or Bridge? Conceptualising the Baltic logic of the EU's neighbourhood", *Geopolitics*, vol. 12, issue 1

Galeotti, Mark (2022a) *The Moscow Kremlin: Russia's fortified heart*, Oxford: Osprey

Galeotti, Mark (2022b) *Putin's Wars: from Chechnya to Ukraine*, Oxford: Osprey

Galimova, Natal'ia; Zhermeleva, Ol'ga and Shishkunova, Elena (2012) "Vladimir Putin Vybiraet mezhdu Belorussiei i Kazakhstanom", *Izvestiia*, May 15

Gall, Carlotta and de Waal, Thomas (1997) *Chechnya: a small victorious war*, London: Pan

Gamov, Aleksandr (2012) "Aleksandr Lukashenko—Vladimiru Putinu: 'Vash Vizit Vazhnee Mnogikh Ekonomicheskikh Dogovorennostei'", *Komsomol'skaia Pravda*, June 2

Gamova, Svetlana (2014) "V Soiuznom Gosudarstve Poiavliaetsia Granitsa", *Nezavisimaia Gazeta*, December 10

Gapova, Elena (2002) "On Nation, Gender, and Class Formation in Belarus…and Elsewhere in the Post-Soviet World", *Nationalities Papers*, vol. 30, issue 4

Garner, Ian (2023) *Z Generation: into the heart of Russia's fascist youth*, London: Hurst

Gasiuk, Aleksandr (2022) "Zapadnye SMI Soobshchili, chto Budet v Otvete SShA o Garantiiakh Bezopasnosti", *Rossiiskaia Gazeta*, January 26. https://rg.ru/2022/01/26/zapadnye-smi-soobshchili-chto-budet-v -otvete-ssha-o-garantiiah-bezopasnosti.html (accessed July 21, 2024)

Gatrell, Peter (2019) *The Unsettling of Europe: the great migration, 1945 to the present*, London: Allen Lane

Gavrish, Oleg and Serov, Mikhail (2013) "Pol'sha Sdelala Iavnoe Glasnym", *Kommersant (Ukraine)*, July 2

Gel'man, Vladimir (2008) "Out of the Frying Pan, into the Fire? Post-Soviet regime changes in comparative perspective", *International Political Science Review*, vol. 29, issue 2

Gel'man, Vladimir (2023) "Escape from Political Freedom: the constitutional crisis of 1993 and Russia's Political Trajectory", *Russian History*, vol. 50, issue 1-2

"Gen. Skrzypczak: Na Białorusi Będzie Powstanie: przygotujmy się" (2023) *Polsatnews.pl*, May 23. https://www.polsatnews.pl/wiadomosc/20 23-05-23/gen-skrzypczak-nia-bialorusi-bedzie-powstanie-przygotuj my-sie/ (accessed July 24, 2024)

Gentile, Michael and Kragh, Martin (2022) "The 2020 Belarusian Presidential Election and Conspiracy Theories in the Russo-Ukrainian Conflict", *International Affairs*, vol. 98, issue 3

Gerasimov, Il'ia (2003) "'Kutezh Trekh Kniazei v Zelenom Dvorike': ili rozhdenie 'liberal'noi imperii'", *Ab Imperio*, issue 3

"Germany Calls for Setting Up UN Peacekeeping Mission in Ukraine before Russian Election" (2018) *Radio Free Europe/Radio Liberty*, January 4. https://www.rferl.org/a/germany-gabriel-calls-setting-up-un-pe acekeeping-mission-ukraine-before-russian-presidential-election/28 954057.html (accessed July 11, 2024)

Gerovitch, Slava (2015) *Soviet Space Mythologies: public images, private memories, and the making of a cultural identity*, Pittsburgh, PA: UPP

Gerwarth, Robert and Horne, John (2012) "Bolshevism as Fantasy: fear of revolution and counter-revolutionary violence, 1917-1923" in *War in Peace: paramilitary violence in Europe after The Great War*, Oxford: OUP; eds. Robert Gerwarth and John Horne

Gessen, Masha (2014) *Words Can Break Cement: the passion of Pussy Riot*, London: Granta

Getzler, Israel (2002) "The Communist Leaders' Role in the Kronstadt Tragedy of 1921 in the Light of Recently Published Archival Documents", *Revolutionary Russia*, vol. 15, issue 1

Gherghina, Sergiu and Klymenko, Lina (2012) "Why Look Back? Citizens' attitudes toward the communist regime in Belarus, Russia, and Ukraine", *Problems of Post-Communism*, vol. 59, issue 1

Gigin, Vadim (2023) "Vneshnepoliticheskii Reid Belorusskogo Lidera", *Belarus' Segodnia*, December 5. https://www.sb.by/articles/vneshne politicheskiy-reyd-belorusskogo-lidera.html (accessed July 25, 2024)

Giles, Keir (2024) *Russia's War on Everybody: and what it means for you*, London: Bloomsbury

Gilman, Martin (2010) *No Precedent, No Plan: inside Russia's 1998 default*, Cambridge, MA: MIT

Giner-Sorolla, Roger and Sabo, John (2016) "Disgust in the Moral Realm: do all roads lead to character?" in *Purity and Danger Now: new perspectives*, Abingdon: Routledge; eds. Robbie Duschinsky, Simone Schnall and Daniel Weiss

Ginsburg, Tom (2020) "Authoritarian International Law?" *American Journal of International Law*, vol. 114, issue 2

Giusti, Serena (2023) "The EU's Tripartite Approach towards Belarus and the Limits of Resilience", *Europe-Asia Studies*, vol. 75, issue 8

Givens, John and Mistur, Evan (2021) "The Sincerest Form of Flattery: nationalist emulation during the COVID-19 pandemic", *Journal of Chinese Political Science*, vol. 26, issue 1

Glantz, David and House, Jonathan (2015) *When Titans Clashed: how the Red Army stopped Hitler*, Lawrence, KS: UPK

"Glava Belorusskoi Pravoslavnoi Tserkvi Nazval Samozvantsami Initsiatorov Avtokefalii v Strane" (2019) *TASS*, January 5. https://tass.ru/obs chestvo/5976749 (accessed August 10, 2024)

"Glava MID Rossii Prizval Belorussiiu Otkazat'sia ot Smertnoi Kazni" (2012) *Ekonomicheskie Novosti*, March 20

"Glava MID Ukrainy Uvidel Riski dlia Kieva v Ucheniiakh 'Zapad-2021'" (2021) *Interfax*, September 11. https://www.interfax.ru/world/ 789696 (accessed August 11, 2024)

318 UNCANNY ALLIES

"Glavnyi Efir. 14.03.2021" (2021) *ATN: Novosti Belarusi i mira*, March 14. https://www.youtube.com/watch?v=0yFEFhCIXAI (accessed July 18, 2024)

"Glavnyi Efir. 09.04.2023" (2023) *TVR.by*, April 9. https://www.tvr.by/videogallery/informatsionno-analiticheskie/glavnyy-efir/itogi-per egovorov-prezidentov-rossii-i-belarusi-soyuznaya-kooperatsiya-bel arusi-i-rossii-sud-nad-eks/ (accessed August 11, 2024)

Glenn, John (2003) "The Economic Transition in Central Asia: implications for democracy", *Democratization*, vol. 10, issue 3

Głowacki, Albin and Lebedeva, Natalia (2015) "Poland between the Soviet Union and Germany, 1939-1941: the Red Army invasion and the fourth partition of Poland" in *White Spots – Black Spots: difficult matters in Polish-Russian relations, 1918-2008*, Pittsburgh, PA: UPP; eds. Adam Rotfeld and Anatoly Torkunov

Gnedina, Elena (2015) "'Multi-Vector' Foreign Policies in Europe: balancing, bandwagoning or bargaining?" *Europe-Asia Studies*, vol. 67, issue 7

Godzimirski, Jakub (2000) "Russian National Security Concepts 1997 and 2000: a comparative analysis", *European Security*, vol. 9, issue 4

Goh, Evelyn (2005) "Nixon, Kissinger, and the 'Soviet Card' in the U.S. Opening to China, 1971-1974", *Diplomatic History*, vol. 29, issue 3

Golan, Galia (2004) "Russia and the Iraq War: was Putin's policy a failure?" *Communist and Post-Communist Studies*, vol. 37, issue 4

Goldfrank, David (2020) "Christianity in Rus' and Muscovy" in *The Oxford Handbook of Russian Religious Thought*, Oxford: OUP; eds. Caryl Emerson, George Pattison and Randall Poole

Goldman, Marshall (2009) "Russia: a petrostate in a time of worldwide economic recession and political turmoil", *Social Research*, vol. 76, issue 1

Golts, Alexander (2013) "Lukashenko Exploits Putin's Weakness", *The Moscow Times*, September 30. https://www.themoscowtimes.com/2013/09/30/lukashenko-exploits-putins-weakness-a28137 (accessed August 7, 2024)

Gol'ts, Aleksandr (2021) "Nasil'stvennaia Deportatsiia v Mir Vladimira Putina", *Ezhednevnyi Zhurnal*, June 7. https://www.ej.ru/?a=note &id=36189 (accessed August 11, 2024)

Gompert, David; Binnendijk, Hans and Lin, Bonny (2014) *Blinders, Blunders, and Wars: what America and China can learn*, Santa Monica, CA: Rand

Gontmakher, Evgenii (2020) "Politicheskie Uroki Demografii", *Moskovskii Komsomolets*, September 8

Goode, J. (2012) "Nationalism in Quiet Times: ideational power and post-Soviet hybrid regimes", *Problems of Post-Communism*, vol. 59, issue 3

BIBLIOGRAPHY 319

Goode, J. (2016) "Eyes Wide Shut: democratic reversals, scientific closure, and the study of politics in Eurasia", *Social Science Quarterly*, vol. 97, issue 4

Gorbachev, Mikhail (1987) *Perestroika: new thinking for our country and the world*, New York: Harper and Row

Gorbachev, Ruslan (2012) "Kto Vy, Gospodin Rumas?" *Salidarnasts'*, January 31. https://gazetaby.com/post/kto-vy-gospodin-rumas/42167/ (accessed July 11, 2024)

Götz, Elias (2024) "Takeover by Stealth: the curious case of Russia's Belarus policy", *Problems of Post-Communism*, vol. 71, issue 3

Goujon, Alexandra (2010) "Memorial Narratives of WWII Partisans and Genocide in Belarus", *East European Politics and Societies*, vol. 24, issue 1

Gould-Davies, Nigel (2020) "Belarus and Russian Policy: patterns of the past, dilemmas of the present", *Survival*, vol. 62, issue 6

Gould-Davies, Nigel (2022) "Belarus, Russia, Ukraine: three lessons for a post-war order", *Survival*, vol. 64, issue 5

Gozzi, Laura and Scarr, Francis (2024) "Russian Election: why Putin's fifth term as president was never in doubt", *BBC News*, March 17. https://www.bbc.co.uk/news/world-europe-68505228 (accessed July 26, 2024)

Grant, Susan (2022) *Soviet Nightingales: care under communism*, Ithaca, NY: Cornell UP

Gray, Nataliia and Cameron, David (2019) "Fighting Unemployment the Soviet Way: Belarus' law against social parasites", *Eastern European Economics*, vol. 57, issue 6

Gray, William (2016) "Paradoxes of 'Ostpolitik': revisiting the Moscow and Warsaw treaties, 1970", *Central European History*, vol. 49, issue 3-4

Greene, Samuel (2022) "You Are What You Read: media, identity, and community in the 2020 Belarusian uprising", *Post-Soviet Affairs*, vol. 38, issue 1-2

Gregory, Paul (1994) *Before Command: an economic history of Russia from emancipation to the first five-year*, Princeton, NJ: PUP

Grishin, Aleksandr (2023) "Odin Den' Miatezha: kto na camom dele spas Rossiiu i ostanovil kolonny Prigozhina", *Komsomol'skaia Pravda*, June 25. https://www.kp.ru/daily/27520.5/4783913/ (accessed July 24, 2024)

Grossman, Vasily (2020) *Stalingrad*, London: Vintage

Gryl', Ianka (2018) "Vse iz-za Babicha?" *BelGazeta*, August 2. http://www.belgazeta.by/ru/1155/event/37409/ (accessed August 10, 2024)

Gudziak, Borys (1998) *Crisis and Reform: the Kyivan Metropolitanate, the Patriarchate of Constantinople, and the genesis of the Union of Brest*, Cambridge, MA: Harvard UP

Gugushvili, Alexi (2015) "Self-Interest, Perceptions of Transition and Welfare Preferences in the New Eastern Europe and the South Caucasus", *Europe-Asia Studies*, vol. 67, issue 5

Gushchin, Aleksandr (2015) "Kart-Blansh: zvezdnyi chas Minska", *Nezavisimaia Gazeta*, February 20

Gustafson, Kristian; Lomas, Dan; Wagner, Steven; Abdalla, Neveen and Davies, Philip (2024) "Intelligence Warning in the Ukraine War, Autumn 2021—Summer 2022", *Intelligence and National Security*, vol. 39, issue 3

Guzzini, Stefano (2000) "A Reconstruction of Constructivism in International Relations", *European Journal of International Relations*, vol. 6, issue 2

Hadano, Takamitsu (2020) "Multipolarity and the Future of Multilateralism: towards 'thick' peacekeeping in the Donbas conflict", *Global Policy*, vol. 11, issue 2

Haerpfer, Christian (2008) "Support for Democracy and Autocracy in Russia and the Commonwealth of Independent States, 1992-2002", *International Political Science Review*, vol. 29, issue 4

Hafner, Gerhard (2018) "The 'Soviet' Intervention in Czechoslovakia (1968)", *Austrian Review of International and European Law*, vol. 21, issue 1

Hagen, J. (2003) "Redrawing the Imagined Map of Europe: the rise and fall of the 'center'", *Political Geography*, vol. 22, issue 5

Hale, Henry (2006) "Democracy or Autocracy on the March? The coloured revolutions as normal dynamics of patronal presidentialism", *Communist and Post-Communist Studies*, vol. 39, issue 3

Hale-Dorrell, Aaron (2021) *Corn Crusade: Khrushchev's farming revolution in the post-Stalin Soviet Union*, Oxford: OUP

Hall, Stephen (2023) "The End of Adaptive Authoritarianism in Belarus", *Europe-Asia Studies*, vol. 75, issue 1

Halperin, Charles (2019) *Ivan the Terrible: free to reward and free to punish*, Pittsburgh, PA: UPP

Halperin, Charles (2022) *The Rise and Demise of the Myth of the Rus' Land*, Baltimore, MD: Arc Humanities

Halperin, Sandra and Heath, Oliver (2017) *Political Research: methods and practical skills (2nd ed.)*, Oxford: OUP

Hansbury, Paul (2023) *Belarus in Crisis: from domestic unrest to the Russia-Ukraine War*, London: Hurst

Harbatsevich, Artsem (2015) "Iak Nashyia Uskhodniia Saiuzniki 'Dynamiats'' Belaruskae Voiska", *Nasha Niva*, November 14. https://nashaniva.com/159715 (accessed August 9, 2024)

Harbatsevich, Artsem (2016) "Kanal ANT Praishousia pa Pravaslaunykh 'Patryiatychnykh' Letnikakh, Iakiia Arhanizouvaiuts' Ruskiia Natsysty dlia Belaruskikh Padletkau", *Nasha Niva*, August 2. https://nashaniva.com/174677 (accessed August 9, 2024)

Harbatsevich, Artsem (2018a) "Setka: iak Rasiia stvarae u Belarusi Rehiianal'nyia saity na baze autarau z 'Rumola' i NODa", *Nasha Niva*, May 20. https://nashaniva.com/207674 (accessed August 10, 2024)

Harbatsevich, Artsem (2018b) "U Sinodze RPTs, Iaki Zbiaretstsa u Paniadzelak u Minsku, Ne Zasiadae Nivodny Belarus", *Nasha Niva*, October 14. https://nashaniva.com/217559 (accessed August 10, 2024)

Harrison, Hope (2003) *Driving the Soviets up the Wall: Soviet-East German relations, 1953-1961*, Princeton, NJ: PUP

Hartmann, Hauke (2001) "US Human Rights Policy under Carter and Reagan, 1977-1981", *Human Rights Quarterly*, vol. 23, issue 2

Hartwell, Christopher (2022) "Part of the Problem? The Eurasian Economic Union and environmental challenges in the former Soviet Union", *Problems of Post-Communism*, vol. 69, issue 4-5

Hasegawa, Tsuyoshi (2017) *The February Revolution, Petrograd, 1917: the end of the tsarist regime and the birth of dual power*, Leiden: Brill

Haslam, Jonathan (2011) *Russia's Cold War: from the October Revolution to the fall of the Wall*, New Haven, CT: Yale UP

Haydock, Michael (1999) *City under Siege: the Berlin Blockade and Airlift, 1948-1949*, Washington, DC: Brassey's

Haynes, Rebecca (2020) *Moldova: a history*, London: Bloomsbury

Heinzig, Dieter (2003) *The Soviet Union and Communist China 1945-1950: the arduous road to the alliance*, Armonk, NY: M.E. Sharpe

Hellmeier, Sebastian and Weidmann, Nils (2020) "Pulling the Strings? The strategic use of pro-government mobilization in authoritarian regimes", *Comparative Political Studies*, vol. 53, issue 1

Hellquist, Elin (2016) "Either with Us or against Us? Third-country alignment with EU sanctions against Russia/Ukraine", *Cambridge Review of International Affairs*, vol. 29, issue 3

Hellquist, Elin (2019) "Ostracism and the EU's Contradictory Approach to Sanctions at Home and Abroad", *Contemporary Politics*, vol. 25, issue 4

Henig, Ruth (2010) *The League of Nations*, London: Haus

Henry, Étienne (2020) "The Road to Collective Security: Soviet Russia, the League of Nations, and the emergence of the *ius contra bellum* in the aftermath of the Russian Revolution (1917-1934)", *Journal of the History of International Law*, vol. 22, issue 2-3

Henry, Laura and Plantan, Elizabeth (2022) "Activism in Exile: how Russian environmentalists maintain voice after exit", *Post-Soviet Affairs*, vol. 38, issue 4

Herd, Graeme (2005) "Colorful Revolutions and the CIS: 'manufactured' versus 'managed' democracy?" *Problems of Post-Communism*, vol. 52, issue 2

Herranz-Surralles, Anna (2024) "The EU Energy Transition in a Geopoliticizing World", *Geopolitics*, online first

Hervouet, Ronan (2021) "The Moral Economy of the Kolkhoz Worker, or Why the Protest Movement in Belarus Does Not Seem to Concern the Collectivized Countryside", *Slavic Review*, vol. 80, issue 1

Hill, William (2018) *No Place for Russia: European security institutions since 1989*, New York: Columbia UP

Hillion, Christophe (2000) "Institutional Aspects of the Partnership between the European Union and the Newly Independent States of the Former Soviet Union: case studies of Russia and Ukraine", *Common Market Law Review*, vol. 37, issue 5

Hillman, Arye and Ursprung, Heinrich (2000) "Political Culture and Economic Decline", *European Journal of Political Economy*, vol. 16, issue 2

Hofbauer, Martin (2010) "The Battle of Tannenberg in 1410: strategic interests and tactical implementation", *Journal of Military and Strategic Studies*, vol. 13, issue 1

Högselius, Per (2013) *Red Gas: Russia and the origins of European energy dependence*, Basingstoke: Palgrave Macmillan

Hollis, Martin and Smith, Steve (1990) *Explaining and Understanding International Relations*, Oxford: Clarendon

Holm, Michael (2017) *The Marshall Plan: a New Deal for Europe*, Abingdon: Routledge

Holquist, Peter (2003) "State Violence as Technique: the logic of violence in Soviet totalitarianism" in *Stalinism: the essential readings*, Oxford: Blackwell; ed. David Hoffmann

"Hometown" (2024) *President of the Republic of Belarus*. https://president.gov.by/en/president/bez-galstuka/malaya-rodina (accessed July 11, 2024)

Hopf, Ted (2002) *Social Construction in International Politics: identities and foreign policies, Moscow, 1955 and 1999*, Ithaca, NY: Cornell UP

BIBLIOGRAPHY 323

Hormel, Leontina and Southworth, Caleb (2006) "Eastward Bound: a case study of post-Soviet labour migration from a rural Ukrainian town", *Europe-Asia Studies*, vol. 58, issue 4

Hornát, Jan; Šlosarčík, Ivo; Tomalová, Eliška and Váška, Jan (2023) "International Organisations as Status Enhancers: the case of the Czech Republic", *Europe-Asia Studies*, vol. 75, issue 10

Hornsby, Robert (2013) *Protest, Reform and Repression in Khrushchev's Soviet Union*, Cambridge: CUP

Hornsby, Robert (2019) "Strengthening Friendship and Fraternal Solidarity: Soviet youth tourism to Eastern Europe under Khrushchev and Brezhnev", *Europe-Asia Studies*, vol. 71, issue 7

Hornsby, Robert (2023) *The Soviet Sixties*, New Haven, CT: Yale UP

Horowitz, Shale (2003) "War after Communism: effects on political and economic reform in the former Soviet Union and Yugoslavia", *Journal of Peace Research*, vol. 40, issue 1

Horror Fiction in the Global South: cultures, narratives and representations (2012) London: Bloomsbury; eds. Ritwick Bhattacharjee and Saikat Ghosh

Hort, Sven and Zakharov, Nikolay (2019) "An Authoritarian-Populist Welfare State? Reassessing the 'Belarusian model' in comparative perspective" in *Globalizing Welfare: an evolving Asian-European dialogue*, Cheltenham: Edward Elgar; eds. Stein Kuhnle, Per Selle and Sven Hort

Hosking, Geoffrey (2006) *Rulers and Victims: the Russians in the Soviet Union*, Cambridge, MA: Harvard UP

Hosking, Geoffrey (2012) *Russia and the Russians: a history (2nd ed.)*, London: Penguin

Hosking, Geoffrey (2014) *Trust: a history*, Oxford: OUP

Hughes, Lindsey (1998) *Russia in the Age of Peter the Great*, New Haven, CT: Yale UP

Hughes, Lindsey (2002) *Peter the Great: a biography*, New Haven, CT: Yale UP

Hülsemann, Laura and Busvine, Douglas (2023) "Wagner Boss Prigozhin Spotted at Russia-Africa Summit", *Politico*, July 27. https://www.politico.eu/article/russia-africa-summit-wagner-yevgeny-prigozhin/ (accessed July 24, 2024)

"Hundreds Attend Protest against Russian Air Base in Belarus" (2015) *Radio Free Europe/Radio Liberty*, October 4. https://www.rferl.org/a/belarus-russia-air-base-protest/27287417.html (accessed August 9, 2024)

Hurak, Ihor and D'Anieri, Paul (2022) "The Evolution of Russian Political Tactics in Ukraine", *Problems of Post-Communism*, vol. 69, issue 2

Hurnevich, Dz'mitry (2022) "'Navat 'Yabats'ki' Suprats' Udzelu Belarusau u Chuzhoi Vaine': dyskusiia Vusava i Tsygankova", *Radyio Svaboda*, January 6. https://www.svaboda.org/a/31642483.html (accessed July 21, 2024)

Hurnevich, Dz'mitry (2023) "'Pamezhnyi Voiny': chamu Pol'shcha stala voraham No 1 dlia Lukashenki", *Radyio Svaboda*, February 9. https://www.svaboda.org/a/32263985.html (accessed July 24, 2024)

Iakovlevskii, Roman (2016) "Voennaia Diplomatiia na Marshe", *Khartyia '97*, December 12. https://charter97.org/be/news/2016/12/12/234097/ (accessed August 9, 2024)

"Idet Gibridnaia Voina protiv Belarusi, i My Dolzhny Zhdat' Pakostei s Lioboi Storony" (2020) *Belta*, August 6. https://www.belta.by/president/view/lukashenko-idet-gibridnaja-vojna-protiv-belarusi-i-my-dolzhny-zhdat-pakostej-s-ljuboj-storony-401625-2020/ (accessed August 11, 2024)

Ilchenko, Sergei (1998) "Ukraina-Rossiia: edinozhdy predav", *Pravda*, February 18

Il'iash, Igor' (2019) "Chto Takoe Uglublennaia Integratsiia Rossii i Belorussii—i Pochemu Sami Belorusy Ee Opasaiutsia?" *Meduza*, December 10. https://meduza.io/feature/2019/12/10/chto-takoe-uglublennaya-integratsiya-rossii-i-belorussii-i-pochemu-sami-belorusy-ee-opasayutsya (accessed August 10, 2024)

Inozemtsev, Vladislav (2015) "Rossiia kak Fon", *Moskovskii Komsomolets*, May 26

"Instruktory ChVK 'Vagner' Uzhe v Belarusi" (2023) *YouTube*, July 14. https://www.youtube.com/watch?v=wfQsautwdmU (accessed July 24, 2024)

"Interpol Decides to Declare Kerimov Internationally Wanted—TV" (2013) *Interfax*, September 3

"Interv'iu Prezidenta Tsentral'nym SMI Kitaia" (2012) *Belarus' Segodnia*, January 20

Ioffe, Grigory (2003) "Understanding Belarus: Belarusian identity", *Europe-Asia Studies*, vol. 55, issue 8

Ioffe, Grigory (2003b) "Understanding Belarus: questions of language", *Europe-Asia Studies*, vol. 55, issue 7

Ioffe, Grigory (2004) "Understanding Belarus: economy and political landscape", *Europe-Asia Studies*, vol. 56, issue 1

Ioffe, Grigory (2007a) "Culture Wars, Soul Searching, and Belarusian Identity", *East European Politics and Societies*, vol. 21, issue 2

Ioffe, Grigory (2007b) "Nation-Building in Belarus: a rebuttal", *Eurasian Geography and Economics*, vol. 48, issue 1

Ioffe, Grigory (2007c) "Unfinished Nation-Building in Belarus and the 2006 Presidential Election", *Eurasian Geography and Economics*, vol. 48, issue 1

Ioffe, Grigory (2013) "Geostrategic Interest and Democracy Promotion: evidence from post-Soviet space", *Europe-Asia Studies*, vol. 65, issue 7

Ioffe, Grigory and Yarashevich, Viachaslau (2011) "Debating Belarus: an economy in comparative perspective", *Eurasian Geography and Economics*, vol. 52, issue 6

Isakava, Volha (2017) "Between the Public and the Private: Svetlana Aleksievich interviews Ales' Adamovich. Translator's preface", *Canadian Slavonic Papers*, vol. 59, issue 3-4

Isoaho, Mari (2006) *The Image of Aleksandr Nevskiy in Medieval Russia*, Leiden: Brill

Ito, Ryuta (2023) "A Neoclassical Realist Model of Overconfidence and the Japan-Soviet Neutrality Pact in 1941", *International Relations*, online first

Iusin, Maksim (1998) "Belorussiia Popadaet v Mezhdunarodnuiu Izoliatsiiu", *Izvestiia*, July 15

Ivanov, Aleksei (2019) "Mikhail Babich: Zapad Tratit Sotni Millionov Evro na Obrabotku Zhitelei Belorussii", *Komsomol'skaia Pravda*, February 12

Ivanov, Igor (2002) *The New Russian Diplomacy*, Washington, DC: Brookings Institution

Ivzhenko, Tat'iana (2013) "Minsk i Kiev Sozdaiut Situativnuiu Koalitsiiu", *Nezavisimaia Gazeta*, September 27

Ivzhenko, Tat'iana (2017) "Lukashenko Zaverit Poroshenko v Bezopasnosti Uchenii 'Zapad-2017'", *Nezavisimaia Gazeta*, July 21

Jalalzai, Farida and Jurek, Steven (2023) "The 'Accidental Candidate' versus Europe's Longest Dictator: Belarus's unfinished revolution for women", *Politics and Governance*, vol. 11, issue 1

James, M. (2013) *Collected Ghost Stories*, Oxford: Oxford World Classics

Jang, Woojeong (2024) "The Contestation of International Ties and Regime Transitions: evidence from the former Soviet republics", *Democratization*, vol. 31, issue 1

Janos, Andrew (1996) "What Was Communism: a retrospective in comparative analysis", *Communist and Post-Communist Studies*, vol. 29, issue 1

Jirušek, Martin and Kuchyňková, Petra (2018) "The Conduct of Gazprom in Central and Eastern Europe: a tool of the Kremlin, or just an adaptable player?" *East European Politics and Societies*, vol. 32, issue 4

Johnson, Juliet (2016) *Priests of Prosperity: how central bankers transformed the postcommunist world*, Ithaca, NY: Cornell UP

Johnson, Juliet and Köstem, Seçkin (2016) "Frustrated Leadership: Russia's economic alternative to the West", *Global Policy*, vol. 7, issue 2

Josticova, Hana and Aliyev, Huseyn (2024) "There Won't Be a Free Belarus without a Free Ukraine: motivations of Belarusian volunteers fighting for Ukraine in the Russo-Ukrainian War", *Post-Soviet Affairs*, vol. 40, issue 3

Jozwiak, Rikard (2017) "NATO Chief Says Alliance Assessing Whether All Russian Troops Left Belarus", *Radio Free Europe/Radio Liberty*, October 5. https://www.rferl.org/a/nato-russia-ukraine-belarus-zapad-exe rcises-stoltenberg/28775940.html (accessed August 9)

Jukes, Geoffrey (2002) *The First World War: the eastern front, 1914-1918*, Oxford: Osprey

Junisbai, Barbara (2012) "Improbable but Potentially Pivotal Oppositions: privatization, capitalists, and political contestation in the post-Soviet autocracies", *Perspectives on Politics*, vol. 10, issue 4

"K Predstoiashchemu Rabochemu Vizitu Ministra Inostrannykh Del Rossiiskoi Federatsii S.V. Lavrova v Respubliki Belorussiia" (2023) *Ministerstvo Inostrannykh Del Rossiiskoi Federatsii*, January 18. https://mid.ru/ru/foreign_policy/news/1848375/ (accessed July 24, 2024)

Kagan, Vladislav (2012) "Aleksandr Lukashenko Vmeshalsia vo Vnutrennie Slova Posla", *Kommersant*, June 16

Kagarlitsky, Boris (2015) *Empire of the Periphery: Russia and the World System*, London: Pluto

Kakhishvili, Levan and Kupatadze, Alexander (2023) "End of the Post-Soviet Era in Georgia's Foreign Policy? Georgia's relations with former Soviet republics" in *Georgia's Foreign Policy in the 21st Century: challenges for a small state*, London: Bloomsbury; eds. Tracey German, Stephen Jones and Kornely Kakachia

Kaiser, Claire (2022) *Georgian and Soviet: entitled nationhood and the specter of Stalin in the Caucasus*, Ithaca, NY: Cornell UP

Kaiser, Robert (1994) *The Geography of Nationalism in Russia and the USSR*, Princeton, NJ: PUP

Kalinovsky, Artemy (2009) "Decision-Making and the Soviet War in Afghanistan", *Journal of Cold War Studies*, vol. 11, issue 4

Kaltenthaler, Karl; Ceccoli, Stephen and Michta, Andrew (2006) "Explaining Individual-Level Support for Privatization in European Post-Soviet Economies", *European Journal of Political Research*, vol. 45, issue 1

Kamakin, Andrei (2015) "Zapadnye Druz'ia Kremlia: kto oni i kak dorogo obkhodiatsia Rossii", *Moskovskii Komsomolets*, August 21

Kamakin, Andrei (2020) "Lukashenko i Pustota", *Moskovskii Komsomolets*, September 18

Kananovich, Uladzimir (2016) "Heroes and Villains: politics and historical memory in late medieval East Europe: the case study of the land of Navahrudak", *Russian History*, vol. 43, issue 1

Kappeler, Andreas (2001) *The Russian Empire: a multiethnic history*, Harlow: Pearson

Karavaev, Aleksandr (2014) "Prakticheskaia Realizatsiia Miunkhenskoi Rechi", *Politkom.ru*, March 19. https://www.politcom.ru/17351.html (accessed August 7, 2024)

Karbalevich, Valer (2022) "Prymus da Udzelu u Agresii? Havoshta Lukashenku vyklikali u Maskvu", *Radyio Svoboda*, March 11. https://www.svaboda.org/a/31748665.html (accessed July 22, 2024)

Karbalevich, Valerii (2001) "The Belarusian Model of Transformation: Alaksandr Lukashenka's regime and the nostalgia for the Soviet past", *International Journal of Sociology*, vol. 31, issue 4

Karbalevich, Valerii (2021) "Lukashenko Privez Putinu Proekt Konstitutsii, chtoby Vyslushat' Otsenku Rossiiskogo Lidera", *Salidarnasts'*, September 14. https://gazetaby.com/post/karbalevich-lukashenko-privez-putinu-proekt-konsti/179509/ (accessed July 19, 2024)

Karbalevich, Valerii (2022) "'Proiskhodit Rutinizatsiia Idei Voiny, EE Vozmozhnosti': pochemu Lukashenko govorit o voine kak o neizbezhnom?" *Nasha Niva*, January 26. https://nashaniva.com/ru/283641 (accessed August 11, 2024)

Karbalevich, Valerii (2024) "Rezhim Vyryvaet Belarus' iz Evropeiskogo Konteksta: v 2024-m kurs na Aziiu i Global'noi Iug prodolzhitsia", *Pozirk*, January 2. https://pozirk.online/ru/longreads/58739/ (accessed July 26, 2024)

Karelin, Sergei (1998) "Rossiia i Belorussiia Gotovy k Sozdaniiu Konfederatsii", *Nezavisimaia Gazeta*, December 26

Karpekova, Svetlana (1998) "Diplomatov Vyseliaiut", *Izvestiia*, June 10

Karpovich, Oleg (2017) "Glazami Khudozhnika: NTV — v formate absoliutnoi poshlosti", *Belarus' Segodnia*, December 1. https://www.sb.by/articles/ntv-v-formate-absolyutnoy-poshlosti.html (accessed August 10, 2024)

Kaszeta, Dan (2023) *The Forest Brotherhood: Baltic resistance against the Nazis and Soviets*, London: Hurst

Kaufman, Philip (1983) *The Right Stuff*, Burbank, CA: Warner Brothers

Kazakevich, Andrei (2022) "The Belarusian Soviet 'Nomenklatura': a political history, 1947-1994" in *Moscow and the Non-Russian Republics in the Soviet Union: nomenklatura, intelligentsia, and centre-periphery relations*, Abingdon: Routledge; eds. Li Bennich-Björkman and Saulius Grybkauskas

"Kazakh, Belarusian Presidents Differ on Some Integration Issues" (2013) *Interfax*, December 24

Kazharski, Aliaksei and Makarychev, Andrey (2015) "Suturing the Neighbourhood? Russia and the EU in conflictual intersubjectivity", *Problems of Post-Communism*, vol. 62, issue 6

Kazharski, Aliaksei and Makarychev, Andrey (2021) "Belarus, Russia, and the Escape from Geopolitics", *Political Geography*, vol. 89

Kelly, Aileen (2016) *The Discovery of Chance: the life and thought of Alexander Herzen*, Cambridge, MA: Harvard UP

Kemp-Welch, A. (2008) *Poland under Communism: a Cold War history*, Cambridge: CUP

Kempe, Frederick (2011) *Berlin 1961: Kennedy, Khrushchev, and the most dangerous place on Earth*, New York: G.P. Putnam's

Kenez, Peter (2017) *A History of the Soviet Union from the Beginning to Its Legacy (3rd ed.)*, Cambridge: CUP

Kengor, Paul (2007) *The Crusader: Ronald Reagan and the fall of communism*, New York: Harper Perennial

Kent, Neil (2008) *A Concise History of Sweden*, Cambridge: CUP

"KGB Chief Views Belarus as Barrier to Terrorism, Extremism" (2012) *Interfax*, October 5

"Khabamol'sk—Furgalovsk" (2020) *Telegram*, August 15. https://t.me/Khabamolsk/2657 (accessed July 16, 2024)

Khalezin, Nikolai (2012) "Otkat Vnaklon", *Khartyia '97*, April 6. https://charter97.org/be/news/2012/4/6/50437/ (accessed August 6, 2024)

Khalip, Irina (2018) "V Ritme Kaleidoskopa", *Khartyia '97*, December 30. https://charter97.link/ru/news/2018/12/30/318256 (accessed July 10, 2024)

Khalip, Irina (2020) "Iz Zhizni Otdykhaiushchikh: dlia koro Lukashenko ustroil spektakl' s ChVK pod Minskom?" *Novaia Gazeta*, July 29. https://novayagazeta.ru/articles/2020/07/29/86446-iz-zhizni-otd yhayuschih (accessed July 16, 2024)

Khimshiashvili, Polina; Rozhdestvenskii, Il'ia and Makarenko, Georgii (2017) "I Kreml' Stroit Stenu: kak Rossiia i Belorussiia doshli do vosstanovleniia pogranpunktov", *RBC.ru*, February 2. https://www.rbc.ru/newspaper/2017/02/03/589300f49a79471d0bc4add9 (accessed July 9, 2024)

Khislavski, Grigori (2021) "Das 'Schisma von 1054' als mikro- und makrohistorisches Ereignis: Überlegungen zu einem theologisch-kirchenpolitischen Erklärungsmodell", *Milennium*, vol. 18, issue 1

Khodarkovsky, Michael (2002) *Russia's Steppe Frontier: the making of a colonial empire, 1500-1800*, Bloomington, IN: IUP

Khodasevich, Anton (2012a) "Belorussii Prochat Novyi Krizis", *Nezavisimaia Gazeta*, April 5

Khodasevich, Anton (2012b) "Otlozhennyi Konflikt", *Nezavisimaia Gazeta*, January 18

Khodasevich, Anton (2012c) "Vybory s Boikotom i bez", *Nezavisimaia Gazeta*, September 4

Khodasevich, Anton (2014a) "Integratsiia i Obidy Lukashenko", *Nezavisimaia Gazeta*, October 20

Khodasevich, Anton (2014b) "Lukashenko Gotovit Skandal", *Nezavisimaia Gazeta*, April 29

Khodasevich, Anton (2015) "Na Belorussiiu Posypalsia Dozhd' iz Iuanei", *Nezavisimaia Gazeta*, May 13

Khodasevich, Anton (2016a) "Lukashenko Ne Khochet Byt' Mal'chikom na Pobegushkakh", *Nezavisimaia Gazeta*, April 22

Khodasevich, Anton (2016b) "Lukashenko Prodemonstriroval Voennuiu Moshch'", *Nezavisimaia Gazeta*, July 4

Khodasevich, Anton (2017a) "Belorussiiu Gotovy Priniat' v VTO Uzhe v Kontse Goda", *Nezavisimaia Gazeta*, January 24. https://www.ng.ru/cis/2017-01-24/7_6911_belorus.html (accessed August 10, 2024)

Khodasevich, Anton (2017b) "Lukashenko Voiuet s Nesoglasnymi", *Nezavisimaia Gazeta*, March 27. https://www.ng.ru/cis/2017-03-27/6_6958_minsk.html (accessed August 9, 2024)

Khodasevich, Anton (2017c) "Soiuznoe Gosudarstvo Nachinaet Razvod", *Nezavisimaia Gazeta*, February 3. https://www.ng.ru/cis/2017-02-03/1_6920_razvod.html (accessed July 9, 2024)

Khodasevich, Anton (2018) "Lukashenko Obviniaet Rossiiu v Kontrabande", *Nezavisimaia Gazeta*, July 18

Khodasevich, Anton (2021a) "Belorussiia Zhdet Ustupok ot Zapada", *Nezavisimaia Gazeta*, September 12. https://www.ng.ru/cis/2021-09-12/5_8249_belorussia.html (accessed July 19, 2024)

Khodasevich, Anton (2021b) "Lukashenko Usilit Pravitel'stvo Chekistami", *Nezavisimaia Gazeta*, March 12

Khodasevich, Anton (2021c) "Minsk Ulichili v Torgovle Liud'mi", *Nezavisimaia Gazeta*, July 4. https://www.ng.ru/cis/2021-07-04/5_8189_belorussia.html (accessed July 19, 2024)

"Khotiat li Zhenshchiny Sluzhit' i Gotoviatsia li k Voine v Belarusi? Rasskazal Leonid Kasinskii" (2022) STVBY, March 6. https://www.youtube.com/watch?v=owU-h5ZbNnc&t=1s (accessed July 20, 2024)

"Khrenin Rasskazal o Gruppirovke VSU 'Chislennost'iu 112-114 Tysiach Chelovek' na Granitse s Belarus'iu i Poobeshchal Sbivat' Aviatsiiu NATO" (2024) *Zerkalo*, February 22. https://news.zerkalo.io/econ omics/61754.html?c (accessed July 26, 2024)

Khromeychuk, Olesya (2021) *A Loss: the story of a dead soldier told by his sister*, Stuttgart: ibidem

Khrushchev, Nikita (1971) *Khrushchev Remembers*, London: Sphere

Kiaupienė, Jūratė (2001) "The Grand Duchy and the Grand Dukes of Lithuania in the Sixteenth Century: reflections on the Lithuanian political nation and the Union of Lublin" in *The Polish-Lithuanian Monarchy in European Context c. 1500-1795*, Basingstoke: Palgrave; ed. Richard Butterwick

Kirpichevskaia, Marina (2012) "Rossiia Poteriaet 480 Mlrd Rublei iz-za Belorusskikh Tamozhennikov", *Izvestiia*, December 6

Kiva, Aleksei (2018) "Eshche Shest' Let s Vladimirom Putinym", *Nezavisimaia Gazeta*, February 5

Kivelson, Valerie and Suny, Ronald (2017) *Russia's Empires*, Oxford: OUP

Klaskovskii, Aleksandr (2016) "Lukashenko Obostriaet Igru s Kremlem", *Naviny.by*, December 26. https://naviny.by/article/20161226/1482 773295-lukashenko-obostryaet-igru-s-kremlem (accessed July 7, 2024)

Klaskovskii, Aleksandr (2017) "Pochemu Putin Podobrel k Lukashenko?" *Naviny.by*, April 3. http://naviny.by/article/20170403/1491251616-pochemu-putin-podobrel-k-lukashenko (accessed July 9, 2024)

Klaskovskii, Aleksandr (2022) "'Lukashenko do Poslednego Nadeialsia, chto do Nastoiashchei Voiny ne Doidet': kak napadenie Rossii na Ukrainu otrazitsia na Belarusi? Chero zhdat'?" *Nasha Niva*, February 24. https://nashaniva.com/?c=ar&i=285355&lang=ru (accessed July 22, 2024)

Klaskovskii, Aleksandr (2023a) "Lukashenko Topit za Peredyshku dlia Putina Da i Sam Ne Proch' Zarisovat'sia Golubem Mira", *Telegra.ph*, August 18. https://telegra.ph/Lukashenko-topit-za-peredyshku-dl ya-Putina-da-i-sam-ne-proch-zarisovatsya-golubem-mira-08-18 (accessed July 24, 2024)

Klaskovskii, Aleksandr (2023b) "Rezhim Lukashenko Delaet Belorusov Zalozhnikami Kremlevskogo Iadernogo Shantazha", *Telegra.ph*, March 26. https://telegra.ph/Rezhim-Lukashenko-delaet-belorusov-zaloz hnikami-kremlevskogo-yadernogo-shantazha-03-26-2 (accessed July 24, 2024)

Klaskovskii, Alexander (2023c) "Stalinskaia Khvatka: v Belarusi stroitsia sistema pozhestve pozdnesovetskoi", *Telegra.ph*, October 2. https://telegra.ph/Stalinskaya-hvatka-V-Belarusi-stroitsya-sistema-pozhest che-pozdnesovetskoj-10-02 (accessed July 24, 2024)

Klaskovskii, Aleksandr (2024) "'Otvel ot Propasti' — i Zavel v Dzhungli: za 30 let Lukashenko rassorilsia s sosediami, ostalas' Afrika", *Pozirk*, July 10. https://pozirk.online/ru/longreads/94819/ (accessed July 26, 2024)

Klimov, Elem (1985) *Idi i Smotri*, Minsk and Moscow: Belarusfilm and Mosfilm

Klinke, Ian (2013) "What Is to Be Done? Marx and Mackinder in Minsk", *Cooperation and Conflict*, vol. 48, issue 1

Kluge, Janis (2022) "Russia's Economy Is Much More Than a 'Big Gas Station': under sanctions, that's now its biggest problem", *Bulletin of the Atomic Scientists*, vol. 78, issue 6

Klymenko, Lina (2016) "Narrating the Second World War: history textbooks and nation building in Belarus, Russia, and Ukraine", *Journal of Educational Media, Memory and Society*, vol. 8, issue 2

Kłysiński, Kamil; Menkiszak, Marek and Strzelecki, Jan (2018) "Russia Puts Pressure on Belarus", *OSW*, December 14. https://www.osw.waw.pl/en/publikacje/analyses/2018-12-14/russia-puts-pressure-belarus (accessed July 11, 2024)

Knobel', Aleksandr (2015) "Ispytanie EAES", *Vedomosti*, February 17

Knobel, Alexander; Lipin, Andrey; Malokostov, Andrey; Tarr, David and Turdyeva, Natalia (2019) "Deep Integration in the Eurasian Economic Union: what are the benefits of successful implementation or wider liberalization?" *Eurasian Geography and Economics*, vol. 60, issue 2

Knoll, Paul (2008) "The Most Unique Crusader State: The Teutonic Order in the development of the political culture of Northeastern Europe during the Middle Ages" in *The Germans and the East*, West Lafayette, IN: Purdue UP; eds. Charles Ingrao and Franz Szabo

Kobierecka, Anna and Kobierecki, Michał (2023) "Enforced Ostracism? Analysis of the international sports organizations' reactions to the 2022 Russian invasion of Ukraine", *The International Journal of the History of Sport*, vol. 40, issue 14

Kocho-Williams, Alastair (2011) *Russian and Soviet Diplomacy, 1900-39*, Basingstoke: Palgrave Macmillan

Kolesnikov, Andrei (2018a) "O Natsional'noi Gordosti Belorossov", *Kommersant*, October 13

Kolesnikov, Andrei (2018b) "Zdes' Russkii Dukh, Zdes' Belarus'iu Pakh-net", *Kommersant*, December 25. https://www.kommersant.ru/doc/3843000 (accessed July 11, 2024)

Kollmann, Nancy (2017) *The Russian Empire 1450-1801*, Oxford: OUP

Kolossov, Vladimir and Turovsky, Rostislav (2001) "Russian Geopolitics at the Fin-de-siecle", *Geopolitics*, vol. 6, issue 1

"Kommentarii Ofitsial'nogo Predstavitelia MID Rossii M.V. Zakharovoi v Sviazi s Sobytiiami vokrug Posadki v Minske Samoleta 'Ryanair'", *Mid.ru*, May 24. https://archive.mid.ru/ru/foreign_policy/news/-/asset_publisher/cKNonkJE02Bw/content/id/4742118 (accessed July 18, 2024)

König, Helmut (1996) "Wohin steuert Rußland? Zur Situation nach den Wahlen vom Dezember 1995", *Osteuropa*, vol. 46, issue 11

Konoga, Polina (2023) "Nam Nado Sokhranit' Nezavisimost', chtoby No-vye Pokoleniia Nikogda Ne Khodili pod Pletkoi", *Belarus' Segodnia*, September 1. https://www.sb.by/articles/lukashenko-nam-nado-sokhranit-nezavisimost-chtoby-novye-pokoleniya-nikogda-ne-kho dili-pod-pletkoy.html (accessed July 24, 2024)

Kononovich, Evgenii (2015) "Vsegda Otkrytyi Format", *Belarus' Segodnia*, August 5

Kononovich, Evgenii (2023) "Lukashenko i Raisi Podpisali Dorozhnuiu Kartu Vsestoronnego Sotrudnichestva na 2023-2026 Gody", *Belarus' Segodnia*, March 13. https://www.sb.by/articles/lukashenko-i-raisi-podpisali-dorozhnuyu-kartu-vsestoronnego-sotrudnichestva-na-20 23-2026-gody.html (accessed July 25, 2024)

Kononovich, Evgenii and Kriat, Dmitrii (2014) "Nash Vzgliad na Mirou-stroistvo", *Belarus' Segodnia*, July 18

"Konsolidatsiia bez Flaga: belorusskoe obshchestvo khorosho derzhitsia pered rossiiskoi propagandoi—issledovaniia", *Nasha Niva*, October 22. https://nashaniva.com/ru/328453 (accessed July 24, 2024)

Korolev, Alexander (2018) "Theories of Non-Balancing and Russia's Foreign Policy", *Journal of Strategic Studies*, vol. 41, issue 6

Korosteleva, Elena (2009) "The Limits of EU Governance: Belarus's response to the European Neighbourhood Policy", *Contemporary Politics*, vol. 15, issue 2

Korosteleva, Elena (2010) "Moldova's European Choice: 'between two stools?'" *Europe-Asia Studies*, vol. 62, issue 8

Korosteleva, Elena (2011) "Change of Continuity: is the Eastern Partnership an adequate tool for the European neighbourhood?" *International Relations*, vol. 25, issue 2

Korosteleva, Elena (2016) "The European Union and Belarus: democracy promotion by technocratic means?" *Democratization*, vol. 23, issue 4

Korosteleva, Elena and Petrova, Irina (2022) "What Makes Communities Resilient in Times of Complexity and Change", *Cambridge Review of International Affairs*, vol. 35, issue 2

Korosteleva, Elena and Petrova, Irina (2023) "Power, People, and the Political: understanding the many crises in Belarus", *Nationalities Papers*, vol. 51, issue 4

Korosteleva, Julia and White, Stephen (2006) "'Feeling European': the view from Belarus, Russia and Ukraine", *Contemporary Politics*, vol. 12, issue 2

Korsunskaya, Darya; Kobzeva, Oksana and Khalmetov, Damir (2018) "Russia to Suspend Light, Heavy Oil Product Exports to Belarus from November", *Reuters*, October 11. https://www.reuters.com/article/markets/currencies/exclusive-russia-to-suspend-light-heavy-oil-pr oduct-exports-to-belarus-from-no-idUSKCN1ML242/ (accessed August 10, 2024)

Kotkin, Stephen (1997) *Magnetic Mountain: Stalinism as a civilization*, Berkeley, CA: UCP

Kotkin, Stephen (2016) "Russia's Perpetual Geopolitics: Putin returns to the historical pattern", *Foreign Affairs*, vol. 95, issue 3

Kozlova, Dar'ia (2020) "Ketchupom Mazali v Podvorotne, potom Vybegali", *Novaia Gazeta*, August 14

Kramer, Mark (1998) "The Czechoslovak Crisis and the Brezhnev Doctrine" in *1968: the world transformed*, Cambridge: CUP; eds. Carole Fink, Philipp Gassert and Detlef Junker

Kramer, Mark (2008) "Russian Policy toward the Commonwealth of Independent States: recent trends and future prospects", *Problems of Post-Communism*, vol. 55, issue 6

Kramer, Mark (2014) "Stalin, the Split with Yugoslavia, and Soviet-East European efforts to reassert control, 1948-1953" in *Stalin and Europe: imitation and domination, 1928-1953*, Oxford: OUP; eds. Timothy Snyder and Ray Brandon

Kranz, Kathrin (2016) "European Union Arms Embargoes: the relationship between institutional design and norms", *Cambridge Review of International Affairs*, vol. 29, issue 3

"Krasnaia Zelen'" (2021) *YouTube*. https://www.youtube.com/watch?v=qhKjFaZz7AI (accessed July 16, 2024)

Kratochwil, Friedrich (2000) "Constructing a New Orthodoxy? Wendt's 'Social Theory of International Politics' and the constructivist challenge", *Millennium*, vol. 29, issue 1

Kravchenko, Vladimir (2012) "Evrosoiuz 'Sanktsioniroval' Lukashenko", *Zerkalo Nedeli*, October 20

Krawatzek, Félix and Frieß, Nina (2023) "A Foundation for Russia? Memories of World War II for young Russians", *Nationalities* Papers, vol. 51, issue 6

"Kreml' Nazval Razmeshchenie Iadernogo Oruzhiia v Belorussii Otvetom na Rasshirenie NATO" (2023) *Interfax*, April 6. https://www.interfax.ru/russia/894751 (accessed August 11, 2024)

Kriat, Dmitrii (2012) "Novye Diplomaticheskie Litsa", *Belarus' Segodnia*, February 21

Krait, Dmitrii (2015) "Trebuetsia Polnaia Otdacha", *Belarus' Segodnia*, December 8

Kriat, Dmitrii (2016) "Rabotat' Pridetsia po Edinym Pravilam", *Belarus' Segodnia*, February 10

Kriat, Dmitrii (2018) "Sviashchennyi Sinod Russkoi Pravoslavnoi Tserkvi Vpervye Sobralsia v Minske", *Sovetskaia Belorussiia*, October 16. https://www.sb.by/articles/nasha-sila-v-edinstve-cerkov.html (accessed July 11, 2024)

Kriat, Dmitrii (2023) "Lukashenko Oproverg Feiki o Tom, chto ChVK 'Vagner' Ukhodit iz Belarusi", *Belarus' Segodnia*, August 25. https://www.sb.by/articles/lukashenko-oproverg-feyki-o-tom-chto-chvk-vagner-ukhodit-iz-belarusi.html (accessed July 24, 2024)

Krickovic, Andrej (2014) "Imperial Nostalgia or Prudent Geopolitics? Russia's efforts to reintegrate the post-Soviet space in geopolitical perspective", *Post-Soviet Affairs*, vol. 30, issue 6

Kristensen, Hans; Korda, Matt; Johns, Eliana and Knight, Mackenzie (2023a) "Nuclear Weapons Sharing, 2023", *Bulletin of the Atomic Scientists*, vol. 79, issue 6

Kristensen, Hans; Korda, Matt; Johns, Eliana and Knight, Mackenzie (2024) "Russian Nuclear Weapons, 2024", *Bulletin of the Atomic Scientists*, vol. 80, issue 2

Kristensen, Hans; Korda, Matt and Reynolds, Eliana (2023b) "Russian Nuclear Weapons, 2023", *Bulletin of the Atomic Scientists*, vol. 79, issue 3

Kriviakina, Elena (2017) "Aleksandr Lukashenko: O Nefti, Gosgranitse i Druzhbe s Rossiei", *Komsomol'skaia Pravda*, February 4

Krivosheev, Kirill (2016) "Minsk ne Pretenduet na Bosfor i Dardanelly", *Kommersant*, November 12

Krivosheev, Kirill (2020) "I Natovtsy Ego Terzali, i 'Vagnerovtsy'", *Kommersant*, August 6. https://www.kommersant.ru/doc/4443733?from=main_2 (accessed July 16, 2024)

Krivosheev, Kirill and Shimanov, Matvei (2020) "V Belorussii Ob''iavleno Chvkchainoe Polozhenie", *Kommersant*, July 30. https://www.kommersant.ru/doc/4435185 (accessed July 16, 2024)

Kříž, Zdeněk (2023) "The Costly Gamble: how Russia's invasion of Ukraine weakened its role as a balancing power", *Defense and Security Analysis*, vol. 39, issue 3

Kropatcheva, Elena (2011) "Playing Both Ends against the Middle: Russia's geopolitical energy games with the EU and Ukraine", *Geopolitics*, vol. 16, issue 3

"Kto v Okruzhenii Lukashenko Vystupal za Vstuplenie v Voinu, a Kto Byl Protiv" (2023) *Nasha Niva*, March 8. https://nashaniva.com/ru/311735 (accessed July 24, 2024)

Kubik, Jan and Bernhard, Michael (2014) "A Theory of the Politics of Memory" in *Twenty Years after Communism*, Oxford: OUP; eds. Michael Bernhard and Jan Kubik

Kucera, Joshua (2013) "CSTO Planning Joint Air Forces", *Eurasianet*, April 17. https://eurasianet.org/csto-planning-joint-air-forces (accessed July 7, 2024)

Kukushkina, Diana (2016) "Rossiia Usilivaet Gruppirovku Voisk u Zapadnykh Granits iz-za Aktivnosti NATO", *Novye Izvestiia*, June 3

Kulagin, Vladimir (2023) "Rossiia Gotovitsia k Razmeshcheniiu Iadernogo Oruzhiia v Belorussii", *Vedomosti*, March 26. https://www.vedomosti.ru/politics/articles/2023/03/27/968186-rossiya-gotovitsya-k-razmescheniyu-yadernogo-oruzhiya-v-belorussii (accessed July 24, 2024)

Kulakevich, Tatsiana (2014) "Twenty Years in the Making: understanding the difficulty for change in Belarus", *East European Politics and Societies*, vol. 28, issue 4

Kulakevich, Tatsiana and Augsburger, Aaron (2021) "Contested Elections, Protest, and Regime Stability: comparing Belarus and Bolivia", *Canadian Slavonic Papers*, vol. 63, issue 3-4

Kulakevich, Tatsiana and Kubik, Jan (2023) "Anti-Authoritarian Learning: prospects for democratization in Belarus based on a study of Polish Solidarity", *Nationalities Papers*, vol. 51, issue 4

Kuleszewicz, Anna (2017) "Between Russia and the West: Belarus as a challenge for European stability and security", *Polish Political Science Yearbook*, vol. 46, issue 1

Kumar, Krishan (2021) *Empires: a historical and political sociology*, Cambridge: Polity

Kunadze, Georgii (2021) "Put' Izgoia: kuda vedet vneshniaia politika Rossii", *Novaia Gazeta*, July 3. https://novayagazeta.ru/articles/2021/07/03/put-izgoia (accessed July 19, 2024)

Kupchan, Charles (2020) *Isolationism: a history of America's efforts to shield itself from the world*, Oxford: OUP

Kurak, Anna (2024) "Aleksandr Lukashenko: 30 let doveriia grazhdan i upravleniia gosudarstvom", *Belarus' Segodnia*, July 11. https://www.sb.by/articles/verno-sluzhit-narodu.html (accessed July 26, 2024)

Kurilla, Ivan (2023) "Understanding the Immortal Regiment: memory dualism in a social movement", *Europe-Asia Studies*, vol. 75, issue 8

Kuus, Merje (2004) "Europe's Eastern Expansion and the Reinscription of Otherness in East-Central Europe", *Progress in Human Geography*, vol. 28, issue 4

Kuzio, Taras (2003) "National Identities and Virtual Foreign Policies among the Eastern Slavs", *Nationalities Papers*, vol. 31, issue 4

Kuzio, Taras (2005a) "From Kuchma to Yushchenko: Ukraine's 2004 presidential elections and the Orange Revolution", *Problems of Post-Communism*, vol. 52, issue 2

Kuzio, Taras (2005b) "Nation Building, History Writing and Competition over the Legacy of Kyiv Rus in Ukraine", *Nationalities Papers*, vol. 33, issue 1

Kuzio, Taras (2010) "Populism in Ukraine in a Comparative European Context", *Problems of Post-Communism*, vol. 57, issue 6

Kuzio, Taras (2015) "Rise and Fall of the Party of Regions Political Machine", *Problems of Post-Communism*, vol. 62, issue 3

Kuznetsova, Daria (2023) "Broadcasting Messages via Telegram: pro-government social media control during the 2020 protests in Belarus and 2022 anti-war protests in Russia", *Political Communication*, online first

Lagerspetz, Mikko (1999) "Postsocialism as a Return: notes on a discursive strategy", *East European Politics and Societies*, vol. 13, issue 2

Lakstygal, Il'ia and Mishutin, Gleb (2022) "Zapadnykh Diplomatov Otzyvaiut iz Kieva", *Vedomosti*, January 25. https://www.vedomosti.ru/politics/articles/2022/01/24/906206-zapadnih-diplomatov (accessed July 21, 2024)

Lankina, Tomila; Libman, Alexander and Obydenkova, Anastassia (2016) "Authoritarian and Democratic Diffusion in Post-Communist Regimes", *Comparative Political Studies*, vol. 49, issue 12

Lanteigne, Marc (2006-07) "*In Medias Res*: the development of the Shanghai Co-operation Organization as a Security Community", *Pacific Affairs*, vol. 79, issue 4

Larrabee, Stephen (2006) "Ukraine and the West", *Survival*, vol. 48, issue 1

Larsen, Karen (2023) "From Mercenary to Legitimate Actor? Russian discourses on private military companies", *Post-Soviet Affairs*, vol. 39, issue 6

Larson, Deborah (2012) "How Identities Form and Change: supplementing constructivism with social psychology" in *Psychology and Constructivism in International Relations: an ideational alliance*, Ann Arbor, MI: UMP; eds. Vaughn Shannon and Paul Kowert

Larson, Deborah and Shevchenko, Alexei (2019) *Quest for Status: Chinese and Russian foreign policy*, New Haven, CT: Yale UP

Lasmanis, Jānis (2017) "'Zapad 2017' Nograndējis: krievijas spēkiem jāpamet Baltkrievija", *Neatkarīgā*, September 20. https://nra.lv/politika/pasaule/222912-neatkarigas-reportaza-zapad-2017-nograndejis-krievijas-spekiem-japamet-baltkrievija.htm (accessed July 9, 2024)

Latsis, Otto (1998) "Nadolgo Li Prishel Primakov?" *Novye Izvestiia*, September 16

Latynina, Iu. (2013) "Kod Dostupa — 2013-10-26", *Echofm*, October 26. https://echofm.online/archive/code/1614 (accessed August 7, 2024)

Laurila, Juhani (2003) "Transit Transport between the European Union and Russia in Light of Russian Geopolitics and Economics", *Emerging Markets Finance and Trade*, vol. 39, issue 5

Lavnikevich, Denis (2016) "Kitaiskii Zontik Lukashenko", *Gazeta.ru*, October 1. https://www.gazeta.ru/business/2016/09/30/10224275.shtml (accessed August 9, 2024)

Lavnikevich, Denis and Khodarenok, Mikhail (2016) "'Gibridnoe' Opolchenie Lukashenko", *Gazeta.ru*, September 13. https://www.gazeta.ru/army/2016/09/13/10191803.shtml (accessed August 9, 2024)

Leal-Arcas, Rafael; Ríos, Juan and Grasso, Constantino (2015) "The European Union and Its Energy Security Challenges: engagement through and with networks", *Contemporary Politics*, vol. 21, issue 3

"Lebed'ko: Putin Reshil Vospitat' Lukashenko" (2012) *Khartyia '97*, December 6. https://charter97.org/ru/news/2012/12/6/62405/ (accessed August 6, 2024)

Ledeneva, Alena and Seabright, Paul (2000) "Barter in Post-Soviet Societies: what does it look like and why does it matter?" in *The Vanishing Rouble: barter networks and non-monetary transactions in post-Soviet societies*, Cambridge: CUP; ed. Paul Seabright

LeDonne, John (1997) *The Russian Empire and the World, 1700-1917: expansion and containment*, Oxford: OUP

LeDonne, John (2020) *Forging a Unitary State: Russia's management of the Eurasian space 1650-1850*, Toronto: UTP

Leshchenko, Natalia (2004) "A Fine Instrument: two nation-building strategies in post-Soviet Belarus", *Nations and Nationalism*, vol. 10, issue 3

Leukavets, Victoria; Makarychev, Andrey and Beridze, Giorgi (2023) "Electoral Campaigns in Times of Lockdown: post-Soviet experiences", *Europe-Asia Studies*, vol. 75, issue 4

Lewis, Simon (2018) *Belarus – Alternative Visions: nation, memory and cosmopolitanism*, Abingdon: Routledge

Lewis, Simon (2019) "Border Trouble: ethnopolitics and cosmopolitan memory in recent Polish cinema", *East European Politics and Societies*, vol. 33, issue 2

Li, Xiaobing (2017) *The Cold War in East Asia*, Abingdon: Routledge

Libman, Alexander (2011) "Russian Federalism and Post-Soviet Integration: divergence of development paths", *Europe-Asia Studies*, vol. 63, issue 8

Libman, Alexander and Davidzon, Igor (2023) "Military Intervention as Spectacle? Authoritarian regionalism and protests in Kazakhstan", *International Affairs*, vol. 99, issue 3

Libman, Alexander and Obydenkova, Anastassia (2018) "Regional International Organizations as a Strategy of Autocracy: The Eurasian Economic Union and Russian foreign policy", *International Affairs*, vol. 94, issue 5

Libman, Alexander and Vinokurov, Evgeny (2012) "Post-Soviet Integration and the Interaction of Functional Bureaucracies", *Review of International Political Economy*, vol. 19, issue 5

Lieven, Anatol (2002) "The Secret Policemen's Ball: the United States, Russia and the international order after 11 September", *International Affairs*, vol. 78, issue 2

Lieven, Dominic (2000) *Empire: the Russian Empire and its rivals*, London: John Murray

Lieven, Dominic (2009) *Russia against Napoleon: the battle for Europe, 1807 to 1814*, London: Allen Lane

Lieven, Dominic (2015) *Towards the Flame: empire, war and the end of tsarist Russia*, London: Allen Lane

Light, Margot (1996) "Foreign Policy Thinking" in Neil Malcolm, Alex Pravda, Roy Allison and Margot Light, *Internal Factors in Russian Foreign Policy*, Oxford: OUP

Lih, Lars (2007) "1905 and All That: the revolution and its aftermath", *Kritika*, vol. 8, issue 4

Lindner, Rainer and Sahm, Astrid (2000) "'Dialog' ohne Dialog vor 'Wahlen' ohne Wahl? Belarus' am Vorabend der Parlamentswahlen", *Osteuropa*, vol. 50, issue 9

Lipskii, Andrei (2021) "Kholodnyi Mir: vneshniaia politika Kremlia kak instrument sokhraneniia vlasti", *Novaia Gazeta*, January 12. https://novayagazeta.ru/articles/2021/01/12/88660-holodnyy-mir (accessed July 18, 2024)

Lisenkova, Elena (2023) "Beliaev Rasskazal, chto Ozhidaet Pol'shu posle Poteri Vlasti Partii 'Pravo i Spravedlivost'", *Belarus' Segodnya*, December 12. https://www.sb.by/articles/belyaev-rasskazal-chto-ozhidaet-polshu-posle-poteri-vlasti-partii-pravo-i-spravedlivost.html (accessed July 24, 2024)

Liu, Amy; Roosevelt, Megan and Sokhey, Sarah (2017) "Trade and the Recognition of Commercial Lingua Francas: Russian language laws in post-Soviet countries", *Economics and Politics*, vol. 29, issue 1

Locoman, Ecaterina and Papa, Mihaela (2022) "Transformation of Alliances: mapping Russia's close relationships in the era of multivectorism", *Contemporary Security Policy*, vol. 43, issue 2

Loftus, Suzanne (2019) *Insecurity and the Rise of Nationalism in Putin's Russia: keeper of traditional values*, Cham: Palgrave Macmillan

Logvinenko, Igor (2020) "Authoritarian Welfare State, Regime Stability, and the 2018 Pension Reform in Russia", *Communist and Post-Communist Studies*, vol. 53, issue 1

Łomanowski, Andrzej and Szoszyn, Ruslan (2016) "Dyktator czy Partner", *Rzeczpospolita*, March 24. https://archiwum.rp.pl/artykul/1303996-Dyktator-czy-partner.html (accessed August 9, 2024)

Lomb, Samantha (2018) *Stalin's Constitution: Soviet participatory politics and the discussion of the 1936 draft constitution*, Abingdon: Routledge

Longworth, Philip (2005) *Russia's Empires: their rise and fall from prehistory to Putin*, London: John Murray

Lonkin, Claudia (2024) "The Belarusian Chameleons: Pesniary's popularity and the ambiguity of Soviet identities", *Europe-Asia Studies*, vol. 76, issue 3

Lovell, Stephen (2010) *The Shadow of War: the Soviet Union and Russia, 1941 to the present*, Chichester: Wiley-Blackwell

Löwenhardt, John; Hill, Ronald and Light, Margot (2001) "A Wider Europe: the view from Minsk and Chisinau", *International Affairs*, vol. 77, issue 3

Lozka, Katsiaryna and Makarychev, Andrey (2024) "Depoliticization and Necropolitics: a critical examination of Lukashenka's regime", *Problems of Post-Communism*, online first

Lubachko, Ivan (1972) Belorussia: under Soviet rule, 1917-1957, Lexington, KY: UPK

340   UNCANNY ALLIES

Lucas, Edward (2014) *The New Cold War: Putin's Russia and the threat to the West (revised ed.)*, Basingstoke: Palgrave Macmillan

"Lukashenka pra 'Glybokuiu Intehratsyiu': Maskva Khocha Inkarparavats' Belarus' u Sklad Rasii" (2018a) *Nasha Niva*, December 14. https://nashaniva.com/222213 (accessed August 10, 2024)

"Lukashenka pra Rasiiu: Ia Uzho Ne Kazhu 'Bratskaia Dziarzhava'. Budem partnerami" (2018b) *Nasha Niva*, December 12. https://nashaniva.com/222689 (accessed August 10, 2024)

"Lukashenka Sells Out Sovereignty" (2012) *Charter '97*, February 14. https://charter97.org/en/news/2012/2/14/47976/ (accessed August 6, 2024)

"Lukashenka: Uves' Savetski Narod Unes Dastoiny Uklad u Vialikuiu Peramohu, i Dzialits' Iae Nedarechy" (2018c) *Belta*, May 9. https://blr.belta.by/president/view/lukashenka-uves-savetski-narod-unes-dastojny-uklad-u-vjalikuju-peramogu-i-dzjalits-jae-nedarechy-68717-2018/ (accessed August 10, 2024)

Lukashenko, Aleksandr (2012a) "Vse dlia Cheloveka, vo Imia Cheloveka", *Belarus' Segodnia*, July 4

"Lukashenko: Belarus, Kazakhstan Will Always Maintain Good Relations" (2019a) *Belarus.by*, May 28. https://www.belarus.by/en/press-center/news/lukashenko-belarus-kazakhstan-will-always-maintain-good-relations_i_98799.html (accessed August 10, 2024)

"Lukashenko: Belarus' Namerena Ispol'zovat' Vse Rezervy dlia Vosstanovleniia Spokoistviia v Regione" (2019b) *Belta*, July 3. https://www.belta.by/president/view/lukashenko-belarus-namerena-ispolzovat-vse-rezervy-dlja-vosstanovlenija-spokojstvija-v-regione-353760-2019/ (accessed August 10, 2024)

"Lukashenko: Belorusskie Mirotvortsy Gotovy Stat' Mezhdu Konfliktuiushchimi Storonami v Ukraine pri Dogovorennosti mezhdu Poroshenko i Putinym" (2018a) *Belta*, February 10. https://www.belta.by/video_official/getRecord/2891/ (accessed August 10, 2024)

"Lukashenko: Belorussko-Rossiiskie Peregovory v Sochi Byli Tiazhelye, no Rezul'tativnye" (2018b) *Belta*, September 22. https://www.belta.by/president/view/lukashenko-belorussko-rossijskie-peregovory-v-sochi-byli-tjazhelye-no-rezultativnye-318816-2018/ (accessed August 10, 2024)

"Lukashenko: My Sdelali Vse, Chto ot Nas Khotel Zapad" (2015) *Ekonomicheskie Novosti*, October 11

"Lukashenko Predlagali Vziatku v 5 Milliardov Dollarov" (2012b) *Novoe Vremia*, October 18

"Lukashenko: I will not order the border service to protect the European Union from migrants" (2024a) *Belta*, July 2. https://eng.belta.by/president/view/lukashenko-i-will-not-order-the-border-service-to-protect-the-european-union-from-migrants-159523-2024/ (accessed July 26, 2024)

"Lukashenko: Komu-to Neimetsia Privatizirovat' Pobedu v Velikoi Otechestevnnoi Voine" (2018c) *Belta*, June 2. https://www.belta.by/president/view/lukashenko-komu-to-nejmetsja-privatizirovat-pobedu-v-velikoj-otechestvennoj-vojne-305266-2018/ (accessed August 10, 2024)

"Lukashenko Nazval Nenormal'noi Situatsiiu s Tsenami na Rossiiskii Gaz dlia Belorussii" (2020) *Interfaks*, January 9, https://www.interfax.ru/business/690627 (accessed June 18, 2024)

"Lukashenko o ChVK 'Vagner'" (2023) *Telegram*, July 6. https://t.me/pul_1/9398 (accessed July 24, 2024)

"Lukashenko ob Integratsii s Rossiei: My Nikogda Ne Byli protiv Tesneishego Soiuza, no Nas Vsegda Derzhali na Rasstoianii" (2021a) *Belta*, August 9. https://www.belta.by/president/view/lukashenko-ob-integratsii-s-rossiej-my-nikogda-ne-byli-protiv-tesnejshego-sojuza-no-nas-vsegda-454507-2021/ (accessed August 11, 2024)

"Lukashenko Otvetil na Vopros o Budushchem Ukrainy" (2022) *Belarus' Segodnia*, September 1. https://www.sb.by/articles/lukashenko-otvetil-na-vopros-o-budushchem-ukrainy.html (accessed July 21, 2024)

"Lukashenko Pozdravil Kirilla s Desiatiletiem so Dnia Patriarshei Intronizatsii" (2019c) *Belta*, February 1. https://www.belta.by/president/view/lukashenko-pozdravil-kirilla-s-desjatiletiem-so-dnja-patriarshej-intronizatsii-334918-2019/ (accessed August 10, 2024)

"Lukashenko Pozdravil Narod Ukrainy s Dnem Nezavisimosti" (2022) *Belarus' Segodnia*, August 24. https://www.sb.by/articles/pozdravlenie-ukraina-den-nezavisimosti-2022.html (accessed July 22, 2024)

"Lukashenko Predlozhil Gubernatoru Orlovskoi Oblasti RF Pomoshch' 'po Zashchite Mirnogo Naseleniia'" (2024b) April 1. https://pozirk.online/ru/news/76801/ (accessed July 26, 2024)

"Lukashenko Provel Urok v Shkole: ob IT, zavisimosti ot progressa i velosipede Zelenskogo" (2019d) *YouTube*, September 2. https://www.youtube.com/watch?v=1QYnwdF26gE (accessed August 10)

"Lukashenko Rasschityvaet na Vstuplenie Belarusi v ShOS na Sammite v Astane i Blagodarit Rossiiu za Podderzhku" (2024b) *Belta*, June 25. https://www.belta.by/president/view/lukashenko-rasschityvaet-na-vstuplenie-belarusi-v-shos-na-sammite-v-astane-i-blagodarit-rossiju-za-643492-2024/ (accessed August 11, 2024)

"Lukashenko Rasskazal, Mogut li Rossiia i Belorussiia Ob''edinit'sia" (2019e) *RIA Novosti*, February 15. https://ria.ru/20190215/1550 933917.html (accessed August 10, 2024)

"Lukashenko Rasskazal ob Ul'timatume Belarusi: trebuiut, chtoby my stali kak Ukraina" (2021b) *Belarus' Segodnia*, December 3. https://www. sb.by/articles/lukashenko-rasskazal-ob-ultimatume-belarusi-trebu yut-chtoby-my-stali-kak-ukraina.html (accessed July 18, 2024)

"Lukashenko Skazal, chto Peredast Putinu Informatsiiu o Vozmozhnykh Kuratorakh Terakta v 'Krokus Siti Kholle'" (2024c) *Zerkalo*, March 26. https://news.zerkalo.io/economics/64348.html (accessed July 26, 2024)

"Lukashenko Utverzhdaet, chto Belorusy Solidarny s RF, Soperezhivaiut i Gotovy Pomoch' Ei Vsem, chem Mogut" (2024d) *Pozirk*, February 1. https://pozirk.online/ru/news/64381/ (accessed July 26, 2024)

"'Lukashenku Yosts' pra Shto Zadumatstsa': Aliaksandr Frydman pra Hibel' Pryhozhyna" (2023) *YouTube*, August 23. https://www.you tube.com/watch?v=yJtkny7MA0w&t=406s (accessed July 24, 2024)

"Lukashenko Zaproponuvav Viddaty Bilorusi Kontrol' nad Rosi'sko-Ukraiinskym Kordonom" (2018d) *Radio Svoboda*, October 31. https:// www.radiosvoboda.org/a/news-lukashenko-ukraine-russia-border /29575286.html (accessed August 10, 2024)

Luk'ianov, Fedor (2017) "Rossiia i Belorussiia: novyi etap?" *Rossiiskaia Gazeta*, February 8

Lukowski, Jerzy (2014) *A Concise History of Poland (2nd ed.)*, Cambridge: CUP

Lüthi, Lorenz (2008) *The Sino-Soviet Split: Cold War in the communist world*, Princeton, NJ: PUP

Lutskevich, Danila (2024) "Chego Zhdat' ot Vyborov v Rossii i Kak Oni Otraziatsia na Belarusi? Rassuzhdaiut analitiki", *Nasha Niva*, March 13. https://nashaniva.com/ru/338010 (accessed July 26, 2024)

Lysenko, Volodymyr and Desouza, Kevin (2015) "The Use of Information and Communication Technologies by Protesters and the Authorities in the Attempts at Colour Revolutions in Belarus 2001-2010", *Europe-Asia Studies*, vol. 67, issue 4

Maass, Anna-Sophie (2017) *EU-Russia Relations, 1999-2015: from courtship to confrontation*, Abingdon: Routledge

Magid, Mikhail (2021) "Tri Stsenariia na Sluchai Otsutstviia Rosta", *Vedomosti*, January 21. https://www.vedomosti.ru/opinion/articles/ 2021/01/20/854870-stsenariya (accessed July 18, 2024)

Magocsi, Paul (2018) *Historical Atlas of Central Europe (3rd rev. and expanded ed.)*, Toronto: UTP

Mahlstein, Kornel; McDaniel, Christine; Schropp, Simon and Tsigas, Marinos (2022) "Estimating the Economic Effects of Sanctions on Russia: an Allied trade embargo", *The World Economy*, vol. 45, issue 11

Main, Steven (1997) "The Arrest and 'Testimony' of Marshal of the Soviet Union M.N. Tukhachevsky (May-June 1937)", *The Journal of Slavic Military Studies*, vol. 10, issue 1

Makarychev, Andrey and Yatsyk, Alexandra (2017) "Biopower and Geopolitics as Russia's Neighbourhood Strategies: reconnecting people or reaggregating lands?" *Nationalities Papers*, vol. 45, issue 1

"Makei: Belarus' Ne Zhazhdet Vstupleniia v ES, no Khochet Tesno Sotrudnichat'" (2017a) *Belta*, July 14. https://www.belta.by/politics/view/makej-belarus-ne-zhazhdet-vstuplenija-v-es-no-hochet-tesno-sotrud nichat-257401-2017/ (accessed August 10, 2024)

"Makei: Nikomu Ne Udastsia Possorit' Druzhestvennye Belarus' i Rossiiu v Ugodu Merkantil'nym Interesam" (2017b) *Belta*, April 27. https://www.belta.by/politics/view/makej-nikomu-ne-udastsja-possorit-d ruzhestvennye-belarus-i-rossiju-v-ugodu-merkantilnym-interesam-244624-2017/ (accessed August 10, 2024)

"Makei: Novoe Soglashenie Belarusi s ES Budet Skoree Ran'she, chem Pozzhe" (2017c) *Belta*, November 24. https://www.belta.by/politics/view/makej-novoe-soglashenie-belarusi-s-es-budet-skoree-ranshe-chem-pozzhe-277398-2017/ (accessed August 10, 2024)

"Makei Raskryl Podrobnosti Predstoiashchikh Peregovorov s Lavrovym po NATO" (2017d) *Belta*, June 2. https://www.belta.by/politics/vie w/makej-raskryl-podrobnosti-predstojaschih-peregovorov-s-lavrov ym-po-nato-250707-2017/ (accessed August 9, 2024)

Maksimov, Ivan (2013) "'Gazprom' Podgotovil 'Siurpriz' dlia Ukrainy", *Nevskoe Vremia*, April 5

Malinova, Olga (2020) "'Nation' and 'Civilization' as Templates for Russian Identity Construction: a historical overview" in *Russia as Civilization: ideological discourses in politics, media and academia*, Abingdon: Routledge; eds. Kåre Mjør and Sanna Turoma

Malloy, Tove (2022) "Territorial or Non-Territorial Autonomy: the tools for governing diversity" in *The Routledge Handbook of Comparative Territorial Autonomies*, Abingdon: Routledge; eds. Brian Fong and Atsuko Ichijo

Manaev, Oleg (2018) "Media in Post-Soviet Belarus: between democratization and reinforcing authoritarianism" in *Mass Media in the Post-Soviet World: market forces, state actors, and political manipulation in the informational environment after communism*, Stuttgart: ibidem; eds. Peter Rollberg and Marlene Laruelle

Manilyk, Andrei (2014) "Peregovory v Minske", *Rabochaia Gazeta*, August 14

Mann, Michael (2013) *The Sources of Social Power (vol. 4): globalizations, 1945-2011*, Cambridge: CUP

Marandici, Ion and Leşanu, Alexandru (2021) "The Political Economy of the Post-Soviet De Facto States: a paired comparison of Transnistria and the Donetsk People's Republic", *Problems of Post-Communism*, vol. 68, issue 4

March, Luke (2007) "From Moldovanism to Europeanization? Moldova's Communists and nation building", *Nationalities* Papers, vol. 35, issue 4

March, Luke and Herd, Graeme (2006) "Moldova between Europe and Russia: inoculating against the coloured contagion?" *Post-Soviet Affairs*, vol. 22, issue 4

Marková, Alena (2022) *The Path to a Soviet Nation: the policy of Belarusization*, Leiden: Brill

Markus, Ustina (1997) "Russia and Belarus: elusive integration", *Problems of Post-Communism*, vol. 44, issue 5

Marples, David (1999a) *Belarus: a denationalized nation*, Amsterdam: Harwood

Marples, David (1999b) "National Awakening and National Consciousness in Belarus", *Nationalities Papers*, vol. 27, issue 4

Marples, David (2005) "Europe's Last Dictatorship: the roots and perspectives of authoritarianism in 'White Russia'", *Europe-Asia Studies*, vol. 57, issue 6

Marples, David (2006) "Color Revolutions: the Belarus case", *Communist and Post-Communist Studies*, vol. 39, issue 3

Marples, David (2007) "Elections and Nation-Building in Belarus: a comment on Ioffe", *Eurasian Geography and Economics*, vol. 48, issue 1

Marples, David (2008a) "The Energy Dilemma of Belarus: the nuclear power option", *Eurasian Geography and Economics*, vol. 49, issue 2

Marples, David (2008b) "Is the Russia-Belarus Union Obsolete?" *Problems of Post-Communism*, vol. 55, issue 1

Marples, David (2014) *"Our Glorious Past": Lukashenka's Belarus and the Great Patriotic War*, Stuttgart: ibidem

Marples, David (2016) "The 'Minsk Phenomenon': demographic development in the Republic of Belarus", *Nationalities Papers*, vol. 44, issue 6

Marples, David (2020) *Understanding Ukraine and Belarus: a memoir*, Bristol: E-International Relations. https://www.e-ir.info/2020/06/30/understanding-ukraine-and-belarus-a-memoir/ (accessed August 5, 2024)

Marples, David and Laputska, Veranika (2020) "Kurapaty: Belarus' continuing debates", *Slavic Review*, vol. 79, issue 3

Marples, David and Laputska, Veranika (2022) "Maly Traścianiec in the Context of Current Narratives on the Holocaust in the Republic of Belarus", *Europe-Asia Studies*, vol. 74, issue 1

Marten, Kimberly (2019) "Russia's Use of Semi-State Security Forces: the case of the Wagner Group", *Post-Soviet Affairs*, vol. 35, issue 3

Martin, Janet (2006) "North-eastern Russia and the Golden Horde (1246-1359)" in *The Cambridge History of Russia (vol. 1): from early Rus' to 1689*, Cambridge: CUP; ed. Maureen Perrie

Martin, Janet (2007) *Medieval Russia 980-1584 (2nd ed.)*, Cambridge: CUP

Martin, Janet (2023) "Unintended Consequences", *Canadian-American Slavic Studies*, vol. 57, issue 3-4

Martin, Terry (2001) *The Affirmative Action Empire: nations and nationalism in the Soviet Union, 1923-1939*, Ithaca, NY: Cornell UP

Martinovich, Viktor (2014) "Krym-Briule: kogo podderzhit Minsk v rossi-isko-ukrainskom konflikte?" *BelGazeta*, March 10. https://www.belgazeta.by/ru/2014_03_10/topic_week/28500/ (accessed August 7, 2024)

Martinsen, Kaare (2002) "The Russian Takeover of Belarus", *Comparative Strategy*, vol. 21, issue 5

Martynov, Kirill (2021) "Kto v Zalozhnikakh u Lukashenko? Chto ob-shchego y Marii Zakharovoi i Sof'i Sapegi, krome rossiiskogo pas-porta", *Novaia Gazeta*, May 29. https://novayagazeta.ru/articles/2021/05/29/kto-v-zalozhnikakh-u-lukashenko (accessed July 19, 2024)

Mastny, Vojtech (1999) "The Soviet Non-Invasion of Poland in 1980-1981 and the End of the Cold War", *Europe-Asia Studies*, vol. 51, issue 2

Matsuzato, Kimitaka (2004) "A Populist Island in an Ocean of Clan Politics: the Lukashenka regime as an exception among CIS countries", *Europe-Asia Studies*, vol. 56, issue 2

Matveeva, Anna (2018) "Russia's Power Projection after the Ukraine Crisis", *Europe-Asia Studies*, vol. 70, issue 5

Maurer, John (2022) *Competitive Arms Control: Nixon, Kissinger, and SALT, 1969-1972*, New Haven, CT: Yale UP

Mayo, P. (1978) "Byelorussian Orthography: from the 1933 reform to the present day", *Journal of Belarusian Studies*, vol. 4, issue 2

McAllister, Ian and White, Stephen (2015) "Electoral Integrity and Support for Democracy in Belarus, Russia, and Ukraine", *Journal of Elections, Public Opinion and Parties*, vol. 25, issue 1

McAllister, Ian and White, Stephen (2016) "Lukashenka and His Voters", *East European Politics and Societies*, vol. 30, issue 2

McFaul, Michael (1999) "Authoritarian and Democratic Responses to the Financial Meltdown in Russia", *Problems of Post-Communism*, vol. 46, issue 4

McGlynn, Jade (2023) *Russia's War*, London: Bloomsbury

McGuckin, John (2020) *The Eastern Orthodox Church: a new history*, New Haven, CT: Yale UP

McMahon, Robert (2021) *The Cold War: a very short introduction (2nd ed.)*, Oxford: OUP

Mearsheimer, John (2015) "Why Is Ukraine the West's Fault?" *YouTube*, September 25. https://www.youtube.com/watch?v=JrMiSQAGOS4 (accessed July 19, 2024)

Medetsky, Anatoly (2012) "Belarus Suspected of Evading Duty Payments", *The Moscow Times*, July 19. https://www.themoscowtimes.com/archive/belarus-suspected-of-evading-duty-payments (accessed August 6, 2024)

Medish, Mark (1994) "Russia: lost and found", *Daedalus*, vol. 123, issue 3

Medvedev, Dmitrii (2009) "Rossiia Vpered!", *Kremlin.ru*, September 10. http://kremlin.ru/events/president/news/5413 (accessed August 2, 2024)

"Medvedev Namerenno Vyrval iz Konteksta Slova Lukashenko o 'Ne Nashikh Voinakh'?" (2019a) *YouTube*, November 5. https://www.youtube.com/watch?v=zSdAIh2w6do (accessed August 10, 2024)

"Medvedev Poschital Strannymi Slova Lukashenko o Vtiagivanii v Chuzhie Voiny" (2019b) *Radio Sputnik*, November 4. https://radiosputnik.ru/20191104/1560563190.html (accessed August 10, 2024)

"Medvedev Prigrozil Otmenit' Skidki na Gaz 'Tormoziashchim Integratsiiu' EAES" (2017) *Republic (Slon)*, March 7

"Medvedev Prizval Rabotat' nad Raznymi Putiami Integratsii Rossii i Belorussii" (2019a) *Ria Novosti*, March 6. https://ria.ru/20190306/1551598040.html (accessed July 12, 2024)

Medvedev, Roy (2000) *Post-Soviet Russia: a journey through the Yeltsin era*, New York: Columbia UP

"Medvedev Schitaet Poka Bessmyslennymi Rassuzhdeniia o Nazvanii Valiuty Soiuznogo Gosudarstva" (2019) *TASS*, March 6. https://tass.ru/ekonomika/6192507 (accessed July 12, 2024)

Melnichuk, Tatsiana (2020) "Belarus WW2 Parade Defies Pandemic and Upstages Putin", *BBC News*, May 9. https://www.bbc.co.uk/news/world-europe-52574749 (accessed July 16, 2024)

Mendez, Alvaro; Forcadell, Francisco and Horiachko, Kateryna (2022) "Russia-Ukraine Crisis: China's Belt and Road Initiative at the crossroads", *Asian Business and Management*, vol. 21, issue 4

Merheim-Eyre, Igor (2017) "The Visegrad Countries and Visa Liberalisation in the Eastern Neighbourhood: a *Pan Tadeusz* syndrome?" *East European Politics and Societies*, vol. 31, issue 1

Merriman, John (2019) *A History of Modern Europe: from the Renaissance to the present (4th ed.)*, New York: W.W. Norton

Metcalf, Lee (1997) "The (Re)Emergence of Regional Economic Integration in the Former Soviet Union", *Political Research Quarterly*, vol. 50, issue 3

"MH17 Plane Crash: EU to widen Russia sanctions" (2014) *BBC News*, July 22. https://www.bbc.co.uk/news/uk-28415248 (accessed on July 6, 2024)

Miarka, Agnieszka (2024) "Social Mobilization in Belarus: the Polish perspective", *Problems of Post-Communism*, vol. 71, issue 1

Miazhevich, Galina (2007) "Official Media Discourse and the Self-Representation of Entrepreneurs in Belarus", *Europe-Asia Studies*, vol. 59, issue 8

Miazhevich, Galina (2009) "Hybridisation of Business Norms as Intercultural Dialogue: the case of two post-Soviet countries", *Communist and Post-Communist Studies*, vol. 42, issue 2

"MID Belarusi Vnov' Vystupil s Kritikoi Metodov Raboty Rossiiskogo Posla Babicha" (2019) *Belta*, April 19. https://www.belta.by/politics/view/mid-belarusi-vnov-vystupil-s-kritikoj-metodov-raboty-rossijskogo-posla-babicha-344760-2019/ (accessed August 10, 2024)

"MID Belorussii Zastupilsia za Vladimira Putina" (2014) *Nezavisimaia Gazeta*, June 17

"MID Belorussii: Vopros o Razmeshchenii Aviabazy Rossii Seichas Zakryt" (2016) *RIA Novosti*, April 8. https://ria.ru/20160408/1405257821.html (accessed August 9, 2024)

"MID Rossii" (2021) *x.com*, September 17. https://x.com/MID_RF/status/1438768364353114115 (accessed July 17, 2024)

Mijnssen, Ivo (2021) *Russia's Hero Cities: from postwar ruins to the Soviet hero-archy*, Bloomington, IN: IUP

"Mikhail Babich: Nikto ne predlagal Belorussii vstupat' v sostav Rossii" (2019) *Ria Novosti*, March 14. https://ria.ru/20190314/1551786886.html (accessed July 12, 2024)

Miller, Eric and Toritsyn, Arkady (2005) "Bringing the Leader Back In: internal threats and alignment theory in the Commonwealth of Independent States", *Security Studies*, vol. 14, issue 2

Miller, Michael (2017) "The Strategic Origins of Electoral Authoritarianism", *British Journal of Political Science*, vol. 50, issue 1

Miller, Nicholas and Volpe, Tristan (2023) "The Rise of the Autocratic Nuclear Marketplace", *Journal of Strategic Studies*, vol. 46, issue 6-7

Miłosz, Czesław (2001) *The Captive Mind*, London: Penguin

"Minister Reportedly Says Belarus Should Balance between EU, Russia-led Bloc" (2013) *Belapan*, November 15

"Minoborony—o Iadernom Oruzhii v Belarusi: eto ne razmeshchenie, a vozvrashchenie" (2024) *Zerkalo*, January 29. https://news.zerkalo.io/economics/59897.html?c (accessed July 26, 2024)

"Minsk Hopes to Get Oil in Full Despite Potash Conflict—Lukashenko (Part 2)" (2013) *Interfax*, October 21

"Minsk Ne Samai!" (2018) *Segodnia*, October 23

"Minsk Should Not Be Fifth Wheel on Moscow-Beijing Axis— Lukashenko" (2012) *Interfax*, August 6

"Minsk Udivlen Dannymi o Soglashenii po Uproshcheniiu Vizovogo Rezhima s ES" (2015) *RIA Novosti*, December 10. https://ria.ru/20151210/1339757172.html (accessed August 9, 2024)

Mishutin, Gleb (2020) "'Rossiiskikh Naemnikov' v Belorussii Obvinili v Rabote na Oppozitsiiu", *Vedomosti*, July 30. https://www.vedomosti.ru/politics/articles/2020/07/30/835673-rossiiskih-naemnikov (accessed July 16, 2024)

"Misija Ukraiiny v OON: Genasambleiia Ukhvalyla Rezoliutsiiu Shchodo Krymu—RF Vpershe Nazvano Derzhavoiu-Okupantom" (2016) *5.ua*, November 16. https://www.5.ua/polityka/henasambleia-oon-ukhvalyla-rezoliutsiiu-shchodo-krymu-rosiiu-nazvano-derzhavoiuokupantom-131198.html?fbclid=IwZXh0bgNhZW0CMTEAAR2avxgGA0O7iORWONG7HPiV4Z_BeM-nWvcaJtw8ABm7jcJzUiGj6s3QGys_aem_jd3zuOPvyV3rSupnfMj9AQ (accessed July 7, 2024)

Mitrofanova, Anastasia (2016) "Russian Ethnic Nationalism and Religion Today" in *The New Russian Nationalism: imperialism, ethnicity and authoritarianism 2000-2015*, Edinburgh: EUP; eds. Pål Kolstø and Helge Blakkisrud

Moiseev, Danila (2022) "NATO Otvetilo na Predlozheniia Moskvy Perebroskoi Voisk na Vostok", *Nezavisimaia Gazeta*, January 24. https://www.ng.ru/world/2022-01-24/1_8353_nato.html (accessed July 21, 2024)

Moldashev, Kairat and Hassan, Mohamed (2017) "The Eurasian Union: actor in the making?" *Journal of International Relations and Development*, vol. 20, issue 1

Monday, Chris (2011) "Family Rule as the Highest Stage of Communism", *Asian Survey*, vol. 51, issue 5

The Monster Theory Reader (2020) Minneapolis, MN: UMP; ed. Jeffrey Weinstock

Montgomery, Kathleen and Remington, Thomas (1994) "Regime Transition and the 1990 Soviet Republican Elections", *The Journal of Communist Studies and Transition Politics*, vol. 10, issue 1

Moore, Ben (2023) "The Eyes of the Other: Mary Shelley's Frankenstein and the uncanny" in *The Bloomsbury Handbook to Literature and Psychoanalysis*, London: Bloomsbury; ed. Jeremy Tambling

Moorhouse, Roger (2016) *The Devils' Alliance: Hitler's pact with Stalin, 1939-41*, London: Vintage

Morahan, Christopher (1986) *Clockwise*, London: Moment Films

Morgan, Michael (2018) *The Final Act: the Helsinki Accords and the transformation of the Cold War*, Princeton, NJ: PUP

Morozov, S. (2007) "1934-1935: Germany, Japan and Poland against the USSR", *International Affairs (Moscow)*, vol. 53, issue 2

Morris, Chris (2013) "EU-Russia Rivalry Looms over Vilnius Summit", *BBC News*, November 28

Morris, Marcia (2018) *Writing the Time of Troubles: False Dmitry in Russian literature*, Boston, MA: Academic Studies

Morrison, Kelly; Donno, Daniela; Savun, Burcu and Davutoglu, Perisa (2024) "Competing Judgments: multiple election observers and post-election contention", *The Review of International Organizations*, online first

Moshes, Arkadii (2017) "Pochemu Ne Stoit Zhdat' 'Tsvetnuiu Revoliutsiiu' v Minske", *Ezhednevnaia Delovaia Gazeta RBK*, December 14

"The Most Important Results of the Public Opinion Poll in December 2013" (2015) *IISEPS*, n.d. http://www.iiseps.org/?p=2685&lang=en (accessed August 7, 2024)

"Mozart: Don Giovanni (Halidon Music)" (2023) *YouTube*, March 26. https://www.youtube.com/watch?v=DIvTXv65hyo (accessed July 18, 2024)

Msemburi, William; Karlinsky, Ariel; Knutson, Victoria; Aleshin-Guendel, Serge; Chatterji, Somnath and Wakefield, Jon (2023) "The WHO Estimates of Excess Mortality Associated with the COVID-19 Pandemic", *Nature*, vol. 613

Mudrov, Sergei (2020) "Belarus, Crimea and the Donbass: Belarusian attitudes to the post-Maidan events in Ukraine", *Journal of Contemporary Central and Eastern Europe*, vol. 28, issue 1

Mukhin, Vladimir (2020) "Pol'sha Realizuet v Belorussii Stsenarii 'Krymskoi Vesny'", *Nezavisimaia Gazeta*, August 23. https://www.ng.ru/armies/2020-08-23/2_7944_poland1.html (accessed July 16, 2024)

350 UNCANNY ALLIES

Mukhin, Vladimir (2023) "Takticheskoe Iadernoe Oruzhie Rossii v Evrope Sygraet Strategicheskuiu Rol'", *Nezavisimaia Gazeta*, March 26. https://www.ng.ru/armies/2023-03-26/1_8689_europe.html

Müller, Anna (2022) "Writing Władysław Gomułka's Life: historiographies of Władysław Gomułka's biographies", *East European Politics and Societies*, vol. 36, issue 3

"My Vpervye za Desiatki Let Okazalis' na Poroge Konflikta, Sposobnogo Zatianut' Ves' Kontinent" (2022a) *Belarus' Segodnia*, February 18. https://www.sb.by/articles/lukashenko-my-vpervye-za-desyatki-let-okazalis-na-poroge-konflikta-sposobnogo-zatyanut-ves-kontinent.html (accessed July 20, 2024)

Mykhaylovskiy, Vitaliy (2019) *European Expansion and the Contested Borderlands of Late Medieval Podillya, Ukraine*, Amsterdam: Arc Humanities

"Na Kastrychnitskai Ploshchy u Mensku Praisla Aktsyia za Vyzvalen'ne Palitviaz'niau i Suprats' Vuchen'niau 'Zakhad-2017'" (2017) *Radyio Svaboda*, July 7. https://www.svaboda.org/a/akcyja-suprac-vucenniau-zachad-2017/28602077.html (accessed August 9, 2024)

Naimark, Norman (2019) *Stalin and the Fate of Europe: the postwar struggle for sovereignty*, Cambridge, MA: Harvard UP

"Nas Nachali Napriagat' Vagnerovtsy—Prosiatsia na Zapad" (2023) *Belarus' Segodnya*, July 23. https://www.sb.by/articles/lukashenko-nas-nachali-napryagat-vagnerovtsy-prosyatsya-na-zapad-.html (accessed July 24, 2024)

"Nasha Strana—Nash Vybor" (2015) *Belarus' Segodnia*, October 12

"National Threat Assessment 2023" (2023) *State Security Department of the Republic of Lithuania* and *Defence Intelligence and Security Service under the Ministry of National Defence*, Lithuania: Vilnius. https://www.vsd.lt/wp-content/uploads/2023/03/National-threat-assessment-2023_EN_for_download.pdf (accessed July 25, 2024)

"Nationalist Party Being Set Up in Russia" (2012) *Interfax*, April 21

Natsional'naia Ekonomika Respubliki Belarus': problemy i perspektivy razvitiia (2016) Minsk: Belorusskii Gosudarstvennyi Ekonomicheskii Universitet; ed. G. Korolenok

Navumchyk, Siarhei (2023) "Pastaviu pad Sumnei Svaiu Sdol'nas'ts' Kantraliavats' Vaiskovuiu Sferu i Abaraniaiu Pazytsyiu Maskvy: analis interviiu Lukashenki", *Radyio Svaboda*, August 17. https://www.svaboda.org/a/32552844.html (accessed July 24, 2024)

"'Ne My Razviazali Etu Voinu, u Nas Sovest' Chista': Lukashenko rasskazal o gotovivshemsia napadenii na Belarus'" (2022) *Belarus' Segodnia*, March 11. https://www.sb.by/articles/ne-my-razvyazali-etu-voynu-u-nas-sovest-chista-lukashenko-rasskazal-o-gotovivshemsya-napadenii-na-be.html (accessed July 21, 2024)

"'Ne Po-Bratski': v MID osudili zaderzhanie rossiiskikh zhurnalistov v Minske" (2020) *RIA Novosti*, August 10. https://ria.ru/20200810/1575595643.html?in=t (accessed August 11, 2024)

"Nedelia" (2014) *YouTube*, December 28. https://www.youtube.com/watch?v=RbdFTBCEjJc (accessed August 7, 2024)

Nefedov, Sergei and Ellman, Michael (2019) "The Soviet Famine of 1931-1934: genocide, a result of poor harvests, or the outcome of a conflict between the state and the peasants?" *Europe-Asia Studies*, vol. 71, issue 6

Neiberg, Michael (2015) *Potsdam: the end of World War II and the remaking of Europe*, New York: Basic

Netreba, Petr (2012) "Ottepel' po Kontraktu", *Kommersant*, July 19

Neumann, Iver (2017) "Russia's Return as True Europe, 1991-2017", *Conflict and Society*, vol. 3, issue 1

Nezhdanskii, Kirill (2018) "Posol Spetsnazncheniia", *BelGazeta*, August 10. http://www.belgazeta.by/ru/1156/event/37445/ (accessed August 10, 2024)

"'Nezygar'': Lukashenko ne budet uchastvovat' v sleduiushchikh prezidentskikh vyborakh" (2018) *Nasha Niva*, September 22. https://nashaniva.com/?c=ar&i=216376&lang=ru (accessed July 11, 2024)

"Niama Resursu ni u Rasei, ni u Putsina Zadushyshch' Belarus'" (2012) *Radyio Svaboda*, May 8. https://www.svaboda.org/a/24573735.html (accessed August 6, 2024)

Nietzsche, Friedrich (2017) *The Will to Power*, London: Penguin

Nikolayenko, Olena (2015a) "Marching against the Dictator: Chernobyl Path in Belarus", *Social Movement Studies*, vol. 14, issue 2

Nikolayenko, Olena (2015b) "Youth Movements and Elections in Belarus", *Europe-Asia Studies*, vol. 67, issue 3

Nikonov, Viacheslav (2013) "God Spustia", *Rossiiskaia Gazeta*, May 7

Nitoiu, Cristian (2018) "The European Union's 'Ideal Self' in the Post-Soviet Space", *Europe-Asia Studies*, vol. 70, issue 5

Nizhnikau, Ryhor and Silvan, Kristiina (2022) "From Demobilisation to Civic Engagement: the post-2014 remodelling of the Belarusian Republican Youth Union", *Europe-Asia Studies*, vol. 74, issue 7

Niziołek, Katarzyna (2022) "'I Remember Little. Almost Nothing': participatory theatre as a means to access subjugated memories", *Memory Studies*, vol. 15, issue 2

Nordstrom, Louise (2023) "Wagner Group's Bloody Year in Ukraine: from murder squad to cannon fodder", *France 24*, February 22. https://www.france24.com/en/europe/20230222-wagner-group-s-bloody-year-in-ukraine-from-murder-squad-to-cannon-fodder (accessed July 24, 2024)

Norris, John (2005) *Collision Course: NATO, Russia, and Kosovo*, Westport, CT: Praeger

Novoprudskii, Semen (2017) "Teper' My Ne Boimsia Togo, Chto Boiatsia Nas", *Gazeta.ru*, January 18. https://www.gazeta.ru/comments/column/novoprudsky/10479647.shtml (accessed August 9, 2024)

Nukusheva, Aigul; Karzhassova, Guldana; Rustembekova, Dinara; Au, Tatyana and Baikenzhina, Kulbagila (2021) "International Nuclear Energy Legal Regulation: comparing the experience of the EU and the CIS countries", *International Environmental Agreements: politics, law and economics*, vol. 21, issue 4

Nuzov, Ilya (2017) "The Dynamics of Collective Memory in the Ukraine Crisis: a transitional justice perspective", *International Journal of Transitional Justice*, vol. 11, issue 1

"O Chem Piat' Chasov Govorili Putin i Lukashenko?" (2022) *SN Plus*, March 11. https://www.sn-plus.com/2022/03/11/o-chem-pyat-chasov-govorili-putin-i-lukashenko/ (accessed July 22, 2024)

"O Vragakh Belarusi, Ubiistvakh Bezhentsev i Gotovnosti Dat' Otpor: Lukashenko vyskazalsia na Temu Voennoi Bezopasnosti" (2021) *Belta*, November 29. https://www.belta.by/president/view/o-vragah-belarusi-ubijstvah-bezhentsev-i-gotovnosti-dat-otpor-lukashenko-vyskazalsja-na-temu-voennoj-472100-2021/ (accessed July 21, 2024)

"Ob Itogakh Vyborov Prezidenta Respubliki Belarus' v 2020 Godu" (2020) *Gov.by*, n.d. https://web.archive.org/web/20200908083130/http://rec.gov.by/sites/default/files/pdf/2020/inf9.pdf (accessed July 14, 2024)

"Obrashchenie Sinoda Belorusskoi Pravoslavnoi Tserkvi (Belorusskogo Ekzarkhata Moskovskogo Patriarkhata) ot 11 Sentiabria 2018 Goda" (2018) *Church.by*, September 11. http://church.by/news/obrashenie-sinoda-belorusskoj-pravoslavnoj-cerkvi-ot-11-sentjabrja-2018-goda (accessed July 11, 2024)

Obydenkova, Anastassia and Libman, Alexander (2012) "The Impact of External Factors on Regime Transition: lessons from the Russian regions", *Post-Soviet Affairs*, vol. 28, issue 3

O'Connor, Kevin (2019) *The House of Hemp and Butter: a history of Old Riga*, Ithaca, NY: Northern Illinois UP

Odom, William (1998) *The Collapse of the Soviet Military*, New Haven, CT: Yale UP

"Ofitsial'noe Zaiavlenie Ministra Oborony Respubliki Belarus'" (2022) *Ministerstvo Oborony Respubliki Belarus'*, January 6. https://www.mil.by/ru/news/143087/#close (accessed July 21, 2024)

O'Hanlon, Michael (2017) *Beyond NATO: a new security architecture for Eastern Europe*, Washington, DC: Brookings Institution

Oldberg, Ingmar (2005) "Foreign Policy Priorities under Putin" in *Russia as a Great Power: dimensions of security under Putin*, Abingdon: Routledge; eds. Jakob Hedenskog, Vilhelm Konnander, Bertil Nygren, Ingmar Oldberg and Christer Pursiainen

O'Loughlin, John; Linke, Andrew; Toal, Gerard and Bakke, Kristin (2024) "Support for Vladimir Putin in Russia's Neighbours: survey evidence from an endorsement experiment in six post-Soviet countries", *Political Geography*, vol. 108

O'Loughlin, John and Talbot, Paul (2005) "Where in the World Is Russia? Geopolitical perceptions and preferences of ordinary Russians", *Eurasian Geography and Economics*, vol. 46, issue 1

O'Loughlin, John and Toal, Gerard (2022) "The Geopolitical Orientations of Ordinary Belarusians: survey evidence from early 2020", *Post-Soviet Affairs*, vol. 38, issue 1-2

Onuch, Olga and Hale, Henry (2022) *The Zelensky Effect*, London: Hurst

Onuch, Olga and Sasse, Gwendolyn (2022) "Anti-Regime Action and Geopolitical Polarization: understanding protester dispositions in Belarus", *Post-Soviet Affairs*, vol. 38, issue 1-2

Onuch, Olga; Sasse, Gwendolyn and Michiels, Sébastien (2023) "Flowers, Tractors, and Telegram: who are the protesters in Belarus? A survey based assessment of anti-Lukashenka protest participants", *Nationalities Papers*, vol. 51, issue 4

Opršal, Zdeněk; Harmáček, Jaromír; Vítová, Pavla; Syrovátka, Miroslav and Jarecka-Stępień, Katarzyna (2021) "Polish and Czech Foreign Aid: a 'mélange' of geopolitical and developmental objectives", *Journal of International Relations and Development*, vol. 24, issue 2

Orenstein, Mitchell (2019) *The Lands in Between: the new politics of Russia's hybrid war*, Oxford: OUP

Orlova, Dariya (2017) "'Europe' as a Normative Model in the Mediatised Discourse of Ukrainian Political Elites", *Europe-Asia Studies*, vol. 69, issue 2

Orwell, George (1989) *Nineteen Eighty-Four*, London: Penguin

354 UNCANNY ALLIES

Orwell, George (2000) *Homage to Catalonia*, London: Penguin

Osipov, Maksim (2016) "Nashi Goroda Dolzhny Byt' Krasivymi", *Belarus' Segodnia*, November 15

Osipov, Maksim (2021) "Otkaz Pol'shi ot Politiki Dobrososedstva: prichiny i posledstviia", *Belarus' Segodnya*, March 13. https://www.sb.by/art icles/proverka-na-razryv-polsha.html (accessed July 18, 2024)

Osipov, Maksim (2023a) "Eksperty—ob Elegantnom Otvete Minska na Iadernyi Shantazh Zapada", *Belarus' Segodnia*, March 26. https:// www.sb.by/articles/eksperty-ob-elegantnom-otvete-minska-na-ya dernyy-shantazh-zapada.html (accessed July 24, 2024)

Osipov, Maksim (2023b) "Gaidukevich: Reshenie o Razmeshchenii Iader-nogo Oruzhiia na Territorii Belarusi Sokhranit Nam Mir", *Belarus' Segodnia*, March 26. https://www.sb.by/articles/gaydukevich-resh enie-o-razmeshchenii-yadernogo-oruzhiya-na-territorii-belarusi-sok hranit-nam-mir.html (accessed July 24, 2024)

Oskanian, Kevork (2021) *Russian Exceptionalism between East and West: the ambiguous empire*, Cham: Springer

"Ostanovit' Neonatsizm, Fashizm, Ksenofobiiu i Rusofobiiu na Ukraine!" (2013) *Pravda*, December 12

Østbø, Jardar (2016) *The New Third Rome: readings of a Russian nationalist myth*, Stuttgart: ibidem

"Otkrytie Memoriala Mirnym Zhiteliam SSSR—Zhertvam Natsistskogo Genotsida v Gody Velikoi Otechestvennoi Voiny" (2024) *Kremlin.ru*, January 27. http://kremlin.ru/events/president/news/73334 (ac-cessed August 11, 2024)

"Otnoshenie Rossiian k Drugim Stranam" (2014) *Levada-Tsentr*, June 5. https://www.levada.ru/2014/06/05/otnoshenie-rossiyan-k-drugi m-stranam-6/ (accessed August 7, 2024)

"Otvet Nachal'nika Upravleniia Informatsii i Tsifrovoi Diplomatii MID Belarusi A. Glaza na Vopros Portala 'TUT.BY'" (2019) *MID Respubliki Belarus'*, April 19. https://mfa.gov.by/press/news_mfa/fdbb89a4 38798052.html (accessed July 12, 2024)

Oukaderova, Lida (2010) "The Sense of Movement in Georgii Daneliia's 'Walking the Streets of Moscow'", *Studies in Russian and Soviet Cin-ema*, vol. 4, issue 1

Pacer, Valerie (2016) *Russian Foreign Policy under Dmitry Medvedev, 2008-2012*, Abingdon: Routledge

Padhol, Uladzimir and Marples, David (2011) "The 2010 Presidential Elec-tion in Belarus", *Problems of Post-Communism*, vol. 58, issue 1

Palivoda, Andrei (2019) "Imenem Rosta Vzaimnoi Torgovli", *Zerkalo Nedeli*, October 12

BIBLIOGRAPHY 355

Panfilova, Viktoriia (2019) "V Ashkhabade Prezidenta Ukrainy Ne Dozhdutsia", *Nezavisimaia Gazeta*, October 10

Pankovets, Zmiter (2017) "Marzaliuk ob NTV: 'Eti Liudi Dolzhny Stat' Personami Non-Grata i Nikogda Ne Peresech' Granits Belarusi'", *Nasha Niva*, December 4. https://nashaniva.com/ru/articles/201357/ (accessed August 10, 2024)

Panteleev, Sergei (2021) "Vtoroe Dykhanie Evraziiskoi Integratsii", *Vedomosti*, September 13. https://www.vedomosti.ru/opinion/articles /2021/09/13/886287-vtoroe-dihanie (accessed July 19, 2024)

"Parad 'Skorykh': sostoianie Lukashenko ukhudshilos'" (2023) *Khartyia '97*, May 10. https://charter97.org/ru/news/2023/5/10/547391/ (accessed July 24, 2024)

Paratunin, Nikolai (2013) "Pul's EAS: segodnia i zavtra", *Argumenty Nedeli*, December 19

Partlett, William (2019) "Post-Soviet Constitution Making" in *Comparative Constitution Making*, Cheltenham: Edward Elgar; eds. David Landau and Hanna Lerner

Patel, Kiran (2017) "Who Was Saving Whom? The European Community and the Cold War, 1960s-1970s", *The British Journal of Politics and International Relations*, vol. 19, issue 1

"Patriarkh Kirill Prizval Belorusov Ne Reshat' Problemy s Pomoshchiu 'Maidana'" (2021) *Interfax*, January 7. https://www.interfax.ru/world/744272 (accessed August 11, 2024)

Paul, Allen (2010) *Katyń: Stalin's massacre and the triumph of truth*, DeKalb, IL: Northern Illinois UP

Pavlenko, Aneta (2013) "Language Management in the Russian Empire, Soviet Union, and Post-Soviet Countries" in *The Oxford Handbook of Sociolinguistics*, Oxford: OUP; eds. Robert Bayley, Richard Cameron and Ceil Lucas

Pavlova, Elena (2021) "The EU-Russia Relationship through the Lens of Postcolonial Theory" in *The Routledge Handbook of EU-Russia Relations*, Abingdon: Routledge; eds. Tatiana Romanova and Maxine David

Payne, Stanley (2004) *The Spanish Civil War, the Soviet Union, and Communism*, New Haven, CT: Yale UP

Penttilä, Risto (2003) "The Role of the G8 in International Peace and Security", *The Adelphi Papers*, vol. 43, issue 355

"Peramovy Belarusi i Kitaia Zatsiahnulisiia: shto zdarylasia?" (2023) *YouTube*, December 4. https://www.youtube.com/watch?v=YXBOg TXjy6o&t=738s (accessed July 25, 2024)

"Peremennaia Kerimova" (2013) *Vedomosti*, September 3

"'Peremeny Dolzhny Byt' v Ramkakh Zakona': Lukashenko ob aktivizatsii raboty nad obnovleniem Konstitutsii" (2020) *Belta*, August 19. https://www.belta.by/video_official/getRecord/6240/ (accessed August 11, 2024)

Perrie, Maureen and Pavlov, Andrei (2003) *Ivan the Terrible*, Abingdon: Routledge

Pershái, Alexander (2010) "Minor Nation: the alternative modes of Belarusian nationalism", *East European Politics and Societies*, vol. 24, issue 3

Person, Robert (2016) "The Deep Impact of Economic Collapse on Democratic Support", *Problems of Post-Communism*, vol. 63, issue 5-6

Pertsev, Andrei (2023) "'Bylo Oshchushchenie, chto Posle Bunta On Plokho Zakonchit. Takogo Ne Proshchaiut": krushenie samoleta Prigozhina—chto o vozmozhnoi gibeli glavy ChVK Vagnera govoriat istochniki 'Meduzy', blizkie k Kremliu", *Meduza*, August 23. https://meduza.io/feature/2023/08/23/bylo-oschuschenie-chto-posle-bunta-on-ploho-zakonchit-takogo-ne-proschayut (accessed July 24, 2024)

"Peskov Nadeetsia, chto 'Belorusskii Stsenarii' v Rossii ne Povtoritsia" (2020a) *Novye Izvestiia*, September 10

"Peskov Zaiavil, chto Oligarkhov v Rossii Ne Sushchestvuet" (2020b) *TASS*, June 10. https://tass.ru/ekonomika/8694057 (accessed August 11, 2024)

Peterson, Christian (2012) "'Confronting' Moscow: the Reagan administration, human rights, and the Final Act", *The Historian*, vol. 74, issue 1

Petersson, Bo (2014) "Still Embodying the Myth? Russia's recognition as a great power and the Sochi Winter Games", *Problems of Post-Communism*, vol. 61, issue 1

Petrov, Gennadii (2021a) "Evropeitsy Ishchut Sposoby Ukroshcheniia Minska: ES sobiraetsia zashchishchat' granitsu s pomoshch'iu sanktsii, Ukrainy i Rossii", *Nezavisimaia Gazeta*, November 10. https://www.ng.ru/world/2021-11-10/6_8297_sanctions.html (accessed July 18, 2024)

Petrov, Gennadii (2021b) "Russkie s Kitaitsami Opiat' Reshili Stat' Brat'iami Navek", *Nezavisimaia Gazeta*, July 4. https://www.ng.ru/world/2021-07-04/1_8189_brothers.html (accessed July 19, 2024)

Petrov, Gennadii (2022) "Lavrov Trebuet ot Zapada Vernut'sia k Real'nosti", *Nezavisimaia Gazeta*, January 26. https://www.ng.ru/world/2022-01-26/6_8355_lavrov.html (accessed July 21, 2024)

Petrov, Nikita (2021) "The Soviet Past and the 1945 Victory Cult as Civil Religion in Contemporary Russia" in *The Future of the Soviet Past: the politics of history in Putin's Russia*, Bloomington, IN: IUP; eds. Anton Weiss-Wendt and Nanci Adler

Petrova, Svetlana (2024) "Vote of No Confidence: how artificial intelligence proved that Russia's 2018 presidential election was stolen", *Novaya Gazeta Europa*, March 14. https://novayagazeta.eu/articles/2024/03/14/vote-of-no-confidence-en (accessed July 11, 2024)

Petrova, Tsveta and Pospieszna, Paulina (2021) "Democracy Promotion in Times of Autocratization: the case of Poland, 1989-2019", *Post-Soviet Affairs*, vol. 37, issue 6

Phillips, Ian (2022) "Belarus Admits Russia's War 'Drags On'", *Associated Press*, May 5. https://apnews.com/article/belarus-alexander-lukashenko-ap-interview-9bc1f6524eb65841b924883705684b7f (accessed July 21, 2024)

Pieper, Moritz (2021) *The Making of Eurasia: competition and cooperation between China's Belt and Road Initiative and Russia*, London: Bloomsbury

Pipes, Richard (1997) *The Formation of the Soviet Union: communism and nationalism, 1917-1923*, Cambridge, MA: Harvard UP

Pittman, Avril (1992) *From Ostpolitik to Reunification: West German-Soviet political relations since 1974*, Cambridge: CUP

Plokhy, Serhii (2006) *The Origins of the Slavic Nations: premodern identities in Russia, Ukraine, and Belarus*, Cambridge: CUP

Plokhy, Serhii (2010) *Yalta: the price of peace*, New York: Viking

Plokhy, Serhii (2012) *The Cossack Myth: history and nationhood in the age of empires*, Cambridge: CUP

Plokhy, Serhii (2014) *The Last Empire: the final days of the Soviet Union*, New York: Basic

Plokhy, Serhii (2018) *Chernobyl: history of a tragedy*, London: Allen Lane

Plokhy, Serhii (2021) *Nuclear Folly: a new history of the Cuban Missile Crisis*, London: Allen Lane

Plokhy, Serhii (2023) *The Russo-Ukrainian War*, London: Penguin

Plugatarev, Igor' (2002) "Belorussiia Stanet 90-m Sub''ektom Federatsii: Vladimir Putin predlozhil Lukashenko bezal'ternativnyi vybor", *Nezavisimaia Gazeta*, August 15

"Pochemu Minskaia Militsiia 'Ne Zametila' Avtoprobeg 'Koloradskoi' Kolonny" (2017) *Khartyia '97*, September 19. https://charter97.link/ru/news/2017/9/19/263411/ (accessed August 9, 2024)

Podvig, Pavel (2017) "Did Star Wars Help End the Cold War? Soviet response to the SDI program", *Science and Global Security*, vol. 25, issue 1

358   Uncanny Allies

Poe, Edgar (2004) *The Selected Writings*, New York: W.W. Norton

Poe, Marshall (2003) *The Russian Moment in World History*, Princeton, NJ: PUP

Pogodina, Viktoria (2017) "The Minsk Process and the Settlement of the Ukraine Conflict: dances of interests", *International Affairs (Moscow)*, vol. 63, issue 6

"Polemika Ekspertov iz Belorussii: 'EAES Nuzhny Novye Draivery Rosta'" (2015) *RSMD*, October 27. https://russiancouncil.ru/analytics-and-comments/analytics/polemika-ekspertov-iz-belorussii-eaes-nuzhn y-novye-drayvery-/ (accessed August 9, 2024)

Polonsky, Antony (2013) *The Jews in Poland and Russia: a short history*, Liverpool: LUP

"Polskie Radio Kluczowym Środkiem Przekazu Podczas Wybuchu Wojny" (2023) *Polskie Radio Rzeszów*, September 1. https://radio.rze szow.pl/40213/polskie-radio-kluczowym-srodkiem-przekazu-pod-czas-wybuchu-wojny/#:~:text=Ca%C5%82e%20nasze%20%C5%BC ycie%20publiczne%20i,%E2%80%93%20walka%20a%C5%BC%20do %20zwyci%C4%99stwa%E2%80%9D (accessed July 20, 2024)

Ponzio, Richard and Siddiqui, Muznah (2023) "Peacekeeping, Disarmament, and the New Agenda for Peace", *Global Governance*, vol. 29, issue 2

Poplavskii, Aleksei (2021) "'Sorval Dzhekpot': chto grozit Lukashenko posle intsidenta s samoletom Ryanair", *Gazeta.ru*, May 24. https://www.gazeta.ru/politics/2021/05/24_a_13605620.shtml (accessed July 18, 2024)

Popov, Dmitrii (2020) "Lukashenko Pereshel Chertu Russkogo Mira: sdaet nashikh Ukraine", *Moskovskii Komsomolets*. August 6. https://www.mk.ru/politics/2020/08/06/lukashenko-pereshel-chertu-russkogo-mira-sdaet-nashikh-ukraine.html (accessed July 16, 2024)

Popov, Dmitrii (2023) "Iadernaia Sensatsiia: Putin ustroil Amerike khudshii moment v istorii", *Moskovskii Komsomolets*, March 26. https://www.mk.ru/politics/2023/03/26/yadernaya-sensaciya-putin-ustr oil-amerike-khudshiy-moment-v-istorii.html (accessed July 24, 2024)

Popova, Nadezhda (2016) "Ba-bakh! 'Rosatom' uronil iadernyi reaktor", *Nasha Versiia*, August 8

Portela, Clara (2016) "Are European Union Sanctions 'Targeted'?" *Cambridge Review of International Affairs*, vol. 29, issue 3

Portnikov, Vitalii (2015) "Belorusskii Flirt: o chem Lukashenko mozhet dogovorit'sia s Zapadom?" *Republic (Slon)*, October 13

Portnov, Andrii (2015) "Post-Maidan Europe and the New Ukrainian Studies", *Slavic Review*, vol. 74, issue 4

Pospieszna, Paulina and Galus, Aleksandra (2020) "Promoting Active Youth: evidence from Polish NGO's civic education programme in Eastern Europe", *Journal of International Relations and Development*, vol. 23, issue 1

Pospieszna, Paulina and Pietrzyk-Reeves, Dorota (2022) "Responses of Polish NGOs Engaged in Democracy Promotion to Shrinking Civic Space", *Cambridge Review of International Affairs*, vol. 35, issue 4

Postnikova, Ekaterina (2021) "Pozadi—Minsk: kak zhivut bezhentsy na granitse Belorussii i Pol'shi", *Izvestiia*, November 11. https://iz.ru/1248006/ekaterina-postnikova/pozadi-minsk-kak-zhivut-bezhentcy-na-granitce-belorussii-i-polshi (accessed July 18, 2024)

Postnikova, Ekaterina and Baikova, Tat'iana (2022) "Otkaznoe Pis'mo: kak SShA i NATO otvetili na trebovaniia RF po garantiiam", *Izvestiia*, January 26. https://iz.ru/1282801/ekaterina-postnikova-tatiana-baikova/otkaznoe-pismo-kak-ssha-i-nato-otvetili-na-trebovaniia-rf-po-garantiiam (accessed July 21, 2024)

"'Poteria Nadezhdy na Svobodu na Blizhaishie Desiatiletiia': chitateli 'Zerkala'—o priezde Prigozhina v Belarus'", *Zerkalo*, June 25. https://news.zerkalo.io/life/42225.html?c (accessed July 24, 2024)

Pouliot, Vincent (2010) *International Security in Practice: the politics of NATO-Russia diplomacy*, Cambridge: CUP

Powell, Bill (1996) "Russian Roulette", *Newsweek*, June 17

"The Power of the Powerless Today" (2018) *East European Politics and Societies*, vol. 32, issue 2; eds. James Krapfl and Barbara Falk

"President Denies Belarus Losing Sovereignty to Russia-led Regional Unions" (2012a) *Belapan*, December 11

"President Says Belarus Needs to Study China's Experience" (2012b) *Interfax*, November 12

"Press-Konferentsiia Ministra Inostrannykh Del Rossiiskoi Federatsii S.V. Lavrova po Problematike Evropeiskoi Bezopasnosti, Moskva, 1 Dekabria 2022 Goda" (2022) *Mid.ru*, December 1. https://mid.ru/ru/foreign_policy/news/1841407/ (accessed August 11, 2024)

"Prezidentskie Vybory v Rossii i Zoloto Domrachevoi: glavnoe za Voskresen'e" (2018) *Sovetskaia Belorussiia*, March 19. https://www.sb.by/articles/prezidentskie-vybory-v-rossii-i-zoloto-domrachevoy-glavnoe-za-voskresene.html (accessed July 11, 2024)

Pridham, G. (2001) "Uneasy Democratizations: pariah regimes, political conditionality and reborn transitions in Central and Eastern Europe", *Democratization*, vol. 8, issue 4

360   UNCANNY ALLIES

"Prinimat' Reshenie Posylat' Voiska, Tol'ko Potomy Chto 'Nas Pozvali' —
   Eto Otmazka dlia Detskogo Sada" (2022) *Salidarnasts'*, January 6.
   https://gazetaby.com/post/gulak-prinimat-reshenie-posylat-vojs
   ka-tolko-potom/182433/ (accessed July 21, 2024)

"Progressing Recession Deteriorates Quality of Debts" (2015) *Belarus Digest*, November 6. https://belarusdigest.com/story/progressing-re
   cession-deteriorates-quality-of-debts-belarus-economy-digest/   (accessed August 9, 2024)

Prokshin, Konstantin (2012) "Rossiia Zapodozrila Belorussiiu v Moshen-
   nichestve s Neft'iu", *Izvestiia*, June 14

"Protesty protiv Napadeniia na Ukrainu Zatmili Referendum: ocheredi na
   uchastkakh nabliudalis' tol'ko v to vremia, v kotoroe prizyvala golo-
   sovat' oppozitsiia" (2022) *Nasha Niva*, February 27. https://nas
   haniva.com/?c=ar&i=285487&lang=ru (accessed July 21, 2024)

Prozorov, Sergei (2022) *The Biopolitics of Stalinism: ideology and life in Soviet
   socialism*, Edinburgh: EUP

"Pugaiushchie Assotsiatsii" (2013) *Vedomosti*, September 4

"Putin Nazval Pobedu Lukashenko na Vyborakh Svidetel'stvom Ego
   Vysokogo Politicheskogo Avtoriteta" (2015) *Ekonomicheskie Novosti*,
   October 12

"Putin Raspravitsia s Lukashenko za Uchastie v Miatezhe Prigozhina"
   (2023) *Khartyia '97*, August 26. https://charter97.org/ru/news/
   2023/8/26/561277/ (accessed July 24, 2024)

"Putin Repeats Ukraine Nazi Claims at Leningrad Siege Memorial" (2024)
   The Moscow Times, January 27. https://www.themoscowtimes.com/
   2024/01/27/putin-repeats-ukraine-nazi-claims-at-leningrad-siege-
   memorial-a83877 (accessed July 26, 2024)

Putin, Vladimir (2021) "Article by Vladimir Putin 'On the Historical Unity
   of Russians and Ukrainians'", *Kremlin.ru*, July 12. http://en.kremlin.
   ru/events/president/news/66181 (accessed July 19, 2024)

"Putin's Palace: history of world's largest bribe" (2021) *YouTube*, January
   19.   https://www.youtube.com/watch?v=ipAnwilMncI   (accessed
   July 12, 2024)

"Rabochii Vizit v Rossiiskuiu Federatsiyu: peregovory s Vladimirom
   Putinym" (2021) *Prezident Respubliki Belarus'*, April 22. https://presid
   ent.gov.by/ru/events/aleksandr-lukashenko-sovershit-rabochiy-vi
   zit-v-rossiyskuyu-federaciyu (accessed July 18, 2024)

Rad, Pavlo (2024) "Ukraine-Belarus Relations in the Context of the Russo-
   Ukrainian War", *Wilson Center*, June 27. https://www.wilsoncenter.
   org/blog-post/ukraine-belarus-relations-context-russo-ukrainian-
   war (accessed July 26, 2024)

Radnitz, Scott (2010) "The Color of Money: privatization, economic dispersion, and the post-Soviet 'revolutions'", *Comparative Politics*, vol. 42, issue 2

Radzikhovskii, Leonid (2012) "Razvodiashchii Brat", *Nezavisimaia Gazeta*, November 16

Radzikhovskii, Leonid (2020) "Bratskoe Partnerstvo", *Rossiiskaia Gazeta*, September 22

Raffensperger, Christian (2012) *Reimagining Europe: Kievan Rus' in the medieval world*, Cambridge, MA: Harvard UP

Ragsdale, Hugh (2004) *The Soviets, the Munich Crisis, and the Coming of World War II*, Cambridge: CUP

Raleigh, Donald (2018) "'I Speak Frankly Because You Are My Friend': Leonid Ilich Brezhnev's personal relationship with Richard M. Nixon", *The Soviet and Post-Soviet Review*, vol. 45, issue 2

Ramani, Samuel (2023) *Putin's War on Ukraine: Russia's campaign for global counter-revolution*, London: Hurst

"Raseia Zaiavila, Shto Budze Dapamahats' Belarusi Zmahatstsa z Karanavirusam, 'Iak i Ranei'" (2020) *Radyio Svaboda*, April 22. https://www.svaboda.org/a/30569741.html (accessed August 11, 2024)

Rasizade, Alec (2008) "Putin's Mission in the Russian Thermidor", *Communist and Post-Communist Studies*, vol. 41, issue 1

"Rasporiazhenie" (2015) *Pravo.gov.ru*, September 18. http://publication.pravo.gov.ru/document/0001201509190001 (accessed August 9, 2024)

Razumovskii, V. (1996) "Is G7 Becoming G8?" *International Affairs (Moscow)*, vol. 42, issue 5-6

"Reaktsiia Minska" (2014) *Komsomol'skaia Pravda*, January 23

Recknagel, Charles (2014) "Money Troubles: Russia's weak ruble pulls down neighbors' currencies", *Radio Free Europe/Radio Liberty*, December 11. https://www.rferl.org/a/russia-ruble-effects-neighboring-countries/26738229.html (accessed on July 5, 2024)

Reid, Anna (2022) "Putin's War on History: the thousand-year struggle over Ukraine", *Foreign Affairs*, vol. 101, issue 3

Remchukov, Konstantin and Rodin, Ivan (2023) "Prigozhinskii Miatezh Perekvalifitsirovan vo Vnutrielitnyi Konflikt", *Nezavisimaia Gazeta*, June 25. https://www.ng.ru/politics/2023-06-25/1_8756_rebellion.html (accessed July 24, 2024)

Remnick, David (1993) *Lenin's Tomb: the last days of the Soviet empire*, London: Vintage

Rentea, Simona (2016) "Introduction" in *The Routledge Handbook of Biopolitics*, Abingdon: Routledge; eds. Sergei Prozorov and Simona Rentea

"Resolution ES-11/1 adopted" (2022) *X.com*, March 2. https://x.com/UN_PGA/status/1499067097711886340 (accessed July 21, 2024)

Revell, Stephen and White, Stephen (2002) "The USSR and Its Diplomatic Partners, 1917-91", *Diplomacy and Statecraft*, vol. 13, issue 1

Rey, Marie-Pierre (2012) *Alexander I: the tsar who defeated Napoleon*, DeKalb, IL: NIUP

Reynolds, David and Pechatnov, Vladimir (2018) *The Kremlin Letters: Stalin's wartime correspondence with Churchill and Roosevelt*, New Haven, CT: Yale UP

"RF Ne Propustila iz Belorussii 360 Tonn Ovoshchei iz-za Ogranichenii" (2014) *RIA Novosti*, November 28. https://ria.ru/20141128/1035 618579.html (accessed August 7, 2024)

Riabov, Oleg and Riabova, Tatiana (2014) "The Remasculinization of Russia? Gender, nationalism, and the legitimation of power under Vladimir Putin", *Problems of Post-Communism*, vol. 61, issue 2

Rich, Vera (1990) "Byelorussia Awakens", *The World Today*, vol. 46, issue 11

Rich, Vera (1997) "Belarus Turns on Soros", *The Times Higher Education Supplement*, May 9

Rieber, Alfred (2014) *The Struggle for the Eurasian Borderlands: from the rise of early modern empires to the end of the First World War*, Cambridge: CUP

Riga, Liliana (2012) *The Bolsheviks and the Russian Empire*, Cambridge: CUP

Risch, William (2015) "A Soviet West: nationhood, regionalism, and empire in the annexed western borderlands", *Nationalities Papers*, vol. 43, issue 1

The Rise and Fall of the Grand Alliance, 1941-45 (1995) Basingstoke: Macmillan; eds. Ann Lane and Howard Temperley

Rivera, David and Rivera, Sharon (2009) "Yeltsin, Putin, and Clinton: presidential leadership and Russian democratization in comparative perspective", *Perspectives on Politics*, vol. 7, issue 3

Roberts, Geoffrey (2007) *Stalin's Wars: from world war to cold war, 1939-1953*, New Haven, CT: Yale UP

Roberts, Sean (2017) "The Eurasian Economic Union: the geopolitics of authoritarian cooperation", *Eurasian Geography and Economics*, vol. 58, issue 4

Roberts, Sean and Moshes, Arkady (2016) "The Eurasian Economic Union: a case of reproductive integration?" *Post-Soviet Affairs*, vol. 32, issue 6

Robertson, Graeme (2022) "Protest, Platforms, and the State in the Belarus Crisis", *Post-Soviet Affairs*, vol. 38, issue 1-2

Robin, Ron (2017) *The Cold World They Made: the strategic legacy of Roberta and Albert Wohlstetter*, Cambridge, MA: Harvard UP

Rohava, Maryia (2018) "Identity in an Autocratic State: or what Belarusians talk about when they talk about national identity", *East European Politics and Society*, vol. 32, issue 3

Rojansky, Matthew and King, Harrison (2012) "Putin's Platform", *Carnegie Endowment for International Peace*, February 28. https://carnegieendo wment.org/research/2012/02/putins-platform?lang=en#foreignpo licy (accessed on June 29, 2024)

Rojo-Labaien, Ekain (2018) "The Baku 2015 European Games as a National Milestone of Post-Soviet Azerbaijan", *Nationalities Papers*, vol. 46, issue 6

Romanchuk, Iaroslav (2016) "Bratskii Trolling", *BelGazeta*, November 5. http://www.belgazeta.by/ru/1070/topic_week/33646/ (accessed August 9, 2024)

Romero, George (1978) *Dawn of the Dead*, United Film and Titanus

Rosenberg, Steve (2024) "Why Is Russia Trying to Frame Ukraine for Concert Massacre?" *BBC News*, April 8. https://www.bbc.co.uk/ne ws/world-europe-68759150 (accessed July 26, 2024)

Rosenfeldt, Niels (2006) *Stalin: diktaturets anatomi*, København: Høst og Søn

"Rossiia i Belorussiia Podpisali Neskol'ko Dokumetov o Sotrudichestve" (2015) *Ria Novosti*, March 3. https://ria.ru/20150303/1050690708. html (accessed August 8, 2024)

"Rossiia Ne u Del: konets mirovoi ekspansii" (2019) *Gazeta.ru*, April 11. https://www.gazeta.ru/comments/2019/04/11_e_12296461.shtml (accessed August 10, 2024)

"Rosiia Rospochala Viinu proti Ukraiiny" (2022a) *Poltavshchyna*, February 22. https://poltava.to/news/64867/ (accessed July 20, 2024)

"Rossiia v OBSE" (2022b) *Mid.ru*, December 2. https://mid.ru/ru/foreign _policy/vnesnepoliticeskoe-dos-e/dvustoronnie-otnosenij-rossii-s-inostrannymi-gosudarstvami/rossia-i-diskussii-o-budusem-obse/ (accessed August 11, 2024)

"Rossiia Vozrozhdaet Divizii" (2016) *Izvestiia*, May 10

"Rossiiskie SMI: Belarus' Vybrala Katastrofu" (2012) *Khartyia '97*, September 27. https://charter97.org/ru/news/2012/9/27/59079/ (accessed August 6, 2024)

"Rossiiskii Posol Preupredil Minsk o Trudnostiakh pri Vstuplenii v VTO" (2016) *Interfax*, March 31. https://www.interfax.ru/business/501322 (accessed August 9, 2024)

"Rost Dokhodov—Glavnaia Soderzhatel'naia Povestka Sleduiushchikh Vyborov" (2019) *Nezavisimaia Gazeta*, May 29. https://www.ng. ru/editorial/2019-05-29/2_7585_red.html (accessed July 12, 2024)

Rostovskii, Mikhail (2020) "U Lukashenko Sorvalo Rez'bu: zachem Bat'ke shou s 'diversantami'", *Moskovskii Komsomolets*, July 30. https://www.mk.ru/politics/2020/07/30/u-lukashenko-sorvalo-rezbu-zachem-batke-shou-s-diversantami.html (accessed July 16, 2024)

Rostovskii, Mikhail (2020) "Uskol'zashchaia Belorussiia", *Moskovskii Komsomolets*, July 23

Rostovskii, Mikhail (2021) "Spasitel' ot Riadovogo Lukashenko: kak Rossii pobedit' v voine razvodok", *Moskovskii Komsomolets*, November 14, 2021. https://www.mk.ru/politics/2021/11/14/spastis-ot-ryadovogo-lukashenko-kak-rossii-pobedit-v-voyne-razvodok.html (accessed July 18, 2024)

Rostovskii, Mikhail (2023) "Prigozhin Uedet, Problemy Ostanutsia: glubinnye politicheskie posledstviia neudavshegosia putcha", *Moskovskii Komsomolets*, June 25. https://www.mk.ru/politics/2023/06/25/prigozhin-uedet-problemy-ostanutsya-glubinnye-politicheskie-posledstviya-neudavshegosya-putcha.html (accessed July 24, 2024)

Roth, Andrew (2018) "Vladimir Putin Secures Record Win in Russian Presidential Election", *The Guardian*, March 19. https://www.theguardian.com/world/2018/mar/19/vladimir-putin-secures-record-win-in-russian-presidential-election (accessed July 10, 2024)

Roth, Andrew (2020) "'We Will Perish': embattled Lukashenko sends SOS to Putin", *The Guardian*, August 16. https://www.theguardian.com/world/2020/aug/16/we-will-perish-embattled-lukashenko-sends-sos-to-putin (accessed July 16, 2024)

Roth, Andrew and Sauer, Pjotr (2024) "Russia Lauding Torture Was Unthinkable—Now It Is Proud to Do So", *The Guardian*, March 25. https://www.theguardian.com/world/2024/mar/25/russian-officials-lauding-torture-was-unthinkable-now-it-is-proud-to-do-so (accessed July 26, 2024)

The Routledge Handbook of Russian International Relations Studies (2023) Abingdon: Routledge; eds. Maria Lagutina, Natalia Tsvetkova and Alexander Sergunin

Rowland, Richard (2003a) "Nationality Population Trends in Belarus during the Recent Intercensal Period, 1989-1999", *Eurasian Geography and Economics*, vol. 44, issue 7

Rowland, Richard (2003b) "Population Trends in Belarus and the Impact of Chernobyl', 1989-2002", *Eurasian Geography and Economics*, vol. 44, issue 4

Rowland, Robert and Jones, John (2016) "Reagan's Strategy for the Cold War and the Evil Empire Address", *Rhetoric and Public Affairs*, vol. 19, issue 3

BIBLIOGRAPHY   365

Rubenstein, Joshua (2011) *Leon Trotsky: a revolutionary's life*, New Haven, CT: Yale UP

Rublee, Maria (2015) "Fantasy Counterfactual: a nuclear-armed Ukraine", *Survival*, vol. 57, issue 2

Rudakova, Anastasiia (2012) "Tamozhennyi Soiuz Poka Ne Dal Rezul'tatov", *Izvestiia*, July 26

Rudling, Per (2014) *The Rise and Fall of Belarusian Nationalism, 1906-1931*, Pittsburgh, PA: UPP

"'Ruskiia—Heta Fashysty': iak interv'iuerka Lukashenki peraabuvalas' Prosta Padchas Vainy" (2023) *Nasha Niva*, August 18. https://nashaniva.com/324334 (accessed July 24, 2024)

"Russia More Responsible for Potash Row Than Belarus, Says Envoy" (2013) *Belapan*, December 27

"Russia Unhappy with Belarusian Plans to Assemble Chinese Cars—Envoy" (2012) *Belapan*, June 6

"Russian Airbase to Be Established in Belarus in 2014—Shoigu" (2013a) *Interfax*, December 10

"Russian Deputy PM Calls Detention of Potash Firm Chief in Minsk 'Inadequate'" (2013b) *Interfax*, August 26

"Russian Envoy Urges Belarus to Conduct Privatization, Introduce Single Currency" (2012) *Interfax*, June 13

"Russian Govt Closely Watching Situation with Baumgartner's Detention—Dvorkovich (part 2)" (2013c) *Interfax*, August 29

"'Russkii Vopros' 7 05 2014" (2014) *YouTube*, May 10. https://www.youtube.com/watch?v=SaSAvKjz06k (accessed August 7, 2024)

Rutland, Peter (2008) "Russia as an Energy Superpower", *New Political Economy*, vol. 13, issue 2

Ruvinskii, Vladimir (2018) "Ekonomicheskii Konflikt Moskvy i Minska na Politicheskoi Pochve", *Vedomosti*, December 25. https://www.vedomosti.ru/opinion/articles/2018/12/25/790381-moskvi-minska (accessed July 11, 2024)

Ruvinskii, Vladimir (2019) "Chernye Ochki Chetvertogo Sroka", *Vedomosti*, May 30. https://www.vedomosti.ru/opinion/articles/2019/05/30/802826-chernie-ochki (accessed July 12, 2024)

"Rynochnuiu Ideologiiu Nam Podkinuli…" (2012) *Sovetskaia Rossiia*, October 18

Rzeczkowski, Grzegorz (2021) "Po Włamaniu u Dworczyka: czego chcą od PiS ludzie Putina?" *Polityka*, June 10. https://www.polityka.pl/tygodnikpolityka/kraj/2121903,1,po-wlamaniu-u-dworczyka-czego-chca-od-pis-ludzie-putina.read (accessed August 11, 2024)

Safarov, B. (2017) "Ukraina Vybrala Svoi Put'", *Ekho*, August 25

Sagramoso, Domitilla (2020) *Russian Imperialism Revisited: from disengagement to hegemony*, Abingdon: Routledge

Saivetz, Carol (2012) "The Ties That Bind? Russia's evolving relations with its neighbors", *Communist and Post-Communist Studies*, vol. 45, issue 3-4

Sakhnin, Aleksei (2021a) "Pochemu Rossiiskaia Miagkaia Sila Slabee Zapadnoi", *Vedomosti*, May 16. https://www.vedomosti.ru/opinion/articles/2021/05/16/869923-rossiiskaya-sila (accessed July 19, 2024)

Sakhnin, Aleksei (2021b) "V Gore i v Kreposti: kak Rossii ne povtorit' sud'bu SSSR", *Vedomosti*, March 23. https://www.vedomosti.ru/opinion/articles/2021/03/22/862654-gore-kreposti (accessed July 18, 2024)

Sakovich, Asia (2024) "V Administratsii Lukashenko Priznali Slozhnosti s Eksportom", *Belsat*, April 29. https://belsat.eu/ru/news/29-04-2024-v-administratsii-lukashenko-priznali-slozhnosti-s-eksportom (accessed July 26, 2024)

Sakwa, Richard (2011) "Russia's Identity: between the 'domestic' and the 'international'", *Europe-Asia Studies*, vol. 63, issue 6

Sakwa, Richard (2015) *Frontline Ukraine: crisis in the borderlands*, London: I.B. Tauris

Sakwa, Richard (2024) "From the Customs Union to the Eurasian Economic Union" in *The Elgar Companion to the Eurasian Economic Union*, Cheltenham: Edward Elgar; eds. Alexander Libman and Evgeny Vinokurov

Sakwa, Richard and Webber, Mark (1999) "The Commonwealth of Independent States, 1991-1998: stagnation and survival", *Europe-Asia Studies*, vol. 51, issue 3

Sanchez-Sibony, Oscar (2014) *Red Globalization: the political economy of the Soviet Cold War from Stalin to Khrushchev*, Cambridge: CUP

Sannikov, Andrei (2023) "Zaiavlenie Glavy Delegatsii Respubliki Belarus' na Peregovorakh po Iadernomu Razoruzheniiu", *Khartyia '97*, March 26. https://charter97.org/ru/news/2023/3/26/541517/ (accessed July 24, 2024)

Sarotte, M. (2021) *Not One Inch: America, Russia, and the making of post-Cold War stalemate*, New Haven, CT: Yale UP

Sasunkevich, Olga (2016) *Informal Trade, Gender and the Border Experience: from political borders to social boundaries*, Abingdon: Routledge

Savchenko, Andrew (2009) *Belarus: a perpetual borderland*, Leiden: Brill

Sayle, Timothy (2009) "Andropov's Hungarian Complex: Andropov and the lessons of history", *Cold War History*, vol. 9, issue 3

Sayle, Timothy (2019) *Enduring Alliance: a history of NATO and the postwar global order*, Ithaca, NY: Cornell UP

Scaliger, Charles (2022) "Russia vs. Ukraine: is it our fight?" *The New American*, vol. 38, issue 3

Scarborough, Isaac (2023) *Moscow's Heavy Shadow: the violent collapse of the USSR*, Ithaca, NY: Cornell UP

Šćepanović, Janko (2024) "Still a Great Power? Russia's status dilemmas post-Ukraine War", *Journal of Contemporary European Studies*, vol. 32, issue 1

Schattenberg, Susanne (2021) *Brezhnev: the making of a statesman*, London: I.B. Tauris

Schenk, Frithjof (2010) "Attacking the Empire's Achilles Heels: railroads and terrorism in tsarist Russia", *Jahrbücher für Geschichte Osteuropas*, vol. 58, issue 2

Schlögel, Karl (2023) *The Soviet Century: archaeology of a lost world*, Princeton, NJ: PUP

Schoenborn, Benedikt and Niedhart, Gottfried (2016) "Erfurt and Kassel, 1970" in *Transcending the Cold War: summits, statecraft, and the dissolution of bipolarity in Europe, 1970-1990*, Oxford: OUP; eds. Kristina Spohr and David Reynolds

Schwarz, Hans-Peter (2010) "The Division of Germany, 1945-1949" in *The Cambridge History of the Cold War (vol. 1): origins*, Cambridge: CUP; eds. Melvyn Leffler and Odd Westad

Sebestyen, Victor (2006) *Twelve Days: revolution 1956 – how the Hungarians tried to topple their Soviet masters*, London: Weidenfeld and Nicolson

Sebestyen, Victor (2009) *Revolution 1989: the fall of the Soviet empire*, London: Weidenfeld and Nicolson

"Segodnia" (2019) *NTV*, January 14. https://www.ntv.ru/peredacha/segodnya/m23700/o531117 (accessed August 10, 2024)

Sejersen, Mikkel (2019) "Democratic Sanctions Meet Black Knight Support: revisiting the Belarusian case", *Democratization*, vol. 26, issue 3

Selart, Anti (2015) *Livonia, Rus' and the Baltic Crusades in the Thirteenth Century*, Leiden: Brill

Sell, Louis (2016) *From Washington to Moscow: US-Soviet relations and the collapse of the USSR*, Durham, NC: Duke UP

Semyonov, Alexander (2009) "'The Real and Live Ethnographic Map of Russia': the Russian Empire in the mirror of the State Duma" in *Empire Speaks Out: languages of rationalization and self-description in the Russian Empire*, Leiden; Brill; eds. Ilya Gerasimov, Jan Kusber and Alexander Semyonov

Semyonov, Alexander and Smith, Jeremy (2017) "Nationalism and Empire before and after 1917", *Studies in Ethnicity and Nationalism*, vol. 17, issue 3

Senf, Carol (1979) "*Dracula*: the unseen face in the mirror", *The Journal of Narrative Technique*, vol. 9, issue 3

Sergeev, Mikhail (2020) "Razryv s Belorussiei Budet Stoit' RF Bolee 20 Milliardov Dollarov", *Nezavisimaia Gazeta*, August 6. https://www.ng.ru/economics/2020-08-06/1_7931_minsk.html (accessed July 16, 2024)

Service, Robert (2015) *The End of the Cold War: 1985-1991*, London: Pan

Service, Robert (2020) *The Penguin History of Modern Russia: from tsarism to the twenty-first century (5th ed.)*, London: Penguin

Sever, Natal'ia (2023) "Shraibman: Teper' Kreml', Veroiatno, Budet Eshche Aktivnee Podderzhivat' Lukashenko i ne Davat' Emu Poteriat' Vlast'", *Salidarnasts'*, June 14. https://gazetaby.com/post/shrajbman-teper-kreml-veroyatno-budet-eshhe-aktivn/192139/ (accessed July 24, 2024)

Sharafutdinova, Gulnaz (2020) *The Red Mirror: Putin's leadership and Russia's insecure identity*, Oxford: OUP

Sharipzhan, Merhat (2018) "Lukashenka Says Belarus Will Never Be Part of Russia", *Radio Free Europe/Radio Liberty*, December 14. https://www.rferl.org/a/lukashenka-says-belarus-will-never-be-part-of-russia/29656460.html (accessed July 10, 2024)

Shatz, Howard and Reach, Clint (2023) "The Cost of the Ukraine War for Russia", *RAND Research Report*, Santa Monica, CA: RAND. https://www.rand.org/content/dam/rand/pubs/research_reports/RRA2400/RRA2421-1/RAND_RRA2421-1.pdf (accessed July 26, 2024)

Shavel', Roman (2023) "Aleksandr Klaskovskii: Risk vstupleniia Belarusi v voinu vozrastaet", *Belsat*, April 18. https://belsat.eu/ru/news/18-04-2023-aleksandr-klaskovskij-risk-vstupleniya-belarusi-v-vojnu-vozrastaet?fbclid=IwAR20sM7dKPo7hu3eOhTjmgT55-3TB_39c4q52rBOlb5cFdQwGXdm0LT5ors (accessed July 25, 2024)

Shchipanov, Mikhail (2012) "Chas Iks, Kogda Ischeznet Russkii Rubl', Nastupit Iavno Ne Zavtra", *Vechernaia Moskva*, January 20

Shearer, David (2013) "Stalinist Modernity, and the Social Engineering Argument" in *The Anatomy or Terror: political violence under Stalin*, Oxford: OUP; ed. James Harris

Shelley, Mary (2021) *Frankenstein*, New York: W.W. Norton

Sheremet, Pavel (2012) "Vsepogloshchaiushchaia Druzhba", *Novoe Vremia*, June 4

Sherr, James (1997) "Russia-Ukraine Rapprochement? The Black Sea Fleet accords", *Survival*, vol. 39, issue 3

Shevel, Oxana (2009) "The Politics of Citizenship Policy in New States", *Comparative Politics*, vol. 41, issue 3

Shevtsova, Lilia (2014) "The Maidan and Beyond: the Russia factor", *Journal of Democracy*, vol. 25, issue 3

Shiyan, Roman (2011) "The 'Rumour of Betrayal' and the 1668 Anti-Russian Uprising in Left-bank Ukraine", *Canadian Slavonic Papers*, vol. 53, issue 2-4

Shnirelman, Victor (2020) "Russia between a Civilization and a Civic Nation: secular and religious uses of civilizational discourse during Putin's third term" in *Russia as Civilization: ideological discourses in politics, media and academia*, Abingdon: Routledge; eds. Kåre Mjør and Sanna Turoma

Shraibman, Artem (2022) "Kak Mozhet i Ne Mozhet Zakonchits'ia Eta Voina", *Telegra.ph*, March 12. https://telegra.ph/Kak-mozhet-i-ne-mozhet-zakonchitsya-ehta-vojna-03-12 (accessed July 22, 2024)

Shraibman, Artem (2023) "Lukashenko Sozdaet Bazu, Chtoby Belorusy Khoteli ot Nego Izbavit'sia po Prichine, po Kotoroi Ego Vybrali", *Zerkalo*, March 26. https://news.zerkalo.io/economics/35436.html?utm_source=news.zerkalo.io&utm_medium=news-right-block&utm_campaign=popular-news (accessed July 24, 2024)

"Shraibman pra Sanktsyi, Paz'niaka i Intehrats'iu" (2021) *Radyio Svaboda*, September 15. https://www.svaboda.org/a/31460936.html (accessed July 19, 2024)

Shubin, Aleksandr (2006) *Predannaia Demokratiia: SSSR i neformaly, 1986-1989*, Moskva: Evropa

Shulman, Stephen (2005) "Ukrainian Nation-Building under Kuchma", *Problems of Post-Communism*, vol. 52, issue 5

Shushkevich, Stanislau (2004) "Belarus Will Soon Be Liberated", *Demokratizatsiya*, vol. 12, issue 1

Shushkevich, Stanislau (2013) "Belavezha Forest Viskuli December 7-8, 1991", *Demokratizatsiya*, vol. 21, issue 3

Shustov, V. (1997) "A Charter on European Security", *International Affairs (Moscow)*, vol. 43, issue 6

Shyrokykh, Karina (2022) "Human Rights Sanctions and the Role of Black Knights: evidence from the EU's post-Soviet neighbours", *Journal of European Integration*, vol. 44, issue 3

Sidorskii, Sergei and Siul'zhina, Aelita (2013) "EEP: nastroika agrarnogo rynka", *Soiuz Belarus'-Rossiia*, June 20

Silitski, Vitali (2009) "The Milk Spilt by the Milk War", *Politico*, June 24. https://www.politico.eu/article/the-milk-split-by-the-milk-war/ (accessed August 3, 2024)

Silitski, Vitali (2010) "'Survival of the Fittest': domestic and international dimensions of the authoritarian reaction in the former Soviet Union following the coloured revolutions", *Communist and Post-Communist Studies*, vol. 43, issue 4

Silvan, Kristiina (2020) "From *Komsomol* to the Republican Youth Union: building a pro-presidential mass youth organisation in post-Soviet Belarus", *Europe-Asia Studies*, vol. 72, issue 8

Simonyan, Artur (2024) "International Lawyers in Post-Soviet Eurasia: decoding the divisibility", *The European Journal of International Law*, vol. 35, issue 1

Sinel'nikova, Raissa (2010) "Reformbedürftig: die Betreuung der Kriegsgeneration in Belarus", *Osteuropa*, vol. 60, issue 5

Sinitsyn, Andrei (2015) "Bitva za Belorussiiu", *Vedomosti*, January 27

"Situation of Human Rights in Belarus in the Run-up to the 2020 Presidential Election and in Its Aftermath" (2023) *United Nations Human Rights Office of the High Commissioner*, February 3. https://www.ohchr.org/en/documents/country-reports/ahrc5268-belarus-run-2020-pr esidential-election-and-its-aftermath-report (accessed July 16, 2024)

Skak, Mette (2019) "Russian Strategic Culture: the generational approach and the counter-intelligence state thesis" in *Routledge Handbook of Russian Security*, Abingdon: Routledge; ed. Roger Kanet

Skey, Michael (2023) "Sportswashing: media headline or analytic concept?" *International Review for the Sociology of Sport*, vol. 58, issue 5

Skinner, Barbara (2019) "Orthodox Missions to the 'Ancient Orthodox' Lands in Belarus and the 1839 Uniate Conversion", *Canadian-American Slavic Studies*, vol. 53, issue 3

Skosyrev, Vladimir (1998) "Primakov Prizyvaet Sozdat' Aziatskii Treugol'nik", *Izvestiia*, December 22

Skrypchenko, Maksym (2023) "The Wagner Rebellion Revealed Putin's Weakness", *Al-Jazeera*, June 25. https://www.aljazeera.com/opinio ns/2023/6/25/the-wagner-rebellion-revealed-putins-weakness#:~: text=Therefore%2C%20Putin%20will%20likely%20%E2%80%9Cpla y,and%20foreign%20allies%20and%20adversaries (accessed July 24, 2024)

Slezkine, Yuri (2017) *The House of Government: a saga of the Russian Revolution*, Princeton, NJ: PUP

Słojewska, Anna (2014) "Na Ratunek Partnerstwu", February 10. https://www.rp.pl/swiat/art12637671-na-ratunek-partnerstwu (accessed August 7, 2024)

"Smerts' Prygozhyna Robits' Samoha Lukashenku u Neikai Stupeni 'Novym Prygozhynym'", *Nasha Niva*, August 24. https://nashaniva.com/324797 (accessed July 24, 2024)

Smirnov, Dmitrii (2013) "Putin Postavil Zadachi FSB", *Komsomol'skaia Pravda*, February 15

Smirnov, Dmitrii (2014) "Aleksandr Lukashenko: Ia Skazal: 'Volodia, Nas Vtiagivaiut v Etu Voinu…'", *Komsomol'skaia Pravda*, October 18

Smith, Hanna (2016) "Statecraft and Post-Imperial Attractiveness: Eurasian integration and Russia as a great power", *Problems of Post-Communism*, vol. 63, issue 3

Smith, Jeremy (2013) *Red Nations: the nationalities experience in and after the USSR*, Cambridge: CUP

Smith, Karen (2005) "The Outsiders: The European Neighbourhood Policy", *International Affairs*, vol. 81, issue 4

Smith, Kathleen (2017) *Moscow 1956: the silenced spring*, Cambridge, MA: Harvard UP

Smith, S. (2017) *Russia in Revolution: an empire in crisis, 1890 to 1928*, Oxford: OUP

Snyder, Timothy (1998) "The Polish-Lithuanian Commonwealth since 1989: national narratives in relations among Poland, Lithuania, Belarus and Ukraine", *Nationalism and Ethnic Politics*, vol. 4, issue 3

Snyder, Timothy (2011) *Bloodlands: Europe between Hitler and Stalin*, London: Vintage

Snyder, Timothy (2015) *Black Earth: the Holocaust as history and warning*, London: Bodley Head

Sobol, Valeria (2022) *Haunted Empire: gothic and the Russian imperial uncanny*, Ithaca, NY: Cornell UP

Socher, Johannes (2021) *Russia and the Right to Self-Determination in the Post-Soviet Space*, Oxford: OUP

Sodaro, Michael (1992) *Moscow, Germany, and the West from Khrushchev to Gorbachev*, Ithaca, NY: Cornell UP

"Soglashenie o Sozdanii Zony Svobodnoi Torgovli" (1994) *Sajt Ispolkoma SNG*, April 15. (https://cis.minsk.by/reestrv2/doc/321#text) (accessed June 28, 2024)

372 UNCANNY ALLIES

Solovei, Igor (2017) "Vykradennia Rosiis'kymy Spetssluzhbamy Pavla Hryba v Bilorusi: iak tse poznachytsia na ukraiin'sko-bilorus'kykh vidnosynakh", *LB.ua*, September 13. https://lb.ua/world/2017/09/13/376411_pohishchenie_rossiyskimi_spetssluzhbami.html (accessed August 9, 2024)

Sorokin, Vladimir (2018) *Day of the Oprichnik*, London: Penguin

"Sovmestnoe Zaiavlenie Ministrov Inostrannykh Del Respubliki Belarus' i Rossiiskoi Federatsii po Obshchim Vneshnepoliticheskim Prioritetam Rossii i Belarusi" (2023) *Ministerstvo Inostrannykh Del Respubliki Belarusi*, May 17. https://mfa.gov.by/press/news_mfa/ced85451b9ff421b.html (accessed July 24, 2024)

"Sovmestnoe Zaiavlenie Predsedatelia Pravitel'stva Rossiiskoi Federatsii i Prem'er-Ministra Respubliki Belarus' o Tekushchem Razvitii i Dal'neishikh Shagakh po Ugubleniiu Integratsionnykh Protsessov v Ramkakh Soiuznogo Gosudarstva" (2021) *Government.ru*, September 10. http://government.ru/news/43234/ (accessed July 19, 2024)

Sozaev-Gur'ev, Egor (2015) "ShOS Rasshiriaetsia, BRIKS Ukrepliaetsia", *Izvestiia*, July 13

Sozaev-Gur'ev, Egor (2017) "Prezidenty Rossii i Belorussii Obsudiat Energeticheskoe Sotrudnichestvo", *Izvestiia*, February 2. https://iz.ru/news/661441#ixzz4YAuTogsF (accessed July 9, 2024)

Sozaev-Gur'ev, Yegor (2018) "Glaz na Gaz: RF i Belorussiia provedut eshche odnu vstrechu do Novogo Goda", *Izvestiia*, December 26. https://iz.ru/827823/nataliia-portiakova-egor-sozaev-gurev/glaz-da-gaz-rf-i-belorussiia-provedut-eshche-odnu-vstrechu-do-novogo-goda (accessed July 11, 2024)

"Spasatel'nyi Krug dlia Strany i Rol' Lichnosti: institutu prezidenstva v Belarusi ispolnilos' 30 let" (2024) *Belta*, July 10. https://www.belta.by/society/view/spasatelnyj-krug-dlja-strany-i-rol-lichnosti-institutu-prezidentstva-v-belarusi-ispolnilos-30-let-646819-2024/ (accessed July 26, 2024)

Spechler, Dina and Spechler, Martin (2009) "A Reassessment of the Burden of Eastern Europe on the USSR", *Europe-Asia Studies*, vol. 61, issue 9

Splidsboel-Hansen, Flemming (2002) "Past and Future Meet: Aleksandr Gorchakov and Russian foreign policy", *Europe-Asia Studies*, vol. 54, issue 3

Stalin, I. (1930) "Golovokruzhenie ot Uspekhov", *Pravda*, March 2

"Stanislav Shushkevich: Rossiia Izvlechet Svoi Vygody, no Lukashenko Ne Spaset", *Khartyia '97*, March 5. https://charter97.org/ru/news/2012/3/5/48893/ (accessed August 6, 2024)

"Statement by Boris Yeltsin" (1999) *Kremlin.ru*, December 31. http://www.en.kremlin.ru/events/president/transcripts/24080 (accessed July 29, 2024)

"Statement by the Holy Synod of the Russian Orthodox Church Concerning the Encroachment of the Patriarchate of Constantinople on the Canonical Territory of the Russian Church" (2018) *Mospat.ru*, October 15. https://mospat.ru/en/news/47059/ (accessed July 11, 2024)

Statiev, Alexander (2014) "Soviet Partisan Violence against Soviet Civilians: targeting their own", *Europe-Asia Studies*, vol. 66, issue 9

Stepanenko, Oleg (2012a) "Amerikanskii Aktsent Vladimira Putina", *Pravda*, February 17

Stepanenko, Oleg (2012b) "Strategiia Ostaetsia Prezhnei", *Pravda*, May 11

Stern, Eric and Sundelius, Bengt (1992) "Managing Asymmetrical Crisis: Sweden, the USSR, and *U-137*", *International Studies Quarterly*, vol. 36, issue 2

Stevens, Christopher (2020) "Russia-Kazakhstan Relations in the Early Post-Soviet Era: explaining the roots of cooperation", *Europe-Asia Studies*, vol. 72, issue 7

Stognei, Anastasia (2024) "Russians Back Vladimir Putin in Blaming Ukraine for Concert Hall Terror Attack", *Financial Times*, March 31. https://www.ft.com/content/e5b52757-1faf-4e6c-9adf-5c018dbf24e6 (accessed July 26, 2024)

Stoker, Bram (2021) *Dracula*, New York: W.W. Norton

Strokan', Sergei (2021) "Pristup Bezhenstva: migratsionnyi krizis nanes novyi udar po otnosheniiam Moskvy s Zapadom", *Kommersant*, November 14. https://www.kommersant.ru/doc/5077372 (accessed July 18, 2024)

Strokan', Sergei (2022) "Podzhigateli Volny: situatsiia vokrug Ukrainy stanovitsia predvoennoi", *Kommersant*, January 24. https://www.kommersant.ru/doc/5181247 (accessed July 21, 2024)

Stulberg, Adam (2012) "Strategic Bargaining and Pipeline Politics: confronting the credible commitment problem in Eurasian energy transit", *Review of International Political Economy*, vol. 19, issue 5

Stykow, Petra (2023) "Making Sense of a Surprise: perspectives on the 2020 'Belarusian Revolution'", *Nationalities Papers*, vol. 51, issue 4

Subtelny, Orest (2009) *Ukraine: a history (4th ed.)*, Toronto: UTP

Suesse, Marvin (2018) "Breaking the Unbreakable Union: nationalism, disintegration and the Soviet economic collapse", *The Economic Journal*, vol. 128, issue 615

374 UNCANNY ALLIES

Sukhov, Ivan (2015) "Russia Is Slamming Door after Door on the West", *The Moscow Times*, March 12. https://www.themoscowtimes.com/2015/03/12/russia-is-slamming-door-after-door-on-the-west-a44703 (accessed August 9, 2024)

"Summary of the Day in Court: 17 November 2022—judgment" (2022) *District Court of the Hague*, November 17. https://www.courtmh17.com/en/insights/news/2022/summary-of-the-day-in-court-17-november-2022-judgment/ (accessed on July 6, 2024)

Suny, Ronald (2010) *The Soviet Experiment: Russia, the USSR, and the successor states (2nd ed.)*, Oxford: OUP

"Surikov: Ob''edinenie MAZa i KamAZa Bylo By na Pol'zu Nashikh Narodov" (2016) *Belta*, March 31. https://www.belta.by/economics/view/surikov-objedinenie-maza-i-kamaza-bylo-by-na-polzu-nashih-narodov-187718-2016/ (accessed August 9, 2024)

Surovell, Jeffrey (2005) "Yevgenii Primakov: 'hard-liner' or casualty of the conventional wisdom?" *The Journal of Communist Studies and Transition Politics*, vol. 21, issue 2

Surovell, Jeffrey (2012) "The Grand Deception: post-Soviet Russia and the wars in the former Yugoslavia", *The Journal of Slavic Military Studies*, vol. 25, issue 3

Suslov, Mikhail (2012) "Geographical Metanarratives in Russia and the European East: contemporary pan-Slavism", *Eurasian Geography and Economics*, vol. 53, issue 5

Sussman, Gerald (2006) "The Myths of 'Democracy Assistance': U.S. political intervention in post-Soviet Eastern Europe", *Monthly Review*, vol. 58, issue 7

Suzdal'tsev, A. (2012) "Belorusskii Politicheskii Klass v Usloviiakh Ekonomicheskogo Krizisa 2011 g.", *Mirovaia Ekonomika i Mezhdunarodnye Otnosheniia*, March 31

Suzdaltsev, Andrey (2023) "The Presidentialization of Belarusian Political Parties" in *The Presidentialization of Political Parties in Russia, Kazakhstan and Belarus*, Basingstoke: Palgrave; eds. Marina Glaser, Ivan Krivushin and Mara Morini

Svanidze, Nikolai (2019) "Itogi Goda, Kak Ostat'sia?" *Ezhednevnyi Zhurnal*, January 7. https://www.ej.ru/?a=note&id=33284 (accessed August 10, 2024)

"Sviatlana Tsikhanouskaya: Lukashenka is dragging us back to the past, to notorious Soviet Union. It is his childhood dream to live in single state with Russia" (2024) *Tsikhanouskaya.org*, July 23. https://tsikha nouskaya.org/en/news/sviatlana-tsikhanouskaya-lukashenka-is-d ragging-us-back-to-the-past-to-notorious-soviet-union-it-is-his-chil dhood-dream-to-live-in-single-state-with-russia.html (accessed July 26, 2024)

Svoboda, Karel (2019) "On the Road to Maidan: Russia's economic state-craft towards Ukraine in 2013", *Europe-Asia Studies*, vol. 71, issue 10

Svoboda, Karel (2021) "Norms as a Political Weapons? Sanitary, phytosan-itary, and technical norms as Russia's foreign trade tool", *Problems of Post-Communism*, vol. 68, issue 1

Swain, Amanda (2015) "Commemorating the 'Living Torch of Freedom': searching for a usable past in Romas Kalanta's 1972 self-immolation", *Ab Imperio*, issue 2

Swain, Geoffrey (2022) "The Bolsheviks and World Revolution" in *The Bloomsbury Handbook of the Russian Revolution*, London: Bloomsbury; eds. Geoffrey Swain, Charlotte Alston, Michael Hickey, Boris Kolonitskii and Franziska Schedewie

Sweeney, John (2012) "Were Executed Minsk Metro Bombers framed?" *BBC News*, July 30

Szabo, Franz (2008) *The Seven Years War in Europe, 1756-1763*, Harlow: Pearson

Szostek, Joanna (2015) "Russian Influence on News Media in Belarus", *Communist and Post-Communist Studies*, vol. 48, issue 2-3

Szostek, Joanna (2018) "The Mass Media and Russia's 'Sphere of Interests': mechanisms of regional hegemony in Belarus and Ukraine", *Geopoli-tics*, vol. 23, issue 2

Szporluk, Roman (1979) "West Ukraine and West Belorussia: historical tra-dition, social communication, and linguistic assimilation", *Soviet Studies*, vol. 31, issue 1

Tabata, Shinichiro (2002) "Russian Revenues from Oil and Gas Exports: flow and taxation", *Eurasian Geography and Economics*, vol. 43, issue 8

Talentino, Andrea (2004) "The Two Faces of Nation-Building: developing function and identity", *Cambridge Review of International Affairs*, vol. 17, issue 3

"Taliban Urge Restraint in Russia-Ukraine Conflict" (2022) *Arab News*, Feb-ruary 25. https://www.arabnews.com/node/2031816/world (ac-cessed July 21, 2024)

"Tbilisi Declaration and Resolutions Adopted by the OSCE Parliamentary Assembly" (2016) *OSCEPA*, July 1 to 5. https://www.oscepa.org/en/documents/all-documents/annual-sessions/2016-tbilisi/declaration-24/3371-tbilisi-declaration-eng/file (accessed August 9, 2024)

Tekin, Ali and Williams, Paul (2009) "EU-Russian Relations and Turkey's Role as an Energy Corridor", *Europe-Asia Studies*, vol. 61, issue 2

Temby, Owen (2015) "What Are Levels of Analysis and What Do They Contribute to International Relations Theory?" *Cambridge Review of International Affairs*, vol. 28, issue 4

Temper, Elena (2008) "Konflikte um Kurapaty: geteilte Erinnerung im postsowjetischen Belarus", *Osteuropa*, vol. 58, issue 6

Terent'eva, Aleksandra (2013) "Chelovek Nedeli: Vladislav Baumgertner", *Vedomosti*, September 2

Thatcher, Ian (2011) "Khrushchev as Leader" in *Khrushchev in the Kremlin: policy and government in the Soviet Union, 1953-1964*, Abingdon: Routledge; eds. Melanie Ilic and Jeremy Smith

Thompson, Michael (2017) "Autonomy and Common Good: interpreting Rousseau's General Will", *International Journal of Philosophical Studies*, vol. 25, issue 2

Tiberg, Erik (1995) *Moscow, Livonia and the Hanseatic League 1487-1550*, Stockholm: AUS

"Tikhanovskaia Obratilas' k Narodu i Prezidentu Ukrainy: v Belarusi zapushcheno Antivoennoe Dvizhenie" (2022) *YouTube*, March 3. https://www.youtube.com/watch?v=-fuGGl-G-Vc (accessed July 21, 2024)

Tikhonov, Aleksandr (2017) "'Zapad-2017' Ne Ugrozhaet Zapadu", *Krasnaia Zvezda*, August 30

Tikhonov, Aleksandr (2021) "Voennuiu Bezopasnost' Ukrepliaem Soobshcha" (2021) *Krasnaia Zvezda*, October 22

Tikhonov, Aleksandr; Nikol'skii, Aleksei; Gasymov, Nurlan and Mukhametshina, Elena (2023) "Chem Zakonchitsia dlia 'Vagnera' Pokhod na Stolitsu", *Vedomosti*, June 26. https://www.vedomosti.ru/politics/articles/2023/06/26/982255-chem-zakonchitsya-dlya-vagnera-pohod-na-stolitsu (accessed July 24, 2024)

Titova, Anna (2021) "Nalog na Velichie: kak Kreml' za 20 let potratil 46 trln rublei na geopoliticheskie spetsoperatsii", *Novaia Gazeta*, January 27. https://novayagazeta.ru/articles/2021/01/27/88901-nalog-na-velichie (accessed July 18, 2024)

Tolstrup, Jakob (2009) "Studying a Negative External Actor: Russia's management of stability and instability in the 'Near Abroad'", *Democratization*, vol. 16, issue 5

Tolstrup, Jakob (2015) "Black Knights and Elections in Authoritarian Regimes: why and how Russia supports authoritarian incumbents in post-Soviet states", *European Journal of Political Research*, vol. 54, issue 4

Tolz, Vera (2001) *Russia*, London: Arnold

Tolz, Vera (2002) "Rethinking Russian-Ukrainian Relations: a new trend in nation-building in post-communist Russia?" *Nations and Nationalism*, vol. 8, issue 2

Tolz, Vera (2010) "The West" in *A History of Russian Thought*, Cambridge: CUP; eds. William Leatherbarrow and Derek Offord

"Tragediia v Podmoskov'e: udastsia li pravosudiiu dotianut'sia do zakazchikov i pochemu s pomoshch'iu terakta ne udalos' raskachat' obshchestvo" (2024) *Tvr.by*, March 29. https://www.tvr.by/news/obshchestvo/tragediya_v_podmoskove_udastsya_li_pravosudiyu_dotyanutsya_do_zakazchikov_i_pochemu_s_pomoshchyu_ter/ (accessed July 26, 2024)

"'Traktor Vylechit Vsekh': kak zashchishchat'sia ot koronavirusa. Sovety Aleksandra Lukashenko" (2020) *Meduza*, March 17. https://meduza.io/shapito/2020/03/17/traktor-vylechit-vseh (accessed July 18, 2024)

Treisman, Daniel (2011) *The Return: Russia's journey from Gorbachev to Medvedev*, New York: Free

Trenin, Dmitri (2002) *The End of Eurasia: Russia on the border between geopolitics and globalization*, Washington, DC: Carnegie Endowment

Trotsky, Leon (2004) *The Revolution Betrayed*, Mineola, NY: Dover

Troyat, Henri (2001) *Ivan the Terrible*, London: Phoenix

Trudoliubov, Maksim (2014) "Politika Vneshnikh Shokov", *Vedomosti*, January 24

Trushkov, Viktor (2012) "Gosudarstvennye Skrepy Soiuza Narodov", *Pravda*, December 14

Tsarik, Iurii (2016) "Natsisty i Fashisty ne Dolzhny Imet' Dostupa k Belorusskim Detiam i uzh Tem Bolee—Byt' Ikh Nastavnikami", *Belarus' Segodnia*, June 1. https://www.sb.by/articles/vopros-seryeznyy.html (accessed August 9, 2024)

Tsarik, Iurii (2019) "Rossiiskie Media v Belarusi", *Riddle*, October 30. https://ridl.io/ru/rossijskie-media-v-belarusi/ (accessed August 10, 2024)

"Tseremoniia Vrucheniia Veritel'nykh Gramot" (2022) *Kremlin.ru*, September 20. http://kremlin.ru/events/president/news/69379 (accessed August 11, 2024)

Tsipko, Alexander (1994) "A New Russian Identity or Old Russia's Reintegration?" *Security Dialogue*, vol. 25, issue 4

Tsikhanouskaya, Sviatlana (2023) "The Criminal Prigozhin Won't Be Missed in Belarus", *X.com*, August 23. https://x.com/Tsihanouskaya/status/1694442779751882804 (accessed July 24, 2024)

Tsipko, Aleksandr (2020) "Druzhit' s Lukashenko ili s Narodom Belarusi?" *Moskovskii Komsomolets*, September 22

Tsygankov, Andrei (2000) "Defining State Interests after Empire: national identity, domestic structures and foreign trade policies of Latvia and Belarus", *Review of International Political Economy*, vol. 7, issue 1

Tsygankov, Andrei (2006) "If Not by Tanks, Then by Banks? The role of soft power in Putin's foreign policy", *Europe-Asia Studies*, vol. 58, issue 7

Tsygankov, Andrei (2008) "Russia's International Assertiveness: what does it mean for the West?" *Problems of Post-Communism*, vol. 55, issue 2

Tsygankov, Andrei (2012) *Russia and the West from Alexander to Putin: honor in international relations*, Cambridge: CUP

Tsygankov, Andrei (2014) *The Strong State in Russia: development and crisis*, Oxford: OUP

Tsygankov, Andrei (2022a) "Russia, Eurasia and the Meaning of Crimea", *Europe-Asia Studies*, vol. 74, issue 9

Tsygankov, Andrei (2022b) *Russia's Foreign Policy: change and continuity in national identity (6th ed.)*, Lanham, MD: Rowman and Littlefield

Tudoroiu, Theodor (2011) "The Neo-Communist Regime of Present-Day China", *Journal of Chinese Political Science*, vol. 16, issue 4

Tuliakov, Oleg (2018) "Rossiia bez Kul'ta Lichnosti?" *Literaturnaia Gazeta*, January 24

Turkowski, Andrzej (2023) "A Return to Prometheanism: the space of opinion on Polish-Russian relations in postcommunist Poland", *Europe-Asia Studies*, vol. 75, issue 4

"U Militsyi Nia Vedaiuts', tsi Padpadaiuts' Hramadziane Rasei pad Status 'Inshazemtsau' u Belarusi" (2017) *Radyio Svaboda*, October 2. https://www.svaboda.org/a/28768543.html (accessed August 9, 2024)

"U Vitsebsku Ustaliavali Pomnik Kniaziu Al'herdu" (2014) *Narodnyia Naviny Vitsebska*, June 24. https://viciebsk.cc/2014/06/24/u-vitsebsku-wstalyavali-pomnik-knyazyu-algerdu-fotarepartazh/ (accessed July 5, 2024)

Uhl, Matthias (2012) "Soviet and Warsaw Pact Military Strategy from Stalin to Brezhnev: the transformation from 'strategic defense' to 'unlimited nuclear war', 1945-1968" in *Blueprints for Battle: planning for war in Central Europe, 1948-1968*, Lexington, KY: UPK; eds. Jan Hoffenaar and Dieter Krüger

"Ukraina Nikogda s Nami Ne Budet Voevat', ved' Voina Prodlitsia Maksimum Tri-Chetyre Dnia" (2022) *Belta*, February 5. https://www.belta.by/president/view/lukashenko-ukraina-nikogda-s-nami-ne-budet-voevat-ved-vojna-prodlitsja-maksimum-tri-chetyre-dnja-483158-2022/ (accessed July 21, 2024)

"Ukraine Conflict Updates" (2024) *Institute for the Study of War*, July 20 (updated daily). https://www.understandingwar.org/backgrounder/ukraine-conflict-updates (accessed July 20, 2024)

"Ukrainian Intellectuals Protest Arrest and Imprisonment of Their Colleagues in Ukraine" in *Ukrainian Dissidents: an anthology of texts* (2021) Stuttgart: ibidem; eds. Oleksii Sinchenko, Dmytro Stus and Leonid Finberg

"Ukrainian Lawmakers Back President's Move to Obtain Autocephalous Status for Orthodox Church" (2018) *Radio Free Europe / Radio Liberty*, April 19. https://www.rferl.org/a/ukraine-lawmakers-back-president-move-to-obtain-autocephalous-status-for-orthodox-church/29176970.html (accessed August 10, 2024)

Ullrich, Volker (2016) *Hitler: a biography (2 vols.)*, London: Vintage

Umpirovich, Dmitrii (2022) "Lukashenko: Nikakie Ukraintsy Ne Natsiki, Krome Praviashchei Verkhushki", *Belarus' Segodnia*, August 26. https://www.sb.by/articles/lukashenko-nikakie-ukraintsy-ne-natsiki-krome-pravyashchey-verkhushki.html (accessed July 22, 2024)

"United States and Allies Target Russia and Belarus with Sanctions and Other Economic Measures" (2022) *American Journal of International Law*, vol. 116, issue 3

Urban, Michael (1989) *An Algebra of Soviet Power: elite circulation in the Belorussian Republic 1966-86*, Cambridge: CUP

"Uriad Vnis y Verkhovnu Radu Zakonoproekt 'Pro Mobilizatsiinu Pidhotovku ta Mobilizatsiiu'" (2017) *Narodna Armiia*, June 15

"Ushakov: Vstrecha Putina i Lukashenko Vazhna dlia Vyborov v Belorussii" (2015) *RIA Novosti*, September 11. https://ria.ru/20150911/1243637796.html (accessed August 9, 2024)

"V Belarusi Planiruetsia Reguliarno Organizovyvat' dlia Shkol'nikov Ekskursii k Pravoslavnym Sviatyniam" (2015) *Belta*, November 3. https://www.belta.by/society/view/v-belarusi-planiruetsja-reguljarno-organizovyvat-dlja-shkolnikov-ekskursii-k-pravoslavnym-svjatynjam-168864-2015/ (accessed August 9, 2024)

"V Gosdume Nazvali Rezul'tat Lukashenko na Vyborakh Sfal'sifitsirovannym" (2020) *Gazeta.ru*, August 10. https://www.gazeta.ru/politics/news/2020/08/10/n_14780737.shtml?updated (accessed July 14, 2024)

"V KGB Zaiavili, chto Vozmozhen Yadernyi Udar Po Belarusi" (2022) *Zerkalo*, October 12. https://news.zerkalo.io/life/23803.html (accessed July 21, 2024)

"V Kremle Prokommentirovali Vozmozhnoe Vvedenie Belorusskikh Mirotvortsev v Donbass" (2019a) *TASS*, September 26. https://tass.ru/politika/6931687 (accessed August 10, 2024)

"V Kremle s Ponimaniem Otneslis' k Emotsional'nym Vyskazyvaniiam Lukashenko" (2019) *Interfax*, April 11. https://www.interfax.ru/russia/657831 (accessed August 10, 2024)

Val'chenko, Sergei (2023) "Eksperty Otsenili Vydvizhenie Iadernykh 'Iskanderov' v Otvet na Ugrozy NATO", *Moskovskii Komsomolets*, March 26. https://www.mk.ru/politics/2023/03/26/eksperty-ocenili-vydvizhenie-yadernykh-iskanderov-v-otvet-na-ugrozy-nato.html (accessed July 24, 2024)

Val'samaki, Alisa (2012) "Lukashenko Zapretil Uvol'niat'sia bez Razresheniia Rukovodstva", *Radio Azattyk*, December 11. https://rus.azattyq.org/a/forced-labor-lukashenka-decree/24794639.html (accessed August 6, 2024)

Van Ham, Peter (2008) "Place Branding: the state of the art", *The Annals of the American Academy of Political and Social Science*, vol. 616

Van Ree, Erik (1998) "Socialism in One Country: a reassessment", *Studies in East European Thought*, vol. 50, issue 2

Vanderhill, Rachel (2014) "Promoting Democracy and Promoting Authoritarianism: comparing the cases of Belarus and Slovakia", *Europe-Asia Studies*, vol. 66, issue 2

Vardul', Nikolai (2013) "Kalii Razdora", *Novaia Gazeta*, August 30

Vasil'eva, Kira (2012) "Lukashenko Snial Glavu KGB iz-za Samoubiistva Podchinennogo", *Izvestiia*, November 13

Vasilevskii, Sergei (2024) "Chetvertyi Zalet 'Shakhedov' na Territoriiu Belarusi Uzhe Ne Vygliadit Sluchainost'iu: eto Sistema", *Salidarnasts'*, July 16. https://gazetaby.com/post/chetvertyj-zalet-shaxedov-na-territoriyu-belarusi-uzhe-ne-vyglyadit-sl/201772/

Vatlin, Alexander and Smith, Stephen (2014) "The Comintern" in *The Oxford Handbook of the History of Communism*, Oxford: OUP; ed. Stephen Smith

Verhoeven, Claudia (2009) *The Odd Man Karakozov: imperial Russia, modernity, and the birth of terrorism*, Ithaca, NY: Cornell UP

"Videoobrashchenie k Uchastnikam Plenarnogo Zasedaniia Odinnatsotogo Foruma Regionov Rossii i Belorussii" (2024) *Kremlin.ru*, June 28. http://kremlin.ru/events/president/news/74430 (accessed August 11, 2024)

Vieira, Alena (2014) "The Politico-Military Alliance of Russia and Belarus: re-examining the role of NATO and the EU in light of the intra-alliance security dilemma", *Europe-Asia Studies*, vol. 66, issue 4

Vieira, Alena (2016) "Eurasian Integration: elite perspectives before and after the Ukraine crisis", *Post-Soviet Affairs*, vol. 32, issue 6

Vieira, Alena (2021) "The European Union's 'Potential We' between Acceptance and Contestation: assessing the positioning of six Eastern Partnership countries", *Journal of Common Market Studies*, vol. 59, issue 2

Vogel, Ezra (2011) *Deng Xiaoping and the Transformation of China*, Cambridge, MA: Belknap

"Vol'fovich Nazval Plany Pol'shi po Novoi Divizii u Granits Belarusi Agressivnym Shagom po Otnosheniiu k ODKB" (2023) *Zerkalo*, January 10. https://news.zerkalo.io/economics/30040.html (accessed July 24, 2024)

"Volodymyr Zelen'skyi Zustrivsia z Oleksandrom Lukashenkom u Ramkakh Druhoho Forumu Rehioniv Ukraiiny ta Bilorusi v Zhytomyri" (2019) *President.gov.ua*, October 4. https://www.president.gov.ua/news/volodimir-zelenskij-zustrivsya-z-oleksandrom-lukashenkom-u-r-57601 (accessed July 12, 2024)

Von Seth, Rutger (2018) "All Quiet on the Eastern Front? Media images of the West and Russian foreign political identity", *Europe-Asia Studies*, vol. 70, issue 3

Vorotnikov, Vladislav (2015) "Russia Threatens to Implement Ukraine Food Embargo", *Food Navigator*, November 18. https://www.foodnavigator.com/Article/2015/11/18/Russia-threatens-to-implement-Ukraine-food-embargo (accessed July 6, 2024)

"Vremia Pokazhet" (2015) *Pervyi Kanal*, June 17. https://www.1tv.ru/shows/vremya-pokazhet/vypuski/vremya-pokazhet-vypusk-ot-17-06-2015 (accessed August 8, 2024)

Vuolteenaho, Jani and Basik, Sergei (2024) "Mobilities of Toponymic Place Branding in an Autocratic Post-Soviet City: the Mayak Minska (*the Lighthouse of Minsk*) and the Minsk-Mir (*the Minsk-World*) megaprojects", *Eurasian Geography and Economics*, vol. 65, issue 4

"Vystupleniia na Zasedanii Vyshego Gossoveta Soiuznogo Gosudarstva Rossii i Belorussii" (2013) *Kremlin.ru*, March 15. http://kremlin.ru/events/president/transcripts/17686 (accessed August 7, 2024)

"Vystuplenie Ministra Inostrannykh Del Belarusi S. Aleinika na Zasedanii Soveta Bezopasnosti OON po situatsii v Ukraine (20 sentiabria 2003 g., g. Niu-Iork)" (2023a) *Ministerstva Inostrannykh Del Respubliki Belarus'*, September 21. https://mfa.gov.by/press/news_mfa/b47593 17427c6e4c.html (accessed July 24, 2024)

"Vystuplenie Ministra Inostrannykh Del Rossiiskoi Federatsii S.V. Lavrova v Khode 30-go Zasedaniia SMID OBSE, Skop'e, 30 Noiabria 2023 Goda" (2023b) *Mid.ru*, November 30. https://mid.ru/ru/foreign_policy/news/1918477/ (accessed August 11, 2024)

Wade, Rex (2017) *The Russian Revolution, 1917 (3rd ed.)*, Cambridge: CUP

"Wagner Boss Prigozhin Slams Russian Officials from a Field of Corpses" (2023) *YouTube*, May 5. https://www.youtube.com/watch?v=j-bALDPCp4w (accessed July 24, 2024)

Wagner, Izabela (2020) *Bauman: a biography*, Cambridge: Polity

Waligórska, Magdalena (2016) "Jewish Heritage and the New Belarusian National Identity Project", *East European Politics and Societies*, vol. 30, issue 2

Walker, Charlie (2022) "Remaking a 'Failed' Masculinity: working-class young men, breadwinning, and morality in contemporary Russia", *Social Politics*, vol. 29, issue 4

Walker, Charlie (2023) "Welfare in Russia and Eurasia in the Context of the COVID-19 Pandemic", *Europe-Asia Studies*, vol. 75, issue 2

Walker, Mark (2003) *The Strategic Use of Referendums: power, legitimacy, and democracy*, Basingstoke: Palgrave Macmillan

Walker, Shaun (2017) "Unequal Russia: is anger stirring in the global capital of inequality?" *The Guardian*, April 25. https://www.theguardian.com/inequality/2017/apr/25/unequal-russia-is-anger-stirring-in-the-global-capital-of-inequality (accessed July 16, 2024)

Walker, Shaun (2018) *The Long Hangover: Putin's new Russia and the ghosts of the past*, Oxford: OUP

Wanner, Catherine (2004) "Missionaries of Faith and Culture: Evangelical encounters in Ukraine", *Slavic Review*, vol. 63, issue 4

War against the Peasantry, 1927-1930: the tragedy of the Soviet countryside (2005) New Haven, CT: Yale UP; eds. Lynne Viola, V. Danilov, N. Ivnitskii and Denis Kozlov

Warf, Barney (2009) "The Rapidly Evolving Geographies of the Eurasian Internet", *Eurasian Geography and Economics*, vol. 50, issue 5

Way, Lucan (2005) "Authoritarian State Building and the Sources of Regime Competitiveness in the Fourth Wave: the cases of Belarus, Moldova, Russia, and Ukraine", *World Politics*, vol. 57, issue 2

Way, Lucan (2012a) "Deer in Headlights: incompetence and weak authoritarianism after the Cold War", *Slavic Review*, vol. 71, issue 3

Way, Lucan (2012b) "The Sources of Authoritarian Control after the Cold War: East Africa and the former Soviet Union", *Post-Soviet Affairs*, vol. 28, issue 4

BIBLIOGRAPHY 383

Way, Lucan (2015) "The Limits of Autocracy Promotion: the case of Russia in the 'near abroad'", *European Journal of Political Research*, vol. 54, issue 4

Way, Lucan (2020) "How a Dictator Became Vulnerable", *Journal of Democracy*, vol. 31, issue 4

Way, Lucan and Levitsky, Steven (2006) "The Dynamics of Autocratic Coercion after the Cold War", *Communist and Post-Communist Studies*, vol. 39, issue 3

Way, Lucan and Levitsky, Steven (2007) "Linkage, Leverage, and the Post-Communist Divide", *East European Politics and Societies*, vol. 21, issue 1

Way, Lucan and Tolvin, Amelie (2023) "Why the 2020 Belarusian Protests Failed to Oust Lukashenka", *Nationalities Papers*, vol. 51, issue 4

Weber, Patrick and Stępień, Beata (2020) "Conform or Challenge? Adjustment strategies of sanction-torn companies", *The World Economy*, vol. 43, issue 11

Weeks, Theodore (2015) *Vilnius between Nations, 1795-2000*, Ithaca, NY: Cornell UP

Wegren, Stephen; Nikulin, Alexander and Trotsuk, Irina (2017) "The Russian Variant of Food Security", *Problems of Post-Communism*, vol. 64, issue 1

Weiss, Tomáš (2018) "Building Leverage at the EU Level? Specialisation and coherence in Czech policy on Eastern European transition", *Journal of International Relations and Development*, vol. 21, issue 1

Wendt, Alexander (1999) *Social Theory of International Politics*, Cambridge: CUP

Wengle, Susanne (2020) "The New Plenty: why are some post-Soviet farms thriving?" *Governance*, vol. 33, issue 4

"West and Russia Need Belarus—Lukashenka" (2016) *ITAR-TASS*, September 12

Westad, Odd (2005) *The Global Cold War*, Cambridge: CUP

Wettig, Gerhard (2017) "Aufrüstung, Grenzschließung und Besatzungsstatus der DDR: sowjetische Deutschland-Politik im Umbruch 1951 bis 1954", *Militärgeschichtliche Zeitschrift*, vol. 76, issue 1

White, Allison (2024) "Policymaking in Personalist Dictatorships: a theory of outbidding", *Policy Studies*, vol. 45, issue 1

White, Stephen (2011) "Debating Belarus: a framing comment", *Eurasian Geography and Economics*, vol. 52, issue 6

White, Stephen; Biletskaya, Tania and McAllister, Ian (2016) "Belarusians between East and West", *Post-Soviet Affairs*, vol. 32, issue 1

White, Stephen; Korosteleva, Julia and McAllister, Ian (2008) "A Wider Europe? The view from Russia, Belarus and Ukraine", *Journal of Common Market Studies*, vol. 46, issue 2

White, Stephen and McAllister, Ian (2007) "Turnout and Representation Bias in Post-Communist Europe", *Political Studies*, vol. 55, issue 3

White, Stephen; McAllister, Ian and Feklyunina, Valentina (2010) "Belarus, Ukraine and Russia: east or west?" *The British Journal of Politics and International Relations*, vol. 12, issue 3

White, Stephen; McAllister, Ian and Light, Margot (2002a) "Enlargement and the New Outsiders", *Journal of Common Market Studies*, vol. 40, issue 1

White, Stephen; McAllister, Ian; Light, Margot and Löwenhardt, John (2002b) "A European or a Slavic Choice? Foreign policy and public attitudes in post-Soviet Europe", *Europe-Asia Studies*, vol. 54, issue 2

Whitmore, Brian (2021) "Lukashenko Goes All In with Putin", *The Atlantic*, August 25. https://www.atlanticcouncil.org/blogs/belarusalert/lu kashenka-goes-all-in-with-putin/ (accessed July 19, 2024)

Wickham, Chris (2009) *The Inheritance of Rome: a history of Europe from 400 to 1000*, London: Allen Lane

Wigell, Mikael and Vihma, Antto (2016) "Geopolitics versus Geoeconomics: the case of Russia's geostrategy and its effects on the EU", *International Affairs*, vol. 92, issue 3

Wijermars, Mariëlle and Lokot, Tetyana (2022) "Is Telegram a 'Harbinger of Freedom'? The performance, practices, and perception of platforms as political actors in authoritarian states", *Post-Soviet Affairs*, vol. 38, issue 1-2

Wilcox, Mark (2011) "Russia and the Treaty on Conventional Armed Forces in Europe (CFE Treaty)—a paradigm change?" *The Journal of Slavic Military Studies*, vol. 24, issue 4

Wilke, Manfred (2014) *The Path to the Berlin Wall: critical stages in the history of divided Germany*, New York: Berghahn

Williams, Kieran (1997) *The Prague Spring and Its Aftermath: Czechoslovak politics, 1968-1970*, Cambridge: CUP

Wilson, Andrew (2002) "Elements of a Theory of Ukrainian Ethno-National Identities", *Nations and Nationalism*, vol. 8, issue 1

Wilson, Andrew (2014) *Ukraine Crisis: what it means for the world*, New Haven, CT: Yale UP

Wilson, Andrew (2016) "Belarus: from a social contract to a security contract?" *Journal of Belarusian Studies*, vol. 8, issue 1

Wilson, Andrew (2021) *Belarus: the last European dictatorship (new ed.)*, New Haven, CT: Yale UP

Wilson, James (2014) *The Triumph of Improvisation: Gorbachev's adaptability, Reagan's engagement, and the end of the Cold War*, Ithaca, NY: Cornell UP

Wise, Charles and Brown, Trevor (1998) "The Consolidation of Democracy in Ukraine", *Democratization*, vol. 5, issue 1

Wójcik-Żołądek, Monika (2023) "The Myth of the Great Patriotic War in Kaliningrad Oblast", *Europe-Asia Studies*, vol. 75, issue 1

Wolfe, Sven (2023) "Between the Minor and the Intimate: encountering the authoritarian (extra)ordinary in Russia, Belarus and Ukraine", *Geopolitics*, vol. 28, issue 2

"Women Tear Balaclavas Off Security Officers amid Mass Arrests in Belarus" (2020) *YouTube*, September 17. https://www.youtube.com/watch?v=McRs76J-QYI (accessed July 16, 2024)

Woodward, Bob (2002) *Bush at War*, New York: Simon and Schuster

Woolhiser, Curt (2014) "The Russian Language in Belarus: language use, speaker identities and metalinguistic discourse" in *The Russian Language outside the Nation*, Edinburgh: EUP; ed. Lara Ryazanova-Clarke

Wyman, Matthew; Miller, Bill; White, Stephen and Heywood, Paul (1995) "Parties and Voters in Elections" in *Elections and Political Order in Russia: the implications of the 1993 elections to the Federal Assembly*, Budapest: Central European UP; ed. Peter Lentini

X (George Kennan) (1946-47) "The Sources of Soviet Conduct", *Foreign Affairs*, vol. 25, issue 4

Yakouchyk, Katsiaryna (2016) "The Good, the Bad, and the Ambitious: democracy and autocracy promoters competing in Belarus", *European Political Science Review*, vol. 8, issue 2

Yanchenko, Kostiantyn and Zulianello, Mattia (2024) "'Not Fighting Corruption, but Defeating It': the populism of Zelensky's Servant of the People in comparative perspective", *European Societies*, vol. 26, issue 2

Yanık, Lerna and Subotić, Jelena (2021) "Cultural Heritage as Status Seeking: the international politics of Turkey's restoration wave", *Cooperation and Conflict*, vol. 56, issue 3

Yarashevich, Viachaslau (2013) "External Debt of Post-Communist Countries", *Communist and Post-Communist Studies*, vol. 46, issue 2

Yarashevich, Viachaslau (2014) "Political Economy of Modern Belarus: going against mainstream?" *Europe-Asia Studies*, vol. 66, issue 10

Yeltsin, Boris (2000) *Midnight Diaries*, London: Weidenfeld and Nicolson

"Yeltsin Resigns; In Boris Yeltsin's words: 'I have made a decision'" (2000) *The New York Times*, January 1

Yemel'ianenkov, Aleksandr (2020) "70 Let Nazad Moskva Ob''iavila o Nalichii Sobstvennogo Iadernogo Oruzhiia", *Rossiiskaia Gazeta*, March 8. https://rg.ru/2020/03/08/70-let-nazad-moskva-obiavila-o-nalichii-sobstvennogo-iadernogo-oruzhiia.html (accessed July 26, 2024)

Yost, David (1993) "Europe and Nuclear Deterrence", *Survival*, vol. 35, issue 3

Yost, David (2015) "The Budapest Memorandum and Russia's Intervention in Ukraine", *International Affairs*, vol. 91, issue 3

Yudina, Natalia and Verkhovsky, Alexander (2019) "Russian Nationalist Veterans of the Donbas War", *Nationalities Papers*, vol. 47, issue 5

Zabortseva, Yelena (2014) "Rethinking the Economic Relationship between Kazakhstan and Russia", *Europe-Asia Studies*, vol. 66, issue 2

Zadora, Anna (2016) "La Grande Guerre Patriotique Comme Pilier de L'Identité Nationale: une étude biélorusse", *Revue d'Études Comparatives Est-Ouest*, vol. 47, issue 1-2

Zagorski, Andrei (1992) "Post-Soviet Nuclear Proliferation Risks", *Security Dialogue*, vol. 23, issue 3

Zaharchenko, Tatiana and Goldenman, Gretta (2004) "Accountability in Governance: the challenge of implementing the Aarhus Convention in Eastern Europe and Central Asia", *International Environmental Agreements: politics, law and economics*, vol. 4, issue 3

"Zaiavlenie MID Rossii v Sviazi s Vyborami v Respublike Belarusi" (2024) *Mid.ru*, February 26. https://www.mid.ru/ru/foreign_policy/news/1934993/ (accessed July 26, 2024)

Zamoyski, Adam (2007) *Rites of Peace: the fall of Napoleon and the Congress of Vienna*, New York: Harper Collins

Zaporozhchenko, Ruslan (2024) "The End of Russian Hegemony in the Post-Soviet Space? War in Ukraine and disintegration processes in Eurasia", *Europe-Asia Studies*, online first

Zaprudskii, Sergei (2018) "V Konflikte s Zapadom Rossiia o Belarusi ne Zabudet", *Thinktanks.pro*, March 19. https://thinktanks.pro/publication/2018/03/19/v-konflikte-s-zapadom-rossiya-o-belarusi-ne-zabudet.html (accessed August 10, 2024)

Zaremba, Marcin (2019) *Communism-Legitimacy-Nationalism: nationalist legitimization of the communist regime in Poland*, Berlin: Peter Lang

Zaretsky, Robert (2019) *Catherine and Diderot: the empress, the philosopher, and the fate of the Enlightenment*, Cambridge, MA: Harvard UP

Zhuchkova, Yulia (2015) "Russia Is Losing Friends and Alienating People", *The Moscow Times*, January 19. https://www.themoscowtimes.com/2015/01/19/russia-is-losing-friends-and-alienating-peoples-a43008 (accessed August 8, 2024)

Zhukova, Ekatherina (2017) "Foreign Aid and Identity after the Chernobyl Nuclear Disaster: how Belarus shapes relations with Germany, Europe, Russia, and Japan", *Cooperation and Conflict*, vol. 52, issue 4

Zhukova, Ekatherina (2018) "Chernobyl, Responsibility and National Identity: positioning Europe and Russia in the media of Belarus and Ukraine", *Europe-Asia Studies*, vol. 70, issue 7

Zhurzhenko, Tatiana (2004) "Cross-Border Cooperation and Transformation of Regional Identities in the Ukrainian-Russian Borderlands: towards a Euroregion 'Slobozhanshchyna'? Part 2", *Nationalities Papers*, vol. 32, issue 2

Zielonka, Jan (2012) "Empires and the Modern International System", *Geopolitics*, vol. 17, issue 3

Zimmerman, William (2009) "Russian National Interests, Use of Blood and Treasure, and Energy Price Assessments: 2008-2009", *Post-Soviet Affairs*, vol. 25, issue 3

Zimmerman, William (2016) *Ruling Russia: authoritarianism from the revolution to Putin*, Princeton, NJ: PUP

Zubok, Vladislav (2000) "The Case of Divided Germany, 1953-1964" in *Nikita Khrushchev*, New Haven, CT: Yale UP; eds. William Taubman, Sergei Khrushchev and Abbott Gleason

Zubok, V. (2002) "Gorbachev and the End of the Cold War: perspectives on history and personality", *Cold War History*, vol. 2, issue 2

Zubok, Vladislav and Pleshakov, Constantine (1996) *Inside the Kremlin's Cold War: from Stalin to Khrushchev*, Cambridge, MA: Harvard UP

Zygar, Mikhail (2023) *War and Punishment: the story of Russian oppression and Ukrainian resistance*, London: Weidenfeld and Nicolson

Zysk, Katarzyna (2017) "Nonstrategic Nuclear Weapons in Russia's Evolving Military Doctrine", *Bulletin of the Atomic Scientists*, vol. 73, issue 5

Zyuganov, Gennady (1997) *My Russia: the political autobiography*, Armonk, NY: M.E. Sharpe

SOVIET AND POST-SOVIET POLITICS AND SOCIETY

Edited by Dr. Andreas Umland | ISSN 1614-3515

1   *Андреас Умланд (ред.)* | Воплощение Европейской конвенции по правам человека в России. Философские, юридические и эмпирические исследования | ISBN 3-89821-387-0

2   *Christian Wipperfürth* | Russland – ein vertrauenswürdiger Partner? Grundlagen, Hintergründe und Praxis gegenwärtiger russischer Außenpolitik | Mit einem Vorwort von Heinz Timmermann | ISBN 3-89821-401-X

3   *Manja Hussner* | Die Übernahme internationalen Rechts in die russische und deutsche Rechtsordnung. Eine vergleichende Analyse zur Völkerrechtsfreundlichkeit der Verfassungen der Russländischen Föderation und der Bundesrepublik Deutschland | Mit einem Vorwort von Rainer Arnold | ISBN 3-89821-438-9

4   *Matthew Tejada* | Bulgaria's Democratic Consolidation and the Kozloduy Nuclear Power Plant (KNPP). The Unattainability of Closure | With a foreword by Richard J. Crampton | ISBN 3-89821-439-7

5   *Марк Григорьевич Меерович* | Квадратные метры, определяющие сознание. Государственная жилищная политика в СССР. 1921 – 1941 гг | ISBN 3-89821-474-5

6   *Andrei P. Tsygankov, Pavel A. Tsygankov (Eds.)* | New Directions in Russian International Studies | ISBN 3-89821-422-2

7   *Марк Григорьевич Меерович* | Как власть народ к труду приучала. Жилище в СССР – средство управления людьми. 1917 – 1941 гг. | С предисловием Елены Осокиной | ISBN 3-89821-495-8

8   *David J. Galbreath* | Nation-Building and Minority Politics in Post-Socialist States. Interests, Influence and Identities in Estonia and Latvia | With a foreword by David J. Smith | ISBN 3-89821-467-2

9   *Алексей Юрьевич Безугольный* | Народы Кавказа в Вооруженных силах СССР в годы Великой Отечественной войны 1941-1945 гг. | С предисловием Николая Бугая | ISBN 3-89821-475-3

10   *Вячеслав Лихачев и Владимир Прибыловский (ред.)* | Русское Национальное Единство, 1990-2000. В 2-х томах | ISBN 3-89821-523-7

11   *Николай Бугай (ред.)* | Народы стран Балтии в условиях сталинизма (1940-е – 1950-е годы). Документированная история | ISBN 3-89821-525-3

12   *Ingmar Bredies (Hrsg.)* | Zur Anatomie der Orange Revolution in der Ukraine. Wechsel des Elitenregimes oder Triumph des Parlamentarismus? | ISBN 3-89821-524-5

13   *Anastasia V. Mitrofanova* | The Politicization of Russian Orthodoxy. *Actors and Ideas* | With a foreword by William C. Gay | ISBN 3-89821-481-8

14   *Nathan D. Larson* | Alexander Solzhenitsyn and the Russo-Jewish Question | ISBN 3-89821-483-4

15   *Guido Houben* | Kulturpolitik und Ethnizität. Staatliche Kunstförderung im Russland der neunziger Jahre | Mit einem Vorwort von Gert Weisskirchen | ISBN 3-89821-542-3

16   *Leonid Luks* | Der russische „Sonderweg"? Aufsätze zur neuesten Geschichte Russlands im europäischen Kontext | ISBN 3-89821-496-6

17   *Евгений Мороз* | История «Мёртвой воды» – от страшной сказки к большой политике. Политическое неоязычество в постсоветской России | ISBN 3-89821-551-2

18   *Александр Верховский и Галина Кожевникова (ред.)* | Этническая и религиозная интолерантность в российских СМИ. Результаты мониторинга 2001-2004 гг. | ISBN 3-89821-569-5

19   *Christian Ganzer* | Sowjetisches Erbe und ukrainische Nation. Das Museum der Geschichte des Zaporoger Kosakentums auf der Insel Chortycja | Mit einem Vorwort von Frank Golczewski | ISBN 3-89821-504-0

20   *Эльза-Баир Гучинова* | Помнить нельзя забыть. Антропология депортационной травмы калмыков | С предисловием Кэролайн Хамфри | ISBN 3-89821-506-7

21   *Юлия Лидерман* | Мотивы «проверки» и «испытания» в постсоветской культуре. Советское прошлое в российском кинематографе 1990-х годов | С предисловием Евгения Марголита | ISBN 3-89821-511-3

22   *Tanya Lokshina, Ray Thomas, Mary Mayer (Eds.)* | The Imposition of a Fake Political Settlement in the Northern Caucasus. The 2003 Chechen Presidential Election | ISBN 3-89821-436-2

23   *Timothy McCajor Hall, Rosie Read (Eds.)* | Changes in the Heart of Europe. Recent Ethnographies of Czechs, Slovaks, Roma, and Sorbs | With an afterword by Zdeněk Salzmann | ISBN 3-89821-606-3

24 *Christian Autengruber* | Die politischen Parteien in Bulgarien und Rumänien. Eine vergleichende Analyse seit Beginn der 90er Jahre | Mit einem Vorwort von Dorothée de Nève | ISBN 3-89821-476-1

25 *Annette Freyberg-Inan with Radu Cristescu* | The Ghosts in Our Classrooms, or: John Dewey Meets Ceauşescu. The Promise and the Failures of Civic Education in Romania | ISBN 3-89821-416-8

26 *John B. Dunlop* | The 2002 Dubrovka and 2004 Beslan Hostage Crises. A Critique of Russian Counter-Terrorism | With a foreword by Donald N. Jensen | ISBN 3-89821-608-X

27 *Peter Koller* | Das touristische Potenzial von Kam''janec'–Podil's'kyj. Eine fremdenverkehrsgeographische Untersuchung der Zukunftsperspektiven und Maßnahmenplanung zur Destinationsentwicklung des „ukrainischen Rothenburg" | Mit einem Vorwort von Kristiane Klemm | ISBN 3-89821-640-3

28 *Françoise Daucé, Elisabeth Sieca-Kozlowski (Eds.)* | Dedovshchina in the Post-Soviet Military. Hazing of Russian Army Conscripts in a Comparative Perspective | With a foreword by Dale Herspring | ISBN 3-89821-616-0

29 *Florian Strasser* | Zivilgesellschaftliche Einflüsse auf die Orange Revolution. Die gewaltlose Massenbewegung und die ukrainische Wahlkrise 2004 | Mit einem Vorwort von Egbert Jahn | ISBN 3-89821-648-9

30 *Rebecca S. Katz* | The Georgian Regime Crisis of 2003-2004. A Case Study in Post-Soviet Media Representation of Politics, Crime and Corruption | ISBN 3-89821-413-3

31 *Vladimir Kantor* | Willkür oder Freiheit. Beiträge zur russischen Geschichtsphilosophie | Ediert von Dagmar Herrmann sowie mit einem Vorwort versehen von Leonid Luks | ISBN 3-89821-589-X

32 *Laura A. Victoir* | The Russian Land Estate Today. A Case Study of Cultural Politics in Post-Soviet Russia | With a foreword by Priscilla Roosevelt | ISBN 3-89821-426-5

33 *Ivan Katchanovski* | Cleft Countries. Regional Political Divisions and Cultures in Post-Soviet Ukraine and Moldova| With a foreword by Francis Fukuyama | ISBN 3-89821-558-X

34 *Florian Mühlfried* | Postsowjetische Feiern. Das Georgische Bankett im Wandel | Mit einem Vorwort von Kevin Tuite | ISBN 3-89821-601-2

35 *Roger Griffin, Werner Loh, Andreas Umland (Eds.)* | Fascism Past and Present, West and East. An International Debate on Concepts and Cases in the Comparative Study of the Extreme Right | With an afterword by Walter Laqueur | ISBN 3-89821-674-8

36 *Sebastian Schlegel* | Der „Weiße Archipel". Sowjetische Atomstädte 1945-1991 | Mit einem Geleitwort von Thomas Bohn | ISBN 3-89821-679-9

37 *Vyacheslav Likhachev* | Political Anti-Semitism in Post-Soviet Russia. Actors and Ideas in 1991-2003 | Edited and translated from Russian by Eugene Veklerov | ISBN 3-89821-529-6

38 *Josette Baer (Ed.)* | Preparing Liberty in Central Europe. Political Texts from the Spring of Nations 1848 to the Spring of Prague 1968 | With a foreword by Zdeněk V. David | ISBN 3-89821-546-6

39 *Михаил Лукьянов* | Российский консерватизм и реформа, 1907-1914 | С предисловием Марка Д. Стейнберга | ISBN 3-89821-503-2

40 *Nicola Melloni* | Market Without Economy. The 1998 Russian Financial Crisis | With a foreword by Eiji Furukawa | ISBN 3-89821-407-9

41 *Dmitrij Chmelnizki* | Die Architektur Stalins | Bd. 1: Studien zu Ideologie und Stil | Bd. 2: Bilddokumentation | Mit einem Vorwort von Bruno Flierl | ISBN 3-89821-515-6

42 *Katja Yafimava* | Post-Soviet Russian-Belarussian Relationships. The Role of Gas Transit Pipelines | With a foreword by Jonathan P. Stern | ISBN 3-89821-655-1

43 *Boris Chavkin* | Verflechtungen der deutschen und russischen Zeitgeschichte. Aufsätze und Archivfunde zu den Beziehungen Deutschlands und der Sowjetunion von 1917 bis 1991 | Ediert von Markus Edlinger sowie mit einem Vorwort versehen von Leonid Luks | ISBN 3-89821-756-6

44 *Anastasija Grynenko in Zusammenarbeit mit Claudia Dathe* | Die Terminologie des Gerichtswesens der Ukraine und Deutschlands im Vergleich. Eine übersetzungswissenschaftliche Analyse juristischer Fachbegriffe im Deutschen, Ukrainischen und Russischen | Mit einem Vorwort von Ulrich Hartmann | ISBN 3-89821-691-8

45 *Anton Burkov* | The Impact of the European Convention on Human Rights on Russian Law. Legislation and Application in 1996-2006 | With a foreword by Françoise Hampson | ISBN 978-3-89821-639-5

46 *Stina Torjesen, Indra Overland (Eds.)* | International Election Observers in Post-Soviet Azerbaijan. Geopolitical Pawns or Agents of Change? | ISBN 978-3-89821-743-9

47 *Taras Kuzio* | Ukraine – Crimea – Russia. Triangle of Conflict | ISBN 978-3-89821-761-3

48 *Claudia Šabić* | „Ich erinnere mich nicht, aber L'viv!" Zur Funktion kultureller Faktoren für die Institutionalisierung und Entwicklung einer ukrainischen Region | Mit einem Vorwort von Melanie Tatur | ISBN 978-3-89821-752-1

49 *Marlies Bilz* | Tatarstan in der Transformation. Nationaler Diskurs und Politische Praxis 1988-1994 | Mit einem Vorwort von Frank Golczewski | ISBN 978-3-89821-722-4

50 *Марлен Ларюэль (ред.)* | Современные интерпретации русского национализма | ISBN 978-3-89821-795-8

51 *Sonja Schüler* | Die ethnische Dimension der Armut. Roma im postsozialistischen Rumänien | Mit einem Vorwort von Anton Sterbling | ISBN 978-3-89821-776-7

52 *Галина Кожевникова* | Радикальный национализм в России и противодействие ему. Сборник докладов Центра «Сова» за 2004-2007 гг. | С предисловием Александра Верховского | ISBN 978-3-89821-721-7

53 *Галина Кожевникова и Владимир Прибыловский* | Российская власть в биографиях I. Высшие должностные лица РФ в 2004 г. | ISBN 978-3-89821-796-5

54 *Галина Кожевникова и Владимир Прибыловский* | Российская власть в биографиях II. Члены Правительства РФ в 2004 г. | ISBN 978-3-89821-797-2

55 *Галина Кожевникова и Владимир Прибыловский* | Российская власть в биографиях III. Руководители федеральных служб и агентств РФ в 2004 г.| ISBN 978-3-89821-798-9

56 *Ileana Petroniu* | Privatisierung in Transformationsökonomien. Determinanten der Restrukturierungs-Bereitschaft am Beispiel Polens, Rumäniens und der Ukraine | Mit einem Vorwort von Rainer W. Schäfer | ISBN 978-3-89821-790-3

57 *Christian Wipperfürth* | Russland und seine GUS-Nachbarn. Hintergründe, aktuelle Entwicklungen und Konflikte in einer ressourcenreichen Region| ISBN 978-3-89821-801-6

58 *Togzhan Kassenova* | From Antagonism to Partnership. The Uneasy Path of the U.S.-Russian Cooperative Threat Reduction | With a foreword by Christoph Bluth | ISBN 978-3-89821-707-1

59 *Alexander Höllwerth* | Das sakrale eurasische Imperium des Aleksandr Dugin. Eine Diskursanalyse zum postsowjetischen russischen Rechtsextremismus | Mit einem Vorwort von Dirk Uffelmann | ISBN 978-3-89821-813-9

60 *Олег Рябов* | «Россия-Матушка». Национализм, гендер и война в России XX века | С предисловием Елены Гощило | ISBN 978-3-89821-487-2

61 *Ivan Maistrenko* | Borot'bism. A Chapter in the History of the Ukrainian Revolution | With a new Introduction by Chris Ford | Translated by George S. N. Luckyj with the assistance of Ivan L. Rudnytsky | Second, Revised and Expanded Edition ISBN 978-3-8382-1107-7

62 *Maryna Romanets* | Anamorphosic Texts and Reconfigured Visions. Improvised Traditions in Contemporary Ukrainian and Irish Literature | ISBN 978-3-89821-576-3

63 *Paul D'Anieri and Taras Kuzio (Eds.)* | Aspects of the Orange Revolution I. Democratization and Elections in Post-Communist Ukraine | ISBN 978-3-89821-698-2

64 *Bohdan Harasymiw in collaboration with Oleh S. Ilnytzkyj (Eds.)* | Aspects of the Orange Revolution II. Information and Manipulation Strategies in the 2004 Ukrainian Presidential Elections | ISBN 978-3-89821-699-9

65 *Ingmar Bredies, Andreas Umland and Valentin Yakushik (Eds.)* | Aspects of the Orange Revolution III. The Context and Dynamics of the 2004 Ukrainian Presidential Elections | ISBN 978-3-89821-803-0

66 *Ingmar Bredies, Andreas Umland and Valentin Yakushik (Eds.)* | Aspects of the Orange Revolution IV. Foreign Assistance and Civic Action in the 2004 Ukrainian Presidential Elections | ISBN 978-3-89821-808-5

67 *Ingmar Bredies, Andreas Umland and Valentin Yakushik (Eds.)* | Aspects of the Orange Revolution V. Institutional Observation Reports on the 2004 Ukrainian Presidential Elections | ISBN 978-3-89821-809-2

68 *Taras Kuzio (Ed.)* | Aspects of the Orange Revolution VI. Post-Communist Democratic Revolutions in Comparative Perspective | ISBN 978-3-89821-820-7

69 *Tim Bohse* | Autoritarismus statt Selbstverwaltung. Die Transformation der kommunalen Politik in der Stadt Kaliningrad 1990-2005 | Mit einem Geleitwort von Stefan Troebst | ISBN 978-3-89821-782-8

70 *David Rupp* | Die Rußländische Föderation und die russischsprachige Minderheit in Lettland. Eine Fallstudie zur Anwaltspolitik Moskaus gegenüber den russophonen Minderheiten im „Nahen Ausland" von 1991 bis 2002 | Mit einem Vorwort von Helmut Wagner | ISBN 978-3-89821-778-1

71 *Taras Kuzio* | Theoretical and Comparative Perspectives on Nationalism. New Directions in Cross-Cultural and Post-Communist Studies | With a foreword by Paul Robert Magocsi | ISBN 978-3-89821-815-3

72 *Christine Teichmann* | Die Hochschultransformation im heutigen Osteuropa. Kontinuität und Wandel bei der Entwicklung des postkommunistischen Universitätswesens | Mit einem Vorwort von Oskar Anweiler | ISBN 978-3-89821-842-9

73 *Julia Kusznir* | Der politische Einfluss von Wirtschaftseliten in russischen Regionen. Eine Analyse am Beispiel der Erdöl- und Erdgasindustrie, 1992-2005 | Mit einem Vorwort von Wolfgang Eichwede | ISBN 978-3-89821-821-4

74 *Alena Vysotskaya | Russland, Belarus und die EU-Osterweiterung.* Zur Minderheitenfrage und zum Problem der Freizügigkeit des Personenverkehrs | Mit einem Vorwort von Katlijn Malfliet | ISBN 978-3-89821-822-1

75 *Heiko Pleines (Hrsg.) | Corporate Governance in post-sozialistischen Volkswirtschaften |* ISBN 978-3-89821-766-8

76 *Stefan Ihrig | Wer sind die Moldawier?* Rumänismus versus Moldowanismus in Historiographie und Schulbüchern der Republik Moldova, 1991-2006 | Mit einem Vorwort von Holm Sundhaussen | ISBN 978-3-89821-466-7

77 *Galina Kozhevnikova in collaboration with Alexander Verkhovsky and Eugene Veklerov | Ultra-Nationalism and Hate Crimes in Contemporary Russia.* The 2004-2006 Annual Reports of Moscow's SOVA Center | With a foreword by Stephen D. Shenfield | ISBN 978-3-89821-868-9

78 *Florian Küchler | The Role of the European Union in Moldova's Transnistria Conflict |* With a foreword by Christopher Hill | ISBN 978-3-89821-850-4

79 *Bernd Rechel | The Long Way Back to Europe.* Minority Protection in Bulgaria | With a foreword by Richard Crampton | ISBN 978-3-89821-863-4

80 *Peter W. Rodgers | Nation, Region and History in Post-Communist Transitions.* Identity Politics in Ukraine, 1991-2006 | With a foreword by Vera Tolz | ISBN 978-3-89821-903-7

81 *Stephanie Solywoda | The Life and Work of Semen L. Frank.* A Study of Russian Religious Philosophy | With a foreword by Philip Walters | ISBN 978-3-89821-457-5

82 *Vera Sokolova | Cultural Politics of Ethnicity.* Discourses on Roma in Communist Czechoslovakia | ISBN 978-3-89821-864-1

83 *Natalya Shevchik Ketenci | Kazakhstani Enterprises in Transition.* The Role of Historical Regional Development in Kazakhstan's Post-Soviet Economic Transformation | ISBN 978-3-89821-831-3

84 *Martin Malek, Anna Schor-Tschudnowskaja (Hgg.) | Europa im Tschetschenienkrieg.* Zwischen politischer Ohnmacht und Gleichgültigkeit | Mit einem Vorwort von Lipchan Basajewa | ISBN 978-3-89821-676-0

85 *Stefan Meister | Das postsowjetische Universitätswesen zwischen nationalem und internationalem Wandel.* Die Entwicklung der regionalen Hochschule in Russland als Gradmesser der Systemtransformation | Mit einem Vorwort von Joan DeBardeleben | ISBN 978-3-89821-891-7

86 *Konstantin Sheiko in collaboration with Stephen Brown | Nationalist Imaginings of the Russian Past.* Anatolii Fomenko and the Rise of Alternative History in Post-Communist Russia | With a foreword by Donald Ostrowski | ISBN 978-3-89821-915-0

87 *Sabine Jenni | Wie stark ist das „Einige Russland"?* Zur Parteibindung der Eliten und zum Wahlerfolg der Machtpartei im Dezember 2007 | Mit einem Vorwort von Klaus Armingeon | ISBN 978-3-89821-961-7

88 *Thomas Borén | Meeting-Places of Transformation.* Urban Identity, Spatial Representations and Local Politics in Post-Soviet St Petersburg | ISBN 978-3-89821-739-2

89 *Aygul Ashirova | Stalinismus und Stalin-Kult in Zentralasien.* Turkmenistan 1924-1953 | Mit einem Vorwort von Leonid Luks | ISBN 978-3-89821-987-7

90 *Leonid Luks | Freiheit oder imperiale Größe?* Essays zu einem russischen Dilemma | ISBN 978-3-8382-0011-8

91 *Christopher Gilley | The 'Change of Signposts' in the Ukrainian Emigration.* A Contribution to the History of Sovietophilism in the 1920s | With a foreword by Frank Golczewski | ISBN 978-3-89821-965-5

92 *Philipp Casula, Jeronim Perovic (Eds.) | Identities and Politics During the Putin Presidency.* The Discursive Foundations of Russia's Stability | With a foreword by Heiko Haumann | ISBN 978-3-8382-0015-6

93 *Marcel Viëtor | Europa und die Frage nach seinen Grenzen im Osten.* Zur Konstruktion ‚europäischer Identität' in Geschichte und Gegenwart | Mit einem Vorwort von Albrecht Lehmann | ISBN 978-3-8382-0045-3

94 *Ben Hellman, Andrei Rogachevskii | Filming the Unfilmable.* Casper Wrede's 'One Day in the Life of Ivan Denisovich' | Second, Revised and Expanded Edition | ISBN 978-3-8382-0044-6

95 *Eva Fuchslocher | Vaterland, Sprache, Glaube.* Orthodoxie und Nationenbildung am Beispiel Georgiens | Mit einem Vorwort von Christina von Braun | ISBN 978-3-89821-884-9

96 *Vladimir Kantor | Das Westlertum und der Weg Russlands.* Zur Entwicklung der russischen Literatur und Philosophie | Ediert von Dagmar Herrmann | Mit einem Beitrag von Nikolaus Lobkowicz | ISBN 978-3-8382-0102-3

97 *Kamran Musayev | Die postsowjetische Transformation im Baltikum und Südkaukasus.* Eine vergleichende Untersuchung der politischen Entwicklung Lettlands und Aserbaidschans 1985-2009 | Mit einem Vorwort von Leonid Luks | Ediert von Sandro Henschel | ISBN 978-3-8382-0103-0

98 *Tatiana Zhurzhenko | Borderlands into Bordered Lands.* Geopolitics of Identity in Post-Soviet Ukraine | With a foreword by Dieter Segert | ISBN 978-3-8382-0042-2

99   *Кирилл Галушко, Лидия Смола (ред.)* | Пределы падения – варианты украинского буду-
щего. Аналитико-прогностические исследования | ISBN 978-3-8382-0148-1

100 *Michael Minkenberg (Ed.)* | Historical Legacies and the Radical Right in Post-Cold War Central
and Eastern Europe | With an afterword by Sabrina P. Ramet | ISBN 978-3-8382-0124-5

101 *David-Emil Wickström* | Rocking St. Petersburg. Transcultural Flows and Identity Politics in the St. Petersburg
Popular Music Scene | With a foreword by Yngvar B. Steinholt | Second, Revised and Expanded Edition |
ISBN 978-3-8382-0100-9

102 *Eva Zabka* | Eine neue „Zeit der Wirren"? Der spät- und postsowjetische Systemwandel 1985-2000 im Spiegel
russischer gesellschaftspolitischer Diskurse | Mit einem Vorwort von Margareta Mommsen | ISBN 978-3-8382-0161-0

103 *Ulrike Ziemer* | Ethnic Belonging, Gender and Cultural Practices. Youth Identitites in Contemporary Russia |
With a foreword by Anoop Nayak | ISBN 978-3-8382-0152-8

104 *Ksenia Chepikova* | ‚Einiges Russland` - eine zweite KPdSU? Aspekte der Identitätskonstruktion einer post-
sowjetischen „Partei der Macht" | Mit einem Vorwort von Torsten Oppelland | ISBN 978-3-8382-0311-9

105 *Леонид Люкс* | Западничество или евразийство? Демократия или идеократия? Сборник статей
об исторических дилеммах России | С предисловием Владимира Кантора | ISBN 978-3-8382-0211-2

106 *Anna Dost* | Das russische Verfassungsrecht auf dem Weg zum Föderalismus und zurück. Zum
Konflikt von Rechtsnormen und -wirklichkeit in der Russländischen Föderation von 1991 bis 2009 | Mit einem Vorwort von Ale-
xander Blankenagel | ISBN 978-3-8382-0292-1

107 *Philipp Herzog* | Sozialistische Völkerfreundschaft, nationaler Widerstand oder harmloser Zeit-
vertreib? Zur politischen Funktion der Volkskunst im sowjetischen Estland | Mit einem Vorwort von Andreas Kappeler | ISBN
978-3-8382-0216-7

108 *Marlène Laruelle (Ed.)* | Russian Nationalism, Foreign Policy, and Identity Debates in Putin's
Russia. New Ideological Patterns after the Orange Revolution | ISBN 978-3-8382-0325-6

109 *Michail Logvinov* | Russlands Kampf gegen den internationalen Terrorismus. Eine kritische Bestands-
aufnahme des Bekämpfungsansatzes | Mit einem Geleitwort von Hans-Henning Schröder und einem Vorwort von Eckhard Jesse
| ISBN 978-3-8382-0329-4

110 *John B. Dunlop* | The Moscow Bombings of September 1999. Examinations of Russian Terrorist Attacks at
the Onset of Vladimir Putin's Rule | Second, Revised and Expanded Edition | ISBN 978-3-8382-0388-1

111 *Андрей А. Ковалёв* | Свидетельство из-за кулис российской политики I. Можно ли делать добро
из зла? (Воспоминания и размышления о последних советских и первых послесоветских годах) | With a foreword by Peter
Reddaway | ISBN 978-3-8382-0302-7

112 *Андрей А. Ковалёв* | Свидетельство из-за кулис российской политики II. Угроза для себя и окру-
жающих (Наблюдения и предостережения относительно происходящего после 2000 г.) | ISBN 978-3-8382-0303-4

113 *Bernd Kappenberg* | Zeichen setzen für Europa. Der Gebrauch europäischer lateinischer Sonderzeichen in der
deutschen Öffentlichkeit | Mit einem Vorwort von Peter Schlobinski | ISBN 978-3-89821-749-1

114 *Ivo Mijnssen* | The Quest for an Ideal Youth in Putin's Russia I. Back to Our Future! History, Modernity, and
Patriotism according to Nashi, 2005-2013 | With a foreword by Jeronim Perović | Second, Revised and Expanded Edition |
ISBN 978-3-8382-0368-3

115 *Jussi Lassila* | The Quest for an Ideal Youth in Putin's Russia II. The Search for Distinctive Conformism in
the Political Communication of Nashi, 2005-2009 | With a foreword by Kirill Postoutenko | Second, Revised and Expanded Edi-
tion | ISBN 978-3-8382-0415-4

116 *Valerio Trabandt* | Neue Nachbarn, gute Nachbarschaft? Die EU als internationaler Akteur am Beispiel ihrer
Demokratieförderung in Belarus und der Ukraine 2004-2009 | Mit einem Vorwort von Jutta Joachim | ISBN 978-3-8382-0437-6

117 *Fabian Pfeiffer* | Estlands Außen- und Sicherheitspolitik I. Der estnische Atlantizismus nach der wiedererlang-
ten Unabhängigkeit 1991-2004 | Mit einem Vorwort von Helmut Hubel | ISBN 978-3-8382-0127-6

118 *Jana Podßuweit* | Estlands Außen- und Sicherheitspolitik II. Handlungsoptionen eines Kleinstaates im Rah-
men seiner EU-Mitgliedschaft (2004-2008) | Mit einem Vorwort von Helmut Hubel | ISBN 978-3-8382-0440-6

119 *Karin Pointner* | Estlands Außen- und Sicherheitspolitik III. Eine gedächtnispolitische Analyse estnischer Ent-
wicklungskooperation 2006-2010 | Mit einem Vorwort von Karin Liebhart | ISBN 978-3-8382-0435-2

120 *Ruslana Vovk* | Die Offenheit der ukrainischen Verfassung für das Völkerrecht und die europäi-
sche Integration | Mit einem Vorwort von Alexander Blankenagel | ISBN 978-3-8382-0481-9

121 *Mykhaylo Banakh* | Die Relevanz der Zivilgesellschaft bei den postkommunistischen Transformationsprozessen in mittel- und osteuropäischen Ländern. Das Beispiel der spät- und postsowjetischen Ukraine 1986-2009 | Mit einem Vorwort von Gerhard Simon | ISBN 978-3-8382-0499-4

122 *Michael Moser* | Language Policy and the Discourse on Languages in Ukraine under President Viktor Yanukovych (25 February 2010–28 October 2012) | ISBN 978-3-8382-0497-0 (Paperback edition) | ISBN 978-3-8382-0507-6 (Hardcover edition)

123 *Nicole Krome* | Russischer Netzwerkkapitalismus Restrukturierungsprozesse in der Russischen Föderation am Beispiel des Luftfahrtunternehmens „Aviastar" | Mit einem Vorwort von Petra Stykow | ISBN 978-3-8382-0534-2

124 *David R. Marples* | 'Our Glorious Past'. Lukashenka's Belarus and the Great Patriotic War | ISBN 978-3-8382-0574-8 (Paperback edition) | ISBN 978-3-8382-0675-2 (Hardcover edition)

125 *Ulf Walther* | Russlands „neuer Adel". Die Macht des Geheimdienstes von Gorbatschow bis Putin | Mit einem Vorwort von Hans-Georg Wieck | ISBN 978-3-8382-0584-7

126 *Simon Geissbühler (Hrsg.)* | Kiew – Revolution 3.0. Der Euromaidan 2013/14 und die Zukunftsperspektiven der Ukraine | ISBN 978-3-8382-0581-6 (Paperback edition) | ISBN 978-3-8382-0681-3 (Hardcover edition)

127 *Andrey Makarychev* | Russia and the EU in a Multipolar World. Discourses, Identities, Norms | With a foreword by Klaus Segbers | ISBN 978-3-8382-0629-5

128 *Roland Scharff* | Kasachstan als postsowjetischer Wohlfahrtsstaat. Die Transformation des sozialen Schutzsystems | Mit einem Vorwort von Joachim Ahrens | ISBN 978-3-8382-0622-6

129 *Katja Grupp* | Bild Lücke Deutschland. Kaliningrader Studierende sprechen über Deutschland | Mit einem Vorwort von Martin Schulz | ISBN 978-3-8382-0552-6

130 *Konstantin Sheiko, Stephen Brown* | History as Therapy. Alternative History and Nationalist Imaginings in Russia, 1991-2014 | ISBN 978-3-8382-0665-3

131 *Elisa Kriza* | Alexander Solzhenitsyn: Cold War Icon, Gulag Author, Russian Nationalist? A Study of the Western Reception of his Literary Writings, Historical Interpretations, and Political Ideas | With a foreword by Andrei Rogatchevski | ISBN 978-3-8382-0589-2 (Paperback edition) | ISBN 978-3-8382-0690-5 (Hardcover edition)

132 *Serghei Golunov* | The Elephant in the Room. Corruption and Cheating in Russian Universities | ISBN 978-3-8382-0570-0

133 *Manja Hussner, Rainer Arnold (Hgg.)* | Verfassungsgerichtsbarkeit in Zentralasien I. Sammlung von Verfassungstexten | ISBN 978-3-8382-0595-3

134 *Nikolay Mitrokhin* | Die „Russische Partei". Die Bewegung der russischen Nationalisten in der UdSSR 1953-1985 | Aus dem Russischen übertragen von einem Übersetzerteam unter der Leitung von Larisa Schippel | ISBN 978-3-8382-0024-8

135 *Manja Hussner, Rainer Arnold (Hgg.)* | Verfassungsgerichtsbarkeit in Zentralasien II. Sammlung von Verfassungstexten | ISBN 978-3-8382-0597-7

136 *Manfred Zeller* | Das sowjetische Fieber. Fußballfans im poststalinistischen Vielvölkerreich | Mit einem Vorwort von Nikolaus Katzer | ISBN 978-3-8382-0757-5

137 *Kristin Schreiter* | Stellung und Entwicklungspotential zivilgesellschaftlicher Gruppen in Russland. Menschenrechtsorganisationen im Vergleich | ISBN 978-3-8382-0673-8

138 *David R. Marples, Frederick V. Mills (Eds.)* | Ukraine's Euromaidan. Analyses of a Civil Revolution | ISBN 978-3-8382-0660-8

139 *Bernd Kappenberg* | Setting Signs for Europe. Why Diacritics Matter for European Integration | With a foreword by Peter Schlobinski | ISBN 978-3-8382-0663-9

140 *René Lenz* | Internationalisierung, Kooperation und Transfer. Externe bildungspolitische Akteure in der Russischen Föderation | Mit einem Vorwort von Frank Ettrich | ISBN 978-3-8382-0751-3

141 *Juri Plusnin, Yana Zausaeva, Natalia Zhidkevich, Artemy Pozanenko* | Wandering Workers. Mores, Behavior, Way of Life, and Political Status of Domestic Russian Labor Migrants | Translated by Julia Kazantseva | ISBN 978-3-8382-0653-0

142 *David J. Smith (Eds.)* | Latvia – A Work in Progress? 100 Years of State- and Nation-Building | ISBN 978-3-8382-0648-6

143 *Инна Чувычкина (ред.)* | Экспортные нефте- и газопроводы на постсоветском пространстве. Анализ трубопроводной политики в свете теории международных отношений | ISBN 978-3-8382-0822-0

144 *Johann Zajaczkowski* | Russland – eine pragmatische Großmacht? Eine rollentheoretische Untersuchung russischer Außenpolitik am Beispiel der Zusammenarbeit mit den USA nach 9/11 und des Georgienkrieges von 2008 | Mit einem Vorwort von Siegfried Schieder | ISBN 978-3-8382-0837-4

145 *Boris Popivanov* | Changing Images of the Left in Bulgaria. The Challenge of Post-Communism in the Early 21st Century | ISBN 978-3-8382-0667-7

146 *Lenka Krátká* | A History of the Czechoslovak Ocean Shipping Company 1948-1989. How a Small, Landlocked Country Ran Maritime Business During the Cold War | ISBN 978-3-8382-0666-0

147 *Alexander Sergunin* | Explaining Russian Foreign Policy Behavior. Theory and Practice | ISBN 978-3-8382-0752-0

148 *Darya Malyutina* | Migrant Friendships in a Super-Diverse City. Russian-Speakers and their Social Relationships in London in the 21st Century | With a foreword by Claire Dwyer | ISBN 978-3-8382-0652-3

149 *Alexander Sergunin, Valery Konyshev* | Russia in the Arctic. Hard or Soft Power? | ISBN 978-3-8382-0753-7

150 *John J. Maresca* | Helsinki Revisited. A Key U.S. Negotiator's Memoirs on the Development of the CSCE into the OSCE | With a foreword by Hafiz Pashayev | ISBN 978-3-8382-0852-7

151 *Jardar Østbø* | The New Third Rome. Readings of a Russian Nationalist Myth | With a foreword by Pål Kolstø | ISBN 978-3-8382-0870-1

152 *Simon Kordonsky* | Socio-Economic Foundations of the Russian Post-Soviet Regime. The Resource-Based Economy and Estate-Based Social Structure of Contemporary Russia | With a foreword by Svetlana Barsukova | ISBN 978-3-8382-0775-9

153 *Duncan Leitch* | Assisting Reform in Post-Communist Ukraine 2000–2012. The Illusions of Donors and the Disillusion of Beneficiaries | With a foreword by Kataryna Wolczuk | ISBN 978-3-8382-0844-2

154 *Abel Polese* | Limits of a Post-Soviet State. How Informality Replaces, Renegotiates, and Reshapes Governance in Contemporary Ukraine | With a foreword by Colin Williams | ISBN 978-3-8382-0845-9

155 *Mikhail Suslov (Ed.)* | Digital Orthodoxy in the Post-Soviet World. The Russian Orthodox Church and Web 2.0 | With a foreword by Father Cyril Hovorun | ISBN 978-3-8382-0871-8

156 *Leonid Luks* | Zwei „Sonderwege"? Russisch-deutsche Parallelen und Kontraste (1917-2014). Vergleichende Essays | ISBN 978-3-8382-0823-7

157 *Vladimir V. Karacharovskiy, Ovsey I. Shkaratan, Gordey A. Yastrebov* | Towards a New Russian Work Culture. Can Western Companies and Expatriates Change Russian Society? | With a foreword by Elena N. Danilova | Translated by Julia Kazantseva | ISBN 978-3-8382-0902-9

158 *Edmund Griffiths* | Aleksandr Prokhanov and Post-Soviet Esotericism | ISBN 978-3-8382-0963-0

159 *Timm Beichelt, Susann Worschech (Eds.)* | Transnational Ukraine? Networks and Ties that Influence(d) Contemporary Ukraine | ISBN 978-3-8382-0944-9

160 *Mieste Hotopp-Riecke* | Die Tataren der Krim zwischen Assimilation und Selbstbehauptung. Der Aufbau des krimtatarischen Bildungswesens nach Deportation und Heimkehr (1990-2005) | Mit einem Vorwort von Swetlana Czerwonnaja | ISBN 978-3-89821-940-2

161 *Olga Bertelsen (Ed.)* | Revolution and War in Contemporary Ukraine. The Challenge of Change | ISBN 978-3-8382-1016-2

162 *Natalya Ryabinska* | Ukraine's Post-Communist Mass Media. Between Capture and Commercialization | With a foreword by Marta Dyczok | ISBN 978-3-8382-1011-7

163 *Alexandra Cotofana, James M. Nyce (Eds.)* | Religion and Magic in Socialist and Post-Socialist Contexts. Historic and Ethnographic Case Studies of Orthodoxy, Heterodoxy, and Alternative Spirituality | With a foreword by Patrick L. Michelson | ISBN 978-3-8382-0989-0

164 *Nozima Akhrarkhodjaeva* | The Instrumentalisation of Mass Media in Electoral Authoritarian Regimes. Evidence from Russia's Presidential Election Campaigns of 2000 and 2008 | ISBN 978-3-8382-1013-1

165 *Yulia Krasheninnikova* | Informal Healthcare in Contemporary Russia. Sociographic Essays on the Post-Soviet Infrastructure for Alternative Healing Practices | ISBN 978-3-8382-0970-8

166 *Peter Kaiser* | Das Schachbrett der Macht. Die Handlungsspielräume eines sowjetischen Funktionärs unter Stalin am Beispiel des Generalsekretärs des Komsomol Aleksandr Kosarev (1929-1938) | Mit einem Vorwort von Dietmar Neutatz | ISBN 978-3-8382-1052-0

167 *Oksana Kim* | The Effects and Implications of Kazakhstan's Adoption of International Financial Reporting Standards. A Resource Dependence Perspective | With a foreword by Svetlana Vlady | ISBN 978-3-8382-0987-6

168 *Anna Sanina* | Patriotic Education in Contemporary Russia. Sociological Studies in the Making of the Post-Soviet Citizen | With a foreword by Anna Oldfield | ISBN 978-3-8382-0993-7

169 *Rudolf Wolters* | Spezialist in Sibirien Faksimile der 1933 erschienenen ersten Ausgabe | Mit einem Vorwort von Dmitrij Chmelnizki | ISBN 978-3-8382-0515-1

170 *Michal Vit, Magdalena M. Baran (Eds.)* | Transregional versus National Perspectives on Contemporary Central European History. Studies on the Building of Nation-States and Their Cooperation in the 20th and 21st Century | With a foreword by Petr Vágner | ISBN 978-3-8382-1015-5

171 *Philip Gamaghelyan* | Conflict Resolution Beyond the International Relations Paradigm. Evolving Designs as a Transformative Practice in Nagorno-Karabakh and Syria | With a foreword by Susan Allen | ISBN 978-3-8382-1057-5

172 *Maria Shagina* | Joining a Prestigious Club. Cooperation with Europarties and Its Impact on Party Development in Georgia, Moldova, and Ukraine 2004–2015 | With a foreword by Kataryna Wolczuk | ISBN 978-3-8382-1084-1

173 *Alexandra Cotofana, James M. Nyce (Eds.)* | Religion and Magic in Socialist and Post-Socialist Contexts II. Baltic, Eastern European, and Post-USSR Case Studies | With a foreword by Anita Stasulane | ISBN 978-3-8382-0990-6

174 *Barbara Kunz* | Kind Words, Cruise Missiles, and Everything in Between. The Use of Power Resources in U.S. Policies towards Poland, Ukraine, and Belarus 1989–2008 | With a foreword by William Hill | ISBN 978-3-8382-1065-0

175 *Eduard Klein* | Bildungskorruption in Russland und der Ukraine. Eine komparative Analyse der Performanz staatlicher Antikorruptionsmaßnahmen im Hochschulsektor am Beispiel universitärer Aufnahmeprüfungen | Mit einem Vorwort von Heiko Pleines | ISBN 978-3-8382-0995-1

176 *Markus Soldner* | Politischer Kapitalismus im postsowjetischen Russland. Die politische, wirtschaftliche und mediale Transformation in den 1990er Jahren | Mit einem Vorwort von Wolfgang Ismayr | ISBN 978-3-8382-1222-7

177 *Anton Oleinik* | Building Ukraine from Within. A Sociological, Institutional, and Economic Analysis of a Nation-State in the Making | ISBN 978-3-8382-1150-3

178 *Peter Rollberg, Marlene Laruelle (Eds.)* | Mass Media in the Post-Soviet World. Market Forces, State Actors, and Political Manipulation in the Informational Environment after Communism | ISBN 978-3-8382-1116-9

179 *Mikhail Minakov* | Development and Dystopia. Studies in Post-Soviet Ukraine and Eastern Europe | With a foreword by Alexander Etkind | ISBN 978-3-8382-1112-1

180 *Aijan Sharshenova* | The European Union's Democracy Promotion in Central Asia. A Study of Political Interests, Influence, and Development in Kazakhstan and Kyrgyzstan in 2007–2013 | With a foreword by Gordon Crawford | ISBN 978-3-8382-1151-0

181 *Andrey Makarychev, Alexandra Yatsyk (Eds.)* | Boris Nemtsov and Russian Politics. Power and Resistance | With a foreword by Zhanna Nemtsova | ISBN 978-3-8382-1122-0

182 *Sophie Falsini* | The Euromaidan's Effect on Civil Society. Why and How Ukrainian Social Capital Increased after the Revolution of Dignity | With a foreword by Susann Worschech | ISBN 978-3-8382-1131-2

183 *Valentyna Romanova, Andreas Umland (Eds.)* | Ukraine's Decentralization. Challenges and Implications of the Local Governance Reform after the Euromaidan Revolution | ISBN 978-3-8382-1162-6

184 *Leonid Luks* | A Fateful Triangle. Essays on Contemporary Russian, German and Polish History | ISBN 978-3-8382-1143-5

185 *John B. Dunlop* | The February 2015 Assassination of Boris Nemtsov and the Flawed Trial of his Alleged Killers. An Exploration of Russia's "Crime of the 21st Century" | ISBN 978-3-8382-1188-6

186 *Vasile Rotaru* | Russia, the EU, and the Eastern Partnership. Building Bridges or Digging Trenches? | ISBN 978-3-8382-1134-3

187 *Marina Lebedeva* | Russian Studies of International Relations. From the Soviet Past to the Post-Cold-War Present | With a foreword by Andrei P. Tsygankov | ISBN 978-3-8382-0851-0

188 *Tomasz Stępniewski, George Soroka (Eds.)* | Ukraine after Maidan. Revisiting Domestic and Regional Security | ISBN 978-3-8382-1075-9

189 *Petar Cholakov* | Ethnic Entrepreneurs Unmasked. Political Institutions and Ethnic Conflicts in Contemporary Bulgaria | ISBN 978-3-8382-1189-3

190 *A. Salem, G. Hazeldine, D. Morgan (Eds.)* | Higher Education in Post-Communist States. Comparative and Sociological Perspectives | ISBN 978-3-8382-1183-1

191 *Igor Torbakov* | After Empire. Nationalist Imagination and Symbolic Politics in Russia and Eurasia in the Twentieth and Twenty-First Century | With a foreword by Serhii Plokhy | ISBN 978-3-8382-1217-3

192 *Aleksandr Burakovskiy* | Jewish-Ukrainian Relations in Late and Post-Soviet Ukraine. Articles, Lectures and Essays from 1986 to 2016 | ISBN 978-3-8382-1210-4

193 *Natalia Shapovalova, Olga Burlyuk (Eds.)* | Civil Society in Post-Euromaidan Ukraine. From Revolution to Consolidation | With a foreword by Richard Youngs | ISBN 978-3-8382-1216-6

194 *Franz Preissler* | Positionsverteidigung, Imperialismus oder Irredentismus? Russland und die „Russischsprachigen", 1991–2015 | ISBN 978-3-8382-1262-3

195 *Marian Madeła* | Der Reformprozess in der Ukraine 2014-2017. Eine Fallstudie zur Reform der öffentlichen Verwaltung | Mit einem Vorwort von Martin Malek | ISBN 978-3-8382-1266-1

196 *Anke Giesen* | „Wie kann denn der Sieger ein Verbrecher sein?" Eine diskursanalytische Untersuchung der russlandweiten Debatte über Konzept und Verstaatlichungsprozess der Lagergedenkstätte „Perm'-36" im Ural | ISBN 978-3-8382-1284-5

197 *Victoria Leukavets* | The Integration Policies of Belarus and Ukraine vis-à-vis the EU and Russia. A Comparative Analysis Through the Prism of a Two-Level Game Approach | ISBN 978-3-8382-1247-0

198 *Oksana Kim* | The Development and Challenges of Russian Corporate Governance I. The Roles and Functions of Boards of Directors | With a foreword by Sheila M. Puffer | ISBN 978-3-8382-1287-6

199 *Thomas D. Grant* | International Law and the Post-Soviet Space I. Essays on Chechnya and the Baltic States | With a foreword by Stephen M. Schwebel | ISBN 978-3-8382-1279-1

200 *Thomas D. Grant* | International Law and the Post-Soviet Space II. Essays on Ukraine, Intervention, and Non-Proliferation | ISBN 978-3-8382-1280-7

201 *Slavomír Michálek, Michal Štefansky* | The Age of Fear. The Cold War and Its Influence on Czechoslovakia 1945–1968 | ISBN 978-3-8382-1285-2

202 *Iulia-Sabina Joja* | Romania's Strategic Culture 1990–2014. Continuity and Change in a Post-Communist Country's Evolution of National Interests and Security Policies | With a foreword by Heiko Biehl | ISBN 978-3-8382-1286-9

203 *Andrei Rogatchevski, Yngvar B. Steinholt, Arve Hansen, David-Emil Wickström* | War of Songs. Popular Music and Recent Russia-Ukraine Relations | With a foreword by Artemy Troitsky | ISBN 978-3-8382-1173-2

204 *Maria Lipman (Ed.)* | Russian Voices on Post-Crimea Russia. An Almanac of Counterpoint Essays from 2015–2018 | ISBN 978-3-8382-1251-7

205 *Ksenia Maksimovtsova* | Language Conflicts in Contemporary Estonia, Latvia, and Ukraine. A Comparative Exploration of Discourses in Post-Soviet Russian-Language Digital Media | With a foreword by Ammon Cheskin | ISBN 978-3-8382-1282-1

206 *Michal Vít* | The EU's Impact on Identity Formation in East-Central Europe between 2004 and 2013. Perceptions of the Nation and Europe in Political Parties of the Czech Republic, Poland, and Slovakia | With a foreword by Andrea Petö | ISBN 978-3-8382-1275-3

207 *Per A. Rudling* | Tarnished Heroes. The Organization of Ukrainian Nationalists in the Memory Politics of Post-Soviet Ukraine | ISBN 978-3-8382-0999-9

208 *Kaja Gadowska, Peter Solomon (Eds.)* | Legal Change in Post-Communist States. Progress, Reversions, Explanations | ISBN 978-3-8382-1312-5

209 *Pawel Kowal, Georges Mink, Iwona Reichardt (Eds.)* | Three Revolutions: Mobilization and Change in Contemporary Ukraine I. Theoretical Aspects and Analyses on Religion, Memory, and Identity | ISBN 978-3-8382-1321-7

210 *Pawel Kowal, Georges Mink, Adam Reichardt, Iwona Reichardt (Eds.)* | Three Revolutions: Mobilization and Change in Contemporary Ukraine II. An Oral History of the Revolution on Granite, Orange Revolution, and Revolution of Dignity | ISBN 978-3-8382-1323-1

211 *Li Bennich-Björkman, Sergiy Kurbatov (Eds.)* | When the Future Came. The Collapse of the USSR and the Emergence of National Memory in Post-Soviet History Textbooks | ISBN 978-3-8382-1335-4

212 *Olga R. Gulina* | Migration as a (Geo-)Political Challenge in the Post-Soviet Space. Border Regimes, Policy Choices, Visa Agendas | With a foreword by Nils Muižnieks | ISBN 978-3-8382-1338-5

213 *Sanna Turoma, Kaarina Aitamurto, Slobodanka Vladiv-Glover (Eds.)* | Religion, Expression, and Patriotism in Russia. Essays on Post-Soviet Society and the State. ISBN 978-3-8382-1346-0

214 *Vasif Huseynov* | Geopolitical Rivalries in the "Common Neighborhood". Russia's Conflict with the West, Soft Power, and Neoclassical Realism | With a foreword by Nicholas Ross Smith | ISBN 978-3-8382-1277-7

215 *Mikhail Suslov* | Geopolitical Imagination. Ideology and Utopia in Post-Soviet Russia | With a foreword by Mark Bassin | ISBN 978-3-8382-1361-3

216 *Alexander Etkind, Mikhail Minakov (Eds.)* | Ideology after Union. Political Doctrines, Discourses, and Debates in Post-Soviet Societies | ISBN 978-3-8382-1388-0

217 *Jakob Mischke, Oleksandr Zabirko (Hgg.)* | Protestbewegungen im langen Schatten des Kreml. Aufbruch und Resignation in Russland und der Ukraine | ISBN 978-3-8382-0926-5

218 *Oksana Huss* | How Corruption and Anti-Corruption Policies Sustain Hybrid Regimes. Strategies of Political Domination under Ukraine's Presidents in 1994-2014 | With a foreword by Tobias Debiel and Andrea Gawrich | ISBN 978-3-8382-1430-6

219 *Dmitry Travin, Vladimir Gel'man, Otar Marganiya* | The Russian Path. Ideas, Interests, Institutions, Illusions | With a foreword by Vladimir Ryzhkov | ISBN 978-3-8382-1421-4

220 *Gergana Dimova* | Political Uncertainty. A Comparative Exploration | With a foreword by Todor Yalamov and Rumena Filipova | ISBN 978-3-8382-1385-9

221 *Torben Waschke* | Russland in Transition. Geopolitik zwischen Raum, Identität und Machtinteressen | Mit einem Vorwort von Andreas Dittmann | ISBN 978-3-8382-1480-1

222 *Steven Jobbitt, Zsolt Bottlik, Marton Berki (Eds.)* | Power and Identity in the Post-Soviet Realm. Geographies of Ethnicity and Nationality after 1991 | ISBN 978-3-8382-1399-6

223 *Daria Buteiko* | Erinnerungsort. Ort des Gedenkens, der Erholung oder der Einkehr? Kommunismus-Erinnerung am Beispiel der Gedenkstätte Berliner Mauer sowie des Soloveckij-Klosters und -Museumsparks | ISBN 978-3-8382-1367-5

224 *Olga Bertelsen (Ed.)* | Russian Active Measures. Yesterday, Today, Tomorrow | With a foreword by Jan Goldman | ISBN 978-3-8382-1529-7

225 *David Mandel* | "Optimizing" Higher Education in Russia. University Teachers and their Union "Universitetskaya solidarnost'" | ISBN 978-3-8382-1519-8

226 *Mikhail Minakov, Gwendolyn Sasse, Daria Isachenko (Eds.)* | Post-Soviet Secessionism. Nation-Building and State-Failure after Communism | ISBN 978-3-8382-1538-9

227 *Jakob Hauter (Ed.)* | Civil War? Interstate War? Hybrid War? Dimensions and Interpretations of the Donbas Conflict in 2014–2020 | With a foreword by Andrew Wilson | ISBN 978-3-8382-1383-5

228 *Tima T. Moldogaziev, Gene A. Brewer, J. Edward Kellough (Eds.)* | Public Policy and Politics in Georgia. Lessons from Post-Soviet Transition | With a foreword by Dan Durning | ISBN 978-3-8382-1535-8

229 *Oxana Schmies (Ed.)* | NATO's Enlargement and Russia. A Strategic Challenge in the Past and Future | With a foreword by Vladimir Kara-Murza | ISBN 978-3-8382-1478-8

230 *Christopher Ford* | Ukapisme – Une Gauche perdue. Le marxisme anti-colonial dans la révolution ukrainienne 1917-1925 | Avec une préface de Vincent Présumey | ISBN 978-3-8382-0899-2

231 *Anna Kutkina* | Between Lenin and Bandera. Decommunization and Multivocality in Post-Euromaidan Ukraine | With a foreword by Juri Mykkänen | ISBN 978-3-8382-1506-8

232 *Lincoln E. Flake* | Defending the Faith. The Russian Orthodox Church and the Demise of Religious Pluralism | With a foreword by Peter Martland | ISBN 978-3-8382-1378-1

233 *Nikoloz Samkharadze* | Russia's Recognition of the Independence of Abkhazia and South Ossetia. Analysis of a Deviant Case in Moscow's Foreign Policy | With a foreword by Neil MacFarlane | ISBN 978-3-8382-1414-6

234 *Arve Hansen* | Urban Protest. A Spatial Perspective on Kyiv, Minsk, and Moscow | With a foreword by Julie Wilhelmsen | ISBN 978-3-8382-1495-5

235 *Eleonora Narvselius, Julie Fedor (Eds.)* | Diversity in the East-Central European Borderlands. Memories, Cityscapes, People | ISBN 978-3-8382-1523-5

236 *Regina Elsner* | The Russian Orthodox Church and Modernity. A Historical and Theological Investigation into Eastern Christianity between Unity and Plurality | With a foreword by Mikhail Suslov | ISBN 978-3-8382-1568-6

237 *Bo Petersson* | The Putin Predicament. Problems of Legitimacy and Succession in Russia | With a foreword by J. Paul Goode | ISBN 978-3-8382-1050-6

238 *Jonathan Otto Pohl* | The Years of Great Silence. The Deportation, Special Settlement, and Mobilization into the Labor Army of Ethnic Germans in the USSR, 1941–1955 | ISBN 978-3-8382-1630-0

239 *Mikhail Minakov (Ed.)* | Inventing Majorities. Ideological Creativity in Post-Soviet Societies | ISBN 978-3-8382-1641-6

240 *Robert M. Cutler* | Soviet and Post-Soviet Foreign Policies I. East-South Relations and the Political Economy of the Communist Bloc, 1971–1991 | With a foreword by Roger E. Kanet | ISBN 978-3-8382-1654-6

241 *Izabella Agardi* | On the Verge of History. Life Stories of Rural Women from Serbia, Romania, and Hungary, 1920–2020 | With a foreword by Andrea Pető | ISBN 978-3-8382-1602-7

242 *Sebastian Schäffer (Ed.)* | Ukraine in Central and Eastern Europe. Kyiv's Foreign Affairs and the International Relations of the Post-Communist Region | With a foreword by Pavlo Klimkin and Andreas Umland| ISBN 978-3-8382-1615-7

243 *Volodymyr Dubrovskyi, Kalman Mizsei, Mychailo Wynnyckyj (Eds.)* | Eight Years after the Revolution of Dignity. What Has Changed in Ukraine during 2013–2021? | With a foreword by Yaroslav Hrytsak | ISBN 978-3-8382-1560-0

244 *Rumena Filipova* | Constructing the Limits of Europe Identity and Foreign Policy in Poland, Bulgaria, and Russia since 1989 | With forewords by Harald Wydra and Gergana Yankova-Dimova | ISBN 978-3-8382-1649-2

245 *Oleksandra Keudel* | How Patronal Networks Shape Opportunities for Local Citizen Participation in a Hybrid Regime A Comparative Analysis of Five Cities in Ukraine | With a foreword by Sabine Kropp | ISBN 978-3-8382-1671-3

246 *Jan Claas Behrends, Thomas Lindenberger, Pavel Kolar (Eds.)* | Violence after Stalin Institutions, Practices, and Everyday Life in the Soviet Bloc 1953–1989 | ISBN 978-3-8382-1637-9

247 *Leonid Luks* | Macht und Ohnmacht der Utopien Essays zur Geschichte Russlands im 20. und 21. Jahrhundert | ISBN 978-3-8382-1677-5

248 *Iuliia Barshadska* | Brüssel zwischen Kyjiw und Moskau Das auswärtige Handeln der Europäischen Union im ukrainisch-russischen Konflikt 2014-2019 | Mit einem Vorwort von Olaf Leiße | ISBN 978-3-8382-1667-6

249 *Valentyna Romanova* | Decentralisation and Multilevel Elections in Ukraine Reform Dynamics and Party Politics in 2010–2021 | With a foreword by Kimitaka Matsuzato | ISBN 978-3-8382-1700-0

250 *Alexander Motyl* | National Questions. Theoretical Reflections on Nations and Nationalism in Eastern Europe | ISBN 978-3-8382-1675-1

251 *Marc Dietrich* | A Cosmopolitan Model for Peacebuilding. The Ukrainian Cases of Crimea and the Donbas | With a foreword by Rémi Baudouï | ISBN 978-3-8382-1687-4

252 *Eduard Baidaus* | An Unsettled Nation. Moldova in the Geopolitics of Russia, Romania, and Ukraine | With forewords by John-Paul Himka and David R. Marples | ISBN 978-3-8382-1582-2

253 *Igor Okunev, Petr Oskolkov (Eds.)* | Transforming the Administrative Matryoshka. The Reform of Autonomous Okrugs in the Russian Federation, 2003–2008 | With a foreword by Vladimir Zorin | ISBN 978-3-8382-1721-5

254 *Winfried Schneider-Deters* | Ukraine's Fateful Years 2013–2019. Vol. I: The Popular Uprising in Winter 2013/2014 | ISBN 978-3-8382-1725-3

255 *Winfried Schneider-Deters* | Ukraine's Fateful Years 2013–2019. Vol. II: The Annexation of Crimea and the War in Donbas | ISBN 978-3-8382-1726-0

256 *Robert M. Cutler* | Soviet and Post-Soviet Russian Foreign Policies II. East-West Relations in Europe and the Political Economy of the Communist Bloc, 1971–1991 | With a foreword by Roger E. Kanet | ISBN 978-3-8382-1727-7

257 *Robert M. Cutler* | Soviet and Post-Soviet Russian Foreign Policies III. East-West Relations in Europe and Eurasia in the Post-Cold War Transition, 1991–2001 | With a foreword by Roger E. Kanet | ISBN 978-3-8382-1728-4

258 *Paweł Kowal, Iwona Reichardt, Kateryna Pryshchepa (Eds.)* | Three Revolutions: Mobilization and Change in Contemporary Ukraine III. Archival Records and Historical Sources on the 1990 Revolution on Granite | ISBN 978-3-8382-1376-7

259 *Mikhail Minakov (Ed.)* | Philosophy Unchained. Developments in Post-Soviet Philosophical Thought. | With a foreword by Christopher Donohue | ISBN 978-3-8382-1768-0

260 *David Dalton* | The Ukrainian Oligarchy After the Euromaidan. How Ukraine's Political Economy Regime Survived the Crisis | With a foreword by Andrew Wilson | ISBN 978-3-8382-1740-6

261 *Andreas Heinemann-Grüder (Ed.)* | Who Are the Fighters? Irregular Armed Groups in the Russian-Ukrainian War since 2014 | ISBN 978-3-8382-1777-2

262 *Taras Kuzio (Ed.)* | Russian Disinformation and Western Scholarship. Bias and Prejudice in Journalistic, Expert, and Academic Analyses of East European, Russian and Eurasian Affairs | ISBN 978-3-8382-1685-0

263 *Darius Furmonavicius* | LithuaniaTransforms the West. Lithuania's Liberation from Soviet Occupation and the Enlargement of NATO (1988–2022) | With a foreword by Vytautas Landsbergis | ISBN 978-3-8382-1779-6

264 *Dirk Dalberg* | Politisches Denken im tschechoslowakischen Dissens. Egon Bondy, Miroslav Kusý, Milan Šimečka und Petr Uhl (1968-1989) | ISBN 978-3-8382-1318-5

265 *Леонид Люкс* | К столетию «философского парохода». Мыслители «первой» русской эмиграции о русской революции и о тоталитарных соблазнах XX века | ISBN 978-3-8382-1775-8

266 *Daviti Mtchedlishvili* | The EU and the South Caucasus. European Neighborhood Policies between Eclecticism and Pragmatism, 1991-2021 | With a foreword by Nicholas Ross Smith | ISBN 978-3-8382-1735-2

267 *Bohdan Harasymiw* | Post-Euromaidan Ukraine. Domestic Power Struggles and War of National Survival in 2014–2022 | ISBN 978-3-8382-1798-7

268 *Nadiia Koval, Denys Tereshchenko (Eds.)* | Russian Cultural Diplomacy under Putin. Rossotrudnichestvo, the "Russkiy Mir" Foundation, and the Gorchakov Fund in 2007–2022 | ISBN 978-3-8382-1801-4

269 *Izabela Kazejak* | Jews in Post-War Wrocław and L'viv. Official Policies and Local Responses in Comparative Perspective, 1945-1970s | ISBN 978-3-8382-1802-1

270 *Jakob Hauter* | Russia's Overlooked Invasion. The Causes of the 2014 Outbreak of War in Ukraine's Donbas | With a foreword by Hiroaki Kuromiya | ISBN 978-3-8382-1803-8

271 *Anton Shekhovtsov* | Russian Political Warfare. Essays on Kremlin Propaganda in Europe and the Neighbourhood, 2020-2023 | With a foreword by Nathalie Loiseau | ISBN 978-3-8382-1821-2

272 *Андреа Пето* | Насилие и Молчание. Красная армия в Венгрии во Второй Мировой войне | ISBN 978-3-8382-1636-2

273 *Winfried Schneider-Deters* | Russia's War in Ukraine. Debates on Peace, Fascism, and War Crimes, 2022–2023 | With a foreword by Klaus Gestwa | ISBN 978-3-8382-1876-2

274 *Rasmus Nilsson* | Uncanny Allies. Russia and Belarus on the Edge, 2012-2024 | ISBN 978-3-8382-1288-3

275 *Anton Grushetskyi, Volodymyr Paniotto* | War and the Transformation of Ukrainian Society (2022–23). Empirical Evidence | ISBN 978-3-8382-1944-8

276 *Christian Kaunert, Alex MacKenzie, Adrien Nonjon (Eds.)* | In the Eye of the Storm. Origins, Ideology, and Controversies of the Azov Brigade, 2014–23 | ISBN 978-3-8382-1750-5

277 *Gian Marco Moisé* | The House Always Wins. The Corrupt Strategies that Shaped Kazakh Oil Politics and Business in the Nazarbayev Era | With a foreword by Alena Ledeneva | ISBN 978-3-8382-1917-2

278 *Mikhail Minakov* | The Post-Soviet Human | Philosophical Reflections on Social History after the End of Communism | ISBN 978-3-8382-1943-1

279 *Natalia Kudriavtseva, Debra A. Friedman (Eds.)* | Language and Power in Ukraine and Kazakhstan. Essays on Education, Ideology, Literature, Practice, and the Media | With a foreword by Laada Bilaniuk | ISBN 978-3-8382-1949-3

280 *Paweł Kowal, Georges Mink, Iwona Reichardt (Eds.)* | The End of the Soviet World? Essays on Post-Communist Political and Social Change | With a foreword by Richardt Butterwick-Pawlikowski | ISBN 978-3-8382-1961-5

281 *Kateryna Zarembo, Michèle Knodt, Maksym Yakovlyev (Eds.)* | Teaching IR in Wartime. Experiences of University Lecturers during Russia's Full-Scale Invasion of Ukraine | ISBN 978-3-8382-1954-7

282 *Oleksiy V. Kresin* | The United Nations General Assembly Resolutions. Their Nature and Significance in the Context of the Russian War Against Ukraine | Edited by William E. Butler | ISBN 978-3-8382-1967-7

283 *Jakob Hauter* | Russlands unbemerkte Invasion. Die Ursachen des Kriegsausbruchs im ukrainischen Donbas im Jahr 2014 | Mit einem Vorwort von Hiroaki Kuromiya | ISBN 978-3-8382-2003-1

284 „Alles kann sich ändern". Letzte Worte politisch Angeklagter vor Gericht in Russland | Herausgegeben von Memorial Deutschland e.V. | ISBN 978-3-8382-1994-3

285 *Nadiya Kiss, Monika Wingender (Eds.)* | Contested Language Diversity in Contemporary Ukraine. National Minorities, Language Biographies, and Linguistic Landscape | ISBN 978-3-8382-1966-0

286 *Richard Ottinger (Ed.)* | Religious Elements in the Russian War of Aggression Against Ukraine. Propaganda, Religious Politics and Pastoral Care, 2014–2024 | ISBN 978-3-8382-1981-3

287 *Yuri Radchenko* | Helping in Mass Murders. Auxiliary Police, Indigenous Administration, SD, and the Shoa in the Ukrainian-Russian-Belorussian Borderlands, 1941–43 | With forewords by John-Paul Himka and Kai Struve | ISBN 978-3-8382-1878-6

288 *Zsofia Maria Schmidt* | Hungary's System of National Cooperation. Strategies of Framing in Pro-Governmental Media and Public Discourse, 2010–18 | With a foreword by Andreas Schmidt-Schweizer | ISBN 978-3-8382-1983-7

ibidem.eu